PART SECOND

OF THE

Mystery of Edwin Drood.

BY THE SPIRIT-PEN OF

CHARLES DICKENS,

THROUGH A MEDIUM.

Embracing, also, that part of the Work which was published prior to the termination of the Author's Earth-Life.

"COGITO, ERGO SUM."

BRATTLEBORO, VT.:
PUBLISHED BY T. P. JAMES.
1873.

To the Poor,

THE HONEST POOR OF EVERY LAND,
WHO ARE NOW HELD BY THE IRON HAND OF POVERTY,
BUT WHO SHALL ONE DAY STAND SIDE BY SIDE
WITH THE HIGHEST ON EARTH,

THESE PAGES ARE DEDICATED,

BY THE AUTHOR,

WITH THE ASSURANCE THAT THE HAPPIEST HOURS
OF HIS EARTHLY EXISTENCE
WERE THOSE THAT WITNESSED THE SUCCESS OF HIS EFFORTS
TO MAKE THEIR LIVES LESS BURDENSOME,
OR WHEN HE HAD
CONTRIBUTED BY WORD OR DEED
TO THEIR
WELFARE AND HAPPINESS.

MEDIUM'S PREFACE.

To gratify public curiosity, in a measure, it was deemed advisable to publish some extracts from this book before the work was finished, that the public might have an opportunity of judging, beforehand, whether it really did emanate from the source which was claimed for it.

The result was what would naturally be expected: Some could identify those characteristics which stamped it as the production of Mr. Dickens' pen, while others could not perceive anything about it that bore the least resemblance to the great author's writings. One individual affirmed, "The verbs are not in the least like Dickens';" but when requested to cite an instance, could not remember any particular case; he only knew they were not, because some one told him so! Most worthy representative of a class; but vastly more entitled to respect than that other class,—and a very small class, in every sense of the word, I am glad to say,—who, finding nothing of any importance to exist in those extracts which would warrant a just condemnation, conceived the brilliant idea that, by attacking me, public attention would be directed from the book, and in that way they could "kill it."

But, unfortunately for the latter class, the public generally were not to be influenced by any such superficial device, and could not be made to believe that an untoward event in my early life would add to or detract from the merits of this book, one iota.

For some wise purpose, no doubt, the Creator saw fit to place upon the earth a class of people who regard every thing *they* do or say as perfectly right and proper, and every thing other folks do or say as all wrong. They have a supreme opinion of their own ideas, and a poor opinion of other people's. Such persons always appear bareheaded in the argumentative field, and have no difficulty in finding a hat which will fit them nicely, even though it may not be so pleasant to wear. It would be supposed, however, that, after selecting the hat and putting it on voluntarily, they would be content to wear it, or discard it, and say nothing; but, instead, they go howling about, disgusted with themselves, and making everybody else disgusted with them.

In Mr. Dickens' Preface to this book, which was published as an extract, will be found, figuratively speaking, two hats, —one labeled "owl-like wisdom," and the other "ignorant bigots," and it was highly edifying to observe with what ease the above mentioned class of individuals discovered that those hats would fit them. This fact leads me to believe that there is a class of people in the world who will admit,—whatever they think of the other characters in this work,—that the character of Mr. Sapsea is not overdrawn.

To give the reader some idea of the ridiculous statements that were made concerning the authorship of this work, and which,—notwithstanding they were far more unreasonable than the true statement which affirmed this book to be the production of a spirit-pen,—were accepted as facts by quite a number of persons, I will cite one or two of them in this Preface.

One statement was, that the manuscript of this Second Part was left completed by Mr. Dickens at the time of his decease, and that one of his heirs, with a view to creating a sensation, thought it would be a capital plan to send it to this country and have it published in this way, and had selected me as his agent to carry out the project.

Another theory,—and the most popular of any,—was that the Evil One was at the bottom of the whole business; and it was said that, at a certain hour every night, his Satanic Majesty could be seen emerging from the chimney of my house and flying away into space, leaving behind him such a strong odor of brimstone that one could smell it for an hour afterwards; and, I suppose, no chimney ever attracted so much attention, or inspired such feelings of awe as that one did, in consequence of this libel upon its fair bricks and mortar.

I am knowing to one instance where two or three of the more superstitious stationed themselves near my house, and patiently awaited the phenomenal or diabolical (whichever you please) display; and yet these very people would not believe it possible that the departed spirit of some loved friend could return to earth, even when they could obtain satisfactory evidence of the fact, with much less trouble.

Concerning the merits of this book, it would ill-become me to speak. I can say this, however, that it is given to the public, word for word, as it came to me. An uneducated man myself, I am not qualified to deny or admit the existence of grammatical errors in its composition. Of course, I could easily have prevented their appearance, had I been solicitous on that score, by employing some person of experience to go over the manuscript, discover deficiencies, and remove them. I preferred, however, to let it go before the public as they find it—a counterpart of the original.

By those who are acquainted with the principles of spiritualism, (and those who are not, can easily understand them by adopting Mr. Dickens' suggestions, as given in his Preface to this work,) it will be easily understood that the first production of a spirit pen would be very liable to contain some imperfections; and more especially would that be the case, where both the medium and the spirit by whom he is controlled, are lacking in experience, and consequently development; but I believe future works, which are to come from the spirit-pen of Mr. Dickens, will be entirely free from imperfections, even if any such exist in the present volume.

Were I to judge from some criticisms which were passed upon this present work, *before it had made its appearance*, I might infer that, on the part of some, condemnation was a foregone conclusion. But, be that as it may, I trust that future criticism will be given in gentlemanly terms; and, above all, that prejudice will not be permitted to influence a verdict.

I am happy to announce that the first chapter of the next work,—"The Life and Adventures of Bockley Wickleheap,"—is finished; and, opening with all the peculiar characteristics of its author, bids fair to equal anything from his pen while on earth.

Finally, I desire to state that the origin of this work does *not* rest upon my "unsupported word," as some have stated. As truthful people as any who stand upon the earth, can testify to the truth of my assertions, for they have "seen whereof they affirm."

With a heart full of gratitude toward those friends who have stood by me during the trials and fatiguing labors of the past eight months, and who have sustained me by their encouraging words when I felt that I must "sink by the wayside," and with a sincere wish that my calumniators may find some good in Mr. Dickens' book, if they cannot find any in his medium, it only remains for me to thank the reader for his attention, and say farewell.

THOS. P. JAMES.

BRATTLEBORO, VT., *September* 25, 1873.

AUTHOR'S PREFACE.

DURING the progress of this work, as with all others on which I was engaged during my earth-life, I have felt a great desire to know the comments which would be bestowed upon it by its readers, and so have been glad when the last line was written, that I could obtain the different opinions which were to determine its success.

If I was apprehensive then, while on earth, it will be easily understood that I was still more so, when attempting to give the public a work, every word of which could only be placed on paper through the agency of earthly hands, used by me as the operator uses the instrument which transmits words thousands of miles by the power of electricity. The day is not far distant when this wonderful science will be better understood by millions who now believe it a delusion; and when that day comes, the world will be the better for it, and thousands who are in this happier world, and those who are yet to come, will be glad to know that the dear ones they have left behind regard their absence as a blessing certain, and so abandon the harrowing thought that it is possible a dear mother, father, sister, brother, wife, child or friend may be engulfed in a flaming sea which is to burn them for ever and ever. How little such people know of the wisdom and goodness of that dear Creator who made all things for a wise purpose; who has placed before the eyes of his earthly children so many evidences by which to convince them that nothing in nature is ever totally destroyed,—much less human souls, which are a part of Himself.

It has not been my intention, in any portion of this work, to strive to influence any living person to change his opinion. I would be glad, however, if my personal friends on earth would seek to investigate the truths which this science—religious science, I should say, perhaps—contains, for I feel confident they would be the happier for it in the end.

No man has a moral right to denounce a theory till he has had opportunity of seeing its workings, and has tangible evidence — the evidence of his senses — that it is not a consistent or reasonable one. These evidences are within your reach, if you will only seek them. But if you are satisfied as you are, and do not care to know more, for fear you will compromise your dignity,—at least have some regard for the feelings of those loved ones who have gone before, and do not ridicule that which, to them, is a living truth, or condemn that of which you know nothing, and of which you have no desire to learn.

Since the fact of this work being in preparation was first made public, I have been pained to observe the ridicule which was apparent in some published articles, but I have also found cause for considerable amusement in witnessing the owl-like wisdom displayed by those poor ignorant bigots who believe "the world was made for the people, and we are the people." We here are filled with pity for those bigots, but our consolation is, that they will be sufficiently punished for their obstinacy when they leave the world, where they now think themselves of such great importance, and learn for a certainty how different a world and life they are to enter upon.

I would fain hope that honest, candid men and women who read this work, will be satisfied that it is not a "delusion," as some have claimed,—even before an opportunity had been given them to read a line of it, and so form any opinion of its merits, —but will recognize in its pages the same desire which animated the author while living,—the desire to make his readers the happier for following the fortunes of those who were his "players;" and if I have succeeded, in even one instance, in making any reader happier, if not better, for the perusal of this work, I shall be content.

I cannot close this page without assuring the dear ones to whom I was so much attached on earth,—family and friends,— how anxiously I await their coming, that they may realize, by experience, how truly I speak concerning this other life. May God help and protect you all, is the earnest prayer of

THE AUTHOR.

Mystery of Edwin Drood.

COMPLETE.

CHAPTER I.

THE DAWN.

An ancient English Cathedral Tower! How can the ancient English Cathedral Tower be here! The well-known massive gray square tower of its old Cathedral? How can that be here! There is no spike of rusty iron in the air, between the eye and it, from any point of the real prospect. What is the spike that intervenes, and who has set it up? Maybe it is set up by the Sultan's orders for the impaling of a horde of Turkish robbers, one by one. It is so, for cymbals clash, and the Sultan goes by to his palace in long procession. Ten thousand cimeters flash in the sunlight, and thrice ten thousand dancing-girls strew flowers. Then follow white elephants, caparisoned in countless gorgeous colors, and infinite in number and attendants. Still the Cathedral Tower rises in the background, where it cannot be, and still no writhing figure is on the grim spike. Stay! Is the spike so low a thing as the rusty spike on the top of a post of an old bedstead that has tumbled all awry? Some vague period of drowsy laughter must be devoted to the consideration of this possibility.

Shaking from head to foot, the man whose scattered consciousness has thus fantastically pieced itself together at length rises, supports his trembling frame upon his arms and looks around. He is in the meanest and closest of small rooms. Through the ragged window-curtain, the light of early day steals in from a miserable court. He lies, dressed, across a large unseemly bed, upon a bedstead that has indeed given way under the weight upon it. Lying, also dressed and also across the bed, not long-wise, are a Chinaman, a Lascar, and a haggard woman. The first two are in a sleep or stupor; the last is blowing at a kind of pipe, to kindle it. And as she blows, and, shading it with her lean hand, concentrates its red spark of light, it serves in the dim morning as a lamp to show him what he sees of her.

"Another?" says this woman, in a querulous, rattling whisper. "Have another?"

He looks about him, with his hand to his forehead.

"Ye've smoked as many as five since ye come in at midnight," the woman goes on, as she chronically complains. "Poor me, poor me, my head is so bad! Them two come in after ye. Ah, poor me, the business is slack, is slack! Few Chinamen about the Docks, and fewer Lascars, and no ships coming in, these say! Here's another ready for ye, deary. Ye'll remember, like a good soul, won't ye, that the market price is dreffle high just now? More nor three shillings and sixpence for a thimblefull! And ye'll remember that nobody but me (and Jack Chinaman t'other side the court; but he can't do it as well as me) has the true secret of mixing it? Ye'll pay up according, deary, won't ye?"

She blows at the pipe as she speaks, and, occasionally bubbling at it, inhales much of its contents.

"O me, O me, my lungs is weak, my lungs is bad! It's nearly ready for ye, deary. Ah, poor me, poor me, my poor hand shakes like to drop off! I see ye coming-to, and I ses to my poor self, 'I'll have another ready for him, and he'll bear in mind the market price of opium, and pay according.' O my poor head! I makes my pipes of old penny ink-bottles, ye see, deary—this is one—and I fits in a mouthpiece, this way, and I takes my mixter out of this thimble with this little horn-spoon; and so I fills, deary. Ah, my poor nerves! I got Heavens-hard drunk for sixteen year afore I took to this; but this don't hurt me, not to speak of. And it takes away the hunger as well as wittles, deary."

She hands him the nearly-emptied pipe, and sinks back, turning over on her face.

He rises unsteadily from the bed, lays the pipe upon the hearthstone, draws back the ragged curtain, and looks with repugnance at his three companions. He notices that the woman has opium-smoked herself into a strange likeness of the Chinaman. His form of cheek, eye and temple, and his color, are repeated in her. Said Chinaman convulsively wrestles with one of his many Gods, or Devils, perhaps, and snarls horribly. The Lascar laughs and dribbles at the mouth. The hostess is still.

"What visions can *she* have?" the waking man muses, as he turns her face toward him, and stands looking down at it. "Visions of many butchers' shops and public-houses, and much credit? Of an increase of hideous customers, and this horrible bedstead set upright again, and this horrible court swept clean? What can she rise to, under any quantity of opium, higher than that!—Eh?"

He bends down his ear, to listen to her mutterings.

"Unintelligible!"

As he watches the spasmodic shoots and darts that break out of her face and limbs, like fitful lightning out of a dark sky, some contagion in them seizes upon him, insomuch that he has to withdraw himself to a lean arm-chair by the hearth—placed there, perhaps, for such emergencies—and to sit in it, holding tight, until he has got the better of this unclean spirit of imitation.

Then he comes back, pounces on the Chinaman, and, seizing him with both hands by the throat, turns him violently on the bed. The Chinaman clutches the aggressive hands, resists, gasps, and protests.

"What do you say?"

A watchful pause.

"Unintelligible!"

Slowly loosening his grasp as he listens to the incoherent jargon with an attentive frown, he turns to the Lascar and fairly drags him forth upon the floor. As he falls, the Lascar starts into a half-risen attitude, glares with his eyes, lashes about him fiercely with his arms, and draws a phantom knife. It then becomes apparent that the woman has taken possession of the knife, for safety's sake; for, she too starting up, and restraining and expostulating with him, the knife is visible in her dress, not in his, when they drowsily drop back, side by side.

There has been chattering and clattering enough between them, but to no purpose. When any distinct word has been flung into the air, it has had no sense or sequence. Wherefore "unintelligible!" is again the comment of the watcher, made with some reassured nodding of his head, and a gloomy smile. He then lays certain silver money on the table, finds his hat, gropes his way down the broken stairs, gives a good-morning to some rat-ridden doorkeeper, in bed in a black hutch beneath the stairs, and passes out.

That same afternoon, the massive gray square tower of an old Cathedral rises before the sight of a jaded traveller. The bells are going for daily vesper service, and he must needs attend it, one would say, from his haste to reach the open Cathedral door. The choir are getting on their sullied white robes, in a hurry, when he arrives among them, gets on his own robe, and falls into the procession filing in to service. Then the Sacristan locks the iron-barred gates that divide the sanctuary from the chancel, and all of the procession, having scuttled into their places, hide their faces; and then the intoned words, "WHEN THE WICKED MAN—" rise among groins of arches and beams of roof, awakening muttered thunder.

CHAPTER II.

A DEAN, AND A CHAPTER ALSO.

WHOSOEVER has observed that sedate and clerical bird, the rook, may perhaps have noticed that when he wings his way homeward toward nightfall, in a sedate and clerical company, two rooks will suddenly detach themselves from the rest, will retrace their flight for some distance, and will there poise and linger, conveying to mere men the fancy that it is of some occult importance to the body politic that this artful couple should pretend to have renounced connection with it.

Similarly, service being over in the old cathedral with the square tower, and the choir scuffling out again, and divers venerable persons of rook-like aspect dispersing, two of these latter retrace their steps, and walk together in the echoing Close.

Not only is the day waning, but the year. The low sun is fiery and yet cold behind the monastery ruin, and the Virginia creeper on the cathedral wall has showered half its deep-red leaves down on the pavement. There has been rain this afternoon, and a wintry shudder goes among the little pools on the cracked, uneven flag-stones, and through the giant elm-trees as they shed a gust of tears. Their fallen leaves lie strewn thickly about. Some of these leaves, in a timid rush, seek sanctuary within the low-arched cathedral door; but two men, coming out, resist them, and cast them forth again with their feet; this done, one of the two locks the door with a goodly key, and the other flits away with a folio music book.

"Mr. Jasper, was that Tope?"

"Yes, Mr. Dean."

"He has stayed late."

"Yes, Mr. Dean. I have stayed for him, your Reverence. He has been took a little poorly."

"Say 'taken,' Tope—to the Dean," the younger rook interposes in a low tone with this touch of correction, as who should say: "You may offer bad grammar to the laity, or the humbler clergy, not to the Dean."

Mr. Tope, Chief Verger and Showman, and accustomed to be high with excursion parties, declines with a silent loftiness to perceive that any suggestion has been tendered to him.

"And when and how has Mr. Jasper been taken—for, as Mr. Crisparkle has remarked, it is better to say taken—taken—" repeats the Dean; "when and how has Mr. Jasper been taken—"

"Taken, sir," Tope deferentially murmurs.

"—Poorly, Tope?"

"Why, sir, Mr. Jasper was that breathed—"

"I wouldn't say 'that breathed,' Tope," Mr. Crisparkle interposes, with the same touch as before. "Not English—to the Dean."

"Breathed to that extent," the Dean (not unflattered by this indirect homage) condescendingly remarks, "would be preferable."

"Mr. Jasper's breathing was so remarkably short," thus discreetly does Mr. Tope work his way round the sunken rock; "when he came in, that it distressed him mightily to get his notes out; which was, perhaps, the cause of his having a kind of fit on him after a little. His memory grew DAZED." Mr. Tope, with his eyes on the Reverend Mr. Crisparkle, shoots this word out, as defying him to improve upon it; "and a dimness and giddiness crept over him as strange as ever I saw; though he didn't seem to mind it particularly, himself. However, a little time and a little water brought him out of his DAZE." Mr. Tope repeats the word and its emphasis, with the air of saying, "As I *have* made a success, I'll make it again."

"And Mr. Jasper has gone home quite himself, has he?" asked the Dean.

"Your Reverence, he has gone home quite himself. And I'm glad to see he's having his fire kindled up, for it's chilly after the wet, and the Cathedral had both a damp feel and a damp touch this afternoon, and he was very shivery."

They all three looked toward an old stone gatehouse crossing the Close, with an arched thoroughfare passing beneath it. Through its latticed window, a fire shines out upon the fast-darkening scene, involving in shadow the pendent masses of ivy and creeper covering the building's front. As the deep Cathedral bell strikes the hour, a ripple of wind goes through these at their distance, like a ripple of the solemn sound that hums through tomb and tower, broken niche and defaced statue, in the pile close at hand.

"Is Mr. Jasper's nephew with him?" the Dean asks.

"No, sir," replies the Verger, "but expected. There's his own solitary shadow betwixt his two windows—the one looking this way, and the one looking down into the High Street—drawing his own curtains now."

"Well, well," says the Dean, with a sprightly air of breaking up the little conference, "I hope Mr. Jasper's heart may not be too much set upon his nephew. Our affections, however laudable, in this transitory world, should never master us; we should guide them, guide them. I find I am not disagreeably reminded of my dinner, by hearing my dinner-bell. Perhaps Mr. Crisparkle you will, before going home, look in on Jasper?"

"Certainly, Mr. Dean. And tell him that you had the kindness to desire to know how he was."

"Ay, do so, do so. Certainly. Wished to know how he was. By all means. Wished to know how he was."

With a pleasant air of patronage, the Dean as nearly cocks his quaint hat as a Dean in good spirits may, and directs his comely gaiters toward the ruddy dining-room of the snug old red-brick house, where he is at present "in residence" with Mrs. Dean and Miss Dean.

Mr. Crisparkle, Minor Canon, fair and rosy, and perpetually pitching himself head foremost into all the deep running water in the surrounding country; Mr. Crisparkle, Minor Canon, early riser, musical, classical, cheerful, kind, good-natured, social, contented, and boy-like; Mr. Crisparkle, Minor Canon and good man, lately "Coach" upon the chief Pagan high-roads, but since promoted by a patron (grateful for a well-taught son) to his present Christian beat; betakes himself to the gate-house, on his way home to his early tea.

"Sorry to hear from Tope that you have not been well, Jasper."

"Oh, it was nothing, nothing!"

"You look a little worn."

"Do I? Oh, I don't think so. What is better, I don't feel so. Tope has made too much of it, I suspect. It's his trade to make the most of every thing appertaining to the Cathedral, you know."

"I may tell the Dean—I call expressly from the Dean—that you are all right again?"

The reply, with a slight smile, is "Certainly; with my respects and thanks to the Dean."

"I'm glad to hear that you expect young Drood."

"I expect the dear fellow every moment."

"Ah! He will do you more good than a doctor, Jasper."

"More good than a dozen doctors; for I love him dearly, and I don't love doctors, or doctors' stuff."

Mr. Jasper is a dark man of some six-and-twenty, with thick, lustrous, well-arranged black hair and whisker. He looks older than he is, as dark men often do. His voice is deep and good, his face and figure are good, his manner is a little sombre. His room is a little sombre, and may have had its influence in forming his manner. It is mostly in shadow. Even when the sun shines brilliantly, it seldom touches the grand piano in the recess, or the folio music-books on the stand, or the bookshelves on the wall, or the unfinished picture of a blooming school-girl hanging over the chimney-piece; her flowing brown hair tied with a blue ribbon, and her beauty remarkable for a quite childish, almost babyish touch of saucy discontent, comically conscious of itself. (There is not the least artistic merit in this picture, which is a mere daub; but it is clear that the painter has made it humorously—one might almost say, revengefully—like the original.)

"We shall miss you, Jasper, at the 'Alternate Musical Wednesdays' to-night; but no doubt you are best at home. Good-night. God bless you! 'Tell me, shep-herds, te-e-ell me; tell me-e-e, have you seen, (have you seen, have you seen, have you seen) my y-y Flo-o-ora-a pass this way?'" Melodiously good Minor Canon the Reverend Septimus Crisparkle thus delivers himself, in musical rhythm, as he withdraws his amiable face from the doorway and conveys it down-stairs.

Sounds of recognition and greeting pass between the Reverend Septimus and somebody else, at the stair-foot. Mr. Jasper listens, starts from his chair, and catches a young fellow in his arms, exclaiming—

"My dear Edwin!"

"My dear Jack! So glad to see you!"

"Get off your great-coat, bright boy, and sit down here in your own corner. Your feet are not wet? Pull your boots off. Do pull your boots off."

"My dear Jack, I am as dry as a bone. Don't moddley-coddley, there's a good fellow. I like any thing better than being moddley-coddleyed."

With the check upon him of being unsympathetically restrained in a genial outburst of enthusiasm, Mr. Jasper stands still, and looks on intently at the young fellow, divesting himself of his outer coat, hat, gloves, and so forth. Once for all a look of intentness, and intensity—a look of hungry, exacting, watchful, and yet devoted affection—is always, now and ever afterward, on the Jasper face whenever the Jasper face is addressed in this direction. And whenever it is so addressed, it is never, on this occasion or on any other, dividedly addressed; it is always concentrated.

"Now I am right, and now I'll take my corner, Jack. Any dinner, Jack?"

Mr. Jasper opens a door at the upper end of the room, and discloses a small inner room pleasantly lighted and prepared, wherein a comely dame is in the act of setting dishes on table.

"What a jolly old Jack it is!" cries the young fellow, with a clap of his hands. "Look here, Jack; tell me; whose birthday is it?"

"Not yours, I know," Mr. Jasper answers, pausing to consider.

"Not mine, you know? No; not mine, *I* know! Pussy's!"

Fixed as the look the young fellow meets is, there is yet in it some strange power of suddenly including the sketch over the chimney-piece.

"Pussy's, Jack! We must drink many happy returns to her. Come, uncle, take your dutiful and sharp-set nephew in to dinner."

As the boy (for he is little more) lays a hand on Jasper's shoulder, Jasper cordially and gayly lays a hand on *his* shoulder, and so Marseillaise-wise they go in to dinner.

"And Lord! Here's Mrs. Tope!" cries the boy. "Lovelier than ever!"

"Never you mind me, Master Edwin," retorts the Verger's wife, "I can take care of myself."

"You can't. You're much too handsome. Give me a kiss, because it's Pussy's birthday."

"I'd Pussy you, young man, if I was Pussy, as you call her," Mrs. Tope blushingly retorts, after being saluted. "Your uncle's too much wrapped up in you, that's where it is. He makes so much of you, that it's my opinion you think you've only to call your Pussys by the dozen, to make 'em come."

"You forget, Mrs. Tope," Mr. Jasper interposes, taking his place at table with a genial smile, "and so do you, Ned, that Uncle and Nephew are words prohibited here by common consent and express agreement. For what we are going to receive His holy name be praised!"

"Done like the Dean! Witness Edwin Drood! Please to carve, Jack, for I can't."

This sally ushers in the dinner. Little to the present purpose, or to any purpose, is said, while it is in course of being disposed of. At length the cloth is drawn, and a dish of walnuts and a decanter of rich-colored sherry are placed upon the table.

"I say! Tell me, Jack," the young fellow then flows on: "do you really and truly feel as if the mention of our relationship divided us at all? *I* don't."

"Uncles as a rule, Ned, are so much older than their nephews," is the reply, "that I have that feeling instinctively."

"As a rule? Ah, maybe! But what is a difference in age of half a dozen years or so? And some uncles in large families are even younger than their nephews. By George, I wish it was the case with us!"

"Why?"

"Because if it was, I'd take the lead with you, Jack, and be as wise as Begone dull care that turned a young man gray, and begone dull care that turned an old man to clay. Halloa, Jack! Don't drink."

"Why not?"

"Asks why not, on Pussy's birthday, and no Happy Returns proposed! Pussy, Jack, and many of 'em. Happy returns, I mean."

Laying an affectionate and laughing touch on the boy's extended hand, as if it were at once his giddy head and his light heart, Mr. Jasper drinks the toast in silence.

"Hip, hip, hip, and nine times nine, and one to finish with, and all that, understood. Hooray, hooray, hooray! And now, Jack, let's have a little talk about Pussy. Two pairs of nut-crackers? Pass me one and take the other." Crack. "How's Pussy getting on, Jack?"

"With her music? Fairly."

"What a dreadfully conscientious fellow you are, Jack! But *I* know, Lord bless you! Inattentive, isn't she?"

"She can learn anything, if she will."

"*If* she will? Egad that's it. But if she won't?"

Crack. On Mr. Jasper's part.

"How's she looking, Jack?"

Mr. Jasper's concentrated face again includes the portrait as he returns, "Very like your sketch indeed."

"I *am* a little proud of it," says the young fellow, glancing up at the sketch with complacency, and then shutting one eye, and taking a corrected prospect of it over a level bridge of nut-cracker in the air: "Not badly hit off from memory. But I ought to have caught that expression pretty well, for I have seen it often enough."

Crack. On Edwin Drood's part.

Crack. On Mr. Jasper's part.

"In point of fact," the former resumes, after some silent dipping among his fragments of walnut with an air of pique, "I see it whenever I go to see Pussy. If I don't find it on her face, I leave it there.—You know I do, Miss Scornful Pert. Booh!" With a twirl of the nut-crackers at the portrait.

Crack. Crack. Crack. Slowly, on Mr. Jasper's part.

Crack. Sharply, on the part of Edwin Drood.

Silence on both sides.

"Have you lost your tongue, Jack?"

"Have you found yours, Ned?"

"No, but really—isn't it, you know, after all?"

Mr. Jasper lifts his dark eyebrows inquiringly.

"Isn't it unsatisfactory to be cut off from choice in such a matter? There, Jack! I tell you! If I could choose, I would choose Pussy from all the pretty girls in the world."

"But you have not got to choose."

"That's what I complain of. My dead-and-gone father and Pussy's dead-and-gone father must needs marry us together by anticipation. Why the—Devil, I was going to say, if it had been respectful to their memory—couldn't they leave us alone?"

"Tut, tut, dear boy," Mr. Jasper remonstrates, in a tone of gentle deprecation.

"Tut, tut? Yes, Jack, it's all very well for *you*. *You* can take it easily. *Your* life is not laid down to scale, and lined and dotted out for you like a surveyor's plan. *You* have no uncomfortable suspicion that you are forced upon anybody, nor has anybody any uncomfortable suspicion that she is forced upon you, or that you are forced upon her. *You* can choose for yourself. Life, for *you*, is a plum with the natural bloom on; it hasn't been over-carefully wiped off for *you*—"

"Don't stop, dear fellow. Go on."

"Can I anyhow have hurt your feelings, Jack?"

"How can you have hurt my feelings?"

"Good Heaven, Jack, you look frightfully ill! There's a strange film come over your eyes."

Mr. Jasper, with a forced smile, stretches out his right hand, as if at once to disarm apprehension and gain time to get better. After a while he says faintly:

"I have been taking opium for a pain—an agony—that sometimes overcomes me. The effects of the medicine steal over me like a blight or a cloud, and pass. You see them in the act of passing; they will be gone directly. Look away from me. They will go all the sooner."

With a scared face the younger man complies, by casting his eyes downward at the ashes on the hearth. Not relaxing his own gaze at the fire, but rather strengthening it with a fierce, firm grip upon his elbow-chair, the elder sits for a few moments rigid, and then, with thick drops standing on his forehead, and a sharp catch of his breath, becomes as he was before. On his so subsiding in his chair, his nephew gently and assiduously tends him while he quite recovers. When Jasper is restored, he lays a tender hand upon his nephew's shoulder, and, in a tone of voice less troubled than the purport of his words—indeed, with something of raillery or banter in it—thus addresses him:

"There is said to be a hidden skeleton in every house; but you thought there was none in mine, dear Ned."

"Upon my life, Jack, I did think so. However, when I come to consider that even in Pussy's house—if she had one—and in mine—if I had one—"

"You were going to say (but that I interrupted you in spite of myself) what a quiet life mine is. No whirl and uproar around me, no distracting commerce or calculation, no risk, no change of place, myself devoted to the art I pursue, my business, my pleasure."

"I really was going to say something of the kind, Jack; but you see, you, speaking of yourself, almost necessarily leave out much that I should have put in. For instance: I should have put in the foreground, your being so much respected as Lay Precentor, or Lay Clerk, or whatever you call it, of this Cathedral; your enjoying the reputation of having done such wonders with the choir; your choosing your society, and holding such an independent position in this queer old place; your gift of teaching (why, even Pussy, who don't like being taught, says there never was such a Master as you are!) and your connection."

"Yes; I saw what you were tending to. I hate it."

"Hate it, Jack?" (Much bewildered.)

"I hate it. The cramped monotony of my existence grinds me away by the grain. How does our service sound to you?"

"Beautiful! Quite celestial!"

"It often sounds to me quite devilish. I am so weary of it! The echoes of my own voice among the arches seem to mock me with my daily drudging round. No wretched monk who droned his life away in that gloomy place, before me, can have been more tired of it than I am. He could take for relief (and did take) to carving demons out of the stalls and seats and desks. What shall I do? Must I take to carving them out of my heart?"

"I thought you had so exactly found your niche in life, Jack," Edwin Drood returns, astonished, bending forward in his chair to lay a sympathetic hand on Jasper's knee, and looking at him with an anxious face.

"I know you thought so. They all think so."

"Well; I suppose they do," says Edwin, meditating aloud. "Pussy thinks so."

"When did she tell you that?"

"The last time I was here. You remember when—three months ago."

"How did she phrase it?"

"Oh! She only said that she had become your pupil, and that you were made for your vocation."

The younger man glances at the portrait. The elder sees it in him.

"Anyhow, my dear Ned," Jasper resumes, as he shakes his head with a grave cheerfulness, "I must subdue myself to my vocation, which is much the same thing outwardly. It's too late to find another now. This is a confidence between us."

"It shall be sacredly preserved, Jack."

"I have reposed it in you, because—"

"I feel it, I assure you. Because we are fast friends, and because you love and trust me, as I love and trust you. Both hands, Jack."

As each stands looking into the other's eyes, and as the uncle holds the nephew's hands, the uncle thus proceeds:

"You know now, don't you, that even a poor monotonous chorister and grinder of music, in his niche, may be troubled with some stray sort of ambition, aspiration, restlessness, dissatisfaction—what shall we call it?"

"Yes, dear Jack."

"And you will remember?"

"My dear Jack, I only ask you, am I likely to forget what you have said with so much feeling?"

"Take it as a warning, then."

In the act of having his hands released, and of moving a step back, Edwin pauses for an instant to consider the application of these last words. The instant over, he says, sensibly touched—

"I am afraid I am but a shallow, surface kind of fellow, Jack, and that my head-piece is none of the best. But I needn't say I am young; and perhaps I shall not grow worse as I grow older. At all events, I hope I have something impressible within me, which feels—deeply feels—the disinterestedness of your painfully laying your inner self bare, as a warning to me."

Mr. Jasper's steadiness of face and figure becomes so marvellous that his breathing seems to have stopped.

"I couldn't fail to notice, Jack, that it cost you a great effort, and that you were very much moved, and very unlike your usual self. Of course, I knew that you were extremely fond of me, but I really was not prepared for your, as I may say, sacrificing yourself to me in that way."

Mr. Jasper, becoming a breathing man again, without the smallest stage of transition between the two extreme states, lifts his shoulders, laughs, and waves his right arm.

"No; don't put the sentiment away, Jack; please don't; for I am very much in earnest. I have no doubt that that unhealthy state of mind which you have so powerfully described is attended with some real suffering, and is hard to bear. But let me reassure you, Jack, as to the chances of its overcoming Me. I don't think I am in the way of it. In some few months less than another year, you know, I shall carry Pussy off from school as Mrs. Edwin Drood. I shall then go engineering into the East, and Pussy with me. And, although we have our little tiffs now, arising out of a certain unavoidable flatness that attends our love-making, owing to its end being all settled beforehand, still I have no doubt of our getting on capitally then, when it's done and can't be helped. In short, Jack, to go back to the old song I was freely quoting at dinner (and who knows old songs better than you!), my wife shall dance and I will sing, so merrily pass the day. Of Pussy's being beautiful there cannot be a doubt; and when you are good besides, Little Miss Impudence," once more apostrophizing the portrait, "I'll burn your comic likeness and paint your music master another."

Mr. Jasper, with his hand to his chin, and with an expression of musing benevolence on his face, has attentively watched every animated look and gesture attending the delivery of these words. He remains in that attitude after they are spoken, as if in a kind of fascination attendant on his strong interest in the youthful spirit that he loves so well. Then he says, with a quiet smile—

"You won't be warned, then?"

"No, Jack."

"You can't be warned, then?"

"No, Jack; not by you. Besides that I don't really consider myself in danger, I don't like your putting yourself in that position."

"Shall we go and walk in the church-yard?"

"By all means. You won't mind my slipping out of it for half a moment to the Nuns' House, and leaving a parcel there? Only gloves for Pussy; as many pairs of gloves as she is years old to-day. Rather poetical, Jack?"

Mr. Jasper, still in the same attitude, murmurs, "'Nothing half so sweet in life,' Ned!"

"Here's the parcel in my great-coat pocket. They must be presented to-night, or the poetry is gone. It's against regulations for me to call at night, but not to leave a packet. I am ready, Jack!"

Mr. Jasper dissolves his attitude, and they go out together.

CHAPTER III.

THE NUNS' HOUSE.

For sufficient reasons, which this narrative will itself unfold as it advances, a fictitious name must be bestowed upon the old Cathedral town. Let it stand in these pages as Cloisterham. It was once possibly known to the Druids by another name, and certainly to the Romans by another, and to the Saxons by another, and to the Normans by another; and a name more or less in the course of many centuries can be of little moment to its dusty chronicles.

An ancient city Cloisterham, and no meet dwelling-place for any one with hankerings after the noisy world. A monotonous, silent city, deriving an earthly flavor throughout, from its cathedral-crypt, and so abounding in vestiges of monastic graves, that the Cloisterham children grow small salad in the dust of abbots and abbesses, and make dirt-pies of nuns and friars; while every ploughman in its outlying fields renders to once puissant Lord Treasurers, Archbishops, Bishops, and such-like, the attention which the Ogre in the story-book desired to render to his unbidden visitor, and grinds their bones to make his bread.

A drowsy city Cloisterham, whose inhabitants seem to suppose, with an inconsistency more strange than rare, that all its changes lie behind it, and that there are no more to come. A queer moral to derive from antiquity, yet older than any traceable antiquity. So silent are the streets of Cloisterham (though prone to echo on the smallest provocation), that, of a summer day, the sunblinds of its shops scarce dare to flap in the south wind; while the sun-browned tramps, who pass along and stare, quicken their limp a little, that they may the sooner get beyond the confines of its oppressive respectability. This is a feat not difficult of achievement, seeing that the streets of Cloisterham city are little more than one narrow street by which you get into it and get out of it: the rest being mostly disappointing yards with pumps in them and no thoroughfare—exception made of the Cathedral-close, and a paved Quaker settlement, in color and general conformation very like a Quakeress's bonnet, up in a shady corner.

In a word, a city of another and a by-gone time is Cloisterham, with its hoarse Cathedral-bell, its hoarse rooks hovering about the Cathedral tower, its hoarser and less distinct rooks in the stalls far beneath. Fragments of old wall, saints' chapel, chapter-house, convent, and monastery, have got incongruously or obstructively built into many of its houses and gardens, much as kindred jumbled notions have become incorporated into many of its citizens' minds. All things in it are of the past. Even its single pawnbroker takes in no pledges, nor has he for a long time, but offers vainly an unredeemed stock for sale, of which the costlier articles are dim and pale old watches apparently in a slow perspiration, tarnished sugar-tongs with ineffectual legs, and odd volumes of dismal books. The most abundant and the most agreeable evidences of progressing life in Cloisterham are the evidences of vegetable life in its many gardens; even its drooping and despondent little theatre has its poor strip of garden, receiving the foul fiend, when he ducks from its stage into the infernal regions, among scarlet beans or oyster-shells, according to the season of the year.

In the midst of Cloisterham stands the Nuns' House; a venerable dark edifice whose present appellation is doubtless derived from the legend of its conventual uses. On the trim gate enclosing its old court-yard is a resplendent brass plate flashing forth the legend: "Seminary for Young Ladies. Miss Twinkleton." The house-front is so old and worn, and the brass plate is so shining and staring, that the general result has reminded imaginative strangers of a battered old beau with a large modern eye-glass stuck in his blind eye.

Whether the nuns of yore, being of a submissive rather than a stiff-necked generation, habitually bent their contemplative heads to avoid collision with the beams in the low ceilings of the many chambers of their House; whether they sat in its long low windows, telling their beads for their mortification instead of making necklaces of them for their adornment; whether they were ever walled up alive in odd angles and jutting gables of the building for having some ineradicable leaven of busy mother Nature in them which has kept the fermenting world alive ever since: these may be matters of interest to its haunting ghosts (if any), but constitute no item in Miss Twinkleton's half-yearly accounts. They are neither of Miss Twinkleton's inclusive regulars, nor of her extras. The lady who undertakes the poetical department of the establishment at so much (or so little) a quarter, has no pieces in her list of recitals bearing on such unprofitable questions.

As, in some cases of drunkenness, and in others of animal magnetism, there are two states of consciousness which never clash, but each of which pursues its separate course as though it were continuous instead of broken (thus, if I hide my watch when I am drunk, I must be drunk again before I can remember where), so Miss Twinkleton has two distinct and separate phases of being. Every night, the moment the young ladies have retired to rest, does Miss Twinkleton smarten up her curls a little, brighten up her eyes a little, and become a sprightlier Miss Twinkleton than the young ladies have ever seen. Every night, at the same hour, does Miss Twinkleton resume the topics of the previous night, comprehending the tenderer scandal of Cloisterham, of which she has no knowledge whatever by day, and references to a certain season at Tunbridge Wells (airily called by Miss Twinkleton, in this state of her existence, "The Wells"), notably the season wherein a certain finished gentleman (compassionately called by Miss Twinkleton, in this state of her existence, "Foolish Mr. Porters") revealed a homage of the heart, whereof Miss Twinkleton, in her scholastic state of existence, is as ignorant as a granite pillar. Miss Twinkleton's companion in both states of existence, and equally adaptable to either, is one Mrs. Tisher, a deferential widow with a weak back, a chronic sigh, and a suppressed voice, who looks after the young ladies' wardrobes, and leads them to infer that she has seen better days. Perhaps this is the reason why it is an article of faith with the servants, handed down from race to race, that the departed Tisher was a hair-dresser.

The pet pupil of the Nuns' House is Miss Rosa Bud, of course called Rosebud; wonderfully pretty, wonderfully childish, wonderfully whimsical. An awkward interest (awkward because romantic) attaches to Miss Bud in the minds of the young ladies, on account of its being known to them that a husband has been chosen for her by will and bequest, and that her guardian is bound down to bestow her on that husband when he comes of age. Miss Twinkleton, in her seminarial state of existence, has combated the romantic aspect of this destiny by affecting to shake her head over it behind Miss Bud's dimpled shoulders, and to brood on the unhappy lot of that doomed little victim. But with no better effect—possibly some unfelt touch of foolish Mr. Porters has undermined the endeavor—than to evoke from the young ladies a unanimous bedchamber cry of "Oh, what a pretending old thing Miss Twinkleton is, my dear!"

The Nuns' House is never in such a state of flutter as when this allotted husband calls to see little Rosebud. (It is unanimously understood by the young ladies that he is lawfully entitled to this privilege, and that if Miss Twinkleton disputed it she would be instantly taken up and transported.) When his ring at the gate-bell is expected, or takes place, every young lady who can, under any pretence, look out of window, looks out of window; while every young lady who is "practising" practises out of time; and the French class becomes so demoralized that the Mark goes round as briskly as the bottle at a convivial party in the last century.

On the afternoon of the day next after the dinner of two at the Gate House, the bell is rung with the usual fluttering results.

"Mr. Edwin Drood to see Miss Rosa."

This is the announcement of the parlor-maid in chief. Miss Twinkleton, with an exemplary air of melancholy on her, turns to the sacrifice, and says, "You may go down, my dear." Miss Bud goes down, followed by all eyes.

Mr. Edwin Drood is waiting in Miss Twinkleton's own parlor, a dainty room, with nothing more directly scholastic in it than a terrestial and a celestial globe. These expressive machines imply (to parents and guardians) that even when Miss Twinkleton retires into the bosom of privacy, duty may at any moment compel her to become a sort of Wandering Jewess, scouring the earth and soaring through the skies in search of knowledge for her pupils.

The last new maid, who has never seen the young gentleman Miss Rosa is engaged to, and who is making his acquaintance between the hinges of the open door, left open for the purpose, stumbles guiltily down the kitchen-stairs, as a charming little apparition, with its face concealed by a little silk apron thrown over its head, glides into the parlor.

"Oh! It *is* so ridiculous!" says the apparition, stopping and shrinking. "Don't, Eddy!"

"Don't what, Rosa?"

"Don't come any nearer, please. It *is* so absurd."

"What is absurd, Rosa?"

"The whole thing is. It *is* so absurd to be an engaged orphan; and it *is* so absurd to have the girls and the servants scuttling about after one, like mice in the wainscot; and it *is* so absurd to be called upon."

The apparition appears to have a thumb in the corner of its mouth while making this complaint.

"You give me an affectionate reception, Pussy, I must say."

"Well, I will in a minute, Eddy, but I can't just yet. How are you?" (Very shortly.)

"I am unable to reply that I am much the better for seeing you, Pussy, inasmuch as I see nothing of you."

This second remonstrance brings a dark, bright, pouting eye out from a corner of the apron; but it swiftly becomes invisible again, as the apparition exclaims, "Oh! Good Gracious, you have had half your hair cut off!"

"I should have done better to have had my head cut off, I think," says Edwin, rumpling the hair in question, with a fierce glance at the looking-glass, and giving an impatient stamp. "Shall I go?"

"No, you needn't go just yet, Eddy. The girls would all be asking questions why you went."

"Once for all, Rosa, will you uncover that ridiculous little head of yours and give me a welcome?"

The apron is pulled off the childish head as its wearer replies, "You're very welcome, Eddy. There! I'm sure that's nice. Shake hand. No, I can't kiss you, because I've got an acidulated drop in my mouth."

"Are you at all glad to see me, Pussy?"

"Oh, yes, I'm dreadfully glad.—Go and sit down.—Miss Twinkleton."

It is the custom of that excellent lady when these visits occur, to appear every three minutes, either in her own person or in that of Mrs. Tisher, and lay an offering on the shrine of Propriety by affecting to look for some desiderated article. On the present occasion, Miss Twinkleton, gracefully gliding in and out, says, in passing, "How do you do, Mr. Drood? Very glad indeed to have the pleasure. Pray excuse me. Tweezers. Thank you!"

"I got the gloves last evening, Eddy, and I like them very much. They are beauties."

"Well, that's something," the affianced replies, half grumbling. "The smallest encouragement thankfully received. And how did you pass your birthday, Pussy?"

"Delightfully! Everybody gave me a present. And we had a feast. And we had a ball at night."

"A feast and a ball, eh? These occasions seem to go off tolerably well without me, Pussy."

"De-lightfully!" cries Rosa, in a quite spontaneous manner, and without the least pretence of reserve.

"Hah! And what was the feast?"

"Tarts, oranges, jellies, and shrimps."

"Any partners at the ball?"

"We danced with one another, of course, sir. But some of the girls made game to be their brothers. It *was* so droll!"

"Did anybody make game to be—"

"To be you? O dear, yes!" cries Rosa, laughing with great enjoyment. "That was the first thing done."

"I hope she did it pretty well," says Edwin, rather doubtfully.

"Oh! It was excellent!—I wouldn't dance with you, you know."

Edwin scarcely seems to see the force of this; begs to know if he may take the liberty to ask why?

"Because I was so tired of you," returns Rosa. But she quickly adds, and pleadingly, too, seeing displeasure on his face: "Dear Eddy, you were just as tired of me, you know."

"Did I say so, Rosa?"

"Say so! Do you ever say so? No, you only showed it. Oh, she did it so well!" cries Rosa, in a sudden ecstasy with her counterfeit betrothed.

"It strikes me that she must be a devilish impudent girl," says Edwin Drood. "And so, Pussy, you have passed your last birthday in this old house."

"Ah, yes!" Rosa clasps her hands, looks down with a sigh, and shakes her head.

"You seem to be sorry, Rosa."

"I am sorry for the poor old place. Somehow, I feel as if it would miss me, when I am gone so far away, so young."

"Perhaps we had better stop short, Rosa?"

She looks up at him with a swift, bright look; next moment shakes her head, sighs, and looks down again.

"That is to say, is it, Pussy, that we are both resigned?"

She nods her head again, and, after a short silence, quaintly bursts out with, "You know we must be married, and married from here, Eddy, or the poor girls will be so dreadfully disappointed!"

For the moment there is more of compassion, both for her and for himself, in her affianced husband's face, than there is of love. He checks the look, and asks, "Shall I take you out for a walk, Rosa dear?"

Rosa dear does not seem at all clear on this point, until her face, which has been comically reflective, brightens. "Oh, yes, Eddy; let us go for a walk! And I tell you what we'll do. You shall pretend that you are engaged to somebody else, and I'll pretend that I am not engaged to anybody, and then we shan't quarrel."

"Do you think that will prevent our falling out, Rosa?"

"I know it will. Hush! Pretend to look out of window—Mrs. Tisher!"

Through a fortuitous concourse of accidents, the matronly Tisher heaves in sight, says, in rustling through the room like the legendary ghost of a dowager in silken skirts, "I hope I see Mr. Drood well; though I needn't ask, if I may judge from his complexion? I trust I disturb no one; but there *was* a paper-knife—oh, thank you, I am sure!" and disappears with her prize.

"One other thing you must do, Eddy, to oblige me," says Rosebud. "The moment we get into the street, you must put me outside, and keep close to the house yourself—squeeze and graze yourself against it."

"By all means, Rosa, if you wish it. Might I ask why?"

"Oh, because I don't want the girls to see you."

"It's a fine day; but would you like me to carry an umbrella up?"

"Don't be foolish, sir. You haven't got polished-leather boots on," pouting, with one shoulder raised.

"Perhaps that might escape the notice of the girls, even if they did see me," remarks Edwin, looking down at his boots with a sudden distaste for them.

"Nothing escapes their notice, sir. And then I know what would happen. Some of them would begin reflecting on me by saying (for *they* are free) that they never will on any account engage themselves to lovers without polished-leather boots. Hark! Miss Twinkleton. I'll ask for leave."

That discreet lady being indeed heard without, inquiring of nobody in a blandly-conversational tone as she advances, "Eh? Indeed! Are you quite sure you saw my mother-of-pearl button-holder on the work-table in my room?" is at once solicited for walking-leave, and graciously accords it. And soon the young couple go out of the Nuns' House, taking all precautions against the discovery of the so vitally-defective boots of Mr. Edwin Drood—precautions, let us hope, effective for the peace of Mrs. Edwin Drood, that is to be.

"Which way shall we take, Rosa?"

Rosa replies, "I want to go to the Lumps-of-Delight shop."

"To the—"

"A Turkish sweetmeat, sir. My gracious me! don't you understand anything? Call yourself an Engineer, and not know *that?*"

"Why, how should I know it, Rosa?"

"Because I am very fond of them. But oh! I forgot what we are to pretend. No, you needn't know any thing about them; never mind."

So he is gloomily borne off to the Lumps-of-Delight shop, where Rosa makes her purchase, and, after offering some to him (which he rather indignantly declines), begins to partake of it with great zest, previously taking off and rolling up a pair of little pink gloves, like rose-leaves, and occasionally putting her little pink fingers to her rosy lips, to cleanse them from the Dust of Delight that comes off the Lumps.

"Now, be a good-tempered Eddy, and pretend. And so you are engaged?"

"And so I am engaged."

"Is she nice?"

"Charming."

"Tall?"

"Immensely tall!" (Rosa being short.)

"Must be gawky, I should think," is Rosa's quiet commentary.

"I beg your pardon; not at all," contradiction rising in him. "What is termed a fine woman, a splendid woman."

"Big nose, no doubt," is the quiet commentary again.

"Not a little one certainly," is the quick reply. (Rosa's being a little one.)

"Long pale nose, with a red nob in the middle. *I* know the sort of nose," says Rosa, with a satisfied nod, and tranquilly enjoying the Lumps.

"You *don't* know the sort of nose, Rosa," with some warmth; "because it's nothing of the kind."

"Not a pale nose, Eddy?"

"No." Determined not to assent.

"A red nose? Oh! I don't like red noses. However, to be sure, she can always powder it."

"She would scorn to powder it," says Edwin, becoming heated.

"Would she? What a stupid thing she must be! Is she stupid in everything?"

"No. In nothing."

After a pause, in which the whimsically wicked face has not been unobservant of him, Rosa says:

"And this most sensible of creatures likes the idea of being carried off to Egypt; does she, Eddy?"

"Yes. She takes a sensible interest in triumphs of engineering skill, especially when they are to change the whole condition of an undeveloped country."

"Lor!" says Rosa, shrugging her shoulders with a little laugh of wonder.

"Do you object," Edwin inquires with a majestic turn of his eyes downward upon the fairy figure—"do you object, Rosa, to her feeling that interest?"

"Object? My dear Eddy! But really. Doesn't she hate boilers and things?"

"I can answer for her not being so idiotic as to hate Boilers," he returns, with angry emphasis; "though I cannot answer for her views about things, really not understanding what Things are meant."

"But don't she hate Arabs, and Turks, and Fellahs, and people?"

"Certainly not," very firmly.

"At least she *must* hate the Pyramids? Come, Eddy?"

"Why should she be such a little—tall, I mean—goose, as to hate the Pyramids, Rosa?"

"Ah! you should hear Miss Twinkleton," often nodding her head, and much enjoying the Lumps, "bore about them, and then you wouldn't ask. Tiresome old burying-grounds! Isises, and Ibises, and Cheopses, and Pharaohses; who cares about them? And then there was Belzoni or somebody, dragged out by the legs, half-choked with bats and dust. All the girls say serve him right, and hope it hurt him, and wish he had been quite choked."

The two youthful figures, side by side, but not now arm in arm, wander discontentedly about the old Close; and each sometimes stops and slowly imprints a deeper footstep in the fallen leaves.

"Well!" says Edwin, after a lengthy silence. "According to custom. We can't get on, Rosa."

Rosa tosses her head, and says she don't want to get on.

"That's a pretty sentiment, Rosa, considering."

"Considering what?"

"If I say what, you'll go wrong again."

"*You'll* go wrong, you mean, Eddy. Don't be ungenerous."

"Ungenerous! I like that!"

"Then I *don't* like that, and so I tell you plainly," Rosa pouts.

"Now, Rosa, I put it to you. Who disparaged my profession, my destination—"

"You are not going to be buried in the Pyramids, I hope?" she interrupts, arching her delicate eyebrows. "You never said you were. If you are, why haven't you mentioned it to me? I can't find out your plans by instinct."

"Now, Rosa, you know very well what I mean, my dear."

"Well, then, why did you begin with your detestable red-nosed giantesses? And she would, she would, she would, she would, she WOULD powder it!" cries Rosa, in a little burst of comical contradictory spleen.

"Somehow or other, I never can come right in these discussions," says Edwin, sighing and becoming resigned.

"How is it possible, sir, that you ever can come right when you're always wrong? And as to Belzoni, I suppose he's dead—I'm sure I hope he is—and how can his legs, or his chokes, concern you?"

"It is nearly time for your return, Rosa. We have not had a very happy walk, have we?"

"A happy walk? A detestably unhappy walk, sir. If I go upstairs the moment I get in and cry till I can't take my dancing-lesson, you are responsible, mind!"

"Let us be friends, Rosa."

"Ah!" cries Rosa, shaking her head and bursting into real tears. "I wish we *could* be friends! It's because we can't be friends, that we try one another so. I am a young little thing, Eddy, to have an old heartache; but I really, really have, sometimes. Don't be angry. I know you have one yourself, too often. We should both of us have done better, if What is to be had been left, What might have been. I am quite a serious little thing now, and not teasing you. Let each of us forbear, this one time, on our own account, and on the other's!"

Disarmed by this glimpse of a woman's nature in the spoilt child, though for an instant disposed to resent it as seeming to involve the enforced infliction of himself upon her, Edwin Drood stands watching her as she childishly cries and sobs, with both hands to the handkerchief at her eyes, and then—she becoming more composed, and indeed beginning in her young inconstancy to laugh at herself for having been so moved—leads her to a seat hard by under the elm-trees.

"One clear word of understanding, Pussy dear. I am not clever out of my own line—now I come to think of it, I don't know that I am particularly clever in it—but I want to do right. There is not—there may be—I really don't see my way to what I want to say, but I must say it before we part—there is not any other young—"

"O no, Eddy! It's generous of you to ask me; but no, no, no!"

They have come very near to the Cathedral-windows, and at this moment the organ and the choir sound out sublimely. As they sit listening to the solemn swell, the confidence of last night rises in young Edwin Drood's mind, and he thinks how unlike this music is to that discordance.

"I fancy I can distinguish Jack's voice," is his remark, in a low tone in connection with the train of thought.

"Take me back at once, please," urges his affianced, quickly laying her light hand upon his wrist. "They will all be coming out directly; let us get away. O what a resounding chord! But don't let us stop to listen to it; let us get away!"

Her hurry is over, as soon as they have passed out of the Close. They go, arm in arm now, gravely and deliberately enough, along the old High Street, to the Nuns' House. At the gate, the street being within sight empty, Edwin bends down his face to Rosebud's.

She remonstrates, laughing, and is a childish school-girl again.

"Eddy, no! I'm too sticky to be kissed. But give me your hand, and I'll blow a kiss into that."

He does so. She breathes a light breath into it, and asks, retaining it and looking into it—

"Now say, what do you see?"

"See, Rosa?"

"Why, I thought you Egyptian boys could look into a hand and see all sorts of phantoms? Can't you see a happy Future?"

For certain, neither of them sees a happy Present, as the gate opens and closes, and one goes in and the other goes away.

CHAPTER IV.

MR. SAPSEA.

Accepting the Jackass as the type of self-sufficient stupidity and conceit—a custom, perhaps, like some few other customs, more conventional than fair—then the purest Jackass in Cloisterham is Mr. Thomas Sapsea, Auctioneer.

Mr. Sapsea "dresses at" the Dean; has been bowed to for the Dean, in mistake; has even been spoken to in the street as My Lord, under the impression that he was the Bishop come down unexpectedly, without his chaplain. Mr. Sapsea is very proud of this, and of his voice, and of his style. He has even (in selling landed property) tried the experiment of slightly intoning in his pulpit, to make himself more like what he takes to be the genuine ecclesiastical article. So, in ending a Sale by Public Auction, Mr. Sapsea finishes off with an air of bestowing a benediction on the assembled brokers, which leaves the real Dean—a modest and worthy gentleman—far behind.

Mr. Sapsea has many admirers; indeed, the proposition is carried by a large local majority, even including non-believers in his wisdom, that he is a credit to Cloisterham. He possesses the great qualities of being portentous and dull, and of having a roll in his speech, and another roll in his gait; not to mention a certain gravely-flowing action with his hands, as if he were presently going to Confirm the individual with whom he holds discourse. Much nearer sixty years of age than fifty, with a flowing outline of stomach, and horizontal creases in his waistcoat; reputed to be rich; voting at elections in the strictly respectable interest; morally satisfied that nothing but he himself has grown since he was a baby; how can dunder-headed Mr. Sapsea be otherwise than a credit to Cloisterham, and society?

Mr. Sapsea's premises are in the High Street, over against the Nuns

House. They are of about the period of the Nuns' House, irregularly modernized here and there, as steadily deteriorating generations found, more and more, that they preferred air and light to Fever and the Plague. Over the doorway, is a wooden effigy, about half life-size, representing Mr. Sapsea's father, in a curly wig and toga, in the act of selling. The chastity of the idea, and the natural appearance of the little finger, hammer, and pulpit, have been much admired.

Mr. Sapsea sits in his dull ground-floor sitting-room, gazing first on his paved back-yard, and then on his railed-off garden. Mr. Sapsea has a bottle of port-wine on a table before the fire—the fire is an early luxury, but pleasant on the cool chilly autumn evening—and is characteristically attended by his portrait, his eight-day clock, and his weather-glass. Characteristically, because he would uphold himself against mankind, his weather-glass against weather, and his clock against time.

By Mr. Sapsea's side on the table are a writing-desk and writing materials. Glancing at a scrap of manuscript, Mr. Sapsea reads it to himself with a lofty air, and then, slowly pacing the room with his thumbs in the arm holes of his waistcoat, repeats it from memory: so internally, though with much dignity, that the word "Ethelinda" is alone audible.

There are three wine-glasses in a tray on the table. His serving-maid entering, and announcing "Mr. Jasper is come, sir," Mr. Sapsea waves "Admit him," and draws two wine-glasses from the rank, as being claimed.

"Glad to see you, sir. I congratulate myself on having the honor of receiving you here for the first time." Mr. Sapsea does the honors of his house in this wise.

"You are very good. The honor is mine and the self-congratulation is mine."

"You are pleased to say so, sir. But I do assure you that it is a satisfaction to me to receive you in my humble home. And that is what I would not say to everybody." Ineffable loftiness on Mr. Sapsea's part accompanies these words, as leaving the sentence to be understood: "You will not easily believe that your society can be a satisfaction to a man like myself; nevertheless, it is."

"I have for some time desired to know you, Mr. Sapsea."

"And I, sir, have long known you by reputation as a man of taste. Let me fill your glass. I will give you, sir," says Mr. Sapsea, filling his own,

"When the French come over,
May we meet them at Dover!"

This was a patriotic toast in Mr. Sapsea's infancy, and he is therefore fully convinced of its being appropriate to any subsequent era.

"You can scarcely be ignorant, Mr. Sapsea," observes Jasper, watching the auctioneer with a smile as the latter stretches out his legs before the fire, "that you know the world."

"Well, sir," is the chuckling reply, "I think I know something of it; something of it."

"Your reputation for that knowledge has always interested and surprised me, and made me wish to know you. For, Cloisterham is a little place. Cooped up in it myself, I know nothing beyond it, and feel it to be a very little place."

"If I have not gone to foreign countries, young man," Mr. Sapsea begins, and then stops: "You will excuse my calling you young man, Mr. Jasper? You are much my junior."

"By all means."

"If I have not gone to foreign countries, young man, foreign countries have come to me. They have come to me in the way of business, and I have improved upon my opportunities. Put it that I take an inventory, or make a catalogue. I see a French clock. I never saw him before in my life, but I instantly lay my finger on him and say 'Paris!' I see some cups and saucers of Chinese make, equally strangers to me personally: I put my finger on them, then and there, and I say 'Pekin, Nankin, and Canton.' It is the same with Japan, with Egypt, and with bamboo and sandal-wood from the East Indies; I put my finger on them all. I have put my finger on the North Pole before now, and said, 'Spear of Esquimaux make, for half a pint of pale sherry!'"

"Really? A very remarkable way, Mr. Sapsea, of acquiring a knowledge of men and things."

"I mention it, sir," Mr. Sapsea rejoins, with unspeakable complacency, "because, as I say, it don't do to boast of what you are; but show how you came to be it, and then you prove it."

"Most interesting. We were to speak of the late Mrs. Sapsea."

"We were, sir." Mr. Sapsea fills both glasses, and takes the decanter into safe keeping again. "Before I consult your opinion as a man of taste on this little trifle"—holding it up—"which is *but* a trifle, and still has required some thought, sir, some little fever of the brow, I ought perhaps to describe the character of the late Mrs. Sapsea, now dead three-quarters of a year."

Mr. Jasper, in the act of yawning behind his wine-glass, puts down that screen, and calls up a look of interest. It is a little impaired in its expressiveness by his having a shut-up gape still to dispose of, with watering eyes.

"Half a dozen years ago, or so," Mr. Sapsea proceeds, "when I had enlarged my mind up to—I will not say to what it now is, for that might seem to aim at too much, but up to the pitch of wanting another mind to be absorbed in it—I cast my eye about me for a nuptial partner. Because, as I say, it is not good for man to be alone."

Mr. Jasper appears to commit this original idea to memory.

"Miss Brobity at that time kept, I will not call it the rival establishment to the establishment at the Nuns' House opposite, but I will call it the other parallel establishment down town. The world did have it that she showed a passion for attending my sales, when they took place on half-holidays, or in vacation time. The world did put it about, that she admired my style. The world did notice that, as time flowed by, my style became traceable in the dictation-exercises of Miss Brobity's pupils. Young man, a whisper even sprang up in obscure malignity, that one ignorant and besotted Churl (a parent) so committed himself as to object to it by name. But I do not believe this. For, is it likely that any human creature in his right senses would so lay himself open to be pointed at, by what I call the finger of scorn?"

Mr. Jasper shakes his head. Not in the least likely. Mr. Sapsea, in a grandiloquent state of absence of mind, seems to refill his visitor's glass, which is full already; and does really refill his own, which is empty.

"Miss Brobity's Being, young man, was deeply imbued with homage to mind. She revered Mind, when launched, or, as I say, precipitated, on an extensive knowledge of the world. When I made my proposal, she did me the honor to be so overshadowed with a species of Awe, as to be able to articulate only the two words, 'Oh Thou!'—meaning myself. Her limpid blue eyes were fixed upon me, her semi-transparent hands were clasped together, pallor overspread her aquiline features, and, though encouraged to proceed, she never did proceed a word further. I disposed of the parallel establishment, by private contract, and we became as nearly one as could be expected under the circumstances. But she never could, and she never did, find a phrase satisfactory to her perhaps-too-favorable estimate of my intellect. To the very last (feeble action of liver), she addressed me in the same unfinished terms."

Mr. Jasper has closed his eyes as the auctioneer has deepened his voice. He now abruptly opens them, and says, in unison with the deepened voice, "Ah!"—rather as if stopping himself on the extreme verge of adding—"men!"

"I have been since," says Mr. Sapsea, with his legs stretched out, and solemnly enjoying himself with the wine and the fire, "what you behold me; I have been since a solitary mourner; I have been since, as I say, wasting my evening conversation on the desert air. I will not say that I have reproached myself; but there have been times when I have asked myself the question: What if her husband had been nearer on a level with her? If she had not had to look up quite so high, what might the stimulating action have been upon the liver?"

Mr. Jasper says, with an appearance of having fallen into dreadfully low spirits, that "he supposes it was to be."

"We can only suppose so, sir," Mr. Sapsea coincides. "As I say, Man proposes, Heaven disposes. It may or may not be putting the same thought in another form; but that is the way I put it."

Mr. Jasper murmurs assent.

"And now, Mr. Jasper," resumes the auctioneer, producing his scrap of manuscript, "Mrs. Sapsea's monument having had full time to settle and dry, let me take your opinion, as a man of taste, on the inscription I have (as I before remarked, not without some little fever of the brow) drawn out for it. Take it in your own hand. The setting-out of the lines requires to be followed with the eye, as well as the contents with the mind."

Mr. Jasper complying, sees and reads as follows:

ETHELINDA,
Reverential Wife of
MR. THOMAS SAPSEA,
AUCTIONEER, VALUER, ESTATE AGENT, ETC.,
OF THIS CITY,
Whose Knowledge of the World,
Though somewhat extensive,
Never brought him acquainted with
A SPIRIT
More capable of
LOOKING UP TO HIM.
STRANGER PAUSE
And ask thyself the Question,
CANST THOU DO LIKEWISE?
If not,
WITH A BLUSH RETIRE.

Mr. Sapsea having risen and stationed himself with his back to the fire, for the purpose of observing the effect of these lines on the countenance of a man of taste, consequently has his face toward the door, when his serving-maid, again appearing, announces, "Durdles is come, sir!" He promptly draws forth and fills the third wine-glass, as being now claimed, and replies, "Show Durdles in."

"Admirable!" quoth Mr. Jasper, handing back the paper.

"You approve, sir?"

"Impossible not to approve. Striking, characteristic, and complete."

The auctioneer inclines his head, as one accepting his due and giving a receipt; and invites the entering Durdles to take off that glass of wine (handing the same), for it will warm him.

Durdles is a stone-mason; chiefly in the gravestone, tomb, and monument way, and wholly of their color from head to foot. No man is better known in Cloisterham. He is the chartered libertine of the place. Fame trumpets him a wonderful workman—which, for aught that anybody knows, he may be (as he never works); and a wonderful sot—which everybody knows he is. With the Cathedral crypt he is better acquainted than any living authority; it may even be than any dead one. It is said that the intimacy of this acquaintance began in his habitually resorting to that secret place, to lock out the Cloisterham boy-populace, and sleep off the fumes of liquor: he having ready access to the Cathedral, as contractor for rough repairs. Be this as it may, he does know much about it, and in the demolition of impedimental fragments of wall, buttress, and pavement, has seen strange sights. He often speaks of himself in the third person; perhaps being a little misty as to his own identity when he narrates; perhaps impartially adopting the Cloisterham nomenclature in reference to a character of acknowledged distinction. Thus he will say, touching his strange sights: "Durdles come upon the old chap," in reference to a buried magnate of ancient time and high degree, "by striking right into the coffin with his pick. The old chap gave Durdles a look with his open eyes, as much as to say, 'Is your name Durdles? Why, my man, I've been waiting for you a Devil of a time!' And then he turned to powder." With a two-foot rule always in his pocket, Durdles goes continually sounding and tapping all about and about the Cathedral; and whenever he says to Tope: "Tope, here's another old 'un in here!" Tope announces it to the Dean as an established discovery.

In a suit of coarse flannel with horn buttons, a yellow neckerchief with draggled ends, an old hat more russet-colored than black, and laced boots of the hue of his stony calling, Durdles leads a hazy, gypsy sort of life, carrying his dinner about with him in a small bundle, and sitting on all manner of tombstones to dine. This dinner of Durdles's has become quite a Cloisterham institution: not only because of his never appearing in public without it, but because of its having been, on certain renowned occasions, taken into custody along with Durdles (as drunk and incapable), and exhibited before the Bench of Justices at the Town Hall. These occasions, however, have been few and far apart; Durdles being as seldom drunk as sober. For the rest, he is an old bachelor, and he lives in a little antiquated hole of a house that was never finished: supposed to be built, so far, of stones stolen from the city wall. To this abode there is an approach, ankle-deep in stone-chips, resembling a petrified grove of tombstones, urns, draperies, and broken columns, in all stages of sculpture. Herein, two journeymen incessantly chip, while other two journeymen, who face each other, incessantly saw stone; dipping as regularly in and out of their sheltering sentry-boxes, as if they were mechanical figures emblematical of Time and Death.

To Durdles, when he has consumed his glass of port, Mr. Sapsea intrusts that precious effort of his Muse. Durdles unfeelingly takes out his two-foot rule, and measures the lines calmly, alloying them with stone-grit.

"This is for the monument, is it, Mr. Sapsea?"

"The Inscription. Yes." Mr. Sapsea waits for its effect on a common mind.

"It'll come in to a eighth of a inch," says Durdles. "Your servant, Mr. Jasper. Hope I see you well."

"How are you, Durdles?"

"I've got a touch of the Tombatism on me, Mr. Jasper, but that I must expect."

"You mean the Rheumatism," says Sapsea, in a sharp tone. (He is nettled by having his composition so mechanically received.)

"No, I don't. I mean, Mr. Sapsea, the Tombatism. It's another sort from Rheumatism. Mr. Jasper knows what Durdles means. You get among them Tombs afore it's well light on a winter morning, and keep on, as the Catechism says, a-walking in the same all the days of your life, and *you*'ll know what Durdles means."

"It is a bitter cold place," Mr. Jasper assents, with an antipathetic shiver.

"And if it's bitter cold for you, up in the chancel, with a lot of live breath smoking out about you, what the bitterness is to Durdles, down in the crypt among the earthy damps there, and the dead breath of the old 'uns," returns that individual, "Durdles leaves you to judge.—Is this to be put in hand at once, Mr. Sapsea?"

Mr. Sapsea, with an Author's anxiety to rush into publication, replies that it cannot be out of hand too soon.

"You had better let me have the key, then," says Durdles.

"Why, man, it is not to be put inside the monument!"

"Durdles knows where it's to be put, Mr. Sapsea; no man better. Ask 'ere a man in Cloisterham whether Durdles knows his work."

Mr. Sapsea rises, takes a key from a drawer, unlocks an iron safe let into the wall, and takes from it another key.

"When Durdles puts a touch or a finish upon his work, no matter where, inside or outside, Durdles likes to look at his work all round, and see that his work is a-doing him credit," Durdles explains, doggedly.

The key proffered him by the bereaved widower being a large one, he slips his two-foot-rule into a side-pocket of his flannel trousers made for it, and deliberately opens his flannel coat, and opens the mouth of a large breast-pocket within it before taking the key to place it in that repository.

"Why, Durdles!" exclaims Jasper, looking on amused. "You are undermined with pockets!"

"And I carries weight in 'em, too, Mr. Jasper. Feel those;" producing two other large keys.

"Hand me Mr. Sapsea's likewise. Surely this is the heaviest of the three."

"You'll find 'em much of a muchness, I expect," says Durdles. "They all belong to monuments. They all open Durdles's work. Durdles keeps the keys of his work mostly. Not that they're much used."

"By-the-by," it comes into Jasper's mind to say, as he idly examines the keys: "I have been going to ask you, many a day, and have always forgotten. You know they sometimes call you Stony Durdles, don't you?"

"Cloisterham knows me as Durdles, Mr. Jasper."

"I am aware of that, of course. But the boys sometimes—"

"Oh! If you mind them young Imps of boys—" Durdles gruffly interrupts.

"I don't mind them, any more than you do. But there was a discussion the other day among the Choir, whether Stony stood for Tony;" clinking one key against another.

("Take care of the wards, Mr. Jasper.")

"Or whether Stony stood for Stephen;" clinking with a change of keys.

("You can't make a pitch-pipe of 'em, Mr. Jasper.")

"Or whether the name comes from your trade. How stands the fact?"

Mr. Jasper weighs the three keys in his hand, lifts his head from his idly-stooping attitude over the fire, and delivers the keys to Durdles with an ingenuous and friendly face.

But the stony one is a gruff one likewise, and that hazy state of his is always an uncertain state, highly conscious of its dignity, and prone to take offence. He drops his two keys back into his pocket one by one, and buttons them up; he takes his dinner-bundle from the chair-back on which he hung it when he came in; he distributes the weight he carries, by tying the third key up in it, as though he were an Ostrich, and liked to dine off cold iron; and he gets out of the room, deigning no word of answer.

Mr. Sapsea then proposes a hit at backgammon, which, seasoned with his own improving conversation, and terminating in a supper of cold roast-beef and salad, beguiles the golden evening until pretty late. Mr. Sapsea's wisdom being, in its delivery to mortals, rather of the diffuse than the epigrammatic order, is by no means expended even then; but his visitor intimates that he will come back for more of the precious commodity on future occasions, and Mr. Sapsea lets him off for the present, to ponder on the instalment he carries away.

John Jasper, on his way home through the Close, is brought to a stand-still by the spectacle of Stony Durdles, dinner-bundle and all, leaning his back against the iron railing of the burial-ground enclosing it from the old cloister-arches; and a hideous small boy in rags flinging stones at him as a well-defined mark in the moonlight. Sometimes the stones hit him, and sometimes they miss him, but Durdles seems indifferent to either fortune. The hideous small boy, on the contrary, whenever he hits Durdles, blows a whistle of triumph through a jagged gap convenient for the purpose, in the front of his mouth, where half his teeth are wanting; and whenever he misses him, yelps out "Mulled agin!" and tries to atone for the failure by taking a more correct and vicious aim.

"What are you doing to the man?" demands Jasper, stepping out into the moonlight from the shade.

"Making a cock-shy of him," replies the hideous small boy.

"Give me those stones in your hand."

"Yes, I'll give 'em you down your throat, if you come a-ketching hold of me," says the small boy, shaking himself loose, and backing. "I'll smash your eye, if you don't look out!"

"Baby-Devil that you are, what has the man done to you?"

"He won't go home."

"What is that to you?"

"He gives me a 'apenny to pelt him home if I ketches him out too late," says the boy. And then chants, like a little savage, half stumbling and half dancing among the rags and laces of his dilapidated boots:

> "Widdy widdy wen!
> I—ket—ches—Im—out—ar—ter—ten,
> Widdy widdy wy!
> Then—E—don't—go—then—I—shy—
> Widdy Widdy Wake-cock warning!"

—with a comprehensive sweep on the last word, and one more delivery at Durdles.

This would seem to be a poetical note of preparation, agreed upon, as a caution to Durdles to stand clear if he can, or to betake himself homeward.

John Jasper invites the boy with a beck of his head to follow him (feeling it hopeless to drag him, or coax him) and crosses to the iron railing where the Stony (and stoned) One is profoundly meditating.

"Do you know this thing, this child?" asks Jasper, at a loss for a word that will define this thing.

"Deputy," says Durdles, with a nod.

"Is that it's—his—name?"

"Deputy," assents Durdles.

"I'm man-servant up at the Travellers' Twopenny in Gas Works Garding," this thing explains. "All us man-servants at Travellers' Lodgins is named Deputy. When we're chock full and the Travellers is all a-bed I come out for my 'elth." Then withdrawing into the road, and taking aim, he resumes:

> "Widdy widdy wen!
> I—ket—ches—Im—out—ar—ter—"

"Hold your hand," cries Jasper, "and don't throw while I stand so near him, or I'll kill you!—Come, Durdles; let me walk home with you to-night. Shall I carry your bundle?"

"Not on any account," replies Durdles, adjusting it. "Durdles was making his reflections here when you come up, sir, surrounded by his works, like a poplar author.—Your own brother-in-law;" introducing a sarcophagus within the railing, white and cold in the moonlight. "Mrs. Sapsea;" introducing the monument of that devoted wife. "Late Incumbent;" introducing the Reverend Gentleman's broken column. "Departed Assessed Taxes;" introducing a vase and towel, standing on what might represent the cake of soap. "Former pastry-cook and muffin-maker, much respected;" introducing gravestone. "All safe and sound here, sir, and all Durdles's work! Of the common

3

folk that is merely bundled up in turf and brambles, the less said, the better. A poor lot, soon forgot."

"This creature, Deputy, is behind us," says Jasper, looking back. "Is he to follow us?"

The relations between Durdles and Deputy are of a capricious kind; for, on Durdles's turning himself about with the slow gravity of beery soddenness, Deputy makes a pretty wide circuit into the road, and stands on the defensive.

"You never cried Widdy Warning before you begun to-night," says Durdles, unexpectedly reminded of, or imagining, an injury.

"Yer lie, I did," says Deputy, in his only form of polite contradiction.

"Own brother, sir," observes Durdles, turning himself about again, and as unexpectedly forgetting his offence as he had recalled or conceived it; "own brother to Peter the Wild Boy! But I gave him an object in life."

"At which he takes aim?" Mr. Jasper suggests.

"That's it, sir," returns Durdles, quite satisfied; "at which he takes aim. I took him in hand and gave him an object. What was he before? A destroyer. What work did he do? Nothing but destruction. What did he earn by it? Short terms in Cloisterham Jail. Not a person, not a piece of property, not a winder, not a horse, nor a dog, nor a cat, nor a bird, nor a fowl, nor a pig, but what he stoned, for want of an enlightened object. I put that enlighted object before him, and now he can turn his honest half-penny by the three penn'orth a week."

"I wonder he has no competitors."

"He has plenty, Mr. Jasper, but he stones 'em all away. Now, I don't know what this scheme of mine comes to," pursues Durdles, considering about it with the same sodden gravity; "I don't know what you may precisely call it. It ain't a sort of a—scheme of a—National Education?"

"I should say not," replies Jasper.

"*I* should say not," assents Durdles; "then we won't try to give it a name."

"He still keeps behind us," repeats Jasper, looking over his shoulder; "is he to follow us?"

"We can't help going round by the Travellers' Twopenny, if we go the short way, which is the back way," Durdles answers, "and we'll drop him there."

So they go on; Deputy, as a rear-rank of one, taking open order, and invading the silence of the hour and place by stoning every wall, post, pillar, and other inanimate object, by the deserted way.

"Is there any thing new down in the crypt, Durdles?" asks John Jasper.

"Any thing old, I think you mean," growls Durdles. "It ain't a spot for novelty."

"Any new discovery on your part, I meant."

"There's a old 'un under the seventh pillar on the left as you go down the broken steps of the little underground chapel as formerly was; I make him out (so fur as I've made him out yet) to be one of them old 'uns with a crook. To judge from the size of the passages in the walls, and of the steps and doors, by which they come and went, them crooks must have been a good deal in the way of the old 'uns! Two on 'em meeting promiscuous must have hitched one another by the mitre, pretty often, I should say."

Without any endeavor to correct the literality of this opinion, Jasper surveys his companion—covered from head to foot with old mortar, lime, and stone grit—as though he, Jasper, were getting imbued with a romantic interest in his weird life.

"Your's is a curious existence."

Without furnishing the least clew to the question, whether he receives this as a compliment or as quite the reverse, Durdles gruffly answers: "Yours is another."

"Well! Inasmuch as my lot is cast in the same old earthy, chilly, never-changing place, Yes. But there is much more mystery and interest in your connection with the Cathedral than in mine. Indeed, I am beginning to have some idea of asking you to take me on as a sort of student, or free 'prentice, under you, and to let me go about with you sometimes, and see some of these odd nooks in which you pass your days."

The Stony One replies, in a general way, All right. Every body knows where to find Durdles, when he's wanted. Which, if not strictly true, is approximately so, if taken to express that Durdles may always be found in a state of vagabondage somewhere.

"What I dwell upon most," says Jasper, pursuing his subject of romantic interest, "is the remarkable accuracy with which you would seem to find out where people are buried.—What is the matter? That bundle is in your way; let me hold it."

Durdles has stopped and backed a little (Deputy, attentive to all his movements, immediately skirmishing into the road) and was looking about for some ledge or corner to place his bundle on, when thus relieved of it.

"Just you give me my hammer out of that," says Durdles, "and I'll show you."

Clink, clink. And his hammer is handed him.

"Now lookee here. You pitch your note, don't you, Mr. Jasper?"

"Yes."

"So I sound for mine. I take my hammer, and I tap." (Here he strikes the pavement, and the attentive Deputy skirmishes at a rather wider range, as supposing that his head may be in requisition.) "I tap, tap, tap. Solid! I go on tapping. Solid still! Tap again. Halloa! Hollow! Tap again, persevering. Solid in hollow! Tap, tap, tap, to try it better. Solid in hollow; and inside solid, hollow again! There you are! Old 'un crumbled away in stone coffin, in vault!"

"Astonishing!"

"I have even done this," says Durdles, drawing out his two-foot rule (Deputy meanwhile skirmishing nearer, as suspecting that Treasure may be about to be discovered, which may somehow lead to his own enrichment, and the delicious treat of the discoverers being hanged by the neck, on his evidence, until they are dead). "Say that hammer of mine's a wall—my work. Two; four; and two is six," measuring on the pavement. "Six foot inside that wall is Mrs. Sapsea."

"Not really Mrs. Sapsea?"

"Say Mrs. Sapsea. Her wall's thicker, but say Mrs. Sapsea. Durdles taps that wall represented by that hammer and says, after good sounding: 'Something betwixt us!' Sure enough, some rubbish has been left in that same six-foot space by Durdles's men!"

Jasper opines that such accuracy "is a gift."

"I wouldn't have it at a gift," returns Durdles, by no means receiving the observation in good part. "I worked it out for myself. Durdles comes by *his* knowledge through grubbing deep for it, and having it up by the roots when it don't want to come.—Halloa you Deputy!"

"Widdy!" is Deputy's shrill response, standing off again.

"Catch that ha'penny. And don't let me see any more of you tonight, after we come to the Travellers' Twopenny."

"Warning!" returns Deputy, having caught the halfpenny, and appearing by this mystic word to express his assent to the arrangement.

They have but to cross what was once the vineyard, belonging to what was once the Monastery, to come into the narrow back lane wherein stands the crazy wooden house of two low stories currently known as the Travellers' Twopenny:—a house all warped and distorted, like the morals of the travellers, with scant remains of a lattice-work porch over the door, and also of a rustic fence before its stamped-out garden; by reason of the travellers being so bound to the premises by a tender sentiment (or so fond of having a fire by the roadside in the course of the day), that they never can be persuaded or threatened into departure, without violently possessing themselves of some wooden forget-me-not, and bearing it off.

The semblance of an inn is attempted to be given to this wretched place by fragments of conventional red curtaining in the windows, which rags are made muddily transparent in the night-season by feeble lights of rush or cotton dip burning dully in the close air of the inside. As Durdles and Jasper come near, they are addressed by an inscribed paper lantern over the door, setting forth the purport of the house. They are also addressed by some half-dozen other hideous small boys—whether twopenny lodgers or followers or hangers-on of such, who knows!—who, as if attracted by some carrion-scent of Deputy in the air, start into the moonlight, as vultures might gather in the desert, and instantly fall to stoning him and one another.

"Stop, you young brutes," cries Jasper angrily, "and let us go by!"

This remonstrance being received with yells and flying stones, according to a custom of late years comfortably established among the police regulations of our English communities, where Christians are stoned on all sides, as if the days of Saint Stephen were revived, Durdles remarks of the young savages with some point, that "they haven't got an object," and leads the way down the lane.

At the corner of the lane, Jasper, hotly enraged, checks his companion and looks back. All is silent. Next moment, a stone coming rattling at his hat, and a distant yell of "Wake-cock Warning!" followed by a crow, as from some infernally-hatched Chanticleer, apprising him under whose victorious fire he stands, he turns the corner into safety, and takes Durdles home: Durdles stumbling among the litter of his stony yard as if he were going to turn head foremost into one of the unfinished tombs.

John Jasper returns by another way to his gate-house, and entering softly with his key, finds his fire still burning. He takes from a locked press, a peculiar-looking pipe which he fills—but not with tobacco—and, having adjusted the contents of the bowl, very carefully, with a little instrument, ascends an inner staircase of only a few steps, leading to two rooms. One of these is his own sleeping-chamber: the other, is his nephew's. There is a light in each.

His nephew lies asleep, calm and untroubled. John Jasper stands looking down upon him, his unlighted pipe in his hand, for some time, with a fixed and deep attention. Then, hushing his footsteps, he passes to his own room, lights his pipe, and delivers himself to the Spectres it invokes at midnight.

CHAPTER V.

PHILANTHROPY IN MINOR CANON CORNER.

The Reverend Septimus Crisparkle (Septimus, because six little brother Crisparkles before him went out, one by one, as they were born, like six weak little rushlights, as they were lighted) having broken the thin morning ice near Cloisterham Weir with his amiable head, much to the invigoration of his frame, was now assisting his circulation by boxing at a looking-glass with great science and prowess. A fresh and healthy portrait the looking-glass presented of the Reverend Septimus, feinting and dodging with the utmost artfulness, and hitting out from the shoulder with the utmost straightness, while his radiant features teemed with innocence, and soft-hearted benevolence beamed from his boxing-gloves.

It was scarcely breakfast-time yet, for Mrs. Crisparkle—mother, not wife of the Reverend Septimus—was only just down, and waiting for the urn. Indeed, the Reverend Septimus left off at this very moment to take the pretty old lady's entering face between his boxing-gloves and kiss it. Having done so with tenderness, the Reverend Septimus turned to again, countering with his left, and putting in his right, in a tremendous manner.

"I say, every morning of my life, that you'll do it at last, Sept," remarked the old lady, looking on; "and so you will."

"Do what, Ma dear?"

"Break the pier-glass, or burst a blood-vessel."

"Neither, please God, Ma dear. Here's wind, Ma. Look at this!"

In a concluding round of great severity, the Reverend Septimus administered and escaped all sorts of punishment, and wound up by getting the old lady's cap into Chancery—such is the technical term used in scientific circles by the learned in the Noble Art—with a lightness of touch that hardly stirred the lightest lavender or cherry ribbon on it. Magnanimously releasing the defeated, just in time to get his gloves into a drawer, and feign to be looking out of window in a contemplative state of mind when a servant entered, the Reverend Septimus then gave place to the urn and other preparations for breakfast. These completed, and the two alone again, it was pleasant to see (or would have been, if there had been any one to see it, which there never was) the old lady standing to say the Lord's Prayer aloud, and her son, Minor Canon nevertheless, standing with bent head to hear it, he being within five years of forty: much as he had stood to hear the same words from the same lips when he was within five months of four.

What is prettier than an old lady—except a young lady—when her eyes are bright, when her figure is trim and compact, when her face is cheerful and calm, when her dress is as the dress of a china shepherdess: so dainty in its colors, so individually assorted to herself, so neatly moulded on her? Nothing is prettier, thought the good Minor Canon frequently, when taking his seat at table opposite his long-widowed mother. Her thought at such times may be condensed into the two words that oftenest did duty together in all her conversations: "My Sept!"

They were a good pair to sit breakfasting together in Minor Canon Corner, Cloisterham. For Minor Canon Corner was a quiet place in the shadow of the Cathedral, which the cawing of the rooks, the echoing footsteps of rare passers, the sound of the Cathedral bell, or the roll of the Cathedral organ, seemed to render more quiet than absolute silence. Swaggering fighting-men had had their centuries of ramping and raving about Minor Canon Corner, and beaten serfs had had their centuries of drudging and dying there, and powerful monks had had their centuries of being sometimes useful and sometimes harmful there, and behold they were all gone out of Minor Canon Corner, and so much the better. Perhaps one of the highest uses of their ever having been there, was, that there might be left behind that blessed air of tranquillity which pervaded Minor Canon Corner, and that serenely romantic state of the mind—productive for the most part of pity and forbearance—which is engendered by a sorrowful story that is all told, or a pathetic play that is played out.

Red-brick walls harmoniously toned down in color by time, strong-rooted ivy, latticed windows, panelled rooms, big oaken beams in little places, and stoned-walled gardens where annual fruit yet ripened upon monkish trees, were the principal surroundings of pretty old Mrs. Crisparkle and the Reverend Septimus as they sat at breakfast.

"And what, Ma dear," inquired the Minor Canon, giving proof of a wholesome and vigorous appetite, "does the letter say?"

The pretty old lady, after reading it, had just laid it down upon the breakfast-cloth. She handed it over to her son.

Now the old lady was exceedingly proud of her bright eyes being so clear that she could read writing without spectacles. Her son was also so proud of the circumstance, and so dutifully bent on her deriving the utmost possible gratification from it, that he had invented the pretence that he himself could *not* read writing without spectacles. Therefore he now assumed a pair, of grave and prodigious proportions, which not only seriously inconvenienced his nose and his breakfast, but seriously impeded his perusal of the letter. For he had the eyes of a microscope and a telescope combined, when they were unassisted.

"It's from Mr. Honeythunder, of course," said the old lady, folding her arms.

"Of course," assented her son. He then lamely read on:

"HAVEN OF PHILANTHROPY,
"CHIEF OFFICES, LONDON, WEDNESDAY.

"DEAR MADAM,

"'I write in the—' In the what's this? What does he write in?"

"In the chair," said the old lady.

The Reverend Septimus took off his spectacles, that he might see her face, as he exclaimed—

"Why, what should he write in?"

"Bless me, bless me, Sept," returned the old lady, "you don't see the context! Give it back to me, my dear."

Glad to get his spectacles off (for they always made his eyes water) her son obeyed, murmuring that his sight for reading manuscript got worse and worse daily.

"'I write,'" his mother went on, reading very perspicuously and precisely, "'from the chair, to which I shall probably be confined for some hours.'"

Septimus looked at the row of chairs against the wall, with a half-protesting and half-appealing countenance.

"'We have,'" the old lady read on with a little extra emphasis, "'a meeting of our Convened Chief Composite Committee of Central and District Philanthropists, at our Head Haven as above; and it is their unanimous pleasure that I take the chair.'"

Septimus breathed more freely, and muttered, "Oh! If he comes to *that*, let him."

"'Not to lose a day's post, I take the opportunity of a long report being read, denouncing a public miscreant—'"

"It is a most extraordinary thing," interposed the gentle Minor Canon, laying down his knife and fork to rub his ear in a vexed manner, "that these Philanthropists are always denouncing somebody. And it is another most extraordinary thing that they are always so violently flush of miscreants!"

"'Denouncing a public miscreant!'"—the old lady resumed, "'to get our little affair of business off my mind. I have spoken with my two wards, Neville and Helena Landless, on the subject of their defective education, and they give in to the plan proposed; as I should have taken good care they did, whether they liked it or not.'"

"And it is another most extraordinary thing," remarked the Minor Canon in the same tone as before, "that these Philanthropists are so given to seizing their fellow-creatures by the scruff of the neck, and (as one may say) bumping them into the paths of peace.—I beg your pardon, Ma dear, for interrupting."

"'Therefore, dear Madam, you will please prepare your son, the Rev. Mr. Septimus, to expect Neville, as an inmate to be read with, on Monday next. On the same day Helena will accompany him to Cloisterham, to take up her quarters at the Nuns' House, the establishment recommended by yourself and son jointly. Please likewise to prepare for her reception and tuition there. The terms in both cases are understood to be exactly as stated to me in writing by yourself, when I opened a correspondence with you on this subject, after the honor of being introduced to you at your sister's house in town here. With compliments to the Rev. Mr. Septimus, I am, Dear Madam, Your affectionate brother (In Philanthropy), LUKE HONEYTHUNDER.'"

"Well, Ma," said Septimus, after a little more rubbing of his ear, "we must try it. There can be no doubt that we have room for an inmate, and that I have time to bestow upon him, and inclination too. I must confess to feeling rather glad that he is not Mr. Honeythunder himself. Though that seems wretchedly prejudiced—does it not?—for I never saw him. Is he a large man, Ma?"

"I should call him a large man, my dear," the old lady replied, after some hesitation, "but that his voice is so much larger."

"Than himself?"

"Than anybody."

"Hah!" said Septimus. And finished his breakfast as if the flavor of the Superior Family Souchong, and also of the ham and toast and eggs, were a little on the wane.

Mrs. Crisparkle's sister, another piece of Dresden china, and matching her so neatly that they would have made a delightful pair of ornaments for the two ends of any capacious old-fashioned chimney-piece, and by right should never have been seen apart, was the childless wife of a clergyman holding Corporation preferment in London City. Mr. Honeythunder, in his public character of Professor of Philanthropy, had come to know Mrs. Crisparkle during the last rematching of the china ornaments (in other words during her last annual visit to her sister), after a public occasion of a philanthropic nature, when certain devoted orphans of tender years had been glutted with plum buns and plump bumptiousness. These were all the antecedents known in Minor Canon Corner of the coming pupils.

"I am sure you will agree with me, Ma," said Mr. Crisparkle, after thinking the matter over, "that the first thing to be done, is, to put these young people as much at their ease as possible. There is nothing disinterested in the notion, because we cannot be at our ease with them unless they are at their ease with us. Now, Jasper's nephew is down here at present; and like takes to like, and youth takes to youth. He is a cordial young fellow, and we will have him to meet the brother and sister at dinner. That's three. We can't think of asking him, without asking Jasper. That's four. Add Miss Twinkleton and the fairy bride that is to be, and that's six. Add our two selves, and that's eight. Would eight at a friendly dinner at all put you out, Ma?"

"Nine would, Sept," returned the old lady, visibly nervous.

"My dear Ma, I particularize eight."

"The exact size of the table and the room, my dear."

So it was settled that way; and when Mr. Crisparkle called with his mother upon Miss Twinkleton, to arrange for the reception of Miss Helena Landless at the Nuns' House, the two other invitations having reference to that establishment were proffered and accepted. Miss Twinkleton did, indeed, glance at the globes, as regretting that they were not formed to be taken out into society; but became reconciled to leaving them behind. Instructions were then dispatched to the Philanthropist for the departure and arrival, in good time for dinner, of Mr. Neville and Miss Helena; and stock for soup became fragrant in the air of Minor Canon Corner.

In those days there was no railway to Cloisterham, and Mr. Sapsea said there never would be. Mr. Sapsea said more; he said there never should be. And yet, marvellous to consider, it has come to pass, in these days, that Express Trains don't think Cloisterham worth stopping at, but yell and whirl through it on their larger errands, casting the dust off their wheels as a testimony against its insignificance. Some remote fragment of Main Line to somewhere else, there was, which was going to ruin the Money Market if it failed, and Church and State if it succeeded, and (of course) the Constitution, whether or no; but even that had already so unsettled Cloisterham traffic, that the traffic, deserting the high-road, came sneaking in from an unprecedented part of the country by a back stableway, for many years labelled at the corner: "Beware of the Dog."

To this ignominious avenue of approach, Mr. Crisparkle repaired, awaiting the arrival of a short squat omnibus, with a disproportionate heap of luggage on the roof—like a little elephant with infinitely too much Castle—which was then the daily service between Cloisterham and external mankind. As this vehicle lumbered up, Mr. Crisparkle could hardly see any thing else of it for a large outside passenger seated on the box, with his elbows squared, and his hands on his knees, compressing the driver into a most uncomfortably small compass, and glowering about him with a strongly-marked face.

"Is this Cloisterham?" demanded the passenger, in a tremendous voice.

"It is," replied the driver, rubbing himself as if he ached, after throwing the reins to the ostler. "And I never was so glad to see it."

"Tell your master to make his box-seat wider then," returned the passenger. "Your master is morally bound—and ought to be legally, under ruinous penalties—to provide for the comfort of his fellow-man."

The driver instituted, with the palms of his hands, a superficial perquisition into the state of his skeleton; which seemed to make him anxious.

"Have I sat upon you?" asked the passenger.

"You have," said the driver, as if he didn't like it at all.

"Take that card, my friend."

"I think I won't deprive you on it," returned the driver, casting his eyes over it with no great favor, without taking it. "What's the good of it to me?"

"Be a Member of that Society," said the passenger.

"What shall I get by it?" asked the driver.

"Brotherhood," returned the passenger, in a ferocious voice.

"Thankee," said the driver, very deliberately, as he got down; "my mother was contented with myself, and so am I. I don't want no brothers."

"But you must have them," replied the passenger, also descending, "whether you like it or not. I am your brother."

"I say!" expostulated the driver, becoming more chafed in temper; "not too fur! The worm *will*, when—"

But here Mr. Crisparkle interposed, remonstrating aside, in a friendly voice, "Joe, Joe, Joe! Don't forget yourself, Joe, my good fellow!" and then, when Joe peaceably touched his hat, accosting the passenger with, "Mr. Honeythunder?"

"That is my name, sir."

"My name is Crisparkle."

"Rev. Mr. Septimus? Glad to see you, sir. Neville and Helena are inside. Having a little succumbed of late, under the pressure of my public labors, I thought I would take a mouthful of fresh air, and come down with them, and return at night. So you are the Rev. Mr. Septimus, are you?" surveying him on the whole with disappointment, and twisting a double eyeglass by its ribbon, as if he were roasting it; but not otherwise using it. "Hah! I expected to see you older, sir."

"I hope you will," was the good-humored reply.

"Eh?" demanded Mr. Honeythunder.

"Only a poor little joke. Not worth repeating."

"Joke? Ay; I never see a joke," Mr. Honeythunder frowningly retorted. "A joke is wasted upon me, sir. Where are they? Helena and Neville, come here! Mr. Crisparkle has come down to meet you."

An unusually handsome lithe young fellow, and an unusually handsome lithe girl; much alike; both very dark, and very rich in color; she of almost the gypsy type; something untamed about them both; a certain air upon them of hunter and huntress; yet withal a certain air of being the objects of the chase, rather than the followers. Slender, supple, quick of eye and limb; half shy, half defiant; fierce of look; an indefinable kind of pause coming and going on their whole expression, both of face and form, which might be equally likened to the pause before a crouch, or a bound. The rough mental notes made in the first five minutes by Mr. Crisparkle would have read thus, *verbatim.*

He invited Mr. Honeythunder to dinner, with a troubled mind (for the discomfiture of the dear old china shepherdess lay heavy on it), and gave his arm to Helena Landless. Both she and her brother, as they walked all together through the ancient streets, took great delight in what he pointed out of the Cathedral and the Monastery-ruin, and wondered—so his notes ran on—much as if they were beautiful barbaric captives brought from some wild tropical dominion. Mr. Honeythunder walked in the middle of the road, shouldering the natives out of his way, and loudly developing a scheme he had, for making a raid on all the unemployed persons in the United Kingdom, laying them every one by the heels in jail, and forcing them, on pain of prompt extermination, to become philanthropists.

Mrs. Crisparkle had need of her own share of philanthropy when she beheld this very large and very loud excrescence on the little party. Always something in the nature of a Boil upon the face of society, Mr. Honeythunder expanded into an inflammatory Wen in Minor Canon Corner. Though it was not literally true, as was facetiously charged against him by public unbelievers, that he called aloud to his fellow-creatures, "Curse your souls and bodies, come here and be blessed!" still his philanthropy was of that gunpowderous sort that the difference between it and animosity was hard to determine. You were to abolish military force, but you were first to bring all commanding officers who had done their duty, to trial by court-martial for that offence, and shoot them. You were to abolish war, but were to make converts by making war upon them, and charging them with loving war as the apple of their eye. You were to have no capital punishment, but were first to sweep off the face of the earth all legislators, jurists, and judges who were of the contrary opinion. You were to have universal concord, and were to get it by eliminating all the people who wouldn't, or conscientiously couldn't, be concordant. You were to love your brother as yourself, but after an indefinite interval of maligning him (very much as if you hated him), and calling him all manner of names. Above all things, you were to do nothing in private, or on your own account. You were to go to the offices of the Haven of Philanthropy, and put your name down as a Member and a Professing Philanthropist. Then you were to pay up your subscription, get your card of membership, and your ribbon and medal, and were evermore to live upon a platform, and evermore to say what Mr. Honeythunder said, and what the Treasurer said, and what the sub-Treasurer said, and what the Committee said, and what the sub-Committee said, and what the Secretary said, and what the Vice-Secretary said. And this was usually said in the unanimously-carried resolution under hand and seal, to the effect: "That this assembled body of Professing Philanthropists views, with indignant scorn and contempt, not unmixed with utter detestation and loathing abhorrence"—in short, the baseness of all those who do not belong to it, and pledges itself to make as many obnoxious statements as possible about them, without being at all particular as to facts.

The dinner was a most doleful breakdown. The philanthropist deranged the symmetry of the table, sat himself in the way of the waiting, blocked up the thoroughfare, and drove Mr. Tope (who assisted the parlor-maid) to the verge of distraction by passing plates and dishes on, over his own head. Nobody could talk to anybody, because he held forth to everybody at once, as if the company had no individual existence, but were a Meeting. He impounded the Reverend Mr. Septimus, as an official personage to be addressed, or kind of human peg to hang his oratorical hat on, and fell into the exasperating habit, common among such orators, of impersonating him as a wicked and weak opponent. Thus, he would ask, "And will you, sir, now stultify yourself by telling me"—and so forth, when the innocent man had not opened his lips, nor meant to open them. Or he would say, "Now see, sir, to what a position you are reduced. I will leave you no escape. After exhausting all the resources of fraud and falsehood, during years upon years; after exhibiting a combination of dastardly meanness with ensanguined daring, such as the world has not often witnessed; you have now the hypocrisy to bend the knee before the most degraded of mankind, and to sue, and whine, and howl for mercy!" Whereat the unfortunate Minor Canon would look, in part indignant, and in part perplexed; while his worthy mother sat bridling, with tears in her eyes, and the remainder of the party lapsed into a sort of gelatinous state, in which there was no flavor or solidity, and very little resistance.

But the gush of philanthropy that burst forth when the departure of Mr. Honeythunder began to impend must have been highly gratifying to the feelings of that distinguished man. His coffee was produced, by the special activity of Mr. Tope, a full hour before he wanted it. Mr. Crisparkle sat with his watch in his hand, for about the same period, lest he should overstay his time. The four young people were unanimous in believing that the Cathedral clock struck three quarters, when it actually struck but one. Miss Twinkleton estimated the distance to the omnibus at five-and-twenty minutes' walk, when it was really five. The affectionate kindness of the whole circle hustled him into his great-coat, and shoved him out into the moonlight, as if he were a fugitive traitor with whom they sympathized, and a troop of horse were at the back door. Mr. Crisparkle and his new charge, who took him to the omnibus, were so fervent in their apprehensions of his catching cold, that they shut him up in it instantly and left him, with still half an hour to spare.

"I know very little of that gentleman, sir," said Neville, to the Minor Canon as they turned back.

"You know very little of your guardian?" the Minor Canon repeated.

"Almost nothing."

"How came he—"

"To *be* my guardian? I'll tell you, sir. I suppose you know that we come (my sister and I) from Ceylon."

"Indeed, no."

"I wonder at that. We lived with a stepfather there. Our mother died there, when we were little children. We have had a wretched existence. She made him our guardian, and he was a miserly wretch who grudged us food to eat, and clothes to wear. At his death, he passed us over to this man; for no better reason that I know of, than his being a friend or connection of his, whose name was always in print and catching his attention."

"That was lately, I suppose?"

"Quite lately, sir. This stepfather of ours was a cruel brute as well as a grinding one. It was well he died when he did, or I might have killed him."

Mr. Crisparkle stopped short in the moonlight and looked at his hopeful pupil in consternation.

"I surprise you, sir?" he said, with a quick change to a submissive manner.

"You shock me; unspeakably shock me."

The pupil hung his head for a little while as they walked on, and then said, "You never saw him beat your sister. I have seen him beat mine, more than once or twice, and I never forgot it."

"Nothing," said Mr. Crisparkle, "not even a beloved and beautiful sister's tears under dastardly ill-usage"—he became less severe, in spite of himself, as his indignation rose—"could justify those horrible expressions that you used."

"I am sorry I used them, and especially to you, sir. I beg to recall them. But permit me to set you right on one point. You spoke of my sister's tears. My sister would have let him tear her to pieces, before she would have let him believe that he could make her shed a tear."

Mr. Crisparkle reviewed those mental notes of his, and was neither at all surprised to hear it, nor at all disposed to question it.

"Perhaps you will think it strange, sir"—this was said in a hesitating voice—"that I should so soon ask you to allow me to confide in you, and to have the kindness to hear a word or two from me in my defence?"

"Defence?" Mr. Crisparkle repeated. "You are not on your defence, Mr. Neville."

"I think I am, sir. At least I know I should be, if you were better acquainted with my character."

"Well, Mr. Neville," was the rejoinder, "what if you leave me to find it out?"

"Since it is your pleasure, sir," answered the young man, with a quick change in his manner to sullen disappointment; "since it is your pleasure to check me in my impulse, I must submit."

There was that in the tone of this short speech which made the conscientious man to whom it was addressed uneasy. It hinted to him that he might, without meaning it, turn aside a trustfulness beneficial to a misshapen young mind, and perhaps to his own power of directing and improving it. They were within sight of the lights in his windows, and he stopped.

"Let us turn back and take a turn or two up and down, Mr. Neville, or you may not have time to finish what you wish to say to me. You are hasty in thinking that I mean to check you. Quite the contrary, I invite your confidence."

"You have invited it, sir, without knowing it, ever since I came here. I say 'ever since,' as if I had been here a week! The truth is, we came here (my sister and I) to quarrel with you, and affront you, and break away again."

"Really?" said Mr. Crisparkle, at a dead loss for anything else to say.

"You see, we could not know what you were beforehand, sir; could we?"

"Clearly not," said Mr. Crisparkle.

"And, having liked no one else with whom we have ever been brought into contact, we had made up our minds not to like you."

"Really?" said Mr. Crisparkle again.

"But we do like you, sir, and we see an unmistakable difference between your house and your reception of us, and anything else we have ever known. This—and my happening to be alone with you—and every thing around us seeming so quiet and peaceful after Mr. Honeythunder's departure—and Cloisterham being so old and grave and beautiful, with the moon shining on it—these things inclined me to open my heart."

"I quite understand, Mr. Neville. And it is salutary to listen to such influences."

"In describing my own imperfections, sir, I must ask you not to suppose that I am describing my sister's. She has come out of the disadvantages of our miserable life as much better than I am as that Cathedral tower is higher than those chimneys."

Mr. Crisparkle in his own breast was not so sure of this.

"I have had, sir, from my earliest remembrance, to suppress a deadly and bitter hatred. This has made me secret and revengeful. I have been always tyrannically held down by the strong hand. This has driven me, in my weakness, to the resource of being false and mean. I have been stinted of education, liberty, money, dress, the very necessaries of life, the commonest pleasures of childhood, the commonest possessions of youth. This has caused me to be utterly wanting in I don't know what emotions, or remembrances, or good instincts—I have not even a name for the thing, you see!—that you have had to work upon in other young men to whom you have been accustomed."

"This is evidently true. But this is not encouraging," thought Mr. Crisparkle, as they turned again.

"And to finish with, sir: I have been brought up among abject and servile dependants, of an inferior race, and I may easily have contracted some affinity with them. Sometimes, I don't know but that it may be a drop of what is tigerish in their blood."

"As in the case of that remark just now," thought Mr. Crisparkle.

"In a last word of reference to my sister, sir (we are twin children), you ought to know, to her honor, that nothing in our misery ever subdued her, though it often cowed me. When we ran away from it (we ran away four times in six years, to be soon brought back and cruelly punished), the flight was always of her planning and leading. Each time she dressed as a boy, and showed the daring of a man. I take it we were seven years old when we first decamped; but, I remember, when I lost the pocket-knife with which she was to have cut her hair short, how desperately she tried to tear it out, or bite it off. I have nothing further to say, sir, except that I hope you will bear with me and make allowance for me."

"Of that, Mr. Neville, you may be sure," returned the Minor Canon. "I don't preach more than I can help, and I will not repay your confidence with a sermon. But I entreat you to bear in mind, very seriously and steadily, that, if I am to do you any good, it can only be with your own assistance; and that you can only render that, efficiently, by seeking aid from Heaven."

"I will try to do my part, sir."

"And, Mr. Neville, I will try to do mine. Here is my hand on it. May God bless our endeavors!"

They were now standing at his house-door, and a cheerful sound of voices and laughter was heard within.

"We will take one more turn before going in," said Mr. Crisparkle, "for I want to ask you a question. When you said you were in a changed mind concerning me, you spoke, not only for yourself, but for your sister, too."

"Undoubtedly I did, sir."

"Excuse me, Mr. Neville, but I think you have had no opportunity of communicating with your sister since I met you. Mr. Honeythunder was very eloquent; but perhaps I may venture to say, without ill-nature, that he rather monopolized the occasion. May you not have answered for your sister without sufficient warrant?"

Neville shook his head with a proud smile.

"You don't know, sir, yet, what a complete understanding can exist between my sister and me, though no spoken word—perhaps hardly as much as a look—may have passed between us. She not only feels as I have described, but she very well knows that I am taking this opportunity of speaking to you, both for her and for myself."

Mr. Crisparkle looked in his face, with some incredulity; but his face expressed such absolute and firm conviction of the truth of what he said, that Mr. Crisparkle looked at the pavement, and mused, until they came to his door again.

"I will ask for one more turn, sir, this time," said the young man, with a rather heightened color rising in his face. "But for Mr. Honeythunder's—I think you called it eloquence, sir?" (somewhat slyly.)

"I—yes, I called it eloquence," said Mr. Crisparkle.

"But for Mr. Honeythunder's eloquence, I might have had no need to ask you what I am going to ask you. This Mr. Edwin Drood, sir: I think that's the name?"

"Quite correct," said Mr. Crisparkle. "D-r-double o-d."

"Does he—or did he—read with you, sir?"

"Never, Mr. Neville. He comes here visiting his relation, Mr. Jasper."

"Is Miss Budd his relation too, sir?"

("Now, why should he ask that, with sudden superciliousness?" thought Mr. Crisparkle.) Then he explained, aloud, what he knew of the little story of their betrothal.

"Oh! *That's* it, is it?" said the young man. "I understand his air of proprietorship now!"

This was said so evidently to himself, or to anybody rather than Mr. Crisparkle, that the latter instinctively felt as if to notice it would be almost tantamount to noticing a passage in a letter which he had read by chance over the writer's shoulder. A moment afterward they re-entered the house.

Mr. Jasper was seated at the piano as they came into his drawing-room, and was accompanying Miss Rosebud while she sang. It was a consequence of his playing the accompaniment without notes, and of her being a heedless little creature, very apt to go wrong, that he followed her lips most attentively, with his eyes as well as hands, carefully and softly hinting the key-note from time to time. Standing with an arm drawn round her, but with a face far more intent on Mr. Jasper than on her singing, stood Helena, between whom and her brother an instantaneous recognition passed, in which Mr. Crisparkle saw, or thought he saw, the understanding that had been spoken of flash out. Mr. Neville then took his admiring station, leaning against the piano, opposite the singer; Mr. Crisparkle sat down by the china shepherdess; Edwin Drood gallantly furled and unfurled Miss Twinkleton's fan; and that lady passively claimed that sort of exhibitor's proprietorship in the accomplishment on view, which Mr. Tope, the Verger, daily claimed in the Cathedral service.

The song went on. It was a sorrowful strain of parting, and the fresh young voice was very plaintive and tender. As Jasper watched the pretty lips, and ever and again hinted the one note, as though it were a low whisper from himself, the voice became less steady, until all at once the singer broke into a burst of tears, and shrieked out, with her hands over her eyes, "I can't bear this! I am frightened! Take me away!"

With one swift turn of her lithe figure, Helena laid the little beauty on a sofa, as if she had never caught her up. Then, on one knee beside her, and with one hand upon her rosy mouth, while with the other she appealed to all the rest, Helena said to them, "It's nothing; it's all over; don't speak to her for one minute, and she is well!"

Jasper's hands had, in the same instant, lifted themselves from the keys, and were now poised above them, as though he waited to resume. In that attitude he yet sat quiet, not even looking round, when all the rest had changed their places and were reassuring one another.

"Pussy's not used to an audience: that's the fact," said Edwin Drood. "She got nervous, and couldn't hold out. Besides, Jack, you are such a conscientious master, and require so much, that I believe you make her afraid of you. No wonder."

"No wonder," repeated Helena.

"There, Jack, you hear! You would be afraid of him, under similar circumstances, wouldn't you, Miss Landless?"

"Not under any circumstances," returned Helena.

Jasper brought down his hands, looked over his shoulder, and begged to thank Miss Landless for her vindication of his character. Then he fell to dumbly playing, without striking the notes, while his little pupil was taken to an open window for air, and was otherwise petted and restored. When she was brought back, his place was empty. "Jack's gone, Pussy," Edwin told her. "I am more than half afraid he did'nt like to be charged with being the Monster who had frightened you." But she answered never a word, and shivered, as if they had made her a little too cold.

Miss Twinkleton now opining that indeed these were late hours, Mrs. Crisparkle, for finding ourselves outside the walls of the Nuns' House, and that we who undertook the formation of the future wives and mothers of England (the last words in a lower voice, as requiring to be communicated in confidence) were really bound (voice coming up again) to set a better example than one of rakish habits, wrappers were put in requisition, and the two young cavaliers volunteered to see the ladies home. It was soon done, and the gate of the Nuns' House closed upon them.

The boarders had retired, and only Mrs. Tisher in solitary vigil awaited the new pupil. Her bedroom being within Rosa's, very little introduction or explanation was necessary, before she was placed in charge of her new friend, and left for the night.

"This is a blessed relief, my dear," said Helena. "I have been dreading all day, that I should be brought to bay at this time."

"There are not many of us," returned Rosa, "and we are good-natured girls; at least the others are; I can answer for them."

"I can answer for you," laughed Helena, searching the lovely little face with her dark fiery eyes, and tenderly caressing the small figure. "You will be a friend to me, won't you?"

"I hope so. But the idea of my being a friend to you seems too absurd, though."

"Why?"

"Oh! I am such a mite of a thing, and you are so womanly and handsome. You seem to have resolution and power enough to crush me. I shrink into nothing by the side of your presence even."

"I am a neglected creature, my dear, unacquainted with all accomplishments, sensitively conscious that I have every thing to learn, and deeply ashamed to own my ignorance."

"And yet you acknowledge every thing to me!" said Rosa.

"My pretty one, can I help it? There is a fascination in you."

"Oh! Is there, though?" pouted Rosa, half in jest and half in earnest. "What a pity Master Eddy doesn't feel it more!"

Of course, her relations toward that young gentleman had been already imparted in Minor Canon Corner.

"Why, surely, he must love you with all his heart!" cried Helena, with an earnestness that threatened to blaze into ferocity if he didn't.

"Eh? O well, I suppose he does," said Rosa, pouting again; "I am sure I have no right to say he doesn't. Perhaps it's my fault. Perhaps I am not as nice to him as I ought to be. I don't think I am. But it *is* so ridiculous!"

Helena's eyes demanded what was.

"*We* are," said Rosa, answering as if she had spoken. "We are such a ridiculous couple! And we are always quarrelling."

"Why?"

"Because we both know we are ridiculous, my dear!" Rosa gave that answer as if it were the most conclusive answer in the world.

Helena's masterful look was intent upon her face for a few moments, and then she impulsively put out both her hands and said—

"You will be my friend and help me?"

"Indeed, my dear, I will," replied Rosa, in a tone of affectionate childishness that went straight and true to her heart; "I will be as good a friend as such a mite of a thing can be to such a noble creature as you. And be a friend to me, please; for I don't understand myself; and I want a friend who can understand me, very much indeed."

Helena Landless kissed her, and, retaining both her hands, said—"Who is Mr. Jasper?"

Rosa turned aside her head in answering, "Eddy's uncle, and my music-master."

"You do not love him?"

"Ugh!" She put her hands up to her face, and shook with fear or horror.

"You know that he loves you?"

"Oh, don't, don't, don't!" cried Rosa, dropping on her knees, and clinging to her new resource. "Don't tell me of it! He terrifies me. He haunts my thoughts, like a dreadful ghost. I feel that I am never safe from him. I feel as if he could pass in through the wall when he is spoken of." She actually did look round, as if she dreaded to see him standing in the shadow behind her.

"Try to tell me more about it, darling."

"Yes, I will, I will. Because you are so strong. But hold me the while, and stay with me afterward."

"My child! You speak as if he had threatened you in some dark way."

"He has never spoken to me about—that. Never."

"What has he done?"

"He has made a slave of me with his looks. He has forced me to understand him, without his saying a word; and he has forced me to keep silence, without his uttering a threat. When I play, he never moves his eyes from my hands. When I sing, he never moves his eyes from my lips. When he corrects me, and strikes a note, or a chord, or plays a passage, he himself is in the sounds, whispering that he pursues me as a lover, and commanding me to keep his secret. I avoid his eyes, but he forces me to see them without looking at them. Even when a glaze comes over them (which is sometimes the case), and he seems to wander away into a frightful sort of dream, in which he threatens most, he obliges me to know it, and to know that he is sitting close at my side, more terrible to me then than ever."

"What is this imagined threatening, pretty one? What is threatened?"

"I don't know. I have never even dared to think or wonder what it is."

"And was this all, to-night?"

"This was all; except that to-night when he watched my lips so closely as I was singing, besides feeling terrified, I felt ashamed and passionately hurt. It was as if he kissed me, and I couldn't bear it, but cried out. You must never breathe this to any one. Eddy is devoted to him. But you said to-night that you would not be afraid of him, under any circumstances, and that gives me—who am so much afraid of him—courage to tell only you. Hold me! Stay with me! I am too frightened to be left by myself."

The lustrous gypsy-face drooped over the clinging arms and bosom, and the wild black hair fell down protectingly over the childish form. There was a slumbering gleam of fire in the intense dark eyes, though they were then softened with compassion and admiration. Let whosoever it most concerned look well to it!

CHAPTER VI.

DAGGERS DRAWN.

THE two young men, having seen the damsels, their charges, enter the court-yard of the Nuns' House, and, finding themselves coldly stared at by the brazen door-plate, as if the battered old beau with the glass in his eye were insolent, look at one another, look along the perspective of the moonlit street, and slowly walk away together.

"Do you stay here long, Mr. Drood?" says Neville.

"Not this time," is the careless answer. "I leave for London again to-morrow. But I shall be here, off and on, until next Midsummer; then I shall take my leave of Cloisterham, and England too; for many a long day, I expect."

"Are you going abroad?"

"Going to wake up Egypt a little," is the condescending answer.

"Are you reading?"

"Reading!" repeats Edwin Drood, with a touch of contempt. "No. Doing, working, engineering. My small patrimony was left a part of the capital of the Firm I am with, by my father, a former partner; and I am a charge upon the Firm until I come of age; and then I step into my modest share in the concern. Jack—you met him at dinner—is, until then, my guardian and trustee."

"I heard from Mr. Crisparkle of your other good fortune."

"What do you mean by my other good fortune?"

Neville has made his remark in a watchfully advancing, and yet furtive and shy manner, very expressive of that peculiar air already noticed, of being at once hunter and hunted. Edwin has made his retort with an abruptness not at all polite. They stop and interchange a rather heated look.

"I hope," says Neville, "there is no offence, Mr. Drood, in my innocently referring to your betrothal?"

"By George!" cries Edwin, leading on again at a somewhat quicker pace. "Everybody in this chattering old Cloisterham refers to it. I wonder no public-house has been set up, with my portrait for the sign of the Betrothed's Head. Or Pussy's portrait. One or the other."

"I am not accountable for Mr. Crisparkle's mentioning the matter to me, quite openly," Neville begins.

"No; that's true; you are not," Edwin Drood assents.

"But," resumes Neville, "I am accountable for mentioning it to you. And I did so, on the supposition that you could not fail to be highly proud of it."

Now, there are these two curious touches of human nature working the secret springs of this dialogue. Neville Landless is already enough impressed by little Rosebud to feel indignant that Edwin Drood (far below her) should hold his prize so lightly. Edwin Drood is already enough impressed by Helena, to feel indignant that Helena's brother (far below her) should dispose of him so coolly, and put him out of the way so entirely.

However, the last remark had better be answered. So, says Edwin—

"I don't know, Mr. Neville" (adopting that mode of address from Mr. Crisparkle), "that what people are proudest of they usually talk most about; I don't know either, that what they are proudest of they most like other people to talk about. But I live a busy life, and I speak under correction by you readers, who ought to know every thing, and I dare say do."

By this time they had both become savage; Mr. Neville out in the open; Edwin Drood under the transparent cover of a popular tune, and a stop now and then to pretend to admire picturesque effects in the moonlight before him.

"It does not seem to me very civil in you," remarks Neville, at length, "to reflect upon a stranger who comes here, not having had your advantages, to try to make up for lost time. But, to be sure, *I* was not brought up in 'busy life,' and my ideas of civility were formed among Heathens."

"Perhaps the best civility, whatever kind of people we are brought up among," retorts Edwin Drood, "is to mind our own business. If you will set me the example, I promise to follow it."

"Do you know that you take a great deal too much upon yourself," is the angry rejoinder; "and that in the part of the world I come from, you would be called to account for it?"

"By whom, for instance?" asked Edwin Drood, coming to a halt, and surveying the other with a look of disdain.

But here a startling right hand is laid on Edwin's shoulder, and Jasper stands between them. For it would seem that he, too, has strolled round by the Nuns' House, and has come up behind them on the shadowy side of the road.

"Ned, Ned, Ned!" he says. "We must have no more of this. I don't like this. I have overheard high words between you two. Remember, my dear boy, you are almost in the position of host to-night. You belong, as it were, to the place, and in a manner represent it toward a stranger. Mr. Neville is a stranger, and you should respect the obligations of hospitality. And, Mr. Neville," laying his left hand on the inner shoulder of that young gentleman, and thus walking on between them, hand to shoulder on either side, "you will pardon me; but I appeal to you to govern your temper too. Now, what is amiss? But why ask! Let there be nothing amiss, and the question is superfluous. We are all three on a good understanding, are we not?"

After a silent struggle between the two young men who shall speak last, Edwin Drood strikes in with, "So far as I am concerned, Jack, there is no anger in me."

"Nor in me," says Neville Landless, though not so freely, or perhaps so carelessly. "But if Mr. Drood knew all that lies behind me, far away from here, he might know better how it is that sharp-edged words have sharp edges to wound me."

"Perhaps," said Jasper, in a smoothing manner, "we had better not qualify our good understanding. We had better not say anything having the appearance of a remonstrance or condition; it might not seem generous. Frankly and freely, you see there is no anger in Ned. Frankly and freely, there is no anger in you, Mr. Neville?"

"None at all, Mr. Jasper." Still, not quite so frankly or so freely; or, be it said once again, not quite so carelessly perhaps.

"All over then! Now, my bachelor gate-house is a few yards from here, and the heater is on the fire, and the wine and glasses are on the table, and it is not a stone's throw from Minor Canon Corner. Ned, you are up and away to-morrow. We will carry Mr. Neville in with us, to take a stirrup-cup."

"With all my heart, Jack."

"And with all mine, Mr. Jasper." Neville feels it impossible to say less, but would rather not go. He has an impression upon him that he has lost hold of his temper; feels that Edwin Drood's coolness, so far from being infectious, makes him red-hot.

Mr. Jasper, still walking in the centre, hand to shoulder on either side, beautifully turns the Refrain of a drinking-song, and they all go up to his rooms. There, the first object visible, when he adds the light of the lamp to that of the fire, is the portrait over the chimney-piece. It is not an object calculated to improve the understanding between the two young men, as rather awkwardly reviving the subject of their difference. Accordingly, they both glance at it consciously, but say nothing. Jasper, however (who would appear from his conduct to have gained but an imperfect clew to the cause of their late high words), directly calls attention to it.

"You recognize that picture, Mr. Neville?" shading the lamp to throw the light upon it.

"I recognize it, but it is far from flattering the original."

"O, you are hard upon it! It was done by Ned, who made me a present of it."

"I am sorry for that, Mr. Drood." Neville apologizes, with a real intention to apologize; "if I had known I was in the artist's presence—"

"O, a joke, sir, a mere joke," Edwin cuts in, with a provoking yawn. "A little humoring of Pussy's points! I'm going to paint her gravely, one of these days, if she's good."

The air of leisurely patronage and indifference with which this is said, as the speaker throws himself back in a chair and clasps his hands at the back of his head, as a rest for it, is very exasperating to the excitable and excited Neville. Jasper looks observantly from the one to the other, slightly smiles, and turns his back to mix a jug of mulled wine at the fire. It seems to require much mixing and compounding.

"I suppose, Mr. Neville," says Edwin, quick to resent the indignant protest against himself in the face of young Landless, which is fully as visible as the portrait, or the fire, or the lamp, "I suppose that if you painted the picture of your lady-love—"

"I can't paint," is the hasty interruption.

"That's your misfortune, and not your fault. You would if you could. But if you could, I suppose you would make her (no matter what she was in reality) Juno, Minerva, Diana, and Venus, all in one. Eh?"

"I have no lady-love, and I can't say."

"If I were to try my hand," says Edwin, with a boyish boastfulness getting up in him, "on a portrait of Miss Landless—in earnest, mind you; in earnest—you should see what I could do!"

"My sister's consent to sit for it being first got, I suppose! As it never will be got, I am afraid I shall never see what you can do. I must bear the loss."

Jasper turns round from the fire, fills a large goblet glass for Neville, fills a large goblet glass for Edwin, and hands each his own; then fills for himself, saying:

"Come, Mr. Neville, we are to drink to my Nephew, Ned. As it is his foot that is in the stirrup—metaphorically—our stirrup-cup is to be devoted to him. Ned, my dearest fellow, my love!"

Jasper sets the example of nearly emptying his glass, and Neville follows it. Edwin Drood says, "Thank you both very much," and follows the double example.

"Look at him!" cries Jasper, stretching out his hand admiringly and tenderly, though rallyingly too. "See where he lounges so easily, Mr. Neville! The world is all before him where to choose. A life of stirring work and interest, a life of change and excitement, a life of domestic ease and love! Look at him!"

Edwin Drood's face has become quickly and remarkably flushed by the wine; so has the face of Neville Landless. Edwin still sits thrown back in his chair, making that rest of clasped hands for his head.

"See how little he heeds it all!" Jasper proceeds in a bantering vein. "It is hardly worth his while to pluck the golden fruit that hangs ripe on the tree for him. And yet consider the contrast, Mr. Neville. You and I have no prospect of stirring work and interest, or of change and excitement, or of domestic ease and love. You and I have no prospect (unless you are more fortunate than I am, which may easily be) but the tedious, unchanging round of this dull place."

"Upon my soul, Jack," says Edwin, complacently, "I feel quite apologetic for having my way smoothed as you describe. But you know what I know, Jack, and it may not be so very easy as it seems, after all. May it, Pussy?" To the portrait, with a snap of his thumb and finger. "We have got to hit it off yet; haven't we, Pussy? You know what I mean, Jack."

His speech has become thick and indistinct. Jasper, quiet and self-possessed, looks to Neville, as expecting his answer or comment. When Neville speaks, *his* speech is also thick and indistinct.

"It might have been better for Mr. Drood to have known some hardships," he says, defiantly.

"Pray," retorts Edwin, turning merely his eyes in that direction, "pray why might it have been better for Mr. Drood to have known some hardships?"

"Ay," Jasper assents with an air of interest; "let us know why?"

"Because they might have made him more sensible," says Neville, "of good fortune that is not by any means necessarily the result of his own merits."

Mr. Jasper quickly looks to his nephew for his rejoinder.

"Have *you* known hardships, may I ask?" says Edwin Drood, sitting upright.

Mr. Jasper quickly looks to the other for his retort.

"I have."

"And what have they made *you* sensible of?"

Mr. Jasper's play of eyes between the two holds good throughout the dialogue, to the end.

"I have told you once before to-night."

"You have done nothing of the sort."

"I tell you I have. That you take a great deal too much upon yourself."

"You added something else to that, if I remember."

"Yes, I did say something else."

"Say it again."

"I said that in the part of the world I come from you would be called to account for it."

"Only there?" cries Edwin Drood, with a contemptuous laugh. "A long way off, I believe? Yes; I see! That part of the world is at a safe distance."

"Say here, then," rejoins the other, rising in a fury. "Say anywhere! Your vanity is intolerable, your conceit is beyond endurance, you talk as if you were some rare and precious prize, instead of a common boaster. You are a common fellow, and a common boaster."

"Pooh, pooh," says Edwin Drood, equally furious, but more collected; "how should you know? You may know a black common fellow, or a black common boaster, when you see him (and no doubt you have a large acquaintance that way); but you are no judge of white men."

This insulting allusion to his dark skin infuriates Neville to that violent degree that he flings the dregs of his wine at Edwin Drood, and is in the act of flinging the goblet after it when his arm is caught in the nick of time by Jasper.

"Ned, my dear fellow!" he cries, in a loud voice; "I entreat you, I command you, to be still!" There has been a rush of all the three, and a clattering of glasses and overturning of chairs. "Mr. Neville for shame! Give this glass to me. Open your hand, sir. I WILL have it!"

But Neville throws him off, and pauses for an instant, in a raging passion, with the goblet yet in his uplifted hand. Then, he dashes it down under the grate, with such force that the broken splinters fly out again in a shower; and he leaves the house.

When he first emerges into the night air, nothing around him is still or steady; nothing around him shows like what it is; he only knows that he stands with a bare head in the midst of a blood-red whirl, waiting to be struggled with, and to struggle to the death.

But, nothing happening, and the moon looking down upon him as if he were dead after a fit of wrath, he holds his steam-hammer beating head and heart, and staggers away. Then he becomes half conscious of having heard himself bolted and barred out, like a dangerous animal; and thinks what shall he do?

Some wildly passionate ideas of the river dissolve under the spell of the moonlight on the Cathedral and the graves, and the remembrance of his sister, and the thought of what he owes to the good man who has but that very day won his confidence and given him his pledge. He repairs to Minor Canon Corner, and knocks softly at the door.

It is Mr. Crisparkle's custom to sit up last of the early household, very softly touching his piano and practising his favorite parts in concerted vocal music. The south wind that goes where it lists, by way of Minor Canon Corner on a still night, is not more subdued than Mr. Crisparkle at such times, regardful of the slumbers of the China shepherdess.

His knock is immediately answered by Mr. Crisparkle himself. When he opens the door, candle in hand, his cheerful face falls, and disappointed amazement is in it.

"Mr. Neville! In this disorder! Where have you been?"

"I have been to Mr. Jasper's, sir. With his nephew."

"Come in."

The Minor Canon props him by the elbow with a strong hand (in a strictly scientific manner, worthy of his morning trainings), and turns him into his own little book-room, and shuts the door.

"I have begun ill, sir. I have begun dreadfully ill."

"Too true. You are not sober, Mr. Neville."

"I am afraid I am not, sir, though I can satisfy you at another time that I have had very little indeed to drink, and that it overcame me in the strangest and most sudden manner."

"Mr. Neville, Mr. Neville," says the Minor Canon, shaking his head with a sorrowful smile, "I have heard that said before."

"I think—my mind is much confused, but I think—it is equally true of Mr. Jasper's nephew, sir."

"Very likely," is the dry rejoinder.

"We quarrelled, sir. He insulted me most grossly. He had heated that tigerish blood I told you of to-day, before then."

"Mr. Neville," rejoins the Minor Canon, mildly, but firmly, "I request you not to speak to me with that clinched right hand. Unclinch it, if you please."

"He goaded me, sir," pursues the young man, instantly obeying, "beyond my power of endurance. I cannot say whether or no he meant it at first, but he did it. He certainly meant it at last. In short, sir," with an irrepressible outburst, "in the passion into which he lashed me, I would have cut him down, if I could, and I tried to do it."

"You have clinched that hand again," is Mr. Crisparkle's quiet commentary.

"I beg your pardon, sir."

"You know your room, for I showed it to you before dinner; but I will accompany you to it once more. Your arm, if you please. Softly, for the house is all a-bed."

Scooping his hand into the same scientific elbow-rest as before, and backing it up with the inert strength of his arm, as skillfully as a Police Expert, and with an apparent repose quite unattainable by novices, Mr. Crisparkle conducts his pupil to the pleasant and orderly old room prepared for him. Arrived there, the young man throws himself into a chair, and, flinging his arms upon his reading-table, rests his head upon them with an air of wretched self-reproach.

The gentle Minor Canon has had it in his thoughts to leave the room, without a word. But, looking round at the door, and seeing this dejected figure, he turns back to it, touches it with a mild hand, and says, "Good-night!" A sob is his only acknowledgment. He might have had many a worse; perhaps could have had few better.

Another soft knock at the outer door attracts his attention as he goes down-stairs. He opens it to Mr. Jasper, holding in his hand the pupil's hat.

"We have had an awful scene with him," says Jasper, in a low voice.

"Has he been so bad as that?"

"Murderous!"

Mr. Crisparkle remonstrates. "No, no, no. Do not use such strong words."

"He might have laid my dear boy dead at my feet. It is no fault of his that he did not. But that I was, through the mercy of God, swift and strong with him, he would have cut him down on my hearth."

The phrase smites home.

"Ah!" thinks Mr. Crisparkle. "His own words!"

"Seeing what I have seen to-night, and hearing what I have heard," adds Jasper, with great earnestness, "I shall never know peace of mind when there is danger of those two coming together with no one else to interfere. It was horrible. There is something of the tiger in his dark blood."

"Ah!" thinks Mr. Crisparkle. "So he said."

"You, my dear sir," pursues Jasper, taking his hand, "even you have accepted a dangerous charge."

"You need have no fear for me, Jasper," returns Mr. Crisparkle, with a quiet smile. "I have none for myself."

"I have none for myself," returns Jasper, with an emphasis on the last pronoun, "because I am not, nor am I in the way of being, the object of his hostility. But you may be, and my dear boy has been. Good-night!"

Mr. Crisparkle goes in, with the hat that has so easily, so almost imperceptibly, acquired the right to be hung up in his hall, hangs it up, and goes thoughtfully to bed.

CHAPTER VII.

BIRDS IN THE BUSH.

Rosa, having no relation that she knew of in the world, had, from the seventh year of her age, known no home but the Nuns' House, and no mother but Miss Twinkleton. Her remembrance of her own mother was of a pretty little creature like herself (not much older than herself, it seemed to her), who had been brought home in her father's arms, drowned. The fatal accident had happened at a party of pleasure. Every fold and color in the pretty summer dress, and even the long wet hair, with scattered petals of ruined flowers still clinging to it, as the dead young figure, in its sad, sad beauty lay upon the bed, were fixed indelibly on Rosa's recollection. So were the wild despair and the subsequent bowed-down grief of her poor young father, who died broken-hearted on the first anniversary of that hard day.

The betrothal of Rosa grew out of the soothing of his year of mental distress by his fast friend and old college companion, Drood: who likewise had been left a widower in his youth. But he, too, went the silent road into which all earthly pilgrimages merge, some sooner and some later; and thus the young couple had come to be as they were.

The atmosphere of pity surrounding the little orphan girl when she first came to Cloisterham had never cleared away. It had taken brighter hues as she grew older, happier, prettier; now it had been golden, now roseate, and now azure; but it had always adorned her with some soft light of its own. The general desire to console and caress her had caused her to be treated in the beginning as a child much younger than her years; the same desire had caused her to be still petted when she was a child no longer. Who should be her favorite? who should anticipate this or that small present? who should take her home for the holidays? who should write to her the oftenest when they were separated? and whom she would most rejoice to see again when they were reunited—even these gentle rivalries were not without their slight dashes of bitterness in the Nuns' House. Well for the poor nuns in their day, if they hid no harder strife under their veils and rosaries.

Thus Rosa had grown to be an amiable, giddy, willful, winning little creature; spoilt, in the sense of counting upon kindness from all around her; but not in the sense of repaying it with indifference. Possessing an exhaustless well of affection in her nature, its sparkling waters had freshened and brightened the Nuns' House for years, and yet its depths had never yet been moved: what might betide when that came to pass; what developing changes might fall upon the heedless head and light heart then, remained to be seen.

By what means the news that there had been a quarrel between the two young men over-night, involving even some kind of onslaught by Mr. Neville upon Edwin Drood, got into Miss Twinkleton's establishment before breakfast, it is impossible to say. Whether it was brought in by the birds of the air, or came blowing in with the very air itself, when the casement windows were set open; whether the baker brought it kneaded into the bread, or the milkman delivered it as part of the adulteration of his milk; or the housemaids, beating the dust out of their mats against the gate-posts, received it in exchange deposited on the mats by the town atmosphere; certain it is that the news permeated every gable of the old building before Miss Twinkleton was down, and that Miss Twinkleton herself received it through Mrs. Tisher, while yet in the act of dressing; or (as she might have expressed the phrase to a parent or guardian of a mythological turn) of sacrificing to the Graces.

Miss Landless's brother had thrown a bottle at Mr. Edwin Drood.

Miss Landless's brother had thrown a knife at Mr. Edwin Drood.

A knife became suggestive of a fork, and Miss Landless's brother had thrown a fork at Mr. Edwin Drood.

As in the governing precedent of Peter Piper, alleged to have picked the peck of pickled pepper, it was held physically desirable to have evidence of the existence of the peck of pickled pepper which Peter Piper was alleged to have picked, so, in this case, it was held psychologically important to know, Why Miss Landless's brother threw a bottle, knife, or fork—or bottle, knife, *and* fork—for the cook had been given to understand it was all three—at Mr. Edwin Drood?

Well, then. Miss Landless's brother had said he admired Miss Bud. Mr. Edwin Drood had said to Miss Landless's brother that he had no business to admire Miss Bud. Miss Landless's brother had then "up'd" (this was the cook's exact information) with the bottle, knife, fork, and decanter (the decanter now coolly flying at everybody's head, without the least introduction), and thrown them all at Mr Edwin Drood.

Poor little Rosa put a forefinger into each of her ears when these rumors began to circulate, and retired into a corner beseeching not to be told any more; but Miss Landless, begging permission of Miss Twinkleton to go and speak with her brother, and pretty plainly showing that she would take it if it were not given, struck out the more definite course of going to Mr. Crisparkle's for accurate intelligence.

When she came back (being first closeted with Miss Twinkleton, in order that anything objectionable in her tidings might be retained by that discreet filter), she imparted to Rosa only what had taken place, dwelling with a flushed cheek on the provocation her brother had received, but almost limiting it to that last gross affront as crowning "some other words between them," and, out of consideration for her new friend, passing lightly over the fact that the other words had originated in her lover's taking things in general so very easily. To Rosa direct, she brought a petition from her brother that she would forgive him; and, having delivered it with sisterly earnestness, made an end of the subject.

It was reserved for Miss Twinkleton to tone down the public mind of the Nuns' House. That lady, therefore, entering in a stately manner what plebeians might have called the school-room, but what, in the patrician language of the head of the Nuns' House, was euphuistically, not to say round-aboutedly, denominated "the apartment allotted to study," and saying with a forensic air, "Ladies!" all rose. Mrs. Tisher at the same time grouped herself behind her chief, as representing Queen Elizabeth's first historical female friend at Tilbury Fort. Miss Twinkleton then proceeded to remark that Rumor, Ladies, had been represented by the Bard of Avon—needless were it to mention the immortal SHAKESPEARE, also called the Swan of his native river, not improbably with some reference to the ancient superstition that that bird of graceful plumage (Miss Jennings will please stand upright) sang sweetly on the approach of death, for which we have no ornithological authority—Rumor, Ladies, has been represented by that bard—hem!—

"who drew
The celebrated Jew,"

as painted full of tongues. Rumor in Cloisterham (Miss Ferdinand will honor me with her attention) was no exception to the great limner's portrait of Rumor elsewhere. A slight *fracas* between two young gentlemen occurring last night within a hundred miles of these peaceful walls (Miss Ferdinand, being apparently incorrigible, will have the kindness to write out this evening, in the original language, the first four fables of our vivacious neighbor, Monsieur La Fontaine) had been very grossly exaggerated by Rumor's voice. In the first alarm and anxiety arising from our sympathy with a sweet young friend, not wholly to be dissociated from one of the gladiators in the bloodless arena in question (the impropriety of Miss Reynolds's appearing to stab herself in the band with a pin, is far too obvious, and too glaringly unladylike, to be pointed out), we descended from our maiden elevation to discuss this uncongenial and this unfit theme. Responsible inquiries having assured us that it was but one of those "airy nothings" pointed at by the Poet (whose name and date of birth Miss Giggles will supply within half an hour), we would now discard the subject, and concentrate our minds upon the grateful labors of the day.

But the subject so survived all day, nevertheless, that Miss Ferdinand got into new trouble by surreptitiously clapping on a paper moustache at dinner-time, and going through the motions of aiming a water-bottle at Miss Giggles, who drew a table-spoon in defence.

Now, Rosa thought of this unlucky quarrel a great deal, and thought of it with an uncomfortable feeling that she was involved in it, as cause, or consequence, or what not, through being in a false position altogether as to her marriage-engagement. Never free from such uneasiness when she was with her affianced husband, it was not likely that she would be free from it when they were apart. To-day, too, she was cast in upon herself, and deprived of the relief of talking freely with her new friend, because the quarrel had been with Helena's brother, and Helena undisguisedly avoided the subject as a delicate and difficult one to herself. At this critical time, of all times, Rosa's guardian was announced as having come to see her.

Mr. Grewgious had been well selected for his trust, as a man of incorruptible integrity, but certainly for no other appropriate quality discernible on the surface. He was an arid, sandy man, who, if he had been put into a grinding-mill, looked as if he would have ground immediately into high-dried snuff. He had a scanty flat crop of hair, in color and consistency like some very mangy yellow fur tippet; it was so unlike hair, that it must have been a wig, but for the stupendous improbability of anybody's voluntarily sporting such a head. The little play of feature that his face presented was cut deep into it, in a few hard curves that made it more like work; and he had certain notches in his forehead, which looked as though Nature had been about to touch them into sensibility or refinement, when she had impatiently thrown away the chisel, and said, "I really cannot be worried to finish off this man; let him go as he is."

With too great length of throat at his upper end, and too much ankle-bone and heel at his lower; with an awkward and hesitating manner; with a shambling walk, and with what is called a near sight—which perhaps prevented his observing how much white-cotton stocking he displayed to the public eye, in contrast with his black suit—Mr. Grewgious still had some strange capacity in him of making on the whole an agreeable impression.

Mr. Grewgious was discovered by his ward, much discomfited by being in Miss Twinkleton's company in Miss Twinkleton's own sacred room. Dim forebodings of being examined in something, and not coming well out of it, seemed to oppress the poor gentleman when found in these circumstances.

"My dear, how do you do? I am glad to see you. My dear, how much improved you are! Permit me to hand you a chair, my dear."

Miss Twinkleton rose at her little writing-table, saying, with general sweetness, as to the polite Universe, "Will you permit me to retire?"

"By no means, madam, on my account. I beg that you will not move."

"I must entreat permission to *move*," returned Miss Twinkleton, repeating the word with a charming grace; but I will not withdraw, since you are so obliging. If I wheel my desk to this corner-window, shall I be in the way?"

"Madam! In the way!"

"You are very kind. Rosa, my dear, you will be under no restraint, I am sure."

Here Mr. Grewgious, left by the fire with Rosa, said again, "My dear, how do you do? I am glad to see you, my dear." And, having waited for her to sit down, sat down himself.

"My visits," said Mr. Grewgious, "are like those of the angels—not that I compare myself to an angel."

"No, sir," said Rosa.

"Not by any means," assented Mr. Grewgious. "I merely refer to my visits, which are few and far between. The angels are, we know very well, up-stairs."

Miss Twinkleton looked round with a kind of stiff stare.

"I refer, my dear," said Mr. Grewgious, laying his hand on Rosa's, as the possibility thrilled through his frame of his otherwise seeming to take the awful liberty of calling Miss Twinkleton my dear, "I refer to the other young ladies."

Miss Twinkleton resumed her writing.

Mr. Grewgious, with a sense of not having managed his opening-point quite as neatly as he might have desired, smoothed his head from back to front as if he had just dived, and were pressing the water out—this smoothing action, however superfluous, was habitual with him—and took a pocket-book from his coat-pocket, and a stump of black lead-pencil from his waistcoat-pocket.

"I made," he said, turning the leaves; "I made a guiding memorandum or so—as I usually do, for I have no conversational powers whatever—to which I will, with your permission, my dear, refer. 'Well and happy.' Truly, you are well and happy, my dear? You look so."

"Yes, indeed, sir," answered Rosa.

"For which," said Mr. Grewgious, with a bend of his head toward the corner-window, "our warmest acknowledgments are due, and I am sure are rendered, to the maternal kindness and the constant care and consideration of the lady whom I have now the honor to see before me."

This point, again, made but a lame departure from Mr. Grewgious, and never got to its destination; for, Miss Twinkleton, feeling that the courtesies required her to be by this time quite outside the conversation, was biting the end of her pen, and looking upward, as waiting for the descent of an idea from any member of the Celestial Nine who might have one to spare.

Mr. Grewgious smoothed his smooth head again, and then made another reference to his pocket-book, lining out "well and happy" as disposed of.

"'Pounds, shillings, and pence,' is my next note. A dry subject for a young lady, but an important subject too. Life is pounds, shillings, and pence. Death is—" A sudden recollection of the death of her two parents seemed to stop him, and he said in a softer tone, and evidently inserting the negative as an after-thought, "Death is *not* pounds, shillings, and pence."

His voice was as hard and dry as himself, and Fancy might have ground it straight, like himself, into high-dried snuff. And yet, through the very limited means of expression that he possessed, he seemed to express kindness. If Nature had but finished him off, kindness might have been recognizable in his face at this moment. But, if the notches in his forehead wouldn't fuse together, and if his face would work and couldn't play, what would he do, poor man!

"'Pounds, shillings, and pence.' You find your allowance always sufficient for your wants, my dear?"

Rosa wanted for nothing, and therefore it was ample.

"And you are not in debt?"

Rosa laughed at the idea of being in debt. It seemed, to her inexperience, a comical vagary of the imagination. Mr. Grewgious stretched his near sight to be sure that this was her view of the case. "Ah!" he said, as comment, with a furtive glance toward Miss Twinkleton, and lining out "pounds, shillings, and pence," "I spoke of having got among the angels! So I did!"

Rosa felt what his next memorandum would prove to be, and was blushing and folding a crease in her dress with one embarrassed hand long before he found it.

"'Marriage.' Hem!" Mr. Grewgious carried his smoothing-hand down over his eyes and nose, and even chin, before drawing his chair a little nearer, and speaking a little more confidentially: "I now touch, my dear, upon the point that is the direct cause of my troubling you with the present visit. Otherwise, being a particularly Angular man, I should not have intruded here. I am the last man to intrude into a sphere for which I am so entirely unfitted. I feel, on these premises, as if I was a bear—with the cramp—in a youthful Cotillon."

His ungainliness gave him enough of the air of his simile to set Rosa off laughing heartily.

"It strikes you in the same light," said Mr. Grewgious, with perfect calmness. "Just so. To return to my memorandum. Mr. Edwin has been to and fro here, as was arranged. You have mentioned that, in your quarterly letters to me. And you like him, and he likes you."

"I *like* him very much, sir," rejoined Rosa.

"So I said, my dear," returned her guardian, for whose ear the timid emphasis was much too fine. "Good. And you correspond."

"We write to one another," said Rosa, pouting, as she recalled their epistolary differences.

"Such is the meaning that I attach to the word 'correspond' in this application, my dear," said Mr. Grewgious. "Good. All goes well, time works on, and at this next Christmas-time it will become necessary, as a matter of form, to give the exemplary lady in the corner-window, to whom we are so much indebted, business-notice of your departure in the ensuing half-year. Your relations with her are far more than business-relations, no doubt; but a residue of business remains in them, and business is business ever. I am a particularly Angular man," proceeded Mr. Grewgious, as if it suddenly occurred to him to mention it, "and I am not used to give any thing away. If, for these two reasons, some competent Proxy would give *you* away, I should take it very kindly."

Rosa intimated, with her eyes on the ground, that she thought a substitute might be found, if required.

"Surely, surely," said Mr. Grewgious. "For instance, the gentleman who teaches Dancing here—he would know how to do it with graceful propriety. He would advance and retire in a manner satisfactory to the feelings of the officiating clergyman, and of yourself, and the bridegroom, and all parties concerned. I am—I am a particularly Angular man," said Mr. Grewgious, as if he had made up his mind to screw it out at last, "and should only blunder."

Rosa sat still and silent. Perhaps, her mind had not got quite so far as the ceremony yet, but was lagging on the way there.

"Memorandum, 'Will.' Now, my dear," said Mr. Grewgious, referring to his notes, disposing of "marriage" with his pencil, and taking a paper from his pocket, "although I have before possessed you with the contents of your father's will, I think it right at this time to leave a certified copy of it in your hands. And, although Mr. Edwin is also aware of its contents, I think it right at this time likewise to place a certified copy of it in Mr. Jasper's hands—"

"Not in his own?" asked Rosa, looking up quickly. "Cannot the copy go to Eddy himself?"

"Why, yes, my dear, if you particularly wish it; but I spoke of Mr. Jasper as being his trustee."

"I do particularly wish it, if you please," said Rosa, hurriedly and earnestly; "I don't like Mr. Jasper to come between us, in any way."

"It is natural, I suppose," said Mr. Grewgious, "that your young husband should be all in all. Yes. You observe that I say, I suppose. The fact is, I am a particularly Unnatural man, and I don't know from my own knowledge."

Rosa looked at him with some wonder.

"I mean," he explained, "that young ways were never my ways.

I was the only offspring of parents far advanced in life, and I half believe I was born advanced in life myself. No personality is intended toward the name you will so soon change, when I remark that, while the general growth of people seem to have come into existence buds, I seem to have come into existence a chip. I was a chip—and a very dry one—when I first became aware of myself. Respecting the other certified copy, your wish shall be complied with. Respecting your inheritance, I think you know all. It is an annuity of two hundred and fifty pounds. The savings upon that annuity, and some other items to your credit, all duly carried to account, with vouchers, will place you in possession of a lump-sum of money, rather exceeding Seventeen Hundred Pounds. I am empowered to advance the cost of your preparations for your marriage out of that fund. All is told."

"Will you please tell me," said Rosa, taking the paper with a prettily-knitted brow, but not opening it, "whether I am right in what I am going to say? I can understand what you tell me so very much better than what I read in law-writings. My poor papa and Eddy's father made their agreement together, as very dear and firm and fast friends, in order that we, too, might be very dear and firm and fast friends after them?"

"Just so."

"For the lasting good of both of us, and the lasting happiness of both of us?"

"Just so."

"That we might be to one another even much more than they had been to one another?"

"Just so."

"It was not bound upon Eddy, and it was not bound upon me by any forfeit, in case—"

"Don't be agitated, my dear. In the case that it brings tears into your affectionate eyes even to picture to yourself—in the case of your not marrying one another—no, no forfeiture on either side. You would then have been my ward until you were of age. No worse would have befallen you. Bad enough, perhaps!"

"And Eddy?"

"He would have come into his partnership derived from his father, and into its arrears to his credit, if any, on attaining his majority, just as now."

Rosa, with her perplexed face and knitted brow, bit the corner of her attested copy, as she sat with her head on one side, looking abstractedly on the floor, and smoothing it with her foot.

"In short," said Mr. Grewgious, "this betrothal is a wish, a sentiment, a friendly project, tenderly expressed on both sides. That it was strongly felt, and that there was a lively hope that it would prosper, there can be no doubt. When you were both children, you began to be accustomed to it, and it *has* prospered. But circumstances alter cases; and I made this visit to-day partly, indeed principally, to discharge myself of the duty of telling you, my dear, that two young people can only be betrothed in marriage (except as a matter of convenience, and therefore mockery and misery) of their own free will, their own attachment, and their own assurance (it may or may not prove a mistaken one, but we must take our chance of that) that they are suited to each other, and will make each other happy. Is it to be supposed, for example, that, if either of your fathers were living now, and had any mistrust on that subject, his mind would not be changed by the change of circumstances involved in the change of your years? Untenable, unreasonable, inconclusive, and preposterous!"

Mr. Grewgious said all this as if he were reading it aloud; or, still more, as if he were repeating a lesson. So expressionless of any approach to spontaneity were his face and manner.

"I have now, my dear," he added, blurring out "Will" with his pencil, "discharged myself of what is doubtless a formal duty in this case, but still a duty in such a case. Memorandum: 'Wishes.' My dear, is there any wish of yours that I can further?"

Rosa shook her head, with an almost plaintive air of hesitation in want of help.

"Is there any instruction that I can take from you with reference to your affairs?"

"I—I should like to settle them with Eddy first, if you please," said Rosa, plaiting the crease in her dress.

"Surely. Surely," returned Mr. Grewgious. "You two should be of one mind in all things. Is the young gentleman expected shortly?"

"He has gone away only this morning. He will be back at Christmas."

"Nothing could happen better. You will, on his return at Christmas, arrange all matters of detail with him; you will then communicate with me, and I will discharge myself (as a mere business acquittance) of my business responsibilities toward the accomplished lady in the corner window. They will accrue at that season." Blurring pencil once again. "Memorandum: 'Leave.' Yes. I will now, my dear, take my leave."

"Could I," said Rosa, rising, as he jerked out of his chair in his ungainly way, "could I ask you most kindly to come to me at Christmas, if I had any thing particular to say to you?"

"Why, certainly, certainly," he rejoined, apparently—if such a word can be used of one who had no apparent lights or shadows about him—complimented by the question. "As a particular Angular man, I do not fit smoothly into the social circle, and consequently I have no other engagement at Christmas-time than to partake, on the twenty-fifth, of a boiled turkey and celery sauce with a—with a particularly Angular clerk I have the good fortune to possess, whose father, being a Norfolk farmer, sends him up (the turkey up), as a present to me, from the neighborhood of Norwich. I should be quite proud of your wishing to see me, my dear. As a professional Receiver of rents, so very few people *do* wish to see me, that the novelty would be bracing."

For his ready acquiescence, the grateful Rosa put her hands upon his shoulders, stood on tiptoe, and instantly kissed him.

"Lord bless me!" cried Mr. Grewgious. "Thank you, my dear. The honor is almost equal to the pleasure. Miss Twinkleton, madam, I have had a most satisfactory conversation with my ward, and I will now release you from the incumbrance of my presence."

"Nay, sir," rejoined Miss Twinkleton, rising with a gracious condescension, "say not incumbrance. Not so, by any means. I cannot permit you to say so."

"Thank you, madam. I have read in the newspapers," said Mr. Grewgious, stammering a little, "that when a distinguished visitor (not that I am one: far from it) goes to a school (not that this is one: far from it), he asks for a holiday, or some sort of grace. It being now the afternoon in the—College—of which you are the eminent head, the young ladies might gain nothing, except in name, by having the rest of the day allowed them. But if there is any young lady at all under a cloud, might I solicit—"

"Ah, Mr. Grewgious, Mr. Grewgious!" cried Miss Twinkleton, with a chastely rallying forefinger. "O you gentlemen, you gentlemen! Fie for shame, that you are so hard upon us poor maligned disciplinarians of our sex, for your sakes! But as Miss Ferdinand is at present weighed down by an incubus"—Miss Twinkleton might have said a pen-and-inkubus of writing out Monsieur La Fontaine—"go to her, Rosa, my dear, and tell her the penalty is remitted, in deference to the intercession of your guardian, Mr. Grewgious."

Miss Twinkleton here achieved a courtesy, suggestive of marvels happening to her respected legs, and which she came out of nobly, three yards behind her starting-point.

As he held it incumbent upon him to call on Mr. Jasper before leaving Cloisterham, Mr. Grewgious went to the Gate-House, and climbed its postern stair. But Mr. Jasper's door being closed, and presenting on a slip of paper the word "Cathedral," the fact of its being service-time was borne into the mind of Mr. Grewgious. So, he descended the stair again, and, crossing the Close, paused at the great western folding-door of the Cathedral, which stood open on the fine and bright, though short-lived, afternoon, for the airing of the place.

"Dear me," said Mr. Grewgious, peeping in, "it's like looking down the throat of Old Time."

Old Time heaved a mouldy sigh from tomb and arch and vault; and gloomy shadows began to deepen in corners; and damps began to rise from green patches of stone; and jewels, cast upon the pavement of the nave from stained glass by the declining sun, began to perish. Within the grill-gate of the chancel, up the steps surmounted loomingly by the fast-darkening organ, white robes could be dimly seen, and one feeble voice, rising and falling in a cracked, monotonous mutter, could at intervals be faintly heard. In the free outer air, the river, the green pastures, and the brown arable lands, the teeming hills and dales, were reddened by the sunset; while the distant little windows in windmills and farm homesteads, shone, patches of bright beaten gold. In the Cathedral, all became gray, murky, and sepulchral, and the cracked, monotonous mutter went on like a dying voice, until the organ and the choir burst forth, and drowned it in a sea of music. Then the sea fell, and the dying voice made another feeble effort, and then the sea rose high, and beat its life out, and lashed the roof, and surged among the arches, and pierced the heights of the great tower; and then the sea was dry, and all was still.

Mr. Grewgious had by that time walked to the chancel-steps, where he met the living waters coming out.

"Nothing is the matter?" Thus Jasper accosted him, rather quickly. "You have not been sent for?"

"Not at all, not at all. I came down of my own accord. I have been to my pretty ward's, and am now homeward bound again."

"You found her thriving?"

"Blooming indeed. Most blooming. I merely came to tell her, seriously, what a betrothal by deceased parents is."

"And what is it—according to your judgment?"

Mr. Grewgious noticed the whiteness of the lips that asked the question, and put it down to the chilling account of the Cathedral.

"I merely came to tell her that it could not be considered binding, against any such reason for its dissolution as a want of affection, or want of disposition to carry it into effect, on the side of either party."

"May I ask, had you any especial reason for telling her that?"

Mr. Grewgious answered somewhat sharply, "The especial reason of doing my duty, sir. Simply that." Then he added, "Come, Mr. Jasper; I know your affection for your nephew, and that you are quick to feel on his behalf. I assure you that this implies not the least doubt of, or disrespect to, your nephew."

"You could not," returned Jasper, with a friendly pressure of his arm, as they walked on side by side, "speak more handsomely."

Mr. Grewgious pulled off his hat to smooth his head, and, having smoothed it, nodded it contentedly, and put his hat on again.

"I will wager," said Jasper, smiling—his lips were still so white that he was conscious of it, and bit and moistened them while speaking—"I will wager that she hinted no wish to be released from Ned."

"And you will win your wager, if you do," retorted Mr. Grewgious. "We should allow some margin for little maidenly delicacies in a young motherless creature, under such circumstances, I suppose; it is not in my line; what do you think?"

"There can be no doubt of it."

"I am glad you say so. Because," proceeded Mr. Grewgious, who had all this time very knowingly felt his way round to action on his remembrance of what she had said of Jasper himself, "because she seems to have some little delicate instinct that all preliminary arrangements had best be made between Mr. Edwin Drood and herself, don't you see? She don't want us, don't you know?"

Jasper touched himself on the breast, and said, somewhat indistinctly, "You mean me."

Mr. Grewgious touched himself on the breast, and said, "I mean us. Therefore, let them have their little discussions and councils together, when Mr. Edwin Drood comes back here at Christmas, and then you and I will step in, and put the final touches to the business."

"So you settled with her that you would come back at Christmas?" observed Jasper. "I see! Mr. Grewgious, as you quite fairly said just now, there is such an exceptional attachment between my nephew and me, that I am more sensitive for the dear, fortunate, happy, happy fellow, than for myself. But it is only right that the young lady should be considered, as you have pointed out, and that I should accept my cue from you. I accept it. I understand that at Christmas they will complete their preparations for May, and that their marriage will be put in final train by themselves, and that nothing will remain for us but to put ourselves in train also, and have every thing ready for our formal release from our trusts on Edwin's birthday."

"That is my understanding," assented Mr. Grewgious, as they shook hands to part. "God bless them both!"

"God save them both!" cried Jasper.

"I said, bless them," remarked the former, looking back over his shoulder.

"I said, save them," returned the latter. "Is there any difference?"

CHAPTER VIII.

SMOOTHING THE WAY.

It has been often enough remarked that women have a curious power of divining the characters of men, which would seem to be innate and instinctive; seeing that it is arrived at through no patient process of reasoning, that it can give no satisfactory or sufficient account of itself, and that it pronounces in the most confident manner even against accumulated observation on the part of the other sex. But it has not been quite so often remarked that this power (fallible, like every other human attribute) is for the most part absolutely incapable of self-revision; and that when it has delivered an adverse opinion which by all human lights is subsequently proved to have failed, it is undistinguishable from prejudice, in respect of its determination not to be corrected. Nay, the very possibility of contradiction or disproof, however remote, communicates to this feminine judgment from the first, in nine cases out of ten, the weakness attendant on the testimony of an interested witness; so personally and strongly does the fair diviner connect herself with her divination.

"Now, don't you think, Ma, dear," said the Minor Canon to his mother one day as she sat at her knitting in his little book-room, "that you are rather hard on Mr. Neville?"

"No, I do *not*, Sept," returned the old lady.

"Let us discuss it, Ma."

"I have no objection to discuss it, Sept. I trust, my dear, I am always open to discussion." There was a vibration in the old lady's cap, as though she internally added, "And I should like to see the discussion that would change *my* mind!"

"Very good, Ma," said her conciliatory son. "There is nothing like being open to discussion."

"I hope not, my dear," returned the old lady, evidently shut to it.

"Well! Mr. Neville, on that unfortunate occasion, commits himself under provocation."

"And under mulled wine," adds the old lady.

"I must admit the wine. Though I believe the two young men were much alike in that regard."

"I don't!" said the old lady.

"Why not, Ma?"

"Because I *don't*," said the old lady. "Still I am quite open to discussion."

"But, my dear Ma, I cannot see how we are to discuss, if you take that line."

"Blame Mr. Neville for it, Sept, and not me," said the old lady, with stately severity.

"My dear Ma! Why Mr. Neville?"

"Because," said Mrs. Crisparkle, retiring on first principles, "he came home intoxicated, and did great discredit to this house, and showed great disrespect to this family."

"That is not to be denied, Ma. He was then, and he is now, very sorry for it.

"But for Mr. Jasper's well-bred consideration in coming up to me next day, after service, in the Nave itself, with his gown still on, and expressing his hope that I had not been greatly alarmed or had my rest violently broken, I believe I might never have heard of that disgraceful transaction," said the old lady.

"To be candid, Ma, I think I should have kept it from you if I could, though I had not decidedly made up my mind. I was following Jasper out to confer with him on the subject, and to consider the expediency of his and my jointly hushing the thing up on all accounts, when I found him speaking to you. Then it was too late."

"Too late, indeed, Sept. He was still as pale as gentlemanly ashes at what had taken place in his rooms overnight."

"If I *had* kept it from you, Ma, you may be sure it would have been for your peace and quiet, and for the good of the young men, and in my best discharge of my duty according to my lights."

The old lady immediately walked across the room and kissed him, saying, "Of course, my dear Sept, I am sure of that."

"However, it became the town-talk," said Mr. Crisparkle, rubbing his ear, as his mother resumed her seat and her knitting, "and passed out of my power."

"And I said then, Sept," returned the old lady, "that I thought ill of Mr. Neville. And I say now that I think ill of Mr. Neville. And I said then, and I say now, that I hope Mr. Neville may come to good, but I don't believe he will." Here the cap vibrated again considerably.

"I am sorry to hear you say so, Ma—"

"I am sorry to say so, my dear," interposed the old lady, knitting on firmly, "but I can't help it."

"—For," pursued the Minor Canon, "it is undeniable that Mr. Neville is exceedingly industrious and attentive, and that he improves apace, and that he has—I hope I may say—an attachment to me."

"There is no merit in the last article, my dear," said the old lady, quickly, "and if he says there is, I think the worse of him for the boast."

"But, my dear Ma, he never said there was."

"Perhaps not," returned the old lady; "still, I don't see that it greatly signifies."

There was no impatience in the pleasant look with which Mr. Crisparkle contemplated the pretty old piece of china as it knitted; but there was, certainly, a humorous sense of its not being a piece of china to argue with very closely."

"Besides, Sept. Ask yourself what he would be without his sister. You know what an influence she has over him; you know what a capacity she has; you know that whatever he reads with you, he reads with her. Give her her fair share of your praise, and how much do you leave for him?"

At these words Mr. Crisparkle fell into a little reverie, in which he thought of several things. He thought of the times he had seen the brother and sister together in deep converse over one of his own old college books; now, in the rimy mornings, when he made those sharpening pilgrimages to Cloisterham Weir; now, in the sombre evenings, when he faced the wind at sunset, having climbed his favorite outlook, a beetling fragment of monastery-ruin; and the two studious figures passed below him along the margin of the river, in which the town fires and lights already shone, making the landscape bleaker. He thought how the consciousness had stolen upon him that, in teaching one, he was teaching two; and how he had almost insensibly adapted his explanations to both minds—that with which his own was daily in contact, and that which he only approached through it. He thought of the gossip that had reached him from the Nuns' House, to the effect that Helena, whom he had mistrusted as so proud and fierce, submitted herself to the fairy-bride (as he called her), and learned from her what she knew. He thought of the picturesque alliance between those two, externally so very different. He thought—perhaps most of all—could it be that these things were yet but so many weeks old, and had become an integral part of his life?"

As, whenever the Reverend Septimus fell a-musing, his good mother took it to be an infallible sign that he "wanted support," the blooming old lady made all haste to the dining-room closet, to produce from it the support embodied in a glass of Constantia and a home-made biscuit. It was a most wonderful closet, worthy of Cloisterham and of Minor Canon Corner. Above it, a portrait of Handel in a flowing wig beamed down at the spectator, with a knowing air of being up to the contents of the closet, and a musical air of intending to combine all its harmonies in one delicious fugue. No common closet with a vulgar door on hinges, openable all at once, and leaving nothing to be disclosed by degrees, this rare closet had a lock in mid-air, where two perpendicular slides met: the one falling down, and the other pushing up. The upper slide, on being pulled down (leaving the lower a double mystery) revealed deep shelves of pickle-jars, jam-pots, tin canisters, spice-boxes, and agreeably outlandish vessels of blue and white, the luscious lodgings of preserved tamarinds and ginger. Every benevolent inhabitant of this retreat had his name inscribed upon his stomach. The pickles, in a uniform of rich brown double-breasted buttoned coat, and yellow or sombre drab continuations, announced their portly forms, in printed capitals, as Walnut, Gherkin, Onion, Cabbage, Cauliflower, Mixed, and other members of that noble family. The jams, as being of a less masculine temperament, and as wearing curl-papers, announced themselves in feminine caligraphy, like a soft whisper, to be Raspberry, Gooseberry, Apricot, Plum, Damson, Apple, and Peach. The scene closing on these charmers, and the lower slide ascending, oranges were revealed, attended by a mighty japanned sugar-box, to temper their acerbity if unripe. Home-made biscuits waited at the Court of these Powers, accompanied by a goodly fragment of plum-cake, and various slender ladies' fingers, to be dipped into sweet wine and kissed. Lowest of all, a compact leaden vault enshrined the sweet wine and a stock of cordials, whence issued whispers of Seville Orange, Lemon, Almond, and Caraway-seed. There was a crowning air upon this closet of closets, of having been for ages hummed through by the Cathedral bell and organ, until those venerable bees had made sublimated honey of everything in store; and it was always observed that every dipper among the shelves (deep, as has been noticed, and swallowing up head, shoulders, and elbows) came forth again mellow-faced, and seeming to have undergone a saccharine transfiguration.

The Reverend Septimus yielded himself up quite as willing a victim to a nauseous medicinal herb-closet, also presided over by the china shepherdess, as to this glorious cupboard. To what amazing infusions of gentian, peppermint, gilliflower, sage, parsley, thyme, rue, rosemary, and dandelion, did his courageous stomach submit itself! In what wonderful wrappers, enclosing layers of dried leaves, would he swathe his rosy and contented face, if his mother suspected him of a toothache! What botanical blotches would he cheerfully stick upon his cheek or forehead, if the dear old lady convicted him of an imperceptible pimple there! Into this herbaceous penitentiary, situated on an upper staircase-landing—a low and narrow whitewashed cell, where bunches of dried leaves hung from rusty hooks in the ceiling, and were spread out upon shelves, in company with portentous bottles—would the Reverend Septimus submissively be led, like the highly-popular lamb who has so long and unresistingly been led to the slaughter, and there would he, unlike that lamb, bore nobody but himself. Not even doing that much, so that the old lady were busy and pleased, he would quietly swallow what was given him, merely taking a corrective dip of hands and face into the great bowl of dried rose-leaves, and into the other great bowl of dried lavender, and then would go out, as confident in the sweetening powers of Cloisterham Weir and a wholesome mind, as Lady Macbeth was hopeless of those of all the seas that roll.

In the present instance the good Minor Canon took his glass of Constantia with an excellent grace, and, so supported to his mother's satisfaction, applied himself to the remaining duties of the day. In their orderly and punctual progress they brought round Vesper Service and twilight. The Cathedral being very cold, he set off for a brisk trot after service; the trot to end in a charge at his favorite fragment of ruin, which was to be carried by storm, without a pause for breath.

He carried it in a masterly manner, and, not breathed even then, stood looking down upon the river. The river at Cloisterham is sufficiently near the sea to throw up oftentimes a quantity of sea-weed. An unusual quantity had come in with the last tide, and this, and the confusion of the water, and the restless dipping and flapping of the noisy gulls, and an angry light out seaward beyond the brown-sailed barges that were turning back, foreshadowed a stormy night. In his mind he was contrasting the wild and noisy sea with the quiet harbor of Minor Canon Corner, when Helena and Neville Landless passed below him. He had had the two together in his thoughts all day, and at once climbed down to speak to them together. The footing was rough in an uncertain light for any tread save that of a good climber; but the Minor Canon was as good a climber as most men, and stood beside them before many good climbers would have been half-way down.

"A wild evening, Miss Landless. Do you not find your usual walk with your brother too exposed and cold for the time of year? Or, at all events, when the sun is down, and the weather is driving in from the sea?"

Helena thought not. It was their favorite walk. It was very retired.

"It is very retired," assented Mr. Crisparkle, laying hold of his opportunity straightway, and walking on with them. "It is a place of all others where one can speak without interruption, as I wish to do.—Mr. Neville, I believe you tell your sister everything that passes between us?"

"Every thing, sir."

"Consequently," said Mr. Crisparkle, "your sister is aware that I have repeatedly urged you to make some kind of apology for that unfortunate occurrence which befel on the night of your arrival here."

In saying it he looked to her, and not to him; therefore, it was she, and not he, that replied—

"Yes."

"I call it unfortunate, Miss Helena," resumed Mr. Crisparkle, "forasmuch as it certainly has engendered a prejudice against Neville. There is a notion about that he is a dangerously passionate fellow, of an uncontrollable and furious temper; he is really avoided as such."

"I have no doubt he is, poor fellow," said Helena, with a look of proud compassion at her brother, expressing a deep sense of his being ungenerously treated. "I should be quite sure of it, from your saying so; but what you tell me is confirmed by suppressed hints and references that I meet with every day."

"Now," Mr. Crisparkle again resumed, in a tone of mild though firm persuasion, "is not this to be regretted, and ought it not to be amended? These are early days of Neville's in Cloisterham, and I have no fear of his outliving such a prejudice, and proving himself to have been misunderstood. But how much wiser to take action at once than to trust to uncertain time! Besides, apart from its being politic, it is right. For there can be no question that Neville was wrong."

"He was provoked," Helena submitted.

"He was the assailant," Mr. Crisparkle submitted.

They walked on in silence, until Helena raised her eyes to the Minor Canon's face, and said, almost reproachfully, "Oh, Mr. Crisparkle, would you have Neville throw himself at young Drood's feet, or at Mr. Jasper's, who maligns him every day? In your heart you cannot mean it. From your heart you could not do it, if his case were yours."

"I have represented to Mr. Crisparkle, Helena," said Neville, with a glance of deference toward his tutor, "that if I could do it from my heart I would. But I cannot, and I revolt from the pretence. You forget, however, that to put the case to Mr. Crisparkle as his own, is to suppose Mr. Crisparkle to have done what I did."

"I ask his pardon," said Helena.

"You see," remarked Mr. Crisparkle, again laying hold of his opportunity, though with a moderate and delicate touch, "you both instinctively acknowledge that Neville did wrong! Then why stop short, and not otherwise acknowledge it?"

"Is there no difference," asked Helena, with a little faltering in her manner, "between submission to a generous spirit, and submission to a base or trivial one?"

Before the worthy Minor Canon was quite ready with his argument in reference to this nice distinction, Neville struck in:

"Help me to clear myself with Mr. Crisparkle, Helena. Help me to convince him that I cannot be the first to make concessions without mockery and falsehood. My nature must be changed before I can do so, and it is not changed. I am sensible of inexpressible affront, and deliberate aggravation of inexpressible affront, and I am angry. The plain truth is, I am still as angry when I recall that night as I was that night."

"Neville," hinted the Minor Canon, with a steady countenance, "you have repeated that former action of your hands, which I so much dislike."

"I am sorry for it, sir, but it was involuntary. I confessed that I was still as angry."

"And I confess," said Mr. Crisparkle, "that I hoped for better things."

"I am sorry to disappoint you, sir, but it would be far worse to deceive you, and I should deceive you grossly if I pretended that you had softened me in this respect. The time may come when your powerful influence will do even that with the difficult pupil whose antecedents you know; but it has not come yet. Is this so, and in spite of my struggles against myself, Helena?"

She, whose dark eyes were watching the effect of what he said on Mr. Crisparkle's face, replied—to Mr. Crisparkle, not to him—"It is so." After a short pause, she answered the slightest look of inquiry conceivable, in her brother's eyes, with as slight an affirmative bend of her own head; and he went on:

"I have never yet had the courage to say to you, sir, what in full openness I ought to have said when you first talked with me on this subject. It is not easy to say, and I have been withheld by a fear of its seeming ridiculous, which is very strong upon me down to this last moment, and might, but for my sister, prevent my being quite open with you even now.—I admire Miss Bud, sir, so very much, that I cannot bear her being treated with conceit or indifference; and even if I did not feel that I had an injury against young Drood on my own account, I should feel that I had an injury against him on hers."

Mr. Crisparkle, in utter amazement, looked at Helena for corroboration, and met in her expressive face full corroboration, and a plea for advice.

"The young lady of whom you speak is, as you know, Mr. Neville, shortly to be married," said Mr. Crisparkle, gravely; "therefore your admiration, if it be of that special nature which you seem to indicate, is outrageously misplaced. Moreover, it is monstrous that you should take upon yourself to be the young lady's champion against her chosen husband. Besides, you have seen them only once. The young lady has become your sister's friend; and I wonder that your sister, even on her behalf, has not checked you in this irrational and culpable fancy."

"She has tried, sir, but uselessly. Husband or no husband, that fellow is incapable of the feeling with which I am inspired, toward the beautiful young creature whom he treats like a doll. I say he is as incapable of it as he is unworthy of her. I say she is sacrificed in being bestowed upon him. I say that I love her, and despise and hate him!" This with a face so flushed, and a gesture so violent, that his sister crossed to his side and caught his arm, remonstrating, "Neville, Neville!"

Thus recalled to himself, he quickly became sensible of having lost the guard he had set upon his passionate tendency, and covered his face with his hand, as one repentant and wretched.

Mr. Crisparkle, watching him attentively, and at the same time meditating how to proceed, walked on for some paces in silence. Then he spoke:

"Mr. Neville, Mr. Neville, I am sorely grieved to see in you more traces of a character as sullen, angry, and wild, as the night now closing in. They are of too serious an aspect to leave me the resource of treating the infatuation you have disclosed as undeserving serious consideration. I give it very serious consideration, and I speak to you accordingly. This feud between you and young Drood must not go on. I cannot permit it to go on any longer, knowing what I now know from you, and you living under my roof. Whatever prejudiced and unauthorized constructions your blind and envious wrath may put upon his character, it is a frank, good-natured character. I know I can trust to it for that. Now, pray observe what I am about to say. On reflection, and on your sister's representation, I am willing to admit that, in making peace with young Drood, you have a right to be met half-way. I will engage that you shall be, and even that young Drood shall make the first advance. This condition fulfilled, you will pledge me the honor of a Christian gentleman that the quarrel is forever at an end on your side. What may be in your heart when you give him your hand can only be known to the Searcher of all hearts; but it will never go well with you if there be any treachery there. So far, as to that; next as to what I must again speak of as your infatuation. I understand it to have been confided to me, and to be known to no other person save your sister and yourself. Do I understand aright?"

Helena answered in a low voice, "It is only known to us three who are here together."

"It is not at all known to the young lady, your friend?"

"On my soul, no!"

"I require you, then, to give me your similar and solemn pledge, Mr. Neville, that it shall remain the secret it is, and that you will take no other action whatsoever upon it than endeavoring (and that most earnestly) to erase it from your mind. I will not tell you that it will soon pass; I will not tell you that it is the fancy of the moment; I will not tell you that such caprices have their rise and fall among the young and ardent every hour; I will leave you undisturbed in the belief that it has few parallels or none, that it will abide with you a long time, and that it will be very difficult to conquer. So much the more weight shall I attach to the pledge I require from you, when it is unreservedly given."

The young man twice or thrice essayed to speak, but failed.

"Let me leave you with your sister, whom it is time you took home," said Mr. Crisparkle. "You will find me alone in my room by-and-by."

"Pray do not leave us yet," Helena implored him. "Another minute."

"I should not," said Neville, pressing his hand upon his face, "have needed so much as another minute, if you had been less patient with me, Mr. Crisparkle, less considerate of me, and less unpretendingly good and true. O, if in my childhood I had known such a guide!"

"Follow your guide now, Neville," murmured Helena, "and follow him to heaven!"

There was that in her tone which broke the good Minor Canon's voice, or it would have repudiated her exaltation of him. As it was, he laid a finger on his lips, and looked toward her brother.

To say that I give both pledges, Mr. Crisparkle, out of my innermost heart, and to say that there is no treachery in it, is to say nothing!" Thus Neville, greatly moved. "I beg your forgiveness for my miserable lapse into a burst of passion."

"Not mine, Neville, not mine. You know with whom forgiveness lies as the highest attribute conceivable. Miss Helena, you and your brother are twin-children. You came into this world with the same dispositions, and passed your younger days together, surrounded by the same adverse circumstances. What you have overcome in yourself, can you not overcome in him? You see the rock that lies in his course. Who but you can keep him clear of it?"

"Who but you, sir?" replied Helena. "What is my influence, or my weak wisdom, compared with yours!"

"You have the wisdom of Love," returned the Minor Canon, "and it was the highest wisdom ever known upon this earth, remember. As to mine—but the less said of that commonplace commodity the better. Good-night!"

She took the hand he offered her, and gratefully and almost reverently raised it to her lips.

"Tut!" said the Minor Canon, softly, "I am much overpaid!" And he turned away.

Retracing his steps toward the Cathedral Close, he tried, as he went along in the dark, to think out the best means of bringing to pass what he had promised to effect, and what must somehow be done. "I shall probably be asked to marry them," he reflected, "and I would they were married and gone! But this presses first." He debated principally, whether he should write to young Drood, or whether he should speak to Jasper. The consciousness of being popular with the whole Cathedral establishment inclined him to the latter course, and the well-timed sight of the lighted gate-house decided him to take it. "I will strike while the iron is hot," he said, "and see him now."

Jasper was lying asleep on a couch before the fire, when, having ascended the postern-stair, and received no answer to his knock at the door, Mr. Crisparkle gently turned the handle and looked in. Long afterward he had cause to remember how Jasper sprang from the couch in a delirious state between sleeping and waking, crying out, "What is the matter? Who did it?"

"It is only I, Jasper. I am sorry to have disturbed you."

The glare of his eyes settled down into a look of recognition, and he moved a chair or two, to make a way to the fireside.

"I was dreaming at a great rate, and am glad to be disturbed from an indigestive after-dinner sleep. Not to mention that you are always welcome."

"Thank you. I am not confident," returned Mr. Crisparkle, as he sat himself down in the easy-chair placed for him, "that my subject will at first sight be quite as welcome as myself; but I am a minister of peace, and I pursue my subject in the interest of peace. In a word, Jasper, I want to establish peace between these two young fellows."

A very perplexed expression took hold of Mr. Jasper's face; a verv perplexing expression too, for Mr. Crisparkle could make nothing of it.

"How?" was Jasper's inquiry, in a low and slow voice, after a silence.

"For the 'How' I come to you. I want to ask you to do me the great favor and service of interposing with your nephew (I have already interposed with Mr. Neville), and getting him to write you a short note, in his lively way, saying that he is willing to shake hands. I know what a good-natured fellow he is, and what influence you have with him. And, without in the least defending Mr. Neville, we must all admit that he was bitterly stung."

Jasper turned that perplexed face toward the fire. Mr. Crisparkle, continuing to observe it, found it even more perplexing than before, inasmuch as it seemed to denote (which could hardly be) some close internal calculation.

"I know that you are not prepossessed in Mr. Neville's favor," the Minor Canon was going on, when Jasper stopped him:

"You have cause to say so. I am not, indeed."

"Undoubtedly, and I admit his lamentable violence of temper, though I hope he and I will get the better of it between us. But I have exacted a very solemn promise from him as to his future demeanor toward your nephew, if you do kindly interpose; and I am sure he will keep it."

"You are always responsible and trustworthy, Mr. Crisparkle. Do you really feel sure that you can answer for him so confidently?"

"I do."

The perplexed and perplexing look vanished.

"Then you relieve my mind of a great dread and a heavy weight," said Jasper; "I will do it."

Mr. Crisparkle, delighted by the swiftness and completeness of his success, acknowledged it in the handsomest terms.

"I will do it," repeated Jasper, "for the comfort of having your guaranty against my vague and unfounded fears. You will laugh—but do you keep a Diary?"

"A line for a day; not more."

"A line for a day would be quite as much as my uneventful life would need, Heaven knows," said Jasper, taking a book from a desk; "but that my Diary is, in fact, a Diary of Ned's life too. You will laugh at this entry; you will guess when it was made:

"'Past midnight.—After what I have just now seen, I have a morbid dread upon me of some horrible consequences resulting to my dear boy, that I cannot reason with or in any way contend against. All my efforts are vain. The demoniacal passion of this Neville Landless, his strength in his fury, and his savage rage for the destruction of its object, appall me. So profound is the impression, that twice since have I gone into my dear boy's room, to assure myself of his sleeping safely, and not lying dead in his blood.'

"Here is another entry next morning:

"'Ned up and away. Light-hearted and unsuspicious as ever. He laughed when I cautioned him, and said he was as good a man as Neville Landless any day. I told him that might be, but he was not as bad a man. He continued to make light of it, but I travelled with him as far as I could, and left him most unwillingly. I am unable to shake off these dark intangible presentiments of evil—if feelings founded upon staring facts are to be so called.'

"Again and again," said Jasper, in conclusion, twirling the leaves of the book before putting it by, "I have relapsed into these moods, as other entries show. But I have now your assurance at my back, and shall put it in my book, and make it an antidote to my black humors."

"Such an antidote, I hope," returned Mr. Crisparkle, "as will induce you before long to consign the black humors to the flames. I ought to be the last to find any fault with you this evening, when you have met my wishes so freely; but I must say, Jasper, that your devotion to your nephew has made you exaggerative here."

"You are my witness," said Jasper, shrugging his shoulders, "what my state of mind honestly was, that night, before I sat down to write, and in what words I expressed it. You remember objecting to a word I used, as being too strong? It was a stronger word than any in my Diary."

"Well, well. Try the antidote," rejoined Mr. Crisparkle, "and may it give you a brighter and better view of the case! We will discuss it no more, now. I have to thank you for myself, and I thank you sincerely."

"You shall find," said Jasper, as they shook hands, "that I will not do the thing you wish me to do by halves. I will take care that Ned, giving way at all, shall give way thoroughly."

On the third day after this conversation, he called on Mr. Crisparkle with the following letter:

"MY DEAR JACK:

"I am touched by your account of your interview with Mr. Crisparkle, whom I much respect and esteem. At once I openly say that I forgot myself on that occasion quite as much as Mr. Landless did, and that I wish that by-gone to be a by-gone, and all to be right again.

"Look here, dear old boy. Ask Mr. Landless to dinner on Christmas Eve (the better the day the better the deed), and let there be only we three, and let us shake hands all round there and then, and say no more about it.

"My dear Jack,

"Ever your most affectionate,

"EDWIN DROOD.

"P. S.—Love to Miss Pussy at the next music-lesson."

"You expect Mr. Neville, then?" said Mr. Crisparkle.

"I count upon his coming," said Mr. Jasper.

CHAPTER IX.

A PICTURE AND A RING.

BEHIND the most ancient part of Holborn, London, where certain gabled-houses some centuries of age still stand looking on the public way, as if disconsolately looking for the Old Bourne that has long run dry, is a little nook composed of two irregular quadrangles, called Staple Inn. It is one of those nooks, the turning into which out of the clashing street imparts to the relieved pedestrian the sensation of having put cotton in his ears and velvet soles on his boots. It is one of those nooks where a few smoky sparrows twitter in smoky trees, as though they called to one another, "Let us play at country," and where a few feet of garden-mould and a few yards of gravel enable them to do that refreshing violence to their tiny understandings. Moreover, it is one of those nooks which are legal nooks; and it contains a little Hall, with a little lantern in its roof; to what obstructive purposes devoted, and at whose expense, this history knoweth not.

In the days when Cloisterham took offence at the existence of a railroad afar off, as menacing that sensitive constitution, the property of us Britons; the odd fortune of which sacred institutions it is to be in exactly equal degrees croaked about, trembled for, and boasted of, whatever happens to anything, anywhere in the world; in those days no neighboring architecture of lofty proportions had arisen to overshadow Staple Inn. The westering sun bestowed bright glances on it, and the southwest wind blew into it unimpeded.

Neither wind nor sun, however, favored Staple Inn, one December afternoon toward six o'clock, when it was filled with fog, and candles shed murky and blurred rays through the windows of all its then-occupied sets of chambers; notably, from a set of chambers in a corner house in the little inner quadrangle, presenting in black and white over its ugly portal the mysterious inscription:

P
J T
1747.

In which set of chambers, never having troubled his head about the inscription, unless to bethink himself at odd times on glancing up at it, that haply it might mean Perhaps John Thomas, or Perhaps Joe Tyler, sat Mr. Grewgious, writing by his fire.

Who could have told, by looking at Mr. Grewgious, whether he had ever known ambition or disappointment? He had been bred to the Bar, and had laid himself out for chamber practice; to draw deeds; "convey, the wise it call," as Pistol says. But Conveyancing and he had made such a very indifferent marriage of it that they had separated by consent—if there can be said to be separation where there has never been coming together.

No. Coy Conveyancing would not come to Mr. Grewgious. She was wooed, not won, and they went their several ways. But an Arbitration being blown toward him by some unaccountable wind, and he gaining great credit in it as one indefatigable in seeking out right and doing right, a pretty fat Receivership was next blown into his pocket by a wind more traceable to its source. So, by chance, he had found his niche. Receiver and Agent now, to two rich estates, and deputing their legal business, in an amount worth having, to a firm of solicitors on the floor below, he had snuffed out his ambition (supposing him to have ever lighted it) and had settled down with his snuffers for the rest of his life under the dry vine and fig-tree of P. J. T., who planted in seventeen-forty-seven.

Many accounts and account-books, many files of correspondence, and several strong boxes, garnished Mr. Grewgious's room. They can scarcely be represented as having lumbered it, so conscientious and precise was their orderly arrangement. The apprehension of dying suddenly, and leaving one fact or one figure with any incompleteness or obscurity attaching to it, would have stretched Mr. Grewgious stone dead any day. The largest fidelity to a trust was the life-blood of the man. There are sorts of life-blood that course more quickly, more gayly, more attractively; but there is no better sort in circulation.

There was no luxury in his room. Even its comforts were limited to its being dry and warm, and having a snug though faded fireside. What may be called its private life was confined to the hearth, and an easy-chair, and an old-fashioned occasional round table that was brought out upon the rug after business hours, from a corner where it elsewise remained turned up like a shining mahogany shield. Behind it, when standing thus on the defensive, was a closet, usually containing something good to drink. An outer room was the clerk's room; Mr. Grewgious's sleeping-room was across the common stair; and he held some not empty cellarage at the bottom of the common stair. Three hundred days in the year, at least, he crossed over to the hotel in Furnival's Inn for his dinner, and after dinner crossed back again, to make the most of these simplicities until it should become broad business day once more, with P. J. T., date seventeen-forty-seven.

As Mr. Grewgious sat and wrote by his fire that afternoon, so did the clerk of Mr. Grewgious sit and write by *his* fire. A pale, puffy-faced, dark-haired person of thirty, with big dark eyes that wholly wanted lustre, and a dissatisfied, doughy complexion, that seemed to ask to be sent to the baker's, this attendant was a mysterious being possessed of some strange power over Mr. Grewgious. As though he had been called into existence, like a fabulous Familiar, by a magic spell which had failed when required to dismiss him, he stuck tight to Mr. Grewgious's stool, although Mr. Grewgious's comfort and convenience would manifestly have been advanced by dispossessing him. A gloomy person with tangled locks, and a general air of having been reared under the shadow of that baleful tree of Java which has given shelter to more lies than the whole botanical kingdom, Mr. Grewgious, nevertheless, treated him with unaccountable consideration.

"Now, Bazzard," said Mr. Grewgious, on the entrance of his clerk, looking up from his papers as he arranged them for the night, "what is in the wind besides fog?"

"Mr. Drood," said Bazzard.

"What of him?"

"Has called," said Bazzard.

"You might have shown him in."

"I am doing it," said Bazzard.

The visitor came in accordingly.

"Dear me!" said Mr. Grewgious, looking round his pair of office candles. "I thought you had called and merely left your name and gone. How do you do, Mr. Edwin? Dear me, you're choking?"

"It's this fog," returned Edwin, "and it makes my eyes smart like cayenne pepper."

"Is it really so bad as that? Pray undo your wrappers. It's fortunate I have so good a fire; but Mr. Bazzard has taken care of me."

"No, I haven't," said Mr. Bazzard, at the door.

"Ah! Then it follows that I must have taken care of myself without observing it," said Mr. Grewgious. "Pray be seated in my chair. No. I beg! Coming out of such an atmosphere, in *my* chair."

Edwin took the easy-chair in the corner; and the fog he had brought in with him, and the fog he took off with his great-coat and neck-shawl, was speedily licked up by the eager fire.

"I look," said Edwin, smiling, "as if I had come to stop."

"—By-the-by," cried Mr. Grewgious, "excuse my interrupting you; do stop. The fog may clear in an hour or two. We can have dinner in from just across Holborn. You had better take your cayenne pepper here than outside; pray stop and dine."

"You are very kind," said Edwin, glancing about him, as though attracted by the notion of a new and relishing sort of gypsy party.

"Not at all," said Mr. Grewgious; "*you* are very kind to join issue with a bachelor in chambers, and take pot-luck. And I'll ask," said Mr. Grewgious, dropping his voice, and speaking with a twinkling eye, as if inspired with a bright thought, "I'll ask Bazzard. He mightn't like it else.—Bazzard!"

Bazzard reappeared.

"Dine presently with Mr. Drood and me."

"If I am ordered to dine, of course I will, sir," was the gloomy answer.

"Save the man!" cried Mr. Grewgious. "You're not ordered; you're invited."

"Thank you, sir," said Bazzard; "in that case I don't care if I do."

"That's arranged. And perhaps you wouldn't mind," said Mr. Grewgious, "stepping over to the hotel in Furnival's, and asking them to send in materials for laying the cloth. For dinner we'll have a tureen of the hottest and strongest soup available, and we'll have the best-made dish that can be recommended, and we'll have a joint (such as a haunch of mutton), and we'll have a goose, or a turkey, or any little stuffed thing of that sort that may happen to be in the bill of fare—in short, we'll have whatever there is on hand."

These liberal directions Mr. Grewgious issued with his usual air of reading an inventory, or repeating a lesson, or doing anything else by rote. Bazzard, after drawing out the round table, withdrew to execute them.

"I was a little delicate, you see," said Mr. Grewgious, in a lower tone, after his clerk's departure, "about employing him in the foraging or commissariat department. Because he mightn't like it."

"He seems to have his own way, sir," remarked Edwin.

"His own way!" returned Mr. Grewgious. "Oh, dear, no! Poor

fellow, you quite mistake him. If he had his own way, he wouldn't be here."

"I wonder where he would be!" Edwin thought. But he only thought it, because Mr. Grewgious came and stood himself with his back to the other corner of the fire, and his shoulder-blades against the chimney-piece, and collected his skirts for easy conversation.

"I take it, without having the gift of prophecy, that you have done me the favor of looking in to mention that you are going down yonder—where I can tell you, you are expected—and to offer to execute any little commission from me to my charming ward, and perhaps to sharpen me up a bit in any proceedings? Eh, Mr. Edwin?"

"I called, sir, before going down, as an act of attention."

"Of attention!" said Mr. Grewgious. "Ah! of course, not of impatience?"

"Impatience, sir?"

Mr. Grewgious had meant to be arch—not that he, in the remotest degree, expressed that meaning—and had brought himself into scarcely supportable proximity with the fire, as if to burn the fullest effect of his archness into himself, as other subtle impressions are burned into hard metals. But his archness suddenly flying before the composed face and manner of his visitor, and only the fire remaining he started, and rubbed himself.

"I have lately been down yonder," said Mr. Grewgious, rearranging his skirts; "and that was what I referred to when I said I could tell you you are expected."

"Indeed, sir! Yes, I knew that Pussy was looking out for me."

"Do you keep a cat down there?" asked Mr. Grewgious.

Edwin colored a little as he explained, "I call Rosa Pussy."

"Oh, really," said Mr. Grewgious, smoothing down his head, "that's very affable."

Edwin glanced at his face, uncertain whether or no he seriously objected to the appellation. But Edwin might as well have glanced at the face of a clock.

"A pet name, sir," he explained again.

"Umps," said Mr. Grewgious, with a nod. But with such an extraordinary compromise between an unqualified assent and a qualified dissent, that his visitor was much disconcerted.

"Did PRosa—" Edwin began, by way of recovering himself.

"PRosa?" repeated Mr. Grewgious.

"I was going to say Pussy, and changed my mind; did she tell you any thing about the Landlesses?"

"No," said Mr. Grewgious. "What is the Landlesses? An estate? A villa? A farm?"

"A brother and sister. The sister is at the Nuns' House, and has become a great friend of P—"

"PRosa's," Mr. Grewgious struck in, with a fixed face.

"She is a strikingly handsome girl, sir," and I thought she might have been described to you, or presented to you, perhaps?"

"Neither," said Mr. Grewgious. "But here is Bazzard."

Bazzard returned, accompanied by two waiters — an immovable waiter and a flying waiter; and the three brought in with them as much fog as gave a new roar to the fire. The flying waiter, who had brought every thing on his shoulders, laid the cloth with amazing rapidity and dexterity; while the immovable waiter, who had brought nothing, found fault with him. The flying waiter then highly polished all the glasses he had brought, and the immovable waiter looked through them. The flying waiter then flew across Holborn for the soup, and flew back again, and then took another flight for the made-dish and flew back again, and then took another flight for the joint and poultry and flew back again, and between whiles took supplementary flights for a great variety of articles, as it was discovered from time to time that the immovable waiter had forgotten them all. But let the flying waiter cleave the air as he might, he was always reproached on his return by the immovable waiter for bringing fog with him, and being out of breath. At the conclusion of the repast, by which time the flying waiter was severely blown, the immovable waiter gathered up the table-cloth under his arm with a grand air, and having sternly (not to say with indignation) looked on at the flying waiter while he set clean glasses around, directed a valedictory glance toward Mr. Grewgious, conveying, "Let it be clearly understood between us that the reward is mine, and that Nil is the claim of this slave," and pushed the flying waiter before him out of the room.

It was like a highly-finished miniature painting representing My Lords of the Circumlocutional Department, Commandership-in-Chief of any sort, Government. It was quite an edifying little picture to be hung on the line in the National Gallery.

As the fog had been the proximate cause of this sumptuous repast, so the fog served for its general sauce. To hear the out-door clerks, sneezing, wheezing, and beating their feet on the gravel was a zest far surpassing Doctor Kitchener's. To bid, with a shiver, the unfortunate flying waiter shut the door before he had opened it, was a condiment of a profounder flavor than Harvey. And here let it be noticed parenthetically that the leg of this young man in its application to the door evinced the finest sense of touch always preceding himself and tray (with something of an angling air about it), by some seconds, and always lingering after he and the tray had disappeared,(like Macbeth's leg when accompanying him off the stage with reluctance to the assassination of Duncan.)

The host had gone below to the cellar, and had brought up bottles of ruby, straw-colored, and golden drinks, which had ripened long ago in lands where no fogs are, and had since lain slumbering in the shade. Sparkling and tingling after so long a nap, they pushed at their corks to help the cork-screw (like prisoners helping rioters to force their gates), and danced out gayly. If P. J. T. in seventeen-forty-seven, or in any other year of his period, drank such wines, then, for a certainty, P. J. T. was Pretty Jolly Too.

Externally, Mr. Grewgious showed no signs of being mellowed by these glowing vintages. Instead of his drinking them, they might have been poured over him in his high-dried snuff form, and run to waste, for any lights and shades they caused to flicker over his face. Neither was his manner influenced. But, in his wooden way, he had observant eyes for Edwin; and when, at the end of dinner, he motioned Edwin back to his own easy-chair in the fireside corner, and Edwin luxuriously sank into it after very brief remonstrance, Mr. Grewgious, as he turned his seat round toward the fire too, and smoothed his head and face, might have been seen looking at his visitor between his smoothing fingers.

"Bazzard!" said Mr. Grewgious, suddenly turning to him.

"I follow you, sir," returned Bazzard, who had done his work of consuming meat and drink, in a workmanlike manner, though mostly in speechlessness.

"I drink to you, Bazzard; Mr. Edwin, success to Mr. Bazzard!"

"Success to Mr. Bazzard!" echoed Edwin, with a totally unfounded appearance of enthusiasm, and with the unspoken addition, "What in, I wonder!"

"And May!" pursued Mr. Grewgious,—"I am not at liberty to be definite—May!—my conversational powers are so very limited that I know I shall not come well out of this—May!—it ought to be put imaginatively, but I have no imagination—May!—the thorn of anxiety is as nearly the mark as I am likely to get—May it come out at last!"

Mr. Bazzard, with a frowning smile at the fire, put a hand into his tangled locks; as if the thorn of anxiety were there; then into his waistcoat, as if it were there; then into his pockets, as if it were there. In all these movements he was closely followed by the eyes of Edwin, as if that young gentleman expected to see the thorn in action. It was not produced, however, and Mr. Bazzard merely said, "I follow you, sir, and I thank you."

"I am going," said Mr. Grewgious, jingling his glass on the table with one hand and bending aside under cover of the other to whisper to Edwin, "to drink to my ward. But I put Bazzard first. He mightn't like it else."

This was said with a mysterious wink; or what would have been a wink, if, in Mr. Grewgious's hands, it could have been quick enough. So Edwin winked responsively without the least idea what he meant by doing so.

"And now," said Mr. Grewgious, "I devote a bumper to the fair and fascinating Miss Rosa. Bazzard, the fair and fascinating Miss Rosa!"

"I follow you, sir," said Bazzard, "and I pledge you!"

"And so do I!" said Edwin.

"Lord bless me!" cried Mr. Grewgious, breaking the blank silence which of course ensued, though why these pauses *should* come upon us when we have performed any small social rite not directly inducive of self-examination or mental despondency who can tell! "I am a particularly Angular man, and yet I fancy (if I may use the word, not having a morsel of fancy) that I could draw a picture of a true lover's state of mind to-night."

"Let us follow you, sir," said Bazzard, "and have the picture."

"Mr. Edwin will correct it where it's wrong," resumed Mr. Grewgious, "and will throw in a few touches from the life. I dare say it is wrong in many particulars, and wants many touches from the life, for I was born a Chip, and have neither soft sympathies nor soft experiences. Well! I hazard the guess that the true lover's mind is completely permeated by the beloved object of his affections. I hazard the guess that her dear name is precious to him, cannot be heard or repeated without emotion, and is preserved sacred. If he has any distinguishing appellation of fondness for her, it is reserved for her, and is not for common ears. A name that it would be a privilege to call her by, being alone with her own bright self, it would be a liberty, a coldness, an insensibility, almost a breach of good faith, to flaunt elsewhere."

It was wonderful to see Mr. Grewgious sitting bolt upright, with his hands on his knees continuously chopping this discourse out of himself, much as a charity-boy with a very good memory might get his catechism said, and evincing no corresponding emotion whatever, unless in a certain occasional little tingling perceptible at the end of his nose.

"My picture," Mr. Grewgious proceeded, "goes on to represent (under correction from you, Mr. Edwin) the true lover as ever impatient to be in the presence or vicinity of the beloved object of his affections, as caring very little for his ease in any other society, and as constantly seeking that. If I was to say seeking that as a bird seeks its nest, I should make an ass of myself, because that would trench upon what I understand to be poetry; and I am so far from trenching upon poetry at any time, that I never to my knowledge got within ten thousand miles of it. And I am besides totally unacquainted with the habits of birds, except the birds of Staple Inn, who seek their nests on ledges and in gutter-pipes and chimney-pots, not constructed for them by the beneficent hand of Nature. I beg, therefore, to be understood as foregoing the bird's-nest. But my picture does represent the true lover as having no existence separable from that of the beloved object of his affections, and as living at once a doubled life and a halved life. And if I do not clearly express what I mean by that, it is either for the reason that having no conversational powers, I cannot express what I mean, or that having no meaning, I do not mean what I fail to express. Which, to the best of my belief, is not the case."

Edward had turned red and turned white as certain points of this picture came into the light. He now sat looking at the fire and bit his lip.

"The speculations of an Angular man," resumed Mr. Grewgious, still sitting and speaking exactly as before, "are probably erroneous on so globular a topic. But I figure to myself (subject as before to Mr. Edwin's correction) that there can be no coolness, no lassitude, no doubt, no indifference, no half-fire and half-smoke state of mind in a real lover. Pray am I at all near the mark in my picture?"

As abrupt in his conclusion as in his commencement and progress, he jerked this inquiry at Edwin, and stopped when one might have supposed him in the middle of his oration.

"I should say, sir," stammered Edwin, "as you refer the question to me—"

"Yes," said Mr. Grewgious, "I refer it to you as an authority."

"I should say then, sir," Edwin went on embarrassed, "that the picture you have drawn is generally correct; but I submit that perhaps you may be rather hard upon the unlucky lover."

"Likely so," assented Mr. Grewgious, "likely so. I am a hard man in the grain."

"He may not show," said Edwin, "all he feels; or he may not—"

There he stopped so long to find the rest of his sentence that Mr. Grewgious rendered his difficulty a thousand times the greater by unexpectedly striking in with—

"No, to be sure; he *may* not!"

After that they all sat silent; the silence of Mr. Bazzard being occasioned by slumber.

"His responsibility is very great though," said Mr. Grewgious, at length, with his eyes on the fire.

Edwin nodded assent, with *his* eyes on the fire.

"And let him be sure that he trifles with no one," said Mr. Grewgious; "neither with himself, nor with any other."

Edwin bit his lip again, and still sat looking at the fire.

"He must not make a plaything of a treasure. Woe betide him if he does! Let him take that well to heart," said Mr. Grewgious.

Though he said these things in short sentences, much as the suppositious charity-boy just now referred to might have repeated a verse or two from the Book of Proverbs, there was something dreamy (for so literal a man) in the way in which he now shook his right forefinger at the live coals in the grate, and again fell silent.

But not for long. As he sat upright and stiff in his chair, he suddenly rapped his knees, like the carved image of some queer Joss or other coming out of its reverie, and said, "We must finish this bottle, Mr. Edwin. Let me help you. I'll help Bazzard, too, though he *is* asleep. He mightn't like it else."

He helped them both, and helped himself, and drained his glass, and stood it bottom upward on the table, as though he had just caught a bluebottle in it.

"And now, Mr. Edwin," he proceeded, wiping his mouth and hands upon his handkerchief, "to a little piece of business. You received from me, the other day, a certified copy of Miss Rosa's father's will. You knew its contents before, but you received it from me as a matter of business. I should have sent it to Mr. Jasper, but for Miss Rosa's wishing it to come straight to you in preference. You received it?"

"Quite safely, sir."

"You should have acknowledged its receipt," said Mr. Grewgious, "business being business all the world over. However, you did not."

"I meant to have acknowledged it when I first came in this evening, sir."

"Not a business-like acknowledgment," returned Mr. Grewgious; "however, let that pass. Now, in that document you have observed a few words of kindly allusion to its being left to me to discharge a little trust, confided to me in conversation, at such time as I in my discretion may think best."

"Yes, sir."

"Mr. Edwin, it came into my mind just now, when I was looking at the fire, that I could, in my discretion, acquit myself of that trust at no better time than the present. Favor me with your attention half a minute."

He took a bunch of keys from his pocket, singled out by the candle-light the key he wanted, and then, with a candle in his hand, went to a bureau or escritoire, unlocked it, touched the spring of a little secret drawer, and took from it an ordinary ring-case made for a single ring. With this in his hand, he returned to his chair. As he held it up for the young man to see, his hand trembled.

"Mr. Edwin, this rose of diamonds and rubies, delicately set in gold, was a ring belonging to Miss Rosa's mother. It was removed from her dead hand, in my presence, with such distracted grief as I hope it may never be my lot to contemplate again. Hard man as I am, I am not hard enough for that. See how bright these stones shine!" opening the case. "And yet the eyes that were so much brighter, and that so often looked upon them with a light and a proud heart, have been ashes among ashes, and dust among dust, some years! If I had any imagination (which it is needless to say I have not), I might imagine that the lasting beauty of these stones was almost cruel."

He closed the case again as he spoke.

"This ring was given to the young lady who was drowned so early in her beautiful and happy career, by her husband, when they first plighted their faith to one another. It was he who removed it from her unconscious hand, and it was he who, when his death drew very near, placed it in mine. The trust in which I received it was, that, you and Miss Rosa growing to manhood and womanhood, and your betrothal prospering and coming to maturity, I should give it to you to place upon her finger. Failing those desired results, it was to remain in my possession."

Some trouble was in the young man's face, and some indecision was in the action of his hand, as Mr. Grewgious, looking steadfastly at him, gave him the ring.

"Your placing it on her finger," said Mr. Grewgious, "will be the solemn seal upon your strict fidelity to the living and the dead. You are going to her, to make the last irrevocable preparations for your marriage. Take it with you."

The young man took the little case and placed it in his breast.

"If any thing should be amiss, if any thing should be even slightly wrong between you, if you should have any secret consciousness that you are committing yourself to this step for no higher reason than because you have long been accustomed to look forward to it; then," said Mr. Grewgious, "I charge you once more, by the living and by the dead, to bring that ring back to me."

Here Bazzard awoke himself by his own snoring; and, as is usual in such cases, sat apoplectically staring at vacancy, as defying vacancy to accuse him of having been asleep.

"Bazzard!" said Mr. Grewgious, harder than ever.

"I follow you, sir," said Bazzard, "and I have been following you."

"In discharge of a trust, I have handed Mr. Edwin Drood a ring of diamonds and rubies. You see?"

Edwin reproduced the little case, and opened it; and Bazzard looked into it.

"I follow you both, sir," returned Bazzard, "and I witness the transaction."

Evidently anxious to get away and be alone, Edwin Drood now resumed his outer clothing, muttering something about time and appointments. The fog was reported no clearer (by the flying waiter, who alighted from a speculative flight in the coffee interest), but he went out into it; and Bazzard, after his manner, "followed" him.

Mr. Grewgious, left alone, walked softly and slowly to and fro for an hour and more. He was restless to-night, and seemed dispirited.

"I hope I have done right," he said. "The appeal to him seemed necessary. It was hard to lose the ring, and yet it must have gone from me very soon."

He closed the empty little drawer with a sigh, and shut and locked the escritoire, and came back to the solitary fireside.

"Her ring," he went on. "Will it come back to me? My mind hangs about her ring very uneasily to-night. But that is explainable. I have had it so long, and I have prized it so much! I wonder—"

He was in a wondering mood as well as a restless; for, though he checked himself at that point and took another walk, he resumed his wondering when he sat down again.

"I wonder (for the ten thousandth time, and what a weak fool I, for what can it signify now!) whether he confided the charge of their orphan child to me because he knew— Good God, how like her mother she has become!

"I wonder whether he ever so much as suspected that some one doted on her at a hopeless, speechless distance when he struck in and won her! I wonder whether it ever crept into his mind who that unfortunate some one was!

"I wonder whether I shall sleep to-night! At all events, I will shut out the world with the bedclothes and try."

Mr. Grewgious crossed the staircase to his raw and foggy bedroom, and was soon ready for bed. Dimly catching sight of his face in the misty looking-glass, he held his candle to it for a moment.

"A likely some one, *you*, to come into anybody's thoughts in such an aspect!" he exclaimed. "There, there! there! Get to bed, poor man, and cease to jabber!"

With that he extinguished his light, pulled up the bedclothes around him, and, with another sigh, shut out the world. And yet there are such unexplored romantic nooks in the unlikeliest men, that even old tinderous and touch-woody P. J. T. Possibly Jabbered Thus, at some odd times, in or about seventeen-forty-seven.

CHAPTER X.

A NIGHT WITH DURDLES.

When Mr. Sapsea has nothing better to do, toward evening, and finds the contemplation of his own profundity becoming a little monotonous in spite of the vastness of the subject, he often takes an airing in the Cathedral Close and thereabouts. He likes to pass the churchyard with a swelling air of proprietorship, and to encourage in his breast a sort of benignant-landlord feeling, in that he has been bountiful toward that meritorious tenant, Mrs. Sapsea, and has publicly given her a prize. He likes to see a stray face or two looking in through the railings, and perhaps reading his inscription. Should he meet a stranger coming from the churchyard with a quick step, he is morally convinced that the stranger is "with a blush retiring," as monumentally directed.

Mr. Sapsea's importance has received enhancement, for he has become Mayor of Cloisterham. Without mayors and many of them, it cannot be disputed that the whole framework of society—Mr. Sapsea is confident that he invented that forcible figure—would fall to pieces. Mayors have been knighted for "going up" with addresses: explosive machines intrepidly discharging shot and shell into the English Grammar. Mr. Sapsea may "go up" with an address. Rise, Sir Thomas Sapsea! Of such is the salt of the earth.

Mr. Sapsea has improved the acquaintance of Mr. Jasper, since their first meeting to partake of port, epitaph, backgammon, beef, and salad. Mr. Sapsea has been received at the Gate House with kindred hospitality; and on that occasion Mr. Jasper seated himself at the piano, and sang to him, tickling his ears—figuratively, long enough to present a considerable area for tickling. What Mr. Sapsea likes in that young man, is, that he is always ready to profit by the wisdom of his elders, and that he is sound, sir, at the core. In proof of which, he sang to

Mr. Sapsea that evening, no kickshaw ditties, favorites with national enemies, but gave him the genuine George the Third home-brewed: exhorting him (as "my brave boys") to reduce to a smashed condition all other islands but this island, and all continents, peninsulas, isthmuses, promontories, and other geographical forms of land soever, besides sweeping the seas in all directions. In short, he rendered it pretty clear that Providence made a distinct mistake in originating so small a nation of hearts of oak, and so many other verminous peoples.

Mr. Sapsea, walking slowly this moist evening near the churchyard with his hands behind him, on the lookout for a blushing and retiring stranger, turns a corner, and comes instead into the goodly presence of the Dean, conversing with the Verger and Mr. Jasper. Mr. Sapsea makes his obeisance, and is instantly stricken far more ecclesiastical than any Archbishop of York, or Canterbury.

"You are evidently going to write a book about us, Mr. Jasper," quoth the Dean; "to write a book about us. Well! We are very ancient, and we ought to make a good book. We are not so richly endowed in possessions as in age; but perhaps you will put *that* in your book, among other things, and call attention to our wrongs."

Mr. Tope, as in duty bound, is greatly entertained by this.

"I really have no intention at all, sir," replies Jasper, "of turning author or archæologist. It is but a whim of mine. And even for my whim, Mr. Sapsea here is more accountable than I am."

"How so, Mr. Mayor?" says the Dean, with a nod of good-natured recognition of his Fetch. "How is that, Mr. Mayor?"

"I am not aware," Mr. Sapsea remarks, looking about him for information, "to what the Very Reverend the Dean does me the honor of referring." And then falls to studying his original in minute points of detail.

"Durdles," Mr. Tope hints.

"Ay!" the Dean echoes; "Durdles, Durdles!"

"The truth is, sir," explains Jasper, "that my curiosity in the man was first really stimulated by Mr. Sapsea. Mr. Sapsea's knowledge of mankind, and power of drawing out whatever is recluse or odd around him, first led to my bestowing a second thought upon the man: though of course I had met him constantly about. You would not be surprised by this, Mr. Dean, if you had seen Mr. Sapsea deal with him in his own parlor, as I did."

"Oh!" cries Sapsea, picking up the ball thrown to him with ineffable complacency and pomposity; "yes, yes. The Very Reverend the Dean refers to that? Yes. I happened to bring Durdles and Mr. Jasper together. I regard Durdles as a Character."

"A character, Mr. Sapsea, that with a few skillful touches you turn inside out," says Jasper.

"Nay, not quite that," returns the lumbering auctioneer. "I may have a little influence over him, perhaps; and a little insight into his character, perhaps. The Very Reverend the Dean will please to bear in mind that I have seen the world." Here Mr. Sapsea gets a little behind the Dean, to inspect his coat-buttons.

"Well!" says the Dean, looking about him to see what has become of his copyist: "I hope, Mr. Mayor, you will use your study and knowledge of Durdles to the good purpose of exhorting him not to break our worthy and respected Choir-Master's neck; we cannot afford it; his head and voice are much too valuable to us."

Mr. Tope is again highly entertained, and, having fallen into respectful convulsions of laughter, subsides into a deferential murmur, importing that surely any gentleman would deem it a pleasure and an honor to have his neck broken, in return for such a compliment from such a source.

"I will take it upon myself, sir," observed Sapsea, loftily, "to answer for Mr. Jasper's neck. I will tell Durdles to be careful of it. He will mind what *I* say. How is it at present endangered?" he inquires, looking about him with magnificent patronage.

"Only by my making a moonlight expedition with Durdles among the tombs, vaults, towers, and ruins," returns Jasper. "You remember suggesting when you brought us together that, as a lover of the picturesque, it might be worth my while?"

"*I* remember!" replies the auctioneer. And the solemn idiot really believes that he does remember.

"Profiting by your hint," pursues Jasper, "I have had some day-rambles with the extraordinary old fellow, and we are to make a moonlight hole-and-corner exploration to-night."

"And here he is," says the Dean.

Durdles, with his dinner-bundle in his hand, is indeed beheld slouching toward them. Slouching nearer, and perceiving the Dean, he pulls off his hat, and is slouching away with it under his arm, when Mr. Sapsea stops him.

"Mind you take care of my friend," is the injunction Mr. Sapsea lays upon him.

"What friend o' yourn is dead?" asks Durdles. "No orders has come in for any friend o' yourn."

"I mean my live friend, there."

"Oh! Him?" says Durdles. "He can take care of himself, can Mister Jarsper."

"But do you take care of him, too," says Sapsea.

Whom Durdles (there being command in his tone) surlily surveys from head to foot.

"With submission to his Reverence the Dean, if you'll mind what concerns you, Mr. Sapsea, Durdles he'll mind what concerns him."

"You're out of temper," says Mr. Sapsea, winking to the company to observe how smoothly he will manage him. "My friend concerns me, and Mr. Jasper is my friend. And you are my friend."

"Don't you get into a bad habit of boasting," retorts Durdles, with a grave, cautionary nod. "It'll grow upon you."

"You are out of temper," says Sapsea again, reddening, but again winking to the company.

"I own to it," returns Durdles; "I don't like liberties."

Mr. Sapsea winks a third wink to the company, as who should say: "I think you will agree with me that I have settled *his* business;" and stalks out of the controversy.

Durdles then gives the Dean a good-evening, and adding, as he puts his hat on, "You'll find me at home, Mister Jarsper, as agreed, when you want me; I'm a-going home to clean myself," soon slouches out of sight. This going home to clean himself is one of the man's incomprehensible compromises with inexorable facts; he, and his hat, and his boots, and his clothes, never showing any trace of cleaning, but being uniformly in one condition of dust and grit.

The lamplighter now dotting the quiet Close with specks of light, and running at a great rate up and down his little ladder with that object—his little ladder under the sacred shadow of whose inconvenience generations had grown up, and which all Cloisterham would have stood aghast at the idea of abolishing—the Dean withdraws to his dinner, Mr. Tope to his tea, and Mr. Jasper to his piano. There, with no light but that of the fire, he sits chanting choir-music in a low and beautiful voice, for two or three hours; in short, until it has been for some time dark, and the moon is about to rise.

Then, he closes his piano softly, softly changes his coat for a pea-jacket, with a goodly wicker-cased bottle in its largest pocket, and, putting on a low-crowned, flat-brimmed hat, goes softly out. Why does he move so softly to-night? No outward reason is apparent for it. Can there be any sympathetic reason crouching darkly within him?

Repairing to Durdles's unfinished house, or hole in the city wall, and seeing a light within it, he softly picks his course among the gravestones, monuments, and stony lumber of the yard, already touched here and there, sidewise, by the rising moon. The two journeymen have left their two great saws sticking in their blocks of stone; and two skeleton journeymen out of the Dance of Death might be grinning in the shadow of their sheltering sentry-boxes, about to slash away at cutting out the grave-stones of the next two people destined to die in Cloisterham. Likely enough, the two think little of that now, being alive, and perhaps merry. Curious, to make a guess at the two—or say, at one of the two!

"Ho! Durdles!"

The light moves, and he appears with it at the door. He would seem to have been "cleaning himself" with the aid of a bottle, jug, and tumbler; for no other cleansing-instruments are visible in the bare brick room, with rafters overhead and no plastered ceiling, into which he shows his visitor.

"Are you ready?"

"I am ready, Mister Jarsper. Let the old 'uns come out if they dare, when we go among their tombs. My spirits is ready for 'em."

"Do you mean animal spirits, or ardent?"

"The one's the t'other," answers Durdles, "and I mean 'em both."

He takes a lantern from a hook, puts a match or two in his pocket wherewith to light it, should there be need, and they go out together, dinner-bundle and all.

Surely an unaccountable sort of expedition! That Durdles himself, who is always prowling among old graves and ruins, like a Ghoul—that he should be stealing forth to climb, and dive, and wander without an object, is nothing extraordinary; but that the Choir Master or any one else should hold it worth his while to be with him, and to study moonlight effects in such company, is another affair. Surely an unaccountable sort of expedition therefore!

"'Ware that there mound by the yard-gate, Mister Jarsper."

"I see it. What is it?"

"Lime."

Mr. Jasper stops, and waits for him to come up, for he lags behind. "What you call quick-lime?"

"Ay!" says Durdles; "quick enough to eat your boots. With a little handy stirring, quick enough to eat your bones."

They go on, presently passing the red windows of the Travellers' Twopenny, and emerging into the clear moonlight of the Monks' Vineyard. This crossed, they come to Minor Canon Corner: of which the greater part lies in shadow until the moon shall rise higher in the sky.

The sound of a closing house-door strikes their ears, and two men come out. These are Mr. Crisparkle and Neville. Jasper, with a strange and sudden smile upon his face, lays the palm of his hand upon the breast of Durdles, stopping him where he stands.

At that end of Minor Canon Corner the shadow is profound in the existing state of the light: at that end, too, there is a piece of old dwarf wall, breast-high, the only remaining boundary of what was once a garden, but is now the thoroughfare. Jasper and Durdles would have turned this wall in another instant; but, stopping so short, stand behind it.

"Those two are only sauntering," Jasper whispers; "they will go out into the moonlight soon. Let us keep quiet here, or they will detain us, or want to join us, or what not."

Durdles nods assent, and falls to munching some fragments from his bundle. Jasper folds his arms upon the top of the wall, and, with his chin resting on them, watches. He takes no note whatever of the Minor Canon, but watches Neville, as though his eye were at the trigger of a loaded rifle, and he had covered him, and were going to fire. A sense of destructive power is so expressed in his face, that even Durdles pauses in his munching, and looks at him, with an unmunched something in his cheek.

Meanwhile Mr. Crisparkle and Neville walk to and fro, quietly talking together. What they say, cannot be heard consecutively; but Mr. Jasper has already distinguished his own name more than once.

"This is the first day of the week," Mr. Crisparkle can be distinctly heard to observe, as they turn back; "and the last day of the week is Christmas Eve."

"You may be certain of me, sir."

The echoes were favorable at those points, but as the two approach, the sound of their talking becomes confused again. The word "confidence," shattered by the echoes, but still capable of being pieced together, is uttered by Mr. Crisparkle. As they draw still nearer, this fragment of a reply is heard: "Not deserved yet, but shall be, sir." As they turn away again, Jasper again hears his own name, in connection with the words from Mr. Crisparkle: "Remember that I said I answered for you confidently." Then the sound of their talk becomes confused again; they halting for a little while, and some earnest action on the part of Neville succeeding. When they move once more, Mr. Crisparkle is seen to look up at the sky, and to point before him. They then slowly disappear: passing out into the moonlight at the opposite end of the Corner.

It is not until they are gone, that Mr. Jasper moves. But then he turns to Durdles, and bursts into a fit of laughter. Durdles, who still has that suspended something in his cheek, and who sees nothing to laugh at, stares at him until Mr. Jasper lays his face down on his arms to have his laugh out. Then Durdles bolts the something, as if desperately resigning himself to indigestion.

Among those secluded nooks there is very little stir or movement after dark. There is little enough in the high-tide of the day, but there is next to none at night. Besides that the cheerfully frequented High Street lies nearly parallel to the spot (the old Cathedral rising between the two), and is the natural channel in which the Cloisterham traffic flows, a certain awful hush pervades the ancient pile, the cloisters, and the churchyard, after dark, which not many people care to encounter. Ask the first hundred citizens of Cloisterham, met at random in the streets at noon, if they believed in Ghosts, they would tell you no; but put them to choose at night between these eerie Precincts and the thoroughfare of shops, and you would find that ninety-nine declared for the longer round and the more frequented way. The cause of this is not to be found in any local superstition that attaches to the Precincts—albeit a mysterious lady, with a child in her arms and a rope dangling from her neck, has been seen flitting about there by sundry witnesses as intangible as herself—but it is to be sought in the innate shrinking of dust with the breath of life in it, from dust out of which the breath of life has passed; also, in the widely diffused, and almost as widely unacknowledged, reflection: "If the dead do, under any circumstances, become visible to the living, these are such likely surroundings for the purpose that I, the living, will get out of them as soon as I can."

Hence, when Mr. Jasper and Durdles pause to glance around them, before descending into the crypt by a small side-door of which the latter has a key, the whole expanse of moonlight in their view is utterly deserted. One might fancy that the tide of life was stemmed by Mr. Jasper's own Gate-house. The murmur of the tide is heard beyond; but no wave passes the archway, over which his lamp burns red behind his curtain, as if the building were a Light-house.

They enter, locking themselves in, descend the rugged steps, and are down in the Crypt. The lantern is not wanted, for the moonlight strikes in at the groined windows, bare of glass, the broken frames for which cast patterns on the ground. The heavy pillars which support the roof engender masses of black shade, but between them there are lanes of light. Up and down these lanes, they walk, Durdles discoursing of the "old uns" he yet counts on disinterring, and slapping a wall, in which he considers "a whole family on 'em" to be stoned and earthed up, just as if he were a familiar friend of the family. The taciturnity of Durdles is for the time overcome by Mr. Jasper's wicker bottle, which circulates freely; in the sense, that is to say, that its contents enter freely into Mr. Durdles's circulation, while Mr. Jasper only rinses his mouth once, and casts forth the rinsing.

They are to ascend the great tower. On the steps by which they rise to the Cathedral, Durdles pauses for new store of breath. The steps are very dark, but out of the darkness they can see the lanes of light they have traversed. Durdles seats himself upon a step. Mr. Jasper seats himself upon another. The odor from the wicker bottle (which has somehow passed into Durdles's keeping) soon intimates that the cork has been taken out; but this is not ascertainable through the sense of sight, since neither can descry the other. And yet, in talking, they turned to one another, as though their faces could commune together.

"This is good stuff, Mr. Jarsper!"

"It is very good stuff, I hope. I bought it on purpose."

"They don't show, you see, the old uns don't, Mr. Jarsper!"

"It would be a more confused world than it is, if they could."

"Well, it *would* lead toward a mixing of things," Durdles acquiesces: pausing on the remark, as if the idea of ghosts had not previously presented itself to him in a merely inconvenient light, domestically, or chronologically. "But do you think there may be ghosts of other things, though not of men and women?"

"What things? Flower-beds and watering-pots? Horses and harness?"

"No. Sounds."

"What sounds?"

"Cries."

"What cries do you mean? Chairs to mend?"

"No, I mean screeches. Now, I'll tell you, Mr. Jarsper. Wait a bit till I put the bottle right." Here the cork is evidently taken out again, and replaced again. "There! *Now* it's right! This time last year, only a few days later, I happened to have been doing what was correct by the season, in the way of giving it the welcome it had a right to expect, when them town-boys set on me at their worst. At length I gave 'em the slip, and turned in here. And here I fell asleep. And what woke me? The ghost of a cry. The ghost of one terrific shriek, which shriek was followed by the ghost of the howl of a dog: a long dismal, woeful howl, such as a dog gives when a person's dead. That was *my* last Christmas Eve."

"What do you mean?" is the very abrupt, and, one might say, fierce retort.

"I mean that I made inquiries everywhere about, and that no living ears but mine heard either that cry or that howl. So I say they was both ghosts; though why they came to me, I've never made out."

"I thought you were another kind of man," says Jasper, scornfully.

"So I thought, myself," answers Durdles with his usual composure; "and yet I was picked out for it."

Jasper had risen suddenly, when he asked him what he meant, and he now says, "Come; we shall freeze here; lead the way."

Durdles complies, not over-steadily; opens the door at the top of the steps with the key he has already used; and so emerges on the Cathedral level, in a passage at the side of the chancel. Here, the moonlight is so very bright again that the colors of the nearest stained-glass window are thrown upon their faces. The appearance of the unconscious Durdles, holding the door open for his companion to follow, as if from the grave, is ghastly enough, with a purple band across his face, and a yellow splash upon his brow; but he bears the close scrutiny of his companion in an insensible way, although it is prolonged while the latter fumbles among his pockets for a key confided to him that will open an iron gate so to enable them to pass to the staircase of the great tower.

"That and the bottle are enough for you to carry," he says, giving it to Durdles; "hand your bundle to me; I am younger and longer-winded than you." Durdles hesitates for a moment between bundle and bottle; but gives the preference to the bottle as being by far the better company, and consigns the dry weight to his fellow-explorer.

Then they go up the winding staircase of the great tower, toilsomely, turning and turning, and lowering their heads to avoid the stairs above, or the rough stone pivot around which they twist. Durdles has lighted his lantern, by drawing from the cold hard wall a spark of that mysterious fire which lurks in every thing, and, guided by this speck, they clamber up among the cobwebs and the dust. Their way lies through strange places. Twice or thrice they emerge into level low-arched galleries, whence they can look down into the moonlit nave; and where Durdles, waving his lantern, shows the dim angels' heads upon the corbels of the roof, seeming to watch their progress. Anon, they turn into narrower and steeper staircases, and the night air begins to blow upon them, and the chirp of some startled jackdaw or frightened rook precedes the heavy beating of wings in a confined space, and the beating down of dust and straws upon their heads. At last, leaving their light behind a stair—for it blows fresh up here—they look down on Cloisterham, fair to see in the moonlight: its ruined habitations and sanctuaries of the dead, at the tower's base: its moss-softened red-tiled roofs and red brick houses of the living, clustered beyond: its river winding down from the mist on the horizon, as though that were its source, and already heaving with a restless knowledge of its approach toward the sea.

Once again, an unaccountable expedition this! Jasper (always moving softly with no visible reason) contemplates the scene, and especially that stillest part of it which the Cathedral overshadows. But he contemplates Durdles quite as curiously, and Durdles is by times conscious of his watchful eyes.

Only by times, because Durdles is growing drowsy. As aeronauts lighten the load they carry, when they wish to rise, similarly Durdles has lightened the wicker bottle in coming up. Snatches of sleep surprise him on his legs, and stop him in his talk. A mild fit of calenture seizes him, in which he deems that the ground, so far below, is on a level with the tower, and would as lief walk off the tower into the air as not. Such is his state when they begin to come down. And as aeronauts make themselves heavier when they wish to descend, similarly Durdles charges himself with more liquid from the wicker bottle, that he may come down the better.

The iron gate attained and locked—but not before Durdles has tumbled twice, and cut an eyebrow open once—they descend into the crypt again, with the intent of issuing forth as they entered. But, while returning among those lanes of light, Durdles becomes so very uncertain, both of foot and speech, that he half-drops, half-throws himself down, by one of the heavy pillars, scarcely less heavy than itself, and indistinctly appeals to his companion for forty winks of a second each.

"If you will have it so, or must have it so," replies Jasper, "I'll not leave you here. Take them, while I walk to and fro."

Durdles is asleep at once; and in his sleep he dreams a dream.

It is not much of a dream, considering the vast extent of the domains of dreamland, and their wonderful productions; it is only remarkable for being unusually restless, and unusually real. He dreams of lying there, asleep, and yet counting his companion's footsteps as he walks to and fro. He dreams that the footsteps die away into distance of time and of space, and that something touches him, and that something falls from his hand. Then something clinks and gropes about, and he dreams that he is alone for so long a time, that the lanes of light take new directions as the moon advances in her course. From succeeding unconsciousness, he passes into a dream of slow uneasiness from cold; and painfully awakes to a perception of the lanes of light —really changed, much as he had dreamed—and Jasper walking among them, beating his hands and feet.

"Holloa!" Durdles cries out, unmeaningly alarmed.

"Awake at last?" says Jasper, coming up to him. "Do you know that your forties have stretched into thousands?"

"No."

"They have though."

"What's the time?"

"Hark! The bells are going in the Tower!"

They strike four quarters, and then the great bell strikes.

"Two!" cries Durdles, scrambling up; "why didn't you try to wake me, Mister Jarsper?"

"I did. I might as well have tried to wake the dead:—your own family of dead, up in the corner there."

"Did you touch me?"

"Touch you? Yes. Shook you."

As Durdles recalls that touching something in his dream, he looks down on the pavement, and sees the key of the crypt door lying close to where he himself lay.

"I dropped you, did I?" he says, picking it up, and recalling that part of his dream. As he gathers himself again into an upright position, or into a position as nearly upright as he ever maintains, he is again conscious of being watched by his companion.

"Well?" says Jasper, smiling, "Are you quite ready? Pray don't hurry."

"Let me get my bundle right, Mister Jarsper, and I'm with you."

As he ties it afresh, he is once more conscious that he is very narrowly observed.

"What do you suspect me of, Mister Jarsper?" he asks, with drunken displeasure. "Let them as has any suspicions of Durdles, name 'em."

"I've no suspicions of you, my good Mr. Durdles; but I have suspicions that my bottle was filled with something stiffer than either of us supposed. And I also have suspicions," Jasper adds, taking it from the pavement, and turning it bottom upward, "that it's empty."

Durdles condescends to laugh at this. Continuing to chuckle when his laugh is over, as though remonstrant with himself on his drinking powers, he rolls to the door and unlocks it. They both pass out, and Durdles relocks it, and pockets his key.

"A thousand thanks for a curious and interesting night," says Jasper, giving him his hand; "you can make your own way home?"

"I should think so!" answers Durdles. "If you was to offer Durdles the affront to show him his way home, he wouldn't go home.

Durdles wouldn't go home till morning,
And *then* Durdles wouldn't go home,

Durdles wouldn't." This, with the utmost defiance.

"Good-night, then."

"Good-night, Mister Jarsper."

Each is turning his own way, when a sharp whistle rends the silence, and the jargon is yelped out:

"Widdy widdy wen!
I—ket—ches—Im—out—ar—ter—ten.
Widdy widdy wy!
Then—E—don't—go—then—I—shy—
Widdy Widdy Wake-cock warning!"

Instantly afterward, a rapid fire of stones rattles at the Cathedral wall, and the hideous small boy is beheld opposite, dancing in the moonlight.

"What! Is that baby-devil on the watch there!" cries Jasper, in a fury: so quickly roused, and so violent, that he seems another devil himself. "I shall shed the blood of that Impish wretch! I know I shall do it!" Regardless of the fire, though it hits him more than once, he rushes at Deputy, collars him, and tries to bring him across. But Deputy is not to be so easily brought across. With a diabolical insight into the strongest part of his position, he is no sooner taken by the throat than he curls up his legs, forces his assailant to hang him as it were, and gurgles in his throat, and screws his body, and twists, as already undergoing the first agonies of strangulation. There is nothing for it but to drop him. He instantly gets himself together, backs over to Durdles, and cries to his assailant, gnashing the great gap in front of his mouth, with rage and malice:

"I'll blind yer, s'elp me! I'll stone yer eyes out, s'elp me! If I don't have yer eye-sight, bellows me!" At the same time dodging behind Durdles, and snarling at Jasper, now from this side of him, and now from that; prepared, if pounced upon, to dart away in all manner of curvilinear directions, and, if run down after all, to grovel in the dust, and cry: "Now, hit me when I'm down! Do it!"

"Don't hurt the boy, Mister Jarsper," urges Durdles, shielding him. "Recollect yourself."

"He followed us to-night, when we first came here!"

"Yer lie, I didn't!" replies Deputy, in his one form of polite contradiction.

"He has been prowling near us ever since!"

"Yer lie, I haven't," returns Deputy, "I'd only jist come out for my 'elth when I see you two a coming out of the Kinfreederel. If—

I—ket—ches—Im—out—ar—ter—ten."

(with the usual rhythm and dance, though dodging behind Durdles), "it ain't *my* fault, is it?"

"Take him home, then," retorts Jasper, ferociously, though with a strong check upon himself, "and let my eyes be rid of the sight of you!"

Deputy, with another sharp whistle, at once expressing his relief, and his commencement of a milder stoning of Mr. Durdles, begins stoning that respectable gentleman home, as if he were a reluctant ox. Mr. Jasper goes to his Gate-house, brooding. And thus, as every thing comes to an end, the unaccountable expedition comes to an end—for the time.

CHAPTER XI.

BOTH AT THEIR BEST.

Miss Twinkleton's establishment was about to undergo a serene hush. The Christmas recess was at hand. What had once, and at no remote period, been called, even by the erudite Miss Twinkleton herself, "the half," but what was now called, as being more elegant, and more strictly collegiate, "the term," would expire to-morrow. A noticeable relaxation of discipline had for some few days pervaded the Nuns' House. Club suppers had occurred in the bed-rooms, and a dressed tongue had been carved with a pair of scissors, and handed round with the curling-tongs. Portions of marmalade had likewise been distributed on a service of plates constructed of curl-paper; and cowslip-wine had been quaffed from the small squat measuring-glass in which little Rickitts (a junior of weakly constitution) took her steel drops daily. The house-maids had been bribed with various fragments of riband, and sundry pairs of shoes more or less down at the heel, to make no mention of crumbs in the beds; the airiest costumes had been worn on these festive occasions; and the daring Miss Ferdinand had even surprised the company with a sprightly solo on the comb-and-curl-paper, until suffocated in her own pillow by two flowing-haired executioners.

Nor were these the only tokens of dispersal. Boxes appeared in the bed-rooms (where they were capital at other times), and a surprising amount of packing took place, out of all proportion to the amount packed. Largess, in the form of odds and ends of cold cream and pomatum, and also of hair-pins, was freely distributed among the attendants. On charges of inviolable secrecy, confidences were interchanged respecting golden youth of England expected to call, "at home," on the first opportunity. Miss Giggles (deficient in sentiment) did indeed profess that she, for her part, acknowledged such homage by making faces at the golden youth; but this young lady was outvoted by an immense majority.

On the last night before a recess, it was always expressly made a point of honor that nobody should go to sleep, and that ghosts should be encouraged by all possible means. This compact invariably broke down, and all the young ladies went to sleep very soon, and got up very early.

The concluding ceremony came off at twelve o'clock on the day of departure; when Miss Twinkleton, supported by Mrs. Tisher, held a Drawing-Room in her own apartment (the globes already covered with brown holland), where glasses of white wine, and plates of cut pound-cake were discovered on the table. Miss Twinkleton then said: Ladies, another revolving year had brought us round to that festive period at which the first feelings of our nature bounded in our—Miss Twinkleton was annually going to add "bosoms," but annually stopped on the brink of that expression, and substituted "hearts." Hearts; our hearts. Hem! Again a revolving year, ladies, had brought us to a pause in our studies—let us hope our greatly advanced studies—and, like the mariner in his bark, the warrior in his tent, the captive in his dungeon, and the traveller in his various conveyances, we yearned for home. Did we say, on such an occasion, in the opening words of Mr. Addison's impressive tragedy—

> "The dawn is overcast, the morning lowers,
> And heavily in clouds brings on the day,
> The great, th' important day—"

Not so. From horizon to zenith all was *couleur de rose*, for all was redolent of our relations and friends. Might *we* find *them* prospering as *we* expected; might *they* find *us* prospering as *they* expected! Ladies, we would now, with our love to one another, wish one another good-by, and happiness, until we meet again. And when the time should come for our resumption of those pursuits which (here a general depression set in all round), pursuits which, pursuits which;—then let us ever remember what was said by the Spartan General, in words too trite for repetition, at the battle it were superfluous to specify.

The handmaidens of the establishment, in their best caps, then handed the trays, and the young ladies sipped and crumbled, and the bespoken coaches began to choke the street. Then, leave-taking was not long about, and Miss Twinkleton, in saluting each young lady's cheek, confided to her an exceedingly neat letter, addressed to her next friend at law, "with Miss Twinkleton's best compliments" in the corner. This missive she handed with an air as if it had not the least connection with the bill, but were something in the nature of a delicate and joyful surprise.

So many times had Rosa seen such dispersals, and so very little did she know of any other home, that she was contented to remain where she was, and was even better contented than ever before, having her latest friend with her. And yet her latest friendship had a blank place in it of which she could not fail to be sensible. Helena Landless, having been a party to her brother's revelation about Rosa, and having entered into that compact of silence with Mr. Crisparkle, shrank from any allusion to Edwin Drood's name. Why she so avoided it was mysterious to Rosa, but she perfectly perceived the fact. But for the fact, she might have relieved her own little perplexed heart of some of its doubts and hesitations, by taking Helena into her confidence. As it was, she had no such vent; she could only ponder on her own difficulties, and wonder more and more why this avoidance of Edwin's name should last, now that she knew—for so much Helena had told her—that a good understanding was to be re-established between the two young men, when Edwin came down.

It would have made a pretty picture, so many pretty girls kissing Rosa in the cold porch of the Nuns' House, and that sunny little creature peeping out of it (unconscious of sly faces carved on spout and gable peeping at her), and waving farewells to the departing coaches, as if she represented the spirit of rosy youth abiding in the place, to keep it bright and warm in its desertion. The hoarse High Street became musical with the cry, in various silvery voices, "Good-by, Rosebud, Darling!" and the effigy of Mr. Sapsea's father over the opposite doorway seemed to say to mankind: "Gentlemen, favor me with your attention to this charming little last lot left behind, and bid with a spirit worthy of the occasion!" Then the staid street, so unwontedly sparkling, youthful, and fresh for a few rippling moments, ran dry, and Cloisterham was itself again.

If Rosebud in her bower now waited Edwin Drood's coming with an uneasy heart, Edwin, for his part, was uneasy too. With far less force of purpose in his composition than the childish beauty, crowned by acclamation fairy queen of Miss Twinkleton's establishment, he had a conscience, and Mr. Grewgious had pricked it. That gentleman's steady convictions of what was right and what was wrong in such a case as his, were neither to be frowned aside nor laughed aside. They would not be moved. But for the dinner in Staple Inn, and but for the ring he carried in the breast-pocket of his coat, he would have drifted into their wedding-day without another pause for real thought, loosely trusting that all would go well, left alone. But that serious putting him on his truth to the living and the dead had brought him to a check. He must either give the ring to Rosa, or he must take it back. Once put into this narrowed way of action, it was curious that he began to consider Rosa's claims upon him more unselfishly than he had ever considered them before, and began to be less sure of himself than he had ever been in all his easy-going days.

"I will be guided by what she says, and by how we get on," was his decision, walking from the Gate-house to the Nuns' House. "Whatever comes of it, I will bear his words in mind, and try to be true to the living and the dead."

Rosa was dressed for walking. She expected him. It was a bright, frosty day, and Miss Twinkleton had already graciously sanctioned fresh air. Thus they got out together before it became necessary for either Miss Twinkleton, or the Deputy High Priest, Mrs. Tisher, to lay even so much as one of those usual offerings on the shrine of Propriety.

"My dear Eddy," said Rosa, when they had turned out of the High Street, and had got among the quiet walks in the neighborhood of the Cathedral and the river, "I want to say something very serious to you. I have been thinking about it for a long, long time."

"I want to be serious with you too, Rosa, dear. I mean to be serious and earnest."

"Thank you, Eddy. And you will not think me unkind because I begin, will you? You will not think I speak for myself only because I speak first? That would not be generous, would it? And I know you are generous!"

He said, "I hope I am not ungenerous to you, Rosa." He called her Pussy no more. Never again.

"And there is no fear," pursued Rosa, "of our quarreling, is there? Because, Eddy," clasping her hand on his arm, "we have so much reason to be very lenient to each other!"

"We will be, Rosa."

"That's a dear good boy! Eddy, let us be courageous. Let us change to brother and sister from this day forth."

"Never be husband and wife?"

"Never!"

Neither spoke again for a little while. But after that pause, he said, with some effort—

"Of course I know that this has been in both our minds, Rosa, and of course I am in honor bound to confess freely that it does not originate with you."

"No, nor with you, dear," she returned, with pathetic earnestness. "It has sprung up between us. You are not truly happy in our engagement; I am not truly happy in it. O, I am so sorry, so sorry!" And there she broke into tears.

"I am deeply sorry, too, Rosa. Deeply sorry for you."

"And I for you, poor boy! And I for you!"

This pure young feeling, this gentle and forbearing feeling of each toward the other, brought with it its reward in a softening light that seemed to shine on their position. The relations between them did not look willful or capricious, or a failure, in such a light; they became elevated into something more self-denying, honorable, affectionate, and true.

"If we knew yesterday," said Rosa, as she dried her eyes, "and we did know yesterday, and on many, many yesterdays, that we were far from right together in those relations which were not of our own choosing, what better could we do to-day than change them? It is natural that we should be sorry, and you see how sorry we both are; but how much better to be sorry now than then!"

"When, Rosa?"

"When it would be too late. And then we should be angry, besides."

Another silence fell upon them.

"And you know," said Rosa, innocently, "you couldn't like me then; and you can always like me now, for I shall not be a drag upon you, or a worry to you. And I can always like you now, and your sister will not tease or trifle with you. I often did when I was not your sister, and I beg your pardon for it."

"Don't let us come to that, Rosa; or I shall want more pardoning than I like to think of."

"No, indeed, Eddy; you are too hard, my generous boy, upon yourself. Let us sit down, brother, on these ruins, and let me tell you how it was with us. I think I know, for I have considered about it very much since you were here last time. You liked me, didn't you? You thought I was a nice little thing?"

"Everybody thinks that, Rosa."

"Do they?" She knitted her brow musingly for a moment, and then flashed out with the bright little induction: "Well; but say they do. Surely it was not enough that you should think of me only as other people did; now, was it?"

The point was not to be got over. It was not enough.

"And that is just what I mean; that is just how it was with us," said Rosa. "You liked me very well, and you had grown used to me, and had grown used to the idea of our being married. You accepted the situation as an inevitable kind of thing, didn't you? It was to be, you thought, and why discuss or dispute it."

It was new and strange to him to have himself presented to himself so clearly, in a glass of her holding up. He had always patronized her, in his superiority to her share of woman's wit. Was that but another instance of something radically amiss in the terms on which they had been gliding toward a life-long bondage?

"All this that I say of you is true of me as well, Eddy. Unless it was, I might not be bold enough to say it. Only, the difference between us was, that by little and little there crept into my mind a habit of thinking about it, instead of dismissing it. My life is not so busy as yours, you see, and I have not so many things to think of. So I thought about it very much, and I cried about it very much too (though that was not your fault, poor boy); when all at once my guardian came down to prepare for my leaving the Nuns' House. I tried to hint to him that I was not quite settled in my mind, but I hesitated and failed, and he didn't understand me. But he is a good, good man. And he put before me so kindly, and yet so strongly, how seriously we ought to consider, in our circumstances, that I resolved to speak to you the next moment we were alone and grave. And if I seemed to come to it easily just now, because I came to it all at once, don't think it was so really, Eddy, for O, it was very, very hard, and O, I am very, very sorry!"

Her full heart broke into tears again. He put his arm about her waist, and they walked by the river side together.

"Your guardian has spoken to me, too, Rosa dear. I saw him before I left London." His right hand was in his breast, seeking the ring; but he checked it as he thought, "If I am to take it back, why should I tell her of it?"

"And that made you more serious about it, didn't it, Eddy? And if I had not spoken to you, as I have, you would have spoken to me? I hope you can tell me so? I don't like it to be *all* my doing, though it *is* so much better for us."

"Yes, I should have spoken; I should have put everything before you; I came intending to do it. But I never could have spoken to you as you have spoken to me, Rosa."

"Don't say you mean so coldly or unkindly, Eddy, please, if you can help it."

"I mean so sensibly and delicately, so wisely and affectionately."

"That's my dear brother." She kissed his hand in a little rapture. "The dear girls will be dreadfully disappointed," added Rosa, laughing, with the dew-drops glistening in her bright eyes. "They have looked forward to it so, poor pets!"

"Ah! But I fear it will be a worse disappointment to Jack," said Edwin Drood, with a start. "I never thought of Jack!"

Her swift and intent look at him as he said the words could no more be recalled than a flash of lightning can. But it appeared as though she would have instantly recalled it, if she could; for she looked down, confused, and breathed quickly.

"You don't doubt it's being a blow to Jack, Rosa?"

She merely replied, and that evasively and hurriedly: Why should she? She had not thought about it. He seemed to her to have so little to do with it.

"My dear child! Can you suppose that any one so wrapped up in another—Mrs. Tope's expression, not mine—as Jack is in me, could fail to be struck all of a heap by such a sudden and complete change in my life? I say sudden, because it will be sudden to *him*, you know."

She nodded twice or thrice, and her lips parted as if she would have assented. But she uttered no sound, and her breathing was no slower.

"How shall I tell Jack!" said Edwin, ruminating. If he had been less occupied with the thought, he must have seen her singular emotion. "I never thought of Jack. It must be broken to him before the town-crier knows it. I dine with the dear fellow to-morrow and next day—Christmas Eve and Christmas Day—but it would never do to spoil his feast days. He always worries about me, and moddley-coddleys in the merest trifles. The news is sure to overset him. How on earth shall this be broken to Jack?"

"He must be told, I suppose?" said Rosa.

"My dear Rosa! Who ought to be in our confidence, if not Jack?"

"My guardian promised to come down, if I should write and ask him. I am going to do so. Would you like to leave it to him?"

"A bright idea!" cried Edwin. "The other trustee. Nothing more natural. He comes down, he goes to Jack, he relates what we have agreed upon, and he states our case better than we could. He has already spoken feelingly to you, he has already spoken feelingly to me, and he'll put the whole thing feelingly to Jack. That's it! I am not a coward, Rosa, but to tell you a secret, I am a little afraid of Jack."

"No, no! You are not afraid of him?" cried Rosa, turning white and clasping her hands.

"Why, Sister Rosa, Sister Rosa, what do you see from the turret?" said Edwin, rallying her. "My dear girl!"

"You frightened me."

"Most unintentionally, but I am as sorry as if I had meant to do it. Could you possibly suppose for a moment, from any loose way of speaking of mine, that I was literally afraid of the dear fond fellow? What I mean is, that he is subject to a kind of paroxysm, or fit—I saw him in it once—and I don't know but that so great a surprise, coming upon him direct from me, who he is so wrapped up in, might bring it on, perhaps. Which—and this is the secret I was going to tell you—is another reason for your guardian's making the communication. He is so steady, precise, and exact, that he will talk Jack's thoughts into shape in no time; whereas, with me, Jack is always impulsive and hurried, and, I may say, almost womanish."

Rosa seemed convinced. Perhaps from her own very different point of view of "Jack," she felt comforted and protected by the interposition of Mr. Grewgious between herself and him.

And now, Edwin Drood's right hand closed again upon the ring in its little case, and again was checked by the consideration: "It is certain, now, that I am to give it back to him, then why should I tell her of it?" That pretty, sympathetic nature which could be so sorry for him in the blight of their childish hopes of happiness together, and could so quietly find itself alone in a new world to weave fresh wreaths of such flowers as it might prove to bear, the old world's flowers being withered, would be grieved by those sorrowful jewels; and to what purpose? Why should it be? They were but a sign of broken joys and baseless projects; in their very beauty, they were (as the unlikeliest of men had said) almost a cruel satire on the loves, hopes, plans of humanity, which are able to forecast nothing, and are so much brittle dust. Let them be. He would restore them to her guardian when he came down; he in his turn would restore them to the cabinet from which he had unwillingly taken them; and there, like old letters or old vows, or other records of old aspirations come to nothing, they would be disregarded, until, being valuable, they were sold into circulation again, to repeat their former round.

Let them be. Let them lie unspoken of in his breast. However distinctly or indistinctly he entertained these thoughts, he arrived at the conclusion, Let them be. Among the mighty store of wonderful chains that are forever forging, day and night, in the vast iron-works of time and circumstance, there was one chain forged in the moment of that small conclusion, riveted to the foundations of heaven and earth, and gifted with invincible force to hold and drag.

They walked on by the river. They began to speak of their separate plans. He would quicken his departure from England, and she would remain where she was, at least as long as Helena remained. The poor dear girls should have their disappointment broken to them gently, and, as the first preliminary, Miss Twinkleton should be confided in by Rosa, even in advance of the reappearance of Mr. Grewgious. It should be made clear in all quarters that she and Edwin were the best of friends. There had never been so serene an understanding between them since they were first affianced. And yet there was one reservation on each side: on hers, that she intended through her guardian to withdraw herself immediately from the tuition of her music-master; on his, that he did already entertain some wandering speculations whether it might ever come to pass that he would know more of Miss Landless.

The bright frosty day declined as they walked and spoke together. The sun dipped in the river far behind them, and the old city lay red before them, as their walk drew to a close. The moaning water cast its sea-weed duskily at their feet, when they turned to leave its margin; and the rooks hovered above them with hoarse cries, darker splashes in the darkening air.

"I will prepare Jack for my flitting soon," said Edwin, in a low voice, "and I will but see your guardian when he comes, and then go before they speak together. It will be better done without my being by. Don't you think so?"

"Yes."

"We know we have done right, Rosa?"

"Yes."

"We know we are better so, even now?"

"And shall be far, far better so by-and-by."

Still, there was that lingering tenderness in their hearts toward the old positions they were relinquishing, that they prolonged their parting. When they came among the elm-trees by the cathedral, where they had last sat together, they stopped, as by consent, and Rosa raised her face to his, as she had never raised it in the old days—for they were old already.

"God bless you, dear! Good-by!"

"God bless you, dear! Good-by!"

They kissed each other fervently.

"Now, please take me home, Eddy, and let me be by myself."

"Don't look round, Rosa," he cautioned her, as he drew her arm through his, and led her away. "Didn't you see Jack?"

"No! Where?"

"Under the trees. He saw us, as we took leave of each other. Poor fellow! he little thinks we have parted. This will be a blow to him, I am much afraid!"

She hurried on, without resting, and hurried on until they had passed under the Gate House into the street; once there, she asked—

"Has he followed us! You can look without seeming to. Is he behind?"

"No. Yes! he is! He has just passed out under the gateway. The dear sympathetic old fellow likes to keep us in sight. I am afraid he will be bitterly disappointed!"

She pulled hurriedly at the handle of the hoarse old bell, and the gate soon opened. Before going in, she gave him one last wide wondering look, as if she would have asked him with imploring emphasis, "Oh! don't you understand?" And out of that look he vanished from her view.

CHAPTER XII.

WHEN SHALL THESE THREE MEET AGAIN?

Christmas Eve in Cloisterham. A few strange faces in the streets; a few other faces, half strange and half familiar, once the faces of Cloisterham children, now the faces of men and women who come back from the outer world at long intervals to find the city wonderfully shrunken in size, as if it had not washed by any means well in the meanwhile. To these, the striking of the cathedral clock, and the cawing of the rooks from the cathedral tower, are like voices of their nursery time. To such as these, it has happened in their dying hours afar off, that they have imagined their chamber floor to be strewn with the autumnal leaves fallen from the elm-trees in the Close; so have the rustling sounds and fresh scents of their earliest impressions revived, when the circle of their lives was very nearly traced, and the beginning and the end were drawing close together.

Seasonable tokens are about. Red berries shine here and there in the lattices of Minor Canon Corner; Mr. and Mrs. Tope are daintily sticking sprigs of holly into the carvings and sconces of the cathedral stalls, as if they were sticking them into the coat-buttonholes of the Dean and Chapter. Lavish profusion is in the shops: particularly in the articles of currants, raisins, spices, candied peel, and moist sugar. An unusual air of gallantry and dissipation is abroad; evinced in an immense bunch of mistletoe hanging in the greengrocer's shop doorway, and a poor little Twelfth Cake, culminating in the figure of a Harlequin—such a very poor little Twelfth Cake, that one would rather call it a Twenty-Fourth Cake, or a Forty-Eighth Cake—to be raffled for at the pastrycook's, terms one shilling per member. Public amusements are not wanting. The Wax-Work which made so deep an impression on the reflective mind of the Emperor of China is to be seen by particular desire during Christmas Week only, on the premises of the bankrupt livery-stable keeper up the lane; and a new grand comic Christmas pantomime is to be produced at the Theatre; the latter heralded by the portrait of Signor Jacksonini the clown, saying "How do you do to-morrow," quite as large as life, and almost as miserably. In short, Cloisterham is up and doing; though from this description the High-School and Miss Twinkleton's are to be excluded. From the former establishment the scholars have gone home, every one of them in love with one of Miss Twinkleton's young ladies (who knows nothing about it); and only the handmaidens flutter occasionally in the windows of the latter. It is noticed, by the by, that these damsels become, within the limits of decorum, more skittish when thus intrusted with the concrete representation of their sex, than when dividing the representation with Miss Twinkleton's young ladies.

Three are to meet at the Gate-House to-night. How does each one of the three get through the day?

Neville Landless, though absolved from his books for the time by Mr. Crisparkle—whose fresh nature is by no means insensible to the charms of a holiday—reads and writes in his quiet room, with a concentrated air, until it is two hours past noon. He then sets himself to clearing his table, to arranging his books, and to tearing up and burning his stray papers. He makes a clean sweep of all untidy accumulations, puts all his drawers in order, and leaves no note or scrap of paper undestroyed, save such memoranda as bear directly on his studies. This done, he turns to his wardrobe, selects a few articles of ordinary wear—among them, change of stout shoes and socks for walking—and packs these in a knapsack. This knapsack is new, and he bought it in the High Street yesterday. He also purchased, at the same time and at the same place, a heavy walking-stick: strong in the handle for the grip of the hand, and iron-shod. He tries this, swings it, poises it, and lays it by, with the knapsack, on a window-seat. By this time his arrangements are complete.

He dresses for going out, and is in the act of going—indeed, has left his room, and has met the Minor Canon on the stair-case, coming out of his bedroom upon the same story—when he turns back again for his walking-stick, thinking he will carry it now. Mr. Crisparkle, who has paused on the stair-case, sees it in his hand on his immediately reappearing, takes it from him, and asks him with a smile how he chooses a stick.

"Really I don't know that I understand the subject," he answers. "I chose it for its weight."

"Much too heavy, Neville; *much* too heavy."

"To rest upon in a long walk, sir?"

"Rest upon?" repeats Mr. Crisparkle, throwing himself into pedestrian form. "You don't rest upon it; you merely balance with it."

"I shall know better, with practice, sir. I have not lived in a walking country, you know."

"True," says Mr. Crisparkle. "Get into a little training, and we will have a few score miles together. I should leave you nowhere now. Do you come back before dinner?"

"I think not, as we dine early."

Mr. Crisparkle gives him a bright nod and a cheerful good-by, expressing (not without intention) absolute confidence and ease.

Neville repairs to the Nuns' House, and requests that Miss Landless may be informed that her brother is there, by appointment. He waits at the gate, not even crossing the threshold; for he is on his parole not to put himself in Rosa's way.

His sister is at least as mindful of the obligation they have taken on themselves, as he can be, and loses not a moment in joining him. They meet affectionately, avoid lingering there, and walk toward the upper inland country.

"I am not going to tread upon forbidden ground, Helena," says Neville, when they have walked some distance and are turning; "you will understand in another moment that I cannot help referring to—what shall I say—my infatuation."

"Had you not better avoid it, Neville? You know that I can hear nothing."

"You can hear, my dear, what Mr. Crisparkle has heard, and heard with approval."

"Yes; I can hear so much."

"Well, it is this. I am not only unsettled and unhappy myself, but I am conscious of unsettling and interfering with other people. How do I know that, but for my unfortunate presence, you, and—and—the rest of that former party, our engaging guardian excepted, might be dining cheerfully in Minor Canon Corner to-morrow? Indeed it probably would be so. I can see too well that I am not high in the old lady's opinion, and it is easy to understand what an irksome clog I must be upon the hospitalities of her orderly house—especially at this time of year—when I must be kept asunder from this person, and there is such a reason for my not being brought into contact with that person, and an unfavorable reputation has preceded me with such another person, and so on. I have put this very gently to Mr. Crisparkle, for you know his self-denying ways; but still I have put it. What I have laid much greater stress upon at the same time, is, that I am engaged in a miserable struggle with myself, and that a little change and absence may enable me to come through it the better. So, the weather being bright and hard, I am going on a walking expedition, and intend taking myself out of everybody's way (my own included, I hope) to-morrow morning."

"When to come back?"

"In a fortnight."

"And going quite alone?"

"I am much better without company, even if there were any one but you to bear me company, my dear Helena."

"Mr. Crisparkle entirely agrees, you say?"

"Entirely. I am not sure but that at first he was inclined to think it rather a moody scheme, and one that might do a brooding mind harm. But we took a moonlight walk, last Monday night, to talk it over at leisure, and I represented the case to him as it really is. I showed him that I do want to conquer myself, and that, this evening well got over, it is surely better that I should be away from here just now than here. I could hardly help meeting certain people walking together here, and that could do no good, and is certainly not the way to forget. A fortnight hence, that chance will probably be over, for the time; and when it again arises for the last time, why, I can again go away. Further, I really do feel hopeful of bracing exercise and wholesome fatigue. You know that Mr. Crisparkle allows such things their full weight in the preservation of his own sound mind in his own sound body, and that his just spirit is not likely to maintain one set of natural laws for himself and another for me. He yielded to my view of the matter, when convinced that I was honestly in earnest, and so, with his full consent, I start to-morrow morning. Early enough to be not only out of the streets, but out of hearing of the bells, when the good people go to church."

Helena thinks it over, and thinks well of it. Mr. Crisparkle doing so, she would do so; but she does originally, out of her own mind, think well of it, as a healthy project, denoting a sincere endeavor, and an active attempt, at self-correction. She is inclined to pity him, poor fellow, for going away solitary on the great Christmas festival; but she feels it much more to the purpose to encourage him. And she does encourage him.

He will write to her?

He will write to her every alternate day, and tell her all his adventures.

Does he send clothes on, in advance of him?

"My dear Helena, no. Travel like a pilgrim, with wallet and staff. My wallet—or my knapsack—is packed, and ready for strapping on; and here is my staff!"

He hands it to her; she makes the same remark as Mr. Crisparkle, that it is very heavy; and gives it back to him, asking what wood it is? Iron-wood.

Up to this point he has been extremely cheerful. Perhaps the having to carry his case with her, and therefore to present it in its brightest aspect, has roused his spirits. Perhaps the having done so with success is followed by a revulsion. As the day closes in, and the city lights begin to spring up before them, he grows depressed.

"I wish I were not going to this dinner, Helena."

"Dear Neville, is it worth while to care much about it? Think how soon it will be over."

"How soon it will be over," he repeats gloomily. "Yes. But I don't like it."

There may be a moment's awkwardness, she cheeringly represents to him, but it can only last a moment. He is quite sure of himself.

"I wish I felt as sure of everything else as I feel of myself," he answers her.

"How strangely you speak, dear! What do you mean?"

"Helena, I don't know. I only know that I don't like it. What a strange dead weight there is in the air!"

She calls his attention to those copperous clouds beyond the river, and says that the wind is rising. He scarcely speaks again, until he takes leave of her, at the gate of the Nuns' House. She does not immediately enter when they have parted, but remains looking after him along the street. Twice he passes the Gate-House, reluctant to enter. At length, the cathedral clock chiming one quarter, with a rapid turn he hurries in.

And so *he* goes up the postern stair.

Edwin Drood passes a solitary day. Something of deeper moment than he had thought has gone out of his life; and in the silence of his own chamber he wept for it last night. Though the image of Miss Landless still hovers in the background of his mind, the pretty little affectionate creature, so much firmer and wiser than he had supposed, occupies its stronghold. It is with some misgiving of his own unworthiness that he thinks of her, and of what they might have been to one another, if he had been more in earnest some time ago; if he had set a higher value on her; if, instead of accepting his fortune in life as an inheritance of course, he had studied the right way to its appreciation and enhancement. And still, for all this, and though there is a sharp heartache in all this, the vanity and caprice of youth sustain that handsome figure of Miss Landless in the background of his mind.

That was a curious look of Rosa's when they parted at the gate. Did it mean that she saw below the surface of his thoughts, and down into their twilight depths? Scarcely that, for it was a look of astonished and keen inquiry. He decides that he cannot understand it, though it was remarkably expressive.

As he only waits for Mr. Grewgious now, and will depart immediately after having seen him, he takes a sauntering leave of the ancient city and its neighborhood. He recalls the time when Rosa and he walked here or there, mere children, full of the dignity of being engaged. Poor children! he thinks, with a pitying sadness.

Finding that his watch has stopped, he turns into the jeweller's shop to have it wound and set. The jeweller is knowing on the subject of a bracelet, which he begs leave to submit, in a general and quite aimless way. It would suit (he considers) a young bride to perfection; especially if of a rather diminutive style of beauty. Finding the bracelet but coldly looked at, the jeweller invites attention to a tray of rings for gentlemen; here is a style of ring now, he remarks, a very chaste signet which gentlemen are much given to purchasing, when changing their condition. A ring of a very responsible appearance. With the date of their wedding-day engraved inside, several gentlemen have preferred it to any other kind of memento.

The rings are as coldly viewed as the bracelet. Edwin tells the tempter that he wears no jewelry but his watch and chain, which were his father's, and his shirt-pin.

"That I was aware of," is the jeweller's reply, "for Mr. Jasper dropped in for a watch-glass the other day, and, in fact, I showed these articles to him, remarking that if he *should* wish to make a present to a gentleman relative, on any particular occasion—but he said with a smile that he had an inventory in his mind of all the jewelry his gentleman relative ever wore; namely, his watch and chain and his shirt-pin." Still (the jeweller considers) that might not apply to all times, though applying to the present time. "Twenty minutes past two, Mr. Drood, I set your watch at. Let me recommend you not to let it run down, sir."

Edwin takes his watch, puts it on, and goes out, thinking, "Dear old Jack! If I were to make an extra crease in my neckcloth, he would think it worth noticing!"

He strolls about and about, to pass the time until the dinner hour. It somehow happens that Cloisterham seems reproachful to him to-day; has fault to find with him, as if he had not used it well; but is far more pensive with him than angry. His wonted carelessness is replaced by a wistful looking at, and dwelling upon, all the old landmarks. He will soon be far away, and may never see them again, he thinks. Poor youth! Poor youth!

As dusk draws on, he paces the Monks' Vineyard. He has walked to and fro, full half an hour by the cathedral chimes, and it has closed in dark, before he becomes quite aware of a woman crouching on the ground near a wicket-gate in a corner. The gate commands a cross by-path, little used in the gloaming; and the figure must have been there all the time, though he has but gradually and lately made it out.

He strikes into that path, and walks up to the wicket. By the light of a lamp near it, he sees that the woman is of a haggard appearance, and that her weazen chin is resting on her hands, and that her eyes are staring—with an unwinking, blind sort of steadfastness—before her.

Always kindly, but moved to be unusually kind this evening, and having bestowed kind words on most of the children and aged people he has met, he at once bends down, and speaks to this woman.

"Are you ill?"

"No, deary," she answers, without looking at him, and with no departure from her strange blind stare.

"Are you blind?"

"No, deary."

"Are you lost, homeless, faint? What is the matter, that you stay here in the cold so long, without moving?"

By slow and stiff efforts, she appears to contract her vision until it can rest upon him; and then a curious film passes over her, and she begins to shake.

He straitens himself, recoils a step, and looks down at her in a dread amazement; for he seems to know her.

"Good Heaven!" he thinks, next moment. "Like Jack that night!"

As he looks down at her, she looks up at him and whimpers, "My lungs is weakly; my lungs is dreffle bad. Poor me, poor me, my cough is rattling dry!" And coughs in confirmation horribly.

"Where do you come from?"

"Come from London, deary." (Her cough still rending her.)

"Where are you going to?"

"Back to London, deary. I came here, looking for a needle in a haystack, and I ain't found it. Look'ee, deary; give me three-and-sixpence, and don't you be afeard for me. I'll get back to London then, and trouble no one. I'm in a business. Ah, me! It's slack, it's slack, and times is very bad!—but I can make a shift to live by it."

"Do you eat opium?"

"Smokes it," she replies with difficulty, still racked by her cough. "Give me three-and-sixpence, and I'll lay it out well, and get back. If you don't give me three-and-sixpence, don't give me a brass farden. And if you do give me three-and-sixpence, deary, I'll tell you something."

He counts the money from his pocket, and puts it in her hand. She instantly clutches it tight, and rises to her feet with a croaking laugh of satisfaction.

"Bless ye! Harkee, dear genl'mn. What's your Chris'en name?"

"Edwin."

"Edwin, Edwin, Edwin," she repeats, trailing off into a drowsy repetition of the word, and then asks suddenly, "Is the short of that name, Eddy?"

"It is sometimes called so," he replies, with the color starting to his face.

"Don't sweethearts call it so?" she asks, pondering.

"How should I know?"

"Haven't you a sweetheart, upon your soul?"

"None."

She is moving away with another "Bless ye, and thank'ee deary!" when he adds, "You were to tell me something; you may as well do so."

"So I was, so I was. Well, then. Whisper. You be thankful that your name ain't Ned."

He looks at her quite steadily, as he asks, "Why?"

"Because it's a bad name to have just now."

"How a bad name?"

"A threatened name. A dangerous name."

"The proverb says that threatened men live long," he tells her, lightly.

"Then Ned—so threatened is he, wherever he may be while I am a talking to you, deary—should live to all eternity!" replies the woman.

She has leaned forward to say it in his ear, with her forefinger shaking before his eyes, and now huddles herself together, and with another "Bless ye, and thank'ee!" goes away in the direction of the Travellers' Lodging House.

This is not an inspiriting close to a dull day. Alone, in a sequestered place, surrounded by vestiges of old time and decay, it rather has a tendency to call a shudder into being. He makes for the better lighted streets, and resolves as he walks on to say nothing of this to-night, but to mention it to Jack (who alone calls him Ned), as an odd coincidence, to-morrow; of course only as a coincidence, and not as anything better worth remembering.

Still, it holds to him, as many things much better worth remembering never did. He has another mile or so to linger out before the dinner-hour; and, when he walks over the bridge and by the river, the woman's words are in the rising wind, in the angry sky, in the troubled water, in the flickering lights. There is some solemn echo of them even in the cathedral chime, which strikes a sudden surprise to his heart as he turns in under the archway of the Gate-House.

And so *he* goes up the postern stair.

John Jasper passes a more agreeable and cheerful day than either of his guests. Having no music-lessons to give in the holiday season, his time is his own, but for the cathedral services. He is early among the shopkeepers, ordering little table luxuries that his nephew likes. His nephew will not be with him long, he tells his provision-dealers, and so must be petted and made much of. While out on his hospitable preparations, he looks in on Mr. Sapsea, and mentions that dear Ned, and that inflammable young spark of Mr. Crisparkle's, are to dine at the Gate-House to-day, and make up their difference. Mr. Sapsea is by no means friendly toward the inflammable young spark. He says that his complexion is "Un-English." And when Mr. Sapsea has once declared any thing to be "Un-English," he considers that thing everlastingly sunk in the bottomless pit.

John Jasper is truly sorry to hear Mr. Sapsea speak thus, for he knows right well that Mr. Sapsea never speaks without a meaning, and that he has a subtle trick of being right. Mr. Sapsea (by a very remarkable coincidence) is of exactly that opinion.

Mr. Jasper is in beautiful voice this day. In the pathetic supplication to have his heart inclined to keep this law, he quite astonishes his fellows by his melodious power. He has never sung difficult music with such skill and harmony as in this day's anthem. His nervous temperament is occasionally prone to take difficult music a little too quickly; to-day his time is perfect.

These results are probably attained through a grand composure of the spirits. The mere mechanism of his throat is a little tender, for he wears, both with his singing-robe and with his ordinary dress, a large black scarf of strong, close-woven silk, slung loosely round his neck. But his composure is so noticeable, that Mr. Crisparkle speaks of it as they come out from vespers.

"I must thank you, Jasper, for the pleasure with which I have heard you to-day. Beautiful! Delightful! You could not have so outdone yourself, I hope, without being wonderfully well."

"I *am* wonderfully well."

"Nothing unequal," says the Minor Canon, with a smooth motion of his hand; "nothing unsteady, nothing forced, nothing avoided; all thoroughly done in a masterly manner, with perfect self-command."

"Thank you. I hope so, if it is not too much to say."

"One would think, Jasper, you had been trying a new medicine for that occasional indisposition of yours."

"No, really? That's well observed; for I have."

"Then stick to it, my good fellow," says Mr. Crisparkle, clapping him on the shoulder with friendly encouragement, "stick to it."

"I will."

"I congratulate you," Mr. Crisparkle pursues, as they come out of the cathedral, "on all accounts."

"Thank you again. I will walk round to the Corner with you, if you don't object; I have plenty of time before my company come; and I want to say a word to you, which I think you will not be displeased to hear."

"What is it?"

"Well. We were speaking, the other evening, of my black humors."

Mr. Crisparkle's face falls, and he shakes his head deploringly.

"I said, you know, that I should make you an antidote to those black humors; and you said you hoped I would consign them to the flames."

"And I still hope so, Jasper."

"With the best reason in the world! I mean to burn this year's Diary at the year's end."

"Because you ——?" Mr. Crisparkle brightens greatly as he thus begins.

"You anticipate me. Because I feel that I have been out of sorts, gloomy, bilious, brain-oppressed, whatever it may be. You said I had been exaggerative. So I have."

Mr. Crisparkle's brightened face brightens still more.

"I couldn't see it then, because I *was* out of sorts; but I am in a healthier state now, and I acknowledge it with genuine pleasure. I made a great deal of a very little; that's the fact."

"It does me good," cries Mr. Crisparkle, "to hear you say it!"

"A man leading a monotonous life," Jasper proceeds, "and getting his nerves, or his stomach, out of order, dwells upon an idea until it loses its proportions. That was my case with the idea in question. So I shall burn the evidence of my case, when the book is full, and begin the next volume with a clearer vision."

"This is better," says Mr. Crisparkle, stopping at the steps of his own door to shake hands, "than I could have hoped!"

"Why, naturally," returns Jasper, "you had but little reason to hope that I should become more like yourself. You are always training yourself to be, mind and body, as clear as crystal, and you always are, and never change; whereas, I am a muddy, solitary, moping weed. However, I have got over that mope. Shall I wait, while you ask if Mr. Neville has left for my place? If not, he and I may walk round together."

"I think," says Mr. Crisparkle, opening the entrance door with his key, "that he left some time ago; at least I know he left, and I think he has not come back. But I'll inquire. You won't come in?"

"My company wait," says Jasper, with a smile.

The Minor Canon disappears, and in a few moments returns. As he thought, Mr. Neville has not come back; indeed, as he remembers now, Mr. Neville said he would probably go straight to the Gate-House.

"Bad manners in a host!" says Jasper. "My company will be there before me! What will you bet that I don't find my company embracing?"

"I will bet—or would, if I ever did bet," returns Mr. Crisparkle—"that your company will have a gay entertainer this evening."

Jasper nods, and laughs Good Night!

He retraces his steps to the cathedral door, and turns down past it to the Gate-House. He sings, in a low voice, and with delicate expression, as he walks along. It still seems as if a false note were not within his power to-night, and as if nothing could hurry or retard him. Arriving thus, under the arched entrance of his dwelling, he pauses for an instant in the shelter to pull off that great black scarf, and hang it in a loop upon his arm. For that brief time, his face is knitted and stern. But it immediately clears, as he resumes his singing, and his way.

And so *he* goes up the postern stair.

The red light burns steadily all the evening in the light-house on the margin of the tide of busy life. Softened sounds and hum of traffic pass it and flow on irregularly into the lonely Precincts; but very little else goes by, save violent rushes of wind. It comes on to blow a boisterous gale.

The Precincts are never particularly well lighted; but the strong blasts of wind blowing out many of the lamps (in some instances shattering the frames too, and bringing the glass rattling to the ground), they are unusually dark to-night. The darkness is augmented and confused by flying dust from the earth, dry twigs from the trees, and great ragged fragments from the rooks' nests up in the tower. The trees themselves so toss and creak, as this tangible part of the darkness madly whirls about, that they seem in peril of being torn out of the earth; while ever and again a crack, and a rushing fall, denote that some large branch has yielded to the storm.

No such power of wind has blown for many a winter night. Chimneys topple in the streets, and people hold to posts and corners, and to one another, to keep themselves upon their feet. The violent rushes abate not, but increase in frequency and fury until at midnight, when the streets are empty, the storm goes thundering along them, rattling at all the latches, and tearing at all the shutters, as if warning the people to get up and fly with it, rather than have the roofs brought down upon their brains.

Still the red light burns steadily. Nothing is steady but the red light.

All through the night the wind blows, and abates not. But early in the morning, when there is barely enough light in the east to dim the stars, it begins to lull. From that time, with occasional wild charges, like a wounded monster dying, it drops and sinks; and at full daylight it is dead.

It is then seen that the hands of the cathedral clock are torn off; that lead from the roof has been stripped away, rolled up, and blown into the Close; and that some stones have been displaced upon the summit of the great tower. Christmas morning though it be, it is necessary to send up workmen to ascertain the extent of the damage done. These, led by Durdles, go aloft; while Mr. Tope and a crowd of early idlers gather down in Minor Canon Corner, shading their eyes and watching for their appearance up there.

This cluster is suddenly broken and put aside by the hands of Mr. Jasper; all the gazing eyes are brought down to the earth by his loudly enquiring of Mr. Crisparkle, at an open window:

"Where is my nephew?"

"He has not been here. Is he not with you?"

"No. He went down to the river last night, with Mr. Neville, to look at the storm, and has not been back. Call Mr. Neville!"

"He left this morning early."

"Left this morning early? Let me in, let me in!"

There is no more looking up at the tower, now. All the assembled eyes are turned on Mr. Jasper, white, half-dressed, panting, and clinging to the rail before the Minor Canon's house.

CHAPTER XIII.

IMPEACHED.

Neville Landless had started so early and walked at so good a pace, that when the church-bells began to ring in Cloisterham for morning-service, he was eight miles away. As he wanted his breakfast by that time, having set forth on a crust of bread, he stopped at the next roadside tavern to refresh.

Visitors in want of breakfast—unless they were horses or cattle, for which class of guests there was preparation enough in the way of water-trough and hay—were so unusual at the sign of The Tilted Wagon, that it took a long time to get the wagon into the track of tea and toast and bacon, Neville, in the interval, sitting in a sanded parlor, wondering in how long a time after he had gone, the sneezy fagots would begin to make somebody else warm.

Indeed, The Tilted Wagon, as a cool establishment on the top of a hill, where the ground before the door was puddled with damp hoofs and trodden straw; where a scolding landlady slapped a moist baby (with one red sock on and one wanting) in the bar; where the cheese was cast aground upon a shelf, in company with a mouldy table-cloth and a green-handled knife, in a sort of cast-iron canoe; where the pale-faced bread shed tears of crumb over its shipwreck in another canoe; where the family linen, half washed and half dried, led a public life of lying about; where everything to drink was drunk out of mugs, and everything else was suggestive of a rhyme to mugs—The Tilted Wagon, all these things considered, hardly kept its painted promise of providing good entertainment for Man and Beast. However, Man, in the present case, was not critical, but took what entertainment he could get, and went on again after a longer rest than he needed.

He stopped at some quarter of a mile from the house, hesitating whether to pursue the road or to follow a cart-track between two high hedgerows, which led across the slope of a breezy heath, and evidently struck into the road again by-and-by. He decided in favor of this latter track, and pursued it with some toil, the rise being steep, and the way worn into deep ruts.

He was laboring along, when he became aware of some other pedestrians behind him. As they were coming up at a faster pace than his, he stood aside, against one of the high banks, to let them pass. But their manner was very curious. Only four of them passed. Other four slackened speed, and loitered as intending to follow him when he should go on. The remainder of the party (half a dozen perhaps) turned, and went back at a great rate.

He looked at the four behind him, and he looked at the four before him. They all returned his look. He resumed his way. The four in advance went on, constantly looking back; the four in the rear came closing up.

When they all ranged out from the narrow track upon the open slope of the heath, and this order was maintained, let him diverge as he would to either side, there was no longer room to doubt that he was beset by these fellows. He stopped, as a last test; and they all stopped.

"Why do you attend upon me in this way?" he asked the whole body. "Are you a pack of thieves?"

"Don't answer him," said one of the number; he did not see which. "Better be quiet."

"Better be quiet?" repeated Neville. "Who said so?"

Nobody replied.

"It's good advice, whichever of you skulkers gave it," he went on, angrily. "I will not submit to be penned in between four men there, and four men there. I wish to pass, and I mean to pass, those four in front."

They were all standing still, himself included.

"If eight men, or four men, or two men, set upon one," he proceeded, growing more enraged, "the one has no chance but to set his mark upon some of them. And by the Lord I'll do it, if I am interrupted any further!"

Shouldering his heavy stick, and quickening his pace, he shot on to pass the four ahead. The largest and strongest man of the number changed swiftly to the side on which he came up, and dexterously closed with him and went down with him; but not before the heavy stick had descended smartly.

"Let him be!" said this man in a suppressed voice, as they struggled together on the grass. "Fair play! His is the build of a girl to mine, and he's got a weight strapped to his back besides. Let him alone. I'll manage him."

After a little rolling about, in a close scuffle, which caused the faces of both to be besmeared with blood, the man took his knee from Neville's chest, and rose, saying, "There! Now take him arm in arm, any two of you!"

It was immediately done.

"As to our being a pack of thieves, Mr. Landless," said the man, as he spat out some blood, and wiped more from his face, "you know better than that, at mid-day. We wouldn't have touched you, if you hadn't forced us. We're going to take you round to the high-road, anyhow, and you'll find help enough against thieves there, if you want it. Wipe his face, somebody; see how it's a trickling down him!"

When his face was cleansed, Neville recognized in the speaker, Joe, driver of the Cloisterham omnibus, whom he had seen but once, and that on the day of his arrival.

"And what I recommend you for the present is, don't talk, Mr. Landless. You'll find a friend waiting for you at the high-road—gone ahead by the other way when we split into two parties—and you had much better say nothing till you come up with him. Bring that stick along, somebody else, and let's be moving!"

Utterly bewildered, Neville stared around him and said not a word. Walking between his two conductors, who held his arms in theirs, he went on, as in a dream, until they came again into the high-road, and into the midst of a little group of people. The men who had turned back were among the group, and its central figures were Mr. Jasper and Mr. Crisparkle. Neville's conductors took him up to the Minor Canon, and there released him, as an act of deference to that gentleman.

"What is all this, sir? What is the matter? I feel as if I had lost my senses!" cried Neville, the group closing in around him.

"Where is my nephew?" asked Mr. Jasper, wildly.

"Where is your nephew?" repeated Neville. "Why do you ask me?"

"I ask you," retorted Jasper, "because you were the last person in his company, and he is not to be found."

"Not to be found!" cried Neville, aghast.

"Stay, stay," said Mr. Crisparkle. "Permit me, Jasper. Mr. Neville, you are confounded; collect your thoughts; it is of great importance that you should collect your thoughts; attend to me."

"I will try, sir, but I seem mad."

"You left Mr. Jasper's last night, with Edwin Drood?"

"Yes."

"At what hour?"

"Was it at twelve o'clock?" asked Neville, with his hand to his confused head, and appealing to Jasper.

"Quite right," said Mr. Crisparkle; "the hour Mr. Jasper has already named to me. You went down to the river together?"

"Undoubtedly. To see the action of the wind there."

"What followed? How long did you stay there?"

"About ten minutes; I should say not more. We then walked together to your house, and he took leave of me at the door."

"Did he say that he was going down to the river again?"

"No. He said that he was going straight back."

The bystanders looked at one another, and at Mr. Crisparkle. To whom, Mr. Jasper, who had been intensely watching Neville, said, in a low, distinct, suspicious voice, "What are those stains upon his dress?"

All eyes were turned toward the blood upon his clothes.

"And here are the same stains upon this stick!" said Jasper, taking it from the hand of the man who held it. "I know the stick to be his, and he carried it last night. What does this mean?"

"In the name of God, say what it means, Neville!" urged Mr. Crisparkle.

"That man and I," said Neville, pointing out his late adversary, "had a struggle for the stick just now, and you may see the same marks on him, sir. What was I to suppose, when I found myself molested by eight people? Could I dream of the true reason when they would give me none at all?"

They admitted that they had thought it discreet to be silent, and that the struggle had taken place. And yet the very men who had seen it looked darkly at the smears which the bright cold air had already dried.

"We must return, Neville," said Mr. Crisparkle; "of course you will be glad to come back to clear yourself?"

"Of course, sir."

"Mr. Landless will walk at my side," the Minor Canon continued, looking around him. "Come, Neville!"

They set forth on the walk back; and the others, with one exception, straggled after them at various distances. Jasper walked on the other side of Neville, and never quitted that position. He was silent, while Mr. Crisparkle more than once repeated his former questions, and while Neville repeated his former answers; also, while they both hazarded some explanatory conjectures. He was obstinately silent, because Mr. Crisparkle's manner directly appealed to him to take some part in the discussion, and no appeal would move his fixed face. When they drew near to the city, and it was suggested by the Minor Canon that they might do well in calling on the Mayor at once, he assented with a stern nod; but he spake no word until they stood in Mr. Sapsea's parlor.

Mr. Sapsea being informed by Mr. Crisparkle of the circumstances under which they desired to make a voluntary statement before him, Mr. Jasper broke silence by declaring that he placed his whole reliance, humanly speaking, on Mr. Sapsea's penetration. There was no conceivable reason why his nephew should have suddenly absconded, unless Mr. Sapsea could suggest one, and then he would defer. There was no intelligible likelihood of his having returned to the river, and been accidentally drowned in the dark, unless it should appear likely to Mr. Sapsea, and then again he would defer. He washed his hands as clean as he could of all horrible suspicions, unless it should appear to Mr. Sapsea that some such were inseparable from his last companion before his disappearance (not on good terms with previously), and then, once more, he would defer. His own state of mind, he being distracted with doubts, and laboring under dismal apprehensions, was not to be safely trusted; but Mr. Sapsea's was.

Mr. Sapsea expressed his opinion that the case had a dark look; in short (and here his eyes rested full on Neville's countenance), an Un-English complexion. Having made this grand point, he wandered into a denser haze and maze of nonsense than even a mayor might have been expected to disport himself in, and came out of it with the brilliant discovery that to take the life of a fellow-creature was to take something that didn't belong to you. He wavered whether or no he should at once issue his warrant for the committal of Neville Landless to jail, under circumstances of grave suspicion; and he might have gone so far as to do it, but for the indignant protest of the Minor Canon, who undertook for the young man's remaining in his own house, and being produced by his own hands, whenever demanded. Mr. Jasper then understood Mr. Sapsea to suggest that the river should be dragged, that its banks should be rigidly examined, that particulars of his disappearance should be sent to all outlying places and to London, and that placards and advertisements should be widely circulated, imploring Edwin Drood, if for any unknown reason he had withdrawn himself from his uncle's home and society, to take pity on that loving kinsman's sore bereavement and distress, and somehow inform him that he was yet alive. Mr. Sapsea was perfectly understood, for this was exactly his meaning (though he had said nothing about it); and measures were taken toward all these ends immediately.

It would be difficult to determine which was the more oppressed with horror and amazement, Neville Landless or John Jasper. But that Jasper's position forced him to be active, while Neville's forced him to be passive, there would have been nothing to choose between them. Each was bowed down and broken.

With the earliest light of the next morning, men were at work upon the river, and other men—most of whom volunteered for the service—were examining the banks. All the livelong day the search went on; upon the river, with barge and pole, and drag and net; upon the muddy and rushy shore, with jackboot, hatchet, spade, rope, dogs, and all imaginable appliances. Even at night the river was specked with lanterns, and lurid with fires; far-off creeks, into which the tide washed as it changed, had their knots of watchers, listening to the lapping of the stream, and looking out for any burden it might bear; remote shingly causeways near the sea, and lonely points off which there was a race of water, had their unwonted flaring cressets and rough-coated figures when the next day dawned; but no trace of Edwin Drood revisited the light of the sun.

All that day, again, the search went on. Now, in barge and boat; and now ashore among the osiers, or tramping amidst mud and stakes and jagged stones in low-lying places, where solitary water-marks and signals of strange shapes showed like spectres, John Jasper worked and toiled. But to no purpose; for still no trace of Edwin Drood revisited the light of the sun.

Setting his watches for that night again, so that vigilant eyes should be kept on every change of tide, he went home exhausted. Unkempt and disordered, bedaubed with mud that had dried upon him, and with much of his clothing torn to rags, he had but just dropped into his easy-chair, when Mr. Grewgious stood before him.

"This is strange news," said Mr. Grewgious.

"Strange and fearful news."

Jasper had merely lifted up his heavy eyes to say it, and now dropped them again as he drooped, worn out, over one side of his easy-chair.

Mr. Grewgious smoothed his head and face, and stood looking at the fire.

"How is your ward?" asked Jasper, after a time, in a faint, fatigued voice.

"Poor little thing! You may imagine her condition."

"Have you seen his sister?" inquired Jasper, as before.

"Whose?"

The curtness of the counter-question, and the cool, slow manner in which, as he put it, Mr. Grewgious moved his eyes from the fire to his companion's face, might at any other time have been exasperating. In his depression and exhaustion, Jasper merely opened his eyes to say, "The suspected young man's."

"Do you suspect him?" asked Mr. Grewgious.

"I don't know what to think. I cannot make up my mind."

"Nor I," said Mr. Grewgious. "But, as you spoke of him as the suspected young man, I thought you *had* made up your mind.—I have just left Miss Landless."

"What is *her* state?"

"Defiance of all suspicion, and unbounded faith in her brother."

"Poor thing!"

"However," pursued Mr. Grewgious, "it is not of her that I came to speak. It is of my ward. I have a communication to make that will surprise you. At least, it has surprised me."

Jasper, with a groaning sigh, turned wearily in his chair.

"Shall I put it off till to-morrow?" said Mr. Grewgious. "Mind! I warn you, that I think it will surprise you!"

More attention and concentration came into John Jasper's eyes as they caught sight of Mr. Grewgious, smoothing his head again, and again looking at the fire, but now with a compressed and determined mouth.

"What is it?" demanded Jasper, becoming upright in his chair.

"To be sure," said Mr. Grewgious, provokingly slowly and internally, as he kept his eyes on the fire, "I might have known it sooner; she gave me the opening, but I am such an exceedingly Angular man, that it never occurred to me; I took all for granted."

"What is it?" demanded Jasper, once more.

Mr. Grewgious, alternately opening and shutting the palms of his hands as he warmed them at the fire, and looking fixedly at him sideways, and never changing either his action or his look in all that followed, went on to reply:

"This young couple, the lost youth and Miss Rosa, my ward, though so long betrothed, and so long recognizing their betrothal, and so near being married—"

Mr. Grewgious saw a staring white face, and two quivering white lips, in the easy-chair, and saw two muddy hands gripping its sides. But for the hands, he might have thought he had never seen the face.

"—This young couple came gradually to the discovery (made on both sides pretty equally, I think) that they would be happier and better, both in their present and their future lives, as affectionate friends, or say rather as brother and sister, than as husband and wife."

Mr. Grewgious saw a lead-colored face in the easy-chair, and on its surface dreadful starting drops, or bubbles, as if of steel.

"This young couple formed at length the healthy resolution of interchanging their discoveries, openly, sensibly, and tenderly. They met for that purpose. After some innocent and generous talk, they agreed to dissolve their existing, and their intended, relations, forever and ever."

Mr. Grewgious saw a ghastly figure rise, open-mouthed, from the easy-chair, and lift its outspread hands toward its head.

"One of this young couple, and that one your nephew, fearful, however, that in the tenderness of your affection for him you would be bitterly disappointed by so wide a departure from his projected life, forbore to tell you the secret, for a few days, and left it to be disclosed by me, when I should come down to speak to you, and he would be gone. I speak to you, and he is gone."

Mr. Grewgious saw the ghastly figure throw back its head, clutch its hair with its hands, and turn with a writhing action from him.

"I have now said all I have to say, except that this young couple parted, firmly, though not without tears and sorrow, on the evening when you last saw them together."

Mr. Grewgious heard a terrible shriek, and saw no ghastly figure, sitting or standing; saw nothing but a heap of torn and miry clothes upon the floor.

Not changing his action even then, he opened and shut the palms of his hands as he warmed them, and looked down at it.

CHAPTER XIV.

DEVOTED.

When John Jasper recovered from his fit, or swoon, he found himself being tended by Mr. and Mrs. Tope, whom his visitor had summoned for the purpose. His visitor, wooden of aspect, sat stiffly in a chair, with his hands upon his knees, watching his recovery.

"There! You've come to nicely now, sir," said the tearful Mrs. Tope; "you were thoroughly worn out, and no wonder!"

"A man," said Mr. Grewgious, with his usual air of repeating a lesson, "cannot have his rest broken, and his mind cruelly tormented, and his body overtaxed by fatigue, without being thoroughly worn out."

"I fear I have alarmed you?" Jasper apologized faintly, when he was helped into his easy-chair.

"Not at all, I thank you," answered Mr. Grewgious.

"You are too considerate."

"Not at all, I thank you," answered Mr. Grewgious again.

"You must take some wine, sir," said Mrs. Tope, "and the jelly that I had ready for you, and that you wouldn't put your lips to at noon, though I warned you what would come of it, you know, and you not breakfasted; and you must have a wing of the roast fowl that has been put back twenty times if it's been put back once. It shall all be on table in five minutes, and this good gentleman belike will stop and see you take it."

This good gentleman replied with a snort, which might mean yes or no, or anything, or nothing, and which Mrs. Tope would have found highly mystifying, but that her attention was divided by the service of the table.

"You will take something with me?" said Jasper, as the cloth was laid.

"I couldn't get a morsel down my throat, I thank you," answered Mr. Grewgious.

Jasper both ate and drank almost voraciously. Combined with the hurry in his mode of doing it, it was an evident indifference to the taste of what he took, suggesting that he ate and drank to fortify himself against any other failure of the spirits, far more than to gratify his palate. Mr. Grewgious in the mean time sat upright, with no expression in his face, and a hard kind of imperturbably polite protest all over him; as though he would have said, in reply to some invitation to discourse: "I couldn't originate the faintest approach to an observation on any subject whatever, I thank you."

"Do you know," said Jasper, when he had pushed away his plate and glass, and had sat meditating for a few minutes, "do you know that I find some crumbs of comfort in the communication with which you have so much amazed me?"

"*Do* you?" returned Mr. Grewgious; pretty plainly adding the unspoken clause: "I don't, I thank you!"

"After recovering from the shock of a piece of news of my dear boy, so entirely unexpected, and so destructive of all the castles I had built for him; and after having had time to think of it; yes."

"I shall be glad to pick up your crumbs," said Mr. Grewgious dryly.

"Is there not, or is there—if I deceive myself, tell me so, and shorten my pain—is there not, or is there, hope that, finding himself in this new position, and becoming sensitively alive to the awkward burden of explanation, in this quarter, and that, and the other, with which it would load him, he avoided the awkwardness and took to flight?"

"Such a thing might be!" said Mr. Grewgious, pondering.

"Such a thing has been. I have read of cases in which people, rather than face a seven-days' wonder, and have to account for themselves to the idle and impertinent, have taken themselves away, and been long unheard of."

"I believe such things have happened," said Mr. Grewgious, pondering still.

"When I had, and could have, no suspicion," pursued Jasper, eagerly following the new track, "that the dear lost boy had withheld anything from me — most of all, such a leading matter as this — what gleam of light was there for me in the whole black sky? When I supposed that his intended wife was here, and his marriage close at hand, how could I entertain the possibility of his voluntarily leaving this place, in a manner that would be so unaccountable, capricious, and cruel? But, now that I know what you have told me, is there no little chink through which day pierces? Supposing him to have disappeared of his own act, is not his disappearance more accountable and less cruel? The fact of his having just parted from your ward, is in itself a sort of reason for his going away. It does not make his mysterious departure the less cruel to me, it is true; but it relieves it of cruelty to her."

Mr. Grewgious could not but assent to this.

"And, even as to me," continued Jasper, still pursuing the new track, with ardor, and, as he did so, brightening with hope, "he knew that you were coming to me; he knew that you were intrusted to tell me what you have told me; if your doing so has awakened a new train of thought in my perplexed mind, it reasonably follows that, from the same premises, he might have foreseen the inferences that I should draw. Grant that he did foresee them; and even the cruelty to me—and who am I?—John Jasper, Music Master!—vanishes."

Once more, Mr. Grewgious could not but assent to this.

"I have had my distrusts, and terrible distrusts they have been," said Jasper; "but your disclosure, overpowering as it was at first—showing me that my own dear boy had had a great disappointing reservation from me, who so fondly loved him—kindles hope within me. You do not extinguish it when I state it, but admit it to be a reasonable hope. I begin to believe it possible:" here he clasped his hands: "that he may have disappeared from among us of his own accord, and that he may yet be alive and well!"

Mr. Crispa kle came in at the moment. To whom Mr. Jasper repeated:

"I begin to believe it possible that he may have disappeared of his own accord, and may yet be alive and well!"

Mr. Crisparkle taking a seat, and inquiring: "Why so?" Mr. Jasper repeated the arguments he had just set forth. If they had been less plausible than they were, the good Minor Canon's mind would have been in a state of preparation to receive them, as exculpatory of his unfortunate pupil. But he, too, did really attach great importance to the lost young man's having been, so immediately before his disappearance, placed in a new and embarrassing relation toward every one acquainted with his projects and affairs; and the fact seemed to him to present the question in a new light.

"I stated to Mr. Sapsea, when we waited on him," said Jasper: as he really had done: "that there was no quarrel or difference between the two young men at their last meeting. We all know that their first meeting was, unfortunately, very far from amicable; but all went smoothly and quietly when they were last together at my house. My dear boy was not in his usual spirits; he was depressed—I noticed that—and I am bound henceforth to dwell upon the circumstance the more, now that I know there was a special reason for his being depressed: a reason, moreover, which may possibly have induced him to absent himself."

"I pray to Heaven it may turn out so!" exclaimed Mr. Crisparkle.

"*I* pray to Heaven it may turn out so!" repeated Jasper. "You know—and Mr. Grewgious should now know likewise—that I took a great prepossession against Mr. Neville Landless, arising out of his furious conduct on that first occasion. You know that I came to you, extremely apprehensive, on my dear boy's behalf, of his mad violence. You know that I even entered in my Diary, and showed the entry to you, that I had dark forebodings against him. Mr. Grewgious ought to be possessed of the whole case. He shall not, through any suppression of mine, be informed of a part of it, and kept in ignorance of another part of it. I wish him to be good enough to understand that the communication he has made to me has hopefully influenced my mind, in spite of its having been, before this mysterious occurrence took place, profoundly impressed against young Landless."

This fairness troubled the Minor Canon much. He felt that he was not as open in his own dealing. He charged against himself reproachfully that he had suppressed, so far, the two points of a second strong outbreak of temper against Edwin Drood on the part of Neville, and of the passion of jealousy having, to his own certain knowledge, flamed up in Neville's breast against him. He was convinced of Neville's innocence of any part in the ugly disappearance; and yet so many little circumstances combined so woefully against him, that he dreaded to add two more to their cumulative weight. He was among the truest of men; but he had been balancing in his mind, much to its distress, whether his volunteering to tell these two fragments of truth, at this time, would not be tantamount to a piecing together of falsehood in the place of truth.

However, here was a model before him. He hesitated no longer. Addressing Mr. Grewgious, as one placed in authority by the revelation he had brought to bear on the mystery (and surpassingly Angular Mr. Grewgious became when he found himself in that unexpected position), Mr. Crisparkle bore his testimony to Mr. Jasper's strict sense of justice, and, expressing his absolute confidence in the complete clearance of his pupil from the least taint of suspicion, sooner or later, avowed that his confidence in that young gentleman had been formed, in spite of his confidential knowledge that his temper was of the hottest and fiercest, and that it was directly incensed against Mr. Jasper's nephew, by the circumstance of his romantically supposing himself to be enamoured of the same young lady. The sanguine reaction manifest in Mr. Jasper was proof even against this unlooked-for declaration. It turned him paler; but he repeated that he would cling to the hope he had derived from Mr. Grewgious; and that if no trace of his dear boy were found, leading to the dreadful inference that he had been made away with, he would cherish unto the last stretch of possibility, the idea, that he might have absconded of his own wild will.

Now, it fell out that Mr. Crisparkle, going away from this conference still very uneasy in his mind, and very much troubled on behalf of the young man whom he held as a kind of prisoner in his own house, took a memorable night walk.

He walked to Cloisterham Weir.

He often did so, and consequently there was nothing remarkable in his footsteps tending that way. But the preoccupation of his mind so hindered him from planning any walk, or taking heed of the objects he passed, that his first consciousness of being near the Weir, was derived from the sound of the falling water close at hand.

"How did I come here!" was the first thought, as he stopped.

"Why did I come here!" was his second.

Then, he stood intently listening to the water. A familiar passage in his reading, about airy tongues that syllable men's names, rose so unbidden to his ear, that he put it from him with his hand, as if it were tangible.

It was starlight. The Weir was full two miles above the spot to which the young men had repaired to watch the storm. No search had been made up here, for the tide had been running strongly down, at that time of the night of Christmas Eve, and the likeliest places for the discovery of a body, if a fatal accident had happened under such circumstances, all lay—both when the tide ebbed, and when it flowed again—between that spot and the sea. The water came over the Weir, with its usual sound on a cold starlight night, and little could be seen of it; yet Mr. Crisparkle had a strange idea that something unusual hung about the place.

He reasoned with himself: What was it? Where was it? Put it to the proof. Which sense did it address?

No sense reported any thing unusual there. He listened again, and his sense of hearing again checked the water coming over the Weir, with its usual sound on a cold starlight night.

Knowing very well that the mystery with which his mind was occupied, might of itself give the place this haunted air, he strained those hawk's eyes of his for the correction of his sight. He got closer to the Weir, and peered at its well-known posts and timbers. Nothing in the least unusual was remotely shadowed forth. But he resolved that he would come back early in the morning.

The Weir ran through his broken sleep, all night, and he was back again at sunrise. It was a bright frosty morning. The whole composition before him, when he stood where he had stood last night, was clearly discernible in its minutest details. He had surveyed it closely for some minutes, and was about to withdraw his eyes, when they were attracted keenly to one spot.

He turned his back upon the Weir, and looked far away at the sky, and at the earth, and then looked again at that one spot. It caught his sight again immediately, and he concentrated his vision upon it. He could not lose it now, though it was but such a speck in the landscape. It fascinated his sight. His hands began plucking off his coat. For it struck him that at that spot—a corner of the Weir—something glistened, which did not move and come over with the glistening water-drops, but remained stationary.

He assured himself of this, he threw off his clothes, he plunged into the icy water, and swam for the spot. Climbing the timbers, he took from them, caught among their interstices by its chain, a gold watch, bearing engraved upon its back, E. D.

He brought the watch to the bank, swam to the Weir again, climbed it, and dived off. He knew every hole and corner of all the depths, and dived and dived and dived, until he could bear the cold no more. His notion was, that he would find the body; he only found a shirt-pin sticking in some mud and ooze.

With these discoveries he returned to Cloisterham, and, taking Neville Landless with him, went straight to the Mayor. Mr. Jasper was sent for, the watch and shirt-pin were identified. Neville was detained, and the wildest frenzy and fatuity of evil report arose against him. He was of that vindictive and violent nature, that but for his poor sister, who alone had influence over him, and out of whose sight he was never to be trusted, he would be in the daily commission of murder. Before coming to England he had caused to be whipped to death sundry "Natives"—nomadic persons, encamping now in Asia, now in Africa, now in the West Indies, and now at the North Pole—vaguely supposed in Cloisterham to be always black, always of great virtue, always calling themselves Me, and everybody else Massa or Missie (according to sex), and always reading tracts of the obscurest meaning, in broken English, but always accurately understanding them in the purest mother tongue. He had nearly brought Mrs. Crisparkle's gray hairs with sorrow to the grave. (Those original expressions were Mr. Sapsea's.) He had repeatedly said he would have Mr. Crisparkle's life. He had repeatedly said he would have everybody's life, and become in effect the last man. He had been brought down to Cloisterham, from London, by an eminent Philanthropist, and why? Because that Philanthropist had expressly declared: "I owe it to my fellow-creatures that he should be, in the words of BENTHAM, where he is the cause of the greatest danger to the smallest number."

These dropping shots from the blunderbusses of blunderheadedness might not have hit him in the vital place. But he had to stand against a trained and well-directed fire of arms of precision too. He had notoriously threatened the lost young man, and had, according to the showing of his own faithful friend and tutor who strove so hard for him, a cause of bitter animosity (created by himself, and stated by himself), against that ill-starred fellow. He had armed himself with an offensive weapon for the fatal night, and he had gone off early in the morning, after making preparations for departure. He had been found with traces of blood on him; truly, they might have been wholly caused as he represented, but they might not, also. On a search-warrant being issued for the examination of his room, clothes, and so forth, it was discovered that he had destroyed all his papers, and rearranged all his possessions, on the very afternoon of the disappearance. The watch found at the Weir was challenged by the jeweller as one he had wound and set for Edwin Drood, at twenty minutes past two on that same afternoon; and it had run down, before being cast into the water; and it was the jeweller's positive opinion that it had never been rewound. This would justify the hypothesis that the watch was taken from him not long after he left Mr. Jasper's house at midnight, in company with the last person seen with him, and that it had been thrown away after being retained some hours. Why thrown away? If he had been murdered, and so artfully disfigured, or concealed, or both, as that the murderer hoped identification to be impossible, except from something that he wore, assuredly the murderer would seek to remove from the body the most lasting, the best known, and the most easily recognizable, things upon it. Those things would be the watch and shirt-pin. As for his opportunities of casting them into the river; if he were the object of these suspicions, they were easy. For he had been seen by many persons wandering about on that side of the city—indeed on all sides of it—in a miserable and seemingly half-distracted manner. As to the choice of the spot, obviously such criminating evidence had better take its chance of being found anywhere, rather than upon himself, or in his possession. Concerning the reconciliatory nature of the appointed meeting between the two young men, very little could be made of that, in young Landless's favor; for, it distinctly appeared that the meeting originated, not with him, but with Mr. Crisparkle, and that it had been urged on by Mr. Crisparkle; and who could say how unwillingly, or in what ill-conditioned mood, his enforced pupil had gone to it? The more his case was looked into, the weaker it became in every point. Even the broad suggestion that the lost young man had absconded, was rendered additionally improbable on the showing of the young lady from whom he had so lately parted; for, what did she say, with great earnestness and sorrow, when interrogated? That he had, expressly and enthusiastically, planned with her, that he would await the arrival of her guardian, Mr. Grewgious. And yet, be it observed, he disappeared before that gentleman appeared.

On the suspicions thus urged and supported, Neville was detained and re-detained, and the search was pressed on every hand, and Jasper labored night and day. But nothing more was found. No discovery being made, which proved the lost man to be dead, it at length became necessary to release the person suspected of having made away with him. Neville was set at large. Then, a consequence ensued which Mr. Cris parkle had too well foreseen. Neville must leave the place, for the place shunned him and cast him out. Even had it not been so, the dear old china shepherdess would have worried herself to death with fears for her son, and with general trepidation occasioned by their having such an inmate. Even had that not been so, the authority to which the Minor Canon deferred officially, would have settled the point.

"Mr. Crisparkle," quoth the Dean, "human justice may err, but it must act according to its lights. The days of taking sanctuary are past. This young man must not take sanctuary with us."

"You mean that he must leave my house, sir?"

"Mr. Crisparkle," returned the prudent Dean, "I claim no authority in your house. I merely confer with you, on the painful necessity you find yourself under, of depriving this young man of the great advantages of your counsel and instruction."

"It is very lamentable, sir," Mr. Crisparkle represented.

"Very much so," the Dean assented.

"And if it be a necessity—" Mr. Crisparkle faltered.

"As you unfortunately find it to be," returned the Dean.

Mr. Crisparkle bowed submissively. "It is hard to prejudge his case, sir, but I am sensible that—"

"Just so. Perfectly. As you say, Mr. Crisparkle," interposed the Dean, nodding his head smoothly, "there is nothing else to be done. No doubt, no doubt. There is no alternative, as your good sense has discovered."

"I am entirely satisfied of his perfect innocence, sir, nevertheless."

"We-e-ell!" said the Dean, in a more confidential tone, and slightly glancing around him, "I would not say so, generally. Not generally. Enough of suspicion attaches to him to—no, I think I would not say so, generally."

Mr. Crisparkle bowed again.

"It does not become us, perhaps," pursued the Dean, "to be partisans. Not partisans. We clergy keep our hearts warm and our heads cool, and we hold a judicious middle course."

"I hope you do not object, sir, to my having stated in public, emphatically, that he will reappear here, whenever any new suspicion may be awakened, or any new circumstance may come to light in this extraordinary matter?"

"Not at all," returned the Dean. "And yet, do you know, I don't think," with a very nice and neat emphasis on those two words: "I *don't think* I would state it, emphatically. State it? Ye-e-es! But emphatically? No-o-o. I *think* not. In point of fact, Mr. Crisparkle, keeping our hearts warm and our heads cool, we clergy need do nothing emphatically."

So, Minor Canon Row knew Neville Landless no more; and he went whithersoever he would, or could, with a blight upon his name and fame.

It was not until then that John Jasper silently resumed his place in the choir. Haggard and red-eyed, his hopes plainly had deserted him, his sanguine mood was gone, and all his worst misgivings had come back. A day or two afterward, while unrobing, he took his Diary from a pocket of his coat, turned the leaves, and with an impressive look, and without one spoken word, handed this entry to Mr. Crisparkle to read:

"My dear boy is murdered. The discovery of the watch and shirt-pin convinces me that he was murdered that night, and that his jewelry was taken from him to prevent identification by its means. All the delusive hopes I had founded on his separation from his betrothed wife, I give to the winds. They perish before this fatal discovery. I now swear, and record the oath on this page, That I nevermore will discuss this mystery with any human creature, until I hold the clue to it in my hand. That I never will relax in my secrecy or in my search. That I will fasten the crime of the murder of my dear dead boy, upon the murderer. And That I devote myself to his destruction."

CHAPTER XV.

PHILANTHROPY, PROFESSIONAL AND UNPROFESSIONAL.

Full half a year had come and gone, and Mr. Crisparkle sat in a waiting-room in the London chief offices of the Haven of Philanthropy, until he could have audience of Mr. Honeythunder.

In his college days of athletic exercises, Mr. Crisparkle had known professors of the Noble Art of fisticuffs, and had attended two or three of their gloved gatherings. He had now an opportunity of observing that as to the phrenological formation of the backs of their heads, the Professing Philanthropists were uncommonly like the Pugilists. In the development of all those organs which constitute, or attend, a propensity to "pitch into" your fellow-creatures, the Philanthropists were remarkably favored. There were several Professors passing in and out, with exactly the aggressive air upon them of being ready for a turn-up with any Novice who might happen to be on hand, that Mr. Crisparkle well remembered in the circles of the Fancy. Preparations were in progress for a moral little Mill somewhere on the rural circuit, and other Professors were backing this or that Heavy-Weight as good for such or such speech-making hits, so very much after the manner of the sporting publicans that the intended Resolutions might have been Rounds. In an official manager of these displays much celebrated for his platform tactics, Mr. Crisparkle recognized (in a suit of black) the counterpart of a deceased benefactor of his species, an eminent public character, once known to fame as Frosty-faced Fogo, who in days of yore superintended the formation of the magic circle with the ropes and stakes. There were only three conditions of resemblance wanting between these Professors and those. Firstly, the Philanthropists were in very bad training: much too fleshy, and presenting, both in face and figure, a superabundance of what is known to Pugilistic Experts as Suet Pudding. Secondly, the Philanthropists had not the good temper of the Pugilists, and used worse language. Thirdly, their fighting code stood in great need of revision, as empowering them not only to bore their man to the ropes, but to bore him to the confines of distraction; also to hit him when he was down, hit him anywhere and anyhow, kick him, stamp upon him, gouge him, and maul him behind his back without mercy. In these last particulars the Professors of the Noble Art were much nobler than the Professors of Philanthropy.

Mr. Crisparkle was so completely lost in musing on these similarities and dissimilarities, at the same time watching the crowd which came and went by, always, as it seemed, on errands of antagonistically snatching something from somebody, and never giving anything to anybody: that his name was called before he heard it. On his at length responding, he was shown by a miserably shabby and underpaid stipendiary Philanthropist (who could hardly have done worse if he had taken service with a declared enemy of the human race) to Mr. Honeythunder's room.

"Sir," said Mr. Honeythunder in his tremendous voice, like a schoolmaster issuing orders to a boy of whom he had a bad opinion, "sit down."

Mr. Crisparkle seated himself.

Mr. Honeythunder, having signed the remaining few score of a few thousand circulars, calling upon a corresponding number of families without means to come forward, stump up instantly, and be Philanthropists, or go to the Devil, another shabby stipendiary Philanthropist (highly disinterested, if in earnest) gathered these into a basket and walked off with them.

"Now, Mr. Crisparkle," said Mr. Honeythunder, turning his chair half-round toward him when they were alone, and squaring his arms with his hands on his knees, and his brows knitted as if he added, I am going to make short work of *you*,—"now, Mr. Crisparkle, we entertain different views, you and I, sir, of the sanctity of human life."

"Do we?" returned the Minor Canon.

"We do, sir."

"Might I ask you," said the Minor Canon, "what are your views on that subject?"

"That human life is a thing to be held sacred, sir."

"Might I ask you," pursued the Minor Canon as before, "what you suppose to be my views on that subject?"

"By George, sir!" returned the Philanthropist, squaring his arms still more, as he frowned on Mr. Crisparkle: "they are best known to yourself."

"Readily admitted. But you began by saying that we took different views, you know. Therefore (or you could not say so) you must have set up some views as mine. Pray, what views *have* you set up as mine?"

"Here is a man—and a young man," said Mr. Honeythunder, as if that made the matter infinitely worse, and he could have easily borne the loss of an old one: "swept off the face of the earth by a deed of violence. What do you call that?"

"Murder," said the Minor Canon.

"What do you call the doer of that deed, sir?"

"A murderer," said the Minor Canon.

"I am glad to hear you admit so much, sir," retorted Mr. Honeythunder, in his most offensive manner; "and I candidly tell you that I didn't expect it." Here he lowered heavily at Mr. Crisparkle again.

"Be so good as to explain what you mean by those very unjustifiable expressions."

"I don't sit here, sir," returned the Philanthropist, raising his voice to a roar, "to be browbeaten."

"As the only other person present, no one can possibly know that better than I do," returned the Minor Canon very quietly. "But I interrupt your explanation."

"Murder!" proceeded Mr. Honeythunder, in a kind of boisterous revery, with his platform folding of his arms, and his platform nod of abhorrent reflection after each short sentiment of a word. "Bloodshed! Abel! Cain! I hold no terms with Cain. I repudiate with a shudder the red hand when it is offered me."

Instead of instantly leaping into his chair and cheering himself hoarse, as the Brotherhood in public meeting assembled would infallibly have done on this cue, Mr. Crisparkle merely reversed the quiet crossing of his legs, and said mildly, "Don't let me interrupt your explanation—when you begin it."

"The Commandments say no murder. NO murder, sir!" proceeded Mr. Honeythunder, platformally pausing as if he took Mr. Crisparkle to task for having distinctly asserted that they said, You may do a little murder and then leave off.

"And they also say, you shall bear no false witness," observed Mr. Crisparkle.

"Enough!" bellowed Mr. Honeythunder, with a solemnity and severity that would have brought the house down at a meeting, "e—e—nough! My late wards being now of age, and I being released from a trust which I cannot contemplate without a thrill of horror, there are the accounts which you have undertaken to accept on their behalf, and there is a statement of the balance which you have undertaken to receive, and which you cannot receive too soon. And let me tell you, sir, I wish, that as a man and a Minor Canon, you were better employed," with a nod. "Better employed," with another nod. "Bet—ter em—ployed!" with another and the three nods added up.

Mr. Crisparkle rose, a little heated in the face, but with perfect command of himself.

"Mr. Honeythunder," he said, taking up the papers referred to, "my being better or worse employed than I am at present is a matter of taste and opinion. You might think me better employed in enrolling myself a member of your Society."

"Ay, indeed, sir!" retorted Mr. Honeythunder, shaking his head in a threatening manner. "It would have been better for you if you had done that long ago!"

"I think otherwise."

"Or," said Mr. Honeythunder, shaking his head again, "I might think one of your profession better employed in devoting himself to the discovery and punishment of guilt than in leaving that duty to be undertaken by a layman."

"I may regard my profession from a point of view which teaches me that its first duty is toward those who are in necessity and tribulation, who are desolate and oppressed," said Mr. Crisparkle. "However, as I have quite clearly satisfied myself that it is no part of my profession to make professions, I say no more of that. But I owe it to Mr. Neville, and to Mr. Neville's sister (and in a much lower degree to myself), to say to you that I *know* I was in the full possession and understanding of Mr. Neville's mind and heart at the time of this occurrence; and that, without in the least coloring or concealing what was to be deplored in him and required to be corrected, I feel certain that his tale is true. Feeling that certainty, I befriend him. As long as that certainty shall last, I will befriend him. And if any consideration could shake me in this resolve, I should be so ashamed of myself for my meanness that no man's good opinion,—no, nor no woman's,—so gained, could compensate me for the loss of my own."

Good fellow! Manly fellow! And he was so modest, too. There was no more self-assertion in the Minor Canon than in the school-boy who had stood in the breezy playing-fields keeping a wicket. He was simply and stanchly true to his duty alike in the large case and in the small. So all true souls ever are. So every true soul ever was, ever is, and ever will be. There is nothing little to the really great in spirit.

"Then who do you make out did the deed?" asked Mr. Honeythunder, turning on him abruptly.

"Heaven forbid," said Mr. Crisparkle, "that in my desire to clear one man I should lightly criminate another! I accuse no one."

"Tcha!" ejaculated Mr. Honeythunder with great disgust; for this was by no means the principle on which the Philanthropic Brotherhood usually proceeded. "And, sir, you are not a disinterested witness, we must bear in mind."

"How am I an interested one?" inquired Mr. Crisparkle, smiling innocently, at a loss to imagine.

"There was a certain stipend, sir, paid to you for your pupil, which may have warped your judgment a bit," said Mr. Honeythunder, coarsely.

"Perhaps I expect to retain it still?" Mr. Crisparkle returned, enlightened; "do you mean that too?"

"Well, sir," returned the professional Philanthropist, getting up, and thrusting his hands down into his trousers pockets, "I don't go about measuring people for caps. If people find I have any about me that fit 'em, they can put 'em on and wear 'em, if they like. That's their lookout, not mine."

Mr. Crisparkle eyed him with a just indignation, and took him to task thus:

"Mr. Honeythunder, I hoped when I came in here that I might be under no necessity of commenting on the introduction of platform manners or platform manœuvres among the decent forbearances of private life. But you have given me such a specimen of both, that I should be a fit subject for both if I remained silent respecting them. They are detestable."

"They don't suit *you*, I dare say, sir."

"They are," repeated Mr. Crisparkle, without noticing the interruption, "detestable. They violate equally the justice that should belong to Christians, and the restraints that should belong to gentlemen. You assume a great crime to have been committed by one whom I, acquainted with the attendant circumstances, and having numerous reasons on my side, devoutly believe to be innocent of it. Because I differ from you on that vital point, what is your platform resource? Instantly to turn upon me, charging that I have no sense of the enormity of the crime itself, but am its aider and abettor! So, another time—taking me as representing our opponent in other cases—you set up a platform credulity: a moved and seconded and carried unanimously profession of faith in some ridiculous delusion or mischievous imposition. I decline to believe it, and you fall back upon your platform resource of proclaiming that I believe nothing; that because I will not bow down to a false God of your making, I deny the true God! Another time, you make the platform discovery that War is a calamity, and you propose to abolish it by a string of twisted resolutions tossed into the air like the tail of a kite. I do not admit the discovery to be yours in the least, and I have not a grain of faith in your remedy. Again, your platform resource of representing me as revelling in the horrors of a battle-field like a fiend incarnate! Another time, in another of your undiscriminating platform rushes, you would punish the sober for the drunken. I claim consideration for the comfort, convenience, and refreshment of the sober; and you presently make platform proclamation that I have a depraved desire to turn Heaven's creatures into swine and wild beasts! In all such cases your movers, and your seconders, and your supporters—your regular Professors of all degrees—run amuck like so many mad Malays; habitually attributing the lowest and basest motives with the utmost recklessness (let me call your attention to a recent instance in yourself for which you should blush), and quoting figures which you know to be as wilfully one-sided as a statement of any complicated account that should be all Creditor side and no Debtor, or all Debtor side and no Creditor. Therefore it is, Mr. Honeythunder, that I consider the platform a sufficiently bad example and a sufficiently bad school, even in public life; but hold that, carried into private life, it becomes an unendurable nuisance."

"These are strong words, sir!" exclaimed the Philanthropist.

"I hope so," said Mr. Crisparkle. "Good-morning."

He walked out of the Haven at a great rate, but soon fell into his regular brisk pace, and soon had a smile upon his face as he went along, wondering what the china shepherdess would have said if she had seen him pounding Mr. Honeythunder in the late little lively affair. For Mr. Crisparkle had just enough of harmless vanity to hope that he had hit hard, and to glow with the belief that he had trimmed the Philanthropic jacket pretty handsomely.

He took himself to Staple Inn, but not to P. J. T. and Mr. Grewgious. Full many a creaking stair he climbed before he reached some attic rooms in a corner, turned the latch of their unbolted door, and stood beside the table of Neville Landless.

An air of retreat and solitude hung about the rooms, and about their inhabitant. He was much worn, and so were they. Their sloping ceilings, cumbrous rusty locks and grates, and heavy wooden bins and beams, slowly mouldering withal, had a prisonous look, and he had the haggard face of a prisoner. Yet the sunlight shone in at the ugly garret window which had a penthouse to itself thrust out among the tiles; and on the cracked and smoke-blackened parapet beyond, some of the deluded sparrows of the place rheumatically hopped, like little feathered cripples who had left their crutches in their nests; and there was a play of living leaves at hand that changed the air, and made an imperfect sort of music in it that would have been melody in the country.

The rooms were sparely furnished, but with good store of books. Every thing expressed the abode of a poor student. That Mr. Crisparkle had been either chooser, lender, or donor of the books, or that he combined the three characters, might have been easily seen in the friendly beam of his eyes upon them as he entered.

"How goes it, Neville?"

"I am in good heart, Mr. Crisparkle, and working away."

"I wish your eyes were not quite so large and not quite so bright," said the Minor Canon, slowly releasing the hand he had taken in his.

"They brighten at the sight of you," returned Neville. "If you were to fall away from me, they would soon be dull enough."

"Rally, rally!" urged the other, in a stimulating tone. "Fight for it, Neville!"

"If I were dying, I feel as if a word from you would rally me; if my pulse had stopped, I feel as if your touch would make it beat again," said Neville. "But I *have* rallied, and am doing famously."

Mr. Crisparkle turned him with his face a little more toward the light.

"I want to see a ruddier touch here, Neville," he said, indicating his own healthy cheek by way of pattern; "I want more sun to shine upon you."

Neville drooped suddenly as he replied in a lowered voice, "I am not hardy enough for that yet. I may become so, but I cannot bear it yet. If you had gone through those Cloisterham streets as I did; if you had seen, as I did, those averted eyes, and the better sort of people silently giving me too much room to pass, that I might not touch them or come near them, you wouldn't think it quite unreasonable that I cannot go about in the daylight."

"My poor fellow!" said the Minor Canon, in a tone so purely sympathetic that the young man caught his hand: "I never said it was unreasonable; never thought so. But I should like you to do it."

"And that would give me the strongest motive to do it. But I cannot yet. I cannot persuade myself that the eyes of even the stream of strangers I pass in this vast city look at me without suspicion. I feel marked and tainted, even when I go out—as I do only—at night. But the darkness covers me then, and I take courage from it."

Mr. Crisparkle laid a hand upon his shoulder, and stood looking down upon him.

"If I could have changed my name," said Neville, "I would have done so. But as you wisely pointed out to me, I can't do that, for it would look like guilt. If I could have gone to some distant place, I might have found relief in that, but the thing is not to be thought of, for the same reason. Hiding and escaping would be the construction in either case. It seems a little hard to be so tied to a stake, and innocent; but I don't complain."

"And you must expect no miracle to help you, Neville," said Mr. Crisparkle, compassionately.

"No, sir, I know that. The ordinary fullness of time and circumstance is all I have to trust to."

"It will right you at last, Neville."

"So I believe, and I hope I may live to know it."

But perceiving that the despondent mood into which he was falling cast a shadow on the Minor Canon, and (it may be) feeling that the broad hand upon his shoulder was not then quite as steady as its own natural strength had rendered it when it first touched him just now, he brightened and said,—

"Excellent circumstances for study, anyhow! and you know, Mr. Crisparkle, what need I have of study in all ways. Not to mention that you have advised me to study for the difficult profession of the law, specially, and that of course I am guiding myself by the advice of such a friend and helper. Such a good friend and helper!"

He took the fortifying hand from his shoulder, and kissed it. Mr. Crisparkle beamed at the books, but not so brightly as when he had entered.

"I gather from your silence on the subject that my late guardian is adverse, Mr. Crisparkle?"

The Minor Canon answered, "Your late guardian is a—a most unreasonable person, and it signifies nothing to any reasonable person whether he is *ad*verse or *per*verse, or the *re*verse."

"Well for me that I have enough with economy to live upon," sighed Neville, half wearily and half cheerily, "while I wait to be learned and wait to be righted! Else I might have proved the proverb that while the grass grows the steed starves!"

He opened some books as he said it, and was soon immersed in their interleaved and annotated passages, while Mr. Crisparkle sat beside him, expounding, correcting, and advising. The Minor Canon's cathedral duties made these visits of his difficult to accomplish, and only to be compassed at intervals of many weeks. But they were as serviceable as they were precious to Neville Landless.

When they had got through such studies as they had in hand, they stood leaning on the window-sill, and looking down upon the patch of garden. "Next week," said Mr. Crisparkle, "you will cease to be alone, and will have a devoted companion."

"And yet," returned Neville, "this seems an uncongenial place to bring my sister to!"

"I don't think so," said the Minor Canon. "There is duty to be done here; and there are womanly feeling, sense, and courage, wanted here."

"I meant," explained Neville, "that the surroundings are so dull and unwomanly, and that Helena can have no suitable friend or society here."

"You have only to remember," said Mr. Crisparkle, "that you are here yourself, and that she has to draw you into the sunlight."

They were silent for a little while, and then Mr. Crisparkle began anew.

"When we first spoke together, Neville, you told me that your sister had risen out of the disadvantages of your past lives as superior to you as the tower of Cloisterham Cathedral is higher than the chimneys of Minor Canon Corner. Do you remember that?"

"Right well."

"I was inclined to think it at the time an enthusiastic flight. No matter what I think it now. What I would emphasize is, that under the head of Pride your sister is a great and opportune example to you."

"Under *all* heads that are included in the composition of a fine character, she is."

"Say so; but take this one. Your sister has learned how to govern what was proud in her nature. She can dominate it even when it is wounded through her sympathy with you. No doubt she has suffered deeply in those same streets where you suffered deeply. No doubt her life is darkened by the cloud that darkens yours. But bending her pride into a grand composure that is not haughty or aggressive, but is a sustained confidence in you and in the truth, she has won her way through those streets until she passes along them as high in the general respect as any one who treads them. Every day and hour of her life since Edwin Drood's disappearance, she has faced malignity and folly—for you—as only a brave nature well directed can. So it will be with her to the end. Another and weaker kind of pride might sink broken-hearted, but never such a pride as hers: which knows no shrinking, and can get no mastery over her."

The pale cheek beside him flushed under the comparison and the hint implied in it. "I will do all I can to imitate her," said Neville.

"Do so, and be a truly brave man as she is a truly brave woman," answered Mr. Crisparkle, stoutly. "It is growing dark. Will you go my way with me, when it is quite dark? Mind! It is not I who wait for darkness."

Neville replied that he would accompany him directly. But Mr. Crisparkle said he had a moment's call to make on Mr. Grewgious as an act of courtesy, and would run across to that gentleman's chambers, and rejoin Neville on his own doorstep if he would come down there to meet him.

Mr. Grewgious, bolt upright as usual, sat taking his wine in the dusk at his open window; his wineglass and decanter on the round table at his elbow; himself and his legs on the window-seat; only one hinge in his whole body, like a bootjack.

"How do you do, reverend sir?" said Mr. Grewgious, with abundant offers of hospitality which were as cordially declined as made.

"And how is your charge getting on over the way in the set that I had the pleasure of recommending to you as vacant and eligible?"

Mr. Crisparkle replied suitably.

"I am glad you approve of them," said Mr. Grewgious, "because I entertain a sort of fancy for having him under my eye."

As Mr. Grewgious had to turn his eye up considerably, before he could see the chambers, the phrase was to be taken figuratively and not literally.

"And how did you leave Mr. Jasper, reverend sir?" said Mr. Grewgious.

Mr. Crisparkle had left him pretty well.

"And where did you leave Mr. Jasper, reverend sir?"

Mr. Crisparkle had left him at Cloisterham.

"And when did you leave Mr. Jasper, reverend sir?"

That morning.

"Umps!" said Mr. Grewgious. "He didn't say he was coming, perhaps?"

"Coming where?"

"Anywhere, for instance?" said Mr. Grewgious.

"No."

"Because here he is," said Mr. Grewgious, who had asked all these questions with his preoccupied glance directed out at window. "And he don't look agreeable; does he?"

Mr. Crisparkle was craning toward the window, when Mr. Grewgious added,—

"If you will kindly step round here behind me in the gloom of the room, and will cast your eye at the second-floor landing window, in yonder house, I think you will hardly fail to see a slinking individual in whom I recognize our local friend."

"You are right!" cried Mr. Crisparkle.

"Umps!" said Mr. Grewgious. Then he added, turning his face so abruptly that his head nearly came into collision with Mr. Crisparkle's: "What should you say that our local friend was up to?"

The last passage he had been shown in the Diary returned on Mr. Crisparkle's mind with the force of a strong recoil, and he asked Mr. Grewgious if he thought it possible that Neville was to be harassed by the keeping of a watch upon him?

"A watch," repeated Mr. Grewgious, musingly. "Ay!"

"Which would not only of itself haunt and torture his life," said Mr. Crisparkle, warmly, "but would expose him to the torment of a perpetually reviving suspicion, whatever he might do, or wherever he might go?"

"Ay!" said Mr. Grewgious, musingly still. "Do I see him waiting for you?"

"No doubt you do."

"Then *would* you have the goodness to excuse my getting up to see you out, and to go out to join him, and to go the way that you were going, and to take no notice of our local friend?" said Mr. Grewgious. "I entertain a sort of fancy for having *him* under my eye to-night, do you know?"

Mr. Crisparkle, with a significant nod, complied, and, rejoining Neville, went away with him. They dined together, and parted at the yet unfinished and undeveloped railway station: Mr. Crisparkle to get home; Neville to walk the streets, cross the bridges, make a wide round of the city in the friendly darkness, and tire himself out.

It was midnight when he returned from his solitary expedition, and climbed his staircase. The night was hot, and the windows of the staircase were all wide open. Coming to the top, it gave him a passing chill of surprise (there being no rooms but his up there) to find a stranger sitting on the window-sill, more after the manner of a venturesome glazier than an amateur ordinarily careful of his neck; in fact, so much more outside the window than inside, as to suggest the thought that he must have come up by the waterspout instead of the stairs.

The stranger said nothing until Neville put his key in his door; then, seeming to make sure of his identity from the action, he spoke:

"I beg your pardon," he said, coming from the window with a frank and smiling air, and a prepossessing address; "the beans."

Neville was quite at a loss.

"Runners," said the visitor. "Scarlet. Next door at the back."

"Oh!" returned Neville. "And the mignonette and wallflower?"

"The same," said the visitor.

"Pray walk in."

"Thank you."

Neville lighted his candles, and the visitor sat down. A handsome gentleman, with a young face, but an older figure in its robustness and breadth of shoulder; say a man of eight-and-twenty, or at the utmost, thirty: so extremely sunburnt that the contrast between his brown visage and the white forehead shaded out-of-doors by his hat, and the glimpses of white throat below the neckerchief, would have been almost ludicrous but for his broad temples, bright blue eyes, clustering brown hair, and laughing teeth.

"I have noticed," said he; "—my name is Tartar."

Neville inclined his head.

"I have noticed (excuse me) that you shut yourself up a good deal, and that you seem to like my garden aloft here. If you would like a little more of it, I could throw out a few lines and stays between my windows and yours, which the runners would take to directly. And I have some boxes, both of mignonette and wallflower, that I could shove on along the gutter (with a boat-hook I have by me) to your windows, and draw back again when they wanted watering or gardening, and shove on again when they were ship-shape, so that they would cause you no trouble. I could'nt take this liberty without asking your permission, so I venture to ask it. Tartar, corresponding set, next door."

"You are very kind."

"Not at all. I ought to apologize for looking in so late. But having noticed (excuse me) that you generally walk out at night, I thought I should inconvenience you least by awaiting your return. I am always afraid of inconveniencing busy men, being an idle man."

"I should not have thought so, from your appearance."

"No? I take it as a compliment. In fact, I was bred in the Royal Navy and was First Lieutenant when I quitted it. But an uncle, disappointed in the service, leaving me his property on condition that I left the Navy, I accepted the fortune and resigned my commission."

"Lately, I presume?"

"Well, I had had twelve or fifteen years of knocking about first. I came here some nine months before you; I had had one crop before you came. I chose this place because, having served last in a little Corvette, I knew I should feel more at home where I had a constant opportunity of knocking my head against the ceiling. Besides, it would never do for a man who had been aboard ship from his boyhood to turn luxurious all at once. Besides, again: having been accustomed to a very short allowance of land all my life, I thought I'd feel my way to the command of a landed estate by beginning in boxes."

Whimsically as this was said, there was a touch of merry earnestness in it that made it doubly whimsical.

"However," said the Lieutenant, "I have talked quite enough about myself. It is not my way I hope; it has merely been to present myself to you naturally. If you will allow me to take the liberty I have described, it will be a charity, for it will give me something more to do. And you are not to suppose that it will entail any interruption or intrusion on you, for that is far from my intention."

Neville replied that he was greatly obliged, and that he thankfully accepted the kind proposal.

"I am very glad to take your windows in tow," said the Lieutenant. "From what I have seen of you when I have been gardening at mine, and you have been looking on, I have thought you (excuse me) rather too studious and delicate! May I ask, is your health at all affected?"

"I have undergone some mental distress," said Neville, confused, "which has stood me in the stead of illness."

"Pardon me," said Mr. Tartar.

With the greatest delicacy he shifted his ground to the windows again, and asked if he could look at one of them. On Neville's opening it, he immediately sprang out, as if he were going aloft with a whole watch in an emergency, and were setting a bright example.

"For Heaven's sake!" cried Neville, "don't do that! Where are you going, Mr. Tartar? You'll be dashed to pieces!"

"All well!" said the Lieutenant, coolly looking about him on the housetop. "All taut and trim here. Those lines and stay shall be rigged before you turn out in the morning. May I take this short cut home and say, Good-night?"

"Mr. Tartar!" urged Neville. "Pray! It makes me giddy to see you."

But Mr. Tartar, with a wave of his hand and the deftness of a cat, had already dipped through his scuttle of scarlet runners without breaking a leaf, and "gone below."

Mr. Grewgious, his bedroom window-blind held aside with his hand, happened at that moment to have Neville's chambers under his eye for the last time that night. Fortunately his eye was on the front of the house and not the back, or this remarkable appearance and disappearance might have broken his rest as a phenomenon. But Mr. Grewgious seeing nothing there, not even a light in the windows, his gaze wandered from the windows to the stars, as if he would have read in them something that was hidden from him. (Many of us would if we could; but none of us so much as know our letters in the stars yet—or seem likely to do it in this state of existence—and few languages can be read until their alphabets are mastered.)

CHAPTER XVI.

A SETTLER IN CLOISTERHAM.

At about this time a stranger appeared in Cloisterham, a white-haired personage with black eyebrows. Being buttoned up in a tightish blue surtout, with a buff waistcoat and gray trousers, he had something of a military air; but he announced himself at the Crozier (the orthodox hotel, where he put up with a portmanteau) as an idle dog who lived upon his means; and he further announced that he had a mind to take a lodging in the picturesque old city for a month or two, with a view of settling down there altogether. Both announcements were made in the coffee-room of the Crozier, to all whom it might, or might not, concern, by the stranger as he stood with his back to the empty fireplace, waiting for his fried sole, veal cutlet, and pint of sherry. And the waiter (business being chronically slack at the Crozier) represented all whom it might or might not concern, and absorbed the whole of the information.

This gentleman's white head was unusually large, and his shock of white hair was unusually thick and ample. "I suppose, waiter," he said, shaking his shock of hair, as a Newfoundland dog might shake his before sitting down to dinner, "that a fair lodging for a single buffer might be found in these parts, eh?"

The waiter had no doubt of it.

"Something old," said the gentleman. "Take my hat down for a moment from that peg, will you? No, I don't want it; look into it. What do you see written there?"

The waiter read, "Datchery."

"Now you know my name," said the gentleman,—"Dick Datchery. Hang it up again. I was saying something old is what I should prefer, something odd and out of the way; something venerable, architectural, and inconvenient."

"We have a good choice of inconvenient lodgings in the town, sir, I think," replied the waiter, with modest confidence in its resources that way; "indeed, I have no doubt that we could suit you that far, however particular you might be. But a architectural lodging!" That seemed to trouble the waiter's head, and he shook it.

"Any thing Cathedraly, now," Mr. Datchery suggested.

"Mr. Tope," said the waiter brightening, as he rubbed his chin with his hand, "would be the likeliest party to inform in that line."

"Who is Mr. Tope?" inquired Dick Datchery.

The waiter explained that he was the Verger, and that Mrs. Tope had indeed once upon a time let lodgings herself,—or offered to let them; but that as nobody had ever taken them, Mrs. Tope's window-bill, long a Cloisterham Institution, had disappeared; probably had tumbled down one day, and never been put up again.

"I'll call on Mrs. Tope," said Mr. Datchery, "after dinner."

So when he had done his dinner, he was duly directed to the spot, and sallied out for it. But the Crozier being an hotel of a most retiring disposition, and the waiter's directions being fatally precise, he soon became bewildered, and went boggling about and about the Cathedral Tower, whenever he could catch a glimpse of it, with a general impression on his mind that Mrs. Tope's was somewhere very near it, and that, like the children in the game of hot-boiled beans and very good butter, he was warm in his search when he saw the Tower, and cold when he didn't see it.

He was getting very cold indeed when he came upon a fragment of burial-ground in which an unhappy sheep was grazing. Unhappy, because a hideous small boy was stoning it through the railings, and had already lamed it in one leg, and was much excited by the benevolent sportsman-like purpose of breaking its other three legs, and bringing it down.

"'It 'im agin!" cried the boy, as the poor creature leaped, "and made a dint in his wool."

"Let him be!" said Mr. Datchery. "Don't you see you have lamed him?"

"Yer lie," returned the sportsman. "'E went an lamed 'isself. I see 'im do it, and I giv' 'im a shy as a Widdy-warning to 'im not to go a bruisin' 'is master's mutton any more."

"Come here."

"I won't; I'll come when yer can ketch me."

"Stay there, then, and show me which is Mr. Tope's."

"'Ow can I stay here and show you which is Topeseses, when Topeseses is t'other side the Kinfreederal, and over the crossings, and round ever so many corners? Stoo-pid! Ya-a-ah!"

"Show me where it is, and I'll give you something."

"Come on, then!"

This brisk dialogue concluded, the boy led the way, and by and by stopped at some distance from an arched passage, pointing.

"Lookie yonder. You see that there winder and door?"

"That's Tope's?"

"Yer lie; it ain't. That's Jarsper's."

"Indeed?" said Mr. Datchery, with a second look of some interest.

"Yes, and I ain't a-goin' no nearer 'Im, I tell yer."

"Why not?"

"'Cos I ain't a-going to be lifted off my legs and 'ave my braces bust and be choked; not if I knows it and not by 'Im. Wait till I set a jolly good flint a-flyin' at the back o' 'is jolly old 'ed some day! Now look t'other side the harch; not the side where Jarsper's door is; t'other side."

"I see."

"A little way in, o' that side, there's a low door, down two steps. That's Topeseses, with 'is name on a hoval plate."

"Good. See here," said Mr. Datchery, producing a shilling. "You owe me half of this."

"Yer lie; I don't owe yer nothing; I never seen yer."

"I tell you you owe me half of this, because I have no sixpence in my pocket. So the next time you meet me you shall do something else for me, to pay me."

"All right; give us 'old."

"What is your name, and where do you live?"

"Deputy. Travellers' Twopenny, 'cross the green."

The boy instantly darted off with the shilling, lest Mr. Datchery should repent, but stopped at a safe distance, on the happy chance of his being uneasy in his mind about it, to goad him with a demon dance expressive of its irrevocability.

Mr. Datchery, taking off his hat to give that shock of white hair of his another shake, seemed quite resigned, and betook himself whither he had been directed.

Mr. Tope's official dwelling communicating by an upper stair with Mr. Jasper's (hence Mrs. Tope's attendance on that gentleman), was of very modest proportions, and partook of the character of a cool dungeon. Its ancient walls were massive, and its rooms rather seemed to have been dug out of them than to have been designed beforehand with any reference to them. The main door opened at once on a chamber of no describable shape, with a groined roof, which in its turn opened on another chamber of no describable shape, with another groined roof. Their windows small and in the thickness of the walls, these two chambers, close as to their atmosphere and swarthy as to their illumination by natural light, were the apartments which Mrs. Tope had so long offered to an unappreciative city. Mr. Datchery, however, was more appreciative. He found that if he sat with the main door open he would enjoy the passing society of all comers to and fro by the gateway, and would have light enough. He found that if Mr. and Mrs. Tope, living overhead, used for their own egress and ingress a little side stair that came plump into the Precincts by a door opening outward, to the surprise and inconvenience of a limited public of pedestrians in a narrow way, he would be alone, as in a separate residence. He found the rent moderate, and every thing as quaintly inconvenient as he could desire. He agreed therefore to take the lodging then and there, and money down, possession to be had next evening on condition that reference was permitted him to Mr. Jasper as occupying the Gate-House, of which, on the other side of the gateway, the Verger's hole in the wall was an appanage or subsidiary part.

The poor dear gentleman was very solitary and very sad, Mrs. Tope said, but she had no doubt he would "speak for her." Perhaps Mr. Datchery had heard something of what had occurred there last winter?

Mr. Datchery had as confused a knowledge of the event in question, on trying to recall it, as he well could have. He begged Mrs. Tope's pardon when she found it incumbent on her to correct him in every detail of his summary of the facts, but pleaded that he was merely a single buffer getting through life upon his means as idly as he could, and that so many people were so constantly making away with so many other people, as to render it difficult for a buffer of an easy temper to preserve the circumstances of the several cases unmixed in his mind.

Mr. Jasper proving willing to speak for Mrs. Tope, Mr. Datchery, who had sent up his card, was invited to ascend the postern staircase. The Mayor was there, Mrs. Tope said; but he was not to be regarded in the light of company, as he and Mr. Jasper were great friends.

"I beg pardon," said Mr. Datchery, making a leg with his hat under his arm, as he addressed himself equally to both gentlemen; "a selfish precaution on my part and not personally interesting to anybody but myself. But as a buffer living on his means, and having an idea of doing it in this lovely place in peace and quiet, for remaining span of life, beg to ask if the Tope family are quite respectable."

Mr. Jasper could answer for that without the slightest hesitation.

"That is enough, sir," said Mr. Datchery.

"My friend, the Mayor," added Mr. Jasper, presenting Mr. Datchery with a courtly motion of his hand toward that potentate, "whose recommendation is actually much more important to a stranger than that of an obscure person like myself, will testify in their behalf, I am sure."

"The Worshipful the Mayor," said Mr. Datchery, with a low bow, "places me under an infinite obligation."

"Very good people, sir, Mr. and Mrs. Tope," said Mr. Sapsea, with condescension. "Very good opinions. Very well behaved. Very respectful. Much approved by the Dean and Chapter."

"The Worshipful the Mayor gives them a character," said Mr. Datchery, "of which they may indeed be proud. I would ask his Honor (if I might be permitted) whether there are not many objects of great interest in the city which is under his beneficent sway?"

"We are, sir," returned Mr. Sapsea, "an ancient city, and an ecclesiastical city. We are a constitutional city, as it becomes such a city to be, and we uphold and maintain our glorious privileges."

"His Honor," said Mr. Datchery, bowing, "inspires me with a desire to know more of the city, and confirms me in my inclination to end my days in the city."

"Retired from the Army, sir?" suggested Mr. Sapsea.

"His Honor the Mayor does me too much credit," returned Mr. Datchery.

"Navy, sir?" suggested Mr. Sapsea.

"Again," repeated Mr. Datchery, "His Honor the Mayor does me too much credit."

"Diplomacy is a fine profession," said Mr. Sapsea, as a general remark.

"There, I confess, His Honor the Mayor is too many for me," said Mr. Datchery, with an ingenuous smile and bow; "even a diplomatic bird must fall to such a gun."

Now, this was very soothing. Here was a gentleman of a great—not to say a grand—address, accustomed to rank and dignity, really setting a fine example how to behave to a Mayor. There was something in that third-person style of being spoken to, that Mr. Sapsea found particularly recognizant of his merits and position.

"But I crave pardon," said Mr. Datchery. "His Honor the Mayor will bear with me, if for a moment I have been deluded into occupying his time, and have forgotten the humble claims upon my own, of my hotel, the Crozier."

"Not at all, sir," said Mr. Sapsea. "I am returning home, and, if you would like to take the exterior of our cathedral in your way, I shall be glad to point it out."

"His Honor the Mayor," said Mr. Datchery, "is more than kind and gracious."

As Mr. Datchery, when he had made his acknowledgments to Mr. Jasper, could not be induced to go out of the room before the Worshipful, the Worshipful led the way down-stairs, Mr. Datchery following with his hat under his arm, and his shock of white hair streaming in the evening breeze.

"Might I ask His Honor," said Mr. Datchery, "whether that gentleman we have just left is the gentleman of whom I have heard in the neighborhood as being much afflicted by the loss of a nephew, and concentrating his life on avenging the loss."

"That is the gentleman. John Jasper, sir."

"Would His Honor allow me to inquire whether there are strong suspicions of any one?"

"More than suspicions, sir," returned Mr. Sapsea; "all but certainties."

"Only think now!" cried Mr. Datchery.

"But proof, sir, proof, must be built up, stone by stone," said the Mayor. "As I say, the end crowns the work. It is not enough that Justice should be morally certain; she must be immorally certain—legally, that is."

"His Honor," said Mr. Datchery, "reminds me of the nature of the law. Immoral. How true!"

"As I say, sir," pompously went on the Mayor, "the arm of the law is a strong arm, and a long arm. That is the way *I* put it. A strong arm and a long arm."

"How forcible!—And yet, again, how true!" murmured Mr. Datchery.

"And without betraying what I call the secrets of the prison-house," said Mr. Sapsea; "the secrets of the prison-house is the term I use on the bench."

"And what other term than His Honor's would express it!" said Mr. Datchery.

"Without, I say, betraying them, I predict to you, knowing the iron will of the gentleman we have just left (I take the bold step of calling it iron, on account of its strength), that in this case the long arm will reach, and the strong arm will strike.—This is our cathedral, sir. The best judges are pleased to admire it, and the best among our townsmen own to being a little vain of it."

All this time Mr. Datchery had walked with his hat under his arm, and his white hair streaming. He had an odd momentary appearance upon him of having forgotten his hat, when Mr. Sapsea now touched it; and he clapped his hand up to his head as if with some vague expectation of finding another hat upon it.

"Pray be covered, sir," entreated Mr. Sapsea; magnificently implying, "I shall not mind it, I assure you."

"His Honor is very good, but I do it for coolness," said Mr. Datchery.

Then Mr. Datchery admired the cathedral, and Mr. Sapsea pointed it out as if he himself had invented and built it; there were a few details, indeed, of which he did not approve, but those he glossed over, as if the workmen had made mistakes in his absence. The cathedral disposed of, he led the way by the church-yard, and stopped to extol the beauty of the evening—by chance—in the immediate vicinity of Mrs. Sapsea's epitaph.

"And, by-the-by," said Mr. Sapsea, appearing to descend from an elevation to remember it all of a sudden, like Apollo shooting down from Olympus to pick up his forgotten lyre, "*that* is one of our small lions. The partiality of our people has made it so, and strangers have been seen taking a copy of it now and then. I am not a judge of it myself, for it is a little work of my own. But it was troublesome to turn, sir; I may say, difficult to turn with elegance."

Mr. Datchery became so ecstatic over Mr. Sapsea's composition that, in spite of his intention to end his days in Cloisterham, and therefore his probably having in reserve many opportunities of copying it, he would have transcribed it into his pocket-book on the spot, but for the slouching toward them of its material producer and perpetuator, Durdles, whom Mr. Sapsea hailed, not sorry to show him a bright example of behavior to superiors.

"Ah, Durdles!—This is the mason, sir; one of our Cloisterham worthies; everybody here knows Durdles.—Mr. Datchery, Durdles; a gentleman who is going to settle here."

"I wouldn't do it if I was him," growled Durdles. "We're a heavy lot."

"You surely don't speak for yourself, Mr. Durdles," returned Mr. Datchery, "any more than for His Honor."

"Who's His Honor?" demanded Durdles.

"His Honor the Mayor."

"I never was brought afore him," said Durdles, with any thing but the look of a loyal subject of the mayoralty, "and it'll be time enough for me to Honor him when I am. Until which, and when, and where:

'Mr. Sapsea is his name,
England is his nation,
Cloisterham's his dwelling-place,
Aukshneer's his occupation.'"

Here, Deputy (preceded by a flying oyster-shell) appeared upon the scene, and requested to have the sum of threepence instantly "chucked" to him by Mr. Durdles, whom he had been vainly seeking up and down, as lawful wages overdue. While that gentleman, with his bundle under his arm, slowly found and counted out the money, Mr. Sapsea informed the new settler of Durdles's habits, pursuits, abode, and reputation. "I suppose a curious stranger might come to see you, and your works, Mr. Durdles, at any odd time?" said Mr. Datchery upon that.

"Any gentleman is welcome to come and see me any evening if he brings liquor for two with him," returned Durdles, with a penny between his teeth and certain halfpence in his hands. "Or if he likes to make it twice two, he'll be doubly welcome."

"I shall come. Master Deputy, what do you owe me?"

"A job."

"Mind you pay me honestly with the job of showing me Mr. Durdles's house when I want to go there."

Deputy, with a piercing broadside of whistle through the whole gap in his mouth, as a receipt in full for all arrears, vanished.

The Worshipful and the Worshipper then passed on together until they parted, with many ceremonies, at the Worshipful's door; even then, the Worshipper carried his hat under his arm, and gave his streaming white hair to the breeze.

Said Mr. Datchery to himself that night, as he looked at his white hair in the gas-lighted looking-glass over the coffee-room chimney-piece at the Crozier, and shook it out: "For a single buffer, of an easy temper, living idly on his means, I have had a rather busy afternoon!"

CHAPTER XVII.

SHADOW ON THE SUN-DIAL.

Again Miss Twinkleton has delivered her valedictory address, with the accompaniments of white wine and pound cake, and again the young ladies have departed to their several homes. Helena Landless has left the Nuns' House to attend her brother's fortunes, and pretty Rosa is alone.

Cloisterham is so bright and sunny in these summer days that the cathedral and the monastery-ruin show as if their strong walls were transparent. A soft glow seems to shine from within them, rather than upon them from without, such is their mellowness as they look forth on the hot cornfields and the smoking roads that distantly wind among them. The Cloisterham gardens blush with ripening fruit. Time was when travel-stained pilgrims rode in clattering parties through the city's welcome shades; time is when wayfarers, leading a gypsy life between haymaking-time and harvest, and looking as if they were just made of the dust of the earth, so very dusty are they, lounge about on cool doorsteps, trying to mend their unmendable shoes, or giving them to the city kennels as a hopeless job, and seeking others in the bundles that they carry, along with their yet unused sickles swathed in bands of straw. At all the more public pumps there is much cooling of bare feet, together with much bubbling and gurgling of drinking with hand to spout on the part of these Bedouins; the

Cloisterham police meanwhile looking askant from their beats with suspicion, and manifest impatience that the intruders should depart from within the civic bounds, and once more fry themselves on the simmering high-roads.

On the afternoon of such a day, when the last cathedral service is done, and when that side of the High Street on which the Nuns' House stands is in grateful shade, save where its quaint old garden opens to the west between the boughs of trees, a servant informs Rosa, to her terror, that Mr. Jasper desires to see her.

If he had chosen his time for finding her at a disadvantage, he could have done no better. Perhaps he has chosen it. Helena Landless is gone, Mrs. Tisher is absent on leave, Miss Twinkleton (in her amateur state of existence) has contributed herself and a veal-pie to a picnic.

"O, why, why, why did you say I was at home!" cries Rosa, helplessly.

The maid replies that Mr. Jasper never asked the question. That he said he knew she was at home, and begged she might be told that he asked to see her.

"What shall I do? What shall I do?" thinks Rosa, clasping her hands.

Possessed by a kind of desperation, she adds in the next breath that she will come to Mr. Jasper in the garden. She shudders at the thought of being shut up with him in the house; but many of its windows command the garden, and she can be seen as well as heard there, and can shriek in the free air and run away. Such is the wild idea that flutters through her mind.

She has never seen him since the fatal night, except when she was questioned before the Mayor, and then he was present in gloomy watchfulness, as representing his lost nephew and burning to avenge him. She hangs her garden-hat on her arm, and goes out. The moment she sees him from the porch, leaning on the sun-dial, the old horrible feeling of being compelled by him, asserts its hold upon her. She feels that she would even then go back, but that he draws her feet toward him. She cannot resist, and sits down, with her head bent, on the garden-seat beside the sun-dial. She cannot look up at him for abhorrence, but she has perceived that he is dressed in deep mourning. So is she. It was not so at first; but the lost has long been given up, and mourned for, as dead.

He would begin by touching her hand. She feels the intention, and draws her hand back. His eyes are then fixed upon her, she knows, though her own see nothing but the grass.

"I have been waiting," he begins, "for some time, to be summoned back to my duty near you."

After several times forming her lips, which she knows he is closely watching, into the shape of some other hesitating reply, and then into none, she answers, "Duty, sir?"

"The duty of teaching you, serving you as your faithful music-master."

"I have left off that study."

"Not left off, I think. Discontinued. I was told by your guardian that you discontinued it under the shock that we have all felt so acutely. When will you resume?"

"Never, sir."

"Never? You could have done no more if you had loved my dear boy."

"I did love him!" cries Rosa with a flash of anger.

"Yes; but not quite — not quite in the right way, shall I say! Not in the intended and expected way. Much as my dear boy was, unhappily, too self-conscious and self-satisfied (I'll draw no parallel between him and you in that respect) to love as he should have loved, or as any one in his place would have loved; must have loved!"

She sits in the same still attitude, but shrinking a little more.

"Then, to be told that you discontinued your study with me was to be politely told that you abandoned it altogether?" he suggested.

"Yes," says Rosa, with sudden spirit. "The politeness was my guardian's, not mine. I told him that I was resolved to leave off, and that I was determined to stand by my resolution."

"And you still are?"

"I still am, sir. And I beg not to be questioned any more about it. At all events, I will not answer any more; I have that in my power."

She is so conscious of his looking at her with a gloating admiration of the touch of anger on her, and the fire and animation it brings with it, that even as her spirit rises, it falls again, and she struggles with a sense of shame, affront, and fear, much as she did that night at the piano.

"I will not question you any more, since you object to it so much; I will confess."

"I do not wish to hear you, sir," cries Rosa, rising.

This time he does touch her with his outstretched hand. In shrinking from it she shrinks into her seat again.

"We must sometimes act in opposition to our wishes," he tells her in a low voice. "You must do so now, or do more harm to others than you can ever set right."

"What harm?"

"Presently presently. You question *me*, you see, and surely that's not fair when you forbid me to question you. Nevertheless, I will answer the question presently. Dearest Rosa! Charming Rosa!"

She starts up again.

This time he does not touch her. But his face looks so wicked and menacing, as he stands leaning against the sun-dial, — setting, as it were, his black mark upon the very face of day, — that her flight is arrested by horror as she looks at him.

"I do not forget how many windows command a view of us," he says, glancing toward them. "I will not touch you again, I will come no nearer to you than I am. Sit down, and there will be no mighty wonder in your music-master's leaning idly against a pedestal and speaking with you, remembering all that has happened and our shares in it. Sit down, my beloved."

She would have gone once more, — was all but gone, — and once more his face darkly threatening what would follow if she went, has stopped her. Looking at him with the expression of the instant frozen on her face, she sits down on the seat again.

"Rosa, even when my dear boy was affianced to you, I loved you madly; even when I thought his happiness in having you for his wife was certain, I loved you madly; even when I strove to make him more ardently devoted to you, I loved you madly; even when he gave me the picture of your lovely face so carelessly traduced by him, which I feigned to hang always in my sight for his sake, but worshipped in torment for years, I loved you madly. In the distasteful work of the day, in the wakeful misery of the night, girded by sordid realities, or wandering through Paradises and Hells of visions into which I rushed, carrying your image in my arms, I loved you madly."

If anything could make his words more hideous to her than they are in themselves, it would be the contrast between the violence of his look and delivery, and the composure of his assumed attitude.

"I endured it all in silence. So long as you were his, or so long as I supposed you to be his, I hid my secret loyally. Did I not?"

This lie, so gross, while the mere words in which it is told are so true, is more than Rosa can endure. She answers, with kindling indignation: "You were as false throughout, sir, as you are now. You were false to him, daily and hourly. You know that you made my life unhappy by your pursuit of me. You know that you made me afraid to open his generous eyes, and that you forced me, for his own trusting, good, good sake, to keep the truth from him, that you were a bad, bad man!"

His preservation of his easy attitude rendering his working features and his convulsive hands absolutely diabolical, he returns, with a fierce extreme of admiration:

"How beautiful you are! You are more beautiful in anger than in repose. I don't ask you for your love; give me yourself and your hatred; give me yourself and that pretty rage; give me yourself and that enchanting scorn; it will be enough for me."

Impatient tears rise to the eyes of the trembling little beauty, and her face flames; but as she again rises to leave him in indignation, and seek protection within the house, he stretches out his hand toward the porch, as though he invited her to enter it.

"I told you, you rare charmer, you sweet witch, that you must stay and hear me, or do more harm than can ever be undone. You asked me what harm. Stay, and I will tell you. Go, and I will do it!"

Again Rosa quails before his threatening face, though innocent of its meaning, and she remains. Her panting breathing comes and goes as if it would choke her; but with a repressive hand upon her bosom, she remains.

"I have made my confession that my love is mad. It is so mad that, had the ties between me and my dear lost boy been one silken thread less strong, I might have swept even him from your side when you favored him."

A film comes over the eyes she raises for an instant, as though he had turned her faint.

"Even him," he repeats. "Yes, even him! Rosa, you see me and you hear me. Judge for yourself whether any other admirer shall love you and live, whose life is in my hand."

"What do you mean, sir?"

"I mean to show you how mad my love is. It was hawked through the late inquiries by Mr. Crisparkle that young Landless had confessed to him that he was a rival of my lost boy. That is an inexpiable offence in my eyes. The same Mr. Crisparkle knows under my hand that I have devoted myself to the murderer's discovery and destruction, be he whom he might, and that I determined to discuss the mystery with no one until I should hold the clew in which to entangle the murderer as in a net. I have since worked patiently to wind and wind it round him; and it is slowly winding as I speak."

"Your belief, if you believe in the criminality of Mr. Landless, is not Mr. Crisparkle's belief, and he is a good man," Rosa retorts.

"My belief is my own; and I reserve it, worshipped of my soul! Circumstances may accumulate so strongly *even against an innocent man*, that directed, sharpened, and pointed, they may slay him. One wanting link discovered by perseverance against a guilty man proves his guilt, however slight its evidence before, and he dies. Young Landless stands in deadly peril either way."

"If you really suppose," Rosa pleads with him, turning paler, "that I favor Mr. Landless, or that Mr. Landless has ever in any way addressed himself to me, you are wrong."

He puts that from him with a slighting action of his hand and a curled lip.

"I was going to show you how madly I love you. More madly now than ever, for I am willing to renounce the second object that has arisen in my life to divide it with you; and henceforth to have no object in existence but you only. Miss Landless has become your bosom friend. You care for her peace of mind?"

"I love her dearly."

"You care for her good name?"

"I have said, sir, I love her dearly."

"I am unconsciously," he observes, with a smile, as he folds his hands upon the sun-dial and leans his chin upon them, so that his talk would seem from the windows (faces occasionally come and go there) to be of the airiest and playfullest, "I am unconsciously giving offence by questioning again. I will simply make statements, therefore, and not put questions. You do care for your bosom friend's good name, and you do care for her peace of mind. Then remove the shadow of the gallows from her, dear one!"

"You dare propose to me to —"

"Darling, I dare propose to you. Stop there. If it be bad to idolize you, I am the worst of men; if it be good, I am the best. My love for you is above all other love, and my truth to you is above all other truth. Let me have hope and favor, and I am a forsworn man for your sake."

Rosa puts her hands to her temples, and, pushing back her hair, looks wildly and abhorrently at him, as though she were trying to piece together what it is his deep purpose to present to her only in fragments.

"Reckon up nothing at this moment, angel, but the sacrifices that I lay at those dear feet, which I could fall down among the vilest ashes and kiss, and put upon my head as a poor savage might. There is my fidelity to my dear boy after death. Tread upon it!"

With an action of his hands, as though he cast down something precious.

"There is the inexpiable offence against my adoration of you. Spurn it!"

With a similar action.

"There are my labors in the cause of a just vengeance for six toiling months. Crush them!"

With another repetition of the action.

"There is my past and my present wasted life. There is the desolation of my heart and my soul. There is my peace; there is my despair. Stamp them into the dust, so that you take me, were it even mortally hating me!"

The frightful vehemence of the man, now reaching its full height, so additionally terrifies her as to break the spell that has held her to the spot. She swiftly moves toward the porch; but in an instant he is at her side, and speaking in her ear.

"Rosa, I am self-repressed again. I am walking calmly beside you to the house. I shall wait for some encouragement and hope. I shall not strike too soon. Give me a sign that you attend to me."

She slightly and constrainedly moves her hand.

"Not a word of this to any one, or it will bring down the blow, as certainly as night follows day. Another sign that you attend to me."

She moves her hand once more.

"I love you, love you, love you. If you were to cast me off now—but you will not—you would never be rid of me. No one should come between us. I would pursue you to the death."

The handmaid coming out to open the gate for him, he quietly pulls off his hat as a parting salute, and goes away with no greater show of agitation than is visible in the effigy of Mr. Sapsea's father opposite. Rosa faints in going up-stairs, and is carefully carried to her room, and laid down on her bed. A thunder-storm is coming on, the maids say, and the hot and stifling air has overset the pretty dear; no wonder; they have felt their own knees all of a tremble all day long.

Rosa no sooner came to herself than the whole of the late interview was before her. It even seemed as if it had pursued her into her insensibility, and she had not had a moment's unconsciousness of it. What to do, she was at a frightened loss to know; the only clear thought in her mind was, that she must fly from this terrible man.

But where could she take refuge, and how could she go? She had never breathed her dread of him to any one but Helena. If she went to Helena, and told her what had passed, that very act might bring down the irreparable mischief that he threatened he had the power, and that she knew he had the will, to do. The more fearful he appeared to her excited memory and imagination, the more alarming her responsibility appeared: seeing that a slight mistake on her part, either in action or delay, might let his malevolence loose on Helena's brother.

Rosa's mind throughout the last six months had been stormily confused. A half-formed, wholly-unexpressed suspicion tossed in it, now heaving itself up, and now sinking into the deep; now gaining palpability, and now losing it. Jasper's self-absorption in his nephew when he was alive, and his unceasing pursuit of the inquiry how he came by his death, if he were dead, were themes so rife in the place, that no one appeared able to suspect the possibility of foul play at his hands. She had asked herself the question, "Am I so wicked in my thoughts as to conceive a wickedness that others cannot imagine?" Then she had considered, Did the suspicion come of her previous recoiling from him before the fact? And, if so, was not that a proof of its baselessness? Then she had reflected, "What motive could he have, according to my accusation?" She was ashamed to answer in her mind, "The motive of gaining *me!*" And covered her face, as if the lightest shadow of the idea of founding murder on such an idle vanity were a crime almost as great.

She ran over in her mind again all that he had said by the sun-dial in the garden. He had persisted in treating the disappearance as murder, consistently with his whole public course since the finding of the watch and shirt-pin. If he were afraid of the crime being traced out, would he not rather encourage the idea of a voluntary disappearance? He had even declared that, if the ties between him and his nephew had been less strong, he might have swept "even him" away from her side. Was that like his having really done so? He had spoken of laying his six months' labors in the cause of a just vengeance at her feet. Would he have done that, with that violence of passion, if they were a pretence? Would he have ranged them with his desolate heart and soul, his wasted life, his peace, and his despair? The very first sacrifice that he represented himself as making for her was his fidelity to his dear boy after death. Surely these facts were strong against a fancy that scarcely dared to hint itself. And yet he was so terrible a man! In short, the poor girl (for what could she know of the criminal intellect, which its own professed students perpetually misread, because they persist in trying to reconcile it with the average intellect of average men, instead of identifying it as a horrible wonder apart?), could get by no road to any other conclusion than that he *was* a terrible man, and must be fled from.

She had been Helena's stay and comfort during the whole time. She had constantly assured her of her full belief in her brother's innocence, and of her sympathy with him in his misery. But she had never seen him since the disappearance, nor had Helena ever spoken one word of his avowal to Mr. Crisparkle in regard of Rosa, though as a part of the interest of the case it was well known far and wide. He was Helena's unfortunate brother, to her, and nothing more. The assurance she had given her odious suitor was strictly true, though it would have been better (she considered now) if she could have restrained herself from so giving it. Afraid of him as the bright and delicate little creature was, her spirit swelled at the thought of his knowing it from her own lips.

But where was she to go? Anywhere beyond his reach, was no reply to the question. Somewhere must be thought of. She determined to go to her guardian, and to go immediately. The feeling she had imparted to Helena on the night of their first confidence was so strong upon her—the feeling of not being safe from him, and of the solid walls of the old convent being powerless to keep out his ghostly following of her—that no reasoning of her own could calm her terrors. The fascination of repulsion had been upon her so long, and now culminated so darkly, that she felt as if he had power to bind her by a spell. Glancing out at window, even now, as she rose to dress, the sight of the sun-dial on which he had leaned when he declared himself turned her cold, and made her shrink from it, as though he had invested it with some awful quality from his own nature.

She wrote a hurried note to Miss Twinkleton, saying that she had sudden reason for wishing to see her guardian promptly, and had gone to him; also, entreating the good lady not to be uneasy, for all was well with her. She hurried a few quite useless articles into a very little bag, left the note in a conspicuous place, and went out, softly closing the gate after her.

It was the first time she had ever been even in Cloisterham High Street alone. But knowing all its ways and windings very well, she hurried straight to the corner from which the omnibus departed. It was at that very moment going off.

"Stop and take me, if you please, Joe. I am obliged to go to London."

In less than another minute she was on her road to the railway, under Joe's protection. Joe waited on her when she got there, put her safely into the railway carriage, and handed in the very little bag after her, as though it were some enormous trunk, hundredweights heavy, which she must on no account endeavor to lift.

"Can you go round when you get back, and tell Miss Twinkleton, that you saw me safely off, Joe?"

"It shall be done, Miss."

"With my love, please, Joe."

"Yes, Miss—and I wouldn't mind having it myself!" But Joe did not articulate the last clause; only thought it.

Now that she was whirling away for London in real earnest, Rosa was at leisure to resume the thoughts which her personal hurry had checked. The indignant thought that his declaration of love soiled her; that she could only be cleansed from the stain of its impurity by appealing to the honest and true; supported her for a time against her fears, and confirmed her in her hasty resolution. But as the evening grew darker and darker, and the great city impended nearer and nearer, the doubts usual in such cases began to arise. Whether this was not a wild proceeding after all; how Mr. Grewgious might regard it; whether she should find him at the journey's end; how she would act if he were absent; what might become of her, alone, in a place so strange and crowded; how, if she had but waited and taken counsel first; whether, if she could now go back, she would not do it thankfully: a multitude of such uneasy speculations disturbed her, more and more as they accumulated. At length, the train came into London over the housetops; and down below lay the gritty streets with their yet unneeded lamps aglow, on a hot, light, summer night.

"Hiram Grewgious, Esquire, Staple Inn, London." This was all Rosa knew of her destination; but it was enough to send her rattling away again in a cab, through deserts of gritty streets, where many people crowded at the corners of courts and by-ways to get some air, and where many other people walked with a miserably monotonous noise of shuffling feet on hot paving-stones, and where all the people and all their surroundings were so gritty and so shabby.

There was music playing here and there, but it did not enliven the case. No barrel-organ mended the matter, and no big drum beat dull care away. Like the chapel-bells that were also going here and there, they only seemed to evoke echoes from brick surfaces, and dust from every thing. As to the flat wind-instruments, they seemed to have cracked their hearts and souls in pining for the country.

Her jingling conveyance stopped at last at a fast-closed gate-way which appeared to belong to somebody who had gone to bed very early, and was much afraid of house-breakers; Rosa, discharging her conveyance, timidly knocked at this gate-way, and was let in, very little bag and all, by a watchman.

"Does Mr. Grewgious live here?"

"Mr. Grewgious lives there, Miss," said the watchman, pointing further in.

So Rosa went further in, and, when the clocks were striking ten, stood on P. J. T.'s doorsteps, wondering what P. J. T. had done with his street-door.

Guided by the painted name of Mr. Grewgious, she went up-stairs and softly tapped and tapped several times. But no one answering, and Mr. Grewgious's door-handle yielding to her touch, she went in, and saw her guardian sitting on a window-seat at an open window, with a shaded lamp placed far from him on a table in a corner.

Rosa drew near to him in the twilight of the room. He saw her, and he said in an undertone, "Good Heaven!"

Rosa fell upon his neck, with tears, and then he said, returning her embrace:

"My child, my child! I thought you were your mother!"

"But what, what, what," he added, soothingly, "has happened? My dear, what has brought you here? Who has brought you here?"

"No one. I came alone."

"Lord bless me!" ejaculated Mr. Grewgious. "Came alone! Why didn't you write to me to come and fetch you?"

"I had no time. I took a sudden resolution. Poor, poor Eddy!"

"Ah, poor fellow, poor fellow!"

"His uncle has made love to me. I cannot bear it," said Rosa, at once with a burst of tears and a stamp of her little foot; "I shudder with horror of him, and I have come to you to protect me and all of us from him, if you will?"

"I will!" cried Mr. Grewgious, with a sudden rush of amazing energy. "Damn him!

'Confound his politics,
Frustrate his knavish tricks!
On Thee his hopes to fix?
Damn him again!'"

After this most extraordinary outburst, Mr. Grewgious, quite beside himself, plunged about the room, to all appearance undecided whether he was in a fit of loyal enthusiasm, or combative denunciation.

He stopped and said, wiping his face, "I beg your pardon, my dear, but you will be glad to know I feel better. Tell me no more just now, or I might do it again. You must be refreshed and cheered. What did you take last? Was it breakfast, lunch, dinner, tea, or supper? And what will you take next? Shall it be breakfast, lunch, dinner, tea, or supper?"

The respectful tenderness with which, on one knee before her, he helped her to remove her hat, and disentangle her pretty hair from it, was quite a chivalrous sight. Yet who, knowing him only on the surface, would have expected chivalry—and of the true sort, too; not the spurious—from Mr. Grewgious?

"Your rest, too, must be provided for," he went on, "and you shall have the prettiest chamber in Furnival's. Your toilet must be provided for, and you shall have every thing that an unlimited head-chambermaid—by which expression I mean a head-chambermaid not limited as to outlay—can procure. Is that a bag?" He looked hard at it; sooth to say, it required hard looking at to be seen at all in a dimly-lighted room; "and is it your property, my dear?"

"Yes, sir. I brought it with me."

"It is not an extensive bag," said Mr. Grewgious, candidly, "though admirably calculated to contain a day's provision for a canary-bird. Perhaps you brought a canary-bird?"

Rosa smiled, and shook her head.

"If you had he should have been made welcome," said Mr. Grewgious, "and I think he would have been pleased to be hung upon a nail outside and pit himself against our Staple sparrows; whose execution must be admitted to be not quite equal to their intention. Which is the case with so many of us! You didn't say what meal, my dear. Have a nice jumble of all meals."

Rosa thanked him, but said she could only take a cup of tea. Mr. Grewgious, after several times running out, and in again, to mention such supplementary items as marmalade, eggs, water-cresses, salted fish, and frizzled ham, ran across to Furnival's without his hat, to give his various directions. And soon afterward they were realized in practice, and the board was spread.

"Lord bless my soul!" cried Mr. Grewgious, putting the lamp upon it, and taking his seat opposite Rosa, "what a new sensation for a poor old Angular bachelor, to be sure!"

Rosa's expressive little eyebrows asked him what he meant.

"The sensation of having a sweet young presence in the place that whitewashes it, paints it, papers it, decorates it with gilding, and makes it Glorious," said Mr. Grewgious. "Ah me! Ah me!"

As there was something mournful in his sigh, Rosa, in touching him with his tea-cup, ventured to touch him with her small hand, too.

"Thank you, my dear," said Mr. Grewgious. "Ahem! Let's talk."

"Do you always live here, sir?" asked Rosa.

"Yes, my dear."

"And always alone?"

"Always alone; except that I have daily company in a gentleman by the name of Bazzard; my clerk."

"*He* doesn't live here?"

"No, he goes his ways after office-hours. In fact, he is off duty here, altogether, just at present; and a Firm down-stairs, with which I have business-relations, lend me a substitute. But it would be extremely difficult to replace Mr. Bazzard."

"He bears up against it with commendable fortitude, if he is," returned Mr. Grewgious, after considering the matter. "But I doubt if he is. Not particularly so. You see, he is discontented, poor fellow."

"Why isn't he contented?" was the natural inquiry.

"Misplaced," said Mr. Grewgious, with great mystery.

Rosa's eyebrows resumed their inquisitive and perplexed expression.

"So misplaced," Mr. Grewgious went on, "that I feel constantly apologetic toward him. And he feels (though he doesn't mention it) that I have reason to be."

Mr. Grewgious had by this time grown so very mysterious, that Rosa did not know how to go on. While she was thinking about it, Mr. Grewgious suddenly jerked out of himself for the second time:

"Let's talk. We were speaking of Mr. Bazzard. It's a secret, and moreover it is Mr. Bazzard's secret; but the sweet presence at my table makes me so unusually expansive, that I feel I must impart it in inviolable confidence. What do you think Mr. Bazzard has done?"

"O dear!" cried Rosa, drawing her chair a little nearer, and her mind reverting to Jasper, "nothing dreadful, I hope?"

"He has written a play," said Mr. Grewgious, in a solemn whisper. "A tragedy."

Rosa seemed much relieved.

"And nobody," pursued Mr. Grewgious, in the same tone, "will hear, on any account whatever, of bringing it out."

Rosa looked reflective, and nodded her head slowly; as who should say, "Such things are, and why are they!"

"Now, you know," said Mr. Grewgious, "*I* couldn't write a play."

"Not a bad one, sir?" asked Rosa, innocently, with her eyebrows again in action.

"No. If I was under sentence of decapitation, and was about to be instantly decapitated, and an express arrived with a pardon for the condemned convict Grewgious if he wrote a play, I should be under the necessity of resuming the block and begging the executioner to proceed to extremities—meaning," said Mr. Grewgious, passing his hand under his chin, "the singular number, and this extremity."

Rosa appeared to consider what she would do if the awkward suppositious case were hers.

"Consequently," said Mr. Grewgious, "Mr. Bazzard would have a sense of my inferiority to himself under any circumstances; but when I am his master, you know, the case is greatly aggravated."

Mr. Grewgious shook his head seriously, as if he felt the offence to be a little too much, though of his own committing.

"How came you to be his master, sir?" asked Rosa.

"A question that naturally follows," said Mr. Grewgious. "Let's talk. Mr. Bazzard's father, being a Norfolk farmer, would have furiously laid about him with a flail, a pitchfork, and every agricultural implement available for assaulting purposes, on the slightest hint of his son's having written a play. So the son, bringing to me the father's rent (which I receive), imparted his secret, and pointed out that he was determined to pursue his genius, and that it would put him in peril of starvation, and that he was not formed for it."

"For pursuing his genius, sir?"

"No, my dear," said Mr. Grewgious, "for starvation. It was impossible to deny the position that Mr. Bazzard was not formed to be starved, and Mr. Bazzard then pointed out that it was desirable that I should stand between him and a fate so perfectly unsuited to his formation. In that way Mr. Bazzard became my clerk, and he feels it very much."

"I am glad he is grateful," said Rosa.

"I didn't quite mean that, my dear. I mean that he feels the degradation. There are some other geniuses that Mr. Bazzard has become acquainted with, who have also written tragedies, which likewise nobody will on any account whatever hear of bringing out, and these choice spirits dedicate their plays to one another in a highly panegyrical manner. Mr. Bazzard has been the subject of one of these dedications. Now, you know, *I* never had a play dedicated to *me!*"

Rosa looked at him as if she would have liked him to be the recipient of a thousand dedications.

"Which again, naturally, rubs against the grain of Mr. Bazzard," said Mr. Grewgious. "He is very short with me sometimes, and then I feel that he is meditating, 'This blockhead is my master! A fellow who couldn't write a tragedy on pain of death, and who will never have one dedicated to him with the most complimentary congratulations on the high position he has taken in the eyes of posterity!' Very trying, very trying. However, in giving him directions, I reflect beforehand, 'Perhaps he may not like this,' or 'He might take it ill if I asked that,' and so we got on very well. Indeed, better than I could have expected."

"Is the tragedy named, sir?" asked Rosa.

"Strictly between ourselves," answered Mr. Grewgious, "it has a dreadfully appropriate name. It is called The Thorn of Anxiety. But Mr. Bazzard hopes—and I hope—that it will come out at last."

It was not hard to divine that Mr. Grewgious had related the Bazzard history thus fully, at least quite as much for the recreation of his ward's mind from the subject that had driven her there, as for the gratification of his own tendency to be social and communicative. "And now, my dear," he said at this point, "if you are not too tired to tell me more of what passed to-day—but only if you feel quite able—I should be glad to hear it. I may digest it the better, if I sleep on it to-night."

Rosa, composed now, gave him a faithful account of the interview. Mr. Grewgious often smoothed his head while it was in progress, and begged to be told a second time those parts which bore on Helena and Neville. When Rosa had finished, he sat, grave, silent, and meditative, for a while.

"Clearly narrated," was his only remark at last, "and, I hope, clearly put away here," smoothing his head again. "See, my dear," taking her to the open window, "where they live! The dark windows over yonder."

"I may go to Helena to-morrow?" asked Rosa.

"I should like to sleep on that question to-night," he answered, doubtfully. "But let me take you to your own rest, for you must need it."

With that, Mr. Grewgious helped her to get her hat on again, and hung upon his arm the very little bag that was of no earthly use, and led her by the hand (with a certain stately awkwardness, as if he were going to walk a minuet) across Holborn, and into Furnival's inn. At the hotel door, he confided her to the Unlimited head-chambermaid, and said that while she went up to see her room, he would remain below, in case she should wish it exchanged for another, or should find that there was anything she wanted.

Rosa's room was airy, clean, comfortable, almost gay. The Unlimited had laid in every thing omitted from the very little bag (that is to say, every thing she could possibly need), and Rosa tripped down the great many stairs again, to thank her guardian for his thoughtful and affectionate care of her.

"Not at all, my dear," said Mr. Grewgious, infinitely gratified; "it is I who thank you for your charming confidence and for your charming company. Your breakfast will be provided for you in a neat, compact, and graceful little sitting-room (appropriate to your figure), and I will come to you at ten o'clock in the morning. I hope you don't feel very strange, indeed, in this strange place."

"O no, I feel so safe!"

"Yes, you may be sure that the stairs are fire-proof," said Mr. Grewgious, "and that any outbreak of the devouring element would be perceived and suppressed by the watchmen."

"I did not mean that," Rosa replied. "I mean I feel so safe from him."

"There is a stout gate of iron bars to keep him out," said Mr. Grewgious, smiling, "and Furnival's is fire-proof and especially watched and lighted, and *I* live over the way!" In the stoutness of his knight-errantry, he seemed to think the last-named protection all-sufficient. In the same spirit, he said to the gate-porter as he went out, "if some one staying in the hotel should wish to send across the road to me in the night, a crown will be ready for the messenger." In the same spirit, he walked up and down outside the iron gate for the best part of an hour, with some solicitude; occasionally looking in between the bars, as if he had laid a dove in a high roost in a cage of lions, and had it on his mind that she might tumble out.

CHAPTER XVIII.

A RECOGNITION.

NOTHING occurred in the night to flutter the tired dove, and the dove arose refreshed. With Mr. Grewgious, when the clock struk ten in the morning, came Mr. Crisparkle, who had come at one plunge out of the river at Cloisterham.

"Miss Twinkleton was so uneasy, Miss Rosa," he explained to Rosa, "and came round to Ma and me with your note, in such a state of wonder, that, to quiet her, I volunteered on this service by the very first train to be caught in the morning. I wished at the time that you had come to me; but now I think it best that you did *as* you did, and came to your guardian."

"I did think of you," Rosa told him; "but Minor Canon Corner was so near him—"

"I understand. It was quite natural."

"I have told Mr. Crisparkle," said Mr. Grewgious, "all that you told me last night, my dear. Of course I should have written it to him immediately; but his coming was most opportune. And it was particularly kind of him to come, for he had but just gone."

"Have you settled," asked Rosa, appealing to them both, "what is to be done for Helena and her brother?"

"Why really," said Mr. Crisparkle, "I am in great perplexity. If even Mr. Grewgious, whose head is much longer than mine, and who is a whole night's cogitation in advance of me, is undecided, what must I be!"

The Unlimited here put her head in at the door,—after having rapped, and been invited to present herself,—announcing that a gentleman wished for a word with another gentleman named Crisparkle, if any such gentleman were there. If no such gentleman were there, he begged pardon for being mistaken.

"Such a gentleman is here," said Mr. Crisparkle, "but is engaged just now."

"Is it a dark gentleman?" interposed Rosa, retreating on her guardian.

"No, Miss, more of a brown gentleman."

"You are sure not with black hair?" asked Rosa, taking courage.

"Quite sure of that, Miss. Brown hair and blue eyes."

"Perhaps," hinted Mr. Grewgious, with habitual caution, "it might be well to see him, reverend sir, if you don't object. When one is in a difficulty or at a loss, one never knows in what direction a way out of it may chance to open. It is a business principle of mine, in such a case, not to close up any direction, but to keep an eye on every direction that may present itself. I could relate an anecdote in point, but that it would be premature."

"If Miss Rosa will allow me then—? Let the gentleman come in," said Mr. Crisparkle.

The gentleman came in; apologized with a frank but modest grace for not finding Mr. Crisparkle alone; turned to Mr. Crisparkle, and smilingly asked the unexpected question: "Who am I?"

"You are the gentleman I saw smoking under the trees in Staple Inn a few minutes ago."

"True. There I saw you. Who else am I?"

Mr. Crisparkle concentrated his attention on a handsome face, much sunburnt; and the ghost of some departed boy seemed to rise gradually and dimly in the room.

The gentleman saw a struggling recollection lighten up the Minor Canon's features, and smiling again, said, "What will you have for breakfast this morning? You are out of jam."

"Wait a moment!" cried Mr. Crisparkle, raising his right hand. "Give me another instant! Tartar!"

The two shook hands with the greatest heartiness, and then went the wonderful length—for Englishmen—of laying their hands, each on the other's shoulders, and looking joyfully each into the other's face.

"My old fag!" said Mr. Crisparkle.

"My old master!" said Mr. Tartar.

"You saved me from drowning!" said Mr. Crisparkle.

"After which you took to swimming, you know!" said Mr. Tartar.

"God bless my soul!" said Mr. Crisparkle.

"Amen!" said Mr. Tartar.

And then they fell to shaking hands most heartily again.

"Imagine," exclaimed Mr. Crisparkle, with glistening eyes,—"Miss Rosa Bud and Mr. Grewgious,—imagine Mr. Tartar, when he was the smallest of juniors, diving for me, catching me, a big, heavy senior, by the hair of the head, and striking out for the shore with me like a water-giant."

"Imagine my not letting him sink, as I was his fag!" said Mr. Tartar. "But the truth being that he was my best protector and friend, and did me more good than all the masters put together, an irrational impulse seized me rather to pick him up or go down with him."

"Hem! Permit me, sir, to have the honor," said Mr. Grewgious, advancing with extended hand, "for an honor I truly esteem it. I am proud to make your acquaintance. I hope you didn't take cold. I hope you were not inconvenienced by swallowing too much water. How have you been since?"

It was by no means apparent that Mr. Grewgious knew what he said, though it was very apparent that he meant to say something friendly and appreciative.

If Heaven, Rosa thought, had but sent such courage and skill to her poor mother's aid! And he to have been so slight and young then!

"I don't wish to be complicated upon it, I thank you, but I think I have an idea," Mr. Grewgious announced, after taking a jog-trot or two across the room, so unexpected and unaccountable that they had all stared at him, doubtful whether he was choking or had the cramp. "I *think* I have an idea. I believe I have had the pleasure of seeing Mr. Tartar's name as tenant of the top set next the top set in the corner?"

"Yes, sir," returned Mr. Tartar. "You are right so far."

"I am right so far," said Mr. Grewgious. "Tick that off," which he did, with his right thumb on his left. "Might you happen to know the name of your neighbor in the top set on the other side of the party-wall?" coming very close to Mr. Tartar, to lose nothing of his face, in his shortness of sight.

"Landless!"

"Tick that off," said Mr. Grewgious, taking another trot and then coming back. "No personal knowledge, I suppose, sir?"

"Slight, but some."

"Tick that off," said Mr. Grewgious, taking another trot and again coming back. "Nature of knowledge, Mr. Tartar?"

"I thought he seemed to be a young fellow in a poor way, and I asked his leave—only just now—to share my flowers up there with him; that is to say, to extend my flower-gardens to his windows."

"Would you have the kindness to take seats?" said Mr. Grewgious. "I *have* an idea."

They complied; Mr. Tartar more the less readily for being all abroad; and Mr. Grewgious, seated in the centre, with his hands upon his knees, thus stated his idea with his usual manner of having got the statement by heart.

"I cannot as yet make up my mind whether it is prudent to hold open communication under present circumstances, and on the part of the fair member of the present company, with Mr. Neville or Miss Helena. I have reason to know that a local friend of ours (on whom I beg to bestow a passing but a hearty malediction, with the kind permission of my reverend friend) sneaks to and fro, and dodges up and down. When not doing so himself, he may have some informant skulking about, in the person of a watchman, porter, or such-like hanger-on of Staples. On the other hand, Miss Rosa very naturally wishes to see her friend Miss Helena, and it would seem important that at least Miss Helena (if not her brother too—through her) should privately know from Miss Rosa's lips what has occurred and what has been threatened. Am I agreed with generally in the views I take?"

"I entirely coincide with them," said Mr. Crisparkle, who had been very attentive.

"As I have no doubt I should," added Mr. Tartar, smiling, "if I understood them."

"Fair and softly, sir," said Mr. Grewgious; "we shall fully confide in you directly, if you will favor us with your permission. Now, if our local friend should have any informant on the spot, it is tolerably clear that such informant can only be set to watch the chambers in the occupation of Mr. Neville. He reporting to our local friend, who comes and goes there, our local friend would supply for himself, from his own previous knowledge, the identity of the parties. Nobody can be set to watch all Staples, or to concern himself with comers and goers to other sets of chambers, unless, indeed, mine."

"I begin to understand to what you tend," said Mr. Crisparkle, "and highly approve of your caution."

"I needn't repeat that I know nothing yet of the why and wherefore," said Mr. Tartar; "but I, also, understood to what you tend, so let me say at once that my chambers are freely at your disposal."

"There!" cried Mr. Grewgious, smoothing his head triumphantly. "Now we have all got the idea. You have it, my dear?"

"I think I have," said Rosa, blushing a little as Mr. Tartar looked quickly toward her.

"You see, you go over to Staples with Mr. Crisparkle and Mr. Tartar," said Mr. Grewgious; "I going in and out and out and in alone, in my usual way; you go up with those gentlemen to Mr. Tartar's rooms; you look into Mr. Tartar's flower-garden; you wait for Miss Helena's appearance there, or you signify to Miss Helena that you are close by; and you communicate with her freely, and no spy can be the wiser."

"I am very much afraid I shall be—"

"Be what, my dear?" asked Mr. Grewgious, as she hesitated. "Not frightened?"

"No, not that," said Rosa, shyly; "in Mr. Tartar's way. We seem to be appropriating Mr. Tartar's residence so very coolly."

"I protest to you," returned that gentleman, "that I shall think the better of it forevermore if your voice sounds in it only once."

Rosa not quite knowing what to say about that, cast down her eyes, and turning to Mr. Grewgious, dutifully asked if she should put her hat on. Mr. Grewgious being of opinion that she could not do better, she withdrew for the purpose. Mr. Crisparkle took the opportunity of giving Mr. Tartar a summary of the distresses of Neville and his sister. The opportunity was quite long enough for the purpose, as the hat happened to require a little extra fitting.

Mr. Tartar gave his arm to Rosa, and Mr. Crisparkle walked, detached, in front.

"Poor, poor Eddy!" thought Rosa, as they walked along.

Mr. Tartar waved his right hand as he bent his head down over Rosa, talking in his animated way.

"It was not so powerful or so sun-browned when it saved Mr. Crisparkle," thought Rosa, glancing at it; "but it must have been very steady and determined then."

Mr. Tartar told her he had been a sailor, roving everywhere for years and years.

"When are you going to sea again?" asked Rosa.

"Never!"

Rosa wondered what the girls would think if they could see her crossing the wide street on the sailor's arm. And she fancied that the passers-by must think her very little and very helpless contrasted with the strong figure that could have caught her up and carried her out of any danger without resting, miles and miles.

She was thinking further that his far-seeing blue eyes looked as if they had been used to watch danger afar off, and to watch it without flinching, coming nearer and nearer, when happening to raise her own eyes, she found that he seemed to be thinking something about *them.*

This a little confused Rosebud, and may account for her never afterward quite knowing how she ascended (with his help) to his garden in the air, and got into a marvellous country that bloomed like the country on the summit of the magic bean-stalk. May it flourish forever.

CHAPTER XIX.

A GRITTY STATE OF THINGS COMES ON.

Mr. Tartar's chambers were the neatest, the cleanest, and the best-ordered chambers ever seen under the sun, moon, and stars. The floors were scrubbed to that extent that you might have supposed the London blacks emancipated forever and gone out of the land for good. Every inch of brass-work in Mr. Tartar's possession was polished and burnished till it shone like a brazen mirror. No speck, nor spot, nor spatter soiled the purity of any of Mr. Tartar's household gods, large, small, or middle-sized. His sitting-room was like the admiral's cabin, his bath-room was like a dairy, his sleeping-chamber, fitted all about with lockers and drawers, was like a seedsman's shop; and his nicely-balanced cot just stirred in the midst as if it breathed. Every thing belonging to Mr. Tartar had quarters of its own assigned to it; his maps and charts had their quarters; his books had theirs; his brushes had theirs; his boots had theirs; his clothes had theirs; his case-bottles had theirs; his telescopes and other instruments had theirs. Every thing was readily accessible. Shelf, bracket, locker, hook, and drawer were equally within reach, and were equally contrived with a view to avoiding waste of room, and providing some snug inches of stowage for something that would have exactly fitted nowhere else. His gleaming little service of plate was so arranged upon his sideboard as that a slack salt-spoon would have instantly betrayed itself; his toilet implements were so arranged upon his dressing-table as that a toothpick of slovenly deportment could have been reported at a glance. So with the curiosities he had brought home from various voyages. Stuffed, dried, repolished, or otherwise preserved, according to their kind; birds, fishes, reptiles, arms, articles of dress, shells, seaweeds, grasses, or memorials of coral reef; each was displayed in its especial place, and each could have been displayed in no better place. Paint and varnish seemed to be kept somewhere out of sight, in constant readiness to obliterate stray finger-marks wherever any might become perceptible in Mr. Tartar's chambers. No man-of-war was ever kept more spick and span from careless touch. On this bright summer day a neat awning was rigged over Mr. Tartar's flower-garden as only a sailor could rig it; and there was a sea-going air upon the whole effect, so delightfully complete that the flower-garden might have appertained to stern-windows afloat, and the whole concern might have bowled away gallantly with all on board, if Mr. Tartar had only clapped to his lips the speaking-trumpet that was slung in a corner, and given hoarse orders to have the anchor up, look alive there, men, and get all sail upon her!

Mr. Tartar doing the honors of this gallant craft was of a piece with the rest. When a man rides an amiable hobby that shies at nothing and kicks nobody, it is only agreeable to find him riding it with a humorous sense of the droll side of the creature. When the man is a cordial and an earnest man by nature, and withal is perfectly fresh and genuine, it may be doubted whether he is ever seen to greater advantage than at such a time. So Rosa would have naturally thought (even if she hadn't been conducted over the ship with all the homage due to the first Lady of the Admiralty, or First Fairy of the Sea), that it was charming to see and hear Mr. Tartar half laughing at, and half rejoicing in his various contrivances. So Rosa would have naturally thought, anyhow, that the sunburnt sailor showed to great advantage when, the inspection finished, he delicately withdrew out of his admiral's cabin, beseeching her to consider herself its Queen, and waving her free of his flower-garden with the hand that had Mr. Crisparkle's life in it.

"Helena! Helena Landless! Are you there?"

"Who speaks to me? Not Rosa?" Then a second handsome face appearing.

"Yes, my darling."

"Why, how did you come here, dearest?"

"I—I don't quite know," said Rosa, with a blush; "unless I am dreaming!"

Why with a blush? For their two faces were alone with the other flowers. Are blushes among the fruits of the country of the magic beanstalk?

"*I* am not dreaming," said Helena, smiling. "I should take more for granted if I were. How do we come together—or so near together—so very unexpectedly?"

Unexpectedly indeed, among the dingy gables and chimney-pots of P. J. T.'s connection, and the flowers that had sprung from the salt sea. But Rosa, waking, told in a hurry how they came to be together, and all the why and wherefore of that matter.

"And Mr. Crisparkle is here," said Rosa, in rapid conclusion; "and could you believe it? Long ago, he saved his life?"

"I could believe any such thing of Mr. Crisparkle," returned Helena, with a mantling face.

(More blushes in the beanstalk country.)

"Yes, but it wasn't Mr. Crisparkle," said Rosa, quickly putting in the correction.

"I don't understand, love."

"It was very nice of Mr. Crisparkle to be saved," said Rosa, "and he couldn't have shown his high opinion of Mr. Tartar more expressively. But it was Mr. Tartar who saved him."

Helena's dark eyes looked very earnestly at the bright face among the leaves, and she asked, in a slower and more thoughtful tone:

"Is Mr. Tartar with you now, dear?"

"No; because he has given up his rooms to me—to us, I mean. It *is* such a beautiful place!"

"Is it?"

"It is like the inside of the most exquisite ship that ever sailed. It is like—it is like—"

"Like a dream?" suggested Helena.

Rosa answered with a little nod, and smelled the flowers.

Helena resumed, after a short pause of silence, during which she seemed (or it was Rosa's fancy) to compassionate somebody: "My poor Neville is reading in his own room, the sun being so very bright on this side just now. I think he had better not know that you are so near."

"O, I think so too!" cried Rosa, very readily.

"I suppose," pursued Helena, doubtfully, "that he must know by-and-by all you have told me; but I am not sure. Ask Mr. Crisparkle's advice, my darling. Ask him whether I may tell Neville as much or as little of what you have told me as I think best."

Rosa subsided into her state-cabin, and propounded the question. The Minor Canon was for the free exercise of Helena's judgment.

"I thank him very much," said Helena, when Rosa emerged again with her report. "Ask him whether it would be best to wait until any more maligning and pursuing of Neville on the part of this wretch shall disclose itself, or to try to anticipate it: I mean, so far as to find out whether any such goes on darkly about us?"

The Minor Canon found this point so difficult to give a confident opinion on, that, after two or three attempts and failures, he suggested a reference to Mr. Grewgious. Helena acquiescing, he betook himself (with a most unsuccessful assumption of lounging indifference) across the quadrangle to P. J. T.'s, and stated it. Mr. Grewgious held decidedly to the general principle that if you could steal a march upon a brigand or a wild beast you had better do it; and he also held decidedly to the special case that John Jasper was a brigand and a wild beast in combination.

Thus advised, Mr. Crisparkle came back again and reported to Rosa, who in her turn reported to Helena. She, now steadily pursuing her train of thought at her window, considered thereupon.

"We may count on Mr. Tartar's readiness to help us, Rosa?" she inquired.

O yes! Rosa shyly thought so. O yes, Rosa shyly believed she could almost answer for it. But should she ask Mr. Crisparkle? "I think your authority on the point as good as his, my dear," said Helena, sedately, "and you needn't disappear again for that." Odd of Helena!

"You see, Neville," Helena pursued after more reflection, "knows no one else here: he has not so much as exchanged a word with any one else here. If Mr. Tartar should call to see him openly and often; if he would spare a minute for the purpose, frequently; if he would even do so, almost daily; something might come of it."

"Something might come of it, dear?" repeated Rosa, surveying her friend's beauty with a highly-perplexed face. "Something might?"

"If Neville's movements are really watched, and if the purpose really is to isolate him from all friends and acquaintances and wear his daily life out, grain by grain (which would seem to be the threat to you), does it not appear likely," said Helena, "that his enemy would in some way communicate with Mr. Tartar to warn him off from Neville? In which case we might not only know the fact, but might know from Mr. Tartar what the terms of the communication were."

"I see!" cried Rosa. And immediately darted into her state-cabin again.

Presently her pretty face reappeared, with a greatly-heightened color, and she said that she had told Mr. Crisparkle, and that Mr. Crisparkle had fetched in Mr. Tartar, and that Mr. Tartar—"who is waiting now in case you want him," added Rosa, with a half look back, and in not a little confusion, between the inside of the state-cabin and out— had declared his readiness to act as she had suggested, and to enter on his task that very day.

"I thank him from my heart," said Helena. "Pray tell him so."

Again, not a little confused between the flower-garden and the cabin, Rosa dipped in with her message, and dipped out again with more assurances from Mr. Tartar, and stood wavering in a divided state between Helena and him, which proved that confusion is not always necessarily awkward, but may sometimes present a very pleasant appearance.

"And now, darling," said Helena, "we will be mindful of the caution that has restricted us to this interview for the present, and will part. I hear Neville moving too. Are you going back?"

"To Miss Twinkleton's?" asked Rosa.

"Yes."

"O, I could never go there any more; I couldn't, indeed, after that dreadful interview!" said Rosa.

"Then where *are* you going, pretty one?"

"Now I come to think of it, I don't know," said Rosa. "I have settled nothing at all yet, but my guardian will take care of me. Don't be uneasy, dear. I shall be sure to be somewhere."

(It did seem likely.)

"And I shall hear of my Rosebud from Mr. Tartar?" inquired Helena.

"Yes, I suppose so; from—" Rosa looked back again in a flutter, instead of supplying the name. "But tell me one thing before we part, dearest Helena. Tell me that you are sure, sure, sure, I couldn't help it."

"Help it, love?"

"Help making him malicious and revengeful. I couldn't hold any terms with him, could I?"

"You know how I love you, darling," answered Helena, with indignation; "but I would sooner see you dead at his wicked feet."

"That's a great comfort to me! And you will tell your poor brother so, won't you. And you will give him my remembrance and my sympathy? And you will ask him not to hate me?"

With a mournful shake of the head, as if that would be quite a superfluous entreaty, Helena lovingly kissed her two hands to her friend, and her friend's two hands were kissed to her, and then she saw a third hand (a brown one) appear among the flowers and leaves, and help her friend out of sight.

The refection that Mr. Tartar produced in the Admiral's Cabin by merely touching the spring knob in a locker and the handle of a drawer, was a dazzling, enchanted repast. Wonderful macaroons, glittering liqueurs, magically-preserved tropical spices, and jellies of celestial tropical fruits, displayed themselves profusely at an instant's notice. But Mr. Tartar could not make time stand still; and time, with his hard-hearted fleetness, strode on so fast that Rosa was obliged to come down from the Beanstalk country to earth, and her guardian's chambers.

"And now, my dear," said Mr. Grewgious, "what is to be done next? To put the same thought in another form; what is to be done with you?"

Rosa could only look apologetically sensible of being very much in her own way, and in everybody else's. Some passing idea of living, fire-proof, up a good many stairs in Furnival's Inn for the rest of her life was the only thing in the nature of a plan that occurred to her.

"It has come into my thoughts," said Mr. Grewgious, "that as the respected lady, Miss Twinkleton, occasionally repairs to London in the recess, with the view of extending her connection, and being available for interviews with metropolitan parents, if any—whether, until we have time in which to turn ourselves round, we might invite Miss Twinkleton to come and stay with you for a month?"

"Stay where, sir?"

"Whether," explained Mr. Grewgious, "we might take a furnished lodging in town for a month, and invite Miss Twinkleton to assume the charge of you in it for that period?"

"And afterward?" hinted Rosa.

"And afterward," said Mr. Grewgious, "we should be no worse off than we are now."

"I think that might smooth the way," assented Rosa.

"Then let us," said Mr. Grewgious, rising, "go and look for a furnished lodging. Nothing could be more acceptable to me than the sweet presence of last evening for all the remaining evenings of my existence; but these are not fit surroundings for a young lady. Let us set out in quest of adventures, and look for a furnished lodging. In the meantime, Mr. Crisparkle here, about to return home immediately, will no doubt kindly see Miss Twinkleton and invite that lady to co-operate in our plan."

Mr. Crisparkle, willingly accepting the commission, took his departure; Mr. Grewgious and his ward set forth on their expedition.

As Mr. Grewgious's idea of looking at a furnished lodging was to get on the opposite side of the street to a house with a suitable bill in the window, and stare at it, and then work his way tortuously to the back of the house and stare at that; and then not go in, but make similar trials of another house, with the same result, their progress was but slow. At length he bethought himself of a widowed cousin, divers times removed, of Mr. Bazzard's, who had once solicited his influence in the lodger world, and who lived in Southampton Street, Bloomsbury Square. This lady's name, stated in uncompromising capitals of considerable size on a brass door-plate, and yet not lucidly as to sex or condition, was BILLICKIN.

Personal faintness and an overpowering personal candor were the distinguishing features of Mrs. Billickin's organization. She came languishing out of her own exclusive back parlor, with the air of having been expressly brought-to for the purpose from an accumulation of several swoons.

"I hope I see you well, sir," said Mrs. Billickin, recognizing her visitor with a bend.

"Thank you, quite well. And you, ma'am?" returned Mr. Grewgious.

"I am as well," said Mrs. Billickin, becoming aspirational with excess of faintness, "as I hever ham."

"My ward and an elderly lady," said Mr. Grewgious, "wish to find a genteel lodging for a month or so. Have you any apartments available, ma'am?"

"Mr. Grewgious," returned Mrs. Billickin, "I will not deceive you, far from it I *have* apartments available."

This, with the air of adding, "Convey me to the stake, if you will, but while I live I will be candid."

"And now, what apartments, ma'am?" asked Mr. Grewgious, cosily. To tame a certain severity apparent on the part of Mrs. Billickin.

"There is this sitting-room,—which call it what you will, it is the front parlor, miss," said Mrs. Billickin, impressing Rosa into the conversation; "the back parlor being what I cling to and never part with; and there is two bedrooms at the top of the 'ouse with gas laid on. I do not tell you that your bedroom floors is firm, for firm they are not. The gas-fitter himself allowed that to make a firm job, he must go right under your jistes, and it were not worth the outlay as a yearly tenant so to do. The piping is carried above your jistes, and it is best that it should be made known to you."

Mr. Grewgious and Rosa exchanged looks of some dismay, though they had not the least idea what latent horrors this carriage of the piping might involve. Mrs. Billickin put her hand to her heart, as having eased it of a load.

"Well! The roof is all right, no doubt," said Mr. Grewgious, plucking up a little.

"Mr. Grewgious," returned Mrs. Billickin, "if I was to tell you, sir, that to have nothink above you is to have a floor above you, I should put a deception upon you which I will not do. No, sir. Your slates WILL rattle loose at that elewation in windy weather, do your utmost, best or worst! I defy you, sir, be you what you may, to keep your slates tight, try how you can." Here Mrs. Billickin, having been warm with Mr. Grewgious, cooled a little, not to abuse the moral power she held over him. "Consequent," proceeded Mrs. Billickin, more mildly, but still firmly in her incorruptible candor, "consequent it would be worse than of no use for me to trapse and travel up to the top of the 'ouse with you, and for you to say, 'Mrs. Billickin, what stain do I notice in the ceiling, for a stain I do consider it?' and for me to answer, 'I do not understand you, sir.' No, sir; I will not be so underhand. I *do* understand you before you pint it out. It is the wet, sir. It do come in, and it do not come in. You may lay dry there, half your lifetime, but the time will come, and it is best that you should know it, when a dripping sop would be no name for you."

Mr. Grewgious looked much disgraced by being prefigured in this pickle.

"Have you any other apartments, ma'am?" he asked.

"Mr. Grewgious," returned Mrs. Billickin, with much solemnity, "I have. You ask me have I, and my open and my honest answer air, I have. The first and second floors is wacant, and sweet rooms."

"Come, come! There's nothing against *them*," said Mr. Grewgious, comforting himself.

"Mr. Grewgious," replied Mrs. Billickin, "pardon me, there is the stairs. Unless your mind is prepared for the stairs, it will lead to inevitable disappointment. You cannot, miss," said Mrs. Billickin, addressing Rosa, reproachfully, "place a first floor, and far less a second, on the level footing of a parlor. No, you cannot do it, miss; it is beyond your power, and wherefore try?"

Mrs. Billickin put it very feelingly, as if Rosa had shown a headstrong determination to hold the untenable position.

"Can we see these rooms, ma'am?" inquired her guardian.

"Mr. Grewgious," returned Mrs. Billickin, "you can. I will not disguise it from you, sir, you can."

Mrs. Billickin then sent into her back parlor for her shawl (it being a state fiction dating from immemorial antiquity that she could never go anywhere without being wrapped up), and having been enrolled by her attendant, led the way. She made various genteel pauses on the stairs for breath, and clutched at her heart in the drawing-room as if it had very nearly got loose, and she had caught it in the act of taking wing.

"And the second floor?" said Mr. Grewgious, on finding the first satisfactory.

"Mr. Grewgious," replied Mrs. Billickin, turning upon him with ceremony, as if the time had now come when a distinct understanding on a difficult point must be arrived at, and a solemn confidence established, "the second floor is over this."

"Can we see that, too, ma'am?"

"Yes, sir," returned Mrs. Billickin, "it is as open as the day."

That also proving satisfactory, Mr. Grewgious retired into a window with Rosa for a few words of consultation, and then, asking for pen and ink, sketched out a line or two of agreement. In the mean time Mrs. Billickin took a seat, and delivered a kind of Index to, or Abstract of, the general question.

"Five-and-forty shillings per week by the month certain at the time of year," said Mrs. Billickin, "is only reasonable to both parties. It is not Bond Street, nor yet St. James's Palace; but it is not pretended that it is. Neither is it attempted to be denied—for why should it?—that the Arching leads to a Mews. Mewses must exist. Respecting attendance; two is kep' at liberal wages. Words *has* arisen as to tradesmen, but dirty shoes on fresh hearth-stoning was attributable, and no wish for a commission on your orders. Coals is either *by* the fire, or *per* the scuttle." She emphasized the prepositions as marking a subtle but immense difference. "Dogs is not viewed with favor. Besides litter, they gets stole, and snaring suspicions is apt to creep in, and unpleasantness takes place."

By this time Mr. Grewgious had his agreement-lines and his earnest-money ready. "I have signed it for the ladies, ma'am," he said, "and you'll have the goodness to sign it for yourself, Christian and Surname, there, if you please."

"Mr. Grewgious," said Mrs. Billickin, in a new burst of candor, "no, sir! You must excuse the Christian name."

Mr. Grewgious stared at her.

"The door-plate is used as a protection," said Mrs. Billickin, "and acts as such, and go from it I will not."

Mr. Grewgious stared at Rosa.

"No, Mr. Grewgious, you must excuse me. So long as this 'ouse is known indefinite as Billickin's, and so long as it is a doubt with the riff-raff where Billickin may be hidin', near the street door or down the airy, and what his weight and size, so long I feel safe. But commit myself to a solitary female statement, no, miss! Nor would you for a moment wish," said Mrs. Billickin, with a strong sense of injury, "to take that advantage of your sex, if you was not brought to it by inconsiderate example."

Rosa, reddening as if she had made some most disgraceful attempt to overreach the good lady, besought Mr. Grewgious to rest content with any signature. And accordingly, in a baronical way, the sign-manual BILLICKIN got appended to the document.

Details were then settled for taking possession on the next day but one, when Miss Twinkleton might be reasonably expected, and Rosa went back to Furnival's Inn on her guardian's arm.

Behold Mr. Tartar walking up and down Furnival's Inn, checking himself when he saw them coming, and advancing toward them!

"It occurred to me," hinted Mr. Tartar, "that we might go up the river, the weather being so delicious and the tide serving. I have a boat of my own at the Temple Stairs."

"I have not been up the river for this many a day," said Mr. Grewgious, tempted.

"I was never up the river," added Rosa.

Within half an hour they were setting this matter right by going up the river. The tide was running with them, the afternoon was charming. Mr. Tartar's boat was perfect. Mr. Tartar and Lobley (Mr. Tartar's man) pulled a pair of oars. Mr. Tartar had a yacht, it seemed, lying somewhere down by Greenhithe; and Mr. Tartar's man had charge of this yacht and was detached upon his present service. He was a jolly-favored man, with tawny hair and whiskers, and a big red face. He was the dead image of the sun in old woodcuts, his hair and whiskers answering for rays all round him. Resplendent in the bow of the boat, he was a shining sight, with a man-of-war's man's shirt on — or off, according to opinion — and his arms and breast tattooed all sorts of patterns. Lobley seemed to take it easily, and so did Mr. Tartar; yet their oars bent as they pulled, and the boat bounded under them. Mr. Tartar talked as if he were doing nothing, to Rosa, who was really doing nothing, and to Mr. Grewgious, who was doing this much, that he steered all wrong; but what did that matter when a turn of Mr. Tartar's skillful wrist, or a mere grin of Mr. Lobley's over the bow, put all to rights! The tide bore them on in the gayest and most sparkling manner, until they stopped to dine in some everlastingly green garden, needing no matter-of-fact identification here, and then the tide obligingly turned, — being devoted to that party alone for that day; and as they floated idly among some osier-beds, Rosa tried what she could do in the rowing way, and came off splendidly, being much assisted; and Mr. Grewgious tried what he could do, and came off on his back, doubled up with an oar under his chin, being not assisted at all. Then there was an interval of rest under boughs (such rest!) what time Mr. Lobley mopped, and, arranging cushions, stretchers, and the like, danced the tight-rope the whole length of the boat like a man to whom shoes were a superstition and stockings slavery; and then came the sweet return among delicious odors of limes in bloom, and musical ripplings; and all too soon the great black city cast its shadow on the waters, and its dark bridges spanned them as death spans life, and the everlastingly green garden seemed to be left for everlasting, unregainable and far away.

"Cannot people get through life without gritty stages, I wonder!" Rosa thought next day, when the town was very gritty again, and every thing had a strange and an uncomfortable appearance of seeming to wait for something that wouldn't come. No. She began to think that now the Cloisterham school-days had glided past and gone, the gritty stages would begin to set in at intervals and make themselves wearily known!

Yet what did Rosa expect? Did she expect Miss Twinkleton? Miss Twinkleton duly came. Forth from her back parlor issued the Billickin to receive Miss Twinkleton, and War was in the Billickin's eye from that fell moment.

Miss Twinkleton brought a quantity of luggage with her, having all Rosa's as well as her own. The Billickin took it ill that Miss Twinkleton's mind, being sorely disturbed by this luggage, failed to take in her personal identity with that clearness of perception which was due to its demands. Stateliness mounted her gloomy throne upon the Billickin's brow in consequence. And when Miss Twinkleton, in agitation, taking stock of her trunks and packages, of which she had seventeen, particularly counted in the Billickin herself as number eleven, the B. found it necessary to repudiate.

"Things cannot too soon be put upon the footing," said she, with a candor so demonstrative as to be almost obtrusive, "that the person of the 'ouse is not a box nor yet a bundle, nor a carpet-bag. No, I am 'ily obleeged to you, Miss Twinkleton, nor yet a beggar."

This last disclaimer had reference to Miss Twinkleton's distractedly pressing two and sixpence on her instead of the cabman.

Thus cast off, Miss Twinkleton wildly inquired "which gentleman" was to be paid? There being two gentlemen in that position (Miss Twinkleton having arrived with two cabs), each gentleman, on his being paid, held forth his two and sixpence on the flat of his open hand, and with a speechless stare and a dropped jaw displayed his wrong to heaven and earth. Terrified by this alarming spectacle, Miss Twinkleton placed another shilling in each hand, at the same time appealing to the law in flurried accents and recounting her luggage, this time with the two gentlemen in, who caused the total to come out complicated. Meanwhile the two gentlemen, each looking very hard at the last shilling grumblingly, as if it might become eighteenpence if he kept his eyes on it, descended the doorsteps, ascended their carriages, and drove away, leaving Miss Twinkleton on a bonnet-box in tears.

The Billickin beheld this manifestation of weakness without sympathy, and gave directions for "a young man to be got in" to wrestle with the luggage. When that gladiator had disappeared from the arena, peace ensued, and the new lodgers dined.

But the Billickin had somehow come to the knowledge that Miss Twinkleton kept a school. The leap from that knowledge to the inference that Miss Twinkleton set herself to teach *her* something was easy. "But you don't do it," soliloquized the Billickin; "*I* am not your pupil, whatever she," meaning Rosa, "may be, poor thing!"

Miss Twinkleton, on the other hand, having changed her dress and recovered her spirits, was animated by a bland desire to improve the occasion in all ways, and to be as serene a model as possible. In a happy compromise between her two states of existence she had already become, with her work-basket before her, the equally vivacious companion with a slight judicious flavoring of information when the Billickin announced herself.

"I will not hide from you, ladies," said the B., enveloped in the shawl of state, "for it is not my character to hide, neither my motives, nor my actions, that I take the liberty to look in upon you to express a 'ope that your dinner was to your liking. Though not Professed but Plain, still her wages should be a sufficient object to her to stimulate to soar above mere roast and biled."

"We dined very well indeed," said Rosa, "thank you."

"Accustomed," said Miss Twinkleton, with a gracious air which to the jealous ears of the Billickin seemed to add "my good woman,"—"accustomed to a liberal, nutritious, yet plain and salutary diet, we have found no reason to bemoan our absence from the ancient city and the methodical household in which the quiet routine of our lot has been hitherto cast."

"I did think it well to mention to my cook," observed the Billickin, with a gush of candor, "which I 'ope you will agree with, Miss Twinkleton, was a right precaution, that the young lady being used to what we should consider here but poor diet, had better be brought forward by degrees. For, a rush from scanty feeding to generous feeding, and from what you may call messing to what you may call method, do require a power of constitution, which is not often found in youth, particularly when undermined by boarding-school?"

It will be seen that the Billickin now openly pitted herself against Miss Twinkleton, as one whom she had fully ascertained to be her natural enemy.

"Your remarks," returned Miss Twinkleton, from a remote moral eminence, "are well meant, I have no doubt; but you will permit me to observe that they develop a mistaken view of the subject which can only be imputed to your extreme want of accurate information."

"My information," retorted the Billickin, throwing in an extra syllable for the sake of emphasis at once polite and painful: "my information, Miss Twinkleton, were my own experience, which I believe is usually considered to be good guidance. But whether so or not, I was put in youth to a very genteel boarding-school, the mistress being no less a lady than yourself, of about your own age or it may be some years younger, and a poorness of blood flowed from the table which has run through my life."

"Very likely," said Miss Twinkleton, still from her distant eminence; "and very much to be deplored. Rosa, my dear, how are you getting on with your work?"

"Miss Twinkleton," resumed the Billickin, in a courtly manner, "before retiring on the Int, as a lady should, I wish to ask of yourself, as a lady, whether I am to consider that my words is doubted?"

"I am not aware on what ground you cherish such a supposition," began Miss Twinkleton, when the Billickin neatly stopped her.

"Do not, if you please, put suppositions betwixt my lips, where none such have been imparted by myself. Your flow of words is great, Miss Twinkleton, and no doubt is expected from you by your pupils, and no doubt is considered worth the money. *No* doubt, I am sure. But not paying for flows of words and not asking to be favored with them here, I wish to repeat my question."

"If you refer to the poverty of your circulation," began Miss Twinkleton, when again the Billickin neatly stopped her.

"I have used no such expressions."

"If you refer then to the poorness of your blood."

"Brought upon me," stipulated the Billickin, expressly, "at a boarding-school."

"Then," resumed Miss Twinkleton, "all I can say is, that I am bound to believe on your asseveration that it is very poor indeed. I cannot forbear adding, that if that unfortunate circumstance influences your conversation, it is much to be lamented, and it is eminently desirable that your blood were richer. Rosa, my dear, how are you getting on with your work?"

"Hem! Before retiring, Miss," proclaimed the Billickin to Rosa, loftily cancelling Miss Twinkleton, "I should wish it to be understood between yourself and me that my transactions in future is with you alone. I know no elderly lady here, Miss; none older than yourself."

"A highly desirable arrangement, Rosa, my dear," observed Miss Twinkleton.

"It is not, Miss," said the Billickin, with a sarcastic smile, "that I possess the Mill I have heard of, in which old single ladies could be ground up young (what a gift it would be to some of us!) but that I limit myself to you totally."

"When I have any desire to communicate a request to the person of the house, Rosa, my dear," observed Miss Twinkleton, with majestic cheerfulness, "I will make it known to you, and you will kindly undertake, I am sure, that it is conveyed to the proper quarter."

"Good-evening, Miss," said the Billickin, at once affectionately and distantly. "Being alone in my eyes, I wish you good-evening with best wishes, and do not find myself drove, I am truly 'appy to say, into expressing my contempt for any indiwidual, unfortunately for yourself, belonging to you."

The Billickin gracefully withdrew with this parting speech, and from that time Rosa occupied the restless position of shuttlecock between these two battledores. Nothing could be done without a smart match being played out. Thus, on the daily-arising question of dinner, Miss Twinkleton would say, the three being present together:

"Perhaps, my love, you will consult with the person of the house whether she can procure us a lamb's fry; or, failing that, a roast fowl."

On which the Billickin would retort (Rosa not having spoken a word), "If you was better accustomed to butcher's meat, Miss, you would not entertain the idea of a lamb's fry. Firstly, because lambs has long been sheep, and secondly, because there is such things as killing-days, and there is not. As to roast fowls, Miss, why you must be quite surfeited with roast fowls, letting alone your buying, when you market for yourself, the agedest of poultry with the scaliest of legs, quite as if you was accustomed to picking 'em out for cheapness. Try a little inwention, Miss. Use yourself to 'ousekeeping a bit. Come now, think of something else."

To this encouragement, offered with the indulgent toleration of a wise and liberal expert, Miss Twinkleton would rejoin, reddening:

"Or, my dear, you might propose to the person of the house a duck."

"Well, Miss!" the Billickin would exclaim (still no word being spoken by Rosa), "you do surprise me when you speak of ducks! Not to mention that they're getting out of season and very dear, it really strikes to my heart to see you have a duck, for the breast, which is the only delicate cuts in a duck, always goes in a direction which I cannot imagine where, and your own plate comes down so miserably skin-and-bony! Try again, Miss. Think more of yourself and less of others. A dish of sweetbreads now, or a bit of mutton. Somethink at which you can get your equal chance."

Occasionally the game would wax very brisk indeed, and would be kept up with a smartness rendering such an encounter as this quite tame. But the Billickin almost invariably made by far the higher score, and would come in with side hits of the most unexpected and extraordinary description, when she seemed without a chance.

All this did not improve the gritty state of things in London, or the air that London had acquired in Rosa's eyes of waiting for something that never came. Tired of working and conversing with Miss Twinkleton, she suggested working and reading: to which Miss Twinkleton readily assented, as an admirable reader, of tried powers. But Rosa soon made the discovery that Miss Twinkleton didn't read fairly. She cut the love-scenes, interpolated passages in praise of female celibacy, and was guilty of other glaring pious frauds. As an instance in point, take the following passage: "Ever dearest and best adored, said Edward, clasping the dear head to his breast, and drawing the silken hair through his caressing fingers, from which he suffered it to fall like golden rain; ever dearest and best adored, let us fly from the unsympathetic world and the sterile coldness of the stony-hearted, to the rich warm Paradise of Trust and Love." Miss Twinkleton's fraudulent version tamely ran thus: "Ever engaged to me with the consent of our parents on both sides, and the approbation of the silver-haired rector of the district, said Edward, respectfully raising to his lips the taper fingers so skillful in embroidery, tambour, crochet, and other truly feminine arts; let me call on thy papa 'ere to-morrow's dawn has sunk into the west, and propose a suburban establishment, lowly it may be, but within our means, where he will be always welcome as an evening guest, and where every arrangement shall invest economy and constant interchange of scholastic acquirements with the attributes of the ministering angel to domestic bliss."

As the days crept on and nothing happened, the neighbors began to say that the pretty girl at Billickin's who looked so wistfully and so much out of the gritty windows of the drawing-room, seemed to be losing her spirits. The pretty girl might have lost them but for the accident of lighting on some books of voyages and sea-adventure. As a compensation against their romance, Miss Twinkleton, reading aloud, made the most of all the latitudes and longitudes, bearings, winds, currents, offsets, and other statistics (which she felt to be none the less improving because they expressed nothing whatever to her); while Rosa, listening intently, made the most of what was nearest to her heart. So they both did better than before.

CHAPTER XX.

THE DAWN AGAIN.

Although Mr. Crisparkle and John Jasper met daily under the Cathedral roof, nothing at any time passed between them bearing reference to Edwin Drood after the time, more than half a year gone by, when Jasper mutely showed the Minor Canon the conclusion and the resolution entered in his Diary. It is not likely that they ever met, though so often, without the thoughts of each reverting to the subject. It is not likely that they ever met, though so often, without a sensation on the part of each that the other was a perplexing secret to him. Jasper as the denouncer and pursuer of Neville Landless, and Mr. Crisparkle as his consistent advocate and protector, must at least have stood sufficiently in opposition to have speculated with keen interest on the steadiness and next direction of the other's designs. But neither ever broached the theme.

False pretence not being in the Minor Canon's nature, he doubtless displayed openly that he would at any time have revived the subject, and even desired to discuss it. The determined reticence of Jasper, however, was not to be so approached. Impassive, moody, solitary, resolute, so concentrated on one idea, and on its attendant fixed purpose, that he would share it with no fellow-creature, he lived apart from human life. Constantly exercising an Art which brought him into mechanical harmony with others, and which could not have been pursued unless he and they had been in the nicest mechanical relations and unison, it is curious to consider that the spirit of the man was in moral accordance or interchange with nothing around him. This indeed he had confided to his lost nephew before the occasion for his present inflexibility arose.

That he must know of Rosa's abrupt departure, and that he must divine its cause, was not to be doubted. Did he suppose that he had terrified her into silence, or did he suppose that she had imparted to any one—to Mr. Crisparkle himself for instance—the particulars of his last interview with her? Mr. Crisparkle could not determine this in his mind. He could not but admit, however, as a just man, that it was not, of itself, a crime to fall in love with Rosa, any more than it was a crime to offer to set love above revenge.

The dreadful suspicion of Jasper which Rosa was so shocked to have received into her imagination appeared to have no harbor in Mr. Crisparkle's. If it ever haunted Helena's thoughts, or Neville's, neither gave it one spoken word of utterance. Mr. Grewgious took no pains to conceal his implacable dislike of Jasper, yet he never referred it, however distantly, to such a source. But he was a reticent as well as an eccentric man; and he made no mention of a certain evening when he warmed his hands at the Gate House fire and looked steadily down upon a certain heap of torn and miry clothes upon the floor.

Drowsy Cloisterham, whenever it awoke to a passing consideration of a story above six months old and dismissed by the bench of magistrates, was pretty equally divided in opinion whether John Jasper's beloved nephew had been killed by his treacherously-passionate rival, or in an open struggle; or had, for his own purposes, spirited himself away. It then lifted up its head to notice that the bereaved Jasper was still ever devoted to discovery and revenge; and then dozed off again. This was the condition of matters, all round, at the period to which the present history has now attained.

The Cathedral doors have closed for the night, and the Choir Master, on a short leave of absence for two or three services, sets his face toward London. He travels thither by the means by which Rosa travelled, and arrives, as Rosa arrived, on a hot, dusty evening.

His travelling baggage is easily carried in his hand, and he repairs with it, on foot, to a hybrid hotel in a little square behind Aldersgate Street, near the General Post-Office. It is hotel, boarding-house, or lodging-house, at its visitor's option. It announces itself in the new Railway Advertisers as a novel enterprise timidly beginning to spring up. It bashfully, almost apologetically, gives the traveller to understand that it does not expect him, on the good old constitutional hotel plan, to order a pint of sweet blacking for his drinking, and throw it away; but insinuates that he may have his boots blacked instead of his stomach, and maybe also have bed, breakfast, attendance, and a porter up all night, for a certain fixed charge. From these and similar premises many true Britons in the lowest spirits deduce that the times are levelling times, except in the article of high-roads, of which there will shortly be not one in England.

He eats without appetite, and soon goes forth again. Eastward and still eastward through the stale streets he takes his way, until he reaches his destination; a miserable court, specially miserable among many such.

He ascends a broken staircase, opens a door, looks into a dark, stifling room, and says, "Are you alone here?"

"Alone, deary; worse luck for me and better for you," replies a croaking voice. "Come in, come in, whoever you be; I can't see you till I light a match, yet I seem to know the sound of your speaking. I am acquainted with you, ain't I?"

"Light your match, and try."

"So I will, deary, so I will; but my hand that shakes, as I can't lay it on a match all in a moment. And I cough so, that, put my matches where I may, I never find 'em there. They jump and start, as I cough and cough, like live things. Are you off a voyage, deary?"

"No."

"Not sea-faring?"

"No."

"Well, there's land customers and there's water customers. I'm a mother to both. Different from Jack Chinaman t'other side the court. He ain't a father to neither. It ain't in him. And he ain't got the true secret of mixing, though he charges as much as me that has, and more if he can get it. Here's a match, and now where's the candle? If my cough takes me, I shall cough out twenty matches afore I gets a light."

But she finds the candle, and lights it before the cough comes on. It seizes her in the moment of success, and she sits down rocking herself to and fro, and gasping at intervals. "O, my lungs is awful bad, my lungs is wore away to cabbage-nets!" until the fit is over. During its continuance she has had no power of sight, or any other power not absorbed in the struggle; but as it leaves her, she begins to strain her eyes, and as soon as she is able to articulate, she cries, staring,—

"Why, it's you!"

"Are you so surprised to see me?"

"I thought I never should have seen you again, deary. I thought you was dead and gone to Heaven."

"Why?"

"I didn't suppose you could have kept away, alive, so long, from the poor old soul with the real receipt for mixing it. And you are in mourning too! Why didn't you come and have a pipe or two of comfort? Did they leave you money, perhaps, and so you didn't want comfort?"

"No!"

"Who was they as died, deary?"

"A relative."

"Died of what, lovey?"

"Probably, Death."

"We are short to-night!" cries the woman, with a propitiatory laugh. "Short and snappish we are! But we're out of sorts for want of a smoke. We've got the all-overs, haven't us, deary? But this is the place to cure 'em in; this is the place where the all-overs is smoked off!"

"You may make ready, then," replies the visitor, "as soon as you like."

He divests himself of his shoes, loosens his cravat, and lies across the foot of the squalid bed, with his head resting on his left hand.

"Now you begin to look like yourself," says the woman, approvingly. "Now I begin to know my old customer indeed! Been trying to mix for yourself this long time, poppet?"

"I have been taking it now and then in my own way."

"Never take it your own way. It ain't good for trade, and it ain't good for you. Where's my ink-bottle, and where's my thimble, and where's my little spoon? He's going to take it in an artful form now, my deary dear!"

Entering on her process, and beginning to bubble and blow at the faint spark enclosed in the hollow of her hands, she speaks from time to time in a tone of snuffling satisfaction, without leaving off. When he speaks, he does so without looking at her, and as if his thoughts were already roaming away by anticipation.

"I've got a pretty many smokes ready for you, first and last, haven't I, chuckey?"

"A good many."

"When you first come, you was quite new to it; warn't ye?"

"Yes, I was easily disposed of, then."

"But you got on in the world, and was able by-and-by to take your pipe with the best of 'em, warn't ye?"

"Ay. And the worst."

"It's just ready for you. What a sweet singer you was when you first come! Used to drop your head, and sing yourself off, like a bird! It's ready for you now, deary."

He takes it from her with great care, and puts the mouthpiece to his lips. She seats herself beside him, ready to refill the pipe. After inhaling a few whiffs in silence, he doubtingly accosts her with,—

"Is it as potent as it used to be?"

"What do you speak of, deary?"

"What should I speak of, but what I have in my mouth?"

"It's just the same. Always the identical same."

"It doesn't taste so. And it's slower."

"You've got more used to it, you see."

"That may be the case, certainly. Look here." He stops, becomes dreamy, and seems to forget that he has invited her attention. She bends over him, and speaks in his ear.

"I'm attending to you. Says you just now, look here. Says I now, I am attending to ye. We was talking just before of your being used to it."

"I know all that. I was only thinking. Look here. Suppose you had something in your mind; something you were going to do."

"Yes, deary; something I was going to do?"

"But had not quite determined to do."

"Yes, deary."

"Might or might not do, you understand."

"Yes." With the point of a needle she stirs the contents of the bowl.

"Should you do it in your fancy when you were lying here doing this?"

She nods her head. "Over and over again."

"Just like me! I did it over and over again. I have done it hundreds of thousands of times in this room."

"It's to be hoped it was pleasant to do, deary."

"It *was* pleasant to do!"

He says this with a savage air, and a spring or start at her. Quite unmoved, she retouches and replenishes the contents of the bowl with her little spatula. Seeing her intent upon the occupation, he sinks into his former attitude.

"It was a journey, a difficult and dangerous journey. That was the subject in my mind. A hazardous and perilous journey, over abysses where a slip would be destruction. Look down, look down! You see what lies at the bottom there?"

He has darted forward to say it, and to point at the ground, as though at some imaginary object far beneath. The woman looks at him as his spasmodic face approaches close to hers, and not at his pointing. She seems to know what the influence of her perfect quietude will be; if so, she has not miscalculated it, for he subsides again.

"Well; I have told you, I did it, here, hundreds of thousands of times. What do I say? I did it millions and billions of times. I did it so often and through such vast expanses of time that, when it was really done, it seemed not worth the doing, it was done so soon."

"That's the journey you have been away upon?" she quietly remarks.

He glares at her as he smokes, and then, his eyes becoming filmy, answers: "That's the journey."

Silence ensues. His eyes are sometimes closed and sometimes open. The woman sits beside him, very attentive to the pipe, which is all the while at his lips.

"I'll warrant," she observes, when he has been looking fixedly at her for some consecutive moments, with a singular appearance in his eyes of seeming to see her a long way off, instead of so near him,—"I'll warrant you made the journey in a many ways when you made it so often?"

"No, always in one way."

"Always in the same way?"

"Ay."

"In the way in which it was really made at last?"

"Ay."

"And always took the same pleasure in harping on it?"

"Ay."

For the time he appears unequal to any other reply than this lazy monosyllabic assent. Probably to assure herself that it is not the assent of a mere automaton, she reverses the form of her next sentence.

"Did you never get tired of it, deary, and try to call up something else for a change?"

He struggles into a sitting posture, and retorts upon her: "What do you mean? What did I want? What did I come for?"

She gently lays him back again, and, before returning him the instrument he has dropped, revives the fire in it with her own breath; then says to him, coaxingly,—

"Sure, sure, sure! Yes, yes, yes! Now I go along with you. You was too quick for me. I see now. You come o' purpose to take the journey. Why, I might have known it, through its standing by you so."

He answers first with a laugh, and then with a passionate setting of his teeth: "Yes, I came on purpose. When I could not bear my life I came to get the relief, and I got it. It WAS one! It WAS one!" This repetition with extraordinary vehemence, and the snarl of a wolf.

She observes him very cautiously, as though mentally feeling her way to her next remark. It is: "There was a fellow-traveller, deary."

"Ha ha ha!" He breaks into a ringing laugh, or rather yell.

"To think," he cries, "how often fellow-traveller, and yet not know

14

it! To think how many times he went the journey, and never saw the road!"

The woman kneels upon the floor, with her arms crossed on the coverlet of the bed, close by him, and her chin upon them. In this crouching attitude she watches him. The pipe is falling from his mouth. She puts it back, and, laying her hand upon his chest, moves him slightly from side to side. Upon that he speaks, as if she had spoken.

"Yes! I always made the journey first, before the changes of colors and the great landscapes and glittering processions began. They couldn't begin till it was off my mind. I had no room till then for any thing else."

Once more he lapses into silence. Once more she lays her hand upon his chest, and moves him slightly to and fro, as a cat might stimulate a half-slain mouse. Once more he speaks, as if she had spoken.

"What? I told you so. When it comes to be real at last, it is so short that it seems unreal for the first time. Hark!"

"Yes, deary. I'm listening."

"Time and place are both at hand."

He is on his feet, speaking in a whisper, and as if in the dark.

"Time, place, and fellow-traveller," she suggests, adopting his tone, and holding him softly by the arm.

"How could the time be at hand unless the fellow-traveller was? Hush! The journey's made. It's over."

"So soon?"

"That's what I said to you. So soon. Wait a little. This is a vision. I shall sleep it off. It has been too short and easy. I must have a better vision than this; this is the poorest of all. No struggle, no consciousness of peril, no entreaty—and yet I never saw *that* before." With a start.

"Saw what, deary?"

"Look at it! Look, what a poor, mean, miserable thing it is! *That* must be real. It's over!"

He has accompanied this incoherence with some wild, unmeaning gestures; but they trail off into the progressive inaction of stupor, and he lies a log upon the bed.

The woman, however, is still inquisitive. With a repetition of her cat-like action, she slightly stirs his body again, and listens; stirs again, and listens; whispers to it, and listens. Finding it past all rousing for the time, she slowly gets upon her feet, with an air of disappointment, and flicks the face with the back of her hand in turning from it.

But she goes no farther away from it than the chair upon the hearth. She sits in it, with an elbow on one of its arms, and her chin upon her hand, intent upon him. "I heard ye say once," she croaks under her breath—"I heard ye say once, when I was lying where you're lying, and you were making your speculations upon me, 'Unintelligible!' I heard you say so, of two more than me. But don't ye be too sure always; don't ye be too sure, beauty!"

Unwinking, cat-like, and intent, she presently adds: "Not so potent as it once was? Ah! Perhaps not at first. You may be more right there. Practice makes perfect. I may have learned the secret how to make ye talk, deary."

He talks no more, whether or no. Twitching in an ugly way from time to time, both as to his face and limbs, he lies heavy and silent. The wretched candle burns down; the woman takes its expiring end between her fingers, lights another at it, crams the guttering, frying morsel deep into the candlestick, and rams it home with the new candle, as if she were loading some ill-savored and unseemly weapon of witchcraft; the new candle, in its turn, burns down; and still he lies insensible. At length, what remains of the last candle is blown out, and daylight looks into the room.

It has not looked very long, when he sits up, chilled and shaking, slowly recovers consciousness of where he is, and makes himself ready to depart. The woman receives what he pays her with a grateful "Bless ye, bless ye, deary!" and seems, tired out, to begin making herself ready for sleep as he leaves the room.

But seeming may be false or true. It is false in this case, for, the moment the stairs have ceased to creak under his tread, she glides after him, muttering emphatically, "I'll not miss ye twice!"

There is no egress from the court but by its entrance. With a weird peep from the door-way she watches for his looking back. He does not look back before disappearing, with a wavering step. She follows him, peeps from the court, sees him still faltering on without looking back, and holds him in view.

He repairs to the back of Aldersgate Street, where a door immediately opens to his knocking. She crouches in another door-way, watching that one, and easily comprehending that he puts up temporarily at that house. Her patience is unexhausted by hours. For sustenance she can, and does, buy bread within a hundred yards, and milk as it is carried past her.

He comes forth again at noon, having changed his dress, but carrying nothing in his hand, and having nothing carried for him. He is not going back into the country, therefore, just yet. She follows him a little way, hesitates, instantaneously turns confidently, and goes straight into the house he has quitted.

"Is the gentleman from Cloisterham in doors?"

"Just gone out."

"Unlucky. When does the gentleman return to Cloisterham?"

"At six, this evening."

"Bless ye and thank ye. May the Lord prosper a business where a civil question, even from a poor soul, is so civilly answered!"

"I'll not miss ye twice!" repeats the poor soul in the street, and not so civilly. "I lost ye last where that omnibus you got into nigh your journey's end plied betwixt the station and the place. I wasn't so much as certain that you even went right on to the place. Now I know ye did. My gentleman from Cloisterham, I'll be there before ye and bide your coming. I've sworn my oath that I'll not miss ye twice!"

Accordingly, that same evening the poor soul stands in Cloisterham, High Street, looking at the many quaint gables of the Nuns' House, and getting through the time as she best can until nine o'clock; at which hour she has reason to suppose that the arriving omnibus passengers may have some interest for her. The friendly darkness, at that hour, renders it easy for her to ascertain whether this be so or not; and it is so, for the passenger not to be missed twice arrives among the rest.

"Now, let me see what becomes of you. Go on."

An observation addressed to the air. And yet it might be addressed to the passenger, so compliantly does he go along the High Street until he comes to an arched gateway, at which he unexpectedly vanishes. The poor soul quickens her pace; is swift, and close upon him entering under the gateway; but only sees a postern-staircase on one side of it, and on the other side an ancient vaulted room, in which a large-headed, gray-haired gentleman is writing, under the odd circumstance of sitting open to the thoroughfare and eyeing all who pass, as if he were toll-taker of the gateway; though the way is free.

"Halloa!" he cries, in a low voice, seeing her brought to a standstill; "who are you looking for?"

"There was a gentleman passed in here this minute, sir."

"Of course there was. What do you want with him?"

"Where do he live, deary?"

"Live? Up that staircase."

"Bless ye! Whisper. What's his name, deary?"

"Surname Jasper, Christian name John. Mr. John Jasper."

"Has he a calling, good gentleman?"

"Calling? Yes. Sings in the choir."

"In the spire?"

"Choir."

"What's that?"

Mr. Datchery rises from his papers, and comes to his door-step. "Do you know what a cathedral is?" he asks, jocosely.

The woman nods.

"What is it?"

She looks puzzled, casting about in her mind to find a definition, when it occurs to her that it is easier to point out the substantial object itself, massive against the dark-blue sky and the early stars.

"That's the answer. Go in there at seven to-morrow morning, and you may see Mr. John Jasper, and hear him, too."

"Thank ye! Thank ye!"

The burst of triumph in which she thanks him does not escape the notice of the single buffer of an easy temper living idly on his means. He glances at her; clasps his hands behind him, as the wont of such buffers is; and lounges along the echoing precincts at her side.

"Or," he suggests, with a backward hitch of his head, "you can go up at once to Mr. Jasper's rooms there."

The woman eyes him with a cunning smile, and shakes her head.

"Oh! You don't want to speak to him?"

She repeats her dumb reply, and forms with her lips a soundless "No."

"You can admire him at a distance three times a day, whenever you like. It's a long way to come for that, though."

The woman looks up quickly. If Mr. Datchery thinks she is to be so induced to declare where she comes from, he is of a much easier temper than she is. But she acquits him of such an artful thought, as he lounges along, like the chartered bore of the city, with his uncovered gray hair blowing about, and his purposeless hands rattling the loose money in the pockets of his trousers.

The chink of the money has an attraction for her greedy ears. "Wouldn't you help me to pay for my travellers' lodging, dear gentleman, and to pay my way along? I am a poor soul, I am indeed, and troubled with a grievous cough."

"You know the travellers' lodging, I perceive, and are making directly for it," is Mr. Datchery's bland comment, still rattling his loose money. "Been here often, my good woman?"

"Once in all my life."

"Ay, ay?"

They have arrived at the entrance to the Monk's Vineyard. An appropriate remembrance, presenting an exemplary model for imitation, is revived in the woman's mind by the sight of the place. She stops at the gate, and says, energetically:

"By this token, though you mayn't believe it, that a young gentleman gave me three and sixpence as I was coughing my breath away on this very grass. I asked him for three and sixpence, and he gave it me."

"Wasn't it a little cool to name your sum?" hints Mr. Datchery, still rattling. "Isn't it customary to leave the amount open? Mightn't it have had the appearance, to the young gentleman, only the appearance, that he was rather dictated to?"

"Look'ee here, deary," she replies, in a confidential and persuasive tone, "I wanted the money to lay it out on a medicine as does me good, and as I deal in. I told the young gentleman so, and he gave it me, and I laid it out honest to the last brass farden. I want to lay out the same sum in the same way now; and, if you'll give it me, I'll lay it out honest to the last brass farden again, upon my soul!"

"What's the medicine?"

"I'll be honest with you beforehand, as well as after. It's opium."

Mr. Datchery, with a sudden change of countenance, gives her a sudden look.

"It's opium, deary. Neither more nor less. And it's like a human creetur so far, that you always hear what can be said against it, but seldom what can be said in its praise."

Mr. Datchery begins very slowly to count out the sum demanded of him. Greedily watching his hands, she continues to hold forth on the great example set him.

"It was last Christmas Eve, just arter dark, the once that I was here afore, when the young gentleman gave me the three and six."

Mr. Datchery stops in his counting, finds he has counted wrong, shakes his money together, and begins again.

"And the young gentleman's name," she adds, "was Edwin."

Mr. Datchery drops some money, stoops to pick it up, and reddens with the exertion as he asks:

"How do you know the young gentleman's name?"

"I asked him for it, and he told it me. I only asked him the two questions, what was his Chris'en name, and whether he'd a sweetheart? And he answered, Edwin, and he hadn't."

Mr. Datchery pauses with the selected coins in his hand, rather as if he were falling into a brown study of their value, and couldn't bear to part with them. The woman looks at him distrustfully, and with her anger brewing for the event of his thinking better of the gift; but he bestows it on her as if he were abstracting his mind from the sacrifice, and with many servile thanks she goes her way.

John Jasper's lamp is kindled, and his Lighthouse is shining when Mr. Datchery returns alone toward it. As mariners on a dangerous voyage, approaching an iron-bound coast, may look along the beams of the warning light to the haven lying beyond it that may never be reached, so Mr. Datchery's wistful gaze is directed to this beacon, and beyond.

His object in now revisiting his lodging is merely to put on the hat which seems so superfluous an article in his wardrobe. It is half-past ten by the Cathedral clock when he walks out into the Precincts again; he lingers and looks about him, as though, the enchanted hour when Mr. Durdles may be stoned home having struck, he had some expectation of seeing the Imp who is appointed to the mission of stoning him.

In effect, that Power of Evil is abroad. Having nothing living to stone at the moment, he is discovered by Mr. Datchery in the unholy office of stoning the dead, through the railings of the church-yard. The Imp finds this a relishing and piquing pursuit; firstly, because their resting-place is announced to be sacred; and, secondly, because the tall headstones are sufficiently like themselves, on their beat in the dark, to justify the delicious fancy that they are hurt when hit.

Mr. Datchery hails him with: "Halloa, Winks!"

He acknowledges the hail with: "Halloa, Dick!" Their acquaintance seemingly having been established on a familiar footing.

"But, I say," he remonstrates, "don't yer go a-making my name public. I never means to plead to no name, mind yer. When they says to me in the Lock-up, a-going to put me down in the book, 'What's your name?' I says to them, 'Find out.' Likeways when they says, 'What's your religion?' I says, 'Find out.'"

Which, it may be observed in passing, it would be immensely difficult for the State, however statistical, to do.

"Asides which," adds the boy, "there ain't no family of Winkses."

"I think there must be."

"Yer lie, there ain't. The travellers give me the name on account of my getting no settled sleep and being knocked up all night; whereby I gets one eye roused open afore I've shut the other. That's what Winks means. Deputy's the nighest name to indict me by; but yer wouldn't catch me pleading to that, neither."

"Deputy be it always, then. We two are good friends; eh, Deputy?"

"Jolly good."

"I forgave you the debt you owed me when we first became acquainted, and many of my sixpences have come your way since; eh, Deputy?"

"Ah! And what's more, yer ain't no friend o' Jarsper's. What did he go a histing me off my legs for?"

"What, indeed! But never mind him now. A shilling of mine is going your way to-night, Deputy. You have just taken in a lodger I have been speaking to; an infirm woman with a cough."

"Puffer," assents Deputy, with a shrewd leer of recognition, and smoking an imaginary pipe, with his head very much on one side, and his eyes very much out of their places; "Hopeum Puffer."

"What is her name?"

"'Er Royal Highness the Princess Puffer."

"She has some other name than that; where does she live?"

"Up in London. Among the Jacks."

"The sailors?"

"I said so; Jacks. And Chayer men. And hother Knifers."

"I should like to know, through you, exactly where she lives."

"All right. Give us 'old."

A shilling passes; and, in that spirit of confidence which should pervade all business transactions between principals of honor, this piece of business is considered done.

"But here's a lark!" cries Deputy. "Where did yer think 'Er Royal Highness is a-goin' to, to-morrow morning?" Blest if she ain't a-goin' to the KIN-FREE-DER-EL!" He greatly prolongs the word in his ecstasy, and smites his leg, and doubles himself up in a fit of shrill laughter.

"How do you know that, Deputy?"

"Cos she told me so just now. She said she must he hup and hout o' purpose. She ses, 'Deputy, I must 'ave a early wash, and make mysel as swell as I can, for I'm a-goin' to take a turn at the KIN-FREE-DER-EL!'" He separates the syllables with his former zest, and, not finding his sense of the ludicrous sufficiently relieved by stamping about on the pavement, breaks into a slow and stately dance, perhaps supposed to be performed by the Dean.

Mr. Datchery receives the communication with a well-satisfied though a pondering face, and breaks up the conference. Returning to his quaint lodging, and sitting long over the supper of bread and cheese and salad and ale which Mrs. Tope has left prepared for him, he still sits when his supper is finished. At length he rises, throws open the door of a corner cupboard, and refers to a few uncouth chalked strokes on its inner side.

"I like," says Mr. Datchery, "the old tavern way of keeping scores.

Illegible, except to the scorer. The scorer not committed, the scored debited with what is against him. Hum; ha! A very small score this; a very poor score!"

He sighs over the contemplation of its poverty, takes a bit of chalk from one of the cupboard-shelves, and pauses with it in his hand, uncertain what addition to make to the account.

"I think a moderate stroke," he concludes, "is all I am justified in scoring up;" so, suits the action to the word, closes the cupboard, and goes to bed.

A brilliant morning shines on the old city. Its antiquities and ruins are surpassingly beautiful, with the lusty ivy gleaming in the sun, and the rich trees waving in the balmy air. Changes of glorious light from moving boughs, songs of birds, scents from gardens, woods, and fields—or, rather, from one great garden of the whole cultivated island in its yielding time—penetrate into the Cathedral, subdue its earthy odor, and preach the Resurrection and the Life. The cold stone tombs of centuries ago grow warm; and flecks of brightness dart into the sternest marble corners of the building, fluttering there like wings.

Comes Mr. Tope with his large keys, and yawningly unlocks and sets open. Come Mrs. Tope and attendant sweeping sprites. Come, in due time, organist and bellows-boy, peeping down from the red curtains in the loft, fearlessly flapping dust from books up at that remote elevation, and whisking it from stops and pedals. Come sundry rooks, from various quarters of the sky, back to the great tower, who may be presumed to enjoy vibration, and to know that bell and organ are going to give it them. Come a very small and straggling congregation indeed: chiefly from Minor Canon Corner and the Precincts. Come Mr. Crisparkle, fresh and bright; and his ministering brethren, not quite so fresh and bright. Come the Choir in a hurry (always in a hurry, and struggling into their night-gowns at the last moment, like children shirking bed), and comes John Jasper leading their line. Last of all comes Mr. Datchery into a stall, one of a choice empty collection very much at his service, and glancing about him for Her Royal Highness the Princess Puffer.

The service is pretty well advanced before Mr. Datchery can discern Her Royal Highness. But by that time he has made her out, in the shade. She is behind a pillar, carefully withdrawn from the Choirmaster's view, but regards him with the closest attention. All unconscious of her presence, he chants and sings. She grins when he is most musically fervid, and—yes, Mr. Datchery sees her do it!—shakes her fist at him behind the pillar's friendly shelter.

Mr. Datchery looks again to convince himself. Yes, again! As ugly and withered as one of the fantastic carvings on the under brackets of the stall-seats, as malignant as the Evil One, as hard as the big brass eagle holding the sacred books upon his wings (and, according to the sculptor's representation of his ferocious attributes, not at all converted by them), she hugs herself in her lean arms, and then shakes both fists at the leader of the Choir.

And at that moment, outside the grated door of the Choir, having eluded the vigilance of Mr. Tope by shifty resources in which he is an adept, Deputy peeps, sharp-eyed, through the bars, and stares astounded from the threatener to the threatened.

The service comes to an end, and the servitors disperse to breakfast. Mr. Datchery accosts his last new acquaintance outside, when the Choir (as much in a hurry to get their bed-gowns off as they were but now to get them on) have scuffled away.

"Well, mistress. Good-morning. You have seen him?"

"*I*'ve seen him, deary; *I*'ve seen him!"

"And you know him?"

"Know him! Better far than all the Reverend Parsons put together know him."

Mrs. Tope's care has spread a very neat, clean breakfast ready for her lodger. Before sitting down to it, he opens his corner-cupboard door; takes his bit of chalk from its shelf; adds one thick line to the score, extending from the top of the cupboard door to the bottom; and then falls to with an appetite.

CHAPTER XXI.

WHAT THE ORGAN SAID.

THE Choir has taken its departure. The Choir Leader has *not* taken his departure, but remains after the others have gone, as is his wont at times, — only the bellows-boy keeping him company.

He is seated before the organ now and plays one of those sublime sonatas of Beethoven's; and as its cadences rise and fall through the master-touch of his hand, he appears lost in the sweetness of the harmony which his own hands produce. As some strain sweeter than the one preceding it gushes from the instrument, he fancies that the air is filled with sweet voices; anon, when the Melody breaks out in more sonorous chords, he feels that a presence of Something is standing near him, and, with a voice whose tones are like the moaning of the winds, murmurs a name—the name of Edwin Drood!

Still he plays on, seeing naught but the instrument before him, while the Melody still proceeds from its hundred throats.

Now he hears another and yet sweeter voice proceeding from the Melody—a sad, sweet voice—murmuring a name that brings to his mind a fair young girl, who, years before, had wakened from a dream of love to find that she had been deceived and left to die of a broken heart.

Still the Melody goes on;—There is a slight rustle in the aisle—soft steps approach him—but still he hears naught but the voices, and the Melody continues. Softly, yet nearer, approach the footsteps; slyly they betake themselves behind the organ. Possibly the mind of the bellows-boy being so absorbed with the sweet strains of the Melody is the reason that he does not, at first, hear or observe her as she stands beside him. Possibly the mind of *no* bellows-boy ever gave evidence of undergoing greater fear, as, a moment after, his eyes encounter her weird figure. Giving one scream, he is soon out of sight, leaving the Choir Leader gazing on a face that is peering at him, with bleared eyes, from behind the organ,—and he recognizes the Princess Puffer.

Mingled doubt and surprise come upon the Jasper face; astonishment seems to have paralyzed the Jasper lips, for not one word escapes them. The old woman, however, does not appear to share his discomfiture, but with a cunning smile and cat-like step, approaches him. He has risen to his feet now, and, standing by his side, she puts her face close to his and whispers:

"Deary, my poor lungs was that bad that I'd need go for change of air to make 'em better; so I come here to get it. It's many a long year, lovey, since I'd see'd the inside o' holy walls; so I come in here with the rest on 'em; and afore five minutes had gone arter, I see'd ye up here; I was that glad when I know'd it were you that I waved my hand to ye but ye didn't see it—so, says I, I'll wait and maybe I'll git a chance to speak with him, if so be no one is by to see."

John Jasper has recovered himself now, but with a face pale with anger at the familiarity of the woman. He realizes that it will be useless to deny his identity, or to feign ignorance concerning her, and therefore assumes a pleasant tone and asks what her business may be with him.

"All for your good, lamby—all for your good; it's Heaven's mercy that I comed across ye as I 'ave. Ye'll 'ave no need to fear that I'll know ye now, deary—'cos I does. And it's a blessin' for ye; for now ye'll want me to come this way at times, and fetch some of my best with me. I'll be at the Twopenny, you see, and in a quiet way let ye know as I've come. And I'll fetch the best allers, with pipe and mixter—and ye can 'ave it right in your own lodgin's; no more riskin' your precious life climbin' them rickety old stairs, as has nearly been my death at times afore I got used to 'em. I wouldn't do this for every one, deary—and wouldn't for you, only that I've took a interest in ye."

Mr. Jasper does not appear to reciprocate the friendship which the Puffer professes for him; he merely nods his head, and asks—

"What other motive have you in seeking this interview?"

A violent fit of coughing prevents an immediate reply, but after it has subsided, she says:

"Don't say it was motive, deary, for ye know in your heart it wasn't. All chance, my seein' on ye, and that's the truth. But now, as we are here by ourselves, deary, and no one by, it may be as ye'd like to talk some more about the journey beyond the seas. Likely ye may need help afore ye're half done with it, lovey, and I'll stand your friend, never fear."

This last with a sly, cunning look, that spoke more than any words could utter.

Very earnestly did John Jasper gaze into the face of the old woman, as if to read her inmost soul; while she returned his gaze, keeping the same leer upon her features as when she ceased speaking. After a moment he bursts into a hearty laugh. Walking a short distance from her and then returning again, he says:

"My dear woman, the unfortunate habit that I have acquired—the use of opium—has brought me in contact with strange company. It also led me to seek you, which I should never have done had I supposed you the imbecile that you show yourself to be to-day. But I am disposed to be charitable and believe you to be laboring under the effects of a recent debauch. Therefore, I will only say this—Do you go back to London immediately and never let me see you here again, or many a pound that would otherwise go to you will be paid to some one of your rivals. Do you understand me?"

He is looking sternly into her face as he ceases, while she returns the look, still with the cunning smile upon her features.

"Well, well, deary," is her answer, in a conciliatory tone, "I only hope as ye'll forgive an old 'ooman who only thought as she might be of service to ye. I'll not come agin since ye don't wish it, lamby, but I'll allers have the best for ye when ye come to see me. God's blessin' on ye, sir, good-bye;" and is seized with another violent coughing fit, which lasts till she has passed through the Cathedral door.

She proceeds in the direction of the Travellers' Twopenny, and when she reaches a position where she is sure the Music Master cannot perceive her, she shakes her fist at the Cathedral in a savage manner, muttering the while—

"So, so, my jackey-duck! and ye think to rid yourself of me so easily? I know ye now for sure. Ye may deceive some but ye don't me. My time ain't come yet; it will come soon enough. I can afford to wait!" and so passes out of sight.

Mr. Jasper hopes that no one has observed her as she left the Cathedral, lest he may be annoyed with questions. Hence Mr. Jasper gazes eagerly out of window to learn if she is perceived. He follows her with his eyes till she is lost from sight, and is just turning to leave the window, when he hears a voice close outside the door, half chanting a refrain that he had heard before:

Widdy widdy wen!
I—ket—ches—im—out—ar—ter—ten.
Widdy widdy why,
Then—E—don't—go—then—I—shy—
Widdy widdy, Wake-cock warnin!

"Troubles never come singly," is an old adage and proves a true one in Jasper's case, for no sooner had he been relieved of the old woman's presence, and was just flattering himself that she had not been observed, than he turns to whence the voice proceeds and discovers the Deputy, with eyes and mouth wide open, gazing steadily at him through the half-open door.

He walks leisurely towards the boy, and on reaching the door, finds that young gentleman has taken himself to the opposite side of the way from where he is eyeing the Music Master in a very defiant manner, and moreover has armed himself with a good-sized stone which he holds in his hand in such a way that a very proper inference could be drawn of the use he intends to make of it should occasion require.

"What do you mean by disturbing me with your noise, boy?" asks Jasper, and moves nearer to where the boy stands.

"I wan't a-disturbin' on yer," is the answer, retreating a few steps, "and don't yer go a touchin' me, or I'll sling this 'ere flint at yer 'ed; yer bust my braces once, Jarsper, but yer won't do it agin."

"I don't want to hurt you, blockhead," said Jasper, as a sudden thought came to him. Then taking some silver from his pocket, he continued: "I want you to do me a service and I'll reward you."

"What is it?" enquires the Deputy, still eyeing the other doubtfully.

"Come closer to me and I'll tell you," is the answer.

"Yer ain't a-foolin' on me?" enquires the boy, suspiciously.

"Why should I deceive you?" is the reply.

"Say yer 'opes as yer'll be busted if yer fool me," returns the Deputy.

"Well," rejoins Jasper, good-humouredly, "I hope I may be busted."

"All right, Jarsper," returns the boy, and comes over to where the other stands. "Now what do yer want a feller to do?"

"First, I want to know if you saw the person who passed out from the Cathedral a few moments since, and if you would know her again?"

"If I said as I didn't see her, I'd lie," is the answer; "and if I said as I'd know her agin, I'd tell the truth."

"Very good," said Jasper. "Now I want you to follow her, and tell me where she goes, and find out if she returns to London; do this faithfully and you shall have a shilling for the service,—and don't attempt to deceive me," he continues, "or I'll flog the life out of you."

"Jarsper, I don't fool no one," returns the Deputy; "when I says I'll do anythin' I allers does it. But where shall I come for the shillin'?" adds the boy.

"Come to my lodgings in an hour—that will give you time—and if I am convinced that you have been faithful, you will have no cause to complain."

The boy gave one long, shrill whistle; then throwing the stone, which he had continued to hold in his hand, as a precautionary measure, at an imaginary Durdles in the shape of a post on the opposite way, ran briskly off in the direction of the Travellers' Twopenny.

CHAPTER XXII.

A LIGHT BREAKS ON STAPLE INN.

One morning, a few days after the scenes narrated in the preceding chapter, Mr. Grewgious, having just returned from his customary morning call on Rosa, is seated at his desk apparently in deep thought, occasionally casting a glance at Bazzard, who is seated near him at another desk, engaged in writing, and so intent upon his work that he does not raise his eyes therefrom. Several times does Mr. Grewgious seem on the point of addressing his busy companion, and then thinking better of it, falls to meditating again. It was during one of these meditations that a stranger had entered unannounced, and stood midway between the door and Mr. Grewgious ere he was observed by the latter; and he might have remained in that position a much longer time, had he not, in quite a loud voice, enquired if there was "Any one at home?"

For such an exceedingly Angular Man, Mr. Grewgious gave a sudden start, while Bazzard dropped his pen and stared at the new-comer very much as he would have done had he beheld his employer standing on his head. The surprise which his presence had created, caused the new-comer to smile; remarking that he was sorry to cause them annoyance, but that he had knocked at the door some little time, and, no one answering the summons, he had made bold to enter.

"And you did perfectly right, sir," replies Grewgious, approaching the visitor, "perfectly right, sir. The apology should come from us. Should not the apology come from us, Bazzard?"

Being thus appealed to, Mr. Bazzard, who has hardly recovered himself, is heard to say:

"I follow you, sir," and then falls to following the work before him, which had been so suddenly interrupted.

The visitor proves to be no less a personage than Mr. Datchery, who places his hand upon the back of the chair proffered him by Grewgious, and informs that gentleman that he has called on business of a private nature, and could they be alone for a short time?

"Certainly," pleasantly returns Grewgious, but manifesting no little surprise upon his countenance, as he lead the way to an inner apartment.

On entering the room, Datchery begs permission to bolt the door, which, being granted, he proceeds to do, remarking as he does it that he is glad it is a bolt, for keyholes have done a good deal of mischief in their day. Both gentlemen are seated now, and Datchery abruptly introduces himself:

"Mr. Grewgious, my name is Datchery, and I am from Cloisterham."

On hearing Cloisterham mentioned, Mr. Grewgious' mind instantly reverts to the mysterious occurrence of Christmas time and he thinks it possible the visitor is about to impart some information that is to throw light upon it. He bows his head as an intimation that he should be glad to hear more.

"It don't matter," continues Datchery, "at this time, that I should say more about myself. Whatever else I have to say is of a matter that directly concerns you, and one you have under your charge; I am actuated solely by a desire to benefit those who need assistance in their troubles. I think you will understand my position, and will not attribute such questions as I may ask to mere idle curiosity. Do you go along with me, sir?"

Says Mr. Grewgious: "So far as I can with propriety answer your questions, I will. You will allow me to observe, however, that this interview is a little—well, shall I say abrupt? I think you will agree with me. However, presuming that you refer to the disappearance of Edwin Drood, I shall be glad to assist you in any way that I can, or with any facts that I possess."

"You are correct in your surmises, sir," rejoins Datchery, "and now that you *have* inferred what are my motives, we shall get along very comfortably, no doubt."

A pause, and then Datchery:—

"Will you please tell me, Mr. Grewgious, if you have ever settled upon any theory which would account for the sudden taking off of that young man; that is, do you believe, from any knowledge of the circumstances which surrounded him, that his absence is voluntary, or do you believe that there was any person who could have had an interest in putting him out of the way by violence?"

For causes best known to himself, Mr. Grewgious did not immediately reply to his questioner; most probably for the reason that he *had* settled upon a theory which was in no wise complimentary to a certain person he could name. Another reason was, that this Mr. Datchery might only be, after all, acting in the interest of the person he had suspected, and possibly this visit might have been arranged for the express purpose of leading him (Mr. Grewgious) to make some statement in which he should compromise himself.

Mr. Datchery, looking anxiously at Mr. Grewgious, meanwhile, awaiting his reply, finally hears it:

"My dear sir; it would not be doing justice to myself, were I to say that I have settled upon any thing definite in the matter. In fact, I have held so many theories in regard to it, that I have not been able to settle on any one of them. But when I consider, or when others consider, what an exceedingly Angular Man I am by nature, I am not surprised at the unsatisfactory result of my theories, nor do I suppose any one else will wonder thereat."

The speaker, delivering these words with great hesitation, twists about in his chair in a nervous manner, seeming to feel that, notwithstanding his caution, he has possibly compromised himself in what he has said.

Mr. Datchery notices the doubt with which the other regards him, and is a little annoyed thereat, but keeps it to himself, and pleasantly replies, though in earnest tones:

"I regret that you cannot feel sufficient confidence in me to warrant a definite reply to my question. I assure you, sir, that my sole object is to subserve the interests of those whose welfare you seek, and I emphatically repeat that your opinion in this matter will aid materially in solving this mystery. Now, will you kindly favor me with your belief and say if you think Edwin Drood has been murdered, or that he has voluntarily taken himself away?"

The earnestness with which Mr. Datchery prefaced his last question seemed to inspire Mr. Grewgious with more confidence than he had before entertained, and his reply indicated as much:

"As I before remarked, I have held no settled opinion concerning the affair, for I have had no better opportunity of arriving at facts than any one else; nor so good an opportunity as some others have had; for instance, his relative, say—Mr. Jasper; and, if it would not be improper for a person of my Peculiar Habits to venture such a remark, I should say, with all due respect to that Musical Personage, that he would be the proper person, as his kinsman, to set the wheels of investigation in motion, and so grind out the facts."

Mr. Grewgious' reference to John Jasper was put in his most Angular manner, and Mr. Grewgious' eyes had a most Angular expression, as he turned them upon his listener. If his object in introducing that individual's name was to turn the subject of their conversation upon the Music-master, it proved successful, for Datchery immediately said:

"And what do you think of Mr. Jasper? I understand he took the loss of his nephew very much to heart, and has sworn to ferret out, unaided, his assassin."

"My dear sir, pardon me if I do not choose to give my opinion in that direction. I do not deny, mind you, that I *have* an opinion, but I prefer to keep it."

"As you please, sir," returns Datchery, "but allow me to ask you one thing more, and I hope you will feel at liberty to give me a definite reply, for on your answer will depend very much the course I intend to pursue; and, let me add, that I am determined to do all in my power to unravel this mystery. Would John Jasper have any interest in the death of Edwin Drood, and, if so, what?"

The earnest tone and eager look that accompanied the latter portion of the speaker's remark, were not lost upon Grewgious, who gazed steadily at him as he closed the sentence.

Who could this man be, he thought, that seemed so deeply interested in one who was neither kith nor kin to him?

"Well, I will be candid with you," replies Mr. Grewgious, and speaking very earnestly now. "I *do* believe that Edwin Drood has been foully dealt with—by whom I *do not* know. Perhaps it is a bold remark to hazard to a stranger, but I will venture it, notwithstanding; I do believe—believe, mind you—that John Jasper did have an interest in the death of his nephew; though what that interest was I am not prepared to say."

"Thank you for your confidence, sir, and let me assure you it is not misplaced. Once more, and I am done. Has Miss Bud mourned the loss of young Drood? Do you think she ever had any affection for him?"

If Mr. Grewgious was staggered at the former questions of his visitor, he was double-staggered at the last. What possible object could the man have in asking that? He recovers himself in a moment, but makes answer in a somewhat lofty tone:

"Miss Bud, being a young lady of tender sympathies, would very naturally, under the circumstances, grieve for the loss of a young man whose life had been so closely identified with her own up to the time of his taking off. She *does* mourn for him constantly. There is nothing strange in that, I should suppose."

"Far from it, sir," returns the other, "but having heard something of the romance connected with the two, I felt some curiosity to learn the truth of certain statements that I have heard, which declared that no affection existed between them. And now, Mr. Grewgious," continues Datchery, rising from his chair, "permit me to thank you for the courtesy you have shown me, as well as for your confidence. From what I have gathered from you, I can lay my plans for finding out more in another quarter. Good-morning; we shall meet again at no distant day, be sure."

Returning to where they had left Bazzard, Mr. Grewgious instructs that gentleman to show the visitor out, and Bazzard, rising to do so, at the same time making answer, "I follow you, sir," causes Mr. Datchery to look round and utter in a curt tone, that if he (Bazzard) follows him beyond the door, it is more than likely that the person who cooks his dinner will not need to get a plate for him to-day. Which saying, being overheard by Grewgious, causes him to smile at Datchery's mistake, while Bazzard stands with his hand still on the door, undecided whether he ought to apologize to the irate Datchery or otherwise.

Proceeding directly back to Cloisterham, where he arrives in due time, Datchery has nearly reached his lodgings at Tope's, when he perceives approaching him in an opposite direction the form and features of no less a person than the Choir Leader, who is so engrossed with his thoughts that he does not observe his fellow-lodger, but is making straight by him; whereat, Mr. Datchery accosts him, thus:

"An old buffer like me must keep his eyes sharp about him, when such folks as you go along with their heads down," and smiles in a good-humoured way upon Jasper.

The latter, coming to a sudden halt, apologizes for his rudeness, adding: "My mind is occupied with a very unpleasant subject to-day, and I have just started for a walk, thinking to obtain relief."

"A young man's mind should never be occupied with unpleasant subjects, lest the wine of life grows stale ere the bottle is half emptied. Might I enquire the nature of your distress?"

"No new thing," replies Jasper, in a despondent tone; "I presume you have heard how a dear nephew of mine disappeared a few months since, under circumstances that lead to the belief that he was foully dealt with."

"I have heard it mentioned," returns Datchery, with something like a twinkle in his eye, but which is not observed by the other, "and should have taken more interest in it, no doubt, had I been a younger man; but an old buffer like me, that has knocked about most of the world, gets used to those sort of things. You were very much attached to each other, however, and that, of course, alters the case."

"Attached is not the word, sir," replies Jasper, mournfully; "I loved him like my life, which I would gladly have given for him."

"Well, Mr. Jasper," returns Datchery, assuming a tone of sympathy, "I am sorry that you take his loss so hard, for it don't help the matter; but are you quite sure that he is really dead? Is it not possible that, after all, he has gone off in a boyish freak, just to try the affection of his friends; and that he will return, when you least expect him, to laugh at your fears? Cheer up, man; don't give way to melancholy till there is proof positive that he is dead."

"You mean well, I have no doubt," is Jasper's answer, "but so long a time has elapsed since his disappearance, that I feel warranted in believing I shall never see him again."

Mr. Datchery places his hand upon his forehead as though struggling to remember something, and then resumes:

"If I remember aright, there were strong suspicions attached to a young man about his own age. Was it a—yes, I'm sure that's what I heard—a pupil of Mr. Crisparkle's? Was there, do you think, anything on which to base those suspicions?"

Mr. Datchery, while speaking, is staring straight at the heavens; when he ceases speaking he drops his eyes suddenly, and, fixing them upon the Choir Leader, is staring straight in that gentleman's face. Knowing Datchery to be an eccentric person is probably the reason why Jasper does not appear to notice the singular look, but replies to his question:

"Yes, I think there was; at least, enough to satisfy me; but, though every effort was made to discover the traces of his guilt, no positive evidence could be obtained, and he is allowed to go unpunished, when every one is satisfied of his guilt. Even the Mayor, before whom the investigation took place, said it had a dark look. But yet he could not be held upon the evidence. I have tried to believe him innocent, for my conscience would never allow me a moment's peace, if I thought I was accusing an innocent man."

"Well said, sir; well said. In these days, when mankind is so prone to believe every evil word that is spoken of their fellows, without stopping to ascertain the truth, it sounds well to hear a man say that he would not charge upon an innocent person that of which he is not guilty. But did no suspicion attach to other parties?"

Mr. Jasper, looking sharply into his questioner's face and hesitating a moment as if not quite understanding the question, does not reply; whereat Datchery calmly returns the look and repeats the question.

"I do not think that suspicion attached to any other person, nor do I think there was reason to suspect any other than the one just mentioned."

Mr. Datchery hems twice, and then remains silent, as though expecting the Music Master to continue.

"It is a sad subject to me," Jasper adds, after the awkward pause, "as you will readily understand, and one which I strive to avoid; still I am no less determined to ferret it to the bottom, and time will tell whether I accuse any person unjustly. But I must ask you to pardon me if I leave you abruptly; I have an appointment, and the time is near at hand," and proceeds on his way, while Datchery turns into his lodgings, muttering that "the time *is* near at hand, and the *man*, too."

Mr. Datchery's first act, after removing his hat, is to repair to the cupboard-door on which his score was affixed, and add thereto a moderate stroke, remarking at the same time:

"This begins to assume a business-like appearance; it won't be long before the scores are even, and then we will compare pages; it may be some little time yet ere we shall reach that end, but it will surely come, and the reckoning will prove a strange one when it is made. God help the debtor, for he'll need it!"

Then he resumes his hat, and leaving his lodgings, hastens off in the direction of the Crozier. Arriving there, he ascends to a room on the second landing, and knocks softly at the door, which is opened a very little way at first, and then is thrown wide open for Datchery to enter, which he does, the door being quickly closed; and if a passer-by had listened to the shouts of laughter that now and then emanated from that room, he would have concluded that it contained a merry company indeed.

CHAPTER XXIII.

JOHN JASPER HAS AN INTERVIEW WITH AN AGENT, AND THE READER HAS AN INTRODUCTION TO THE PADLERS.

If John Jasper's feelings were not pleasant ones when he fell in with Datchery, they had not mended much when parting from him, were his face to be taken as an index of his mind, for it wears a very cloudy and stern appearance, as he continues his walk with rapid step down the High street of the old city. Never once looking to the right or left, he walks on with the same moody expression on his features, until he reaches a cross street leading directly to the river. Then he glances hastily about him, as though to assure himself that he is not observed; apparently satisfied on that point, he turns the corner, and proceeds with the same rapid step towards his destination.

This street bore anything but an aristocratic air in the appearance of its dwellings, and was in every way decidedly dirty. The crossings were filthy; the footpaths were dilapidated, like the houses which they fronted; and one could hardly have imagined them to be inhabited by anything human, were it not for an occasional smell of onions, or some other savory vegetable, which now and then steamed up from the basements to indicate to the passer-by that if their occupants had forgotten how to be clean, they still recognized the importance of having something to eat.

Cloisterham could boast, it seemed, like its more pretentious neighbor, the Great City, of having poverty in its midst; and though, like its more pretentious neighbor, it tried to shut its eyes to the fact, they would not stay shut, for now and then some circumstance would present itself, which made the fact decidedly convincing. About midway between the High street and the water was one house which commanded more attention than any other, from its kingly tumble-down appearance, and as this narrative could not well go on without an introduction to one of its inmates, we will go in through the street-door, which is seldom closed, and ascend a flight of stairs that once boasted of a railing, but is now shorn of that useful appendage, probably because, at some remote period, coals were not plenty in that neighborhood.

Ascending the stairs and gaining the landing, from some three or four doors we will select the one in the darkest corner and enter. The room was occupied by three persons.

One of these persons was a man, apparently about thirty or thirty-five years of age, with black hair and eyes, and eye-brows so thick and bushy that it was no wonder the eyes beneath them were sunk far into the head, as though they were being crowded by degrees entirely out of sight. He possessed an athletic frame and high cheek bones, and had a slow, awkward motion in all his movements. It would be difficult to determine his nationality were it not that his speech indicated him to be an Englishman. His dress was decidedly slouchy — nothing that he wore seemed to fit him. Although there was a slight sinister expression on his features, there was, at the same time, a pleasant, devil-may-care look so mixed with it, that even a skilled physiognomist would have been puzzled to decide the character of the man from reading his features. He had been christened with the name of Forbes, but as he grew in years his friends and more intimate associates had seen fit, for some reason best known to themselves, to address him as Fopperty, and he continued to hold that cognomen to the present time. Speaking of his first name naturally leads us to his last one, and that was Padler. So, then, we will introduce to you, ladies and gentlemen, Fopperty Padler, and proceed to the next one of the trio.

This was Mrs. Padler, mother of the aforesaid, and if appearances did not deceive, she could not have been far from sixty or seventy, — in fact, an old woman, and a very wicked old woman, if all that the neighbors hinted were true. She was short, thick-set, with stooping shoulders, and nature or disease had caused one of her limbs to be shorter than the other, so that when she walked she reminded one very forcibly of the walking-beam* of a steamer. Her face was of a

* Some "reliable authority" having criticised an extract that was taken from this work prior to its publication in book form, has stated it as *his* opinion that an English reader would fail to comprehend the term here given. With all due respect for the superior judgment of this "reliable authority," whoever he may be, I shall beg to differ with him, and give it as *my* opinion that if, in the United Kingdom, a man, woman, or child can be found who does *not*

dirty white color, and such hair as she had was of nearly the same shade, and as she brushed it back, and made a very small pug, which she fastened to the crown of her head, it resembled more than anything else a very, very small ball of yarn, after the cat has had it to play with for a few hours. At the time we introduce this good soul she seems to be a little out of temper, or a little *into* temper, which is, perhaps, the most correct way of expressing being decidedly cross.

The cause of these unpleasant feelings would seem to have sprung from something that the last of the trio had been doing — a little child, a girl — who might have been ten years old, and who looks so entirely unlike those by whom she is surrounded, that it seems astonishing how she comes to be in their company. Her habiliments, it is true, would show her to be one of the world's poor — one of those little waifs whom nobody cares for, and who soon enough (God help them!) learn to care for nobody. But there is a distinguishing characteristic in the face of this child that stamps her of a nobler nature than the average of this class of children. It is an intelligent face, with large, full, blue eyes, that wear a thoughtful expression, though now the tears are standing in them, for she is weeping.

Her beautiful brown hair falls in dishevelled masses over her shoulders, as though it were kindly striving to shield from vulgar gaze what her poor, ragged dress could not cover. This was Bessie Padler, who called the woman at her side grandmother, but who, the neighbors slyly hinted among themselves, was really no relative. That some hidden mystery surrounded her, they did not doubt. One thing they were sure of — the old woman did not hesitate to beat her, and she had a miserable existence. But it could not be helped, that any one could see, and there the matter ended.

"Ain't ye never goin' to 'ave any sense, or 'ave I took a born idjiot to bring up?" cries the old woman, in the torrent of her wrath, addressing the child. "What's the good in all my talkin' and advisin' on ye if ye don't mean to 'arken to it and live up to it? Do ye think as we've so much gold and siller we ken give some to every little sick brat as 'appens to live hereabouts? Ain't it a good thing, now," addressing Fopperty, "ain't it a nice thing for us to 'ave a good Smarahan — (Mrs. Padler means Samaritan) — in the family, Fopperty; and a barefooted one at that?" Here the old lady gives vent to a series of croaks intended for a laugh of derision. "Givin' her sixpences," continues the beldame, "to strangers as cares nothin' for her, when her

know what a walking (or working) beam is, in connection with marine engines, that man, woman, or child must have first seen the light of day in that country where Sir John Franklin last saw it, and must have been a very recent importation, indeed.

poor old grandmother is sufferin' this blissed minnit for the very money to buy her gin with, which every doctor as is a doctor will say is the only thing as keeps the breath o' life in her; take that, you devil's shadder," and strikes the child in the face with a blow that nearly fells her to the floor, and which she would have repeated had not Fopperty interposed by arresting her uplifted hands.

"Hold hard, mem, hold hard!" and steps between them; "you've reached a pint where the turn comes. Bess hain't done such a dreadful thing, after all, and you know it. Billy Blagut saved her from drowndin' when she tumbled in the river that time, and it's only fair she should do him a good turn now, when he needs it. Another thing, I'm looking for some one every minit, and he musn't see this 'ere girl a-cryin'. Now, mem, as I was saying, you've reached a pint where the turn comes, so be satisfied to stop there, and by-and-by I'll take a turn and bring you a pint of 'alf-and-'alf as will make you wink." This last seems to soften the old lady a bit, and Fopperty lifts the child into a chair beside him, and endeavors to lead her thoughts from herself by speaking of the sick boy.

"I suppose Billy was glad you brought him the orange, Bessie, wasn't he? Dry your eyes now, and tell me all about it."

Glad of an opportunity to be released from the abuse of the old woman, the child proceeded to tell Fopperty that she had been to the house of the sick boy, and had learned from his mother that he was recovering, and that he had expressed a wish for an orange, but that she could not afford to purchase one; and that, after a little time, she had left the house, on her way home, when she found a sixpence, which some one had dropped upon the crossing. That she had hurried off as fast as she could run, and investing the money in the desired fruit, had hastened with it to the bedside of the sick boy.

"And oh, how happy I felt, Fopperty!" she concluded; "you know we poor children don't have such luxuries when we are well, so it must be that God intends them for us when we are sick. Did I do wrong, Fopperty? He saved my life, you know," she added, as though she thought that fact should mitigate the wrong, if there was any.

"Devil a bit," is the reply, and gently stroking the child's forehead; "I'm glad to see you show such a good trait, Bess. Though where you ever learned it, I don't know; certainly not from me or the old woman. You're a good little girl, Bessie, and though I sometimes get one-sided and curse things right and left, and don't always treat you as gentle as I ought, I won't stand by and see others abuse ye, if I know it," and looks at his mother in a meaning way, that would say "You're included mem."

The ancient Padler blood resumes its boiling, and the ancient Padler resumes her feet; with an air of mock-politeness she approaches the child and standing before her, says:

"Miss Padler, I suppose it will be expected, after what my son has just said, that I should humbly ask your parding and promise better manners. P'raps I'd better say, too, now I'm about it, that bein' no use round 'ere, and havin' no business in my own house, is why I ought to ask you, Miss Padler, kindly to allow me to remain, and after this I'll allers give you your own way and say nothink."

"There, mother," interposes Fopperty, "that will do; you know—"

A knock at the door interrupts what else he was about to say, and quickly pushing the child toward his mother, he ejaculates:

"Here, mem, quick; take Bess and go into the other room. The man I'm expectin' has come. Treat her gently now, and no nonsense while he's here, or it'll be the worse for you when he's gone—hurry!"

Thus urged, Mrs. Padler takes the child's arm and leads, or rather see-saws her to the adjoining room just as Fopperty opens the door to Mr. Jasper, and to whom he says:

"I've been some time lookin' for you, sir, and had almost given up your coming. I agreed to wait though, and I've done it."

"Glad to hear it, Padler," is Jasper's answer; "but we will proceed at once with the business that brought me here."

Fopperty placing some chairs, the two are seated, and Jasper resumes:

"Is Bessie—the child for whose father some very foolish people took me—with you now?"

"We are taking care of Bessie yet," is the rejoinder, "and I think the less we say about her father the better. She's a good girl, and deserves a better fâther, whoever he may be."

The Jasper face turns a little red at this, but its owner only says:

"I merely enquired because it's a long time since I've seen you, and probably should not have seen you now, only that I learned, a few days since, while in London, that you had come to this out-of-the-world place to live."

"And did you make an appointment to meet me here, to tell me that only?" asks Fopperty, doggedly.

"Far from it," answers the other, smiling pleasantly to pacify his companion, who evidently had lost his temper. "I will proceed at once to the business that brought me. It is a business that requires great caution in its management, and you will be well-paid therefor." Jasper, evidently at a loss how to proceed, pauses a moment and then continues:

"There lives in Bloomsbury Square a woman by the name of Billickin." Jasper pauses again.

"To which I don't object," returns Fopperty, and waits for the other to continue.

"There is a young lady lodging there through whom I desire to ascertain the whereabouts of another person. What I want you to do is to obtain lodgings in that house if possible and watch the lady; follow her whenever she goes out, and learn if possible if she calls on persons by the name of Landless—a brother and sister—whom I am convinced are located somewhere in the neighborhood. The lady you are to follow is Miss Rosa Bud; do you comprehend the business now, or shall I say more?"

Fopperty has been seated with his elbows resting upon a small table, his chin resting on his hands, and his eyes intently fixed on Jasper's face as though he would read him through and through; as Jasper closes his last sentence, Fopperty's eyebrows come down and his eyes retreat under them for several seconds; then he looks at Jasper again and asks what he is taking all this trouble for.

"Because my nephew was murdered a few months since, and his murderer is suspected to be the person whose whereabouts I want you to discover through this lady, Miss Bud."

"Wouldn't it be better to employ the detective force and have it done kind o' regular like?" asks Fopperty, still eyeing his visitor's face.

"I have my reasons for undertaking this in my own way," replies Jasper, apparently a little nettled by Fopperty's manner. "I have stated the business which brought me. Do you undertake it—yes or no?"

"And how much do you intend to come down,—you ain't told me that yet, you know." And after making this inquiry the speaker's eyes seem to retreat further into his head than before, while his eyebrows take the place of his eyes.

Mr. Jasper makes answer that if Fopperty will meet him in the same place that day week, with the desired information, ten pounds will be his reward.

This proving satisfactory, Fopperty expresses himself to that effect and Jasper rises to go.

"By-the-way," remarks Jasper, as though suddenly reminded of it, "I have not seen your mother or Bessie for so long a time that I should hardly know them. Are they at home?"

"Oh, yes," is the answer, "I'll call them," and Jasper resumes his seat.

Fopperty having called to his mother, who must have occupied a position in the neighborhood of the keyhole, judging from the instantaneous opening of the door, that dear old lady enters the room followed by the child.

Jasper merely nods to the old woman, but looks earnestly at the child whom he greets in affectionate terms, while offering his hand. She does not take it, but retreats towards Fopperty, whom she really loves, notwithstanding his rough manner, and stands by his side.

Mr. Jasper is a little hurt by her refusal to take his hand, and enquires if this is timidity, or if her present behaviour arises from dislike for him.

"Oh, as for that matter," Fopperty returns, tenderly brushing the child's hair from her forehead, "she has her likes and dislikes, like the rest on us. Maybe if she see you oftener she'd feel more at home with you; wouldn't you, Bess?"

"I don't like black eyes when they look like his!" answers Bess, pointing to Jasper as she spoke. "In my dreams,—and I have dreadful ones sometimes,—I always see eyes that look like his, and I'm sure I could never like them. I always see them, when I dream of darling mother. Ask him if he knew her before she died, Fopperty."

All this time she has never once allowed her face to turn toward the Music Master. There was something about him that was repugnant to her, and she seemed to fear him.

"Child," said Jasper after a pause, "I am very sorry that you should dislike me for so foolish a cause as you assign. My eyes are as God made them. You do not find fault with His works, I hope."

Turning slowly towards the speaker she answers: "No; God's works are perfect until they are abused; I think you are a wicked man," she adds with such an old look upon her face that it might have belonged to a person twice her years.

Mrs. Padler, who had been sitting quietly by up to this point, now felt it her duty to interpose a word.

"Bless us and save us," said she, "hear the gal talk. That's a pretty way to speak to the gentleman, ain't it"; then to Jasper—"It's a wonder, as ye don't fly at her and beat her to a jelly. Oh, dear, oh, dear! she don't love anybody; she don't know and she never will know good manners. I've tried and tried to learn her, but it's no use, and I'm tired of tryin'."

It being evident from these derogatory statements concerning the child's disposition that the old lady still entertains feelings of animosity towards her, Fopperty takes it upon himself to reply:

"There, mem, you've wiggled that gin-gulliper of yours about enough; Mr. Jasper didn't come here to-day to admire your precious gummin'."

"Oh, Lor; how very respectful some folks is to their parents to be sure," rejoins the old woman with an air of politeness and a very red face; "it's quite a treat to listen to 'em."

While this affectionate scene was in progress between mother and son, Mr. Jasper had been intently observing the features of the child; finally, addressing Fopperty, he said:

"She resembles her mother far more than when I last saw her; but then she was a very little child. Do you remember your mother, Bess?"

Whatever feelings of dislike the child cherished in her breast for him, or whatever feelings of fear his presence had created in her heart, the last sentence banished all. Turning towards him, with her slight form erect and her large blue eyes fixed upon his, she said in tones that would have touched the sternest heart:

"Yes, yes; I do remember her, and God grant I may never forget her; poor, dear, dead mother! How many times I've wished that I could visit her grave. Did I but know where to look for it, I'd gladly travel miles to reach it, that I might place some little wild flowers upon it, and ask her to look down upon her little girl, who has been, oh, *so* lonely since she went to Heaven, and whose daily prayer is that death will soon unite us!"

Tears and sobs prevent her from uttering more; clinging to Fopperty, she buries her face upon his breast, and gives vent to an agony of grief.

Why does Jasper's face blanch as he beholds the child in this attitude of grief, clinging to the strong man by her side as though for comfort and protection? Does his mind revert to a time when, years before, a loving woman, with a face almost as childish as the one before him, whose features it resembled, in an agony of grief and despair hid *her* face upon the breast of a man who had deceived her, and told him that her shame could no longer be kept from the world, and begged that he would keep his promise by placing on her finger the marriage-ring? Does he see a vision of that confiding, innocent face, which looked upon his for the last time—beaming with joy at his parting words, which told her that the morrow should witness the ceremony,—when he left her forever, to die of a broken heart?

The child has grown calm again, and it would seem that she loved to speak of her mother, for she continues to address Jasper—

"There is not a night when I lay me down to sleep that I do not feel dear mother's arms about my neck as they were the day she died,

—poor thin arms, 'tis true, but dear to me, for I had known a mother's love in their embrace. She told me, I remember—oh, how well—I was her darling helpless child; told me my lot would be a hard one, for I must suffer for the sins of others, and then whispered a prayer that God would watch over and protect me. Then she was so still, that I nestled closer to her, and cried myself to sleep. When they woke me, she still held me in her dear embrace, but they said that she was dead now, and would never speak again, and that I—was an orphan."

Fopperty draws her closer to him as she ceases, offering words of comfort, while the other two gaze with sorrow depicted on their faces for the weeping child, and it is evident that her words have touched a tender chord in their hearts.

Like most old ladies, Mrs. Padler never listens to the trials and misfortunes of others without having a desire to relate her own experience under like circumstances; hence she embraces the present opportunity of edifying her hearers with an account of how she felt at the loss of *her* mother.

"Poor Bessie," she exclaims, "I know how to feel for her. We never know what it is to lose a mother, till we've had it to bear. I know how dreadful I felt when I lost mine; it's awful, Mr. Jasper, awful! It's worse nor toothache, or—or—corns," at a loss for a word to express it; and then looks at Jasper very hard, as meaning to say, "We will listen to your experience now, dear sir."

Mr. Jasper, having sat in a thoughtful mood all this time, and regretting that he had introduced a subject that was fraught with so much grief to the child, proceeded to tell her that he felt sorry that he should have lead her thoughts into such sad channels; that it was with no desire to wound her feelings that had prompted him to mention her mother, and that it spoke well for her that she still loved and cherished her mother's memory.

The child looked up at him a moment, and then asked, suddenly:

"Did you know my mother?"

Rather nonplussed for the moment, Jasper finally makes answer that he knew *of* her.

"Then why did you not help her and make her life a happier one? When I first saw you here to-day, I thought of her, and you shall hear why. One night, when grandmother and I had gone to bed, I had a dream; but, oh! so real, that it seemed as though I must have been awake. I was in a beautiful garden, where there were trees and flowers and green grass, and darling mother was with me. I ran, and played, and plucked the prettiest flowers I could find, and placed them in her hair when she would stoop to kiss me and call me her dear little girl. Oh, I was so happy! How I have wished that I could have died then, and never wakened from that dream. At times I'd hide behind some tree larger than the others, and when mother would miss me and be frightened, I'd run out from my hiding-place, and then we would both laugh so merrily — I, to think how frightened she was; and she, feeling so glad that she had not really lost her little girl. We rambled thus through pleasant groves, where the birds were singing so sweetly and so loud that it seemed as if their little hearts would burst from very joy. So we passed the time away, till, coming to a grove more dense than any other we had seen, we spied a tree with branches hanging low, on which grew, oh! such lovely fruit that nothing could equal it. 'Oh, Mother!' I cried, 'see how good God has been to lead us to this spot, for now we can pick some of this nice fruit.' Dear mother! She gave me one look, so full of affection that I shall remember it while I live, and, reaching up to get what I was so eager for, the tree parted in the middle, and a man whom I do not remember, only that he had eyes like yours—the same black eyes—seized her about the waist and dragged her into the opening. In my fright I screamed and wakened, but not till I had heard her say, 'Child, beware of gaudy baubles; I trusted, was deceived, and now behold my fate!'"

As the child ceases speaking, her listeners gaze upon her with amazement in their faces, and for a few moments no one spoke. Mr. Jasper is the first to break the silence.

"Bessie, it is a great misfortune to you that your mind is allowed to dwell on such absurd visions as you have just described. It is plain to me that you do not enjoy that exercise which one of your years requires. You should study the child's interests, Mrs. Padler," addressing the old lady, "and provide more and better facilities for her health and comfort."

"That's all very well to talk, sir," returns Mrs. Padler; "but who's to furnish the money which is required to do it? Those who ought to, won't, and them as would like to, can't; so, what's a poor old woman to do? What's more, she ain't like other young 'uns, and won't play out o' doors when she might."

"I hope from my heart she will recover from the unhappy state of mind in which I find her," is Jasper's earnest reply; "and it is plain to me that the least said about her mother before her, the better." He takes some silver from his pocket while he is speaking, and handing it to Mrs. Padler, continues: "That is to be used for her only. I shall expect to see a change in her wardrobe, at least, when next I visit you." Then turning to Fopperty, he says:

"I suppose that everything is plain concerning our business?"

"Couldn't be plainer," is the laconic rejoinder.

Taking his hat, Jasper bids them farewell, and proceeds on his way home. On reaching the street, he found it had grown quite late, and the shades of evening were beginning to fall. He is proceeding in the direction of the High Street, and had nearly reached it, when he is startled by hearing a shrill and familiar voice cry out "Widdy!" and on the instant a stone came bounding about his feet, just as the voice cried "Warnin'!" the cry giving way to a very loud, very long, and very shrill whistle.

On turning about, Jasper discovers the Deputy a few rods from him, looking with a great deal of concern manifested on his face as to what the other is going to do next.

"You devil's brat!" cried the Music Master, in a passionate tone, "why do you persist in dogging my footsteps as you do?"

"Yer lie!" returns the boy. "I wan't a doggin' yer. I was only just a takin' a aim at that there post to keep my 'and in."

"I solemnly swear," continues the Choir Leader, "that if you ever come upon me again as you have at different times, I'll tear you to shreds."

"Take care yer don't make no mistake an' git teared to shreds yourself, Jarsper," the boy returns, arming himself with another stone that lies near him. Then breaking out with one of his favorite refrains:

Chudy, Chudy, Chy,
Wink—Wink—pooky, who plays 'igh.
Wuddy, Wuddy, Cho,
Don't—I—ches—'Im—when—'E—plays low,

And disappears through an adjacent area, leaving Jasper to continue his way to the Gate House with such feelings as most men would not envy.

CHAPTER XXIV.

BEGINNING TO FORGE THE CHAIN.

PROBABLY Cloisterham, at no period of its existence, had ever undergone more excitement over any event that had transpired in its midst, or out of it, for that matter, than it did when Edwin Drood had so mysteriously disappeared. For a long time thereafter gossip was at its height, and there were nearly as many causes assigned for his sudden taking off as there were persons to utter them.

As is usual in such cases, localities that he had been wont to visit were regarded with curiosity, mingled with feelings of awe, by the superstitious class; and the more timid Cloisterhamites were impressed with mortal fear when it came to be whispered about that one or two individuals had declared they had actually seen the ghostly form of the missing young man clothed in a full suit of white, as every respectable ghost should be, at some one of the places mentioned. One elderly female, who resided quite a distance from Minor Canon Corner, had also affirmed that she had seen him "as plain as she ever saw anything in her life," looking in at her parlour windows just at dusk; that he wore a very sorrowful look, while pointing to his throat, which, she observed, was cut from ear to ear; and then disappeared in the darkness.

But perhaps the story which Mr. Durdles told, concerning what he had seen, had a more dire effect on the nerves of certain of his hearers, in that he was known to be so much in the company of the dead; and, being so much in their company, was less liable to become a victim to those hallucinations which might be charged upon other people. Mr. Durdles *had* seen the ghost of Edwin Drood just where it was patent to everybody the ghost would be—about the Cathedral—because, when living, he was most often seen in that locality.

And here let us observe that it is a singular fact, and one which none will dispute, that the ghosts of murdered people should prefer to exhibit themselves on the spot where their murder occurred, it being only natural to suppose that they would keep as far away from it as possible, after what befel them there. Perhaps some of the learned scientists of the present century will explain this fact, but it is to be hoped they will arrive at a more satisfactory conclusion than usually attends their investigations upon phenomenal subjects.

Mr. Durdles, having seen the before-mentioned apparition, tells of it thus:

"The next night but one after that there affair happened, Durdles was out on business what concerned him and no one else. Was Durdles sober? Durdles was! He knowed what's o'clock as well as he knows now. Comin' through the Corner, Durdles heerd a noise just when he was along of the Cathedral. Was that noise a natural one, or was it such a noise as stiff 'uns could make?"

"Says I, Durdles, don't be scared, 'cos then you'll run, and if you run, you'll never know what that noise is."

"So Durdles stood still, he did, and a minit after he heerd it agin, and it come right from the Cathedral Tower. When Durdles heerd where it come from, he looked up; he didn't look down, he looked *up;*" this with a deal of emphasis on the last word, as meaning that most people would have looked down. "Then Durdles saw what most men would 'a run from, but Durdles only looked the harder. Settin' right on the edge of the tower was that there unfortnit young man, with 'is 'ed bare, and one side on it all bloody as the moon shined on it. Then Durdles cried out, 'Who's done this ere wicked deed for you, Mr. Drood?' That's what Durdles said. What did It say? That's Durdles' business, and he don't mean to make it anybody else's."

And though repeating this story dozens of times for several weeks after, not one word more could be obtained from him.

As we before said, while a great many superstitious people were greatly impressed with his narrative, the majority regarded it as purely mythical; or that, perphaps, the black bottle that kept company with Durdles always on his nocturnal walks had more to do with what he saw than anything else.

But the affair had become an old story, and like all other startling events had died out, or was only occasionally spoken of. Still there were a few who yet remembered it, and it was as green in their hearts as though it had happened but yesterday, and one of those few was the Minor Canon.

His interest in the Landlesses—Neville and Helena—has never ceased, and he continues his visits to their quarters in Staple Inn, encouraging the brother and sister with words of affection and consolation.

The good old China Shepherdess, who was and had always been his confidant in everything else, he did not think it best to enlighten concerning the whereabouts of the two orphans, and it was, therefore, no wonder that she thought it strange he should visit London so frequently.

"Sept, my dear boy," said she, one day, as they were seated at a cosy tea, "I wish you would tell me what it is that calls you to London so often. Not that I doubt you have some excellent reason, for I feel sure you have; and hence my curiosity is all the more excited to learn the cause."

"All in good time, Ma, dear, all in good time; be patient," he continues, pleasantly, "and don't forget the Mrs. Bluebeard's fate. I have also had *my* curiosity excited for a few weeks past, but so far have been satisfied to leave it ungratified."

"Then if it's anything that I can say that will gratify it, my dear boy, tell me, so that I may set you an example." Both laugh heartily at this rejoinder of the old lady, and after a moment the Minor Canon continues:

"I am perfectly willing you should know what it is, Ma, but I don't think you can help me. I have been wondering for some time who is the white-headed old gentleman calling himself Datchery, and what he can find in this dull and sleepy place to attract him here,—Mrs. Tope's lodger, I mean."

"Haven't you made his acquaintance yet, Sept?" asked his mother.

"Yes—and no; I have met him, of course, and nearly every day, but, beyond a passing recognition, I know nothing about him. I believe, however, that I will go over to Tope's this evening and call on this eccentric personage."

So, tea over, Mr. Crisparkle takes his hat, and, kissing his mother an affectionate good-bye, sallies forth towards the Gate House. It was just twilight, and, looking in the direction of the postern stairs, he discerns a bright light in the room of the Choir Leader. The shutters being open, he is enabled to look into the room and plainly discern objects. One of these objects was the Music Master himself, and as he was at that moment acting in a rather unusual manner, the Minor Canon could not refrain from stopping for a moment to see more.

John Jasper, then, had in his hand a small object that seemed to be the cause of his strange behaviour. He would take it to the window, and, after looking on it for a moment, would dash it upon the floor, raise his arms and clasp his hands above his head, and then bring them down with terrible force, walking the floor meanwhile as though he were suffering the most intense agony. As Jasper approached the window, the Minor Canon could see that his face was perfectly colorless, while a wild light shone in his eyes. Again and again did the excited man take from the floor, where he had thrown it, the before-mentioned object, and as often would he dash it down again.

What could be the meaning of this? thought the Reverend Septimus. Something dreadful must have occurred to rouse this man to such a pitch of frenzy. Jasper grows calmer after a time, and hastens to close the shutters in an impatient manner, as though only just realizing that he had been so much exposed to public gaze. And that was all the Minor Canon saw; but that was enough, for now he knew that something of more than ordinary interest had caused this man to act as he had, and all his old suspicions came back to him stronger than ever.

About to proceed on his way, his mind filled with a hundred reasons for the strange scene which he had just witnessed, it was little wonder that a slight cough from some person very near him caused him to start with surprise, for he had supposed himself to be the only person in the neighborhood of his look-out.

The cough coming first was succeeded by a "hem," and then appeared the individual from whom the sounds had proceeded, in the person of Mr. Datchery, who, as he gained the side of the Minor Canon, said:

"The world seems to move along very comfortably, notwithstanding our young neighbor yonder has been acting pretty much as though it didn't. You've been observing him, and I've been observing him and *you* at the same time; it was quite a treat to me, I assure you, and interested me very much, which is saying considerable for an old buffer like me, who has seen most everything worth seeing, and seldom finds much now-a-days to excite his curiosity. But I trust you will pardon me, Reverend Sir, for the position in which you find me; I really could not help it."

The position in which the Minor Canon found *himself* was one that most men of honor would have felt a little ashamed of, no matter what the circumstances that had led thereto; but to Mr. Crisparkle,— who possessed one of the noblest natures, and who heartily despised anything that savored of a prying disposition, or an idle curiosity to be gratified by taking an underhanded advantage, — the act in which Datchery found him engaged, distressed and mortified him beyond measure, and it was several moments ere he could find words to reply.

Meanwhile, Datchery, — it being a very warm evening, — took off his hat, gave his shock of white hair a toss, wiped his brow with his handkerchief very coolly, and commenced fanning himself with his hat, while waiting for the other to reply.

The Minor Canon broke the silence: "Permit me to say, Mr. Datchery, that the position in which you discovered me here, has overwhelmed me with shame and confusion. Nevertheless, I feel in my heart that I am justified in doing anything that will open a page to that man's character."

"Don't mention it, sir," said Datchery. "I have no doubt your motives were of the best, so oblige me by not speaking of it again. If you are not particularly engaged this evening," he pursued, "I should regard it a favor and an honor if you would spend an hour with me at my lodgings. I dare say you will find it a monotonous hour and decidedly dry, for an old buffer that lives all alone, and seldom goes into society, won't prove a very instructive host, to say the least; but you're nevertheless welcome; and, to be frank with you, I have an object in asking this, which is to ascertain some facts concerning the history of our Living Tableaux yonder, and ascertain, if possible, some trifling matters connected with that history."

"I assure you, dear sir," returned the Minor Canon, "it will give me the greatest pleasure to pass an hour with you; and, to be equally frank, that was in reality my mission over here to-night, when my curiosity was so much excited by witnessing what it appears we both saw in that room."

By this time they had reached the arch-way, and in a few moments were seated in Mr. Datchery's lodgings; whereupon the latter opened the conversation by saying:

"Reverend Sir, I am a plain man, living in an unpretentious way, as you perceive; a rough experience with a rough world has ground me down to that extent that I think I have had all my irregular points pretty well smoothed off, and have no very strong desire to go through that smoothing process again. To illustrate: I feel pretty much as a man would that has worn a tight shoe till it becomes unbearable, and then throws it aside forever.—It don't hurt the shoe, and it does the man a deal of good. So I have settled here on pretty much the same principle—to get away from, or throw off the world. The world's just as well off, and I am a great sight the gainer."

"But, my dear sir," replied Mr. Crisparkle, "did it never occur to you that it is well for us that this world *is* a rough one, as you term it? Do you never think that all the trials, griefs, disappointments and misfortunes that fall to our lot only fit us the better to appreciate that great Rest that eventually comes to all? And do you not think, dear sir, that we also owe a duty to our Maker in this, that by bearing each one of us our burthens patiently and uncomplainingly, we set an example to the faint-hearted that counts so much in our favor in the eyes of our Master in Heaven? Pardon me, Mr. Datchery, if I do not quite coincide with your views, so far as giving the World the cold shoulder is concerned."

"Well, well, Reverend Sir; perhaps I put it a little strong," is Datchery's answer, "but you're a young man yet; when you've lived in the world as many years as I have, perhaps you'll change your views. I do not deny that your views are highly commendable, or that our Master in Heaven is pleased to see us have a care for our fellow-mortals, and help them bear their crosses by our examples and words of encouragement; but that kind of philanthropy is easier preached than practiced; and men have come to regard their own interests first, in all things. Mark me; I don't suppose, of course, that I am going to say anything that will change your views *now*, but one of these days I think you will agree with me; and now, with your leave, we will change the subject.

I desire to ask you a question: If you wanted to take the head out of a barrel, so that you might look at the inside, what would you do first?"

The Minor Canon smiled as he replied, "Why, loosen the hoops, to be sure," and wondering what the man meant by such a droll question, so suddenly propounded.

"*Ex*-actly," with a good deal of emphasis on the first syllable; then continuing: "Now, — with all due respect however, — I know that there is naturally a great curiosity on the part of some people to know what takes an old fellow like me to such a place as this, with no apparent business, and not even an old friend or acquaintance to greet him; and I know, or think, Reverend Sir, that you are among the number who entertain similar thoughts. In order, therefore, to have everything well understood between us, let me say one thing to begin with. I *have* an object in making this visit; my life is *not* entirely aimless. My object is to loosen certain hoops, so that the inside of a certain barrel, figuratively speaking, can be exposed to view."

The Minor Canon betrayed but little surprise at the significance expressed in the closing words of Datchery, though he did feel somewhat amused at the terms which the man had employed to convey his meaning. That Datchery had some hidden cause for appearing in Cloisterham in the sudden way which he had come, was something that he had always believed from the first, though what that cause might be he was not prepared to say. He had surmised of late, however, from some things that had come under his notice, that the disappearance of Edwin Drood had some connection therewith, but it was only surmise; still, that was enough to prepare him for the admission that Datchery had made, and for that reason he did not evince any astonishment at the significance of the latter's words. His reply was:

"I suppose, Mr. Datchery, that you refer to the young man who so suddenly disappeared from our midst some time ago, and who has never been heard from since?"

Mr. Datchery stepped hastily to the door, which he opened, and peering cautiously about for a moment, returned to his seat and said:

"Our Nervous Friend," pointing over his shoulder with his thumb in the direction of Jasper's room, "comes and goes, like other folks; unlike other folks, he is very likely to come when he is least thought of or expected. You will please observe a little caution during our conversation, for it is seldom that I have a caller, and should he hear your voice, it would be just like him to have a little—just a *little*, you know—curiosity to stop and hear what is going on. He's cunning, sir, cunning and deep; but I think he'll touch bottom before many days. Perhaps I'm talking a little open to you, sir, but we may as well understand each other on the start, and I do not think I am mistaken when I say that I believe your opinion of our Nervous Friend yonder is pretty much the same as mine. What do *you* say, sir?"

"If you mean that you think I entertain feelings of distrust towards John Jasper, you are quite right; I may be wrong, and I hope I am for his sake; but there are a great many circumstances in my possession that place him in anything but an enviable position in my eyes. God forgive me if I am mistrusting an innocent man, but I cannot help believing him to be instrumental in causing the disappearance of his nephew."

"Well, we shall know all in good time," said Datchery; "it takes time to sift these things thoroughly. These sly ones have to be dealt with exactly in proportion to their slyness. The only sure way to deal with them is to let them get the rope wound round and round their bodies till they can't get it off, and they become so entangled finally that they hang themselves; in other words, we must get them so firmly immeshed in their own net that there is no possible escape for them; and, now, one word which will change the subject somewhat. Is it possible for any one to gain access to the Cathedral crypt other than those in authority?"

"Certainly not, except by permission, which is sometimes given."

"And do you know, Reverend Sir, if any such permission has been given within a few months to any one?"

"I do not think so,—stop; now you speak of it, I think I heard it said that our Choir Leader made a nocturnal visit therein with the stone-mason Durdles, though that was previous to the affair we were speaking of, and so long ago that it had escaped my mind. But why do you ask?"

"Because," answers Datchery, approaching the Minor Canon closely, and speaking in a low tone, "because that visit was, in my opinion, connected with the disappearance of Edwin Drood—somehow—mind you, I don't say how, but somehow it was; and sooner or later, we shall know in what way."

"I cannot understand how it could have any bearing on the affair," answered the Minor Canon. "Certainly, if he was intending any mischief in that quarter, he would hardly have taken Durdles as a witness, and Durdles, I am sure, accompanied him on his visit."

"If you knew what I do, sir, in connection with that night's adventures, or rather, if you should hear what I have heard, you might be tempted to change your views. But all in good time. I'll start the hoops," he continued, laughing, "and pretty soon you shall behold what there is inside."

"If that time ever comes, and Heaven grant that it speedily may, no one will be more thankful than I; but I fear—good God, what is that noise?" he exclaimed, interrupting himself as a piercing scream, and then another, and another came from the direction of Jasper's rooms. Both started to their feet instantly, and hastened to the door; stepping out, they were met by the Verger and his wife, both very pale, and trembling with fear at the terrible screams which they also had heard.

The Minor Canon, on questioning Mrs. Tope as to where she thought the noise proceeded from, that lady declared that she believed it to come from the room of John Jasper, and thither they all betook themselves in great haste, Mr. Tope making a feint to get ahead of the others in his desire to show his courage, but taking good care to keep close to the Minor Canon, and very kindly allowing that gentleman to be a little in advance all the time.

Arriving at Jasper's door they stopped, and Mr. Datchery applying his ear thereto, endeavored to ascertain if there were evidences of life in the room. Failing in this, he gave three or four double knocks, the last of which might have awakened every sleeping rook for two miles around.

"Who's there?" cried Jasper, as they heard him apparently spring to his feet and approach the door.

"Only your neighbors," replied Datchery.

The door was unlocked and opened, and Jasper stood before them, with a face which looked like a dead man's. It was evident that he had made some hasty attempts at arranging his toilet before coming to the door, but he had succeeded only in a measure, as his cravat was off, and his hair was tossed about in a way that showed he had just left a restless pillow. He looked very greatly surprised on seeing them, but did not show it in his speech as he invited them in.

No change was visible in Mr. Jasper's apartments since the night that Edwin Drood last occupied them with his uncle. Rosa's picture still occupied the same position where it had hung then, and the piano stood open, littered with pages of music. The Verger and his wife looked curiously around, as though they expected to see some terrible thing in the room that would account for the screams they had heard, but they were doomed to disappointment.

"Have you heard no noises up here?" inquired Datchery, after they were seated.

"No," was the reply; "though that is not strange, for I retired early to-night, not feeling well, and your knocking at my door awoke me from a sound sleep. What were the noises like, pray?"

"Well," answered Datchery, "the noises were simply screams, like some one in great fear, or undergoing bodily hurt."

"Is it not possible that you may have been mistaken as to the direction from whence they proceeded? for if you could have heard them in *your* lodgings, I should have supposed they would have awakened me, had they occurred near mine."

"I might have thought myself mistaken, had others not heard the same thing. It is quite impossible that we all should have been deceived."

"I am very thankful," said the Minor Canon, now speaking for the first time, "that there is really nothing amiss with you, Mr. Jasper, for I must confess that I had grave apprehensions when we came here to ascertain the meaning of these dreadful shrieks. I do not pretend to say that they came from your room, but they certainly came from this direction. I regret that we should have so disturbed you, but it was certainly our duty to convince ourselves that you were in no danger."

"Do not mention it, sir," is the Choir Leader's reply. "I do not mind being aroused, and I am grateful that you should be so thoughtful of my welfare. Had I been as thoughtful of my poor boy's welfare, I should not now daily have his loss to mourn. I have thought of him more to-day, it seems to me, than ever. By the way, do you know, dear sir, that I have got some evidence—just a little speck—which leads me to believe that I am at last on track of his murderer?"

Dim recollections of what she had heard concerning Edwin Drood's appearance, in ghostly form arrayed, sprang to the mind of Mrs. Tope, as Jasper mentioned his nephew; and sundry glances towards the windows and remote corners of the room were the consequence of such recollections; there being nothing to see, however, the good lady recovered from her alarm as the Minor Canon answered:

"I sincerely trust that any evidence you have will prove successful in solving the mystery of his disappearance, for it seems to me it would be a relief, even were you to learn for a certainty that he was dead."

"By-the-way," interposed Datchery, as Jasper was about to make some remark, "I was in London yesterday, and fell in with an old acquaintance whom I had not seen for some time, and he asked me where I was located now;—funny that I didn't think to tell you this before, Mr. Jasper,—I meant to." All the time Datchery keeps his eyes on Jasper's face, and never takes them away till he ceases speaking. "As I was saying," he continues, "he desired to know where he should call if he wanted to find me at home, and I mentioned the place — Cloisterham."

"'Indeed,' said he. 'Well, then, you have heard of that young man who so mysteriously disappeared, and who, after being gone so long turned up again.' 'I did hear,' said I, 'that he had gone, but not that he had been heard from.' 'It's a fact,' said he; 'he's alive and well.'"

"It's a lie! a d—d lie!" cried Jasper, springing from his chair, and glaring at Datchery with clenched hands and a face that was almost livid. "How did he know—the fool! How did he dare! What did he see!" and then the Jasper arms drop listlessly at his side, his limbs tremble, his head sinks upon his breast, and he falls to the floor a mass of lifelessness.

The excitement at this moment was very great, and naturally led to confusion on the part of all, so that it was some moments before any assistance was rendered the unconscious man who lay helpless at their feet. The Minor Canon and Datchery were the first to recover themselves, and they raised Jasper and placed him upon the bed, the Verger and his wife nearly dead with fear, looking on without offering any assistance.

The question being asked of Mrs. Tope by the Minor Canon if her lodger was subject to attacks of this kind, the worthy dame affirms that she has known of his being taken so before at divers times, and always when he has been conversing about his nephew; and she further declares it to be her fixed opinion that it is grief for his nephew that has led to the present scene, and that it is shameful so kind and good a gentleman should suffer as he does. How much more she would have said is not known, for at this point Datchery cut her short by sending her for some brandy. When she returns with it she finds Jasper in a sitting position, and apologizing to the two gentlemen for his violent excitement and consequent result.

Taking the brandy from Mrs. Tope and pouring out a glassful, he swallows it and declares that now he feels better and they need entertain no fears for him.

Such thoughts as pervaded the breast of the Minor Canon as he stood watching the Music Master during his recovery, were not of a very complimentary nature, and Jasper seemed to have a suspicion that such was the case, as he addressed the Reverend gentleman:

"I am convinced more and more, Mr. Crisparkle, as time passes by, that the loss of my dear boy has had a more terrible effect on me than I would have believed possible, and though I struggle hard to overcome it, I find it beyond my power to do so. It is my constant thought by day, and fills my mind at night; and I feel sure that, before long, the terrible suspense will kill me. If I could only have help,—some one to whom I could look for assistance; but no, there is no one that can render me any help, and so I go along, day after day, turning this way and that, wandering through long paths of conjecture, to find myself at last just where I started, and no wiser than at first. My poor, poor boy! who had such bright prospects before him,—so much of the flower and sunshine of life to deck his pathway,—to be shut out just as he was entering on the happiest moment that falls to the lot of man. Oh, it was cruel, cruel! Why could it not have been me instead of him. How gladly would I have given my life to save his, for what did I have to live for *but* him; and now that he has gone, I am left alone and desolate."

The Minor Canon's tender heart was touched, and he felt that he could do no less than to utter words of encouragement. When the Music Master ceased speaking he replied in tones of kindness: "Mr. Jasper, I am pained beyond description to see you in the despondent condition in which you are, and to know that the cause of it is one from which there appears to be no loophole of escape. I have no doubt you try to govern your feelings to the best of your ability; but one thing is certain: it will never do for you to brood over this unfortunate affair to the injury of your health; and that your health *is* becoming affected, I can plainly perceive. Something must be done for you, and I will try to think of some plan by which your mind can be diverted from this unpleasant subject, and then we shall see you as you used to be. Another thing, my dear fellow, we don't want to lose that voice, for I am sure we should find it difficult to replace it. No, no; something must be done, and I think I have hit on a method by which we can bring about the desired result. At any rate, I'll take to-morrow to think it over, and if I find it practicable, I'll tell you what it is."

The tones in which the Minor Canon spoke were sufficient evidence that he now felt the kindliest motives towards the person whom he was addressing, and Jasper's face indicated that the knowledge of that fact was most welcome to him, for he took the hand of the Minor Canon, and holding it in his own for a moment, said:

"I thank you, sir, sincerely thank you, for those words of encouragement; but while I appreciate them, I cannot disguise from myself how hard a thing it will be to counteract the feelings engendered in my heart by the unfortunate occurrence of last Christmas. Would to God that I could forget all, or wake to find it a terrible dream, and my dear boy with me here as he was then, with his merry voice and cheery face; but, alas! the stern fact exists, and I shall never see him again. Nevertheless, I will strive to overcome, though I doubt my power to do so, these bitter feelings; for, as you say, I shall only injure myself by a contrary course, and in that case my hopes of unearthing his assassin will be entirely blasted."

"Excuse me," remarked Datchery, as Jasper reseated himself, "excuse me if it has only just occurred to me that I should apologize for any remark that I have made to cause your feelings a shock, but I can only give as a reason that you were mentioning the subject, you know, and so recalled the interview that I—"

"Not another word," interrupted Jasper, pleasantly, "not another word concerning this subject, if you please. There is no one to blame, and no one regrets more than I that you should have witnessed the weakness that I have shown to-night. Rest assured if I could have governed myself I should have done so, but that was impossible. Let us not mention it further."

"As you seem to have entirely recovered," said the Minor Canon, rising to go, "I see no reason for prolonging my stay, and will bid you good-night."

As he moved towards the door, followed by Datchery, Jasper called him back, and taking from his pocket a Diary (the same one that the Reverend gentleman remembered as having seen before), opened to a page, and, passing it to the Minor Canon, asked him to read—and he read:

"I think that I hold a clue in my hand which will fasten the guilt on the one that I suspected from the first. I have just set on foot the necessary preliminaries by which I shall prove the correctness or incorrectness of my suspicions, and firmly believe that my efforts will not be fruitless."

At the bottom of the page was dated September 20, the same day on which Jasper had his interview with Fopperty.

"I sincerely trust that you will not be disappointed, if the person you have in view is the guilty one," was the reply of the Reverend gentleman, as he returned the Diary to Jasper, and once more bidding the Music Master good-night, took his departure, followed by Datchery,—the Verger and his wife bringing up the rear.

The Topes repair directly to their own quarters, while the Minor Canon remains a moment to converse with Datchery at the latter's door.

"Reverend Sir," said Datchery when they were alone, "do you think our friend above stairs is likely to sleep well to-night?"

"Poor man," was the reply, "I hope so, and for that matter, every night to come. I have observed, for some time past, that his health seemed poor, but I never noticed till to-night what a great change there is in his whole appearance. Something must be done for him, and that soon."

"Dear sir, you are quite right. Something must be done, and very soon; but here I am talking in the door-way just like an old buffer that I am, instead of asking you in where you can be comfortable."

"Thank you, sir, but it is already past my bed-time, and you will excuse me if I hasten home. I will take this opportunity, however, to thank you for the attention shown me this evening, and shall avail myself of the first opportunity to call on you again." Bidding each other good-night, the Reverend gentleman wended his way homeward, his mind filled with the strange events of the past two hours, and thinking how he could best serve Jasper in his troubles without compromising the interests of others.

Perhaps Mr. Datchery, however, was the most singularly affected by what had transpired, for after the Minor Canon had left him, he entered his room, and locking the door, indulged in divers fancy steps pertaining to the light fantastic, all in his stocking-feet; after which he sat down and rocked to and fro in his chair, laughing most heartily the while, as though thinking of some capital joke. Presently, he arose, and going to the cupboard door, made five straight marks, remarking as he did so, "Every day brings something new to those who want to learn; and though my little account gets posted late to-day, it's the best lot of figures I have had yet;" and then, disrobing himself, retires for the night.

CHAPTER XXV.

THE READER IS CONVEYED TO BILLICKIN HARBOR, AND MEETS AN OLD ACQUAINTANCE.

The current of daily life at the Billickin mansion flows along pretty much the same with its inmates, as when the reader left them in a previous chapter. Nothing of importance had occurred to vary the monotonous life which Rosa had found from the first to exist there. Mr. Grewgious was a frequent visitor, and would often come early in the day and take his ward to his chambers. During these visits, frequent interviews were held with Helena, and these occasions afforded her the only real pleasure that she experienced. But even that crumb of comfort did not prevent her from growing wan and pale, and it was plain to be seen that unless some definite plan was arranged for the future, and the mysteries of the past could be cleared up, serious consequences, involving loss of health, and possibly life, might be expected to ensue.

The Billickin Frigate had not changed in her course, but still bowled along with all sails set, regardless of the Twinkleton Cutter, with which she came in daily collision, but which had, notwithstanding the daily colliding, so far resulted in no serious damage to the sailing qualities of either.

The Billickin, as an offset for the hatred she bore her adversary, was unremitting in her attention to Rosa, and took every opportunity to evince her good feeling, never failing to impress upon her the fact that it was a great pity that her guardian had not the worldly knowledge that she—Billickin—possessed, for then things would be a great deal better for all parties.

"You may think, Miss," she said to Rosa one day when they were alone together, "you may think, and hall the world may think, if it wants to, that a boardin' school is a proper place for young ladies; or you may think that a precepteress is a proper person to 'ave round where young people air, a-livin' with 'em and a-deceivin' on 'em with their fiddle-de-dee ideas; but *I* will *not* be so taken in. There be things that young folks ought to know, and there be things that they oughtn't to know; and I will not deceive you in what you ought to know—which be that such as that person is not good for to be associated in your pathway, Miss."

Poor Rosa, at such times, could only remain silent. To take sides with Miss Twinkleton would only serve to bring her into the Billickin cauldron of hatred, a calamity which it was very desirable to escape, if possible.

It was a popular method of Mrs. Billickin, when in presence of the two ladies, to address herself to Rosa,—as though Miss Twinkleton was merely a stuffed figure,—and relate some reminiscence of her youthful days, touching the history of some young lady who had entirely lost her health by being imprisoned in one of those "horrid Ladies' Semynaries," adding—"and I will *not* try to hide it from you, Miss, for a prison it be, which others may call it what they may. Interested as some folks air in this, which, hearin' me, may think to drown my voice by their tightenin' of their lips, I scorn to deny my words,—and let them say it now, what they will," and waits for a gun from the Twinkleton Cutter.

The reply comes promptly, and is addressed to Rosa:

"Rosa, dear, it might be well to inform the person with whom we have the misfortune to be brought into daily contact, that although, as a general thing, her remarks are highly amusing, even if not quite so instructive, there are times when it is not desirable to listen to them; and, perhaps, after you have intimated as much to the person, she may understand that you desire to dispense, for the present, with her interesting society." After which the Twinkleton Cutter hoists anchor, and sails majestically away through the realms of thought, leaving her adversary to retreat or follow, as her fancy may dictate. Retreat not constituting, in any manner, the tactics of the Billickin Frigate, the consequence always was that she made it a point to follow and discharge one parting salute, and then sail away with such speed as would place her entirely out of hailing distance.

One morning, a few days after the interview between Jasper and Fopperty, a battle royal between the two ladies had reached a very interesting and exciting point, when Mrs. Billickin was forced to retire on account of a summons from the servant, stating that a gentleman was waiting below to obtain audience with the mistress of the mansion.

On descending to the parlour it was found that the gentleman in question was no other than Mr. Fopperty Padler, who had càlled to look at such lodgings as the lady might have to offer, as per bill tied upon the knocker. After a great deal of talk on the part of Mrs. Billickin, during which the conscientious lady set forth all the disadvantages connected with the vacant rooms, she ended by showing them; one of them proving satisfactory, the next question was concerning the references. Whereat the gentleman boldly declared that references he had none, being a stranger in town and only just arrived that morning from one of the rural districts; but that he was willing and ready, then and there, to pay one month's rent in advance, and this proving satisfactory, the bargain was concluded, and Mr. Padler informed that he could occupy his new quarters as soon as he liked.

Thus it happened that on the afternoon of that same day, a cab drove up to the door of the Billickin establishment, and Mr. Padler alighted, in company with a small portmanteau, entered the house and proceeded to occupy his new lodgings.

"A good suit of clothes and a few pounds in the pockets to make music with, helps a man over a good many rough roads that he'd never reach the end of else," soliloquized Fopperty, as he deposited the luggage and divested himself of his hat and coat. "Now, Fopperty," he continues, "you and I, having had a pretty busy day, will take a wink of the soother;" and, without more ado, he throws himself upon the bed and is soon fast asleep.

Shortly after, comes Mr. Grewgious to take Rosa for a walk; not mentioning where, and not necessary, for Rosa knows that this means a visit to the Admiral's Cabin, and from thence to her fairy-realm, the Beanstalk country.

Several days have elapsed since she has seen Helena, for Mr. Grewgious had decided that the visits to the Enchanted Ground should not be too frequent, and even then made with great caution, and only when he could accompany her, lest by any accident or design she should fall in with Jasper and harm befall her.

Good old man! Carrying in his heart the image of this girl's counterpart for all the many years that had elapsed since fate had decreed that her image was all he could possess, it is little wonder that, while in the presence of her child, he lives anew those happy days, whose existence will dwell in his memory forever. Thank God for this affection that lives beyond the grave—this love that does not die when its object is shut out from mortal view by the covering of the grave, but which burns on, steady and bright, to all eternity; and thank God for the Glorious Promise of that Life to come, where affections are steadfast, and where love is not a mockery! Who shall say that such true affection as burned in this old man's heart, and which is now and then unveiled to the world, is not given as living evidence to us of the Truth of that Glorious Promise?

Perhaps it was because his mind was occupied with some such thoughts as these that he did not hear Rosebud say she was all ready, and his not hearing her causes the young lady to playfully approach him, and, standing on her toes, place her lips close to his ear and cry "Ready," so loud that Mr. Grewgious looks confounded for a moment, all of which causes his ward to laugh heartily as they leave the house together.

They have proceeded but a short distance when they observe an old woman approaching from an opposite direction, who, as they come near her, is suddenly attacked with a violent coughing, which might indicate the worst stages of consumption.

As they are passing her, the cough suddenly stops, and stepping up to Mr. Grewgious, she puts out her hand to him, and says:

"Bless ye, good gentleman, will ye be so kind to a poor old 'ooman that ye would give her a shillin' to get her some medicine that 'as been ordered, and that she is that poor she can't buy?"

"Where do you live, my good woman, and how does it happen that you can employ a physician, but have not the means to purchase his prescriptions?"

"Bless ye, sir, the medicine is the doctor, and the doctor is the medicine. The doctors do not cost, but the medicine it do."

"Rosa, my dear, I don't think I comprehend this woman's meaning. Perhaps my extremely Angular temperament blunts my understanding, and if you can comprehend that last remark of hers, perhaps you can explain it to me by putting it a little more intelligibly."

Rosa was about to question the old woman, but was suddenly interrupted by her with, —

"Rosa, Rosa! yes, that's the name. Don't that name go sometimes with Eddy, dear gentleman? and don't Eddy go with the name of Rosa sometimes, sweet Miss?"

The abrupt manner with which this was said, coupled as it was with the name of one who had been so closely identified with her whole life, came near proving very unfortunate for Rosa, and it was with difficulty that she could abstain from fainting; as it was, she leaned very heavily on the arm of her guardian, who, noticing her agitation, whispered a few cheering words to her; then turning to the old woman (who had, in her cunning way, lost nothing of the effect of her allusion to the missing young man), he said:

"*What* do you know of Eddy, as you term him, and *how* do you know that we are interested in any one of that name?"

"Pardon me, kind sir," she replied, still looking sharply at Rosa, if anything sharp could be said to come from her bleared eyes, "pardon me, kind sir, but it's little I know, and so I've my own ways to get at what I *don't* know. I didn't know then, deary, but I do know now, that you was interested in that name. But I'm a friend to Eddy, for he was good to an old 'ooman once, and answered her civil, and give her something to buy her the medicine that I asks you for now."

Mr. Grewgious was greatly puzzled by all this, and it was several moments before he could sufficiently recover from his surprise to decide how he should dispose of this person.

His first impulse was to leave her without further remark, as an impostor, and then he argued if he took that course there would be no way of ascertaining whether she really had any knowledge of Edwin Drood, for she would of course leave the neighborhood and go he knew not where. He therefore decided to treat her kindly, and perhaps there might be something of importance that could be obtained from her which would throw some light on the great mystery of that night at Cloisterham.

"You say, woman, that you need medicine, and have no money to buy it," said Mr. Grewgious. "Rosa, dear, shall I give her some money to buy this medicine with?" addressing Rosa; then to the old woman, "You are sure that it's medicine and not gin that you want?"

"I'll be honest with ye, dear sir: it's not for gin, for that I never buys. No, I wants to buy what's medicine, and bread, and meat, to me. It's opium, dear sir,—that's what it is; and it's that as tells me what I shouldn't hear without it, and shows me things that else never could be seen by me. Give me only one shillin', dear gentleman, and ye'll never be sorry that ye helped a poor old 'ooman that was in need."

Mr. Grewgious was a little startled when he learned what the particular kind of medicine was; but he had made up his mind to give her the desired sum, and taking the amount from his pocket, said:

"Well, well; I don't think that the medicine, as you call it, is of as much benefit to you as you would have us believe, but I have no doubt *you* think so, and will give you the money on this condition, that you tell me your name, and where you live."

"Bless ye, deary, I can't do that now. I'd like to, but I can't do it now. It would do ye no good to know that, and it might do me harm; but don't be afeard but what ye'll see me again before many days. Where does you live, deary?" she continued, addressing Rosa. "Don't fear me; I'm an old 'ooman as couldn't hurt ye if I would, and wouldn't if I could. Where does ye live, deary?"

Rosa looked to her guardian to answer for her, as she felt rather afraid of her questioner and preferred that Mr. Grewgious should conduct the conversation. That gentleman answered for Rosa, by saying:

"I am this young lady's guardian, and if you have, at any time, reasons for seeing her, come to my chambers yonder," pointing over the way. "My name is Grewgious, and any one will direct you—I am most always at home. Here is the money you asked for, and I hope you will enjoy your medicine." They had turned to leave, when the woman interrupted them, saying:

"Bless ye, and thank ye, dear sir, for your kindness to a poor old 'ooman; but will ye please tell me what is the lady's whole name? Do tell me that, sir, and I'll thank ye kindly."

As Mr. Grewgious sees no good reasons for refusing to gratify the old woman's curiosity, he tells her Rosa's full name.

"Bless ye, and thank ye, good sir," she returns, after repeating the name several times, as though to impress it thoroughly upon her memory, and then continues, addressing Rosa:

"I'll not forget ye, Miss. It's likely no harm will come from my meetin' of ye to-day. Rosa Bud," she repeated again, interrupting herself, as though the name were slipping from her, and she was catching it before it had gone altogether. "Well, lovey, ye're but a bud in all else as well as in name, and it's hard, deary, that the frost have o'ertook ye so soon; but ye'll be bright again, lamby, though ye be drooping now, and the days will soon be that sunny that they'll bring the colour to yer cheeks again. Good-bye, Miss, and good-bye, dear gentleman," and with this parting sentence she hobbles away from them, while they resume their walk to the chambers of Mr. Grewgious.

The reader has, of course, recognized in the old woman the Princess Puffer, who for some reason of her own had strolled to the locality where she had fallen in with Rosa and her guardian. After she had got a short distance away, she stopped and looked after them, muttering slowly the while:

"I thought I'd find her about here, poor thing; she be that pretty that it's wicked to break her heart. He'd do it, though; yes, my fine gentleman, ye'd do it, but ye'll find that I've got a trap that may prevent ye from doing the mischief ye've undertaken; leastwise I think so."

Still muttering to herself, she continued her way in an easterly direction, and was soon lost to view.

Meanwhile, Fopperty Padler, having succeeded in obtaining from the "soother" all the winks that he desired, had risen from his slumbers, donned his wearing apparel, and leaving the house, was sauntering leisurely along in the direction of Staple Inn. A coffee-room close by attracts his attention, and entering, he is soon seated at a table refreshing himself with his favorite beverage of gin and water. He has been engaged in that pleasant occupation but a moment, however, when a hand laid on his shoulder causes him to turn suddenly about to discover himself confronted by John Jasper.

"Bless my eyes!" is Fopperty's first salutation; "you're the last man I should expect to see. Have a seat. Will you join me in a glass?"

"You'll excuse me," is Jasper's reply; "I had some business this way, and noticed you just as you turned in here, and followed. How do you succeed? I am very anxious to know, and was only just wishing I might meet you."

"It ain't to be expected as I've done much in the short time I've been here," returns Fopperty, impatiently. "Don't you be in too great a hurry. I'll do this business in good time, and when it's done I'll let you know."

"I suppose you have not yet seen Mr. Grewgious," said Jasper, drawing his chair closer to Fopperty.

"Not yet," returns the latter, "but I've come out now to take a look around Staple and get a little acquainted with the neighbourhood."

There was quite a number of people in the room where they were seated, and though the conversation between the Music Master and Fopperty was carried on in a low tone, one gentleman who was seated nearest them overheard the name of Grewgious, and he became deeply interested in the two men. Unnoticed by them, he drew a little closer to the table at which they were seated, and listened.

"Of course," resumed Fopperty, "it ain't going to make no difference about the price agreed on whether I discovered this Landless' hiding-place in one day or six, so long as I find it."

"Certainly not," was the reply; "as I told you before, the time to me is of value, and if you succeed in finding him out in one day or one hour, so much the better I shall be satisfied, and I will not abate one farthing from the price named."

The gentleman listener became still more interested as he overheard Neville's name introduced, and leaning against the wall, edged a little closer, with a view of hearing all that he could.

"You must feel pretty sure," said Fopperty, "that this chap is really guilty of the crime you suspect him of, or you wouldn't go so far as you have to discover him."

"I hold so strong a proof, that, if I once get hands on him, he shall die like the dog he is," answered Jasper in a savage whisper. Still unperceived by Jasper or Fopperty, the stranger overhears the whole of this last remark, which was uttered with such vehemence that Fopperty cautioned the other to be careful.

"Oh, I have no fear of eavesdroppers," answered Jasper; "I am a stranger to the people here, and they will feel no interest in what we are saying. Now," he continued, "in regard to this Landless; aside from the fact that I believe him to be the murderer of my dear boy, there are other reasons that I have for pursuing him to the death. He has come between me and something which I had looked forward to for years; something which, during my poor boy's existence, never could have come; but after Ned had gone, and when nothing seemed to prevent the success of my heart's object, this accursed villain springs up to take from me what I had so long coveted, as he had before taken my poor boy's life from him. There was no difference in the cruelty of the two acts, only that Ned died with the stab in his heart, while I am forced to live with a double stab in mine. But I will say no more now, for it is time for me to go. Success to you, and, whatever you do, be very cautious, for old Grewgious is a deep one, and is very suspicious where his ward is concerned."

The stranger, who had overheard the greater part of this conversation, moved quietly towards the door as Jasper rose, and when he had reached the street he hurried across the way to Staple Inn and directly to Mr. Grewgious' chambers. On entering, he found the old gentleman just seating himself, having only returned from Rosa's lodging.

"Ah, Mr. Tartar," says Grewgious. "Glad to see you; but what's the matter. You appear to be laboring under some excitement. No trouble above stairs, I hope"; and rose from his chair.

Catching Mr. Grewgious by the arm, he hurried him to the window, and begged him to look in the direction of Furnival's and see if there was any one about that he recognized. Mr. Grewgious, at first, did not see any one that he was particularly interested in, but a moment afterward he looked at Mr. Tartar, and, nodding his head, said:

"My eyes are getting a little dimmed from age; hence my vision is slightly impaired; not so much, however, but that I can tell a villain when I see him at that distance, and seeing him at that distance enables me to say that the individual in question is a familiar acquaintance of mine, who may have or may not have an interest in our neighbors above stairs. It's my opinion that his skulking about here bodes them no good, and we must both keep our eyes open for danger, lest we are surprised by the gentleman of Musical Proclivities yonder," and Mr. Grewgious wiped his brow with his handkerchief very coolly, though it was evident that he felt quite concerned at the sight of John Jasper.

Having delivered himself of this remark,—which tended all the more to excite the curiosity of Tartar, coupled with what he had before heard at the coffee-room,—Mr. Grewgious turned to his companion, and, motioning him to a seat, begged him to favor him (Mr. Grewgious) with such facts concerning the object of their recent observation as he might possess. Whereupon Tartar repeated such conversation as he had gleaned, declaring at the same time that he felt quite ashamed to act as eavesdropper on any man, but hearing the names of persons mentioned in whom he felt interested, he could not resist the desire to listen.

"I may be mistaken in the man," he continued; "but if ever hatred and murder were stamped on human features, they were plainly discernible on those of the person we just observed from yonder window, when he was speaking of Mr. Landless."

"Mr. Tartar," suddenly ejaculated Grewgious, after a moment's pause, "I have an idea, and I have a suggestion."

Tartar bowed his head in reply, and Grewgious continued:

"My idea is, that from what you have told me, the person we last observed is undoubtedly seeking to obtain the whereabouts of our young friends above stairs; and we must do all in our power to prevent his gaining any such intelligence. My suggestion is, that, as it will do no good to mention this circumstance to the young people, but, on the contrary, would cause them to be very unhappy, with no remedy at hand, we had better keep all we know about it to ourselves, till such time as it may be prudent to mention it."

"I agree with you, sir, perfectly, and I would also suggest, if you will permit me, that greater care than ever should be exercised when your ward visits the brother and sister. If anything is gained by this man, it will be through such visits, and great precaution must be observed."

"You are right," said Grewgious, "quite right. I will take care of that." And so the interview ended, Tartar taking himself to the Admiral's Cabin, very much alarmed for his neighbors over the way, and Mr. Grewgious wondering what will be the result of this new enterprise on the part of Jasper, and what he (Grewgious) could do to frustrate him.

Some three or four days after this occurrence, came Mr. Crisparkle to pay his weekly visit to the orphans and to call on Mr. Grewgious, for the visits would not be complete, were the good old gentleman neglected.

Mr. Crisparkle enters, very rosy, for he has walked fast. His countenance expresses the pleasure it gives him to be once more in the precincts of Staple Inn, for his interest is centered in more than one person dwelling there, and though it would be difficult for the Minor Canon to analyze his feelings were he asked to do so, nevertheless his heart has gone out to the fair girl with the black hair and eyes, whose brother is to a certain extent a prisoner in the Beanstalk country; and they are dear to each other, this black-eyed girl and good Minor Canon, but as yet they know not how dear.

It is probable that the Minor Canon's interest in, or we might say devotion to, her unfortunate brother since his misfortune at Cloisterham, and his subsequent captivity at Staple Inn, has done more to engender tender emotions in the breast of Helena towards his benefactor than anything else; and though these feelings seemed to her but those of gratitude, they were in reality of a much warmer nature. She had learned to look forward to his coming with all the eagerness of a child for its parent. She felt how deeply they were under obligations to him for all the kindness he had bestowed on Neville, and realized how much the efforts put forth by him to assist her brother lightened the burthens which devolved upon her in their present hour of trial and isolation from the world.

As for Mr. Crisparkle, he would have laughed heartily had any one told him that he had any feelings but those of sympathy and pity for Helena, but there were moments when he admitted to himself that it would be a great blow to him should anything happen that would prevent him from seeing the orphans again, though exactly what his feelings were, or whether they had more special reference to Helena than Neville, he did not stop to consider. One thing was certain, however; if he did not see Helena at these visits, and it was frequently the case that he did not, he could but feel that the visit had not been so pleasant a one as he had anticipated.

But this attachment was at present only in the bud, and, therefore, neither had betrayed themselves, and they still met, as they had done in the Cloisterham days, feeling that they were still the warmest friends.

This was the first time that the Minor Canon had seen Mr. Grewgious since the night he had visited Datchery at the Gate House, and as he had several matters that he felt it necessary to consult Mr. Grewgious upon, he had taken this opportunity to call on that gentleman.

"You look as though you had been taking some pretty violent exercise," said Grewgious, "and as a consequence had got pretty warm, or, if you will allow so forcible an expression, devilish hot!" and beams good-naturedly on his visitor, who sat wiping the perspiration from his face.

"As you are aware, I am a pretty fast walker; and, as the distance from the station here is no small walk, you can well say that I have had some pretty good exercise for a hot day like this; but I like it—it will do me good. How are you all?" he continues. "No new developments, I suppose?"

"Softly!" was the reply. "What do you mean by developments?"

"I had reference to anything that you might have learned of the affair which has puzzled us all so long and so bitterly."

"What should you say," rejoined Grewgious slowly, "what should you say, Reverend Sir, if I should tell you that I had some new developments, and that they were of a nature that threatened danger to our young friends yonder?" pointing towards the Beanstalk country, "and also yonder?" pointing in the direction of Rosa's lodgings.

"And may I inquire of what the danger consists, and from whence?" asked the Minor Canon, his face showing the alarm he felt at what the other had said.

"You may," was the reply. "But don't hurry—there's time enough. How does our Local Friend prosper?" was the abrupt inquiry.

"I fear that we have misjudged John Jasper," was the earnest reply of Mr. Crisparkle. "He is in a terrible condition, and unless something occurs to enlighten him as to the fate of Edwin Drood, I dread the consequences;" and Mr. Crisparkle proceeded to relate the scene that had taken place at Jasper's room, and all the particulars pertaining thereto.

Mr. Grewgious listened attentively, never losing a word of the narrative, from the beginning to the close; but when it was finished, there was a frown on his face, and it deepened materially when he brought his hand down quite hard on the desk before him, and ejaculated:

"Damn him!—and so he still declares himself determined to persecute this poor fellow and wear his life out by striving to fasten this crime upon *him!*"

"By-the-way," interrupted the Rev. Septimus, "there is one little circumstance connected with that evening's adventure that I omitted to state to you; and I don't know that I should do so now, only that it was so ridiculous in the ending that you may be as pleased to hear a recital of it as I have since been at the thoughts of it." And he went on to relate what he had seen through the window of Jasper's room on that night when he and Datchery were such interested lookers-on.

"A very small matter has sometimes great weight," was Mr. Grewgious' reply. "I think I perceive a very large current floating into the river of our investigations, that will help materially towards floating our boat into a peaceful harbour at the last. I suppose, now, that our Local Friend did not intimate to you the exact evidence that he had, touching the guilt of our young friend above stairs?"

"No mention was made of what it was, only that he had got something, and on the strength of that something he had made a movement looking to another arrest of Neville. I did not, for various reasons, think it best to argue with him, and if I had it would have been futile. He will never, I am satisfied, be convinced of Neville's innocence till the really guilty ones are discovered. God grant that that time is not far distant, for the peace of mind of all of us depends so much upon it!"

"Amen!" was the earnest reply of Mr. Grewgious; "and no exertion shall be wanting on my part to help that time along."

"Have you any idea, Mr. Grewgious, that Neville's whereabouts are known to any others than ourselves?"

"I do not think any positive knowledge exists on the part of any one as to his whereabouts, but I have good reason to believe that they are strongly suspected. Pray, Reverend Sir, does our Musical Friend often visit London?"

"I think not often, — only occasionally."

"What if I should tell you that I saw him here within a day or two?"

"Here! When?" exclaimed the Minor Canon hastily, his mind filled with apprehension for the safety of his young protegé.

Mr. Grewgious then related what had come under the notice of Tartar, and what his own vision had disclosed to him.

"Now, I don't believe," he continued, addressing the Minor Canon, "I don't believe, mind you, that this John Jasper knows where young Landless is; but I do believe that this person who was seen with him that day is staying somewhere about here for the purpose of making the desired discovery, and unless great precaution is used I have no doubt he will be successful. My only wish in the matter is that the discovery may not be made quite yet, as it would interfere somewhat with certain plans that I have formed in connection with this affair. Still, if we are taken on surprise we must do the best we can. At all events, I can say one thing candidly, and that is, that your visit here to-day, and the relation of the scene you witnessed at Jasper's apartments, gives me a new insight into the matter, which, though it may look a small circumstance to you, I think will help, eventually, to change your opinion of that viper, and cause you to view him with the same feelings that I have always entertained for him since that memorable Christmas time — good and strong English Disgust."

And Mr. Grewgious, who had grown very red in the face as he closed his remarks, stamped his heel at the same time, much as though he intended to imply emphasis, or that he would like to have Jasper under his foot at that moment, or both.

Mr. Crisparkle, stating his determination to call on Neville immediately, and being cautioned by Mr. Grewgious as to the care he must exercise in going to the young man's room, took leave of the old gentleman, promising to call again at an early day, and in the meantime doing all in his power to learn what he could concerning Jasper's movements.

Being left alone, Mr. Grewgious paced back and forth for a few moments, in a thoughtful mood, and then seized his hat and hurriedly took his departure for Rosa's lodgings.

CHAPTER XXVI.

A RECOGNITION AND A MEETING.

The day succeeding that on which the interview had taken place between Jasper and Fopperty, came in bright and fair; the heavens were clothed in their brightest tints of blue, the trees had donned their liveliest shades of green, the birds were carroling their morning songs of praise, and all seem waiting for the sun to rise from his eastern bed; nor have they long to wait, for soon he comes with such a fair and smiling face, that, as his beams are cast on tower and tree, the leaves, dew-covered, rustle their applause, and dance in the morning air right merrily, keeping time to the music of the birds. Of a truth, had the gods issued invitations for a merry-making to-day, nature could not have arrayed herself more charmingly.

Perhaps it was with feelings akin to these which led the Princess Puffer, on this same morning, when rising with the lark, to don ***her*** best apparel, and proceed to make ***herself*** merry regardless of the gods; for, in a short time thereafter, she emerges from the narrow street in which her quarters lay, and hastens with all the speed that she possesses in the direction of the station, from whence she intends to take passage to Cloisterham.

Arriving in due time at Cloisterham station, she peers cautiously about to see if there is any face visible that she can recognize, and having satisfied herself on that point, hobbles slowly towards the old city. She proceeds round by the water-side, and when she has nearly reached the street where resided the worthy Mrs. Padler, she spies two children on the pavement—a boy and girl. As she moves toward them, and is about passing them, she looks at the girl, and in that look appears to recognize features that are familiar to her, as she comes to a halt.

The children having both observed the old woman, shrink from her as she approaches. The girl, on seeing the stranger eye her so closely, naturally feels still more alarmed, and places her hand on the arm of the boy, retreating a little behind him, as if for protection.

"What be your name, lamby?" is the opening salutation of the old woman as she stops to address them with what was intended for a conciliatory smile on her features, but which tended to alarm the girl still more.

"Don't be 'feared of me, deary," continues the Puffer, "I'd not hurt ye for all the gold and silver there be in the Bank of England." Then in a coaxing tone: "I likes little girls if so be they're good ones, and I knows you're a good little girl. Now tell me your name, like a little lady."

Still cautiously looking at her questioner and grasping the boy's arm a little tighter, the child answers "Bessie."

"Bessie?" repeated the Puffer. "That's a little lamb, to answer an old woman so prettily. Bessie—a pretty name, too, ain't it, now? I suppose there's another name goes with it, don't there, deary?"

"Yes," replied the child, dropping her eyes as the old woman waited with evident impatience for the child's answer.

"Of course there be, lovey," the Puffer continues, "of course there be. What may it be, sweety."

"Padler."

On hearing the name the old woman was seized with such a violent fit of coughing that both the children expected to see her expire on the spot, but she soon recovered, and when she had fairly got her breath again, she said:

"I suppose, now, you do live hereabouts."

"Yes," was the answer.

"Do you live with your grandmother, deary?"

On hearing this, the child became somewhat interested in her strange questioner, and wondered how the stranger should know anything about her grandmother. Replying in the affirmative, she made bold to ask the Puffer if she knew her grandmother.

"Better than you do, my dear; better than all Cloisterham do. Show me where you live, deary, and I'll bless ye for it."

Bess approached the old woman, and telling her to follow, she led the way to Mrs. Padler's house.

On the way there, the Puffer indulged in various winks and grins peculiar to her, muttering indistinctly something that no one but herself could understand, now and then giving expression to such words as "Secrets," "Dead," and "She don't think I'm so near."

Presently they arrived at the street-door, and Bessie led the way to her grandmother's apartments.

As they entered the room, Mrs. Padler was discovered seated in a chair, mending some articles of clothing, and did not immediately look up, thinking it was only the child come home; but Bess attracted her attention to the visitor by saying:

"Grandma, here is some one to see you."

Mrs. Padler did not at the moment recognize who the visitor was, and ejaculated:

"Drat the girl, who's she got now to—"

"Polly Padler!" exclaimed the Puffer; "Polly Padler! I'd never believe it on ye that ye'd forgit your old friends so easy! It ain't such a long time, that you need to forget me or the troubles I've had, for I ain't changed much for the wuss, and couldn't if I tried, and that's the truth."

Starting from her chair and approaching a few steps nearer the new comer, Mrs. Padler gazed on the Puffer's features a moment, and then, throwing down her work, she raised her hands and exclaimed:

"Bless us and save us! it ain't never Mrs. Tranders that I beholds; it must be a wision."

And it is very probable that had it been a veritable apparition of the Puffer, Mrs. Padler would not have appeared any more startled or surprised.

"Don't be scared, Polly; don't be scared. You've nothing to fear from me; I've wanted this long time to see ye, so I could find out where the gal was, and I ain't 'stonished to find her here with ye, though for anything I know'd she might be dead and underground long ago, with her poor mother."

"Many and many's the day I thought of ye, Mrs. Tranders, since ye left so suddintly; and we all thought as ye must have died in a fit or the like, and just made our minds up as we'd never set eyes on ye agin. How did ye come to know as we was here?"

"Ah, deary, that's just where it is. I didn't know it, and it's all chance my finding on ye as I have. I've been dreadful poorly lately, and I've a cough that's that bad, it can't be told ye; so I jist took a day for a change of air and came up here. Goin' along the street, and nowhere's partic'lar, I seed this gal, and says I to me, that's Bess, or eyes is deceivin' on me; so I jest finds out her name, and when I heard it I know'd I was gettin' near old friends. Its a long time since I've seed her, but I know'd her face, be sure. 'Tain't like as I'd forgit that."

"And good reasons you 'ave to remember it, Mrs. Tranders, for every day of her life she looks more and more like the poor mother that bore her."

Silently, but with much interest, did Bess listen to the conversation that was carried on by the two old women, and at the mention of her mother her interest increased still more, and her attention to what they had to say was still closer. She had heard enough to convince her that in some way the stranger's visit was connected with herself, and she felt anxious to learn all that she could concerning it. The child could not define her feelings, but from some cause she felt a sympathy for the new comer that she had never felt for any living creature since her mother died, and this fact served to deepen her interest.

Helping herself to a seat, the Puffer looked long and earnestly at the child, and then turning her face quickly away to hide the tears that were trickling down her wrinkled features, she said:

"I've not shed a tear before since her mother died, but the sight o' her brings back all the recollections of that day, and I can't help it." And the poor old woman buried her face in her hands, and swaying her body to and fro, wept till her whole frame trembled with the grief that agitated her.

It is a sad sight to see tears on the face of the aged. When we see the young struck down with grief, and the overladen heart lightening its burdens through flowing tear-drops, we feel that the vigor of youth will sustain them, and that time will heal the wounds that grief has made; but the aged have not this advantage in their favor, and when the pangs of grief attack their hearts, the wounds inflicted there must last till those hearts shall cease to beat.

Poor little Bessie, on witnessing this agitation of the Puffer, could not refrain from crying, too, though why, she did not know; and Mrs. Padler looked from the child to her visitor as though she was uncertain whether to join in tearful company, or change the order of things by driving Bessie from the room. This scene, however, was of short duration, and the Puffer broke the silence by declaring that she felt better now than she had for a twelvemonth.

"Do *he* often come here?" asked the Puffer, after she had recovered from her emotion.

"Not often *here*. When we was in London we see'd him once in a while, and little good came of it, for 'twas little he did for to find wittels and clothes for the gal; and he may as well stayed away altogether. Have you see'd him since we lost sight o' you, Mrs. Tranders?"

"Oftener than he thinks, worse luck for him and better for me. He comes to see me, Polly, and don't know it; and though so long the time had been that I'd seen him, I knowed him a'most at the first; but I knowed him certain afore long, and he'll know it soon enough."

"Where did you go to when you went away so suddintly, Mrs. Tranders?"

"It's a long story, Polly, and hardly worth the tellin'. Ye'll take a deal more interest in what happens the next six months than you would in all that happened me the last six years. Don't think, though, that I hain't had an object in life for all these years, for I have, and I'll live to see the end of it, ye may depend."

"And what's supportin' of ye, Mrs. Tranders?" asked Mrs. Padler, who just at that moment happened to think it possible that the old woman might have an idea of throwing herself on the charity of her new-found friends.

"Lord love ye, Polly, I'm in bus'ness, and a rare bus'ness it be; there's few understand it so well as I, and many there be that knows it. I has my reg'lar customers, Polly, and though there be dull times like most other bus'ness, there be also busy ones, and I gets along very well. How long have you been here, Polly?"

"It will be three months this day week," answered Mrs. Padler, a little more cheerfully, since she had found the Puffer depended on herself for a support. "For myself, I'd rather be in Lunnun than here, but Fopperty thought as we'd all be better here than there, so we come; and miserable I am since. Fopperty says it's better for her, though," pointing to Bess, "and as I ain't no consequence, why, I suppose it's just as well here as anywheres."

"And where is Fopperty, deary," asks the Puffer, assuming once more her coaxing tones and cunning manner.

"Oh dear, don't ask me," was the reply; "he comes and he goes, the same as he used to when you know'd him last, and it's precious little he tells me of his comin's or his goin's. Somewheres in Lunnun, but I don't know where."

"Well, Polly, give him the good wishes of aunt Tranders, and tell him I'll come sometime to see him when he is sure to be at home. Ye'll see me often, deary, I have no doubt; but I must be movin', for I've got to walk some ways yet, and you know I can't hurry as much as I could if I was younger, like this little lady," looking at Bess, whom she now addresses: "Lovey, it would not be best for me to tell you *now* why I feel interested in ye, nor how happy it would make my old heart to have a young face like yours always near me. No, it ain't time yet, sweetheart, to do that; there's justice to be done yet, and I could never perform my work with you at my side. You're bad off enough now, God knows, without my making ye worse. It will all come right in the end, and I won't say more. Show me the way to the street, child," and rising from her chair, and taking the child's hand, the Puffer, after receiving an invitation from Mrs. Padler to call again, left the room, she and the child together.

On reaching the pavement, the Puffer seated herself on one of the door-steps, and drawing the child beside her, said:

"Are you happy here, deary?"

Bess, who had treated the visitor throughout with the utmost respect, and had felt genuine pity for her, replied unhesitatingly that she was not happy.

"How can I be happy," she continued, "with no parents to care for me, nor brothers and sisters to love? What did I ever do that I should be so unhappy, and have so little to live for? Sometimes, when I lie down at night, I ask God to let me awake never again on earth. At other times, I often wonder if every one feels so lonely as I, and if they do, what a dreadful thing to live to be old, and all the time to be so unhappy. No, I am not happy, and I wish I was dead."

No excitement, no passionate childish tears during her reply, but calmly, almost coldly, did she unbosom herself to the Puffer, and unfold to her a heart bowed down, at such a tender age, with woe and neglect.

Possessed of more than the average intelligence of children at her age,—an intelligence that had been born and nourished in the midst of bitter privations and sorrows,—it was no wonder that she should at all times dwell upon her misfortunes, and bewail the fate that had been hers, nor wish that life might cease while she was yet young, and so escape the coming trials that seemed to her inevitable as she grew to womanhood.

How many little waifs there are to-day who, suffering for the sins of others, carry in their bosoms the same sad hearts, while praying day after day that their lives may be taken from them ere the rising of another sun; and, all in silence, mourning their young lives away! And, when they have not one kind friend to whom they can look for cheer and sympathy, God help them! for He only can.

"Ah, deary, deary! you break an old woman's heart to hear you speak so down-like, and it makes my flesh creep to hear so young a child as you talkin' so sober and so grave-like. But ye was allers a old child when a babby, and it's not strange after all that it grows on ye. There be better times comin' yet, deary, so don't be cast down, for that won't help ye. Are the Padlers good to ye, my sweet?"

"Oh, yes; I suppose they do the best they can to make me happy, or at least they think they do. Grandma beats me sometimes when she has been drinking, but it's not often; and Fopperty, though he is rough, is very kind to me. But were they ever so kind I could not be happy, for there is something—I don't know what—that makes me feel sorrowful always, and I cannot drive it off."

"Poor child!" thought the old woman. "If I could only help her; but not yet, not yet." Then to Bess: "Ye'll not forget me, deary, will ye, when I tell ye that there be no one in the whole world that's so dear to me as you? Some day ye'll know why, full well."

As the Puffer uttered these words, the child sat with her elbow resting on her knee, and her face resting on her hand, while her large blue eyes gazed steadily on the other's features, as if she was trying to read the mystery which the old woman's words implied. "No," she answered; "I will never forget you, for I feel that there is love in your heart for me, and I know that there is affection in mine for you, though I never saw you before. I suppose it must be because you cried for my poor mamma, and so knowing that you loved her makes me love you in return."

A deep sigh escaped the Puffer, as Bess mentioned her mother's name. Rising from the step hastily, she said:

"Deary, I must not stay to talk further now. I'll see ye again before long, and trust me I'll not forget your interests when I'm settlin' the business between them as is left here and them as is gone there!" pointing her hand heavenward. Then, smoothing the hair back from the child's brow in a loving manner, she bade her good-bye, leaving Bessie, with a sad look still upon her face, gazing after her till she was lost to view.

The Puffer, on leaving Mrs. Padler's house, wended her way slowly in the direction of Minor Canon Corner, and, passing a short distance up the High Street into which she had turned, was suddenly startled by hearing a terrible screech very much like that produced by a cat undergoing the process of tail-squeezing, and which sounded in such close proximity to the old woman that she thought at first she must have trodden on the tail of some stray Grimalkin. Turning quickly round, she perceived Deputy, who, finding that she had spied him, stood on his hands, head downward, and walked towards her a few feet in this position, all the time giving utterance to a series of whistles and yells, till he really did seem more like some strange animal than a human being.

But this kind of exercise was most too tedious to be indulged in a great while, and in a very few moments the boy had assumed his natural position, and was recognized by the Puffer. She was at first disposed to take umbrage at his strange behaviour, but changed her mind, and after looking at him steadily for a moment, said:

"What be the matter with ye, deary? Ain't ye well?"

"Yah! what do yer call me deary for? Yah!" and made a motion of going through the upside-down business again, but thought better of it, and eyed the Puffer sharply.

"Because ye air; why else, lamby?" returns the Puffer.

"Yer lie! I ain't yer deary, nor yer lamby; and don't yer call me lamby again."

"I means no harm by it, lovey," the old woman replies, in a conciliatory tone. "Does ye live hereabouts?"

"No, I don't. I lives hundurds of miles away from 'ere, I does. I'm a hem-i-*sary* what's got bus'ness 'ere and is a-goin' back to 'is *es*-tates when 'e gits ready. I knows some 'un as wants to see *you*, though."

"To see me, deary!" exclaims the other. "What does they want of me, now?"

"I don'ow and don't care; wait 'till yer see 'em and find out, can't yer?"

"Who is they?" inquired the Puffer.

"Yer won't know if I tell yer. It's Datch-er-*rie!*"

"And what do he want to scratch my eye for, lovey?" asked the Puffer, not exactly understanding the Deputy's remark.

"I didn't say that, yer fool; I said *Datch*-erie."

"And where do he live?"

"By the Kin-free-der-el," answered Deputy, "and he is my 'ticklar friend. Yer go ahead and I'll foller, and when yer gits there, I'll holler."

Doing as the boy bade her, the Puffer continued her way towards the Corner, he following along behind, now and then stopping to walk on his hands, or picking up a stone and motioning as though he were about to throw it at his leader. Just before they reached the Gate House, he broke out in his chanting way:

"Chiddy, Chiddy, Chy,
Wink, Wink, pooky, who plays high.
Chuddy, Chuddy, Cho,
Don't—I—catch—'im—when—'e—plays—low."

It was at this moment that Mr. Datchery, having only just emerged from his lodgings, was about turning into the street from the court which led thereto, and he was not a little astonished to meet the Puffer so suddenly, more especially as he had been a few moments before thinking of her, and hoping that he might be so fortunate as to again have an opportunity to converse with her.

The Deputy, on seeing Datchery, came a little nearer and then stopped; at the same time exclaiming:

"There she be, Datcherie! That's 'er Royal 'ighness, the Princess Puffer; I brought her, I did. I don't owe yer nothin' now," and, as he finished the sentence, came running towards them, alternately whistling and screaming, while his arms were kept in a revolving motion, looking very much like the little savage he was intending to represent, and frightening the old woman to such an extent that she nearly lost her breath as he passed her, continuing on in an opposite direction, and was soon out of sight.

Datchery observes the alarm which the boy has caused the Puffer, and hastens to quiet her:

"I hope you won't allow that young rascal to cause you any uneasiness, mistress. He's a strange boy, I will confess, but he won't hurt you, depend. I suppose, now, you haven't forgotten me?" he inquired.

"Oh dear, no," is the reply, and then, a violent fit of coughing coming on, prevents her from saying more for a moment; recovering, she continues: "I've a dreadful cough, dear sir, and when I gits startled it comes upon me all in an instant. He said as some one hereabouts was wantin' to see me, and it may be as it was you—for I lost the name since the fright he gave me—and if it wasn't you I never shall know as who it was, and that's the truth, or I never spoke it."

Another coughing fit; then takes a handkerchief from her pocket, puts it to her eyes as though to wipe them, and peers over one corner of it at Datchery, who sees the look, but feigns ignorance.

"My good woman, you are right, quite right; it was me, and if I had known where to find you, I should have come to you before this. But, before I tell you why, I desire to ask if you have since seen the man whom you were in search of the day that I met you at the Cathedral yonder?"

"I'll tell ye, truly, sir; I did not see him since that day; has he been away, do you know, since that?" and the handkerchief once more came into service to hide a sly look at Datchery's features, as she asked the question.

"Oh, I don't know as to that," returns Datchery; "he may or he may not have been away. I should not be apt to know, as he keeps his own counsel most likely. Now I beg you will no longer distrust me," he continues, "or misconstrue the motive I have in seeking an interview with you; and let me assure you now, that I am no friend of that man; that I believe you can give me information which I want to obtain concerning him, and this last is my only object in seeking you; so far as your interests are concerned you have nothing to fear from me, but, on the contrary, everything perhaps to gain. Will you believe me and trust me?"

"I suppose I may, deary; I suppose I may; I've lived many a year now in this world, and I've 'ad good reasons to doubt every one, from first to last; but I'll take *your* word in this, as you've a voice, dear gentleman, as is like one I'd trust at any time, only that I know the one I means is hushed forever."

She proceeded to say that she was both ready and willing to give him any information in her possession, and, at the suggestion of Datchery, they proceeded to the Minor Canon's house,—the better to escape observation, and, also, to give the Reverend Septimus an opportunity of hearing what the Puffer had to communicate.

They found the Reverend gentleman at home, and, on being informed of the object of their visit, he bade them enter, and ushering them into his private study, the two gentlemen were soon listening eagerly to the Puffer's narrative.

CHAPTER XXVII.

ANOTHER NIGHT WITH DURDLES.

If John Jasper's outward appearance was any indication of his mental condition, his sufferings must have been great indeed since the disappearance of his nephew. The sunken eyes, the pallid cheeks, and wan expression of the whole countenance, plainly told that the man was daily and hourly suffering from some terrible distress, which was slowly breaking him down with its burdens.

On leaving Fopperty, after the interview at the coffee-house, recorded in a previous chapter, he proceeded directly to Cloisterham, reaching his lodgings just at dusk, and meeting no one whom he knew except Mrs. Tope, who declared that he was looking so tired it was a wonder how he kept on his feet. Assuring the good lady, however, that he never felt better, he proceeded to his room, and throwing himself into a chair sat for several moments, evidently intent on some very important subject. After a little, he arose, and pacing the floor in a nervous manner, with his hands clasped behind him, muttered:

"Oh, if I can only ferret out the hiding-place of that black-skinned dog that stands between me and what I love, I'll show her and him what it is to blast the affections of a love like mine! Yes, I'll show them all, — even the suspicious old fool that she flies to for protection, — that I am not so easily disposed of or trampled under foot without one effort at retaliation. Have I not done everything to gain her? Have I not, by all the attention and affection which a man can show, sought to convince her of my great love for her? — and she knew it — she knew it!—and, but for the appearance of this black-skinned whelp, at the very time when everything pointed to a successful termination of my efforts to gain her, success would have crowned my efforts, and I should not be the miserable man I am to-day!"

Throwing himself into a chair, with threatening brow, he sits for a while in silent meditation.

It is getting late as he rouses himself from this thoughtful attitude. The shadows of evening are beginning to fall on surrounding objects, and so quiet is the time that every sound is magnified tenfold. Why does he start and look about him as though he feared to encounter some terrible thing, when a night-bird near his window pipes out on the still air some note of alarm to its neighboring mate? Even the creaking of the floor beneath his feet, as he steps softly upon it, and which would pass unheeded by another person, causes *him* to hold his breath and stop to listen for a repetition that does not come. Then he smiles to think how foolish are his fears, but stopping to listen again with more eagerness than before.

Now he ascends to his sleeping-room. From a closet therein he brings forth a slouched hat, very dirty, and which shows evidence of being well-worn, a pair of stout boots that would have caused a feeling of pride in the heart of any plough-boy who could have worn them, while a heavy coat, nearly new, and trousers to match, accompanied the boots and hat. Hastily disrobing himself of his finer garments, he proceeds to adopt the rougher ones.

By this time it has become quite dark—so dark that, as he emerges from his room, he is obliged to grope his way cautiously along the landing that leads to the postern stair; this reached, he descends, and casting a hasty look around, proceeds on his way, which lies in the direction of the stone-mason's quarters.

Arriving at that worthy gentleman's dwelling, he does not immediately stop, but proceeds beyond a few rods, and then retracing his steps, comes to his original destination; listening outside the door for a few moments, to satisfy himself that Durdles is alone, he knocks and cries:

"Open to a friend!"

A dim light is burning, and stands on one of the unfinished tombstones as the door opens to the visitor. Durdles acts as though he had been aroused from a sound slumber, for he rubs his eyes very hard and looks at Jasper as though not quite certain whether he (Durdles) may not be asleep even now, and only dreaming.

Looking at his visitor so very hard, and for the reason mentioned, is not pleasant to the Music Master, who returns the look with some contempt in his tones, as he asks:

"You should *know me*, and if you're not drunk, you *do*."

"Did I say as I didn't, Mr. Jasper?" comes the rejoinder, in an excited tone. "If Durdles has had a hard day of it, and is woke suddenly out of a snooze, where's the wonder if he don't happen to be a lively one this 'ere present minit. Durdles know'd as there'd not be much sleep *arter* you come, so he took what he could git *afore.*"

"I cannot blame you for that, certainly, Mr. Durdles," replied the other, in a conciliatory voice, "and I am truly very glad that you did so, for the manner in which you left me to myself at our last expedition was far from pleasant. I prefer to have you keep awake by all means to-night."

"Don't you go to havin' no fear for me, sir," is the reply.

"I suppose you have got everything ready," continues Jasper; "we may want to remain longer than before; your leaving me alone, as you did that night by sleeping so long, prevented me from seeing the half I desired; and to answer a question was an impossibility on your part."

"Well, who's to blame if the brandy was stronger than I thought? Not I; Durdles didn't make the brandy, he didn't."

"No," Jasper replies laughing, "but Durdles drunk it, and drunk too much. I'll carry the bottle to-night, however, and we'll see then if the result does not prove more satisfactory. Are you ready? for it is time we were moving."

Durdles takes his coat down from a dusty shelf and puts it outside of his dusty self; takes a lantern from its accustomed place, and then, feeling in his pockets for his keys, which he finds to be all safe, signifies his readiness to start, though not till he has placed in Jasper's hands—who reminds him of it the second time—the bottle that is a part and parcel of Durdles. They move towards the door and are just going out when Jasper snatches the candle from Durdles, as he is about to extinguish it, saying:

"Wait one moment; I have dropped my pencil, I think, near where I was standing, and I must find it," and leaves Durdles waiting at the door while he crosses the shop and stoops down to look for the missing object. It might have been imagination, but Durdles thought he saw the bottle which he handed Jasper glisten in the candle-light as the latter kneeled in his search. As it was only an instant that he saw it, however, and feeling assured that Jasper could have no possible object in drinking clandestinely therefrom, he concluded that he must have been mistaken.

"Ah, here it is!" cried the Choir Leader, "just where I expected. Now we're all ready," and, reaching the door, the light was extinguished and they take their way to the Cathedral.

"It's nigh a twelvemonth since we made this visit here afore," Durdles says, as they near the grand old pile looming up before them like some gigantic ghost, spreading itself across their pathway, as if to prevent their further progress. "I hope you'll see all there is to see this time, sir, for these ere jobs is what Durdles don't like."

"I regret that my curiosity should cause you inconvenience, Durdles," is the reply of Jasper, "but I hope to obtain all that can be obtained by this visit, and will not again solicit this favor from you."

"This ere night air makes me a little chilly," says Durdles after a moment's pause in the conversation; "suppose you hand me that ere bottle, and I'll see if that won't warm me up a bit."

"Not now," is the answer. "Wait till we get inside, and it will do you all the more good for waiting."

Durdles does not urge the point, and at last they reach the entrance. The door is unlocked by the stone-mason, but just as he is about to open it, Jasper lays his hand quickly on the other's arm, and bids him harken. Both assume a listening attitude, but neither see or hear aught to recompense them for the attempt.

"It must have been the rustling of leaves or my imagination, but I fancied I heard footsteps near us," Jasper whispers while peering into the darkness and eagerly listening for any sound that would give evidence of their being followed.

"Nothin' but the wind in the trees," says Durdles. "I've often heered that ere, and looked sharp out for thinkin' it might be a stiff 'un as was wantin' to run a race with me; no danger of that though, Mr. Jasper. But there's one ghost as Durdles *would* like to see, and would'nt run from if he see'd it—day or night."

They have entered now, and, closing and fastening the door behind them, advance up one of the aisles leading to the chancel. Reaching this point both men stop, and Durdles declares that it will be physically impossible for him to go another step without his bottle keeps him company.

Seeing Jasper still hesitate about giving it him, he declares, in terms more emphatic than elegant, that—

Damned if Durdles would scrape another shoe forward, till he had the desired bottle.

"So be it then," is the other's reply; "here it is,—only don't forget the trouble you made me before by using it too freely."

Durdles sets the lantern upon the floor, and placing the bottle to his lips, is about swallowing some of its contents, when Jasper says:

"Stay—you were saying just now that you would like to see the ghost of some one. You did not say who. Who was it now?"

Durdles, with the bottle still poised, makes answer:

"Your nephew, Edwin Drood."

A scream, that was echoed from every nook of the vast expanse, came from Jasper at the mention of the lost one's name, and with pale face and trembling limbs, he seizes Durdles by the shoulder, or he must have fallen where he stood.

Durdles, who professes to be frightened at nothing, throws a hasty glance about him, to ascertain the cause of his companion's agitation. Seeing nothing unusual, he coolly inquires—

"What's the meanin' of this 'ere?"

Jasper, recovering after a moment, declares the night air must have affected him, for that he felt an acute pain through one of his shoulders which was like a dagger-stab.

"I hope I did not alarm you," he adds.

"When Durdles gets scared, it'll be at what no one ever see'd yet." Then takes a draught from the bottle—the draught that he has been denied so long—Jasper watching him closely as he does it, and never leaving him with his eyes until he has taken the bottle from his lips.

They now proceed towards a door at the side of the chancel, and, passing through, descend to the crypt below. Jasper all the time watches his companion, who must have drank more of the liquor than was good for him, for, ere they had descended half way down the stone steps, he mumbles incoherently, leaning heavily on Jasper. Finally, he staggers about in such a fearful manner that the Music Master catches him by the arm just as the light is falling from his hand.

Quickly grasping the lantern, and steadying Durdles till he has fallen in a safe position, Jasper holds the light to his face, and then, convinced that he is unconscious, smiles as he says:

"I fear, Mr. Durdles, that even *this* brandy was too strong for you."

Turning the unconscious sleeper partly over, he finds his way to the pocket of the coat where the keys are deposited, and, having obtained them, resumes his downward journey.

On reaching the bottom, he unlocks the door leading into the crypt, and holds the lantern above his head, so that its rays may reflect the better on distant objects within; and then, apparently satisfied that he is unobserved, moves in an easterly direction, till he comes to a spot that has the appearance of having recently been the scene of labors on the part of the stone-mason. Cautiously looking about him, and peering as far into the distance as the dim rays of the lantern will permit, to assure himself that no one is observing him, he removes with his foot the loose mortar and stone.

Then he stops, and, again holding the lantern above his head, peers eagerly about him for a moment; then kneels and finds an iron ring, which enables him to raise from its place a good-sized slab.

His movements now are very rapid, and made in a nervous manner. His whole attention is devoted to the work before him. He throws the stone back, clears away the debris that is lying about, and, regardless of the dust that rises from the litter, peers with strained eyes into every corner of a nearly square vault which might some time—perhaps a hundred years before—have been used as a tomb.

At first he does not appear satisfied with what he sees, for he bends still further over, and holds the light so that every nook and corner can be observed by him. Then with blanched cheeks, and trembling from head to foot, like one who has heard some fearful, harrowing news, he sets the lantern down by his side, and, gazing still at the opening before him, exclaims:

"My God! my God! what does this mean?" and, still kneeling, buries his face in his hands.

Only for a moment thus, however; for, as if acting on the impulse of some sudden thought, he hastily rises to his feet, and setting the lantern a little further away, turns to replace the stone. Then his eyes, encountering a sight that almost freezes his blood, fairly protrude from their sockets, as he gazes for an instant at a form completely enveloped in white,—all but the face, which he recognizes to be that of EDWIN DROOD!

He clasps his hands above his head, makes one step forward, as though he would approach It nearer; then murmurs in a dying tone, "Mercy! mercy! mercy!" and falls insensible upon the stone floor, at the feet of the object he has so plainly recognized.

Meanwhile, Durdles has recovered from his lethargy, whether real or feigned, and concluding that Jasper must by this time want company, he proceeds to the landing below. Being familiar with the place, he does not experience that difficulty which another person would, in getting along through the darkness which surrounds him.

The lantern, still standing where Jasper had placed it, continues to emit a feeble light, and in the distance resembles a beacon on a rock-bound coast, to warn the mariner of the dangers that surround him.

Like another mariner, Durdles perceives the light through the hazy blackness of the place, and sails along in a careless manner till he gets near it, though not near enough to perceive objects distinctly and so cries:

"Ho, Mr. Jasper."

There is no reply, and Durdles does not attempt to make his presence known again, but walks leisurely along till he reaches the spot where Jasper is still lying, and breathing heavily, like one whose sleep is disturbed with frightful dreams.

Durdles, nowise disconcerted by the scene before him, merely gave vent to a low whistle, as he gazed at the displaced stone, and then turned again to Jasper, lying prostrate, and then back to the stone again.

"Durdles may have been a fool once," he mutters, "but Durdles ain't never allowed himself to be fooled twice. Though *he* be a sly one," he continues, "there be others as sly, or a little slyer, maybe."

Then placing himself by Jasper's side, he shakes him by the shoulder and cries, "Ho, ho!"

A long-drawn sigh is the first response that greets his efforts, which is followed by a stretching of the limbs and a restless movement of the arms, and then the miserable man slowly opens his eyes to what is about him.

"What has happened?" he asks, as he gazes dreamily at his companion.

"That's what Durdles said to himself a time ago," is the reply, "and that's what Durdles says now, along with you."

The sound of Durdles' voice rouses the Music Master from his stupor, and all in an instant his thoughts revert to the circumstances which have led to his present dilemma.

Rising to his feet, with the old, natural nervousness in his tones, he quickly asks Durdles if he has seen a third person in the crypt?

Durdles replies that he has not; and then looks very hard at the displaced stone, as saying, "Perhaps the third person may be down there!"

Jasper notices the look, and, quickly inferring what is in the other's mind, hastens to explain:

"I think, Mr. Durdles, I have had a very narrow escape for my life to-night."

Durdles merely nods his head, and waits for the other to proceed.

"Had anything occurred to me of a serious nature, I should have you to thank for it." All the time his eyes are wandering in a wild manner about and beyond him, as though he expected again to see the terrible object which had caused him such deadly fear.

"Durdles may be to blame, and then again Durdles may not be to blame," is the reply, given in sullen tones.

"Of course you are to blame," rejoins Jasper, assuming an angry mood. "If you had not disregarded my warnings about the too frequent use of that bottle of yours, you would have been in a condition to accompany me, instead of leaving me alone to fall into such infernal pitfalls as these. I do not think, however, that I have any broken bones," —feeling his limbs as though to assure himself of the fact,—

"but falling on the stone pavement must have stunned me. What are such places for?" he continues, after a moment's pause.

"I've been pretty well over this here place, and thought I'd seen all there was, but here's something what I never did see, so Durdles knows no more about it than you."

"Well, we may as well give up any further discoveries to-night, for this fall has made me so weak that I can hardly stand. Let us replace this stone, and see that we put it back so securely that another person, who has a curiosity to go through here, will not meet with the same misfortune that befel me."

"It's nigh two year since I was in this part of the drawin'-room," Durdles says, as they proceed to put back the stone; "but I'm d—d if I see'd this then, and Durdles is knocked in the head to make it out. Stiff 'uns might do somethin' like this, and then they mightn't, and Durdles thinks they didn't."

Jasper does not reply; and, having arranged the stone, they proceed in the direction of the stairs, ascending which, they pass through the door at the chancel side, and so out from the Cathedral.

"Of course you will keep this to yourself, Mr. Durdles," says Jasper; "for I should feel very unpleasant, and, in fact, rather ashamed, to have it known that I had met with such a ridiculous accident."

"Durdles's mouth is one what don't open every time he breathes, and Durdles knows his bus'ness. Don't you be afeered of me, Mr. Jasper."

At this point, they are both startled by hearing a voice near them cry:

"Widdy!"

Being very dark, it was impossible to distinguish the object from which the sound proceeded, but there was no mistaking the voice, and both men became conscious of the near proximity of Deputy. The effect on Durdles was slight; but Jasper, with his naturally excitable temperament,—rendered ten times more so by the events of the past few hours,—on realizing that the boy was a witness of his being in the company of the stone-mason at such an hour, and in such a place, became perfectly furious, and made a sudden spring towards the spot where he thought the boy likely to be. The suddenness with which it was made, unfortunately for Deputy, resulted in that young gentleman being caught by the collar before he had the slightest idea that his enemy was within reaching distance. Retaining his grasp of the boy, Jasper proceeded to shake him in a most savage manner, cuffing him about the head whenever his victim could not dodge the blows, and threatening to kill him, then and there.

"I told you, you young villain, that I would tear you to shreds if you ever dogged my steps again, and now I swear I'll keep my word," all the time striking savagely at the boy with his clenched fist.

"Let me go!" roared Deputy; "Let me go! I hain't done nuffin to you, Jarsper!" and then gives vent to a series of howls that could have been heard half a mile away, writhing and twisting the while, in his efforts to free himself.

Whether he had become tired from the exertion he had made, or whether he was fearful that Deputy's screams would alarm the neighborhood, only Jasper knew. Certain it is that he finally released his hold of the boy's collar just as the other was making a fierce struggle to escape, and as a consequence the Deputy landed pretty violently on his back. Hastily rising to his feet, he cries out:

"You'll ketch it for this, Jarsper!"

"What do you mean, you whelp, by following me here to-night?" and made as though he was about to do the boy more violence.

"I didn't follow yer here," cried the boy savagely, "and don't yer tech me again, or I'll make yer wish yer hadn't."

"What were you doing here if not to watch and dog me?" asks Jasper.

"I'd only just come out to look for 'im," pointing to Durdles, who stood perfectly unconcerned at what was going forward; "and arter I'd been all round a lookin' for 'im, I kim in this 'ere direction, and see'd the light a-comin' out o' the Ken-free-der-el, and I knowed as he was 'ere. That's all about it, Jarsper, and don't yer tech me again," and stooped to find a stone, which he shifted from one hand to the other, as though undecided whether to throw it or not.

The boy's reply seemed to satisfy the Music Master, for he grew calmer directly the boy had ceased, and told him that the quicker he went to his lodgings and his bed the better it would be for him. He then bade Durdles good-night, and, leaving that worthy to get home whenever he chose, departed for the Gate House.

It might have been fancy, but several times before Jasper reached his lodgings he thought he heard footsteps near him; but, when he stopped to listen, all was still and he continued his way, confident that he was mistaken.

Shortly after Jasper has entered his lodgings, and before the lamp has ceased burning in his room, another person passes down the entrance that leads to the Gate House, and in a very stealthy manner indeed. This person, continuing in the same stealthy manner towards the apartments occupied by Mr. Dick Datchery, enters therein, and, procuring a light, proves to be no other than Datchery himself, who hastily removes his shoes and hat, throws himself into a chair in a manner which indicates fatigue, and then ejaculates:

"D—n him!" Then, after a moment's silence, continues: "For a single buffer, living on his means, I have had a pretty hard time to-night, and have proved true the old saying, that, to learn, a man must labor; and, I think, might have been very properly added, 'Devilish hard;' certainly that's my experience. Well, well; it's only a little time before the fog will settle, and we shall be able to see the picture clear. We can afford to be patient. Meantime, my score continues to grow, and that reminds me that I've something to mark down in addition to-night." And, rising, he goes to the cupboard door and adds three or four straight marks. This finished, he disrobes himself and retires for the night, or rather morning. And so ends Jasper's second visit to the Cathedral crypt, whether for good or evil.

CHAPTER XXVIII.

FOPPERTY'S MISSION AND A SUDDEN DISAPPEARANCE.

On the morning succeeding the night that Fopperty Padler first occupied his new lodgings in Southampton Street, the sun had cast his rays into the apartments of the various occupants of the dwelling, and found the minds of each engrossed with subjects widely at variance.

Rosa, whose thoughts were almost constantly dwelling on the misfortunes that surrounded her, found herself, as usual, thinking of Edwin Drood, and agitated by the same problem which, unfortunately for her, was so difficult of solution.

Miss Twinkleton, who had for some days past been studying how she could, with the best grace, resign her present position, and so return to the classic precincts of the Nuns' House,—whose inmates she felt could no longer dispense with her presence,—was contemplating the effect that her decision would have upon Rosa and her guardian; and so both ladies kept very quiet, saying little, and arranging their morning toilets.

If the sun, however, is a faithful chronicler, and keeps a true record of all that its ray-messengers convey to it when they return to headquarters, it would have recorded that Fopperty Padler had, appearances considered, gone to bed the night before in a drunken condition, and had awoke in such a muddled state that he did not appear to have any definite thoughts of anything,—except, perhaps, that he had a rattling headache, and was not quite certain whether the flash of light that he saw on the floor of his room was day-light or candle-light.

By degrees, however, he began to comprehend the fact that another day had commenced to run its race, and decided that he would get up. Being pretty tired from his adventures of the previous day, he, like many another Fopperty, could not instantly bring to his aid the requisite strength of mind necessary to carry out his resolution, but, instead thereof, would mentally resolve that, in just five minutes, he would get up, and doze off to wake and find that his five minutes had been thirty-five. But this could not last forever. An empty stomach soon warned the gentleman that the inner man was just then a person who must be obeyed; so, crawling out in a rather undecided manner, he proceeded to dress himself. While thus occupied, he revolved in his mind what he should do through the day to further the accomplishment of his mission. It was evident that he must pay a visit to Staple Inn, and he determined to make the visit that very day.

Meanwhile, let us return to Rosa. She has performed her toilet, and stepping to the window, looks out upon the street below, which is now beginning to teem with busy life and animation.

She stands a few moments thus, tapping the panes with her fingers, while, now and then, a deep sigh escapes her. She is feeling more sad than usual this morning, and she cannot drive away the sorrow that fills her heart. It seems as though some new misfortune is about to befall her, and yet she thinks nothing worse can happen than has already occurred; so why should she brood over troubles in perspective, when those of the past are all that she can bear. Then she thinks if her guardian would only come;—dear Mr. Grewgious,—good old man. If he had come then, as she wished, how much misery would have been spared both her and him!

She turns suddenly, and, donning her hat and shawl, tells Miss Twinkleton that she is going out for a walk.

Miss Twinkleton mildly protests, but so mildly that the protest has no effect, and Rosa moves towards the door.

"I shall not go far or stay long," she says; "but I think a walk will do me good; before our breakfast is laid I'll return,"—and, thus saying, leaves the room and passes out into the street.

Poor Rosa! Where is Mr. Grewgious, with his words of counsel, his watchful and attentive care, that he does not come now, above all other times! Could he have foreseen what is to be, how faster than ever bird winged its way to its troubled mate would he have hastened to his charge!

A moment after Rosa had gone, Fopperty, who had arranged his toilet for a morning stroll, also departed from the house, and wended his way in the direction of Mr. Grewgious' chambers. Sauntering along in his usual unconcerned and indolent manner, his attention was attracted to a hackney-coach that was being driven at a very rapid rate; and, although the glance which he obtained of the inside was momentary, he thought he recognized one of the occupants. The coach was soon out of sight, however, and without giving the circumstance any further thought, he continued on his way.

Now it so happened that, just as Fopperty was nearly opposite his destination, Mr. Grewgious was leaving his chambers, on his way to Mrs. Billickin's, and was looking about—as persons often do when they first enter the street—to see if he could recognize a familiar face. On casting his eyes over the way he instantly perceived, in the features of Fopperty, the person he had last seen in company with John Jasper.

Forming a hasty resolution as to what course he should pursue, he waited till the other had crossed over and was entering the Inn, and then retraced his steps, and followed after.

Fopperty, being a stranger, was undecided how to proceed, and had come to a halt; and then it was that Mr. Grewgious touched him on the shoulder and enquired if he was looking for any one in particular.

Hesitating a moment, Fopperty replied that he very likely shouldn't be there if he wasn't looking for some one.

"Right, quite right," is the rejoinder of the old gentleman, assuming a merry tone; "I might have known, if I had stopped to think, that there is nothing about Staple that would be very apt to attract one, aside from business."

"Are you acquainted with the people here?" Fopperty asks, eyeing the other suspiciously.

"Oh, pretty well," is the reply. "What is the name of the person you are in search of?"

Fopperty had not anticipated this question, and therefore had no reply to give, but, on the impulse of the moment, he ejaculated—

"Lawson."

"Lawson!" cries Grewgious; "oh, yes, and a fine fellow he is, and a shrewd one, too! Now I look at you carefully, I believe I perceive a great resemblance between you and Lawson. Come with me, sir; his chambers join mine, and we've been neighbors for years. Come, sir, and I will conduct you directly there."

This was rather more than Fopperty had bargained for, but as he reflected that he could very easily declare it to be another Lawson he was in search of when his guide should bring him in contact with the man, he accompanied Mr. Grewgious without more ado, and was led by him directly to the latter's chambers.

"Have a seat," says Mr. Grewgious, placing a chair. "I don't see Mr. Lawson," he adds, glancing hastily about the room, "but perhaps we shall get along just as well without him," and then steps to the door and locks it, putting the key in his pocket; after which he seats himself and looks very coolly at Fopperty, who regards the old man's proceedings with some curiosity, and no little alarm. This is not lost upon Mr. Grewgious, who continues:

"I have not asked you here because I want to do you a violence. Even were I so disposed, I should be foolish to attempt it, for I am an old man, while you are young and possess twice my strength. Neither do I wish you to imagine that I desire to take any undue advantage of you, by the course I have taken. My sole motive in forcing this interview is to appeal to your heart, and ask you to give me a detailed account of the services you are expected to perform to aid a Villain (perhaps you don't know how much of a Villain) in persecuting a poor, unfortunate youth, who has already suffered beyond description, through the agency of this same Villain."

Fopperty's black eyes recede beneath the overhanging brows, and then make their appearance again to stare at the old man with more surprise than before.

"You may think it strange," Mr. Grewgious continues, "that I should know what you are here for, and in whose interest you are employed; but let me assure you I do know, and it will be useless for you to deny the truth of my assertions. Of course, *you* have no personal interest in the matter further than the compensation which you are to receive for what you do; hence you will find it more for your interest to serve me, for I promise that where you are to receive one pound from that Villain, you shall have two from me."

For reasons which will appear as this narrative proceeds, Fopperty Padler, in his heart, detested John Jasper. In undertaking to act the spy for the Music Master, he was actuated solely by mercenary motives; and though he intended to discover the hiding-place of Neville, if possible, he had also determined to put the unfortunate young man on his guard before carrying the intelligence to Jasper. The reader will not, therefore, be surprised at Fopperty's readiness to fall in with Mr. Grewgious' proposition.

"You talks bus'ness, sir, and right to the pint; and that's what I like. My time's my own, and I've a right to do as I please with it;

but, if I makes any arrangement of this kind with you, of course all's mum?"

"You may depend upon that," answers Grewgious.

"But how am I to know as you'll do the right thing, and not split on me to Jasper?" enquires Fopperty doubtfully.

"Because if I trust you, you can trust me; and rest assured it is not for my interest to let Jasper or any one else know of this interview." A pause, and then Grewgious asks: "Do I understand that you accept my proposition?"

"Well, sir," is Fopperty's answer, "I'll do all I can for you; but you mustn't ask too much, for I tell you, sir, that John Jasper ain't no man's fool, and that I knows."

"Your remark would indicate that you had known our Friend for some time. How long, now?"

"Between seven and eight years; but not much for two years gone."

"And now if you was to express your candid opinion, formed after an acquaintance of eight years, off and on, what would you say was the character of our Friend — very good, very fair, or very bad?"

Again the eyes take counsel, and the brows cover them, and then Fopperty ejaculates, "D—n bad!"

"Ah!" rejoins Grewgious, "you state my convictions exactly. Now, would you have any objections to giving me a little history or statement concerning the life of our Friend with the Bad Character?"

A liberal proposition accompanies the request of Mr. Grewgious as an inducement for the other to proceed. Whereupon, Fopperty leans back in his chair, and, settling himself into a comfortable position, relates what he knows of the Choir Leader:

"Eight years ago, or thereabouts, my mother, who is a widow, occupied a third floor back of a house situated in a narrow court in the neighbourhood of Drury Lane. At the time we moved there, a family was livin' on the floor below, consistin' of a woman and her daughter, by the name of Tranders. They were very poor, and the daughter, then about eighteen years old, supported herself and mother by sewin'. It was a mighty poor livin', tho', and enough to discourage an older one than this young and tender girl. After we had lived in the house a few weeks, my mother and the old woman Tranders 'come acquainted, and in that way we found out somethin' of their history. It appeared that a young man had made the acquaintance of the girl about six months before, and she was engaged to marry him, as soon as he could obtain a position that would enable him to support the family. I used to see him pretty often at their lodgin', and I always noticed that he went in and out as though he was afraid some one *would* see him. I remember one day in partic'lar, I was goin' down stairs, and jest when I got to the landin' I heard voices, and a woman sayin', in a kind of mournful tone, I thought, 'Donald,'—that was the name he went by there—Donald Renlaw,—'Donald, it is life or death with me; and it lays with you which, for the shame would kill me. Why cannot the ceremony be performed to-day?'

"I did not stop to hear his reply; I had heard enough to satisfy me that she would die a broken-hearted girl, and that he would be the cause. It wan't no business of mine, though; and I continued on my way along the landin', he and I lookin' pretty hard at each other as I passed. I had never seen him before, but that look was enough for me to remember him by.

"I *thought* him to be a deep one then; I *know* it now. I did not see him again for weeks together, and he kept away from the house pretty much after that time. One mornin,' early, I was wakened from a sound sleep by hearin' some one takin' on horrid bad—cryin' and moanin'. The sounds came from the floor below, and I thought it likely the poor girl was cryin' for her lover. Of course, I couldn't help her, so I went off to sleep again.

"Next mornin,' mother told me as the young lady below stairs had a baby the night afore, and that she, (the poor young lady,) was very sick, and that the old woman Tranders was all but crazy.

"It's no use my goin' over all that happened for two or three years after that; for there is little I can tell you after a few months followin' the birth of this child. Donald came once that we knew of, and the old woman Tranders said he left them money and had promised to look after them, but the young lady would not see him or allow him to come to the room where she lay sick.

"A little time after that, we took other lodgin's, and, for a long while, knew nothin' more of the Tranders."

"Take time, take time," says Mr. Grewgious, as Fopperty ceased speaking, apparently tired; "not but what I am anxious to hear the conclusion of what you have to say; but, at the same time, I have a consideration for your comfort, and therefore again beg that you take time." And Mr. Grewgious tried to appear as if he was calmly waiting for the other to proceed, but it was a poor attempt at calmness, as he nervously beat the desk before him with the tips of his fingers, and moved about in his chair very uneasily.

"We had nearly forgotten the Tranders," resumed Fopperty, "until one day I was passin' by the old place where we lived, and a thought happened to strike me that I'd like to know if they were still livin' there, and how they got along. Just as I was opposite I see a woman come out, so I hailed her and asked if anybody by the name of Tranders was livin' in the house.

"'Oh yes,' she says, 'and poor things, it's a hard time they're enjoyin' of, I ken tell yer. The neighbors has took pity on 'em or they'd a-starved afore this, and Bessie's mother's a-dyin', if she bean't dead a'ready.'

"'Who's Bessie?' says I; 'for I'd never heard the name before, and thought, after all, it must be some other family the woman was tellin' of.'

"'Oh,' she says, 'Bessie's the grand-daughter of old Mrs. Tranders, and dear sweet little cherub she be, though it's said she be a love child, and if so be that's true, I'd like to twist her father's head off—for it must be as he's a great villain.'"

"Right! right!" exclaimed Mr. Grewgious, jumping from his chair so suddenly that Fopperty was quite startled. Mr. Grewgious, pacing the floor for a few moments, and rubbing his hands nervously together, tells Fopperty not to mind him, for if he didn't walk for a moment he couldn't answer for the consequences. After a little, the old gentleman is calmer again, and, resuming his chair, motions Fopperty to proceed.

"After hearin' this," continues Fopperty, "I went straight up to their rooms,—I hadn't forgotten where they were,—and tapped at the door. Old Mrs. Tranders came and invited me in, and told me that her daughter was dead about half-an-hour since, and she'd be glad to have us come to the funeral, which would be the next day. I asked her if I could see the dead girl's face, for maybe I wouldn't be able to come to the funeral, though I promised her as the old lady should. She opened the door leadin' from the room into a sleeping-closet, and there I see a sight that would have melted a flint, if so be flints could melt. There she lay,—as pretty as ever she was when alive,—a sweet smile on her face that was turned down to that of her little child, who she had held in her arms, so the old woman Tranders told me, all the time that she lay a-dyin'.

"Let me tell you, sir," continued Fopperty, who had stopped to wipe his eyes, from which the tears had started at the recollection of the scene he was describing; "let me tell you that, even if such sights as these are sad, they sometimes do a power of good. I had been a pretty wild chap before that, and I haven't been a 'postle Paul since, but I've reason to think that, after that day, things looked different to me than they ever did before, and I felt somethin' come here," striking his breast, "that's never left there through all the time that's passed since that day!"

Mr. Grewgious again jumps from his chair, but this time to grasp the hand of Fopperty, and, while shaking it heartily, says: "It does you credit, my dear fellow, it does you credit, and I am thankful that you have shown me this part of your nature, for it proves that you have germs in your breast, which, properly nourished, will make you a better man in time to come; and, with God's help, we will try to bring it about."

Mr. Grewgious spoke truly when he declared that he was glad to witness this exhibition of feeling on Fopperty's part, for he felt now that he could trust him. He saw that the naturally good heart of the man before him had been covered with the scum produced by idleness and contamination with vice, until the death-bed scene he had witnessed had cleared one spot upon it that shone out bright and clear, and all the more bright and clear from the corruption that still surrounded it.

Oh! who would dread Death when realizing that the touch of his icy hand not only frees the soul from earth, that it may obtain Eternal Happiness in Heaven, but also helps to purify the hearts of those who are left behind! and who, that ever gazed upon the quiet features of the dead, has not turned away, and felt more love and charity dwelling in his heart towards his fellow-man! Ah, ye who mourn for dear ones, beneath the green sod sleeping, try to realize that Death is but God's Messenger, sent to give rest to His tired children of earth! and remember, that while the bodies of your loved ones are mingling with the Dust of Centuries, in the repose of a dark and silent tomb, where the sun's rays can never come, their souls—in which dwelt all their earthly affections — are basking in the light of a Heavenly Sun, whose warmth and brilliancy shall never die!

Fopperty having rallied from his agitation, and Mr. Grewgious resuming his seat, the former continued his narrative:

"Trying to cheer the old woman with such words as I could, I hastened home and told my mother all the particulars. When the funeral took place she went to the house, and stayed till it was all over. There wan't a large funeral, sir—no one but my mother and old Mrs. Tranders and her grandchild. The infernal devil who had brought so much misery to the dead woman was not there. No, not he! Donald Renlaw knew better than to attempt to look upon her dead face. Then—"

"Stay right there for one moment," said Mr. Grewgious, taking a pen and paper, "while I make an item of that name. There," said he, as he folded the slip of paper—"now, if you please."

"Then," Fopperty resumes, "the question was, what to do with the old woman and her child, for they could not support themselves, and some one must help them, or the poor-house would have to be their home. Mrs. Tranders said if we would take the child to keep for a short time, that she could manage for herself, and perhaps pay something towards the child's support. This was done, and Mrs. Tranders had odd jobs by which, for a time, she managed to support herself and do a little for the child. Two months after the mother's death, Mrs. Tranders, the grandmother, disappeared, and we have never seen her since. About this time I fell in with Renlaw. I told him that the little girl was with us and that it was his duty to help support her, or we should have to send her to the poor-house if he didn't, for we couldn't support her without help. He said it was a sad thing, the whole of it, but we must make the best of it, and treat the child the same as if she were our own, and he would pay all the bills, and then gave me a ten-pound note to start on. That was five years ago, and in that time all he has paid is thirty pounds toward her support, till three or four days since he gave my mother a small sum for to buy her clothing.

"Well, as I was sayin', we had pretty much lost sight of Renlaw altogether, when I happened, a few weeks since, to meet him coming from Aldersgate Street in a great hurry; and, as he had a travellin' bag in his hand, I thought I'd follow him and see where he was headed for. He didn't stop till he got to a station, and from there the train took him (and me, for I followed him) to Cloisterham, and where I found he was settled permanently. Acting on the advice of another party, who I fell in with about that time, and who was greatly interested in the man we're speakin' of, I made up my mind that I would secure quarters there for mother and Bess, and so finally oblige him to do somethin' for the child. Another object I had in view was to benefit the health of the child, who has been poorly for a year past, and I thought a change of air would do her good. After I was settled there and everything fixed as I wanted it, I placed myself in his way one day, pretending that I did not see him, and so let him follow me, knowing very well that when he found out where we lived, he would not be slow in coming to see us, for his own interest. I was right, too. The next day but one he came."

Fopperty then proceeded to relate what took place at that interview —which the reader is already familiar with—and from that time down to the moment when he encountered Mr. Grewgious.

Mr. Grewgious did not speak for several moments after the other had ceased. His mind was agitated with various painful subjects, and among others was the certainty he felt that Jasper was, in some way, responsible for the disappearance of Edwin Drood.

Then he remembered the strange behaviour of Jasper on that day when, at the latter's lodgings, he had called to communicate to him the decision of Rosa and Edwin. He arose and walked the room in silence for a few moments, and then said:

"Mr. Padler,—or Fopperty, if you please, for I can remember that better than the other,—I desire to state three things"—and holds up three fingers of the left hand, with the right hand resting on the top of one of them. "First, I thank you for your confidence, and for the information which your narrative has revealed to me." (Ticking off one finger.) "Second, I assume—though you have not said so—that John Jasper and Donald Renlaw are one and the same person; and, though I had no doubt before that he was a miserable wretch, I did not believe him a person of such total depravity as your statement indicates him to be." (Ticking off another finger.) "Third, and last, though by no means least, I propose to bring this Villain to justice at the earliest possible moment; and, as I shall need the assistance of yourself, will ask if you will favor me with such assistance, with the understanding, of course, that you are to be well paid for all you do in that direction."

And Mr. Grewgious, having put down finger number three, proceeds to put himself down into a chair at his side, and waits for the other's reply.

The Fopperty eyes retreating to take counsel, reappear, and their owner makes answer:

"You can depend upon me, sir; only say what I am to do, and I'll do it."

Mr. Grewgious stops and thinks a moment, as though undecided, and finally says:

"Do you go back to Cloisterham, see Jasper, and tell him that you have found the hiding-place of Mr. Landless. After you have told him this, you are to remember carefully every word that he says; and then, after your interview, come to me for further instructions. Do you follow me?"

"Right straight through," is Fopperty's answer; "and you may depend I'll do my best to serve you."

"Here is some money," placing a five-pound note in Fopperty's hand, "and you'll find I'm no niggard in this matter, but will pay well for services rendered. And now our interview must end for to-day, as I have an engagement that should have been met some hours since."

So Fopperty returns to Mrs. Billickin's for his portmanteau, and starts for Cloisterham to convey the news of his discovery of Neville to John Jasper, while Mr. Grewgious hastens to visit Rosa. Arriving there, the latter is met by Miss Twinkleton, who proceeds to inform him that Miss Bud went for a walk some two hours before, promising to return by the time breakfast was laid, and that she (Miss Twinkleton) supposed, of course, that, as she did not return, she must have stepped in upon him (Mr. Grewgious), and that he had prevailed on her to lunch with him.

"Did she speak of calling on me?" hastily inquired Mr. Grewgious.

"No; I believe she said she was not feeling as well as usual this morning, and would—"

"Oh, bosh! bosh!" interrupts the old gentleman, angrily; "you should have gone with her,—gone with her, madam! This is a very serious affair, Miss Twinkleton. You have, in my estimation, acted very unwisely in allowing Rosa to go out unattended, for I have a feeling that she will not return; in which case the whole blame must be attributed to you," and the old gentleman walks the floor in a very excited state of mind, looking sideways at Miss Twinkleton, now and then, in the most savage manner possible.

Miss Twinkleton does not faint at all this. She does not even appear excited. She calmly observes Mr. Grewgious' furious glances at her, and after he has ceased speaking, replies:

"I beg, Mr. Grewgious, that you will not forget the services already contributed in Miss Rosa Bud's behalf, on the part of myself, or that the circumstances under which they were rendered have been far from enviable. Miss Bud was desirous of taking a morning walk; desired to be alone, of course, as she did not solicit my company; and, as she was free to do as she chose, I cannot see why blame should attach to me for any disaster that may have befallen her."

Mr. Grewgious makes no reply, but still walks the floor with nervous step. There is a tap at the door; Mr. Grewgious springs to open it, thinking possibly it may be Rosa, instead of whom stands Mrs. Billickin, who puts her hand upon her side, as she makes a low bow, and making as though she was losing her breath or catching it, just as Mr. Grewgious preferred, says:

"I 'ope, sir, as you'll not mind my *mis*fortions, sir, as is caused by hefforts made in trying the tops ov these stairs to reach. It may be wrong in me to say it, but I do believe that there is not ground enough as comes with this world, for so be there 'ad been more ground, landin's would never been, and so, of course, no stairs to climb. Hand *'ow* do you do, sir?"

"Have you seen my ward this morning?" asks Mr. Grewgious, abruptly.

"Not understanding *why* I am asked this question, sir, an answer I will not give," is the reply of Billickin, folding her arms and looking defiantly at her questioner, as though she would rather like to have him attempt to force her to give a different reply.

"I ask you the question, my good woman," said Mr. Grewgious, rather amused, notwithstanding his agitation, "because Miss Bud left the house two hours since, for a short stroll; and, as she has not returned, I feel somewhat anxious about her."

"I will not deceive you, sir," says the Billickin, "and tells you plainly I 'ave not seen the young lady. Some there be, who, if she had left their 'ouse at early morning would have knowed it well. But I am not a spyer or a watcher of others; though well I know there be those who would stoop to such meanesses," looking sideways at Miss Twinkleton. "I spurns such hacts, and leave 'em for them as is that low, let them come from Ladies' Semynaries, or wheresoever they will."

Observing that the Billickin blood was already warm, and that a very little word from her adversary would be sufficient to set it boiling, Mr. Grewgious thanked her, and said he would go out and search for the absent young lady, for possibly he might succeed in finding her. He then took his departure, leaving the two ladies to get along as best they might.

Through every street and lane in the vicinity did Mr. Grewgious search for the missing one, but all the time with a heavy heart, for he had a foreboding that some evil had befallen her, and that it would be many days ere he should see her, and perhaps never again alive. That John Jasper was at the bottom of this affair he had no doubt, for it was impossible that Rosa would have voluntarily absented herself, unless—it was a horrid thought but one that, nevertheless, forced itself upon him—she had, perhaps, been brooding over the unfortunate circumstances connected with her life, and so, in a fit of despondency, had conceived the idea of making away with herself! Young people had done such things; and so the old man, filled with apprehension at this suggestion, wandered to the river, thinking it possible some clew might be obtained there, but all in vain. In the different streets through which he wandered in his search, he would enquire of the passers-by if they had seen her,—describing her appearance as well as possible,—but all to no purpose; and so, after many weary hours, he returned to his chambers, and throwing himself into a chair, wept as he never had but once in his life before, and then when a woman,—whose features were a counterpart of Rosa's, vanished from his sight forever, and passed out upon that golden river that leads from earth to heaven.

CHAPTER XXIX.

OPENS THE DOOR FOR MR. BROBITY.

BLUNDERHEADED Sapsea, notwithstanding the greatness of his mind, was possessed, like thousands of ordinary mortals, through relationship, of a brother-in-law. That is, people called Solomon — or Sol Brobity, as he was most often addressed—brother-in-law of Mr. Sapsea, in consequence of Miss Brobity, Sol's sister, marrying that Wonderful Being—that quintescence of wisdom and greatness. But Mr. Sapsea would not allow common customs to apply to him, even in relationship, and so he declared, whenever the subject was mentioned, that Solomon was not brother-in-law to him, but that a relationship of that nature might be allowed, in that Mr. Sapsea himself was the brother-in-law—by no means Solomon.

Sapsea's opinion of the whole Brobity family is not a favorable one. They were not, to use his own expression, a people of—Mind.

If, as it sometimes happened, the Brobitys were mentioned in Sapsea's hearing, he would lean back in his chair, and speak of them somewhat after this fashion :

"There is no depth of reasoning power existing there which enables them to discern—Mind. The Perceptive Faculties are dull. Matter, with them, is of more weight than—Mind. Rotundity of Mind is wanting." Mr. Sapsea always closes his eyes at this point, as intending the listener to infer that this last expression was the result of deep thought on his part. "Ethelinda was the only person bearing the name of Brobity who had the power to discern—Mind. It was that Discerning Faculty that led her to consent to change her name to Sapsea. The inevitable consequence of this lack of intelligence on the one hand, and the possession of it on the other, was what might have been expected,—objection to me from them,—admiration from her. I do not say, however, that even *she* had Mind to correspond with mine,—*no* Brobity could have that; but her redeeming quality lay in this,—that she *appreciated* a Great Mind; and hence Ethelinda Sapsea where what before was Ethelinda Brobity."

Then he would usually wait a moment for his hearers to thoroughly digest the great thoughts to which his words had given expression, and then continue :

"Of Ethelinda's mother, I say nothing—she is a Woman;" this in a tone which implied inferiority in Sapsea's estimation. "I say Woman. Of Ethelinda's brother Solomon, I *will* say this: There is no excuse for him. Perhaps it is wrong for me to speak thus. You may say that the Strong should not trample on the weak. There are times when it cannot be helped. There are times when Mind must assert its superiority, and this is one of those times. And I repeat that there is no excuse for him—he *could* have learned from me but would not."

Now it was pretty generally known that, previous to the deceased Mrs. Sapsea's marriage with that great Mind, Sol Brobity was very frank in his expressions concerning it, and declared that the *name* of Sapsea was enough to object to, if nothing more; but when to the name was coupled such a man, he felt it to be his duty, as a loving brother, to utter a protest. Sapsea was suggestive of sap-head; but as no human head could hold the sap—there being an ocean of it, figuratively—why, sea was substituted for head, and hence Sap-sea.

Mr. Sapsea never forgot the indignity thus cast upon him by Sol, and therefore took occasion at all times to belittle his traducer.

Sol Brobity, as we find him to-day, is a thin, spare gentleman of sixty or thereabouts, with red whiskers on each side of his face that have a tendency to grow pointing towards his nose, as though either side were running a race to see which could reach that point first, or if each would like to embrace the other at the earliest possible moment. His head is also covered with hair of the same color, except that the top is bald and shines in the sun like a glass bottle. He is a bachelor, and, though often bantered thereat, declares that he don't want anything about him that he cannot understand; and as he could never understand a woman, he does not want a wife. He had lived with his mother for sixty years, and he didn't understand *her* yet; and although there was a time when he thought he could comprehend his sister, she threw him all abroad again my marrying Sapsea, and since then he had given up all attempts to study female character, concluding that women were so many Living Enigmas, sent into the world to puzzle the brains of men.

He, with his mother, live in the High Street; she an old lady of eighty-five, at least, who has doted on her son always, and who, to this day, calls him Solly, the same as when she rocked him in his cradle.

Notwithstanding the old lady's years, she retains her faculties to a remarkable degree, except that she has been for many years extremely deaf.

Mother and son are seated at table to-day, only just finished dinner, when the latter says:

"Mother, I think of calling on Sapsea before long."

"Stars and garters!" a favorite expression of the old lady's; "Stars and garters, Solly, what do you want of flaxseed?" not understanding his remark, and looking at him with some alarm betokened upon her features, to discover if he showed signs of being ill.

"Sapsea!" roared Solomon; "I said call on Sapsea!" turning very red in the face from exertion, and then laughing heartily at her mistake.

"Call on Sapsea!" exclaimed the old lady, holding up both hands with astonishment. "Why, it's fit to kill us to live as near him as we do, without putting ourselves in contact with him. Don't do it, Solly; don't do it, my dear."

"It surely can't do no harm, mother, to call on him once in a while, and you know we've not been to his house since Ethel died."

"Very true, Solly, very true; and it ain't hurt us any for want of seeing him. Another thing, he'd not treat you decently if you should go there, and you know it. No, Solly, don't go. He don't want to see us; if he did, he'd come whére we were."

"Because this poor, ignorant man does not act as he should towards us," returns Uncle Sol, "it does not signify that we should neglect our duty as Christians, and set him a good example. I do not like him any more than you do, but I feel I should, as a duty to our dead Ethel, treat him with all the respect that I possibly can."

A rap at the door interrupts any further controversy, and the cause of the rap, showing its head, proves to belong to the servant girl; to whom Solomon:

"Well, Razor," a name of Uncle Sol's inventing in lieu of her own, suggested, no doubt, by her sharp features, "well, Razor, and what's the matter now?"

"Please, sir, there's a little girl below stairs as says, 'Tell uncle Sol that Bessie wants to see him.'"

"Little Bessie Padler; yes, yes. I'll be down directly." And rising, he takes his cane, and kissing the old lady affectionately, descends to meet the child.

The old lady cries out to him as he is about closing the door—

"Remember my words, Solly, and keep away from that 'ere Sapsea!"

"Don't borrow any trouble on that score, mother; I'll remember what you say, depend upon it;" and smilingly leaves her to join the child.

A little garden in the rear of Uncle Sol's house was a source of great enjoyment to him, and he had devoted a great deal of time to its culture for many a year. There was no garden in Cloisterham where the blossoms came so early, or whère the flowers grew with such beautiful colours, or shed such fragrant perfumes as they did in that little garden of Uncle Sol Brobity's.

Many an hour did the old man while away in the prettiest of summer-houses, which stood in the midst of his flower-beds, watching with pride the progress of his pets,—calculating when this one would bud or that one would blossom, and what would be their colours when their petal-faces should be for the first time kissed by the morning sun.

It was on one of these occasions, when the old gentleman was seated among his flower-beds, that Bessie Padler had beheld him from a back window of their lodgings which overlooked the garden; and the child was so pleased with the picture that she determined to make the acquaintance of Uncle Sol, and obtain permission to cull a few of the many flowers that she beheld there.

On seeking him for this purpose, the old man was struck with the precocious traits which the child displayed, and took a great interest in her; and thus it came about that they were very much attached to each other, and passed many happy hours together in company with Uncle Sol's tulips and mignonettes;—he seated in his accustomed place, with her at his side;—she listening to his efforts to entertain her with some pleasant conversation, or he listening to a recital of what she knew concerning her own history.

It had become their habit thus to pass an hour or more directly after Uncle Sol's dinner, and again just before sunset; and so it came about that Bess had just sent word to her old friend that she was waiting for him.

Hurrying along as fast as possible, Uncle Sol joins the child, and, after affectionately kissing her, she puts her hand in his, and they two pass out into the garden together.

Sheltered from the rays of the noon-day sun, by the running vines and branches of trees with which his arbour is surrounded, Uncle Sol's face betokens the happiness that fills his heart to be once more with his floral pets; and Bess, who has anticipated for hours before the pleasure in store for her, sits in silent admiration of the scene, which is rendered all the more perfect by her presence.

"Do you see, my child," the old man says after a short silence, and taking her hand in his; "Do you see that all these flowers grow with their faces turned toward this spot, as though they knew from the first that we should come to keep them company, and so appear to welcome us?"

"Yes," answers Bess; then pointing towards a cluster of pinks, she adds, "and do you see, when the wind blows it, how that pink,—the one more scarlet than the rest, I mean,—nods and bows to us? Perhaps it is the effort to attract our attention that makes its face so much more red than the faces of its sisters."

"It is a beautiful sight to see *all* their pretty faces, child, but it brings a sad thought with it, when we remember that their beauty must fade and themselves die just when they have reached perfection, and that they will then vanish from our sight forever."

The child is silent for a moment, and looks at the flowers in a thoughtful, dreamy way. Then, in a pensive tone, she repeats his words:

"'They look the prettiest just before they die. The nearer they are to perfection the nearer they are to death.' Oh, Uncle Sol," she continues earnestly, "that is not a *sad* thought; we should be thankful that God has so ordained it. Think, if they should live beyond that time, how miserable they would feel to know that they could never more possess their strength and beauty, and would be shunned for their fairer brothers and sisters, who come after them. Think how much better off these little flowers than human beings are. Could men and women die when they are near perfection, instead of living on to grow wicked and ugly, how much happier all would be in this world. I often pray to God that it may be His pleasure to take me to Him while I am young, that I may not live and do wicked things when I am old!"

"Dear Bessie," replied Uncle Sol in a tender tone, and hastily brushing away a tear that was beginning to trickle down his face, "You are too young yet to think of such sad things as death. You will live to grow old, I hope, and I have no fear that you will ever do a wicked act. But we are in a sad mood to-day, child, and must talk about something more cheerful. Do you think that your grandmother would consent to let you come and live with us here and be our own little girl?"

"I do not think that grandma would care, but it would be as Fopperty said."

"Would you like to make a change of this kind, yourself, Bess?"

"Oh, ever so much! then I could be with the flowers all day, and help you in taking care of them, couldn't I, Uncle Sol?"

"Be sure you could, dear child." Meditating a moment, he continued—"Do you think Fopperty is at home now, Bessie?"

"He has not been home for two or three days, but he is likely to come at any time."

"Well, now, suppose I go over to your grandmother's with you, and ascertain if she and Fopperty are willing you should change your home."

"Thank you; if you please, I would like to have you. I should not have much to bring with me," she adds, in a despondent tone, "if I came to live with you. This is my best frock," extending her arms and looking down deprecatingly at her dress, "but perhaps you would not have to buy another, for it may be that I shall not live longer than to wear this out. Perhaps I am as near perfect now as I shall ever be, and that God will hear my prayers and take me, as he does our dear little pinks and pansies."

"You must not speak in this way, child, for you make me feel sad to hear you, and you do not want to make Uncle Sol unhappy."

"I only say what I feel and think," Bess replies; "I always do that. But I do not want to say anything to cause you unhappiness if I can help it. Come, let us go to grandmother's."

Leaving the garden, the two proceed to the lodgings of Mrs. Padler, where they find that lady in the act of swallowing something from a glass, which, judging from a certain smell that pervaded the apartment, could have been nothing more nor less than gin and water, with perhaps a dash of sugar in it.

Rising quickly as they enter the room, the old woman hastily puts away the glass, and limps to meet them; and, though she assumed a smile as she turned toward them, it was plain to Uncle Sol that she was not pleased at their sudden entrance, for he heard her ejaculate, as she closed the cupboard door, "Drat the girl."

"Grandma," said the child, "this is Uncle Sol, who has been so kind to me, and he wanted to visit you, so I brought him with me."

"You're pretty much welcome, sir," Mrs. Padler says, but looking at Uncle Sol with an expression that plainly spoke the contrary. "I'm afeerd ye'll not find us quite so comfortable here as ye're used to. Won't ye 'ave a cheer?" and tenders him one.

"Do not apologize for anything, my good woman," taking the proffered seat; "I hope I see you well."

"Barrin a terrible rheumatics, sir, for which I was only jest a takin' of my med'cine as ye come in, I'm very well, and thank ye. I 'opes you're undergoin' a like enjoyment."

Not quite certain whether the old woman meant enjoyment of rheumatics or good health, Uncle Sol hesitated, and finally said he was very well, indeed. Then there was a few moments' silence, during which the little old clock over the chimney-piece ticked merrily, as though delighted at this opportunity of being heard by the new-comer.

"Mrs. Padler," finally spoke Mr. Brobity, "I trust you will take no offence at my intrusion here to-day, nor at the request I am about to make, which, I assure you, does not proceed from any selfish motive; and if you cannot grant the request, at least please consider my proposition in a friendly spirit. I have taken a great interest in this child, and believing that God has seen fit to bestow upon me more of this world's goods than you possess—not that I deserve them any more, understand, only that it has happened so—I have thought it might be possible that, with me, the superior mind which I have found in her could be better developed, and that it would be in my power to make of her, what, I have no doubt, you would be proud to see her,—a superior woman."

Mrs. Padler makes no reply, but simply nods her head a good many times, though whether in approval or disapproval, or in consequence of rheumatics, Uncle Sol is in some doubt. As she makes no attempt to reply, beyond the nod, Uncle Sol continues:

"It is unnecessary for me to state in detail what I propose to do for her; only that, with God's help, I will make a superior woman of her, and that sums it all up. I believe it lays with you and your son whether I shall do so or not. I have come to-day to get your permission to adopt her; I am a bachelor; she will live with me and my mother, and will be treated as our own flesh and blood would be; and I can only add one thing more—she is anxious to make this change."

Mrs. Padler had listened very attentively, and betrayed no particular emotion until she heard that Bessie desired to leave her; then she broke out into a maudlin fit of weeping, muttering that no one cared for her feelings, and she didn't suppose any one ever would.

"What's the good of all my workin' and a-slavin' for this 'ere gal, if she ain't never goin' to love me. Hain't I been a mother to her and a—a—" Mrs. Padler was going to say father, but thought better of it and substituted grandmother instead—"and done all that could be did for a child; and now to want to leave me without ever so much as offerin' to give me even a five-pun' note for all my trouble. *That's* what seems 'ard, sir, and it makes the tears start."

The adroit manner in which the old woman mentioned the five-pound note was not lost upon Mr. Brobity, and he was on the point of assuring her that he would be willing to recompense her to any reasonable amount, when the door opened and Fopperty entered, having only just returned from London, after his interview with Mr. Grewgious.

He looked rather astonished as he encountered the stranger and saw his mother crying; but Bessie quickly stepped forward to greet him, and after he had kissed her, she led him up to Mr. Brobity and introduced him to that gentleman.

After a few commonplace remarks, Fopperty was informed of the object of Uncle Sol's visit; and an attempt was made to gain his consent to Uncle Sol's proposal concerning Bessie.

No pen could depict the amazement which Fopperty's features expressed as he listened to this proposal. It is safe to state that nothing could be seen of his eyes for full five minutes, and the eyebrows certainly had made up their minds that they should never again resume their natural position. After a little, he recovers from his surprise, and says:

"If you had asked anything of this kind a week since, or even forty-eight hours ago, I should have said No, and thought I was right in doing so. As things looks now, though, I ain't agoin' to do that, but I don't want to hurry about agreein' to it."

"I prefer you take time to think it over," replies Uncle Sol; "it is an important matter, and I should want you to weigh it well, for I should regret to have her come and then be taken away again; you could think it over, and let me know to-morrow, perhaps."

The old woman had been waiting patiently to see if any further mention would be made of certain moneys to be paid, but finding that nothing was likely to be said by Fopperty in that direction, she felt it to be her duty to put in a word at this point:

"Of course, Fopperty, "said she, "if we give him the gal, its nothin' but fair that a few pun' be paid to bind the bargain, or else may-be it mightn't hold; and somethin' belongs to us, besides, for the trouble as we've been to all these years, a-workin' and a-strugglin', and a-counselin' on her. If he should only pay me twenty pun' and you the same, it 'ud do us a power o' good, and only just square us, if it did that," and then winks at Fopperty very hard, who only gazes at her with a look of contempt, as he replies:

"Don't you be in such a hurry to let folks know as your brains don't weigh an ounce, mother. They'll find it out soon enough without your puttin' out a sign." Then turning to Mr. Brobity, he continues: "No, sir; if you had offered money as an inducement to get my consent in this affair, I would have kicked you into the street. I love this child too much to think of my interest before her happiness."

He stoops down and imprints a loving kiss upon Bessie's forehead as he ceases speaking, and Uncle Sol was convinced that he meant all he had said.

"I honor your kind heart," rejoins Mr. Brobity, "and feel assured that if affection were all that was needed to advance the interest of the child, she would not suffer on that score with you by."

There was a pause, during which Fopperty seemed to be meditating the advisability of mentioning a subject that was uppermost in his mind. Finally, he said:

"Perhaps, sir, I may as well tell you now as any time, that so far as blood relation is concerned, this child is no kith nor kin of ours. We took her, in the first place, because there was no one else who would.

She has been with us for a very long time; and though we have done all,—or, perhaps I ought to say, have been disposed to do all—in our power for her, I know that in some respects we have failed to do our duty, partly from poverty, and partly from our own indulgence in evil habits; and, while I consented to take her out of pity, I am disposed to part with for the same reason, knowing that with us she can never receive the training that she should have to make her future life a happy one. I do not wish at this time to state anything concerning her further than this:—Her mother is dead; her father lives; but I do not think he will ever claim her. If you want to adopt her and take the chances of her being some day compelled to leave you, I will give my consent, only asking one condition, and that is that I may be allowed to come and see her once in a while."

"Before answering definitely," replies the old gentleman, "I would like to ask a few questions. Does her father live near here?"

"I cannot answer you any further than this; he does not live a thousand miles from London."

"Do you think it probable that he will attempt at any future time to claim her?"

"I think the chances are just about one in ten thousand. I don't *think* he ever will. I mentioned the fact of his being alive the better to let you know what *might* possibly happen. Not that I believe he *will* ever claim her."

Mrs. Padler, who had listened quietly so far to the conversation, here ventured to remark that in her opinion the better way to overcome all such contingencies was for Mr. Brobity to pay a certain amount, and take a receipt in full of all demands.

This proposition did not seem to meet with that approbation which the speaker had anticipated, no attention being paid to it; Fopperty merely remarking that when her opinion was wanted they'd call on her.

"Well, my friend," said Uncle Sol, "I shall run the risk and thank you for the confidence you place in me. Rest assured that Bessie shall be treated in every respect as my own child, and my utmost endeavors shall be put forward to advance her interests. You spoke of wishing to see her occasionally; come as often as you like. I am satisfied that she will never be the worse for seeing you."

"When would you like her to come, sir," asks Fopperty.

"The sooner the better—to-morrow. I will inform my mother of her coming, on my return, and she will make the necessary preparations."

"Very good, sir; I'll fetch her myself sometime through the day."

Bess,—who had been watching Fopperty very closely while he was speaking,—noticed that, after it was decided that she was really to go on the morrow, his lip quivered and he was struggling very hard to hide his emotion. As he finished the last sentence, he happened to glance at her face, and saw that the tears were chasing each other down her cheeks; he caught her up to him and said:

"Don't you want to go, Bess?"

"Dear Fopperty, don't feel bad about it. I want to go and I want to stay. You have been kind to me, Fopperty, and even if I am living at Uncle Sol's I shall never forget you. I don't think I shall live *anywhere* long, Fopperty; and, if it is not wicked to say so, I hope I may not. Some time,—if we're good, Fopperty, and don't tell lies and get drunk,—we shall all go to a home better than any here, and never be separated again. Darling mother is there, Fopperty; and, when I go to meet her I shall tell her how good Fopperty Padler was to her poor lonely little girl, when there was no one else who cared for her. Do try to live a good life, dear Fopperty!"

With the tears streaming down his cheeks, the strong man assured the child that he would try to be a better man for her sake; and Uncle Sol, also deeply affected at the scene, shook hands with him, and told him he knew that it would not be very difficult, for it was evident that he had a good heart for a foundation to build upon.

After a few moments' further conversation, it was arranged that Bess should go to her new home on the following day, and Uncle Sol arose to depart.

Mrs. Padler,—for whom the conversation had little interest after her last suggestion had met with such a miserable failure,—had wandered into dreamland by slow and easy stages until she finally reached that delightful country, and had evidently found it a very comfortable place indeed. The stir incident to the departure of Uncle Sol, however, brought her back to her native land again. Just as Uncle Sol was bidding them good-bye, the old lady's lips began to move as if struggling to articulate something, and she finally succeeded in ejaculating, at the last moment, "Twenty pun'."

CHAPTER XXX.

INTRODUCES JOE SLOGGERS, AND RELATES HOW JASPER VISITS THE PUFFER'S, AND WHAT COMES OF IT.

NOTWITHSTANDING the monotony by which Dick Datchery finds himself surrounded in the quaint old city, he evinces no disposition to remove therefrom for the balance of his life. It would seem, too, that he finds enough to busy himself with, judging from the regular manner with which he goes to and from his lodgings, and he has come to be regarded by the inhabitants, old and young, as a permanent citizen, and entitled to all the respect and privileges due an old settler.

Almost daily visiting the Minor Canon, and spending much of his time in that gentleman's society, had, it is true, given rise to some comment on the part of a few busybodies (and Cloisterham, like every other locality, was afflicted with this species of poisons, for which Toxicologists have thus far failed to apply a name), but after exhausting all their efforts to attach something wrong to these visits, they had come to release Datchery and fasten their venomous fangs into the character of some other victim.

Although having no apparent motive in so doing, Mr. Datchery also calls often at the Crozier, remaining an hour or more each day; and he has, furthermore, become a great favorite with Deputy and Durdles, the former often passing an evening with the old gentleman at his lodgings. Thus, with frequent rambles about tho ancient city, and an occasional boat-sail upon the river, Mr. Datchery keeps himself pretty well occupied.

Now it came about, that, one morning,—shortly after Jasper and Durdles had made their last visit to the Cathedral crypt,—there issued forth from the Crozier Inn a roughly-dressed young man, with such a very brown face that he must have been exposed to the sun's rays a long time; —perhaps he had only returned from a long journey by land and sea; possibly he has acquired his sun-browned face from laboring in the fields, though that seems hardly likely, for, notwithstanding his rough exterior, his features display a classic cast, and a close observer would perceive an air of refinement in his movements which would hardly attach to a common laborer. But, be that as it may, one thing is certain: he is a stranger in Cloisterham, as shown by the interest with which he observes everything about him, when, with a small bundle, tied securely in a red pocket-handkerchief and fastened to a staff which is slung over his shoulder, he walks slowly in the direction of Minor Canon Corner. As he approaches nearer,—as though he had only just thought of it,—he hastily draws his cap,—a weather-beaten one, indeed,—tightly down, so that the visor nearly conceals the upper portion of his face. Why should this precaution be taken? Surely, the sun can scarcely make the face darker than it now is. Perhaps—and that can be the only reason—he fears the wind, which is blowing strongly from the river to-day, may take liberties with it. Still intently gazing on every object which he passes, he proceeds on his way. If any further evidence was needed that he was a stranger in the place, a series of screams and whistles proceeding from a group of boys, whom he passes, would attest to the fact, (for there is some natural instinct about these street-boys that enables them to distinguish a stranger at first sight.)

The young traveller does not heed them, however, but continues on his way, still interested in everything about him, and finally reaches the arched entrance to the Gate House, which seems to attract his attention more than anything he has yet seen, for he comes to a halt, and gazes about, as though in search of some one who could tell him something of the place and its history.

As no one is to be seen, however, he seats himself upon a loose stone lying beneath the archway, and—perhaps, for want of something better to employ himself about—takes from his pack a piece of bread and a slice of cheese to match, which he proceeds to eat as though it tasted good.

On this same morning, Mr. Tope, service being ended, has finished the duties pertaining to his office, and is wending his way home with the air of a man whose mind is engrossed with deep meditation.

For, be it known, the mind of Mr. Tope has been greatly exercised of late, in that he is conscious of the existence of some uncertainty—a vague something,—to use his own term, a Mistiness,—surrounding the Tope Retreat, or, in other words, the Gate House, which was not wont to exist there prior to Mr. Datchery's occupancy. Hence, the Verger, when not engaged with his daily duties, finds himself struggling to penetrate this Mist and satisfy himself as to what there is behind it.

With his mind thus occupied, he reaches the archway, and, with head down and hands clasped behind him, would no doubt have passed the stranger without seeing him, had not the latter accosted him with a "Good mornin', sir."

It was little wonder that this sudden interruption, combined with the peculiar nature of his meditations, should cause Mr. Tope to start with surprise and astonishment at beholding this unusual object; nor was it anything remarkable that he should ejaculate, "Good Lord, deliver us," as earnestly as he would have responded to the petition—"From all crafts and assaults of the Devil."

The stranger, perceiving Mr. Tope's agitation, hastens to encourage him, and, smiling, says:

"Don't you imagine as I'm goin' to do anybody harm, cos I bean't. I'm searchin' for a uncle o' mine what told me, in a letter I got some days ago, as he lived up this way, and wanted I should come and stay with him a while, as he's all alone here and wants company. I've been tryin' to see some one as I could hinquire of, and as you're the fust, I'll ask you," and takes a letter from the pocket of such a ragged coat, that it was a wonder the pockets had not fallen completely out of it years ago.

Mr. Tope takes the letter, which is in rather a dirty condition, and, after striving to decipher through the dirt something that would indicate its contents, finds at the bottom the signature of the writer, D. Datchery.

Mr. Tope makes no reply as he returns the letter to the other. He simply motions with his finger for the young man to follow him, and so the stranger, being conducted towards the lodgings of Mr. Datchery, arrives there in due time, to be instantly recognized as that gentleman's nephew. Mr. Tope turning to leave, is pressed to remain by Datchery and pass a few moments with him and the aforesaid nephew, whom he introduces as Joe Sloggers, the only child of his (Datchery's) sister. Prompted by curiosity, the Verger remains.

"Why, Joe, my boy," exclaims Datchery, after they had all become seated, "I should know you anywhere! Why, Mr. Tope, he's the image of his mother, sir—the same form, the same hair, the same fine complexion! If you should meet his mother, Mr. Tope, you'd know her in a moment, after seeing him."

Mr. Tope nodded approvingly, but it nevertheless struck him that if Datchery's sister, or any other woman, had a complexion like this young man's, there was great room for improvement.

"Well, Joe," Datchery continues, addressing his nephew, "how did you leave the folks—all well I suppose? I'm glad you've, come! But you must be hungry. We'll have some lunch immediately, for dinner will not be served for some time yet, and you'll get very faint before then."

At this remark, Mr. Tope is reminded that it is time for *his* lunch, and begs to be excused, as he cannot conveniently remain longer, and so takes his departure, but not before he has been instructed to notify Mrs. Tope that she is to prepare two dinners that day, and for days to come. "And, by-the-way, Mr. Tope," adds Datchery, "you will confer a great favor if you will call at Mr. Jasper's room and inform him that my nephew has arrived, and that he must excuse me if I do not take that boat-ride with him this afternoon, as we had arranged."

Mr. Tope says it will give him pleasure to comply, and departs.

After Mr. Tope's departure, both uncle and nephew seem to be greatly amused at something; for, after gazing at each other an instant, they break out into hearty and continued laughing, till Datchery interrupts it by saying:

"Most a fortunate circumstance your meeting with him above all others. It won't be many hours before all Minor Canon Corner will know that Datchery has got a nephew come to visit him; and, best of all, Mr. Jasper will be the first to hear of it."

"And what a description I shall get from the poor man," said Sloggers. "I had hard work to keep from laughing in his face when he saw that signature to your letter, and so became aware that you were the uncle I was in search of. He was so taken back that he could not utter a word, but, like the ghost of Hamlet's father, could only beckon me to follow him," and another burst of merriment proceeded from Joe at the thought of it.

"Ah, but you *didn't* laugh in his face, and that's the best of it. I hope you'll manage to restrain your emotions at all times while you are here, as easily as you have done in this instance." A meaning look accompanies this remark of Datchery's, and the young man seems to understand it, for his countenance immediately assumes an expression of sadness.

Datchery, noticing this, protests against it. "That will never do; you must learn to act unconcerned at whatever happens, or you may spoil the labors of months by the impulse of one moment. But, hush! —is that—yes, there comes Mrs. Tope with lunch; so now you must be again my dear nephew, Joe Sloggers, and do your best to impress the good lady with the idea that the son of Datchery's sister is an honour to the whole family of Datcherys.

Meantime let us look into the lodgings of the Music Master; with the exception that he is, if possible, a little more nervous than when he was first introduced into these chapters, and has grown a shade paler than when we last saw him, he has not changed otherwise; and those who have had an opportunity of observing, declare that he is growing more cheerful, and acting more like himself now than at any time since his nephew's disappearance.

Certain it is, that, as we find him to-day, he seems in good spirits, and it would appear, from the fact that he is packing a small travelling-bag with a few articles of dress, that he is making preparations for a short journey.

Mr. Tope, on leaving Datchery, hastened to announce the arrival of the latter's nephew, and hence his desire to forego the boat-ride till some future time.

John Jasper receives the message pleasantly, and asks, for the sake of saying something, apparently, judging from the careless tone in which he says it.

"Perfect family resemblance, this nephew, hey, Tope?"

"It might be perfecter," at which Jasper laughs at the other's bad English, and asks "how perfecter?"

"Complexion," Tope replies, "and features; but odd lookin', and that's where they're alike."

"I fear, Tope, you have no eye for beauty," Jasper pleasantly remarks; then adds, "well, I shall have a little more time to make ready for my trip to London. You'll have to get on without me for a day or two, Tope. I've got leave of absence, and am going to London to-night."

"You get these leaves often, sir," Tope says.

"None too often," is the answer, and Tope, having nothing more to say, leaves Mr. Jasper to prepare for his journey. An hour later, and he sets out on his way to London. Arriving, as always, in the evening, he proceeds directly to his usual rendezvous, near Aldersgate Street. He seems to be well known by the people here, and a servant immediately shows him to his room.

On entering, Jasper closes the door and makes some hasty changes in his toilet; then retraces his way below for supper, of which he eats heartily. Emerging from the house shortly after, he proceeds in an easterly direction, and hastily walks towards his destination.

He reaches it in due time, and entering the house where we first saw him, ascends the same dilapidated stairway, and makes his way to the room where the Puffer presides. He does not stop to knock at the door, but opens it without ceremony, and calls out, after closing it from the inside:

"Where's the reception committee?"

The first intimation that he receives of a presence here, is a short, crackly cough; and then, slowly rising from a bunk in corner of the room, appears the Puffer. Taking a small lamp in her hand, she approaches him and holds the light to his face for several moments. Then says:

"I don't know ye, deary, but nevertheless ye're welcome; this haint a committee's receptakle, though; it's better nor that—better nor that."

"And so you don't recognize me," Jasper returns, eyeing the old woman with a doubtful look.

Again the horrid cough which brought the tears to her eyes, making their lids redder than ever; then rejoins:

"Never see'd ye afore, good gentleman; leastwise, as I remembers. If I did, I'd forgot it, and that's not to be wondered at since I'm gettin' that old that I can hardly remember myself at times, and my lungs is growin' worser and worser altogether."

"Do you forget *all* your customers so easily?" Jasper doubtingly inquires.

"There be few customers as I sees now; oh dear, oh dear, my lungs will kill me," and then another harrowing cough that Jasper thought would be her last.

She soon recovers, however, and he follows her into the room and seats himself upon the side of the bed that forms a necessary article of convenience for her customers. She replaces the lamp in its former position, all the time coughing and mumbling in a complaining way. He watches her closely all the time, and she is conscious of it, but does not betray the consciousness by look or act.

She has got the light arranged now so that it reflects, as much as such a miserable apology for a light can reflect, its rays upon his face while her own is shaded from it, and then asks:

"How long since I mixed it for ye, deary?"

"It's a long time," he replies; "so long that I cannot remember when."

"Does ye have a good ways to come that ye've let it be so long?" she asks, in a reproachful tone.

"Yes, a long way," he ejaculates, impatiently. "Come, don't stand there talking all night! Get ready and talk less!"

"Don't be vexed, lovey, don't be vexed;" this in a coaxing tone; "I knows ye're all impatience to begin. They allers are after I once mix for 'em, and it's nothin' to wonder at since there's none on 'em can mix it like me. Even the Chinee over the way is tryin' to find out my secret; but no one can git that out on us, eh, deary?" All the time she is fitting the tube to the bowl, which she keeps in a little drawer by the foot of the bed, and which she finally gets ready for use. Then she proceeds to fill; and he, perceiving that she is nearly ready, divests himself of his shoes and coat, throws himself across the bed, and waits impatiently for her to complete the mixing and blowing, incident to the ceremony which he awaits with so much impatience.

She draws a chair to the bedside and blows the spark with such force that her eyes grow red from her efforts; then places the tube to his lips, saying as she does so:

"It's the best I've got, dear sir, and I only keeps this for particklar ones as I knows will thank me for its particklarness."

While she is speaking he inhales the fumes, but the effect is not so instantaneous as he seemed to expect. He frowns slightly as he inhales again, and then, taking the tube from his lips, tells her that she is deceiving him, for it does not affect him in the least.

"By my sacred honor, good gentleman!" she cries, "I would not deceive ye for all the gold and silver in the world." She stirs the contents again with the spatula which she has held in her hand all the time, and tells him to try again. This he does, while she continues to blow softly into the bowl, and watching him with a cat-like look, but which he does not seem to notice, for the drug is beginning to have its effect upon him. Even now he continues to hold the tube to his lips, as though afraid he may lose the influence which is slowly, yet surely, beginning to operate upon his brain. A moment more the tube falls from his hand, and he sinks back upon his side. The old woman does not appear to be satisfied, however, for she takes the tube in her own hand and, placing it again to his lips, holds it there till she becomes satisfied that the drug has really done its work. The rays of the lamp reflect upon his face, which is turned towards it, and she watches his lips to catch the first attempt at articulation that shall show itself. She has not long to wait, for now he begins to mutter something in an indistinct tone. She puts her ear close to his lips, but cannot make out what he says, and still in the same position, she moves him gently from side to side; now she is repaid for her trouble, for she hears him say:

"It's a strange road,—will the end never come?"

"I 'spose there's lots of folks goin' the same road, ain't there, lovey."

"Yes, there's thousands, and thousands of thousands, and millions of millions!"

"Do you know 'em all, deary? of course you don't know 'em all, only some of 'em, does ye, lovey?"

"Of course I don't know them all, you fool! But there's some looking at me from one side that I have seen somewhere, and I can't tell where. What are they stopping for when all the others go so fast?"

He starts and raises himself partly upon his elbow; but the Puffer lays him gently back again, and once more places the tube to his lips. He is quiet again, and she asks:

"Won't they let ye go by 'em, deary?"

"I *do* go by them," he mutters, doggedly; "but how is this, that I keep passing them at every rod, while they do not move as I look upon them?"

"Perhaps it's some others as ye takes for 'em, deary."

"Do you think I don't know *him* and *her* well enough to recognize them in any place or at any time?"

"Shall us try to drive 'em off, lamby?"

"I can do that alone," he whispers hoarsely. A pause for a few seconds, and then the perspiration breaks from his every pore, as he cries, "*He's* gone, but I gave him warning! Did I not give him warning?" savagely clutching her by the wrist.

"Of course ye did, deary; I heerd ye give him warnin' as plain as nothin' at all; but where's them as was with him, deary?"

"Hark!" in a low tone; "'twas a woman that kept him company. She's there yet; she thinks I do not see her. Still, now; not a word! hark! She does not see me now; hush, still, still! *There!* she's *mine* at last! Thank God, thank God! my prize is attained; but what a wretched fool I was when the *other* could have been spared me." Now he begins to tremble, as though undergoing some terrible shock. Now he rolls upon the bed, turning and tossing, and would have fallen upon the floor had the Puffer not kept him by force from doing so.

As he approaches her during one of these struggles, she perceives a small package fall upon the coverlet from an inner pocket of his waistcoat. She catches it up quickly, and once more placing the tube to his lips, he becomes more quiet, and is soon totally unconscious.

Assuring herself that he *is* unconscious, the Puffer takes her prize to the light and finds it to consist of a locket, to which is attached a blue ribbon and a ring. Hastily concealing these baubles, she repairs to the bedside just as the sleeper begins to show symptoms of returning consciousness.

"Ah, my hearty," she ejaculates, with a look of triumph on her features, "I'm thinkin' ye'll find it as strong as ye'd care to have it, and it's a good thing as I was prepared for ye so soon as I was, or I'd a lost a deal by your comin' when I didn't expect ye so suddenly."

She does not leave his side, but, seated on a low stool near the bed, she continues to watch him, always with the old cunning look, listening for any sign that shall indicate an attempt at further verbal expression; occasionally she shakes her fist at him, and mumbles something that is not very complimentary to the sleeper.

"Ye thought I didn't know ye, hey, my bundle of slyness?" she mutters. "Oh, no, I didn't! I'd be pretty apt to forget ye, wouldn't

I? Ye'll know soon enough whether I've forgot ye or no, and worse luck to ye when ye finds it out."

The sleeper now shows signs of waking, and moves about uneasily, whereupon the Puffer leans back, and, laying her head on the foot of the bed, pretends to be asleep.

The other starts up suddenly, as though wondering where he is; and then, passing his hand across his brow, seems to be making an effort to collect his thoughts.

He looks about him in a dreamy way, and discovers his companion apparently asleep. He speaks to her, but she does not move. He leaves the bed softly, for fear of waking her, and puts on his shoes and arranges his toilet in a hurried manner, then dons his coat and hat, and, laying some money where he thinks she will be certain to find it, leaves her, as he believes, unconscious, and passes out into the night.

The Puffer waits till he has closed the door, and then she rises, and hastily snatching up an old shawl, hurries to catch sight of him before he gets too far away. It is now quite late; and, as he does not seem to be in a hurry, it is not difficult for her to keep him in sight. Through lanes and courts, and divers out-of-the-way thoroughfares, he proceeds, but not this time to Aldersgate Street. On reaching Cheapside, he calls a hackney-coach, and, giving the driver some directions, enters, and is driven rapidly away.

The Puffer has no intention, however, of being thwarted in this manner; so, waiting till the coach is fairly under way, she hails the driver of a cab standing near, and directs him to follow it.

"Vere ham I to look for the mopuses as pays for this 'ere lux-u-ary, my queen hof 'arts?"

She quickly produces from her pocket some silver, which she places in his hand, and in another moment is being driven in the direction taken by the coach which contains Jasper.

After a time the cab stops, and the Puffer alighting, the driver points in the direction where the coach has also come to a stop, and by the rays of a neighbouring lamp she perceives Jasper just on the point of moving off. They have stopped on one of the most noisy, crowded, bustling streets of London, and it is little wonder that the old woman feels safe from observation, and runs no risk in being detected.

It has come on to rain since they left the Puffer's, and bids fair to be a wet and gloomy night. Perhaps this is why Jasper quickens his steps, and reaches, ere long, a narrow court, in the neighbourhood of Fleet Street. This court, at all times very muddy, very dirty, and seldom traversed, except by those who reside there, is more muddy and deserted than usual to-night.

It is flanked with rows of antiquated houses, that wear an air of melancholy as they lean dejectedly towards the street, as though meditating self-destruction by falling down bodily, and so putting an end to their miseries; and it would seem that the occupants must be very honest and unsuspecting people, indeed, for the street doors are always left wide open by night and day. One of these houses,—a thought more respectable than its neighbours,—seems to be more carefully guarded from the outside world, in that its street door is closed, and boasts of an ornament in the way of a brass door-plate, on which is inscribed in corpulent letters the name of "Slanduce."

It was before this door that Jasper stopped, and at this door that he gave two or three double knocks, and waited patiently for the summons to be answered.

The Puffer crept close to where the Music Master stood, the darkness enabling her to do so undiscovered, determined to follow him into the house if there was a possible chance of doing so undetected.

After a moment, the bolt was withdrawn and Jasper admitted, though not before there had been quite a lengthy conversation carried on at the door. It appeared that a servant had first waited on Jasper, and she, leaving to inform some other person of his presence, that other person came to the door, and finally they had all disappeared inside the house together.

Now, it chanced that the last person was the mistress of the house, and when she had left the street door to escort the new-comer to an adjoining room, she had called to the servant to fasten the door; the servant, however, did not at first hear the command, and the result was that for several moments the door was left partially open, with no one to watch it.

The Puffer did not fail to notice this fact, and instantly proceeded to take advantage of it. Ascending the steps, and feeling her way carefully along the passage, she caught sight of a light shining through the chink of a door; and, hearing at the same time voices proceeding from that direction, stationed herself as near as she could to the spot.

Near where she stood, she observed that a pair of stairs, leading to a landing above, would be of service to her should she be in danger of discovery, and, with this slight protection, she eagerly listens to what the voices in the adjoining room have to communicate.

The first she heard was Jasper, saying:

"I received your note in due season, Mrs. Slanduce, and I hastened to get the particulars connected with this girl's capture, and to give such instruction concerning the course you are to pursue as circumstances require. I do not think it best for me to see her now, preferring to wait until she shall be reconciled to the circumstances by which she is surrounded."

"The whole thing was exceedingly well managed, Mr. Jasper," is the woman's answer, "as I felt certain it would be if Edgar undertook it. The most I fear is that the girl will not recover from the shock which her nervous system has received. She will not taste food, and has done nothing but moan, crying one moment for some one she calls Grewgious to come to her aid; and, the next moment, wishing she could die and join poor Eddy,—whoever that may be, and—"

"I did not ask you to tell me that," interrupts Jasper, excitedly; "confine your remarks to the details of her abduction, and you will tell me all I care to hear, or know."

If Mrs. Slanduce had replied to him that there might be other things that it would be well for him to know, and that among them was the fact of an old woman standing in the passage at that moment, shaking her fist towards the spot from whence his voice proceeded, the intelligence might have been welcome; but Mrs. Slanduce, not being aware of this circumstance herself, does not impart it to her visitor.

Mrs. Slanduce does not seem put out by the excited tones of her visitor. She is only heard to say that she understands perfectly well what Mr. Jasper wants to know, and if he will give her time, she will relate the particulars to his satisfaction.

"You must know," she continues, "that when Edgar found out all the habits of those people in Southampton Street, he became convinced that the opportunity he should have to secure his bird would be in the morning, before there were many people about, and before it was likely that her guardian had left his lodgings to visit her. He made two or three attempts, on as many occasions, but something prevented at each attempt, until the morning she was brought here. Just as he was driving by the house where she lived, he saw her emerge from the street door and proceed in the direction of Furnival's. His resolutions were instantly taken as to the course he would pursue, and telling the driver to return in the opposite direction for a few rods, he left the carriage and overtook the girl. He asked if her name was Miss Bud, and she answered in the affirmative. He then told her that there was a young gentleman in the carriage yonder that desired an interview with her, and as he had only just recovered from a severe illness, would esteem it a favor if she would come to him, as he was physically unable to leave the carriage.

"She seemed quite interested, and wanted to know if the gentleman gave his name. Edgar replied, 'No.' She said, 'Perhaps it's Eddy;' and hurried back to where the carriage stood. When they arrived there Edgar threw the door open, and, lifting her in his arms, jumped in, closed the door, and the coach was driven with great speed until it reached here in safety.

"She fainted after being placed in the coach, and did not recover till some little time after she was carried to her room, above stairs, and where she now remains, wishing, as I said before, that she might die."

"I suppose you keep her door fastened, of course, to prevent any harm coming to her?" Jasper asks with a smile.

"Oh, yes," is the reply; "would you like to go and see how pleasantly she is situated?" and partly rises to escort Jasper thither.

Jasper says he does not think it best to see her to-night. He prefers to wait till she has had time to realize fully her position, and then he thinks she will be more willing to listen to his proposals.

"I should be pleased if you would step up and see if she is doing well," he adds, "so that I can feel easy about her after I am gone."

As Mrs. Slanduce approaches the door for this purpose, the Puffer hastily compresses herself into an angle to escape observation, and, failing that, determines that if she is discovered she will make short work of the Slanduce by choking her to death on the spot. It does not become necessary, however, for her to carry out this dire plan, as Mrs. Slanduce fails to observe her, and hurriedly takes her way to the landing above, as the Puffer learns, by hearing a lock click and then a door shut. The latter then ascends the stairs, and, crouching as near the door as she can, waits for the mistress of the house to make her exit from the room.

She had not long to wait, for in a few moments the woman made her appearance, and by the rays of the candle, which she carried in her hand, the Princess saw her lock the door and leave the key in the lock.

Waiting till she heard Jasper leave, which he did shortly after, and as soon as the house had become quiet, the old woman moved cautiously to the door where the prisoner was confined, and, unlocking it, entered.

She moves about the room on tip-toe, striving to distinguish some object, but, owing to the darkness, can discover nothing, and ventures a remark:

"Be there any ones here as is in trouble?"

"Who speaks?" asks a voice, in a frightened tone.

"Don't talk loud, deary; it's like if you do it'll make us both trouble, and destroy your only chance for safety. Can you see me, deary?"

"No," is the answer; "but I think I recognize your voice. I have heard it somewhere—I can't tell where—and, oh! if you can take me from this place you shall be well rewarded."

"Never you mind the reward, young Miss; that'll come, never fear,

—worse luck for some folks and better for me. Are ye free to move yourself about, poor dear? Can ye walk?"

"Yes," comes the answer; then adds, in appealing tones, "Oh, let us leave this place if it is possible, for I shall die if I am restrained here another day!"

It was arranged by the two women that they should remove their shoes and steal softly down to the street door, when, if they found any difficulty in unfastening it, they would knock loudly till the servant came to open it, and, after it was open, rush past her and gain the street.

Leaving her hat and shawl behind her,—for it was impossible to find them in the darkness,—Rosa and her companion softly descended the stairs; but when they had reached the landing below, Rosa's strength failed her. Taking Rosa in her arms, the Puffer carried her to the door; on feeling for the key, she had the satisfaction of finding it in its place, and then drawing back the bolts, she turned the key, and, with Rosa lying helpless in her arms, gained the street in safety.

Having gained the street, the Puffer's next thought is as to where she shall convey her charge. She could not carry her a very great distance, and she could think of no other refuge but her own lodgings. While she was yet undecided, Rosa, who had been seated on some steps, with her head supported on the Puffer's shoulder, began to recover herself, and, in a few moments, her strength returned to her. She then declared herself able to walk anywhere that her companion should think best, so that it was a place of safety, but preferred to go directly to Mr. Grewgious.

The Puffer thought it would be better to wait until the next day before returning to Mr. Grewgious, as that gentleman might not be found at his chambers, and meanwhile they would repair to her (the Princess') lodgings.

"They are pretty plain," the old woman said; "but ye'll be a deal better off nor you was a hour ago, and that's the truth."

CHAPTER XXXI.

TREATS OF VARIOUS SUBJECTS, AND THE BETTER TO CARRY THE PRECEDING CHAPTER TO A SUCCESSFUL TERMINATION, INTRODUCES THE READER TO MR. PETER PECKCRAFT.

HAD it not been that certain members of the human family were, from time immemorial, gifted with a faculty of collecting and preserving antiquities of divers kinds and species, it is more than probable that a vast amount of information which is now in possession of the present generation, could never have been obtained; and where we now have tangible proofs of some of the habits and customs of those who, centuries ago, contributed toward the navigation of this Mammoth Ship—the earth—we should only have conjecture. But "their works live after them." When this Mammoth Ship topples its old crew, one by one, into the Sea of Futurity, and takes on its new crew of green hands, it does not lose sight of the importance of retaining some of the old landmarks of mental and physical produce, the better to stimulate improvement by those who come after.

Now it is a fact, which none will dispute, that we are all more or less tinctured with this passion for holding something of so rare a nature that no one else can obtain its like,—perhaps a coin, a piece of furniture, animal or plant,—and although this passion may, as some will declare, arise from selfishness or love of display, there is no doubt that our Creator engrafted it into our natures that we might the better assist Him by retaining the superior productions of each successive age.

Whether Mr. Peter Peckcraft had, in the goodness of his heart, an eye to the welfare of those yet unborn generations, is not positively known, inasmuch as he never gave any proof that he had the welfare of anything but his business at heart; certain it is, however, that for a great many years he had bought and sold curiosities of an antique nature, and kept a clerk; though whether this clerk was a necessary or an ornamental appendage, the customers of Mr. Peckcraft had never been able to decide. They only knew he was a clerk because Mr. Peckcraft, when he said "My clerk," pointed to a very pale young man who always occupied the same position on a high stool, before a high desk, and who seldom spoke to the customers, but when questioned on any point, referred the questioner to his employer by pointing with his pen to that personage.

Mr. Peckcraft has devoted the best part of his life to the business in which he is now engaged, and, being a bachelor, has little else to take his attention but his business. Some of his wares have been in his possession for many years, and they have become so essential to his happiness, from being constantly in sight, that they are to him the same as a family of children would be, and he regards them with as much affection. He has frequently had offers for them, but will only shake his head at such times, and say they are "taken."

It is now thirty years, or thereabouts, since Mr. Peckcraft, with a partner whom he had known from boyhood, first established the business here; and, notwithstanding many changes have transpired since that time, there is no change in him, only that he has grown older. His partner had died in the meantime; but so thoroughly opposed was Mr. Peckcraft to a change of any kind, that he had not removed the firm-name sign from over the door, and it still looked down at the passer-by and told him that the business was still conducted by

DROOD & PECKCRAFT.

They had been highly prospered, this firm,—their business had assumed an importance that few would have supposed, from any evidence that presented itself to public notice,—and, at the time when the senior partner departed this life, they had amassed a handsome competence.

Shortly before his death, Mr. Drood had endeavoured to persuade his partner to assume the guardianship of his only child, Edwin, and there had been many interviews concerning the subject; but Mr. Peckcraft always declared that he was not competent to take such a great responsibility upon him, and kindly but firmly declined.

There being no other friend that he felt at liberty to call upon, and no relative but the younger brother of his deceased wife, Mr. Drood left the guardianship of his boy with his brother-in-law, John Jasper, and so far as was known, the trust had been faithfully performed.

Had Mr. Peckcraft been aware that John Jasper would have this important trust assigned him, in the event of his (Peckcraft's) refusing it, it is more than probable that he would have undertaken it in spite of his assumed incompetency; for he declared, when he ascertained that Jasper had been appointed guardian, that it was the only mistake he ever knew his late partner to make, and he feared harm would come of it. But everything had gone on well, up to the time when young Drood had disappeared, and Peckcraft had come to think that he had been hasty, after all, in his conclusions, and that the selection of a guardian could not have been better made.

Mr. Peckcraft has been kept in ignorance of the young man's sudden taking off, and though he had not seen or heard from him for nearly a year, he was not much surprised, for Edwin had been almost a stranger in the past three years. Shortly after his father's death, the young man had expressed a wish for some profession; and, being encouraged by the old gentleman,—whom he regarded in the light of a counsellor (his guardian being so near his own age),—he had, with Mr. Peckcraft's assistance, taken steps to fit himself for a civil engineer. Engaged in this study, it was no unusual thing for him to be gone for months together; it being understood, that, when he had reached his majority, he should assume, if he preferred so to do, the position which his father's remaining interest in the firm entitled him to, and which interest Mr. Peckcraft had agreed to manage for him during his absence.

Mr. Peckcraft's place of business, then, is in Chancery Lane, and Mr. Stollop's place of business is in Chancery Lane, and his lodgings also, for they are located in the rear of the warehouse, and consist of a good-sized sleeping apartment, comfortably furnished. [It is one of the stipulations entered into with every clerk who has been in the employ of the firm, that he shall occupy these lodgings during his time of service, and never be absent a single night therefrom, on pain of losing his position.]

When quite a small boy, Mr. Stollop had met with a severe misfortune. Not that he had lost an arm, or a leg, or an eye, — it would have been much better for him if he had, instead of the greater misfortune that befel him. Two or three days before this misfortune came upon him, Mr. Stollop had attended one of the Minor Theatres with his mother. The play which he had witnessed was one of the blood and fire kind, and the hero, after escaping all the perils that a human being could escape, and succeeding at last in triumphing over his enemies, and obtaining possession of the castle and vast estates of his ancestors, stood in the centre of the stage, with the pride of his heart clasped in love's embrace, amidst blazing fireworks, shouting in thrilling tones that his enemies were now confined in his deepest dungeon, and naught remained to him and his heart's pride but bliss and happiness,—the curtain descending to the music of two fiddles, a flute, and one drum.

Young Stollop went home impressed. If he could only act like that, he should be happy!

Then came his misfortune: an old woman—a neighbour—called in a few days after, and spoke in glowing terms of the acting of the young man who had personified the hero in the play that Stollop had witnessed.

"How proud the mother of that young man must be, Mrs. Stollop, when she beholds him," exclaims the caller.

Mrs. Stollop looks thoughtfully at her son a moment, and then returns answer:

"All mothers can't be so fort'nit, Mrs. Mollum."

"It don't signify," rejoins Mrs. Mollum, "that *some* can't as I knows on."

Then the two ladies fall to looking at young Stollop very hard for a moment, and the lady caller adds:

"I only know that if *I* had a boy, and he had such a forehead as your boy's got, and sech a strikin' featur' and sech a delicate skin, I'd make a heffort."

It is probable that this woman's sin was forgiven her; but Mr. Stollop was ruined from that day thenceforth and forever. A copy of the Young Actor's Guide, — price one shilling, — and a cheap edition of Shakespeare, were his constant companions by night and day, until he had determined in his own mind that he was sufficiently proficient to make his *debut.* But, unfortunately, the managers could not be made to view the things of this world as Mr. Stollop viewed them. Hence, Mr. Stollop's *debut* has never yet come off; but he still lives in hopes, and to this day improves every opportunity of studying his favorite author. After the shop has been closed for the day, Mr. Stollop will sit thus engaged,—sometimes long after midnight,—as this is the only time he has to devote to it; for be it known that Mr. Stollop has long since come to learn,—and learned it without study, too, as many another poor young man has done,—that in order to exist he must have food, and that food is certain to come through honest toil, while he might starve anticipating future greatness with idle hands.

On that night when the Puffer had rescued Rosa from her captivity, Mr. Stollop's mind was deeply engrossed with the play of Hamlet, which he was reading aloud for the benefit of an imaginary audience, consisting of two casts in plaster perched on a top shelf,—one representing the immortal bard himself, with very melancholy features, and the other intended for some renowned Admiral, whose face, being the opposite of his classic companion's, beams very approvingly on Mr. Stollop's efforts.

We left the Puffer decided to take Rosa to her own lodgings, and they had proceeded through Chancery Lane till they had nearly reached Fleet Street, when they became aware that hasty steps were following them, and they hurried as fast as Rosa's strength would permit. The terrible ordeal through which she had passed, coupled with the fact that she had scarcely tasted food for several days, had resulted in her present weak condition, and the new danger which they both felt so imminent was too much for her. As a consequence, just as they reached the door of Mr. Peckcraft's establishment, she felt that what little strength she had was leaving her,—her limbs tottered, she became dizzy, and, loosing her hold on the Puffer's arm, she sank to the pavement with a low moan, and all consciousness left her.

Mr. Stollop has read to the Ghost scene, and, not being a gentleman of very strong nerve, is greatly startled to hear what sounds to him a groan, just as he reaches the passage where Hamlet's deceased sire says:

"I am thy father's ghost!"

Mr. Stollop instantly springs to his feet and looks with apprehension at his friend Shakespeare. He feels certain that the sound came from that direction. Then Mr. Stollop is impressed with the idea that it is getting late—strange he didn't think of it before—he must go to bed. He thinks he would like to hear the groan repeated, however, to assure himself that he was not mistaken. With his face still anxiously turned upon the bust, and just as he fancies the lips are moving, his attention is attracted to the door, from whence he can distinguish the sound of voices quite plainly, as though the owners of them were greatly excited. As the voices grow louder, he approaches the door and listens.

He does not have to wait long to discover that a man and woman are engaged in some wordy quarrel, and as the woman cries for help he unlocks and opens the door, and finds Rosa lying close at his feet and insensible, while the Puffer is struggling with a stalwart man, who, when Stollop makes his appearance, hastily takes himself away.

Stollop, perceiving that there is no immediate danger, assumes an air of courage which he is far from feeling, and cries out:

"What's the matter here?" and then retreats a few steps in anticipation of an attack.

The Puffer recovers her breath, after a moment, and makes answer:

"Dear gentleman, yer comin' as ye did has saved us more than we shall ever know. There be a poor young lady as is fainted 'ere, and if ye'll kindly help me to put her indoors for a few moments, till she gets better on it, I'll thank ye, and so will she when she comes out on it."

On learning that a young lady needed his assistance, the tender heart of Stollop was touched, and a dozen romantic pictures of the future flashed through his brain in about as many seconds:

"Daughter of some wealthy old gentleman; out walking with an elderly aunt; lose their way and wander to this locality, when they are attacked by foot-pads. Stollop, a poor but deserving young clerk of Mr. Peter Peckcraft, while engaged in studying the poets, hears their cries of distress and rushes to their assistance just in time to save the life of one, and perhaps both. The young lady, brought into the shop, is tenderly cared for by Stollop, who, after she recovers, escorts her home, and is told by the father that from that time thenceforth, Stollop will always be a welcome guest. Result: Stollop goes often; an attachment springs up between the lady and her preserver, and they are married; and everything ends to the satisfaction of all parties concerned."

Having arrived at this happy conclusion, Mr. Stollop assists the Puffer to raise Rosa from her recumbent position; after which she is brought indoors and placed on a sofa, while Stollop hurries to his room for a bottle of brandy.

Rosa soon recovers from the swoon into which she had fallen, and looks about in a confused manner, whereat the Puffer hastens to her side and tells her how it happens that they are thus situated, and that the young man has been so kind as to tender them the assistance of which they stood so much in need.

Rosa turns her eyes upon him and murmurs her thanks; then, having gained a sitting position, with the assistance of the Puffer, thinks they had better depart at once to Mr. Grewgious' chambers.

The Puffer will not consent, but still thinks it best that they repair to her lodgings, unless the young gentleman can suggest a better plan.

Stollop, who was attacked by a fit of bashfulness when Rosa got so she could speak, has not yet fairly recovered, and so does not immediately reply to the old woman; but a happy thought coming to him very suddenly a moment after, he so far recovers his presence of mind as to timidly suggest that if the young lady would find it agreeable, he should be happy if they would occupy his sleeping-room. He knew it was an undesirable position for a young lady, to be sure, but the lateness of the hour precluded the possibility of their obtaining lodgings at any public house, and it certainly was not prudent for the young lady, in his opinion, to undertake a very long walk until she had recovered from the effects of the shock which she had so recently experienced.

After considerable hesitation, Stollop's proposal was accepted, and the Puffer and Rosa took possession of the said sleeping-room, in which,—it being a neat and convenient apartment,—they found themselves very comfortable indeed.

As for Stollop, it is safe to assert that there was not a happier man in London than he, and it would occupy no small space to relate the thoughts which filled his mind till the first rays of the morning sun peeped through the crevices of the shutters, throwing light on everything, except the mind of Stollop, as to how the night's adventure would affect his perspective future, and how long it would be ere he should lead the beautiful young lady to the altar.

Mr. Peckcraft, like a great many other gentlemen who live bachelors, was very particular to rise at five o'clock the year round, and prided himself very much on his ability to follow this rule. His lodgings were in Silver Square and he had occupied them for many years, partly on account of his strong dislike to a change of whatever he had been accustomed to, and partly because the lady with whom he lodged was a person who, like him, did not believe in the "Rolling Stone" business. This lady was known as Miss Keep, and a very precise and prim maiden lady she was indeed.

If Miss Keep should be aroused at any time of the night, and should be asked where the dust-brush was to be found, she would tell you to step into the basement, and behind the door you would see a row of pegs, and on the third peg from the door you would find the brush. No matter what the article, there was a place for it, and it could always be found there, night or day, when not in use.

As we were saying, Mr. Peckcraft arose the year round at five o'clock, and, in the recollection of Miss Keep, he had never deviated from that habit except on one occasion. He had been suffering, the night before, with a violent toothache, and had recourse to laudanum to quiet the pain. The pain was quieted, and so was Mr Peckcraft, for he did not waken the next morning till nearly an hour after his usual time; and when, on referring to his watch, he found that such was the case, he very deliberately put himself back into bed again, and remained there until five o'clock the next morning, thereby nearly frightening Miss Keep out of her seven senses until he had explained the cause to her through the key-hole, just as the two servants were on the point of bursting in his door by command of their mistress.

Miss Keep is rather tall and very slim. She has what was probably intended for a blue eye, but the blueing material evidently ran low; hence it would be difficult to state the color—though Miss Keep's enemies—those of her own sex we mean—every lady has these—said Miss Keep's eyes shaded on the milky. She wears her hair pressed tight to her temples in the form of a half-circle, and an artist with his brush could not carry the curve with a more perfect line. Her chin protrudes to about the same angle with her nose. Add to all this a maiden lady with a great love for poetry, and you behold Miss Keep as she is to-day.

Mr. Peckcraft has risen and is just finishing his toilet, and if we did not know that he had disrobed the night before, we should suppose that he had not been undressed from the fact that every article of clothing is arranged the same, in every particular, as it was the day before. He breakfasts at eight, and spends the intervening time at his place of business.

He leaves his sitting-room now, and on his way down stairs encounters Miss Keep on the landing below (there has not been a morning except one, for fifteen years, that he has not met her exactly in the same place), to whom he says:

"A good morning, Miss Keep;"

And she returns with a rhyme:

"The same to you with feelings deep."

And that is all; she passing on to look after her domestic affairs below stairs, and he passing out into the street.

The same scene having been enacted on this particular morning, Mr. Peckcraft takes his way briskly along until he reaches his own door, when he starts back with astonishment at finding Mr. Stollop standing outside with his hands in his pockets, and his eyes very red from being deprived of his night's rest.

Peckcraft never had known him to show himself before six o'clock, precisely. In fact, it was one of the conditions on which Stollop had been employed, that he should never be seen in the shop before that hour, and not a second later. What could be the meaning of this change in Stollop's habits? Peckcraft halted within a few feet of his clerk, and stared at him in silence for several seconds. Then, in a voice which fairly trembled with excitement, he ejaculated:

"Mr.—Stollop—sir! Mr.—Stollop!"

Stollop observes the excitement of his employer, and, with his face a shade paler than was natural, said:

"Mr. Peckcraft, I beg your pardon, sir; I have a tale to unfold to your astonished ears, that will put to silence the censure which, under any other circumstances, should be my portion."

The old gentleman does not appear satisfied with the explanation of his clerk, for he steps up to him and takes him by the collar, while he vociferates:

"Stollop, you're drunk! Do you understand me? Drunk is, or has been, Stollop!"

"Mr. Peckcraft," returns Stollop, freeing himself from the other's grasp, "you wrong me, sir; but being innocent of what you accuse me, I do not feel so sad at the imputation as I do to know that you have so far forgotten yourself as to make a change in your daily habits by taking a person by the collar in a passionate manner."

Mr. Peckcraft felt the force of this latter remark, and looked very uncomfortable. He adopted a mild tone as he said: "Explain your position, Stollop, and forget my imprudence."

Stollop does not reply, but enters the shop, and is followed by Peckcraft. The flickering rays of a candle, which is just dying out, and which sparkles and sputters on the eve of total dissolution, attracts Peckcraft's attention, and he is now convinced that his clerk has spent the night in the shop, and his curiosity is still more excited to learn the facts.

"Now, Stollop," Peckcraft says, seating himself and leaning back in his chair, with folded arms, " as I said before, explain your position, sir."

"I will, sir," is the reply, and proceeds to relate to Mr. Peckcraft the events of the past night, and concludes by adding:—"I feel assured, sir, that the young lady is a highly respectable person, and I know that you will agree with me when you see her. It's a very singular affair, sir, and I feel it to be so, but I feel that I have done only my duty. I should not be astonished, let me add, if gratitude on the part of this young lady should lead to something more in the end; and, if there is nothing to prevent such an occurrence, she and I may both be Stollops before our lives have undergone a span."

Peckcraft had listened with great interest to his clerk's story, but when he had finished his remarks, said:

"Don't be a fool, Stollop; I should be very sorry to reflect in years to come that I had at any time employed a fool for a clerk. I must see these people and endeavour to learn something as to who they are. How do you, or I, know that this is not some nicely arranged plan to rob me. Good God! It has just struck me," and Peckcraft rises excitedly and hastily glances about him, as though to discover if any object is missing.

"I may be, as you say, a fool, sir, but I am not fool enough to entertain such an absurd supposition as you have just mentioned. Why, sir—"

At this point the door leading to Stollop's sleeping-room opens, and the Puffer and Rosa make their appearance, and approach the two gentlemen. On reaching them, the Puffer says, addressing Stollop:

"Blessin's on ye, dear young sir, for the kindness ye've show'd us. I speak for her and me, and ye'll be well paid for it, never fear."

Mr. Stollop places his hand upon his heart, and, bowing to Rosa, assumes a tender tone, and tells her that he feels grateful that an opportunity has been offered him of assisting her, and that he shall remember the events of the past night as among the happiest of his life. What else he might have said was cut short by Mr. Peckcraft, who interrupts him by addressing the Puffer:

"Madam, if my clerk, here," pointing to Stollop, with such emphasis on the "clerk," that the young man felt no larger than a bee's knee; "if my clerk has rendered you a service by offering the shelter which my premises would afford, I am very glad to know it. But you must not wonder that I am greatly astonished to find such an unusual state of things, and I think you will agree with me in saying that *I* am entitled to some explanation from you."

At this point Rosa stepped forward, and proceeded to relate to Peckcraft all the facts in connection with her abduction; and, though she struggled hard to control her feelings during this recital, the recollection of the cruelty that had been practiced upon her, completely overcame her, and she cried and sobbed like a child.

Mr. Peckcraft, with all his eccentricities, had a tender heart, and he was visibly affected at her grief. But, perhaps, Mr. Stollop's emotions were the most demonstrative of all, for, when Rosa related how she was forced into the hackney-coach, he struck at the air with clenched fists, executing divers movements pertaining to the manly art; and when, at last, Rosa was overcome by her emotions, Mr. Stollop sighed heavily and made a feint of weeping by holding his handkerchief to his eyes.

"And now, sir," continued Rosa, addressing the old gentleman, "I trust you are satisfied with these explanations, and if you will call a coach, which will convey me to my guardian, I shall feel grateful, for I am, oh, so anxious to let him know that I am safe. Dear Mr. Grewgious! how alarmed he must be at my absence."

On hearing her mention the name of her guardian, Mr. Peckcraft thinks he knows the gentleman, and, after learning from Rosa a few more facts, he is sure that he knows him, and begs as a favor that he (Peckcraft) may be permitted to accompany her to Staple Inn and renew the acquaintance.

Rosa says it will be agreeable, and begins to look more like the Rosa of old, probably in anticipation of the pleasure she will experience in joining her old guardian. Stollop, for the first time in his life, wishes that his name was Peckcraft, and that he wore that gentleman's shoes, which reflection is interrupted by Mr. Peckcraft, who orders him to exercise his own shoes and call a coach forthwith.

A moment after and the coach stops at the door; seeing which, the Puffer whispers Rosa that, now she is certain of reaching her friends in safety, there is no further need of her, so she will say good-bye and go her way.

"But, my dear friend," cried Rosa, grasping the old woman's arm, "I cannot, in justice, consent to your leaving me in this abrupt way. Think of the service you have rendered me—perhaps saved my life! You must go with me to my guardian, that you may receive something more than gratitude for the kindness you have shown in my behalf. Please come to Mr. Grewgious with me, and let him propose something by which you will be better off than you now are. I know he will grant whatever you wish when he hears of last night's adventures, and I cannot think of parting with you—never, perhaps, to meet again."

"Listen, my child," returns the Puffer, visibly affected; "do not think as I feels ungrateful for your kind offers to an old 'ooman as is nigh her end; but I've a work to do for myself and a few others, as there is nothing of its like in London can compare with. Ye'll see me again, deary, never fear; and I'll see you, deary, happier than ye be to-day. I don't want aught but your love, my sweet one, and God is good to give the likes of me that; good-bye," and offers her hand.

"Be it as you wish," Rosa returns, taking the proffered hand, "and rest assured that when I do see you, you will be doubly welcome; and if you have a daughter that needs protection as I have needed it, God grant that she may never want for the noble heart and strong courage that I have found in you." Tears start to the old woman's eyes as Rosa utters this last sentence—though why, Rosa did not know. The Puffer turns to go, but Rosa holds her by the hand, and drawing her face down to hers, imprints a kiss upon it; then, promising to see her again ere long, they bid each other good-bye, and while the Puffer seeks her own home, Mr. Peckcraft and Rosa, entering the coach, take an opposite direction and proceed to Staple Inn.

CHAPTER XXXII.

IN WHICH MR. GREWGIOUS TRANSACTS SOME BUSINESS IN HIS WARD'S INTERESTS, AND FOPPERTY RELATES TO JASPER HIS SUCCESS AS AN EMISSARY IN THE LATTER'S INTERESTS.

On returning to his chambers, after the fruitless attempt at discovering the whereabouts of Rosa, Mr. Grewgious, sick at heart and sore of limb, threw himself into a chair, and resting his head upon his hand, was lost in deep meditation concerning Rosa's disappearance, and the course he should pursue to discover her whereabouts. That she had been abducted he had not the shadow of a doubt, and he was also confident that John Jasper was in some way connected with it. Arriving at this conclusion, and reflecting how easy it had been to accomplish this abduction, leads him to cast blame upon himself for not having been more thoughtful of her safety. If, he thought, he had provided an abode for Rosa where she could never, by any accident, have been out of his sight, this last terrible blow would never have befallen them.

But something must be done to find her; and, as it was plain that Jasper had connived at this villainy, he must be the one from whom to look for information.

Knowing something of the man's life in the past, and the violent language he had adopted towards Miss Bud, when he had declared his passion for her in the garden of the Nuns' House, Mr. Grewgious had good reason for arriving at his conclusions. But how to approach Jasper, with not the first connecting circumstance to bring against him? Of course, Jasper, if accused of complicity in the affair, would simply deny all knowledge, and what then? Why, nothing—there was no proof.

Notwithstanding, Mr. Grewgious did form a resolution, then and there, to repair to Cloisterham, at once confront the object of his suspicions, and charge him with the crime. With this end in view, he proceeds to pack a few articles in a small travelling bag, and, looking at his watch, finds that he has just time to call for Miss Twinkleton and reach the train.

Turning to Bazzard, who has been busily writing at his desk, he informs that person, as briefly as possible, of the sad events of the morning, adding:

"It remains for me to go to her assistance. Hence, I am going to Cloisterham, and shall be gone for a day at least. If any one calls, tell them I shall return to-morrow, or the next day at farthest."

"I follow you, sir," is Bazzard's response.

"And tell Mr. Tartar," continues Grewgious, "to say nothing to his neighbours above stairs that Miss Bud has so suddenly disappeared; and tell him (Tartar) I am as much at a loss to account for this disappearance as he will be."

"But have an idea?" Bazzard adds in an inquiring tone.

"You are quite right, Bazzard, and no doubt the same idea will strike him; so we will not say anything about that."

Bazzard, still writing rapidly, reiterates, "I follow you, sir," in the same tone that he might have spoken had he addressed the fly which has just alighted on the paper, and who crawls nervously ahead of the gentleman's pen.

Catching up his hat, Mr. Grewgious quits his chambers, and proceeds directly to the Billickin mansion, where he finds Miss Twinkleton sitting at a window with some light embroidery, and who, as he enters, regards him with as much calmness as some firmly reconciled old Roman matron might have regarded the executioner who was to behead her in twenty minutes, precisely.

Mr. Grewgious proceeds to inform her, without ceremony, that Rosa not being found, and no probability of her returning for some time to come, he has thought it best to relinquish the lodgings now occupied by them; and as he has business in Cloisterham, will, if she is agreeable, escort her (Miss Twinkleton) back to that classic ground where she may once more inhale the study-ladened atmosphere of the Nuns' House.

Miss Twinkleton calmly bows her head in reply, and sets about packing her wardrobe for the journey. While she is thus engaged, Mr. Grewgious goes in search of the lady of the house, to inform her of his determination to relinquish the lodgings and settle for the same.

He finds Mrs. Billickin engaged in a wordy argument with the butcher concerning certain items which he avers to be correct, but which she denies with true Billickin spirit.

Mr. Grewgious heard the voices through the door, and, under ordinary circumstances, would have retired; but just now his business is imperative, so he gives two or three apologetic knocks at the door, and the female voice bids him enter, in the same breath with which she has just closed a sentence addressed to her enemy.

On perceiving Mr. Grewgious, she places a chair for him, and places her arms akimbo, and then continues to address the butcher:

"No, sir, I deny it; that charge is one that must be denied by me, however much I may regret the wounding of your feelings, sir. Had it been fowls, as every Christian knows is fit for invalids—of which I do not deny myself to be one—I should have said it's like you're right. Had it been beef, of which every true Henglishman and woman knows is fit for them as is strong to bear, I might 'ave said, 'Possibly, sir, you're wrong, and possibly, sir, you're right;' for beef is what those as dwells within these walls is deservin' of, and gets when I can find it good. But when you come to put down horrid veal, sir—and its a wonder that to the roof of my mouth my tongue it do not cleave as I speak it—veal, which abear it I never could, when a babby I started first myself to feed, and which it be well known is a kind that nothing but a babby cooked can its equal be;—I say to you, sir, in three words, replying to me notwithstanding what you may—I say in three words,—I IT DENY;" and emphasizing each word by clapping her hands together, all the time looking very hard at Mr. Grewgious, who feels very much like a condemned and sentenced felon whose execution is momentarily expected.

An argument concerning the merits or demerits of that particular article of animal food to which Mrs. Billickin objected, the butcher did not feel himself competent to maintain, and he did not attempt it. So a compromise was effected in that the objective item was to be stricken from the account, which was finally settled, greatly to Mr. Grewgious' satisfaction, no less than the butcher's, and the latter personage took his departure.

"I have called, madam," said Mr. Grewgious, "to tell you that, in view of the calamity that has befallen my ward, I have deemed it necessary to give up the apartments which have been allotted to her use, and they will be left at your disposal within a few moments. If you will inform me the amount of my indebtedness to you, I will settle the same, and hope you will not suffer inconvenience by this sudden relinquishment, which you will perceive is beyond my control."

"It does come upon me suddenly, sir," is the Billickin's reply; "though expect it I might from 'avin' come in contacts with she as is left above; and meaning nothing to you, sir, to whom offence I would not give; certain it is that such persons is far from fit the care of young ladies to 'ave, it being in my mind clear that they were never meant therefor."

Mr. Grewgious does not heed the lady's words, but continues:

"Miss Bud's wardrobe will be packed; but, with your permission, I should like her luggage to remain a day or two till I decide the course I am to pursue concerning her."

The Billickin, apparently having been engaged in a mental calculation of the sum due her while Grewgious was speaking, replies that they can stay as long as he likes, and that the amount her due, reckoning all things, is eight pound four and three-pence.

To which the other does not object, and so the business is concluded, to the relief of Grewgious, who had feared a stormy scene, and which fears would no doubt have been realized had not the bottles of her wrath been pretty well drained during her prior interview with the butcher.

By this time the coach has arrived, and, bidding the Billickin a good-morning, he hastens to escort the Head of the Nuns' House, who is already waiting him. As they descend the steps leading from the house, they are hailed by Billickin, who appears with a small parcel in her hands, which she passes to Grewgious, addressing him, but looking at Miss Twinkleton defiantly:

"I ham 'ighly obliged to some folks as I could name for attemptin' to throw a stigama on this 'ouse by droppin' that upon the landin's which they know it will be found by me, and 'opes it may not be returned to them. Some lodgin'-'ouses, no doubt there be, where hadvantage would be took at times like this, and so no doubt there be semynaries as has their short-comin's, kept mostly in such cases by females hold, 'ard as they may try to deceive; but this 'ouse *scorns* such hactions, and tells you plain, and cover the fact I will not."

Miss Twinkleton smilingly takes the parcel from Grewgious, and remarks in a patronizing way:

"Tell the person, if you please, Mr. Grewgious, that honesty is a virtue to be admired wherever it is found; but, more especially, when found among that class who, from the result of straitened circumstances, not to say poverty, are so much more likely to be tempted and fall."

At this the Billickin turns very red in the face, and, trembling with rage, rejoins:

"Thanking you for your good hopinions, which no one cared for to hear,—leastwise myself,—'appy am I to say that sich as you 'ave been made to know since you come to *this* 'ouse that a good trait is honesty. The poor things as you've the charge hof may get some benefit from your hoccupyin', even for so short a time, the rooms of honest persons"; and so ends the conversation by slamming the door to, while Miss Twinkleton smilingly enters the cab, the driver of which has been highly edified at the scene just enacted, and evinces his delight by placing his forefinger on his left eye, and winking very hard at Billickin with his right, as an encouragement to that lady to stick to.

The same morning on which the scenes narrated in the preceding chapter were being enacted at Mr. Peckcraft's, John Jasper leaves his lodgings in Aldersgate Street and hastens on his way to the station from whence he is to return to Cloisterham; and where he arrives in safety. As he is stepping into the omnibus which is to convey him to Minor Canon Corner, the driver places in his hand a note, rather crumpled in appearance, and which bears, in a decently legible hand, the superscription—"Mr. Jasper."

After seating himself, the Music Master tears open the note, and reads:

"Come to the house; the sooner the better. I've got news for you.
PADLER."

He places the note in his pocket and falls to meditating, which does not cease till he reaches the end of his journey, when he repairs to the Gate House, and is shortly after seated at an open window of his lodgings, gazing upon the river, which is visible from where he sits, and which flows so peacefully as it journeys towards the sea, that he falls to wondering if those who perish in its embrace experience sensations that harmonize with its mood; and, if so, that it would almost be a pleasure to die in its embrace to-day.

Thus lost in reflection, it is little wonder that a knocking at his door should cause him a sudden start; then, hastening to answer the summons, he finds himself confronted by Datchery and Joe Sloggers, whom he welcomes in pleasant tones, and, as they enter, places seats for them.

Mr. Datchery introduces his nephew, and, as Jasper shakes him by the hand, the young man's eyes are bent upon the floor, as though fearing to meet the Music Master's glances; whereat Jasper concludes that Mr. Datchery's nephew is a very bashful young man indeed, and is not used to the society of strangers.

Apologizing for the disordered condition of his room, Mr. Jasper busies himself with arranging some sheets of music which lie scattered about, humming some little air while thus engaged, and which Joe Sloggers thinks very pretty, and whispers his uncle to that effect; the whisper, being audible to the Choir Leader, causes him to remark:

"You have a musical ear, Mr. Sloggers."

At which the young man colors slightly, and answer makes:

"I should never get tired of music, sir."

"Ah, my dear sir," Datchery says, "you should have heard his mother as a singer when she was a girl. Not one in our neighbourhood could compare with her. She was at one time almost tempted to adopt the Lyric stage as a profession, but her mother talked her out of it. Yes, Joe comes honestly enough by his love for music."

Mr. Jasper evidently wishes to do all in his power to please his guests, so when Datchery had concluded, he rose and, stepping to the piano, seated himself and played and sang a serenade, in which some loving swain, regardless of his health and the peace of the neighbourhood, endeavours to persuade his lady-love to open her lattice to him,—and, as the result of his supplication is not made known in the song, it may be presumed that the lady had sense enough to keep her lattice closed, and, with a view to her own comfort, preferred to lie in bed.

The visitors declared themselves greatly pleased with this, and then Mr. Datchery looks very sober for a moment, after which he breaks out:

"This gentleman, Joe, has had a vast deal of trouble—more than you'd think for to look at him." Then to Jasper: "But you're looking a deal better than you were some months since. I suppose, now, you haven't heard from your nephew yet, sir?"

Jasper shakes his head mournfully, and says he has not only not heard from him, but that he never expects to, and looks steadily at Joe as he says it; whereat that young gentleman becomes very much confused and turns red, and drops his eyes, and Datchery comes to the rescue:

"I see, sir; you've decided that it won't do to mourn all the time for what you cannot bring back, so you are going to make the best of it, and try to forget it. Am I correct, sir?"

"In the first statement, yes; in the latter, no. I do not want to entirely forget my dear boy; I loved him too well for that. But I was so often warned by my friends that I should injure my health, and all to no purpose, that I have begun to realize the necessity of heeding their warning; but I can never forget—that is impossible."

Joe Sloggers has not ventured any remark till now, when he says, rather earnestly:

"I should think it would be impossible."

Jasper raises his eyes quickly at the speaker, but sees only a very stolid, almost expressionless, face; then turning to the window, he looks out upon the river with much the same thoughts that occupied him when he gazed upon it a half hour since.

Datchery and his nephew look at each other with a peculiar expression, and at that moment Mr. Tope appears at the door, bringing a letter from Mr. Jasper, which came by the afternoon post.

Then Mr. Datchery and his nephew rise to go, and, at Jasper's request, promising to call again, they leave him as they found him—alone.

On being left to himself, the Music Master hastily breaks the seal of the letter he has just received, and reads:

"The prize has escaped. You had not been gone an hour, when, aided by an old woman, she left the house. You need have no fear of the consequences. You will not be known in the matter, unless you choose to admit it. Nothing will be revealed by us. More particulars when you call. E. S."

With the note tightly clutched in his hand he paces the floor with rapid steps, while his face betokened the feelings of hatred and despair that filled his breast.

"What cursed, tantalizing fiend is this," he mutters, still walking the floor, with moody brow, "that, at every step I take to bring her nearer to me, comes between us and places her further from me than before? No need to fear the consequences! Fool! What could a thousand exposures be to bear, compared with the misery I now experience at being thwarted thus when success had so nearly crowned my efforts! There has been some trickery here; I know it; either the Slanduces have played me false, or my steps are dogged at every turn!"

Then a smile of triumph comes over his face as he bethinks him of the note received from Fopperty, and he continues:

"But fate has not yet entirely deserted me; I feel sure, from the tenor of his note, that Fopperty has found the cover of Neville Landless, and it shall not be my fault if I do not visit upon his head tenfold the sufferings that I endure now!"—and taking his hat, he proceeds, in great haste, to the lodgings of the Padlers.

He does not go there direct, however, but walks once or twice by the street on which they are located, and appears to be satisfying himself that he is not followed or watched. At last he turns the corner of the High Street, and on reaching the house makes his way directly to Fopperty's apartments.

He taps at the door, and is admitted by Mrs. Padler, who informs him, in answer to the question, that Fopperty is at home, and "'opes she sees him 'ealthful and 'appy."

He finds the room so filled with the fumes of tobacco smoke that it is with some difficulty he discerns surrounding objects. A man in a distant corner cries out, "A good-mornin' to ye, sir;" and on approaching the spot from whence the voice proceeds, he discovers Fopperty tilted back in a chair with a clay pipe between his lips, from which at intervals he emits clouds of smoke. The latter does not rise from his seat, but stretches out his hand and pushes a chair near him towards Jasper, and tells him at the same time to be seated. Occasionally a strong smell of gin rises above the odor of tobacco, and the Music Master feels confident that the other has been indulging rather freely in the ardent. He seats himself in the chair which is proffered him, and remarks, good-humouredly:

"Enjoying life, I perceive, Fopperty."

The black eyes go in and out at a fearful rate, and after a few violent pulls at the pipe, he doggedly answers:

"And why not? A man can enjoy life so long as he don't trouble his neighbours, I hope. There's no law in England that prevents that, I believe."

"Certainly not," is Jasper's reply, and evidently annoyed; "but I did not come to argue that point with you. I received your note informing me that you had something to communicate of importance; and, as my time is limited, perhaps you will proceed to the subject at once, and inform me what is the nature of your information."

The eyes again back into their hiding places and stay there while their owner asks:

"Have you got the sinews with you?

"I have sufficient funds—for I suppose that is what you mean by sinews—to keep good my word with you, but I don't propose to part with them till I am first assured that you have earned them."

Fopperty continues to smoke in silence a few moments, and finally says:

"I'm goin' to take your word, but mark me, it will go hard with you if you don't do the even thing with me. I've found that young fellow as you wanted, and can put my hand on him at a moment's notice."

On hearing this, Jasper seizes Fopperty by the hand and shakes it heartily, declaring that this is the best news he has heard for a long time. "And how did you contrive to find out this?" he asks.

Fopperty feels it his duty to make the details as hazardous as possible, the better to impress his hearer with the great risk he has run, and closes his adventure by informing his listener that Neville is to be found at Staple Inn. Jasper's face evinces great delight at the knowledge he has gained. "You have done well, Fopperty," he exclaims, "and I am satisfied with the result of your labors. I'll see now if this skulking dog cannot be made to pay the penalty of his atrocious crime." He then takes from his pocket some money, which he passes to Fopperty. The latter has not forgotten Mr. Grewgious' instructions, for he now proceeds to question Jasper.

"I 'spose," he says, as he places the money in his pocket, "you'll go right to work and have this young cove nabbed, now, won't you?"

"Yes," is Jasper's reply, in a savage tone, "but not nabbed as you mean. Before another week passes I'll have the scoundrel so securely in my power that nothing but death can free him."

"And I suppose it won't be long before he's free'd neither, will it?" asked Fopperty.

Jasper only replies to this with a significant look at the questioner, and there is a moment's silence.

Then Fopperty:—"And when do you mean to strike on him?"

"In a few days,—as soon as I have perfected some business that I have in another direction. I don't want too many irons in the heat at once. I may want your services when the time comes, and will make it worth your while."

"All right," is the rejoinder; "you'll find me ready for anything you want," and proceeds to light his pipe. It seemed to Jasper that his companion was the most remarkable smoker he ever thought of, for the immense volumes of smoke which he blew out after every pull so filled the room that, in a moment, it became almost unbearable.

At this point, Mrs. Padler, who had been in an adjoining room during the interview between the two men, made her appearance and hobbled to a chair. On seating herself, she looked at Jasper in a good-natured manner, and told him that she had a little business with him when he got through with Fopperty.

"You can proceed with it now, then," Jasper replies, "and make it brief, for I should be in another place this moment."

"Oh, well, I'll tell ye as fast as I ken. It won't take long. I wants a little money to buy a few harticles for Bessie."

"But I gave you quite a sum a few days since," replies Jasper; "Have you used that all for her?" he inquires, in a doubting tone.

"Every blessed farden, sir," she tells him.

Jasper's face wears an anxious look as he steps to the window and gazes out upon the court below; but the cause of that look is far different from that surmised by Mrs. Padler, who, to the intense delight of her son, proceeds to draw her countenance out of shape by attempting to imitate the expression on Jasper's face.

The latter turns toward them suddenly, and—observing that Fopperty is asleep—says he must be gone. Tossing a few silver pieces to the old woman, he hastily quits the apartments. He has hardly done so, when Fopperty proceeds to raise the windows and clear away the gin and tobacco, and seems highly amused at the success he has had in deceiving Mr. John Jasper.

On this same day, the evening train from London landed in Cloisterham, an elderly gentleman and a middle-aged lady, and these prove to be no others than Miss Twinkleton and Mr. Grewgious. They enter the omnibus, and are driven directly to the Nuns' House. On being admitted, Miss Twinkleton leads the way to the reception room, which Mr. Grewgious remembers in connection with his last visit to Cloisterham, and for a moment the recollection quite overcomes him.

"Poor child," he thinks, "how little did you anticipate then the unhappiness that was in store for you. Oh, could I have been permitted to know all that has transpired since, how differently would I have done. But it was not to be. I could not save your mother; I could not save you."

While thus meditating on subjects connected with the missing girl, the door opens and Miss Twinkleton enters, with the Minor Canon following immediately after.

Mr. Crisparkle hastens to shake Mr. Grewgious by the hand, and seems as glad to see him as though years had intervened since they last met.

"I only just heard that you had arrived, and took the liberty of calling immediately to invite you to spend your time, while here, with me," said the Rev. Septimus, still holding the other's hand in his own, "for I was fearful lest you might make arrangements to go to the public house, and I could not permit you to do that while it was in my power to entertain you."

"You are very kind, dear sir," returns Mr. Grewgious, "and, if I shall not intrude upon you, I will be most happy to accept your invitation.

I fear, however, you will find my society rather dull, for I am—if an Angular Man may be allowed the expression—in great affliction at the present moment."

The Minor Canon perceives for the first time that the old gentleman's face betrays a careworn look, and he hastens to enquire the cause:

"My dear sir, what is the trouble? for now, that you speak of it, I observe that you are labouring under some mental anxiety. I hope our friends in the Tartar Territory are well, and that nothing has happened to cause them further trouble? Helena—Miss Landless—you left her safe?"

"So far as I know at the present moment," is Mr. Grewgious' reply, "the brother and sister are the same as when you last visited them. I cannot say as much for the poor child whom I so foolishly left in danger without knowing it. My ward, Miss Bud, Reverend Sir," the tears stand in his eyes as he finishes the sentence—"Miss Bud is gone, missing—*dead* for aught I know—and my business here now is to seek some clue to her whereabouts."

"My dear friend, you astonish me beyond expression," exclaims the Minor Canon, alarm and surprise depicted on his face; "pray give me the particulars; Miss Bud gone! What does it mean?"

"I cannot tell you what it means, sir, only that the fact remains." He then proceeded to give an account of the disappearance, so far as he was cognizant of it, while the other listened with breathless interest to the recital. He could not utter a word for several moments, so great was the shock he felt at hearing this news, but at last he enquired if Mr. Grewgious had any idea as to who the persons were that had committed so fiendish an outrage.

"You use the right term," Mr. Grewgious answers; "I have an *idea*—and that is all. Proof, I have none, but I *believe* that there is a person in this neighbourhood who can tell something concerning it, and who in fact *knows* all about it. But we will say no more at present, if you please. I have a plan that I am anxious to put in operation, and, with your assistance, I think it can be done. We will discuss it presently. Shall we go out for a short stroll, sir?"

"With pleasure, if you desire it," is the response, and they rise to depart. Before leaving, however, Mr. Grewgious addresses Miss Twinkleton:

"I trust, Madam, that you will pardon me if I have seemed rude at any time since this blow fell upon me, but I have suffered terribly by this misfortune and have not been responsible for my actions at times, which have been very foolish, I have no doubt. Do we part good friends?" and he holds out his hand to her. She takes the hand, and replies:

"Perhaps I may say, sir, that upon no other person, more than those whose duty it chances to be to instil into the minds of young ladies the Cardinal Virtues, combined with Scholastic Teachings, is the Golden Rule more obligatory. I can sympathize with you, and regret that it was beyond my power to prevent the evil which has resulted from the desire that actuated Miss Bud to go out that morning, solitary and alone. But Miss Bud was not, at the time, under this roof. She was an Independent Being, if I may be allowed the expression, and as such merely assumed the privileges that belong to Independent Beings. I regret it deeply; and sincerely trust that the end will not prove so disastrous as you believe. Meanwhile, you will always be welcome at the Nuns' House, and I hope we shall very soon see Miss Bud here, resuming her studies."

Thanking her for her kind wishes, and bidding her good day, Mr. Grewgious follows the Minor Canon from the house that was once Rosebud's home, but which shall know her no more,—at least as pupil.

Meantime, John Jasper, on his way from the Padler's, proceeds towards his lodgings, his mind filled with schemes for persecuting the man whom he accuses of the murder of his nephew. He is determined now to leave no stone unturned that shall help him to carry out this purpose. He reaches the Gate House in good time, and ascends directly to his apartments. He is somewhat surprised to find that the door leading to his sleeping-room is open, and is quite positive that he had closed it before he went out, but concludes that he could not have done so, as there is no other evidence that the room has been tenanted during his absence. Divesting himself of his coat, he draws a chair to the window, and, seated therein, proceeds to meditate as to the best plan to pursue which will ensure the arrest and conviction of Neville for the murder of Edwin Drood.

All this time his features do not indicate in the slightest degree the character of his thoughts, and the calm, almost happy expression which is depicted on his face would impress the beholder that he was engrossed with some subject of a most pleasant nature.

Ah! well it is for all, that in each mortal's breast is concealed from human view the motives that govern every act and deed of each one's life; for were it not so, how many would care to live, while beholding the selfishness and envy that rankled there, and call their fellow, brother?

John Jasper was human, and John Jasper's heart was consequently a sealed book to all but himself; and though there were a few who felt that he was guilty of gross and wicked actions, even though they had as yet no positive proof, there were others, and the majority, who believed him as pure at heart as the generality of mankind.

While engrossed with a subject that has occupied his mind for so many months, he hears a knock at his door, and, without rising, cries out:

"Come in."

The door opens and he beholds the Minor Canon in company with Mr. Grewgious. He shows surprise for a moment, but it is only for a moment, and then rises to greet them pleasantly, and bids them be seated.

He chats gaily with the Minor Canon, while Mr. Grewgious calmly takes from his pocket a pair of spectacles which he carefully wipes with his handkerchief, and, placing them to his eyes, takes a very earnest look at Jasper's face. Jasper notices the look, but is in no way disturbed, and a moment after directs his conversation to Mr. Grewgious, saying:

"It is a long time, sir, since I have had the pleasure of meeting you; not since the unfortunate calamity that occurred to my dear boy," and his voice trembles at this point, while he takes from his pocket his handkerchief to wipe away the tears which the recollection of Edwin causes to fill his eyes.

Mr. Grewgious does not appear to sympathize with the speaker, if his features were to indicate the state of his feelings, for if ever a human countenance—whether belonging to an Angular Man or otherwise—expressed contempt, the face of Mr. Grewgious does now.

Mr. Jasper's agitation after a moment passes away, and Mr. Grewgious, turning his chair a trifle that he may more directly face the Music Master, says:

"So long as it was consistent or possible for me to do so, I have abstained from visiting you, sir, because I knew that I should not be welcome if I had, in the first place, and because I had no really particular business with you, in the second place. In the first of these reasons, you can no doubt bear me out; in the second, I can bear myself out. It will not, then, create very great surprise on your part when I tell you that my object in visiting you now is not because I have any particular friendship for you, or because, as is often the case with some people, I want to kill time; I have an *object*—one to me of the most serious nature."

Mr. Grewgious pauses here, as though expecting some remark from Jasper, but none comes. His head is bowed and his eyes cast to the floor, and either he is a very attentive listener or a very deep thinker now, and Mr. Grewgious hardly knows which. Mr. Crisparkle does not apparently feel comfortable by witnessing this scene, and when Grewgious ceases speaking he (the Minor Canon) commences drumming with his fingers upon the window-pane, as though feeling it his duty to take some part in the interview, and so fills in the time between the waits; as, at the theater, the orchestra fill the time between the acts. Then Grewgious again:

"When your nephew so mysteriously disappeared from the sight of mankind, (if I may so express it,) I regretted the fact, because I felt that violence had been used to bring about the end. I also felt that, had some facts been known to the world as they were to me at that time, the person interested in his death would have seen the futility of molesting him."

He pauses here, to give the man who sits before him with pale face,—and his black eyes ten times more bright in contrast with the face,—an opportunity to reply, but he does not speak nor move a muscle. The Minor Canon, having commenced another interlude on the window-pane, only has time to finish as Mr. Grewgious once more resumes:

"So fate had decided that the young man should be put out of the way, and fate's mandate must be executed. How, or by whom, probably no one but the person who did it knows. Whether any other person will *ever* know remains to be seen. I *think* it will be made clear to us all some time. I trust you are listening to my words." Jasper sits so still, showing no emotion, that the speaker finds it necessary to add the last sentence, to assure himself that the man is not unconscious.

From lips that are parched and dry, judged from their articulation, comes nervously, "I hear and understand you," and waves his hand spasmodically for the other to proceed.

The window-pane interlude—playing very lively this time—ceases, and then Mr. Grewgious continues:

"Of the young man who was suspected at that time, I have only this to say—I believed him innocent then, and as yet have seen no reason to change my opinion. I will suggest while at this point, however, that if any person thinks it best to persecute or molest him, in connection with that affair, they had better look well to it that they have positive evidence to prove their charge; for, if they have not, he has friends that will call for a bitter reckoning with his traducers."

The Minor Canon's interlude again, while the speaker notices indications of interest displayed on the countenance of the Music Master.

"Having said this much about affairs which really have no direct connection with my business here at the present time, I will now proceed to the business which *did* have reference to this interview. Until within a few days, my ward, Miss Bud, was under the roof that I had provided for her comfort and safety—safety, I mean, from those who I did not believe would dare molest her, living there. Now she is not to be found. I make no charge against any person. I do know something of the cause that led her to come to me for protection when she was persecuted by an individual for whom she entertained feelings of bitter dislike and suspicion. Knowing the cause which led her to seek my protection, I have sought this interview with you, for the purpose of compelling you to impart her present whereabouts; or, failing this, to give you warning that a crisis has been reached when a thorough investigation shall be had concerning all that is now hidden in connection with her and that other person whose loss you claim to mourn so deeply."

The pale face is slowly raised to that of the speaker, and words proceed to fall from bloodless lips, as the window-pane ceases its melody.

"And do you *accuse me* of knowing aught of this outrage against the young lady you mention?"

"I make no direct accusations against any person. I only seek information from you because I have an idea that you can tell me what I want to know. If you cannot give me any information, then our interview is at an end, and—"

"Hold, sir!" interrupts Jasper, passionately, rising from his chair and facing Mr. Grewgious; "I have listened as calmly as it was possible for me to do while you have been making insinuations against me of the vilest nature. It is not enough, sir, that I have suffered for months in mind and body—the result of the terrible uncertainty connected with my lost nephew's fate—have passed anxious days and sleepless nights in my great grief for his—to me—death; and now, when I am beginning to forget in a measure the grief which so nearly cost me my life,—now, when acting on the advice of friends—those who have known more of the dread forebodings I had, long before this terrible calamity fell upon me, than you can have any idea of—acting, as I said, by the advice of friends, I have struggled hard to throw off this nightmare that has so long oppressed me; and just as I have succeeded, in a measure, in so doing, you come upon me in this scandalous manner and hurl me back into the abyss from which I have hardly drawn my feet. It is cruel, sir, cruel; and you will live to repent it, be assured."

He has paced the room with rapid strides while speaking; now, as he ceases, he throws himself into a chair and buries his face in his hands.

The Minor Canon, with his noble heart, touched by this outburst on Jasper's part, is about to say something that will help to soothe him; but Mr. Grewgious raises his finger to indicate that he desires the other will be silent. Then, in a careless tone, he addresses Jasper:

"I am to understand, then, that I have made a mistake in calling on you, but should have taken a different course to obtain information of Miss Bud's whereabouts. In fact, I begin to think you are right; for it seems you prefer to keep what you know concealed in your own breast."

The Minor Canon takes this opportunity of remarking—It is possible Mr. Jasper prefers to be alone with Mr. Grewgious; and if so, he will retire.

"Be seated, sir," says Mr. Grewgious, as the Minor Canon rises; "be seated. I prefer to converse with this gentleman in presence of a third party. It is always better, I have found, to have a third party present at any business transaction, and I see no reason why the rule will not apply in this instance. But it is possible my business is ended here, and so perhaps we had better *both* be going."

"Stay," Jasper remonstrates, as the two make a motion to leave their seats. "Keep your seats for a moment, and I will try and make what I have to say as brief as possible. It is well known to you,—nor would I disguise it if I could,—that about the time Miss Bud left here, I took the liberty of asking her to be my wife. If I had not loved her, I should not have done so. Long before my dear boy disappeared, I had learned to love her in secret. So long as it was in secret, injustice was done no person, and I was happy in loving her, even though with the knowledge that she was betrothed to another. Could I have torn this passion from my heart I would have done it willingly, even though my heart had come with it, out of friendship for the dear fellow whose name I need not mention. When he was gone, and, as I believed—as I now believe—never more to walk this earth, I felt that I could honorably tell her my love; and, should she look kindly upon it, be the happy man which she alone could make me. If she could not love me, why then she could tell me so in a kindly manner, and we could continue as we had been—friends—till I might succeed, with time, in convincing her that I was worthy of her. But what a different result! She construes an honorable proposal into an insult, and passionate entreaties into threats, and so flies from the neighbourhood and seeks her legal protector, who, it appears, encourages her in believing that a man who approaches a woman with a pure motive—that of asking her to be his wife—must be her enemy, and a person she should shun.

"No, sir!" continues Jasper, passionately; "I spurn such reflections upon my honor; I loved Rosa—Miss Bud—dearly; I love her now! I would not harm a thread of her dear hair; nor would I deprive myself of the only happiness I ever knew—that of loving her—for all the guardians in England; nor shall my heart cease to beat with love for her till it has ceased to beat forever! Now, sir, do you believe it possible that I can give you information of the missing girl's whereabouts, or know aught of the circumstances connected with her disappearance?"

Although his remarks have been addressed to Mr. Grewgious, Mr. Jasper has kept his face constantly turned towards the Minor Canon, and it may be that there was something about the speaker's looks that created more sympathy for him than the words he had just uttered, and that it was for this reason that Mr. Crisparkle's features evinced an expression of pity, while those of Mr. Grewgious continued to hold the same stern look of contempt which had shown itself throughout the interview, and which did not relax as he replied:

"It would be most proper, and just as satisfactory, if this information should be obtained even from the man who would brave so many of those legal protectors, of which I am such a poor representative. In fact, I am not sure—perhaps I am wrong, and, if so, please attribute it to my Angularity—I am not sure that the romance of this catastrophe would not be heightened by the admiring but rejected lover acting the part of an unselfish and magnanimous character, and revealing the facts that would be of so much benefit to the young lady and her friends."

It was evident to Jasper, from the tenor of this last remark on the part of Grewgious, that it would be an impossibility to convince that gentleman of his non-complicity in the plot which had resulted in Rosa's disappearance. As he ceased speaking, the old gentleman, who had kept his eyes turned away from the Music Master, now directed them upon the face of that gentleman, and, his spectacles having fallen a little lower on his nose than was convenient for use, he contented himself with resorting to a favorite custom of those persons who wear glasses by looking over them, probably with a view of impressing the object of their gaze that there are four eyes looking at him instead of two.

Hoping that the Minor Canon will say something at this point, which he does not, Mr. Jasper says:

"I am glad to feel that there are those who, knowing something of the miseries which I have suffered so long, can sympathize with me, and regret that I should be made the target of a mistaken man's abuse. When you ascertain the whereabouts of the young lady, sir," addressing

Grewgious, "which I feel sure you will before many days, you will be satisfied how deeply you have wronged me; and I trust that the knowledge will create a better impression concerning my character than you appear to have entertained heretofore."

Mr. Grewgious rises to go; and as he does so says:

"Thank you, sir, for the encouragement held out in your last remark—in that you feel confident I shall see her again. Now, mark me, Mr. Jasper; I did not suppose for an instant, when I sought you, that you would tell me one word that would compromise yourself, or admit any knowledge of Rosa's present whereabouts. Hence I am not disappointed at the result of this interview. I am going to leave you. I believe I shall meet you again at no distant day; but for fear that I should not, I will take the present opportunity of telling you what I *think*—understand me, sir, and you, Reverend Sir. I *think* you are a Deep and Devilish Villain; one who would stop at no crime which would help you in any object you might have in view. That is what I *think*, and if I am wrong you know it, and if I am right you know it, and will give me credit for reading human nature pretty correctly, and I charge nothing for the reading. I shall return to London in the morning. If I find Miss Bud within forty-eight hours, it is well for all of us. If I do not find her by that time, it will not be so well for some of us that I could name!"

He moves slowly towards the door while finishing the sentence; and, the Minor Canon following, they both take their departure after bidding Jasper a formal good day;—leaving him with his face turned toward the river—and once more wondering if beneath its bosom the days and nights are laden with miseries that oppress the traveller who gazes at its calm exterior, and who would give so much to know what is that death-voyage that begins when the journey of life is done, and the weary soul obtains that rest which can only be found on the golden shores of Heaven.

CHAPTER XXXIII.

A HAPPY MEETING.

However much mankind may wish to the contrary, the Great Author of the universe never designed that man should be in two places at the same time; and therefore it fell out that Mr. Grewgious having gone to Cloisterham on the same morning that Peckcraft, in company with Rosa, sought him at Staple Inn, they did not find him there, and were told by Mr. Bazzard why he had gone to Cloisterham, and that he would not return for a day or two at least. On obtaining this information, Rosa expressed her regrets that he should have taken this—as it had turned out—unnecessary trouble on her account, and on being informed by Bazzard that the Landlesses had not been made acquainted with the facts concerning her absence, concluded that she would go directly to Billickin's and await the return of her guardian.

Mr. Bazzard had forgotten to say that Miss Twinkleton had accompanied his employer to Cloisterham, and tells her so now; whereat Rosa declared that she should never dare to go back and stay alone there one night, lest she should be attacked and cut into inch pieces by her enemies; and at this horrid thought she fell to weeping, and wished she had never been born; or, that she had been born in Tartary or some other distant land, where young ladies were not subject to such terrible persecutions as they were in England.

Mr. Peckcraft waited till she had become a little calm, and then told her that he had a plan in his mind, which seemed to him, under the circumstances, a very feasible one.

Rosa didn't think much of plans. There had been a good many plans arranged in regard to her ever since she could remember anything, and they had all proved a disappointment to her and those who had contrived them, and she didn't see any use in trying to get along like other folks, for she knew she couldn't—and then falls to weeping again.

Mr. Peckcraft's experience with young ladies being limited, and Mr. Peckcraft being a purely matter-of-fact gentleman, causes him to reply to her that it's of no use to behave obstinate or unreasonable when a man old enough to be her father—Rosa thought he might have substituted grandfather—had suggestions to make with a view to her comfort.

"Now," said he, "the lady with whom I lodge, and whom I have known for many years, has several vacant apartments, and I am sure would make it very pleasant for you. It is a respectable neighbourhood, and very quiet, and I am sure that you need rest; and there is no place in London that offers better advantages, under the circumstances, than this. You can proceed thither with me, and on your guardian's return, he can call on you there; and perhaps you would find it so pleasant that arrangements satisfactory to all parties could be effected for a permanent stay. I am influenced in making this suggestion from the fact that I do not consider it prudent for you to remain in this vicinity a single hour without protection; and I should not feel that I had done my duty did I permit it.

At this point the door opened and a voice, which was instantly recognized by Rosa, inquired if Mr. Grewgious was present. On being informed by Bazzard that he was not, the person was about closing the door, when Rosa called "Mr. Tartar."

It proving to be no less a personage than that gentleman, he entered the room at being called, and Rosa immediately came towards him and shook him by the hand, at the same time expressing her thankfulness that he had come upon them just at this time, for she wanted advice, and knew of no one that could help her in her present dilemma better than he. She then introduced him to Mr. Peckcraft, and, on hearing the name "Tartar," it struck the old gentleman that it didn't take but one more letter to make it Tartary, and wondered if Rosa's previously expressed wish, that she had been born in that distant country, had been suggested by the similarity of the two names.

Mr. Tartar feels somewhat embarrassed at finding himself in his present position, and says that he will retire and call again if Bazzard will inform him when he shall be most likely to find Mr. Grewgious, unless Miss Bud is very certain that it is in his (Tartar's) power to be of service to her.

Bazzard tells the Pilot of the Admiral's Cabin that the gentleman he seeks will not return for some time, and then Rosa proceeds to give a summary of the facts connected with her abduction and subsequent release, and arrival here to find herself in her present predicament.

Mr. Tartar answers, after a moment, that perhaps it would be as safe for her to proceed directly to the Beanstalk Country, and there quietly remain with Miss Landless until her guardian's return.

Rosa would like nothing better, but there was an obstacle in the way, and that was that Mr. Grewgious had directed that the dwellers of that Magic Land were to be kept in profound ignorance of this affair, and she was afraid it would not be right to go contrary to his expressed wish, as the Landlesses would certainly have to be informed of the circumstances which brought her to them in such a mysterious manner.

At this point Mr. Peckcraft, who had looked at his watch several times, and had become painfully aware that his breakfast hour was near at hand—eight o'clock was his hour, to a second—with a fair chance of going by without his being present to partake of it, repeated his former proposal that the lady should accompany him to Miss Keep's; and Mr. Tartar, expressing his opinion that, under the circumstances, she could do no better, Rosa decided to go, but not until a promise has been exacted from both Bazzard and Tartar that instantly upon the arrival of her guardian he should be made acquainted with her whereabouts.

The coach in which they had come to Staple, having been in waiting all this time, they had nothing to do but descend and enter it, which they did, Rosa being escorted thereto by Mr. Tartar, with Peckcraft following in the rear. On being seated, Mr. Peckcraft gave orders where to drive, and Rosa again requesting Mr. Tartar to be sure and inform her guardian that she was well and where he could find her, and that he must come instantly—though she had no fear of that—the coach was driven rapidly away in the direction of Silver Square.

Arriving in due time, Mr. Peckcraft leads the way directly to the parlour, and begs Rosa to make herself as comfortable as possible while he goes in search of the lady who is the ruling power therein.

He is saved any trouble in that direction, however, for just then Miss Keep's voice is heard in the passage, telling an imaginary servant—as a warning to Mr. Peckcraft that she is coming—that she will "look in the parlour, and see if he is there," and opens the door just as Mr. Peckcraft is placing his hand upon the latch, to open it from the inside.

"Just in time, Miss Keep," he said. "I was about going in search of you. This lady is Miss Bud; Miss Bud, Miss Keep." The ladies shake hands, and Mr. Peckcraft proceeds to relate the particulars of Rosa's abduction, and how it comes about that he has taken the liberty to solicit the hospitality of Miss Keep, until such time as the young lady's guardian shall come for her.

"Are you fond of the Muses?" is the first question always proposed to a new acquaintance, the reply to that question always deciding her likes or dislikes for the person thus addressed. Hence Rosa is somewhat surprised and greatly amused by being asked if *she* is fond of the Muses. Hardly knowing what reply to make, she happens to catch Mr. Peckcraft motioning her to answer in the affirmative, by nodding his head up and down so vehemently that he was in imminent danger of breaking his neck.

Whereat Rosa declares that she is passionately fond of the Muses.

Miss Keep smiles approvingly, and turns to Peckcraft, of whom she asks the hour.

"One minute of eight," is the answer, referring to his watch.

"Tired and faint this poor young Miss must feel,
So we'll descend and take our morning meal."

And escorts Rosa to a side room where she can arrange her toilet; which being done, the trio descend to the dining-room just as the clock over the chimney-piece proclaims the hour of eight; whereat Mr. Peckcraft ejaculates, as they are seated:

"Thank heaven, we are in time!" and falls to with a relish.

Breakfast over, Mr. Peckcraft escorts Rosa back to the parlour, Miss Keep previously telling her that she would soon join her and arrange an apartment for her private use while she remained. Miss Keep has two or three other lodgers besides Mr. Peckcraft, all persons who lay claim to belonging to the "better class," or they would not be there.

Mr. Peckcraft has taken leave of Rosa, assuring her that everything will be done for her comfort, and that she is not to mind Miss Keep's peculiarities, for she is all right at heart. He also promises that he will send Stollop up with some entertaining reading, directly.

She had been seated thus but a few moments when she heard footsteps approaching the room, and also heard the voices of persons engaged in conversation, one of whom she thinks must be a very pretentious individual indeed, judging from the tone of his voice, and one or two remarks which she overhears.

As they enter the room, she perceives that one of these persons is a pale young man, dressed in a plain suit of black, carrying an intelligent, thoughtful face, and apparently an attentive listener to what his companion is saying.

The latter is a stout man, middle-aged, with brown hair cut very short, a square face and coarse features, with such a swagger in his gait, and dressed so flashily, that a stranger would instantly set him down for a prize-fighter who had recently had a streak of luck, or a coal-heaver enjoying his holiday and dressed for the occasion.

As they seat themselves, the younger of the two proceeds to address the stout man, as though replying to something he had said:

"But if a book has merit, Mr. Boalslasher,—if it possesses those requisites which tend to elevate, while assisting to beguile the leisure moments of the masses,—what earthly difference does it make, whether the writer at some time in his life was so unfortunate as to fall into a pit and become so bemired that it took years for him to free himself from the filth; or whether he has always found smooth sailing, escaping the pitfalls of life, and possessing wealth and influence, which in many instances only serves as a screen to cover vilest natures. Is it right, Mr. Boalslasher, to say that a book does not possess merit because the writer happens to have blue eyes, or brown eyes, or black eyes?"

Mr. Boalslasher sees something so exceedingly funny in what the speaker has just said, that he falls to laughing and slapping his hands together, and does not stop for two minutes. At the end of that time, by a great effort, apparently, he recovers himself, and is enabled to reply in tones so coarse and loud that Rosa, who has been looking out of window all this time, turns her face, expecting to find that the pale young man has taken a position on the landing; but, finding him close to the speaker, concludes that he must be very deaf.

"You amuse me highly and immensely, Mr. Medagent, when you make use of the term 'Right' in connection with what appears in the columns of the Bœotian. The public don't want things right, sir; and damme, sir, if they shall have 'em right if they do! We've got our columns to fill, sir, and when I say that the Bœotian's circulation is little less than half a million, and that the public won't eat their breakfasts, but wait with empty stomachs till they have read it, sir, you can judge whether we fill 'em satisfactory or not!" Mr. Medagent looked a little puzzled when the speaker said "fill 'em," as wondering if he meant the stomachs, whereat the Editor repeats his last sentence by way of explanation. "Yes, sir; you can judge if we fill those columns satisfactory or not. Now, sir, concerning the articles to which you take exception, let me say this: We don't care a farthing about you or your book; but we have got a character to sustain. When a new book appears, the public expect we will give an opinion on its merits. The public expect we will tear it to pieces, or else what's the *good* of critics? So we tear 'em to pieces *somehow*. If we can't find anything about the book to condemn, why then, damme, sir, we must tackle the author's character. In that way, sir, we impress the public with the idea that we know *everything*, and get the reputation of being enterprising besides. It's the only thing we can do, sir, to keep alive the interest of our columns. In fact, the stepping-stones to an editor's success are made of ruined reputations laid in the cement of scurrility that flows from his pen! Now, sir, them's the principles on which *I* do business, and, by G—d, I am willing to proclaim it at Charing Cross, if necessary!" And Mr. Boalslasher blows his nose violently and with a very loud noise, which is intended, no doubt, for one of those exclamation points which are always seen at the end of every third sentence of his articles in the Bœotian.

Rosa, who has listened with some interest to what the talented editor has been saying, notices that the face of the young man has the faintest flush upon it while listening to the speaker, and that the flush has grown to be quite a bright one as he closes.

Rising from his chair, Mr. Medagent stands before the great man, and with a look of contempt upon his features, addresses him in these words:

"Of your mode of doing business, or the enterprise, as you term it, which your readers give you credit for, I have nothing to say, only that your admissions have shown me what a fool I have been to expect anything like justice from such a man. But I *will* reply to one or two of the statements you have made; and first, I deny that the public encourages any such abuse of individuals as you assert. There may be a few who, actuated by feelings of envy, or who entertain the same disregard for the feelings of their fellows that you possess, will clap their hands and tell you that you have done your duty manfully; but the majority will despise you; and, if you were not so blind that you *would not* see, the falling off of your subscribers,—which I know is of daily occurrence,—would be sufficient to convince you of the truthfulness of my assertion. Again, I deny that newspapers, as a class, resort to any such contemptible means, as you claim they do, to obtain patronage. I will confess that there are exceptions to the rule,—the same as to anything else,—and that occasionally the editorial profession is forced to bear the pain of carrying a thorn of pollution in its side, when numbering among its ranks men who are so void of all the common decencies of life, and so incapable, for want of brains, of making their journals interesting to the public, that they resort to dirty blackguardism and foul-mouthed slanders, which they call independent journalism,—and it is independent with a vengeance. And now, Mr. Boalslasher, you can go on with your scurrility; you will find it difficult to make respectable people read such trash, or if they do, will sympathize with the victim of your abuse; and so, when you thought to do harm, you have really done good." And waving his hand to the Boalslasher, the pale young man took his departure, leaving the former looking very much astonished that any living mortal should thus dare address *Him.*

Stepping before a mirror to arrange his neckcloth, Mr. Boalslasher was heard by Rosa to mutter:

"D—n him! I'll abuse him all I please, or any one else I've a mind to. It don't cost me anything to do it, for I've got a paper of my own, and it costs those fellows more than they care to pay out for replying through another paper. Ha, ha! That's where I've got em, damme; a half column at least for you to-morrow, my fine fellow;" and donning his hat, he swaggers from the room, coughing and spitting as he goes, in a manner that is quite painful to hear.

Shortly after the two gentlemen had taken their departure comes Miss Keep, carrying in her hand a printed tract, and which she declares, as she seats herself by Rosa's side, has interested her so much in the perusal that she had forgotten everything.

"It gives a detailed account," said Miss Keep, by way of explanation, "of a meeting last Tuesday week of the members of our Grand Haven, called for the purpose of raising funds to carry on the noble work in which it is engaged. Let me read you an extract, that you may have an opportunity to judge how interesting it is," and reads:.

"Mr. Slukers, resuming his seat, is replied to by Mr. Honeythunder: If it is true, as the gentleman who has just spoken says, that the public don't understand that our society is a benefit to them, and an ornament to the British nation, spreading for them—if I may be allowed the phrase—the Butter of Philanthropy upon the Bread of Ignorance, they must be made to understand it, sir, and it must be hammered into them. There have been efforts made to crush us, and obstacles thrown in the way of those who longed to join us and become Brothers; and the consequence is, sir, that we have lost ground; but this state of things must not continue. It is my duty, and I am willing to devote my time, and such talent as I possess, to disseminating the principles of our Haven, far and near, and strengthen the cause by increasing the numbers; and it is the duty of other Brothers to put their hands in their pockets and aid the good work; and so each and all will apply his shoulder, according to his peculiar adaptation.

Mr. Honeythunder took his seat amidst great applause; after it had ended he was replied to by

Mr. Slukers—"The gentleman may be right, but I for one feel that I have done all that it is my duty to do, at least for the present; others may do as they like, but my mind is made up."

Mr. Honeythunder (excitedly)—"Am I to understand the gentleman, then, that he does not intend to work with us and for us any longer?—that he is going to deliberately step out of the Shoes of Philanthropy, which have only just got fitted to his feet, and in their stead put on another pair that will carry him straight to the devil? Can it be possible that he (Mr. Slukers) intends to give us the cold shoulder in this, our hour of need, and throw overboard the benefits that a few petty pounds would retain for the benefit of the human race? Can it be possible that I understand him right?"

"Dear Brother Honeythunder," ejaculates Miss Keep, at this point interrupting herself, and looking towards the door in a reflecting mood, "I can see him now," which causes Rosa to turn her eyes very suddenly towards the door in anticipation of the great man's presence, whereat Miss Keep smiles and adds, "in fancy, child! I can see the look of surprise and sadness which pervaded his noble face as he uttered those feeling words to Mr. Slukers—

What pain was felt in Honeythunder's heart,
When Slukers thus did hurl the cruel dart!

"Ah, Miss Bud, you have no idea of the amount of good that man does in the world. His time is constantly employed for the benefit of the human race. I have known him for a long time, and he is always the same."

Rosa, who has not forgotten Mr. Honeythunder's visit to Cloisterham during the Christmas days, does not doubt that he is always the same, and says so.

"It is almost incredible," continues Miss Keep, "that a man with such talent as he possesses, is willing to devote himself so entirely to the interests of those who have no claim upon him. He is always searching for objects upon whom he can impress the beauties of living a life devoted to the practice of Philanthropy. It is only a short time since he converted to the brotherhood—or I should say sisterhood—a lady who was near the point of death; and, so convinced was she of the correctness of the principles upon which our Haven is founded, that she left a very large sum as a bequest to the society, and a very handsome amount to Mr. Honeythunder personally, for the interest he had taken to convince her of her duty to her fellow-men. She died very happy, and Mr. Honeythunder wrote a very lengthy obituary for one of the magazines, in which the lady's kindness of heart was fully set forth. Now was anything ever more kind than that act on his part,—and what a consolation it must have proved to her friends—for she had been a very penurious woman, for years before her death, and it was said that her own sister—who had the misfortune to be the widow of a very poor man—died for the need of comforts, when a few pounds would have saved her life, but which the rich one refused when solicited. Yes, I really do think it speaks well for Mr. Honeythunder's noble efforts, when he can so far succeed in convincing such persons of the importance of doing good with their money when it cannot be of any more use to them."

As Miss Keep finishes this recital of the Great Moral Pugilist's triumph in the Philanthropic Arena, a very trim-looking servant girl tapped at the door, and Miss Keep says:

"Mary, my dear,
What takes you here?"

The good lady never fails to address the two servants in rhyme when opportunity offers, the better to impress them with the idea that their mistress is of a poetical nature, and equal to any emergency in that line; and there are a great many other people who are guilty of equal absurdity, with this exception—that while Miss Keep confines her talent within her domestic circle, and so gets laughed at by a few, the others make theirs to appear in print, and are laughed at by the public.

"Please, ma'am," is the girl's reply, "Mr. Peckcraft's young man is at the door, and says he has a package as is for the young lady as come with Mr. Peckcraft, this mornin'."

"Well, why did you not take it in,
And let him go away again?"

"That's just what I made offer to do, Miss, but he said as he was to 'and it to the young lady hisself, and so I thought I'd better tell you before showin' of 'im in."

"Miss Bud, my friend, what do you say?
Shall Mary show him in this way?"

Rosa finds it difficult to suppress the merriment which she feels at hearing Miss Keep indulge in her favorite method of conversation, but controls herself, and with as sober a countenance as she can assume, says she does not object.

Miss Keep was on the point of issuing a command to that effect, but the servant, feeling that she had had poetry enough to last her for some time, had left directly she heard Rosa's answer, and the result was that a moment thereafter, Mr. Stollop, with hat in hand, stood bowing at the door in a most graceful manner, and said he hoped he had not intruded upon anybody's sanctity.

Nobody replying to this, he proceeded to inform them that his employer had intrusted to him a package for Miss Bud, and feeling the honor which attached to a mission to any young lady, and more especially, the young lady in question, and as he had been instructed furthermore, to see that the package was placed into her hands without delay, he felt in duty bound to deliver it personally, and so return with a happy consciousness of having done his duty.

"And very praiseworthy of you, sir, to be sure," interposes Miss Keep, and smiles graciously on the young man.

Mr. Stollop, who had intended by his remarks to convey to Rosa that she was the object of great solicitude on his part, and that he would at all times be faithful to her interests or die in the struggle,—Mr. Stollop, with deep design intent, does not appear quite satisfied with the result, for Rosa takes the package from his hand and desires him to say to Mr. Peckcraft that he is very thoughtful, and to carry her thanks to that gentleman for his kindness,—but does not mention thanks for Mr. Stollop.

Mr. Stollop remains standing in the middle of the room, and feels very much annoyed and embarrassed. Things are not as he expected. Fancy had deluded him into the idea that Miss Bud, with feelings of gratitude towards him for the services he had rendered her on the night of her escape from the Slanduces—would spring to take him by the hand,

and insist upon his seating himself by her side; that she would tell him how grateful she felt toward him for rescuing her from perhaps a horrid death. All this, and much more had Mr. Stollop anticipated as the result of an interview with the lady; but, alas, for the vanity of human hopes! Instead of those beautiful pictures of the imagination, Mr. Stollop finds himself confronted by the very plainest print, and he does not feel so happy as he had anticipated.

"I hurried very fast, Miss," he says, in a tone which implied that he thought that ought to carry some weight in his favor.

Miss Keep again:

"Fast sped the youth to his true love's bower,
And—and—"

"Dear me, Miss, *do* you remember the line, for I've forgotten it altogether."

Rosa thought she had never heard it, and Miss Keep, after repeating to herself various lines, is forced to give it up.

Rosa turns to Stollop, for whom she entertains decided feelings of contempt, and while she thinks it her duty to thank him for the part he had taken in aiding her to escape from the hands of her enemies, she felt if she did so, he would misconstrue her motives, and make himself still more ridiculous than he had already done. She observes that he is waiting for her to say something in reply, so she addresses him:

"Mr. Peckcraft is very fortunate in having so faithful a clerk as you, sir, and must appreciate you services in the highest degree. I am sure I should if I were he, but—"

Hope, which had been dashed to earth, now fills the Stollop breast, and he cannot restrain himself from interrupting her at this point, by saying:

"Thank you, Miss; thank you kindly for admitting that I am worthy of your appreciation;" and smiles in his sweetest manner, to indicate that he is a happy man.

"I said, if I were Mr. Peckcraft, which I am not," continued Rosa, showing a little displeasure at the other's haste, "I should appreciate your services as I should those of any faithful servant. I was also about to add, when you interrupted me, that it was barely possible Mr. Peckcraft might appreciate you still more if you were to hurry back as fast as you say you came; and I am glad to know that such an excellent gentleman as Mr. Peckcraft has so good a messenger to perform his missions with so much expedition."

On hearing Rosa utter these words, it struck Mr. Stollop that it was barely possible the young lady did not feel disposed to cultivate that tender regard for him which he had so fully anticipated.

He stood silently gazing at her for a moment after she ceased speaking, whereat Rosa turned her face from him to avoid laughing outright at the singular appearance which he presented. With one foot a little in advance of the other, his arms raised and crooked at the elbows, as though on the point of flying, his face wearing a very melancholy appearance and his eyes in a very watery condition, Mr. Stollop resembled a picture of comic despair.

"Miss Bud," he finally exclaimed, in a dramatic tone, "to use the words of a gentleman who lived many years ago, and who, I have no doubt, suffered in his feelings very much as I do now—to use the words of that gentleman, varying them slightly to fit the present occasion—I can only say, had I but served Mr. Peckcraft with half the zeal I've served Miss Bud, I'd be a happy Stollop;" and bidding her farewell, he rushes frantically from the room, to the great relief of Rosa, and nearly frightening Miss Keep into fits, thinking he must have lost his wits.

"Well," said Miss Keep, after she had recovered a little, "of all the strange-acting gentlemen that I ever did see, he is the strangest. I hope he wont go and destroy himself. I never knew him to behave in such a manner before. He has frequently called here on business for Mr. Peckcraft, but I never knew him to act as he has to-day.

His mind must have been in a fearful state
To have left the room at such a rate."

Rosa replied that she did not think he would do anything very desperate, and proceeded to state to Miss Keep how it happened that she first met him, and, that though she felt very grateful to him for the service he had rendered her in her emergency, she did not dare to express her gratitude, as she should have done to any reasonable person, for fear he would make himself still more ridiculous.

"Poor fellow!" replies Miss Keep, "it's a great misfortune, Miss, to possess such a sanguine disposition as he has got. It's quite plain that he has fallen in love with you, and I hope his disappointment will not result fatally. I know something of his feelings and can sympathize with him.

When cruel fate our love destroys,
It stabs to death all other joys."

Common rumor affirmed that, at an early period of her existence, Miss Keep had set her heart on a certain young linen-draper, who had shown her some attention, and which she, in the innocence of her nature, had construed into an affection; and her present condition in life, it was said, was due to the young man taking some other lady to his heart and making her his other half. Perhaps it was the thought of that disappointment which caused Miss Keep to shed a few tears as she closed her last sentence, and Rosa, who had regarded Mr. Stollop's behaviour as something to laugh at, felt a little embarrassed by Miss Keep's taking the affair so seriously.

"Well," said Rosa, after a moment, "you would not think I had done right to encourage any such foolish whim as he had possessed himself of, and which he had no cause to do. It surely was not my fault if he behaved like a fool, and forced me to treat him in a way which would show him that I was not pleased with such absurdity."

"Oh, no," is the reply; "I do not blame you, my child—far from it. But it is a sad sight to behold a young person encouraging a hope which can never be realized, and which may be the cause of blasting all their future existence. It's a dreadful thing.

Love is a power we can't control,
An influence felt by every soul."

And then sighs deeply, while looking sorrowfully at Rosa.

Having no disposition to carry on a further conversation on this subject, or having said all she had to say, was probably the reason why Miss Keep informed Rosa that she would now show her to a comfortable room, where she could obtain the rest which she stood so much in need of, and led the way thereto, followed by Rosa, who was very glad to embrace the opportunity, not having slept since leaving Mrs. Billickin's house. She is taken to a cozy little sleeping room, and, left to herself, is soon enjoying such slumbers as none but the pure and innocent are permitted to realize; and so we will leave her and follow Mr. Stollop.

On leaving the house, after his interview with the young lady for whom he had conceived so sudden and violent a passion, he walks with rapid and excited steps in the direction of Chancery Lane; but, it being one of those remarkable days when an observant person will perceive that everybody is out of doors and nobody at home, the pavements are crowded with pedestrians, and he runs violently against sundry old women, tumbles two or three young urchins into the gutter, and narrowly escapes the loss of an eye by coming in contact with the corner of a trunk which a porter is carrying on his shoulder. He finally reaches Fleet Street, and is just turning into Chancery Lane, when he is knocked out of his senses by hearing a terrific yell from some person that he has come in collision with, and then is knocked into his senses by receiving a blow in the pit of his stomach. Mr. Stollop, looking wildly about him to discern what it all means, hears a voice crying out, with more force than elegance:

"Damn yer eyes! what do you go runnin' over a feller in that there way for?"

Mr. Stollop places his hands upon his stomach and reply doth make that the said "running over" was not premeditated, but purely accidental. Whereat the irate personage comes a little closer, and Mr. Stollop observes that he is about midway between soberness and drunkenness.

"Durdles ain't no man to pick a quarrel without he has reason. Let's shake hands," and proffers his.

Mr. Stollop was very happy to do so, for two reasons:—First, he had no disposition to engage in the manly art in his present state of mind; and, second, he was satisfied that a battle with this person must result in ignoble defeat, for the other was much the heavier man, and evidently possessed greater powers of strength and endurance. The handshaking over, Mr. Durdles proceeds to inform Stollop that he has come to London, from one of the neighbouring towns, in search of a person for whom he has a letter of some importance, and perhaps he (Mr. Stollop) could give him some information concerning the whereabouts of the individual he was seeking.

Stollop replies that he should be happy to do the gentleman a favour, if in his power so to do, and asks the name of the party in question.

Taking from a side pocket three or four letters, all but one being very dirty and crumpled from being carried a long time, Durdles selects the one that is quite fresh-looking, and reads:

"Mr. Peter Peckcraft, Chancery Lane, formerly Drood & Peckcraft."

Mr. Stollop, glancing at the superscription, is surprised to find that the document is intended for his employer, and proceeds to surprise the other by telling him the fact, and that he (Stollop) is going directly there.

Durdles regards this as such a remarkable circumstance, that he invites Stollop to an adjacent public house to partake of a mug of ale, and declares that he never knew anything quite so odd as that he should tumble into the knowledge of Mr. Peckcraft's whereabouts so suddenly; and this was true, for he had literally tumbled into it.

The two gentlemen, in a few moments, are seated at table, waiting for a pint apiece, which Mr. Durdles has ordered.

"Ain't it a little singular," asks Stollop, as the waiter appears with the glasses, "how things come round?"

Mr. Durdles looks at the ale and then at Stollop, not quite understanding whether the speaker has reference to the beverage or something else. He appears lost for a moment, and then, taking a long draught from his own glass, says:

"What d'ye mean?"

"Why, the way you met me, you know, and I being the one that could take you right to the man you wanted to see."

"I've seen things come round more sin'ular nor that," is the answer; "and having seen 'em Durdles don't feel took back by this little circumstance. I could tell you som'at, young man, as would make you think you never heerd its like. But Durdles knows his bus'ness, Durdles does, and he ain't got nothin' to say till the time comes. Have another one?" meaning ale.

"Strange deeds will rise, though all the earth o'erwhelm them, to men's eyes," says Stollop, quoting from his favourite author, and looks very hard at the glass in his hand, as though he expected to see something strange rise from that. In fact, Mr. Stollop's nerves, at no time very strong, are weaker than usual to-day, from the shock they had experienced a half-hour since at Miss Keep's, and the ale had begun to affect him almost directly he swallowed it.

Mr. Durdles makes no reply to this last remark, but turns his attention to the contents of his glass, and, disposing of half of it, he becomes communicative again, and says:

"I spose you wonder, now, what kind of a message there is in this 'ere letter to your guv'ner, eh?" and winks at Stollop to indicate that he (Durdles) knows the secret, but means to keep it.

"You mistake me, Mr. Turtles," is the rejoinder.

"Durdles, *if* you please," interrupts that gentleman, "*Dur*-dells is my name, and I ain't ashamed of it!"

"Excuse me, Mr. Durdles; I was about to say that you mistook my nature if you thought I would be guilty of prying into the business of my employer. What he tells me I hear and keep to myself, and he knows that nothing could ever draw it from me. No, sir; the secrets of *any* man (here he looks very hard at his companion) confided to me are here," placing his hand upon his heart, "and there they will stay."

Durdles' glass being empty, and, noticing his companion's to be in a like condition, he says; "That's right, Mr. —— oh, that reminds me; we ain't on a even footin', we ain't; you've got the name of my father, but I hain't got a letter o' yourn yet."

"My name is Stollop," replies that gentleman modestly, as though he would like to add that if his companion was not perfectly satisfied with it, he might call him by any other that he chose.

"Stol-lop!" Durdles repeats very slowly, emphasizing each syllable as though he were storing it away, a sentence at a time, in the farthest corner of his mind, the better to remember it. "All straight now, Stollop, my boy; we're on a even footin' now; nothin' like an even footin' among gentlemen. As you was a sayin' on a second ago, you keeps all them air secrets of your friends here," striking his own breast in an emphatic manner; "now," he adds, "suppose, Mr. Stollop, as you puts somethin' here," moving his hand quickly to the pit of his stomach, "to keep the other company, and takes a little gin and water sweetened, and then we'll get along to where I can see this 'ere person as is to have this 'ere letter, and get through with the bus'ness."

Mr. Stollop has an idea that he has drank as much already as he ought to, but is pressed so hard that, before he has an opportunity to decline, utterly, Durdles has ordered the gin, and the two gentlemen are sipping it in a very happy frame of mind.

Now, under ordinary circumstances, Mr. Stollop would have refused emphatically to drink anything stronger than the ale; but, in the state of mind which he was laboring under, in consequence of Rosa's recent cool treatment of him, he had reached that point where it was immaterial, he thought, what became of him. Hence, while Mr. Durdles was having a glorious time, and not suffering any in consequence, Mr. Stollop was becoming decidedly drunk.

By the time that the last potation is half exhausted, he has reached that state of maudlin drunkenness, which leads him to believe that Durdles is the best friend he ever had, and so tells him.

He holds out his hand, which the other takes, and with tears streaming down his face, proceeds to enlighten his companion as to the wretchedness that preys upon his mind.

"Oh, my excellent friend!" he says—the tears streaming down his cheeks, which resemble the color of a sunset sky—"you do not know the misery by which I am surrounded. I love a lady, dearly, sir!"—here he refreshes himself by taking a sip of the gin and water, after which Durdles, much interested, repeats:

"Dearly," as a cue for the other to proceed.

"Dearly, sir!" Stollop reiterates emphatically, and wipes his lips with his coat sleeve.

Mr. Durdles smiles grimly, and nods for his friend to proceed.

"With a passion, sir, that was born in a minute, my fancy soared up—up—" describing the flight by raising the glass in his hand at arm's length, "and I felt, for the first time in my life, that love was a precious thing, sir!"

Mr. Durdles nods approval at this last assertion, and remarks, in a careless tone:

"If it ain't a precious thing my name ain't Durdles. That's where I stand."

Stollop is so pleased with this proof of his friend's coinciding with him, that he finds it desirable to shake hands again, which is done.

Mr. Stollop now proceeds to enlighten Durdles concerning the events which had brought Rosa and himself together; and, while a good portion of the narrative was interspersed with expressions intended to convey to the hearer that the narrator's peace of mind was forever blasted by the fate which had led him to make the acquaintance of an angel, Durdles learned enough to satisfy himself that the angel in question was no other than the Miss Bud who had formerly dwelt at the Nuns' House, and whom he remembered in connection with the missing young man to whom she was betrothed.

This knowledge seemed to impress him with the importance of taking a hasty departure, with a view of delivering the message, which he had for Mr. Peckcraft, at the earliest moment; so, the glasses being emptied, he says they must be going.

Mr. Stollop, however, is just sufficiently conscious to know that he is not in a proper state to appear before his employer, and exclaims, striking the table with his glass:

"Never, sir! I may have lost all my own self-respect, sir, but I will never bring disgrace upon the house—or, I should say, shop—of Peckcraft. Place me, sir, in the silent tomb of my ancestors, if their last resting-place can be found, but never ask me to bring the gray hairs of Peckcraft to the grave; leave me, sir!" and rising, sways to and fro, raising his arm in a theatrical manner for the other to depart; then reseats himself, and, with his eyes half closed, stares at Durdles as though surveying him through a fog.

Stollop's allusion to tombs and graves causes Mr. Durdles to wonder if the speaker has discovered, by any sense of sight or smell, that his (Durdles') business is one that brings him in contact with the dead and gone Cloisterhamites; and is so disgusted at his companion's allusions, that he thinks he should be happy to have an opportunity to stow him (Stollop) snugly away in one of the receptacles that he is so anxious to be placed in. He keeps his thoughts to himself, however, and says:

"Durdles ain't one as stands any nonsense, he ain't. When he says he's got to do any thin' he means it. Now he's got to give up this 'ere letter, and he's got to take you along with him, the better to know who to give it up to. D'ye understand?"

Stollop continues to stare at the speaker, and finally mutters that "love is a precious thing, sir," and is so overcome with this thought that he falls to weeping, and is shook by the shoulder pretty roughly by Durdles, who tells him to get up.

"Get up, fool! lean on me, and when you get out in the air you'll feel better;" and, supporting Stollop to his feet, they proceed towards the door, and reach the pavement, but not before Stollop has stopped one of the customers standing near him, and endeavoured to persuade him that "love is a precious thing."

The wind blowing quite fresh, together with the support he receives from Durdles, aids the intoxicated man in recovering himself after a little, and he gradually begins to comprehend the circumstances which have brought him in company with his companion.

He finally told Durdles that he could get along without assistance, but he must contrive some way to improve his personal appearance, or that Mr. Peckcraft would mistrust that he had been indulging in the ardent, and perhaps take away his situation. Acting on this suggestion, they turn into a mercer's shop a few doors off from Peckcraft's, where a friend of Stollop's is engaged as clerk, and are met by that personage, who says:

"Bless my heart, Stolly, my boy, what's been going wrong with you?"

"To tell you the truth," rejoins Stollop, "I've been sipping the nectar, and not being used to such a luxury, I got a little complicated, so to speak, but I'm all right now. I don't want the old man to know it though, Cotley, so just give me a chance to bathe in some cool and limpid stream, and I'll depart to other scenes."

Mr. Cotley smiles and looks very hard at Durdles, which, being noticed by Stollop, he introduces the two gentlemen.

Mr. Cotley is a young man with a very large head on a very small body, and—possessing a pair of arms which are much too long to be in good proportion, and which are constantly being kept in a swinging motion—it would appear to an observing mind that he must be constructed on the principle of a pump, and that his arms must act as handles to pump every thing that he swallows into his head; and this idea would seem to be further strengthened from the fact that his eyes, protruding from their sockets, seem to have hard work to retain the position that nature had designed for them, and were in constant danger of being pushed out altogether.

He shakes Durdles by the hand, and says he is glad to know him; whereat Durdles affirms, "The same to you, sir;" and then turns to Stollop and tells him that time is precious with him, and the sooner they are on the road to Peckcraft's the better he shall be pleased.

Stollop, being provided with soap and water, soon refreshes himself and presents an improved appearance, Mr. Cotley declaring that he looks "like a prince," which might be a compliment or not, some princes not being notorious for cleanliness or beauty, according to biographers, who, of course, knew more about the moral and physical characteristics of other people than the Creator himself.

Bidding Mr. Cotley a good-day, Mr. Stollop and his companion proceed to the shop of Peckcraft, Stollop wondering what kind of a reception he will meet with for absenting himself so long, but feeling encouraged with the belief that his employer will not be disposed to find so much fault with him, since he is accompanied by a person who brings him a private message, and more especially encouraged when Durdles assures him that he will, by some pretext, take upon himself the blame for Stollop's delay.

They find Mr. Peckcraft decidedly out of temper, pacing the floor with his hands behind him; he does not deign to notice Stollop as he enters, and were it not for a glance of curiosity which he bestows upon Durdles, it would be supposed he was not aware that a second person was within hearing. Stollop approaches him with a timid step and says:

"Mr. Peckcraft, ex—"

Mr. Peckcraft interrupts, in a tone of sarcasm: "You are my clerk, I believe, sir?"

"Beg your pardon, sir," resumes Stollop, "bút—"

Mr. Peckcraft again interrupts by continuing: "And undertook the delivery of a parcel for me this morning, which ordinary men could have accomplished in a half-hour, and something to spare, but which you have seen fit to stretch to three hours or more. Are you not ashamed of it, sir?"

Mr. Stollop asserts that, had not circumstances beyond his control been the occasion of his long absence, he should feel he had not done his duty; but, if Mr. Peckcraft will listen for two minutes, he "will a tale unfold" which shall satisfy that gentleman that, though absent, he has nevertheless been engaged in a matter which may prove of some importance to him (Mr. Peckcraft), and proceeds to state how he had been accosted by Durdles as to the whereabouts of Mr. Peckcraft; that, on being told that he (Stollop) was going directly there, then Mr. Durdles wished him to accompany him to his hotel, in a distant part of the city, to get a message which he had brought, so that he could deliver it expeditiously into his (Peckcraft's) hands.

Having closed his remarks he turns to Durdles, and, with sundry winks, appeals to that personage to say whether he has stated the facts correctly; and Durdles declares it to be all true, and adds that it's a wonder they got here as soon as they had, for the walk was a long one, and he was sure he never could have found his way back to Chancery Lane without a great loss of time; and as he knew the message to be an important one, he did not feel like allowing any unnecessary delay in its delivery.

On hearing this, Mr. Peckcraft permits his anger to cool, and offers Durdles a chair. Passing the letter to the old gentleman, Durdles seats himself while Mr. Peckcraft opens the missive and reads as follows:

"MR. P. PECKCRAFT:

"You will doubtless be surprised to receive this, but I know no other person on whom I can call for aid, in a matter that concerns myself and one other, who is knowing to facts which have a bearing on the case in hand. Will you kindly oblige me by taking an early train to Cloisterham, and bringing with you such papers as you have in your possession that bear reference to my dear father's wishes concerning me and my mother's brother, Mr. John Jasper, whom you will remember as my guardian? I think I have heard it said by some one,—I can't remember who, now,—that my father did leave with you certain written instructions which were to be observed in case my guardian failed in his duties to me, and it is important at this time that they are brought forward. However, if they cannot be found, or if they never did exist, pray do not let that prevent your coming at once. After alighting at the station, the omnibus will take you directly to the Crozier Inn, and I will join you very soon after. As I do not care to have my name mentioned, however, just at this time, will you be so good as to say that you are in search of 'Mr. Datchery,' and the porter at the inn will know just where to call for me? I beg you will not slight my request, for it is of vast importance, and as you would do my dear father a favour, I pray that you, in memory of him, will do as much for "Yours anxiously,

"EDWIN DROOD"

Mr. Peckcraft read this letter, at first, hastily—then moderately—and, at last, slowly; and it was evident that he was greatly surprised at its contents. He could not understand how young Drood came to be in Cloisterham when he supposed him to be in India, perfecting himself in the profession which he had adopted years ago. Still, he might have only just returned. But why was it, if he had returned, and was within so short a distance, he had not called personally upon him, instead of sending a message. Perhaps Edwin was sick, he thought; but then, he reflected, were that the case, he would most likely have mentioned it; and as he did not, why, of course, that could not be the reason.

"When did you leave Cloisterham?" he enquires of Durdles.

"When did I leave? On the night express," is the rejoinder.

"Could you not just as well have taken the afternoon train as to wait till night?" inquires Peckcraft, in a suspicious tone.

"Durdles goes when he is sent, Durdles does," is the answer, given with the least bit of surliness.

"When did you leave Mr. Drood?" continues Mr. Peckcraft.

"Durdles came 'ere to bring that there letter—Durdles didn't come to let any man make game of him, and Durdles has got this 'ere to say: If there's anything a-goin' back to the person as writ that there letter, Durdles wants to know it d—n quick, for bus'ness is bus'ness with Durdles, and he's left his own bus'ness to come and attend to another man's, so make short work and talk less; for, as I said afore, bus'ness is bus'ness, and the sooner we gets on an even footin' the sooner we'll understan' one another. Nothin' like an even footin'."

Although Mr. Peckcraft saw that Durdles' ideas were correct, so far as they related to the latter, the tones in which the man had uttered them caused him to think that were he (Peckcraft) a younger man, he should feel it a great relief to set the "even footin'" one side and adopt an odd footing, by kicking his visitor into the street. He sat silent a few moments, and then, going to his desk, penned the following reply to be conveyed by the messenger back to Cloisterham:

"MR. DROOD:

"My Young Friend,—I am surprised to receive your note. I did not suppose you in this country. In fact, I had so much doubt about this letter being genuine, that I at first decided to let the messenger return empty-handed. As I can see no object that any person could have for deception, however, I will take it for granted that it is really you, and say I will come to-morrow, but can't say the hour; perhaps by noon—at any rate by night.

"God bless you, and believe me the same friend to you that your father was to

"PETER PECKCRAFT."

The letter is sealed and addressed to Edwin Drood, and then passed to Durdles, who places it in his pocket, bids the two gentlemen a gruff good-day, and takes his departure.

That same day an elderly gentleman, very tired, very dusty, and very warm, arrives in London, and takes his way to Staple Inn by cab. This same gentleman alights from the vehicle and proceeds directly to P. J. T., which might indicate Poor Jaded Traveller, so Mr. Grewgious thinks, for *he* is a Poor Jaded Traveller, who has just arrived from Cloisterham, and not quite satisfied with the result of his journey. Entering his chambers, he is met by Bazzard, and to him doth say:

"Bazzard, I haven't found her."

That gentleman does not show any surprise at this, but simply returns, "I didn't suppose you would."

"I have obtained some satisfaction from my visit, however, in that I have had the pleasure of telling a Villain what I think of him."

"Which didn't do him any good, nor you either, since you didn't get the young lady."

"Bazzard, you have had time to think over some plan. What shall be my next move, should you say?"

"Better go where she is," answers Bazzard.

Mr. Grewgious, understanding Bazzard so well, feels confident that something has transpired during his absence to indicate the whereabouts of the missing girl. He is so very confident of this that he replaces his hat upon his head as he asks:

"Where should you say that might be, Bazzard?"

Mr. Bazzard then relates to his employer all the events connected with Rosa's arrival with Mr. Peckcraft, and then going away again to that gentleman's lodgings—the better for Miss Rosa's safety.

"And quite right it was that they did so," replies Mr. Grewgious. "I will go directly there," and, receiving the address from Bazzard, who had taken the precaution to write it down plainly, the old gentleman hastened off to join his ward.

He soon arrives at Silver Square, and, knocking loud at Miss Keep's street door, is admitted by the servant, who escorts him to the parlour, and then goes in search of Miss Keep.

Now Miss Keep had no doubt as to the visitor's identity, but, like a great many other people under such circumstances, she feigns ignorance, and professes great astonishment when her visitor discloses his name and business.

Before notifying Rosa, however, Miss Keep felt it her duty to propound her usual inquiries as to his (Mr. Grewgious) admiration for "the Muses," and, though not exactly understanding what the lady meant, he declared that he believed he was fond of them, so far as he knew. This point being settled, Miss Keep excuses herself while she seeks Miss Bud.

She soon returns with Rosa, who, having obtained refreshing sleep, is greatly improved in consequence.

Mr. Grewgious, all impatience to behold his charge once more in safety, has heard them descending the stairs and steps to the door to meet them. He has only reached it when it is opened by Rosa, and, almost before she knows it, she is clasped in the affectionate embrace of her guardian, who exclaims: "Thank God! you are restored to me, my dear child; and if you are ever again exposed to such perils as I feel confident you have only just escaped, it will be when I have no longer the power to prevent it." He imprints a kiss upon her brow as she turns her face up to his, and lies in his arms like a little child, and almost as helpless, from very joy at being once more under his loving eye and protecting arm.

He leads her to a chair, and as they sit beside each other, showing in their faces the joy they feel at being once more together, a stranger might have thought them father and child indeed, instead of guardian and ward.

It is a blessed sight to see two persons entertain such pure affection,—such unselfish devotion,—as was shown by this young girl and her old guardian. Truly it is, that, at such times as these, we realize the original love which our Heavenly Father implants in the hearts of all his children, but which is too often absorbed by the evil passions of our nature, that become entangled with it and choke its growth.

Rosa holds his hand in hers, and after a little time, she says:

"I did not think, before this terrible parting, how much I was dependent upon you for all that I have to look for in this world; and please do not think me silly or childish at the request I am about to make, for I shall feel the happier if you will consent to what I have to ask. I realize now that, were it not for you, I should be alone in the world, with no living creature that I might call my friend, and no one to whom I could look for protection. With no father to guard me, or mother to teach and lead me, with loving words and tender hands, as most other girls have, I feel alone in this great world, except that I have you; and so I have to ask this favor: that you will hereafter consent to my addressing you as father, and I will try to prove a loving daughter, of whom you may never feel ashamed." She has found it difficult to say all this, with her heart almost bursting and her eyes suffused with tears, and when she has finished she lays her head upon his arm, and gives way to her emotions.

Mr. Grewgious places his hand lightly upon her head, gently smoothing back the hair from her forehead, and waits patiently till her emotion has subsided; but his own eyes were filled with tears, and it is doubtful if he could have replied before.

How many there are to-day, who, possessed of all that wealth can bring, would not gladly barter all their gold and silver to possess one friend who carried in his breast the unselfish heart of this old man for his charge! And how many children there are, of parents living, who would not gladly exchange places with Rosa, for no other reason than that they might know the blessing of feeling such confidence and love as she felt for this old man, who was neither kith nor kin to her!

"My dear child," said Mr. Grewgious, when Rosa had become calm again, "I cannot tell you how happy you have made me by this evidence of your affection; and, for all the years that I have passed alone in the world, cherishing but one object, — the memory of one who has long since gone to a better world, — I have often thought perhaps it was better for her and me that she did not remain here, — I feel that I am amply repaid for all the lonely hours that have fallen to my lot, by hearing you express the wish that you have just given utterance to. And I hope I do no injustice to the dead, if, in looking on your face, and beholding the counterpart of that other who so long ago joined the angels, I say that I feel all the more gratitude to my Heavenly Father that it is you who asks me to grant a request which will make me more happy than you can ever understand! It shall be as you desire, my dear child, — daughter, now, — and so far as an Angular Man like myself can understand his position, you shall find in me a father in deed as well as in name. And now, let us be cheerful, for I have much to say to you. I think you have passed over the roughest part of your life, and that the future will prove much happier to you than the past. If the subject is not too unpleasant to speak of, I would like to learn from you all the particulars of this last villainy on the part of our Musical Friend; and, it's my opinion it will really be his last, for a net is being woven that will very soon hold him in its meshes. I only regret that his villainies do not bring him within the pale of the scaffold, which they might have done, could he have had his own way and succeeded in his plans."

Rosa proceeds to relate all she knows in connection with her abduction, while Mr. Grewgious restrains his feelings as much as he is able during the narration, but now and then breaks out with "knave," "coward," and such like complimentary terms, intended for John Jasper. When she concludes, he says:

"I don't know to what lengths this man may go. Although he is so near his end, it is not impossible that he may resort to some desperate measures to do you more mischief, and I would give little for young Landless' life should an opportunity present itself by which he could take it secretly. For a few weeks, at least, I think you had better remain here, if arrangements can be made with the lady of the house. I have still another plan which, I believe, will be an advantage to all parties. The brother and sister, who have for so long a time been cooped up in their elevated position at Staple, I have no doubt would be glad of a change. The young man, in particular, is looking badly, and I have thought for some time that he should be removed to other quarters, where he could have more exercise and enjoy society to a greater extent than he can there. But, before I proceed further, suppose we call for Miss Keep."

Miss Keep, having left the apartment to Rosa and her guardian during their interview, is now hunted up by Rosa, who soon returns with her.

"I have sent for you," said Mr. Grewgious, after they had all got seated, "because I have a proposition to submit, which, if agreeable, will aid me materially in a plan I have for the comfort and happiness of three young people, in whom I am just now deeply interested. Perhaps my being able to read character somewhat from the physiognomy may have something to do with the favour I have to ask of you, as I perceive from your features that you are a lady who is possessed of a kind heart, with a desire to help those who need your assistance. Do you follow me?"

Miss Keep is greatly flattered at this complimentary delineation of her character, and murmurs, "With pleasure, sir," in the same tone that she would have uttered, "Till death do us part."

"Very good," continues Grewgious; "now suppose you had conveniences for lodging three people—two young ladies who would occupy one room in common, and one young gentleman who would require a separate apartment; all worthy young people, who would be no discredit to your house, and who would be willing to pay a satisfactory remuneration for these accommodations. Would you be willing to oblige them by giving them the shelter of your roof for a short time?"

Miss Keep thinks a moment, and then rejoins:

"If anything that I could do
Would lessen their distress,
What different can I say to you,
But simply answer, yes."

The least bit of a smile appears on Mr. Grewgious' face as he asks: "And *have* you the accommodations I mention, Miss Keep?"

"I have," is the reply.

"And when shall the other two come, for one is already here," pointing to Rosa. To which Miss Keep replies:

"They're welcome, sir, at any time
To occupy this house of mine."

"Good," says Mr. Grewgious, in a happy tone, "and concerning the terms, make them satisfactory to yourself, and they will satisfy us."

This matter being disposed of to the great joy of Mr. Grewgious, he looks at his watch and says he must be going, as he has some matters to dispose of that are important. Miss Keep, thinking it possible that they would prefer to be alone, turns to leave the room, and as she reaches the door, says to Mr. Grewgious:

"When the young people are all here, sir, I beg you will be no stranger, but that you will call often, for you will be always welcome. I am happy at all times to call those my friends who are fond of the Muses.

No matter what their age or sex,
No matter what their station,
If they regard the Muses with
A perfect admiration."

And, having delivered herself of this remarkable production, she bends to him very gracefully and retires.

After the poetic creature had departed, Mr. Grewgious bids Rosa farewell, telling her to be of good cheer, for she shall soon have the society of Miss Landless, and that he shall embrace the earliest opportunity of removing the brother and sister from their hiding-place in the Beanstalk country. Leaving the house, he departs for his chambers with a lighter heart than he has known for many a day, and revolving in his mind many plans for the future—looking to the welfare of her who depends so much upon him for her happiness. Is it any wonder if, in his fancy, a vision of another face like hers seems to smile upon him, as though to help and cheer him in his efforts? So much does this fancy cheer and help him that he feels as though the blood of forty years ago were in his veins, while his heart is as light as the birds in merry Spring-time.

CHAPTER XXXIV.

JOHN JASPER'S NERVES RECEIVE A SHOCK, AND MR. SAPSEA'S DIGNITY RECEIVES ANOTHER.

As some tired and jaded traveller, after reaching his destination in safety, throws his weary body upon the bed, and, drawing the bed-clothes partially over him, takes a hasty survey of surrounding objects, to see if all is right, and then hastily extinguishes his light,—so that daily traveller and constant friend and companion of the human family—the Sun—on that day when Mr. Grewgious held his last interview with John Jasper, reaches *its* destination in safety, and has partially hidden itself behind a heavy bank of clouds, and then, peeping over them to see if all is right, hastily extinguishes *its* light.

An approaching storm is imminent. Such an ominous calmness is there in the air, that its very stillness is oppressive; and when, at intervals, a fitful breeze kisses the leaves of the elms, which abound in Minor Canon Corner, as though to inspire them with confidence, they only tremble at its touch, anticipating the approach of the tempest which will sweep so many of their number from parent-arms, and hurl them, they know not whither, only that it will be to their destruction.

Old people looked, with anxiety depicted on their faces, upon the black mass in the horizon, and shaking their heads in a significant manner, or prophesying the approach of a violent storm, close their shutters and doors with more than usual precaution, and while seated about their firesides, listening to the increasing violence of the winds without—which whistle and howl through cracks and crevices till it would seem that the air was filled with fiend musicians, discoursing fiendish music, to which an army of fiends were advancing, spreading desolation in its track—they bethink them how, on such a night as this, some cruel murder had been done, or how the ghost of some murdered person had appeared to his assassin, causing him to lose his reason from despair and fear, and, leaving a confession of his crime behind him, had been discovered on the morrow, dead.

The evening service at the Cathedral is finished now, and the attendants issue forth and hurry to their several homes, not caring to linger in groups and chat, as is usually their wont, but seeming impressed with some dire foreboding of evil that is about to fall upon them.

The wind blowing from the river at first in fitful gusts, gradually assumes a steady gale, which increases in violence.

Now comes the Minor Canon, in company with Mr. Tope, who waits at the door till the choir have changed their robes and departed, so that he can perform his last duties of the day by locking the doors.

The black mass, now rising above the river, has grown in size, and its mantle is spreading on every side.

"Well, Tope, I should say we were to have a bit of a storm," says Mr. Crisparkle, surveying the threatening clouds.

"You might say a bitter storm, sir, and not miss it," is the answer.

The Minor Canon does not think it worth while to reply, but hurries along towards his own door.

Come the members of the choir, hurrying along as usual, only a little faster now, to gain the shelter of their own roofs; and last of all comes Jasper, pale as usual, and waits for Tope to accompany him.

He glances hurriedly at the heavens, and says to the Verger:

"Sudden change in the weather, Tope; we'll get a rough night, I think."

To which the Verger returns that "we'll know better of that in the morning," and so the two walk hurriedly in the direction of the Gate House.

Bidding Tope good-night, Jasper soon gains his apartments, and trimming a light, prepares to spend the evening in his own room. The wind, now blowing directly against Jasper's windows, causes them to creak and shake in their casings, while the sighing and moaning of the trees, like so many spirits of departed ones, sound ominously to this man, as his ear catches their wailing tones, and he fancies they articulate intelligible words that seem to say,

"As ye sow, ye must reap!"

He steps to the window and looks out upon the clouds that are rolling upon and chasing each other in their wild fury, while the rain-drops beat upon the window-panes like living things that were knocking to him for shelter from the blast.

He turns nervously away, and, seating himself at the piano, endeavors to drown the noise of the elements with the instrument, but cannot drown the words which he so distinctly hears borne upon the storm-winds,—

"As ye sow, ye must reap!"

He ceases playing, and listens again to the wind, which has now attained a fearful height, moaning and sighing through the ancient building, and slamming the shutters with such force that it seemed as though they must be torn from their fastenings.

He does not remember such a night since the one on which Edwin Drood and Neville Landless passed that eventful evening with him, and which had such a disastrous ending.

Whatever was the cause, the violence of the storm or the thoughts of his nephew's fate, he is horribly nervous, and steps to the window again to view the storm; but still he is met by the voices which always seem to repeat the same sentence:

"As ye sow, ye must reap!"

He is startled, now, by hearing a knock at his door, but is so weak from a foreboding of evil that the knock is repeated several times before he answers it. At last he cries out, "Come in!" and Mr. Datchery opens the door part way, and, putting in his head, hopes he does not intrude, but would Mr. Jasper like company?

"Nothing would suit me better, sir," is the reply; "you are doubly welcome, for this is a terrible night, and I hate to be by myself during such a storm as this. Walk in and be seated."

The other enters, and closing the door, takes the chair which is proffered him.

"I didn't know what to do with myself this evening," Datchery remarks, leaning back in his chair, and glancing hurriedly about the room, as though in search of something he wants to see without the other's knowledge. "My nephew, Joe, went over to the Crozier about an hour ago, and, as he did not come back, I got rather dull and thought I would step up and sit with you awhile; you know the old saying, 'Misery likes company,' and though it may be all very well for misery, I can't say so much for its company."

"In this case, at any rate," Jasper says, "the adage will apply, for I was wishing just before you entered that some one would call, as I was feeling extremely dull, and I don't know but what I should have stepped in on you had you not come up."

"Then I'm very glad I came," said Datchery, in such an earnest tone that Jasper noticed it, and concluded his visitor meant exactly what he said.

"I am glad these storms are not of frequent occurrence," Datchery begins, "for if they were—Hark!" he exclaims, interrupting himself, "did you hear a knock?" and before Jasper has time to answer, Mr. Datchery seizes the candle and steps quickly to the door. He has hardly got the door open when the light is extinguished, and they are left in total darkness.

"Lord bless me!" is Datchery's ejaculation, "this wind plays fearful pranks; anybody here?" to ascertain if there was any one at the door, but receives no answer; and Jasper, after a minute's delay, procures another light; whereat Datchery reseats himself, and resumes the conversation as though nothing unpleasant had occurred.

"I don't like to be out during these fearful storms, Mr. Jasper; they are too suggestive of danger from a variety of causes. A man is liable to get hit on the head by a stray brick blown from old chimney-pots, or get drenched to the skin, and the result be a fever that may cost him his life. I have had a little experience, before now, in that way, and don't risk myself out at such times unless obliged to be. I suppose now you never happened out in such a gale, did you?"

"Not I," quickly returns Jasper, "I prefer to be indoors, and find that disagreeable enough. It was something such a night as this when my dear nephew was so suddenly taken away, and I am painfully reminded of it to-night by this same storm."

"Ah, and a mysterious affair that was, Mr. Jasper. You have the sympathy of every body, I perceive, for what you suffered in consequence of that night's mystery. It is a little singular that nothing was ever heard from him afterwards."

"Nothing strange in that," Jasper rejoins, moving uneasily in his chair. "If, as I surmise, his assassin struck him a deadly blow, and then threw his body into the river—they were near the river, we know, for a certainty—the tide of course carried the body swiftly out to sea, and it would never be recovered."

"Oh, well," is the encouraging remark of Datchery; 'murder will out' is the old saying, and time will show who the assassin was." As Datchery utters his last remark, he appears to be looking above and beyond the Music Master, but in reality his eyes are studying the face of the latter, who says:

"I believe that circumstances warrant me in saying, notwithstanding the lack of positive evidence which is wanting to prove my assertions, that I know the assassin, sir."

"And, from the repeated assertions which I have heard you make before, concerning your belief, I have no doubt that you *do* know him well."

"But what *can* I do, sir," asks the Music Master, in an earnest tone,

"I have no proof that would convict him, and do not in fact know where to find him if I had—at least, have not known till quite recently. His whereabouts have recently come to me, and in a few days I propose to put a plan in operation which will decide whether I am wrong or right in accusing him. He has powerful friends, however, among those who are enemies to me, and I do not expect to accomplish much; but I shall try. And, even if I do not succeed, shall have the satisfaction of knowing that I have done my duty."

"And when the Villain is caught," rejoins Datchery, "may he suffer the just reward of his villainies. If men will do wrong, they must suffer the consequences, sooner or later. As ye sow, ye must reap."

John Jasper could not have been more struck with amazement than he was on hearing Datchery give utterance to his last sentence. How, or by what chance was this, that he should hear this man repeat the words that had been borne to his ears on the wings of the wind that night, and which had left such an impression upon him that he could not drive them from his mind? By look or act, however, he does not betray his feelings to his companion, but in a cautious tone he asks:

"Pray tell me what you think the phrase you have just mentioned means, Mr. Datchery?"

"Just what it says," replies Datchery. "If, for instance, you should be guilty of an offence against the laws of God and commit murder, or promised to make a woman your wife, the better to rob her of her honor, you have sown the seed and you shall surely reap the fruit of your villainy, as a consequence of that sowing."

"And why do you tell me this?" asks Jasper, excitedly.

"You asked me to give you a definition of the term, and I merely cited those things the better to illustrate my idea of what the term implies."

The subject appears distasteful to the Music Master, for he drops it and says he hopes the storm will abate by morning, as he is going to London the next day, and prefers pleasant weather for the journey.

Datchery, taking this for a hint to go, says he will not remain longer, for he supposes Jasper wants to retire early, and rises to depart.

Jasper thanks him for his call, and says he would be glad to see him often, and bidding each other a good-night, Datchery descends to his own room, and leaves the other to prepare for a night's rest.

The storm continues with unabated fury, and Jasper, though not so nervous as before Datchery called, still feels uncomfortable, and cannot throw off a feeling as of some approaching danger—some presentiment of evil—which is about to befal him. He is ready to retire now, and, extinguishing the light, is soon turning and twisting upon the bed, striving to sleep; but sleep will not come to him.

Several hours pass by, and still he is awake and listening to the storm without.

He rises and goes to the window once more to view the storm. The lights in the various houses of Minor Canon Corner are all extinguished now, and the scene is a dreary one, indeed, and does not help to drive away the restless feelings that have seized upon him.

He returns again to the bed, and after a time is lost in sleep. It is a very light sleep, however, for he starts up and listens to hear a repetition of some noise that sounded close by him in his own apartment. The door of his sleeping room is directly opposite another which opened to the room formerly occupied by Edwin Drood. He remembers that he had left the door open, and thinks he will rise and close it, but is so weak from fear that he cannot move, and lays with his eyes fixed towards it.

Perhaps it was only the wind, he thinks, and closes his eyes to sleep, but all the time acutely listening for any sound that may come. He has not long to wait. A low moan—something between a sigh and a groan—strikes upon his ear, and his eyes are instantly opened and fixed again upon the landing, from whence the sound appears to come. Another moment, and the inmates of the Gate House are startled from their slumbers by hearing terrible shrieks, which they knew could not proceed from the gale, but were produced by a human voice.

There is a great uproar at the door of Jasper's sitting-room, which is the first thing he hears when recovering the consciousness he had lost after giving vent to the screams of terror which had so startled his neighbours. He hears the knocking at his door, but it is some time before he comprehends his situation, or what has happened. It all comes to him in a moment, however, and with a face of ashy paleness, and trembling limbs, he dresses himself as hastily as possible, and descends to the sitting-room below to answer the summons. He calls out at first to ascertain who is there, and the answer comes, "Datchery"; whereat he unfastens the door, and finds that gentleman with his nephew, Joe Sloggers, with great curiosity depicted on their faces; and he invites them in.

"I didn't think to call a second time in one night," is Datchery's first remark, "but, hearing the noise up here, I concluded you might be in danger, so I told Joe, who only came in a few moments since, and who I was sitting up for, that we had better find out what was the trouble, so here we are," and looks at Jasper as though expecting some explanation.

Jasper explains that the howling of the storm had kept him awake till quite late, and, having just fallen into a doze, he was awakened by hearing some noise. He looked in the direction of the landing through the door of his sleeping-room, which was open, and in a very few seconds he saw the exact counterpart of Edwin Drood—in form and features, and dressed exactly as he was the night of his disappearance—standing with a lighted candle in his hand; and so close was he to him, that he could plainly perceive every lineament of his countenance. The figure stood perfectly still, and turned its face to where he lay, so that he could see every feature of it, and he was so struck dumb with fear that for a moment he could not speak. His first thought was to spring out of bed and try to secure it, but so overcome was he that he could only give utterance to his feelings by one loud scream; and that was all he remembered till he heard the knocking at his door afterwards.

Mr. Datchery is very much interested in this narrative, and says he should like to have seen it. "Of course it wasn't the young man himself," he goes on to say; "it must have been his ghost."

"I don't believe in that kind of nonsense," Jasper replies; "I can only account for the phenomena in one way, and that is, that I was pretty well upset when I went to bed, in consequence of the storm having, I suppose, a depressing influence upon me; and, as I had been thinking of the dear fellow in the course of the evening—you remember we were speaking of him, sir—I suppose I must have fancied that I saw what really did not exist."

"Not impossible," says Datchery; "but I do believe in ghosts, and further, I have seen one, and no man can make me believe that such things ain't, for I know they are."

They are all standing in the middle of the room during this conversation, and the candle, which flickers, and at times almost dies out altogether from the gusts which enter from the open door, throws a fitful light upon the scene, and renders surrounding objects quite visible at one moment, and the next so dim that they appear like shadows. Joe Sloggers,—who stands a little apart from the other two, looking about him in an unconcerned manner, and taking no part in the conversation,—now nudges his uncle and points to the picture of Rosa hanging against the wall, and says:

"You ought to have some pictures, Uncle Dick, on your walls. See what a fine one that is. It's a pretty face, ain't it?"

"Ah! Joe, you're like all the young men, spying out a pretty face the first thing. I'll warrant me now, Mr. Jasper, if you had a picture of some different subject, and painted by one of the old masters, hanging beside that one, he'd still think this the finest, because it's a woman. It's human nature, I suppose; but, when you get to be an old buffer like your uncle, Joe, you'll learn that there's more to be gained from admiring the other beauties in nature, than merely that which is seen in a woman's face, the worshiping of which has, before now, sent many a man's soul to perdition. Am I right, Mr. Jasper?"

"I have no doubt you are, sir," rejoins Jasper. "The sketch which your young friend is so much pleased with, however, is not retained for its beauty, or for any intrinsic value that I set upon it. The subject is the young lady to whom my dear nephew was betrothed, and was sketched by him a long time since. I placed it where it hangs, at his request. It remains because I feel sure that, were he here now, he would be glad to see it there."

"Don't think I meant to be personal, sir," returns Datchery; "my remarks had only a general meaning, and did not refer to any particular case. Above all, not to you, for I feel confident you look to higher objects in life than a pretty face, which don't last long at the best, and which time or disease will soon make sad work with."

"You are right sir," replies Jasper; "when you say I have deeper objects in view; I have."

"I said higher," explains Datchery.

"And I said deeper," returns Jasper. "There may be a difference, but I presume my meaning is the same as yours."

"No doubt of it," says Datchery, carelessly; "but you seem to be doing well now, and, if we can be of no service to you, perhaps we had better return to our own apartments and get a bit of sleep, for it must be near morning."

Jasper glances at his watch and finds it quite morning, so, wishing him pleasant slumbers for the balance of the night, Datchery and his nephew return to their own quarters.

When they had entered the room and closed the door, Mr. Datchery says, addressing Joe: "'It's an ill-wind that blows nobody good.' For 'wind' read 'storm' in this instance, and we can make the application perfect, so far as it concerns us to-night. The man has a pretty good nerve, which I hope will continue good till such time as it is best to lift the veil. I rather fancy this mode of punishment. It keeps him in constant torment, and, if we do not frighten him quite to death, I shall be satisfied to continue the practice."

"The Villain!" muttered Joe, who for some reason has taken a bitter dislike to Jasper. "Did you notice how he gazed at the picture as I called attention to it?—as though he were proud of it, or worshipped the original! I could hardly restrain myself from tearing it down before his face and hurling him through the window!"

"All of which would have done no good, my dear Joe," answers

Datchery, "and would have destroyed a very pretty little plan that we have in contemplation, and which is nearly ready to put in practice." Walking leisurely towards the cupboard door, whereon his score is kept, and opening it, he continues: "A very excellent exhibit, and one that will bear daily inspection. The Debtor and Credit sides all filled up and balanced, little remains now but for those interested to go over the account together, examine the items, and have a final settlement.

Then closing the door and telling Joe he must go to bed now, for he (Datchery) is going to do the same, the young gentleman seeks his own bedroom, and the two are soon in the land of dreams.

Like all other nights, whether pleasant or stormy, this particular one has given place to its sister day; and, the storm having subsided, the sun is struggling to show its face through drifting masses of cloud, which represents the rear-guard of the tempest of the preceding night.

The very Honorable Thomas Sapsea's Mind being of that stupendous nature which required a vast amount of rest, when it had any, it naturally followed that Mr. Sapsea was a very sound sleeper. Such things as winds, violent storms, or even hurricanes, which ordinary mortals regard with some apprehension of personal danger, did not disturb him in the least, for the simple reason that, in his opinion, even the Elements would hardly dare to take liberties with mortals possessing the intellect with which he had been gifted.

Hence the great man had slept during this fearful night, just past, totally unconscious of the warring elements, and slept as peacefully as if a breath of air had not disturbed the leaves upon the trees which shaded the windows of his sleeping apartment.

His toilet being perfected, he raises a window and looks out upon the Precincts to get a breath of pure air, and at the same time to discover if there are any evidences to be seen of the violence of the storm in the way of demolished chimneys or fences. Thoroughly convinced of the inability of any storm to do him an injury, he does not think of such a thing as looking about his own premises for damage done, but contents himself by examining those of his neighbours, and then closes the window to prepare for breakfast. He has hardly done so, when he hears a knock at his door, and upon opening it he finds a servant-maid standing before him, with an air of great concern upon her face, who tells him he had better come down as soon as ever he can, for the horrible storm has made dreadful work with Old Mr. Sapsea.

On hearing these words, which were delivered in a frightened tone and with great rapidity, Mr. Sapsea's first thought was that the violence of the wind must have torn the tenants of the church-yard from their receptacles, and that they were lying around in various parts of the Precincts, waiting patiently for their friends to come and put them back into their former resting-places. But how could it be possible that the Elements would dare to take liberties with a Sapsea? He was positive that a live Sapsea was secure from such liberties, and he had always believed that a dead Sapsea would be just as sacred and secure. He could not believe it; there must be some mistake! He did not doubt that other departed ones had been thus dealt with, but a Sapsea—never!

"How do you know, girl, that my father is in the condition you speak of?" he inquires of the servant, who is still standing on the threshold.

"Because, sir," is the earnest reply, "I have *see'd* him, sir! His head is clean gone; likewise one arm, sir."

"Great God!" exclaims Sapsea, "you don't mean to tell me his head is not with the rest of his body?" and the great man lifts his hands in very horror.

"But I just do, sir," replies the servant; "leastwise it's not gone, for some one has picked it up, and put that and the arm on the top step for safety; but you'd best come and see for yourself, sir."

Ordinary minds would never have possessed a doubt that the news he had heard bore reference to the remains of that elder Sapsea, who had lain peacefully in the church-yard so many years; but the Great Mind, after the first shock was over, happened to think it barely possible that the damage in question might have occurred to the effigy of the old gentleman at the street door, and Mr Sapsea asks for information on that point.

"Bless you, sir! you didn't never think I meant the *real* Old Mr. Sapsea, did you?" asked the girl, laughing at the absurdity of his mistake.

"No levity, Miss!" ejaculates Sapsea in a stern manner, "you should have been more explicit in your statement. I understand now that you have reference to the *statue* of my father, and not to his flesh and bones. It seems hardly probable that even such a thing as this could have occurred, when I have always said that nothing could ever possibly happen to it. This is a grave matter. I will be down in a few moments, and learn from observation the extent of this calamity."

It struck the maid that Mr. Sapsea's misunderstanding in the first instance was truly a grave matter, but she did not dare to tell him so, and hastened below, leaving him to follow as soon as he pleased.

The great man had said "calamity" very much the same as he would have said "insult," and regarded it as an insult on the part of the

Elements thus to take liberty with anything bearing the semblance of a Sapsea.

He descends to his street-door with slow and measured steps, and his face wears such an air of stern pomposity, that one would be disposed to think the identical gust of wind that had done the mischief was still remaining at the door in a defiant attitude, and that Mr. Sapsea was going down to order it from the premises; or, failing that, to annihilate it on the spot. He opens the door, and there, sure enough, he sees the body and legs of the dead and gone Auctioneer's counterpart, the toga well preserved; but the head, on which rested the curly wig, lies at the feet of his son, face down, as though ashamed to be caught in such a predicament.

Mr. Thomas Sapsea is not prepared, even now, to believe such a thing possible. He re-enters the house, closes the door so as to shut the scene from his sight, and proceeds to pinch his arms and slap his hands together, to be sure that he is not the victim of some hallucination; then opens the door, and finds himself again contemplating the humiliating scene.

Mr. Sapsea has become so engrossed with the havoc made with his street-door ornament, that he does not observe a second person who comes upon him at this juncture, and who cries in a loud tone:

"What's been a goin' on here?"

On hearing the voice, Sapsea turns and beholds Durdles looking very much astonished and waiting for an answer. The stone-mason, never proverbial for cleanliness, is uncommonly dirty this morning, and with his hammer in his hand, looks as if he had recently been engaged with some labor pertaining to his profession.

The great man folds his arms across his stomach, as though to prevent himself from bursting, and in a dignified manner asks the stone-mason what *he* thinks of that, pointing to the dismembered effigy.

"Think?" is Durdles' answer, "that it's d—d lucky for the old man as this 'ere thing ain't really him."

"It's something I can hardly realize," continues Sapsea, in a mournful tone. "I do not remember anything like it before."

"Thank your old shoes it ain't you!" is the consoling rejoinder of Durdles. "That 'ere 'ead *can* be put on again with a little trouble, and it's all right. Yours *couldn't* be put on so easy; or if it was, it wouldn't do you no good. Durdles has come to tell you as the storm did more damage nor that last night. Perhaps you've heerd all about it, though?"

"I don't think I have," says Sapsea; "what is it, man? speak out."

"That there moniment o' yourn had a smash-up or a smash-down last night, and lays on the sod, there in the church-yard, with two or three more, lookin' like so many stiff 'uns as has taken a houtside passage." He tosses his hammer into the air and catches it so neatly as it descends, and tells what he has just said so very coolly, and with so little concern, that Sapsea believes the man must be joking him. He stares at Durdles for several moments, and, finding him to be apparently in earnest, enquires if this is a fact, or intended as a joke.

"Did yer ever catch Durdles a-jokin'?" returns the stone-mason, indignantly. "No, sir! his bus'ness hain't one as admits of jokes. When Durdles tells you a thing is so, it's *so!* Come and satisfy yourself, if you can't believe me,"—and they proceed to the church-yard, Durdles taking the lead and Sapsea following after. On reaching the spot, they found quite a group of persons congregated, to view the ruins which had been made by the gale among the memorials of the dead. They do not stop until they reach the monument, erected to the late worshipper of Mr. Sapsea's Mind, which is lying prostrate on the ground and broken in several places. The news of the strange freak of last night's tempest has spread quite rapidly, and has reached the ears of the Gate House tenants, and it is not long before Jasper, with a wild, haggard look, makes his appearance. Elbowing his way through the by-standers, he approaches Sapsea, whom he salutes, and then hurriedly inquires what the matter is.

The heart of Mr. Sapsea is too full to reply in words; he silently points to the ruined memorial of Mrs. Sapsea, and then casts his eyes heavenward, as though waiting for a thunderbolt to descend and crush him out of existence.

It is noticed that Mr. Jasper evinces more concern, and appears more distressed even, than the great man who is directly interested. He examines all the surroundings of the monument, and spying Durdles for the first time, asks that gentleman, in anxious tones, if anything unusual was discovered inside the vault.

"What the devil do you mean?" asks Durdles, with a look of surprise.

"Only this," Jasper returns, with a sickly smile; "you carry the key, you know, which unlocks it, and I thought perhaps you might have laid that bottle of yours in there for safe keeping," and makes such a poor attempt to force a laugh that even Durdles is not deceived, but answers, with a sober countenance,—"that there tomb hain't been opened since the day the inscription was put on the moniment, and folks will do well to be a little careful how they accuse me of making a wine-closet of dead folks' houses."

John Jasper acts very strange now, and does not seem to know what he is saying, or where he is. He turns to the now open door leading to the tomb, and, as he enters the enclosure, cries out, excitedly, "Don't try to deceive me; I know better!" and disappears from their astonished view;—then emerges again through the opening, and with a dead man's face, so pale it is, with the eyes set, staggers towards Durdles, crying, "I *will* not have it so; minion, you are deceiving me,—something has *gone!*" and falls insensible as the marble that lays so near him.

Though greatly astonished at beholding the singular behaviour of Jasper, the lookers-on can attribute it to no other cause than that he is overcome at the sight of such desecration, and, though it occurs to a few, who think anything about it, that his words are of a singular nature, they are soon forgotten in the excitement incident to his fainting fit, and all press forward to lend a helping hand to the stricken man.

While they are resorting to various measures to effect Jasper's restoration, and before it is accomplished, Mr. Datchery, arm in arm with his kinsman, Joe Sloggers, are approaching the scene, and on reaching it, stop a moment to contemplate the miserable man, who lays so helpless before them. They make no attempt to assist in his recovery, but content them with looking at the ruins made by last night's storm. Then, observing that the Music Master is beginning to show signs of consciousness, they move slowly away, arm in arm, as they had come, Mr. Datchery remarking, in a low tone, that "though human justice may be slow, Divine retribution cannot be warded off, and comes with ten-fold force, because at the very time and in a way that we least expect it."

CHAPTER XXXV.

ROSES AND THORNS.

The peaceful, quiet life led by Uncle Sol Brobity and his mother, is not without its effect upon their young charge, and Bessie, who has been with them for a number of weeks, though enjoying the society of the old people, and feeling happier than ever before in her life, seems more thoughtful than formerly. She is often found by Uncle Sol, seated alone in the garden with some little blossom in her hand, and gazing so intently at it that one might think she was communing with it, and listening to some sweet and gentle words that told of the hand that formed it and which sent it forth to help purify a sinful world, to take it back again to that blessed land where it will bloom perpetually, and where death never comes.

Uncle Sol took delight in providing everything that he thought would add to the child's comfort and happiness, and hardly a day passed that some new gift was not bestowed upon her. She would tell him, at such times, that she was sure she could never repay him, and he would answer that he was well paid in seeing her face wear a happy smile instead of the thoughtful, sober look that was so often upon it, and said he should not cease bestowing such gifts till he had driven away that melancholy expression so effectually that it could never return again.

A pretty sleeping chamber overlooking the garden, had been provided for her special use, and, aided by the old lady Brobity—Aunt Brobity, Bess had been instructed to call her—the child had learned to keep it in order, and had proved a proficient pupil indeed in this respect, for no neater room could be found in Cloisterham.

Uncle Sol had deemed it best to undertake her education himself till such time as she should be fitted to enter a school and be classed with children of her own age. With this object in view, he had provided some few books from which she could study at stated hours through the day; and she made such excellent progress that Uncle Sol used to say, often, that he didn't see how it happened that he hadn't been a schoolmaster all these years, instead of spending his time in book-stalls.

Notwithstanding all her progress and all her efforts to appear happy, the watchful eye of the old man perceived that his young charge was sad at heart, often sitting with her hands folded across her breast and tears standing in her eyes—though she tried hard to conceal them when she saw him approach her.

He was determined, however, to persevere in his efforts to dispel this melancholy state of mind, and resorted to every device which he thought would attain to that end.

It was the custom of the Brobitys to have tea at four o'clock every afternoon, the year round; after which, Uncle Sol and little Bess would stroll through the garden, where the old man would beguile the time by telling some pleasant story—something of a cheerful nature—that would tend to take her mind and lead her thoughts from herself.

Thus it came about that on the day when this chapter opens, they were taking their daily ramble. She is always attired at such times in the new gown that had been purchased for her with the money

Jasper had left for that purpose with Mrs. Padler, and, though other dresses had been made for her since she became an inmate of Uncle Sol's house, she cannot be persuaded to wear any other, which causes Uncle Sol to banter her in a playful manner by telling her that she is a proud little girl, and he don't know what he shall do with her when she gets to be a woman. She smiles at such times and tries to appear cheerful by replying to him with some pleasant rejoinder. So it happens, to-day, that Uncle Sol accuses her of being proud, and says he expects it won't be long ere she will refuse to walk with an old curmudgeon with a faded coat and knee-breeches. She looks up in his face pleasantly, and says:

"Uncle Sol, I know you don't mean what you say, but, lest you may think me ungrateful, indeed, for the nice clothes you have given me, I will tell you why I do not wear them; it is because they look so new and fresh and bright, with not a stain upon them, that I feel as though I were not fit to touch them, much less wear them, lest the stain which follows me will attach to them, and make me feel for them the same shame which I feel for the miserable little girl whom they were given to."

"Nay, child," answers the old man, in earnest but loving tones, as they seat themselves in their accustomed place, "nay, child, of what avail are such unhappy thoughts as those to which you have just given utterance? If He who sent us here is satisfied with his work, what right have we to condemn it. See those little sparrows flying yonder; listen to their joyous notes; they do not repine at their lot, but cheerfully praise their Creator, with happy notes of song, for such blessings as he has placed before them; and how much more have we to be thankful for than they."

"I realize, every day," returned the child, "that it is wrong for me to feel as I do. I know that God is good, for I can see His goodness in the trees and shrubs and pretty faces of the flowers, but I cannot drive away my unhappiness. By night or day, waking or sleeping, I see my poor darling mother's face constantly before me, and as time goes on, I realize more and more how much she suffered from the wicked acts of others, and I mourn the sad fate which came upon her so cruelly, and which deprived her child so early of a mother's love. I shall never be happy till I join her there," pointing heavenward, "and once more feel her kiss upon my lips, as on that day she left me I felt her kisses then. I know the time is not far away when she will clasp her little girl once more in her embrace, and that thought, more than any other, gives me a peaceful happiness that nothing else can bring."

Uncle Sol is puzzled how to reply to her, and wonders why it is that at such times their conversation always ends with his feeling as sad as the child whom he thinks to impress with happier thoughts, but who, by giving utterance to the causes which lead to her unhappiness, leads his mind into a channel as gloomy as her own.

Happily for the old man, at this moment the servant Razor approaches them with some haste, and informs Uncle Sol that a white-headed old gentleman has called to see him, and is waiting for him in the parlour.

"And did he give no name, Razor?" queries Mr. Brobity.

"Yes, sir," is the reply; "he said tell Mr. Brobity as Mr. Hatchity or Smashity—I can't just remember which—wants to see him on important business."

"I think it must be Datchery, from the Corner," is Uncle Sol's rejoinder, "but I have no acquaintance with him, and do not see what business he can have with me."

"Perhaps you'd know that sooner if you went where he is," suggested Razor.

"Very sensible remark, Razor; I'll come right along; go and tell him so."

The servant retired, and Uncle Sol turned to Bess and asked her if she would remain in the garden or return with him to the house.

"Perhaps I'd better go in," is the child's answer; "I do not feel quite so well as usual, to-day, and I shall go to bed early, for I think I'm a little tired."

Uncle Sol expressed great anxiety at hearing this, and told her he would instantly go for Dr. Muddle, if she felt ill; but she assured him she was not so sick as that; in fact, not sick at all—only tired.

"So I'll take my little bedfellow," she continues, "and we'll hasten in."

It has been her custom, since residing at Uncle Sol's, to hold some little bud or blossom in her hand when she lay down at night to sleep; so now she stoops and culls a pink; then, placing her hand in his, they leave the garden and enter the house together.

On proceeding directly to the parlour, Mr. Brobity finds not only Mr. Datchery there present, but also Fopperty Padler, who is gazing so intently upon a certain figure in the carpet, that one would suppose he was counting the number of threads that formed it, and who merely raises his face to the host to say good-day, and then resumes his counting again. Mr. Datchery, pacing the floor with slow steps, in a thoughtful manner, advances to meet Uncle Sol, to whom he holds out his hand, and says he hopes he has not put that gentleman to any inconvenience, or disturbed him in the least, by this unusual call, but circumstances have forced him to seek this interview, and, therefore, he has taken the liberty of doing so, regardless of ceremony.

Uncle Sol begs him not to make any apologies, for he is welcome, and hopes he will make himself at home.

"I will state the object of my visit as briefly as possible," says Datchery, seating himself, while addressing Uncle Sol. "My friend here undertook to assist me, so far as he could, in making your acquaintance, and I have to thank him for many other favors which are unnecessary to mention at this point, but which will transpire as I proceed."

"He is a noble fellow," answers Uncle Sol, "a noble fellow, and carries a good heart under his waistcoat, as I have had an opportunity to observe before to-day;" and smiles upon the object of his remarks, who merely acknowledges the compliment bestowed upon him by forcing his eyes to play hide and seek in the odd manner so natural to him, while Datchery continues to address Uncle Sol:

"You will observe, sir, that I have the appearance of a man nearly as old as yourself. I have seen a deal of the world, by land and sea, and have had my share of privations and disappointments. I will not say griefs, for ordinary grief is not the word for the wretchedness that has fallen to my lot. You have, as I learn from our friend here, kindly taken under your care and protection a child who is nearly related to me; and, though I do not wish it understood that I am for an instant casting reproach upon her, it is nevertheless true that that child's existence has been indirectly the cause of more misery to me than I ever knew before, and such misery as I would not care to wish upon my bitterest enemy."

He ceases for a moment, hastily brushing away the tears that are falling down his cheeks while Uncle Sol, out of respect for his grief, makes no remark, but waits, with sympathy upon his face, for the other to proceed, which after a moment he does.

"Ten years ago, sir, I was following the sea in the employ of the East India Company, in whose service I had been engaged from a boy, and in which I grew up till I had earned the position of master of one of their first merchantmen. As I was saying, ten years since I sailed as master of a vessel in the employ of that Company, leaving at home a kind and indulgent mother, and a dear sister,—a gentle, loving girl, the pride of our hearts." Again he is overpowered by his emotion, and is obliged to cease till he can recover himself sufficiently to proceed.

Uncle Sol, anxious to say or do something that will tend to lighten his grief, asks if he shall not go and fetch little Bessie.

"Not now, not now," is the reply. "It's better to wait till some other time. Let me proceed. By careful management, what with my salary and what my darling sister Bess could earn by her needle, we were in a fair way to lay up something handsome for a stormy day; hence, when I left them and proceeded on my last voyage, I felt that they would not be deprived of the comforts of life, unless some unforeseen calamity should fall upon us. I don't know how it was, but on that day, when I bade them good-bye and received a sister's kiss—for the last time as it proved—I felt a presentiment of evil, and was so impressed thereat, that I returned to the house three different times before I had got as many rods away, under the pretext that I had forgotten some slight article that I needed. But this could not last forever,—I must be gone. Tearing myself away, I gained my vessel, and bade farewell to the white cliffs of England. We had been out about two weeks when we encountered a terrible storm. I will not stop to give the details of that fearful night, when our vessel foundered, and we were left to the mercy of the waves. Enough that I had lashed myself to a plank, and after great suffering was picked up by another vessel, which was bound for a Turkish port. Before we had reached our destination, however, we fell in with a Malay pirate. Our vessel was captured, and we were given the choice of walking the plank or consenting to be landed on a desolate island, inhabited by a race of brutal savages, and where we should stand a good chance of helping to make a few meals to stay their canabalistic stomachs. Still we were glad to accept the alternative, and we were put ashore accordingly."

He stops a moment here to take breath, and Uncle Sol says it's no wonder his hair has got so white. To which the other quickly replies—

"Oh, I'm no coward, sir, and would not let fear turn my hair white, be assured; see here," instantly removing from his head a wig of white hair, and rising at the same time, he stands before them a much younger looking man now, with the same features to be sure, but with brown curly locks that lay in clusters upon his forehead, and which change his whole appearance.

It was evident that Fopperty, from the little surprise he evinces at this transformation, was already cognizant of the fact of Datchery's disguise; but Uncle Sol, who had come to know that shock of white hair as being associated with the name of Datchery, could hardly have been more astonished, had he seen the Cathedral tower deliberately jump from its high position and walk into his garden.

"My dear sir," is the first ejaculation of the old gentleman; "I never could have believed it!"

Datchery quietly replaced the wig, remarking, as he did so:

"There will be others I could name, who will be more astonished than you are, dear sir, when they behold what you have, and the time is not far distant which will give them the opportunity." He steps to a mirror to assure himself that his disguise is perfectly arranged, and then reseating himself, proceeds with his narrative:

"As I was saying, we were left on that miserablê island. Contriving to exist on such food as we could obtain from plants that grew wild there, and wandering for miles in search of succor, we fell in with a band of the natives, when all but three of us were slain upon the spot, while we who were left were bound hand and foot, and kept for the purpose, I presume, of furnishing a sumptuous repast at some future time.

"My companions being pretty well exhausted before this new misfortune came, died the next day from exposure and hunger, and I was left alone, caring little how soon I might follow them. The natives, however, saw fit to treat me in a humane manner, and took great care of me; and after I had sufficiently recovered strength, we set out for another part of the island, near the sea, and I was kept a prisoner for nine years, never beholding, in that time, a white man's face, and never allowed to be alone for an instant, fearing I should endeavour to escape.

"One day, when in company with two of the natives, I observed a sail approaching the island. On coming nearer, I perceived that the craft was a British man-of-war, and I thought I could perceive, at the mast-head, a man who might be able to recognize us, for it appeared to me that he held a glass in his hand, as though he were observing us as we stood there. I instantly waved my hat to him as a signal, and he returned the signal by waving his; so I knew that I had been seen. The natives insisted on my leaving with them instantly, but freedom was too near at hand, and I was determined to risk my life in the effort to escape, by the aid of this first opportunity since my captivity. The natives approached to seize me, but I felled one of them to the earth with a blow, and ran from the beach with the remaining savage in hot pursuit. I kept my eyes upon the ship while running, and noticed a boat being lowered, which gave me courage to make a desperate attempt to reach the vessel.

"Without once stopping to look back, I jumped into the sea, and, being a good swimmer, struck out in the direction of my last hope. The native set up a terrific howl as he saw me thus escape, and stood upon the beach, where he was soon joined by others of the tribe, but none of them undertook to follow me.

"The boat, in the meantime, had swung off from the ship, and approached me in an opposite direction, and in half an hour I was pulled into her, so completely exhausted that I became insensible, and did not recover till I found myself in a comfortable berth in the ship's cabin, surrounded by the physician and officers, who watched eagerly for my recovery, and which—they told me afterwards—they had at one time utterly despaired of.

"After an interval of a few weeks I had entirely recovered; and, the ship, being homeward bound when she stopped at the island, continued on her way to England, where she arrived in safety.

"I can never express to you the feelings of joy and gratitude which I felt towards my Heavenly Father that I had once more been permitted to stand upon the shores of my native land, and, as I supposed, once more to embrace those dear ones who had been uppermost in my mind during all those years of captivity and desolation.

"I hastened through the crowded streets of the City, seeing or thinking of nothing but the happiness which was in store for me, at once more beholding those loved faces, and anticipating the pleasure that they would experience at again seeing me, whom they must no doubt have given up as lost to them forever.

"Many changes had taken place in the City during those nine years of torture which I had undergone, but the house I sought stood the same as on that memorable day when I departed from all I held dear; and my heart was so full of gratitude, as I gazed upon its old walls, that I felt like a child, and could have knelt and kissed the very pavement that lay before it.

"I did not know then what was the cause, but I had a foreboding of evil come over me, for the first time since I left the vessel, and felt that I was about to hear bad news—but I should never have thought how bad it was to be, God knows!

"With this foreboding still upon me, I knocked at the street-door, which was opened by a stranger, of whom I enquired for my mother, and stating her name.

"She did not remember such a person, she said; then repeated the name two or three times, as though trying to think if she had heard it before. 'Oh, I remember now,' she said; 'I have heard some of the older neighbours about here, who have been acquainted with the neighbourhood for several years, mention those people. A mother and her daughter, by that name, did live here some years ago, but they came to a sad ending, on account of the young lady being attached to a heartless wretch, who afterwards deserted her; whereupon she took it so much to heart that she died from grief, poor thing, and the mother shortly after disappeared, but nobody knew where.'

"I thought I should have died upon the spot when I heard this woman's words. It seemed as though my brain was on fire. I pressed my hand upon my temples, and, leaning against the door, stared at the woman as though she were some devil who was sent to torment me. I soon recovered myself sufficiently to explain to her that the persons she spoke of were my mother and sister, and hoped she would pardon anything unusual in my conduct; but she could perhaps imagine that what she had told me was of such a terrible nature that, for the moment, I could not control myself. I thanked her for the information she had given me, and, acting on her suggestion, enquired of a family next door for further particulars. From them I ascertained that if I could discover the whereabouts of a family by the name of Padler, they could tell me more of this sad affair than any one else would be apt to know. Discouraged and heartsick, I went in search of that family, and after seeking for two whole days, came upon them at last in the neighbourhood of Drury Lane. There it was that I fell in with this young man," pointing to Fopperty, who now sat with eyes intent upon another figure of the carpet—probably because he had got the threads in the first one all counted—and who did not appear to notice this reference to himself. "I fell in with this young man, and from him I learned, what I wish to God I had died before I had heard it! My darling sister, for whom I had such high anticipations, and whom I loved like the very apple of my eye, was dishonored and dead, and my poor old mother an outcast!" Datchery became so affected at this point that he could not proceed, but buried his face in his hands and wept and sobbed like a little child; nor was he alone, for tears were trickling down the furrows of Uncle Sol's cheeks, from sympathy with the sufferer who sat beside him, and even Fopperty rested from his mathematical calculations, and buried his eyes completely for full two minutes. Recovering himself, Datchery proceeded: "After obtaining the full extent of the wrongs that had been done me and mine, I immediately decided that the balance of my life should be devoted to wreaking upon this man a terrible vengeance, if he were to be found upon the face of the earth.

"Having sufficient means at my disposal, which had lain in bank since I left home, and which had increased to a good round sum, I was able to live without labour, and resolved to use every farthing, if it was necessary, to accomplish the end I had in view. Taking this young man into my confidence, I instructed him to keep a sharp lookout and see if he could not discover the Villain, and, if so, to follow him to his abiding place.

"Several weeks passed on, but we had accomplished nothing, till one day Fopperty brought me the gratifying intelligence that he had discovered the Villain in the eastern part of the City, and had followed him to Cloisterham.

"Meantime, I had been searching to obtain some information of my mother, but failed altogether, and was forced to abandon the search. I therefore decided that I would go to Cloisterham, and thinking it would be better to have Fopperty here, where I could call on him at a moment's notice, arrangements were made to that effect, and he, with his mother and the child, came here immediately.

"Although it was not probable that the Villain would know me, I thought it better to be on the sure side, and so, partially disguising myself by assuming the character of an old man, I came here, and by managing shrewdly was so fortunate as to obtain lodgings under the very roof where the object of my hatred found shelter. I had scarcely got settled, however, and my plans fully matured to carry out the purpose I had in view, when I learned that a nephew of his had mysteriously disappeared, and under suspicious circumstances. Perhaps it was natural, but I instantly mistrusted, from what I could glean, that, notwithstanding the Villain was apparently nearly crazy over the murder—as he persisted in calling it—of his nephew, he, for some reason, had a hand in his disappearance, and I determined to ferret out the secret.

"I do not know that it is necessary at this time to state how far I have succeeded in proving my suspicions to be correct. I do not know that it is proper at this time to state the name of the wretch that I am pursuing, and whom I left but an hour since, suffering all the tortures that a wicked heart can suffer. All these things will make themselves apparent at no distant day. I came to tell you something of the history of a man who bears relationship to the child you have, in the kindness of your heart, taken under the shelter of your roof, and I felt it to be my duty to give you an outline of my own history, that you might the better obtain something of hers. I do not wish to interfere with the philanthropic object you have in view concerning her, but, on the contrary, am thankful that she has found so good a friend, and hope your interest in her will never cease, and that it may redound to her advantage; and I pray to God that you may never know the bitterness of a disappointment that fell to my lot in connection with the mother who bore her!"

As Datchery ceased speaking, a deep sigh escaped him as he thought of his unhappy sister, and for several moments not a word was spoken by either of them. Finally, Uncle Sol broke the silence by saying:

"You have my sympathies, dear sir, in the terrible misfortunes which you have experienced; and, so far as Bessie is concerned, you may be sure that everything in my power will be done for her, the same as I should do for my own daughter. She is a remarkable child, and should she live to attain the age of womanhood, will be a credit and honour to us all."

"Her mother was a superior woman," answered Datchery, in a mournful tone, "and possessed a mind as far superior to the Villain that caused her ruin—d—n him—as the angel's mind is above the brute's. The lily growing pure and white from its native stalk, cannot protect itself from the base worm that eats away its sustaining power; neither could she, in the purity of her heart, understand that this man would prove the destruction of her young life, whose blossom had not fairly matured, and which, like the pure lily, was so soon fated to wither and die."

Uncle Sol proffered any assistance that would be of service to Datchery in the work he had undertaken, but the latter assured him that he was well provided for in that respect.

'We have him," said Datchery, "as completely in our power as I could ask, and he is as thoroughly surrounded by those who know him now for what he is, and as carefully watched, as if he were a prisoner with irons on his hands and feet."

"Would you not like to see and converse with little Bessie?" asked Mr. Brobity.

"I think not now," is the reply; "it is getting somewhat late,"—the shadows were beginning to fall, and it was nearly dark,—"and I have work to do which precludes a longer stay. I shall call on you occasionally, and the next time shall be glad to see and converse with the child; and then, perhaps tell her who I am."

Datchery rises to go as he finishes his last remark, and at Uncle Sol's solicitation promises to come again, when convenient for him to do so. He requests Mr. Brobity to keep his own counsel concerning what has been revealed to him, and then, followed by Fopperty, they emerged from the house together, the latter gentleman obtaining from Mr. Brobity full permission, at a request made on his part, to visit Bess on the morrow, or at any other time that pleases him.

They had gone but a few steps from the house when they heard a shrill whistle proceed from the opposite side of the way, and although it was quite dark, they could discern a human figure descending from a neighbouring lamp-post, and make its way towards them. It was recognized by Datchery as being no other than the Deputy, who, when he had joined them, exclaims:

"Here's a fire-fly, ain't it, hey?"

"Why, fire-fly?" asks Datchery with some curiosity.

"Cos' if I fire's flints at things, I lets 'em fly out 'o my hand, don't I?"

"No doubt," is the answer.

"Very good," and picking up a stone that lay at his feet, he threw it at the shadow of something that was hid in the angle of a fence on the opposite side of the way, and which something proved to be a human form as it stole rapidly away, keeping close to the buildings where it passed, and was soon lost to view.

"Well, then," continued Deputy, "ain't I a fire-fly then?" and indulges in a savage dance which lasts for a full minute. Then coming close up to Datchery, he draws that gentleman's head down to his own, and whispers in his ear:

"The old cove, as was to come to-night, is at the Crozier, and he wants to see Mr. Datch-er-*ie*."

"Ah!" is Datchery's response, "I must hurry then to go and meet him. You're a good boy, Winks, to do your work so faithfully;" then takes some silver from his pocket and tenders Deputy, who snatches it from his hand as though he were fearful the other might change his mind and not give it him at all. He tumbles it into his pocket and, as Datchery is about to move away, the boy exclaims:

"And that 'ere cove as just dodged my Widdy Warnin', he is a chap as *don't want* to see Datchery! yah, yah! He's Jarsper, he is; and didn't I twig him from that there post when I was a-takin' of an airin' for my 'elth, and see'd 'im when he fust come up to twig Datchery, as he don't want to see; yah, yah!" and then becomes so amused at the thought, that he breaks out in the old jargon, but which was a little mixed, perhaps owing to excitement caused by his recent proximity to the Choir Leader:

Widdy widdy wen!
Don't—I—ches—im—out—ar—ter—ten.
Widdy widdy wy,
Don't—I—ketch—'im—when—'e—plays—'igh."

And so Datchery leaves the boy to his own amusement, and, in company with Fopperty, hurries off in the direction of the Crozier Inn, but parts with Fopperty when they arrive at the corner of the street in which is situated the lodgings of the latter.

CHAPTER XXXVI.

A FELLOW-TRAVELLER JOINS THE INVISIBLE HOSTS, AND MR. GREWGIOUS BEHOLDS A PICTURE AND A RING.

WHETHER the atmosphere of the Beanstalk country was of an unhealthy nature, or whether the secluded life that he had led for so long a time, combined with the constant dread of being discovered by John Jasper and subjected to further persecution on the part of that worthy, certain it is that Neville Landless has wasted in flesh, and his face has come to assume the color of a dead man's.

Though uttering no complaint, his friends observe his altered appearance, and they experience the deepest solicitude thereat; but, when questioned as to the cause, he always answers that it is nothing serious—that he shall look like himself again in a few days—and begs that they will not be unhappy on his account, for he is aware of no bodily ailment that should cause himself or them uneasiness.

Notwithstanding these assurances on his part, they determined to summon medical aid, which was accordingly done. An intimate friend of Mr. Grewgious, who was regarded as one of the most skillful physicians in London, was called in, and, after a careful investigation, he gave it as his opinion that medicine would do the young man not a particle of good. He would recommend a change from his present mode of life, as being the only thing that would prove beneficial, and that his life depended on it. This opinion was made in the presence of Helena, Mr. Crisparkle and Mr. Grewgious; but, before the physician left Staple, he took the latter gentleman to one side and informed him confidentially that the young man was a wreck in mind and body, and that his death would be very sudden, and might occur at any hour. A change would help to prolong his life a short time, but nothing could save it.

It will, therefore, be easily understood why Mr. Grewgious was so desirous to obtain lodgings for the orphans under the roof of Miss Keep, and on leaving that lady's house on the day that he had perfected arrangements with her for their coming, he hastened to communicate the intelligence to the brother and sister, who were greatly pleased in consequence, and made hasty preparations for an immediate departure to their new home, and which they reached in safety.

For the first few days after their arrival there, it appeared that Neville had begun to improve, but after the excitement attending the change had passed away, he had settled again into the dull and moody habits that were so ruinous to his health, and it was apparent that unless something more could be done for him, his life was indeed destined to be of short duration.

With a loving sister's watchfulness and devotion, Helena sought every opportunity to cheer and encourage him, and she was willingly aided by Rosa in her affectionate efforts; but Neville seemed to evince no disposition to rally, and once or twice declared that he could see nothing to live for, and might as well die one time as another.

One afternoon, Rosa and Helena are seated alone together, and it is evident that their conversation is not of a pleasant nature, for Rosa is looking very grave and sad, and Helena is weeping bitterly.

It was evident that Neville had been the subject of their conversation, for Rosa says:

"Dear Helena, you must not give way to such forebodings; it will do no good, and I feel confident that Neville's condition is not so bad as to warrant the assumption that he is not going to live. Cheer up, dearest, and don't let me see you feeling sad when there is not, as yet, any real certainty that things are as bad as you expect." The speaker throws her arm about the weeping girl as she finishes her remark, and imprints a tender kiss upon her brow; whereat Helena again bursts into a violent fit of weeping, and lays her head upon Rosa's bosom. Recovering herself after a little, and still clasping the other's hand, she replies:

"Rosa, darling, you do not understand the real cause of my despondency. It is not that I consider my brother to be in immediate danger, or that his death, should that occur, would cause me to mourn as I do, if living, he is to be forced to live such a miserable existence as he has known in the past year. No, dear Rosa, I could look upon death as a blessing under such circumstances, and be thankful that such sufferings as his were terminated even by that dread alternative, though it deprived me of him forever, for that would be the will of God. But to witness the misery that he has endured from day to day,—to know that he has been hunted down like a felon, and forced to live the life of one,—and all to gratify the revenge of a Villain,—who has no more cause to believe in his guilt than you or I, and yet continues to pursue him—when I think of all these things together, and realize that he is no nearer being released from this terrible bondage than he was a year since, I am discouraged and disheartened, and must relieve my sorrow by weeping, or I should go mad. I would not for the world let Neville see me weep; that would only add to his misery, poor fellow. He thinks me strong, and so takes courage from my strength and patience, and bears up under his great misfortunes as he never could were I to show, by look or act, that I could see no happier prospect for him in time to come, which, as God is my judge, I cannot!"

"But," rejoins Rosa in soothing tones "I think your prediction, that there are to be no happier days in store for Neville, is not warranted by the circumstances. There are good friends who are doing everything in their power to solve the mystery of poor Eddy's disappearance, and it only wants that mystery unravelled to release Neville from the persecution of that man, whom I hate to think or speak of. Mr. Crisparkle is not discouraged, neither is my guardian, but, on the contrary, they assure us that the prospect grows brighter every day, and that the darkness will soon be dispelled that has so long surrounded us all. I'm sure, that ought to encourage us. It does me, and I feel certain that Mr. Jasper, horrid wretch! will be punished as he deserves for all the misery he has wrought. But, dear Helena," adds Rosa sadly, "do you know I sometimes think that perhaps I have been the cause of all the misery and persecution that has befallen Neville the past year in that if it had not been for me Mr. Jasper would not have been jealous of your brother and followed him as he has. Do you ever think as I do, Helena, and almost hate me in consequence?" She turned her face to her companion's with such an earnest look upon it that Helena, notwithstanding the tears yet stood in her eyes, could not but smile at the anxiety with which Rosa awaited her reply. She stooped down and kissed her, and drew her closer to her as she said:

"How can you ask me such a foolish question, dear? Of course I do not think you to blame; and, as for hating you, foolish child, I hate you the same as I would were you my own dear sister; and my hatred is so intense that, were I to be deprived of you now, and were never more to hear your darling voice speaking words of comfort to me in my despair, I would take my life as willingly as I would take that of the wretch who has made so many aching hearts, could I but have him here before me now!" The dark face of the girl became tinted with the flush of anger that was in her heart at the recollection of John Jasper, and the black eyes fairly flashed as she gave utterance to her last sentence. As Rosa looked upon her with admiration, blended, it must be confessed, with some degree of fear, she thought that Mr. Jasper would do well to beware of such a beautiful tigress as this, were he to approach her when in such a mood as that which was now upon her.

After a short silence, then Rosa:

"You almost frighten me, dear Helena, when you look and speak as you did just now. I never saw that look upon your face but once before, and then it was at the Nuns' House, when I had told you how that man was annoying me, and you promised to protect me from him." Still holding her hand, she gently draws Helena into the chair beside her, from which she had started in her excitement, and the latter assures Rosa that she has nothing to fear.

"I am a passionate woman, Rosa," she adds, "for good or evil, and for those I love, there are no bounds to my affections, while for my enemies there are no limits to my hatred; an injury inflicted upon me or mine is never forgotten, and though I may have strength to hide it from the gaze of others, it is held and nourished in my heart with such tenacity that nothing but death can break the bonds which hold it there! You have seen me patiently bearing up under the troubles which have surrounded my brother and myself, uttering no complaint, but assuming a cheerful manner, the better to strengthen and encourage him. So long as that object is attained, I am content to remain patient and bide my time; and should this persecution prove no more disastrous than it has already, I can be satisfied with the poor consolation of hating the man who has been our enemy, and let it rest there. But if my poor brother should die under the afflictions which have been brought upon him, from being charged with crime that he is innocent of, simply to gratify the envy of a jealous-hearted coward, let that coward beware of my vengeance, for nothing short of his craven life will atone for the wrong he has done an innocent boy, whose life is worth a thousand recreant lives like his!"

Again the black eyes are illumined with that ominous light that Rosa had noticed in them before, and as she ceased speaking, her arms slightly elevated and her hands tightly clenched, she resembled more an avenging angel than a human being, when compared with the delicate, child-like woman by her side.

Rosa hastens to embrace her, and strives to soothe her by saying:

"Now, darling, you are getting excited again, and you know it frightens me dreadfully to see you so. Be assured that Mr. Jasper will receive his just reward and that Neville is not going to die, but will in a few weeks be freed from this incubus which has so long weighed him down, and be as he was before it all happened. Don't, darling, if you love me, allow yourself to become so agitated again. Oh, dear me, dear me," she adds, despondently, "what a lot of trouble I've been the cause of; I wish I had never been born! If I hadn't, poor Eddy would have been alive and well now, and you and Neville would not have had all this misery to suffer. I don't see what good I've ever been to anybody! I suppose I had to be born, though, but why couldn't I have been a South Sea Islander, or a Hottentot, for then I might have done some good in the world." And is so overcome with thinking what a sad mistake fate had made in selecting a birthplace for her, that she falls to sobbing and weeping; whereat Helena becomes the comforter now, and endeavors to console and calm her by telling her that she don't know yet how much good she may do in the world, for she has not lived in it long enough to know, and that there is no doubt she will yet have an opportunity to do a great deal of good for somebody who will bless her for the doing.

After a little, Rosa is herself again, and by mutual consent they change the conversation and discourse on other subjects until Helena asks Rosa why it is that she appears so anxious to avoid a personal interview with her brother.

"I do not ask this in a complaining spirit, dear," she adds, "but merely to gratify curiosity in a matter which has puzzled me for some time; don't think my question impertinent, darling, and don't answer it if you would rather not, because I have no doubt you have some good reason, but which you may prefer to keep to yourself."

"Are you quite sure," asks Rosa, with some hesitation and coloring slightly, "that I *do* avoid him?"

"I think so," rejoins Helena, "and Neville has noticed it, too, but it would kill him if he thought I had spoken of it. Perhaps I should not have mentioned it, however had he not asked me yesterday if I supposed he was disagreeable to Miss Bud; 'because,' said he, 'I can not converse with her a moment on any subject when we are alone; the instant I begin a conversation on any common-place topic, she will make some pretext for leaving the room, and does not return till you have joined me.' You will remember, dear," continues Helena, "that yesterday we were all sitting in the parlour together, when wanting to say a word to Miss Keep, I left the room, and had not been gone a moment, hardly, to return and find Neville alone, who said you had excused yourself almost directly I had closed the door. He felt terribly about it, and cannot get it out of his head that you believe him guilty of the crime with which that villain charges him; and all my efforts will not make him believe to the contrary."

"My dear Helena," replied Rosa, in a tone of sadness, "I regret very much that your brother should impute such a wicked thought as that to me; and I regret still more that he should have noticed any disinclination that I may have to remain alone in his society; but, as he has, and as you ask me the cause, I will tell you, for I know you will not think the less of me when you hear it. You and I feel confident that Jasper would never have pursued Neville as he has, did he not consider him a rival. Now, as you and I know, dearest,—and as every woman knows, for that matter,—a man has no need to say in so many words that he loves a woman. Every act of his, when in her presence, will show her that, and, if she be an honorable woman, she will not encourage him unless she feels and knows that she can bestow her heart and hand upon him when he comes and asks for them. The fact that Neville and poor lost Eddy quarrelled about me at Cloisterham, was evidence that some words must have passed between them concerning me, and, since this hermit life that Neville has been forced to adopt, I have felt that he was cherishing a hope which never could be realized. Hence, I have endeavoured, by assuming an air of coolness and indifference, to destroy that hope which must end in disappointment; for, Helena,—dear friend, do not blame me that I cannot love your brother,—I know he is worthy of any woman's love—but mine—that cannot be—my heart has gone to another, and I only knew it when it was too late! Pity me, pity me, Helena! for I am wretched, oh, so wretched! for doing what I have no power now to undo, but which was done when a silly girl, and before the troubles of one short year had made me know my own heart!" and, hiding her face in Helena's bosom, she wept bitterly.

Sympathizing with her friend, Helena endeavours to console her, and thinks, while so doing, what a wonderful change has come over her, and what a difference there is in the childish girl of the Nuns' House, as she had first seen her, gathering roses and casting them from her, but retaining the thorns, which then she could not see, and lamenting now, when it is too late, that the roses have all withered and died, and naught but the thorns remain. And how many there are reading these lines who can, like her, look back upon the past and realize, when it is too late, that their lives might have been surrounded with the roses that had strewn their pathway, but which, in their blindness, they have trampled under foot, leaving naught but the thorns of sorrow and regret, which will cling to them until the journey of life is ended.

Rosa has become calmer now, and, a moment after, a tap at the door is answered by Helena, who finds Miss Keep come to tell them that Mr. Crisparkle is waiting below to see them.

"Dear me!" cries Rosa, "what *will* he think to see me, looking as if I had cried my eyes out!" She steps to a mirror and finds her face bearing such evidences of recent grief that she declares she cannot go down now, and would Helena excuse her and go down alone?

"Do not be too sensitive, Rosa dear," is Helena's reply; "Mr. Crisparkle has too much good sense to ridicule any one because they may happen to show signs of having given vent to grief in tears. Let us both go down; I have no doubt we shall feel better, and that his presence may serve to cheer us."

After a great deal of objection on the part of Rosa, and a great deal of persuasion on the part of Helena, the former consents to see the Reverend gentleman, and they descend together to bid him welcome.

They find him patiently awaiting them, and, after kindly greetings have passed between them, he inquires for Neville. Helena proceeds to inform him of the distressed condition of her brother's mind, and that she fears he is not gaining in health, but, on the contrary, is failing rapidly. The Reverend gentleman's face grows very sad on hearing this, and he says:

"I am a little surprised at this information, for I felt confident that he had greatly improved when I last saw him, and had flattered myself that I should find him to-day looking more like his old self than he has looked since he left Cloisterham. But we must not expect to accomplish this desirable end in a moment. I feel sure he will come out all right in time, and I have something to tell him which will help to improve him more than anything else could, and what I have to tell him will be as welcome intelligence to you two ladies as to him."

He smiles upon them as he thinks how pleased and astonished they will be, and they regard him with curiosity on their faces, and wait impatiently to learn what is the nature of the information he brings.

"I must," he continues, "request that you promise me beforehand, that you will not ask me to go into details or make any explanation as to the circumstances which have brought it about, for you will know all that in good time, and must be patient till that time comes."

He intends this request for them both, but he looks at Rosa as he finishes speaking, and while Helena assures him that his request shall be complied with, Rosa, who has an instinctive idea that what he is about to impart to them, is something concerning Edwin Drood, is so overcome that she cannot utter a word, but only nods her head in acquiescence.

Then Mr. Crisparkle again continues:

"Things are not so bad as we had all supposed them, concerning that unfortunate disappearance of last Christmas. God has seen fit to be watchful over us and the young man whose loss we have all deplored, since that terrible morning which brought grief into our hearts and caused so much suffering to come upon an innocent person.

The thorns have been present with us for a time, but now the roses are covering them and hiding them from our sight, and their presence will be more dear to us for coming late, while their perfume will be more intense."

Rosa and Helena are both weeping as he ceases, for now they know what he means by speaking thus. Rosa approaches him, and, with a voice trembling with excitement, asks:

"Does Eddy live?"

He takes her hand in his as though he would give her strength to bear the tidings, while he raises his eyes to heaven, and in a fervid voice, makes answer:

"Thanks to our Heavenly Father's mercy and protection, Edwin Drood is alive and well!"

Almost beside herself with joy, as the words pass from his lips, Rosa claps her hands like a little child, exclaiming:

"Oh, joy! joy! Eddy is alive! he is not dead. I shall see him again! Oh dear, oh dear, what can I do to express my gratitude? Bless you, bless you, Mr. Crisparkle!" and hardly realizing what she is doing, to the great astonishment of the Rev. gentleman, she throws her arms about his neck and kisses him, and then recovering herself, blushes extremely at her impetuous behaviour.

Helena makes no demonstration of joy at what she has heard, but calmly clasping her hands and raising them to heaven in a devotional attitude, murmurs:

"Praise God! Heavenly Father, I thank Thee that my brother stands released of the terrible crime of which he was accused, and that the chain which circumstances had woven about him are broken, even at this late day!"

A silence of a few moments ensues, which is broken by Rosa, who asks:

"But where has he been all this time?"

"There you go, Rosa, breaking your promise so quick," laughingly answers the Minor Canon.

"But surely there can be no harm in our knowing where he has kept himself all this time," interposes Helena, whose curiosity was as great as Rosa's to learn just a *very little* more.

"Perhaps I might be willing to answer that question, Miss Bud, if I myself knew where he had been; but I am as ignorant on that point as either of you. I have been informed of some of the particulars connected with the affair, but am not at liberty to state anything more than what I have told you. Perhaps it may be gratifying to you to learn, however, that Mr. Drood begged me, if I saw you, to present his compliments, and tell you that he should be happy, when the time came, to give you a history of the whole affair. But how very thoughtless we are of Neville's happiness, thus to delay carrying *him* the good news."

"Because our own happiness has caused us to forget his," rejoins Helena. "Poor Neville! I hope this intelligence will help him to rally, but I fear it comes too late. Since yesterday he has been obliged to keep his room, and is so weak that he lays upon the sofa most of the time through the day. Let us repair to him at once."

As she ceases speaking, they start to leave the room, when they are confronted by Miss Keep, who throws open the door, and, wringing her hands, in great agitation, exclaims:

"Oh, go at once to Mr. Neville,
For I've just left him very ill."

Before they can recover from the alarm into which her words have thrown them, the agitated lady continues:—"Good sir and ladies: Something dreadful has come over Mr. Landless. One of my maids was coming from the chamber adjoining his, and just as she got to the head of the landing, she discovered Mr. Neville lying on the top stair in an unconscious state; she hurried to tell me, and we both came to where he lay, and I should thought he was dead, only for his faintly moaning, and then trying to get on his feet. We helped him into his room and placed him on the sofa, and I've come as quick as I could to tell you."

Helena had not waited to hear the whole of Miss Keep's narrative, but had hastened to her brother's assistance at the first intimation that he was in trouble, leaving the others to follow. They are about to do so, when they are detained a moment by Miss Keep, who adds, in a very mournful strain:

"I feel dreadfully for this young man, pining away every day as he is. And what makes me pity him still more," addressing the Minor Canon, "is because he is a lover of the Muses, and consequently must suffer double what he would otherwise." Exactly why this should make any difference in the sufferings of the young man, Miss Keep did not explain, but finished what she had to say by adding a rhyme for the occasion:

"And now Miss Bud, and Reverend Sir,
It makes my heart within me stir
With grief, his sufferings to behold,
For fear that soon he'll leave our fold."

Wishing to treat the lady with all due respect, Mr. Crisparkle waited impatiently for her to finish, and as she uttered the last line, he hastily mounted the stairs, followed by Rosa, and both were soon by the side of the invalid.

Neville turns his eyes upon them as they enter, and his face flushes as he beholds Rosa, while he smiles faintly upon the Minor Canon, who advances and takes his protegé by the hand.

"Neville, my dear fellow," remarks Mr. Crisparkle, in a cheerful tone, "what is this? You have been overdoing. You were getting along so finely at my last visit, that I feel sure you have been neglecting yourself in some way to bring about this change." He beams kindly upon the young man, whose hand he still retains, and is answered with a mournful shake of the head:

"You will not have occasion to worry much longer for me, Mr. Crisparkle. I feel that my life is drawing to a close."

He pauses for a moment, and then placing his disengaged hand upon his heart, says, in a faint tone:

"Oh, there is such distress here!" and then the hand falls listless by his side, while his eyes are filled with tears.

"My dear boy, what can I do for you?" asks the Minor Canon, in a tone that evinces his solicitude for Neville's condition. "Would it not be well for me to summon a physician?"

"No physician can help me," is the answer, still made in a faint tone. "My troubles will soon cease, and only that I deplore the grief that Helena will sustain in that event, I can truly say that I shall welcome death. I have no other object to live for, and could not attain it if I had, tied hand and foot as I am." His voice is so weak as he finishes that it has sunk to a whisper, and his face has become so very colorless that the Minor Canon is alarmed, and hastily asks Rosa to see Miss Keep, and tell her to summon a physician instantly. The invalid smiles sorrowfully, as though he deemed his condition of too hopeless a nature for any physician to remedy. Then whispers Mr. Crisparkle that he would like to converse with him in private, and beckons Helena, who sits near him weeping, to his side, and asks her to retire with Rosa for a little time, that he may be left alone with their visitor. She looks at Mr. Crisparkle as though seeking to know from him if it is necessary, and he nods his head to intimate that he thinks it well to grant the invalid's request. Then bending over and imprinting a kiss upon her brother's forehead, and concealing her grief as far as possible, lest it may affect him, she leaves the Minor Canon alone with the invalid.

The latter turns upon his side that he may the better face his companion, whose hand he still clasps, and, in a faint voice, proceeds to address him:

"Mr. Crisparkle, you are the best friend that I possess, aside from my sister. Knowing this, I feel that you will sympathize with me when I relate to you the cause of the sufferings that fill my heart. I have but a little time to live—nay, do not attempt to encourage me with hopes that can never be realized"—this as the Minor Canon had raised his hand, and was about uttering some cheerful assurance. "I have but a short time to live," proceeds Neville, "and I want you to realize, my dear friend, that you are listening to the words of a dying man, and so accept them as the words of truth."

He ceases for a moment, as though to recover strength to proceed, and then, in an earnest tone, he continues:

"Mr. Crisparkle, when Neville Landless' head lies under the sod, remember that almost the last words you heard him utter were that he was innocent of any wrong done to Edwin Drood!"

The speaker gazes anxiously into the eyes of the Minor Canon, as though he would discover there the faintest look that would indicate a doubt of the truthfulness of his assertion.

Tenderly wiping the perspiration from the brow of Neville, which had gathered there from the exertion attending the efforts he had made to give utterance to his remarks, Mr. Crisparkle replies:

"Neville, I never doubted your innocence when you declared it long ago, nor should I doubt it now, even if I had no other evidence than your word to assure me of the fact. My visit here to-day is mainly to tell you of that which exonerates you of all suspicion, and which will, I trust, help to improve you in body as well as in mind. My dear boy, Edwin Drood is still living."

With a cry of surprise, Neville struggles into a sitting posture, and with the cold dew standing upon his brow, he begs of the Minor Canon to repeat his words again, for it seems as though he were dreaming.

Tenderly laying him back upon the pillow, the Minor Canon assures him that it is no dream, but a joyful reality. It was then that Mr. Crisparkle realized, for the first time, how worn and wasted his pupil had become, and that Neville had spoken truly when he declared that his life was nearly ended. After the invalid had recovered a little, the Minor Canon said:

"No, my boy, you are not dreaming, but are wide awake, and understand aright. Edwin Drood is alive and well, and golden light is breaking through the clouds that have so long hung over you."

With a happy smile upon his face, as he casts his eyes to heaven, the stricken man murmurs:

"Now I can die happy. Now my darling sister will not be forced to live and feel that any one can doubt my innocence, and regard her as the sister of a murderer."

Although convinced of the hopelessness of Neville's recovery, Mr.

Crisparkle feels it his duty to assume a cheerful air, and strives to encourage his pupil by holding out to him assurances of a happy future. So he replies, in cheering tones:

"But, my dear fellow, you are not going to die at present, nor for a long time to come, I hope. Cheer up; don't be down-hearted. A long life comes with a light heart. Now that this incubus has been removed from your pathway, you can look the world in the face, fearing accusation from no man, and we shall yet see you your old self again, and we'll pass many merry hours together."

Neville does not reply, but, smiling his gratitude for the kindly words of the speaker, shakes his head in a desponding manner. Then the Minor Canon was convinced that all hope had fled from the breast of the invalid, and that he had, indeed, spoken truly when he said his hour was near at hand.

At this point, there is a tap at the door, and a moment after Helena enters, followed by the physician. The latter salutes Mr. Crisparkle, whom he has met before, and seats himself at the side of the dying boy. After some few questions, he feels his pulse, and as he does so starts with evident surprise. Who but a loving woman watches the face of the physician, at such times as these, more correctly, or reads more accurately the thoughts that are in his mind, at such dread moments? Thus it is that Helena reads in the physician's face, at that moment, the fate that awaits her brother, and, turning her face away, she bursts into a passionate flood of tears.

The physician rises, and, beckoning to Mr. Crisparkle, the two retire to a distant part of the room, when the doctor informs the Reverend gentleman that the invalid may live to behold the morrow's light, but it is doubtful, for no medical skill in the world can save him.

"There is no duty connected with our profession," he adds, "that is more painful to perform, than that which requires us to state that a case is hopeless, and that the patient must die. Nevertheless, it is a duty, and so I tell you that this young man is liable to die at any moment."

Shortly after, the physician takes his departure, and the Minor Canon, —after requesting Helena to once more join Rosa, which she reluctantly does, after a promise that he will tell her presently what the physician has said,—seats himself by Neville's side, and proceeds to inform him, with choked utterance, of the danger which threatens him.

No agitation, no regrets, no murmurs escape his lips, but instead, a calm and pleasant smile upon his face as he answers:

"Do not fear for me, dear friend; I am not afraid to die. On the contrary, only for the pain at leaving Helena alone in the world, I could be happy for knowing it. Knowing that the time was near at hand, was why I desired to speak with you alone. Now that we are alone again, I will try to say all I have to tell you. My life has been a short one, and, God knows! I have seen so little of the sunshine that falls to the common lot, that I am not anxious to make it longer."

He pauses here and closes his eyes, as though to obtain strength and to collect his thoughts. Mr. Crisparkle patiently waits, with a tearful face, until the sufferer is ready to proceed, and then bends over him to catch his words, which are uttered in a weak tone:

"If I have aspired to that which could never be, and have looked forward to the future with hopes that have been dashed to earth, it has been some pleasure to live in fancy, even if I could not enjoy the reality. I have a few requests to make of you, and which I feel sure you will grant a poor fellow, dying, whom you have helped to encourage so much while living."

He waits, as though expecting the other to promise him. With a sobbing voice, the Minor Canon tells him that he will faithfully perform any trust that may be left with him.

"I would ask first," proceeds Neville, "that you see to my sister's welfare, and comfort her when she is left alone. We have never been separated, as you know, and she will take this blow very hard. Be you her comforter, and endeavour to convince her that I could never be happy living, and that I shall feel, in another world, far happier to know that she regards my death as a Divine blessing, knowing that were I to live for fifty years to come I should never see a happy day."

He is so weak now, and turns so pale, that the Minor Canon is alarmed, and leaves his side for an instant to return with a glass of water, which he places to his lips, and at which he seems to rally, as he continues:

"One little year ago, before all these troubles came upon me, I placed in my heart an idol—the image of a woman—and day and night that idol has remained! Even during the darkest hours that have cast their shadows upon me, I have felt encouraged and sustained by its presence there, and have lived, believing that at some future day she might understand that I loved her, and that she would give me her love in return. I would have told her long ago, had I felt sure that she believed me innocent of the crime that was charged against me; but, with love's watchful eye, I saw that she looked upon me with doubt and suspicion, and that really her heart had been given to one whom we had all thought dead. Still I was content to hope and think it barely possible that a time might come—such things have been—when she would understand me as I was and pity me; and that pity would be followed by an affection born of it."

Again he stops to recover strength, and begs the Minor Canon to step to a bureau drawer and take therefrom a casket which he would find therein, and fetch it him. This done, he asks the Reverend gentleman to open it, and take therefrom a piece of ribbon lying there.

Opening the casket, the Minor Canon finds a faded blue ribbon carefully folded, and which shows signs of having been kept in its position for a long time.

The invalid, taking it eagerly from the other's hand, presses it passionately to his lips, and murmurs:

"A slight thing, sir, but oh, so dear to me!"

The Minor Canon regards him with some curiosity, and wonders what can cause him to evince so much feeling at sight of this slight token, and waits with eagerness to learn.

Still holding the ribbon in his hand, Neville continues:

"She does not know that I have this; she must never know. Poor ribbon,—so worthless to all others, so dear to me—from which I shall never again be parted, in life or death!" He presses it to his lips again, and, after a moment's silence, resumes:

"You remember the evening of my arrival at Cloisterham, when we were all at your house. She had a fainting fit, and with Helena sought the garden for relief. When she went out this ribbon was about her neck, and when she returned it was not there. I noticed the loss—what did I not notice that spoke of her!—and, going out shortly after, found it lying upon the ground. I have always kept it, for it had been hers, and was perhaps all the keepsake that I should ever have; at least I thought so, then,—now, God help me, I know it!"

He pauses again, and Mr. Crisparkle takes the opportunity of asking if he has reference to Miss Bud.

"I know you'll think me a foolish fellow," is the reply, "when I tell you, for I know that I have been foolish to cherish such a hope, but I have loved Miss Bud,—Rosa,—for all the time since we first met at your house, and have kept my secret locked in my breast till now."

The Minor Canon looks his astonishment at these words, and understands now the cause of Neville's continued melancholy and heart-sickness, which has brought him thus early at death's door.

"I am very weak," whispers Neville; "will you please raise a window, that I may obtain a little air?"

The window is raised, as he requests, and the cool September Breezes enter the room and fan the cheek of the dying man. So he rallies again, and proceeds:

"She does not know that I love her, and while I live I do not want she should; but, after it is all over, and my pulse has ceased to beat; when I am laid away beneath the green sod of Cloisterham church-yard—be sure and put me there, for Cloisterham is dearer to me than any other place, in that it was there I first came to love her—when all is over, tell her, then, that Neville Landless died loving her, but would not tell his love, because he knew that she could never return it; that he knew—and who could tell so well as a lover—that her heart had gone to the missing man, and that, being gone, it could never be another's. Tell her I do not blame her, and that I was not sorry I could not live, for it was a happy death to die for her!"

The September Breezes fan again the brow of the dying man, and though their touch is like an angel's breath, they seem to give him strength, and he continues:

"After my body has been put in the coffin, I charge you, by all that is holy, to place this little ribbon in my hand, so it may bear me company to my last resting-place, that the lost Neville, and the memento of his lost love may go down to the dust together. But do not tell *her* that; only ask her to come sometimes and place some little flower upon my grave, and tell her that my heart was hers on earth, and that I will keep it for her in heaven; and, if my spirit can return to earth, I'll watch over her with a love as pure as that I bear her now. Promise me this, for it is the last favor you can do your unfortunate friend."

Again the mild September Breezes come softly through the open casement, and, with their kisses on his brow, strive to sustain the sinking man.

With a sad heart, and in tones that bore evidence of his grief, the Minor Canon assured Neville that he would faithfully perform all that he had asked.

Neville faintly smiled his gratitude, and whispered he would like to see his sister now.

Hastening to gratify this wish, the Minor Canon finds Helena impatiently waiting tidings of her brother, and he conducts her to the chamber of the dying boy. As they enter with light step, Neville turns his face to them, and greets his sister with a loving smile as she hurries to his side and bestows a passionate kiss upon his lips. She is frightened at the change which has taken place in him since she left him, and tells Mr. Crisparkle that she thinks they had better send for the doctor again.

Neville takes her hand, and, pressing it in his own, assures her that there is no need of that now.

"Helena," he continues, faintly, "I am going to leave you, dear; I am going to take the journey that we must both take, only it is God's will that I perform it first. I have told our kind friend here what my wishes were concerning myself and you when I am gone, and he has promised to stand our friend in time to come as in time gone by."

Throwing her arms about his neck in a passionate embrace, she exclaims:

"Oh, my dear brother, I cannot bear this! I cannot have it so! You must live now to enjoy what you have so long been deprived of. We can be *happy*, now, dear! The pall has been removed from your life, and the sun is once more enabled to shine upon us, with nothing left to cast a shadow upon our happiness."

She is silent for a moment, and then, turning suddenly to the Minor Canon, she exclaims:

"Why do you not summon a physician, Mr. Crisparkle? It is cruel to let him lie here and suffer, when he needs medical aid so much"—and then she falls to weeping bitterly.

The September Breezes again float through the open casement, moving the curtain with zephyr fingers as they enter, that a sunbeam may bear them company. But the sunbeam does not remain; it goes out instantly, as though lacking courage to witness the sorrow within, while the Breezes once more fan, with loving breath, the brow of the dying brother.

The Minor Canon, his heart filled with grief at the sad scene before him, strives with words of kindness and consolation to comfort the stricken girl, and breaks to her, as gently as he can, the sad fate which is so soon to deprive her of the loved one; but she will not have it so, and still insists that the efforts of the medical man may yet save him. So the physician, once more summoned, soon enters the room again, and takes his place by the bedside.

Helena, who is seated by the bed with Neville's hand clasped in her own, entreats the doctor to save her brother's life.

"My dear child," the physician returns, in a compassionate tone, "he is beyond the power of medical skill, and an hour, at the longest, must terminate his existence. I would gladly help him if I could, but it is not in the power of mortal man to give him aid."

Neville, who has lain in a semi-conscious state for several minutes, now rallies a little and recognizes his sister; he begs of her, in a faint voice, to be reconciled to the blow which is so soon to separate them, and charges her to remember, always, the kindness of the Minor Canon, and to consider him as the best friend she has on earth.

He tries to impress upon her how much happier he shall be in the other world than he can ever be here, and tells her he is glad that he has not long to remain here, where he has known nothing but trouble and misery.

"A better future awaits you, dear sister." He speaks now in a stronger voice, which assumes a prophetic tone as he continues:

"You will miss me, darling, and your grief will be intense; but you will become more reconciled as time goes on, and, being surrounded by those who have a claim upon your affections, will help to soften your grief. But you will never forget me, dear sister, and I shall be the happier for knowing that your love for other dear ones yet to come will not crowd out from a corner of your heart the affection you bear a dead brother, but that you will treasure a brother's love for you, which was all the legacy he had to give."

He appears exhausted now, and closes his eyes, as if to rest; then brightens again, and murmurs something which they cannot understand, only that they can hear the words, "another's," "innocent," "dear sister." He closes his eyes again and turns so pale that they are startled, and beg the physician to tell them if he lives. The physician is about to place his hand upon the heart, to learn if there is life there, when Neville opens his eyes, and, with a slight flush upon his face, gazes with a fixed look upon some object that he fancies is before him, and murmurs:

"Dead, but not forgotten! had I lived she might have forgotten me. So, better death than life. Oh, how happy I might have been could she have given me her heart! But it was not hers to give;—I heard her tell Helena so, and it has killed me. How fondly had I looked forward to the future, when, with her as all my own, we should commence our pleasant journey down life's river. How happy I should have been, while cheering her when trials beset our pathway, and how her dear voice would strengthen and encourage me to bear or overcome all troubles or temptations that might present themselves to check our onward course. But it is all over now; those happy anticipations can never be realized; so death alone can bring relief! Please draw the curtain," he whispers, faintly; "I would like to see the trees and birds and sky once more."

They do as he requests, and, with Mr. Crisparkle's assistance, Helena raises and supports him in a sitting position, the better that he can look out upon the world of life he is so soon to leave.

There comes at this moment a little sparrow, who alights upon the window-sill, and it must have been a very tame one, too, for it does not fly away at seeing them, but hops inside, and remains perched upon the window-seat. While the others have observed it, the dying youth does not seem to notice it, but gazes earnestly at the sunset sky, as though waiting patiently till the door of heaven was opened, and his spirit bade to enter there.

His face now lights up with a radiant smile upon it, and he clasps his hands, as though in an ecstacy of happiness, while he murmurs:

"They're coming now; they will not wait for me to go alone; the door is opened, and an angel—oh, so beautiful—is coming to bear me in its arms. I can almost see the face; it comes nearer—there—it's almost here; I see the face now! It's a childish, happy face. It beckons me to meet it. Listen! what sweet music! good-bye all—kiss me, Helena. God bless and keep you, my sister!" His voice sinks so low now that they can only hear him by placing their ears to his lips, to catch the last words which escape them. "Tell Rosa that her face is just as fresh in my memory now as in the old days that have fled forever, and that her name shall be the theme of my song in Heaven!"

The September Breezes come again through the open casement. They are lighter now, and seem to come with softer touch, the better to convey the escaping spirit to its Maker, just as it had left its earthly tabernacle; and so they bear it away upon their peaceful bosoms!

The little sparrow flies away as the last word escapes the dying brother, perchance as a messenger to bear the tidings of the trembling spirit's approach to its blissful home, and so prepare the hosts upon the other shore to welcome it with words of love and outstretched arms.

The living are left to perform the last sad rites, and mourn the loss of the loved one. Helena, in her great grief, has thrown herself at her brother's side, upon the bed, and with her arm about his neck, while imprinting kisses upon the lips that never more will return them, begs of him to speak once more to her. The Minor Canon, with trembling lips, strives to comfort her, while the physician, used as he is to death bed scenes, is overcome at the mournful one before him. And so the journey over the new road is taken at last, and those who are left to continue theirs over the old road must proceed as before, with only the dead man's memory to bear them company.

Leaving Helena to the care of Rosa and Miss Keep, the Minor Canon hastens to bear the mournful intelligence of Neville's death to Mr. Grewgious, and to consult with him as to the arrangements for the young man's burial at Cloisterham.

While the scene just narrated was transpiring at the house of Miss Keep, and long before Mr. Crisparkle had set out on his way to Mr. Grewgious' chambers, that very lively old lady, known in these pages as the Princess Puffer, had arrayed herself in what she termed her Business Coverers, meaning thereby a miserable bonnet and faded shawl, and which she only wears when in the street,—hence, Coverers, and Business, because she never goes upon the street except on special business,—and leaving the miserable abode which she inhabits, proceeds in the direction of Staple Inn. Threading her way through the courts and lanes which abound in the miserable locality of Lincoln's Inn Fields, until she has reached the better portion of Drury Lane, she turns in a westerly direction, and, then with a more rapid step, proceeds towards her destination.

Usually stealthy and cat-like in her movements, she seems doubly so to-day, and holds in her hand something which is kept close there, and, the better to prevent its being observed by curious eyes, carries the hand in the pocket of her dress.

Although having reached a more respectable portion of the City, she does not relax her efforts to discover if she is being followed or observed, but stops frequently, as though looking at some passing object, but in reality the better to make a careful scrutiny of such pedestrians as chance to come behind her, and then continues a short distance to again repeat her manœuvre.

She finally arrives at Staple, and, after some enquiries, finds her way to the chambers of Mr. Grewgious, and knocks at his door. As she waits an answer to her summons, she spies the initials P. J. T., and is greatly puzzled to understand their meaning; but when she reflects that her present business with Mr. Grewgious is of a nature that may result in something pretty serious for a certain person, she smiles as she asks herself why they will not answer for Punish Jasper Thoroughly. Her thoughts are soon interrupted, however, by the door opening, and Mr. Grewgious,—who does not recognize her,—asking her business.

Still keeping her hand concealed in her dress-pocket, together with her strange, uncouth appearance, leads Mr. Grewgious to fear she may have escaped from some mad-house, and that probably her concealed hand may hold some deadly weapon with which to avenge some fancied insult. This dire suspicion is not lessened when she moves a step nearer him and assumes her cunning smile, the better to quicken his memory and inspire confidence, but, failing in this, she concludes to resort to her vocal powers, and ejaculates:

"Bless ye, dear gentleman, it can't be as ye've forgot a poor old 'ooman as has such lungs as was never know'd afore, and as coughs so bad at times that it a'most takes her breath."

He is reminded now; her last attempt at recognition has the desired effect, and he bids her enter. After she is seated he begs that she will pardon his forgetfulness, for it was a long time since he had met her.

"I have often wondered," he adds, "that you did not keep the promise made at that time to call on me, and, if I had known where you were to be found, it is very probable that I should have made you a visit ere this."

She shakes her head in a meaning way as she makes answer: "If I've been a long time comin', 'tain't for the reason as I've been idle, deary; and it's like that when you comes to know the work I've done, ye'll think it a wonder as an old 'ooman could 'a done it so soon, and that it might 'a taken a younger a deal longer, if they could 'a done it anyways. Is the young lady with ye now, good sir?"

"Not with me here," is the answer, "but where I know she is just as safe from annoyance, or safer."

"I suppose there's no tidings yet from the young gentleman as was called Eddy?" She asks this question with such a look of anxiety accompanying it, that Mr. Grewgious notices it, and wonders what possible object she now has in speaking of the young man, whether dead or alive, and so asks her.

She does not reply to his question, however, but inquires again if the young gentleman's uncle has died from grief, or if he still lives to mourn the loss of his nephew.

Mr. Grewgious answers that, so far as he knows, Jasper is still in the land of the living, and then waits for her to proceed, that he may ascertain to what those questions on her part tend.

The Puffer glances nervously about the room, while the hand which has been concealed in her pocket all this time,—never once withdrawn—now moves uneasily there, and seems very undecided whether to remain or come forth.

Mr. Grewgious glances, with evident curiosity, at her singular behaviour; and, with some apprehension still lingering about him as to his personal safety, he feels that he should enjoy her visit a deal more if she would remove that hand, and he be convinced that it did not contain some deadly weapon which could do him a mischief.

Still undecided, she glances at the door, and asks him would he bolt it, so that they may the better be safe from intrusion. She assures him, when he shows hesitancy in granting this request, that he will be convinced of the importance of this precautionary measure when she comes to tell him what is the object of her visit.

"Ye need have no fear of me, dear gentleman," she adds, a little impatiently; "it don't follows that as I've not fine clothes, I hain't a honest heart and good purpose. And it may be as this old gown as I'm a wearin' on has got that concealed about it that the sight of it will cause ye more happiness and comfort nor the finest clothes or richest jewels in all England."

It is nothing dangerous, then, which is concealed in the pocket where she has kept her hand all this time,—but something of value that the eyes of a third party must not behold.

He is satisfied now, and the door is made secure.

She waits till he has become seated again, and is ready to give her his whole attention, and then says:

"It's narrow roads as sometimes leads to broad and roomy fields; it's little things as sometimes shows us the way to great ones." She pauses a moment,—Mr. Grewgious thinks, perhaps, to indulge in the old cough; but now he thinks of it, he does not remember to have heard the cough, which before had been such a source of complaint with her; nor does he hear it throughout the interview, which appears to him a singular circumstance.

She withdraws her hand from its hiding-place now, and holds in her palm a locket, which her companion gazes at intently, but which he does not appear to recognize. She notices this, and holds it out for him to take, saying at the same time:

"Look at it closely, dear sir, and tell me if you never see'd it afore, and who ye think it really belongs to."

He observes, as he looks closer at it, that some letters are engraved upon the case, and they are so small that he takes his glasses, the better to decipher them, and then reads, "Ned's Pussy." The lettering had evidently been done by an unskilled hand, but there was no difficulty in making out the characters that formed the words. Mr. Grewgious examines it several times before replying, and finally answers:

"I have no doubt that this belonged at some time to the missing young man you were speaking of; but where did you obtain it?"

"And if the missing young man took a journey with another gentleman, and had this about him when he started, but never came back from his journey, and the other gentleman as went with him did come back, and brought this with him, what should ye say then, deary?"

Mr. Grewgious had opened the locket as the Puffer finished, and, so absorbed was he with the face that he beheld there, it was several minutes before he replied. The face was that of Rosa, and represented her as she was about two years before, although the features and expression were not unlike the Rosa of to-day. But Mr. Grewgious' mind was not upon the girl, whom this picture was intended to represent. He was wandering away back into the dead past, and beholding the face of another, who bore to this so great a resemblance, and whose fate—

living and dead—had been the cause of his life of solitude, and whose memory he had cherished, and kept a green spot in his heart that would remain there in all its brightness, till that heart should cease to beat.

He replies to the Puffer, after a moment, that there might be an inference not very complimentary to the one that came back from the journey, but there would be no proof of guilt, as the gem might have been given to hold in trust, and so been in that person's possession a long time previous to the catastrophe.

"Lack-a-day, good gentleman! It's well that all folks ain't women, and 'specially old 'uns, for we'd get strange thoughts in our 'eds. It's a good thing now as the men are so much wiser. Ye'd better keep that, for it's better with you nor with me." He places it in a drawer of his desk, while she puts her hand in her pocket again, and takes therefrom a ring, so thickly studded with diamonds and rubies, and so brilliantly flashing, that it is almost painful to look upon them as she holds them in the sun's rays. Mr. Grewgious springs to take it from her, and is so excited that, could he have seen himself as the Puffer saw him, he would hardly have given himself credit for being such a remarkably Angular Man, after all.

"Softly, and ye'll have it, maybe, all in good time. No need for ye to take it closer to ye, for I see as ye remembers it. So answer me this: what would ye say of the person as 'ad this in his keepin' a'most a year after the missing man was gone."

"I would say," exclaimed Mr. Grewgious, still greatly excited, "I would say he had the heart of a murderer, and with that ring could prove what I said! Edwin Drood was the last person that had it in his keeping before his disappearance, and whoever had it after must have obtained it by force."

"Bless God to hear ye say so, good gentleman!" cried the Puffer, now also excited. "Bless ye and thank ye for the words! Take the ring and use it for that, and I'll bless ye all my days for puttin' the noose about the neck of a villain as caused the death of my poor daughter, and forced me to live the life I 'ave for years, the better that I might 'ave my revenge, which will be just as sweet, though it's been so long in the comin'."

"And who may this man be?" enquires Mr. Grewgious, who has been listening attentively to her words.

"John Jasper," she instantly replies. "Ha! ha!" laughing in a triumphant tone. "He little thought as I'd unriddled him, or knew him for any other but what he called himself, but I did; and I'll live to see him hung like the dog he is, and then I'll be content to die!"

She then proceeds to give her astonished hearer an account of the manner by which the two articles came into her possession, all of which interested Mr. Grewgious very much. Just as she had finished, and while he was thinking what was the proper course to pursue in the matter, a sharp knock is heard at the door. Placing the ring with the locket, Mr. Grewgious opens the door, and is astonished to find the Minor Canon standing before him, looking very pale and sad and very tired, and whom he invites to enter and be seated.

"You have come in good time, Reverend Sir," Mr. Grewgious says, addressing the new comer. "At last we have got substantial evidence that will sustain the accusation which young Drood has to bring against his uncle. Disguise on the part of Edwin Drood is no longer necessary, as the proof we have so long been waiting for has appeared within the past hour, and concealment on the part of young Landless is also unnecessary, for John Jasper's power to persecute him further is at an end. We have nothing to do now but arrest him for the dastardly attack upon his nephew's life, and have him transported, and I only regret that the punishment for his crime will not hang him."

Although the Minor Canon expresses thankfulness for the proof which will aid in the conviction of the Music Master, his face still wears a sad look; whereat Mr. Grewgious wonders greatly, but his wonder ceases when the other adds, in a mournful tone:

"But I have tidings that place it beyond the power of mortal man to further persecute Neville Landless. He is dead!"

"Dead!" exclaimed Mr. Grewgious, starting to his feet with surprise; "Neville Landless dead? Tell me about it. When did it happen?"

Mr. Crisparkle, with choked utterance, related to the old gentleman the details connected with the death of the young man. There was a silence for several moments after he had ceased, which was broken by Mr. Grewgious, who said:

"Poor fellow! I had expected it, and yet I had no idea that it would come so soon. It will kill his sister, I fear. I wish he could have lived long enough to have seen justice done him, and his enemy punished! But we must not remain here; let us repair at once to Miss Keep's, and do all in our power to console Helena, poor child," and the good old man, with the tears standing in his eyes as he thinks of the grief that must fill the sister's heart, rises and prepares to accompany the Minor Canon. A thought seems to strike him, as he asks, suddenly:

"How long a time will it take, think you, to arrange for his funeral, and lay him to rest in the spot where he desired to be buried?"

"Very likely the day after to-morrow, at the farthest. I will return with you to Miss Keep's, and do what I can towards comforting Miss Landless, and we will consult her as to any wishes she may have in the matter; after which I shall take a late train and go back to Cloisterham to-night, so that proper arrangements may be made at the earliest moment."

Mr. Grewgious, addressing the Puffer, now continues:

"You desire to see justice done, you say?"

"Lord love ye, dear sir, ye might a know'd that without me tellin' on ye."

"Good!" returns Grewgious. "Now, would you be willing to go to Cloisterham with this gentleman, and there remain quietly till such time as I may want to communicate with you, and are you prepared to go to-night, if necessary?"

"'Taint many preparations as an old 'ooman like me needs to git ready to go anywheres—even to the church-yard; tell me when I'm to go and I'll be ready, if it's this blessed minit."

Mr. Grewgious consults with the Minor Canon, and finds that gentleman willing to accompany the Puffer on his return; and says, furthermore, that he will undertake to lodge her in some private family, the better that she may escape observation on the part of Jasper.

The Puffer, apprised of this last, bethinks her of the fact that Mrs. Padler is located there, who would, no doubt, be willing to give her shelter for a few days, as she is a relative of the child whom she has in her possession, and proceeds to give them a few facts connected with that relationship, something of which had already been made known to the Minor Canon on the night when, in company with Datchery, she had visited him, but she had not stated, during that interview, that the child was in the neighbourhood of Cloisterham.

Though deeply sympathizing with her, and assuring her of their future assistance, they feel that they have no time to inquire into all the particulars, and telling her to be sure and meet the Minor Canon at the station, in season for the midnight train, she departs with a lighter heart than she has known for many a year, in anticipation of Jasper's downfall; while Mr. Grewgious and his companion take their departure a moment after, in the direction of Miss Keep's, with heavier hearts than they have known for many a year, thinking of the sad calamity which has fallen upon Helena Landless.

CHAPTER XXXVII.

TELLS OF MR. PECKCRAFT'S PILGRIMAGE TO CLOISTERHAM AND WHAT CAME OF IT, AND ALLOWS EDWIN DROOD TO RISE AND EXPLAIN.

For persons who have selected for themselves a groove into which they deposit their lives, and in which they intend those lives to run forever after, until they reach the end from which they will drop into the grave, an absence from home of only one day is regarded as an epoch by them, from which, for years after, they will date succeeding events.

Mr. Peckcraft, being a gentleman who moves on groove principles, it is little wonder that for the balance of the day, after promising Edwin Drood that he would come to Cloisterham on the morrow, he should feel very uneasy in his mind, in consequence, and wish every quarter-hour that he had not consented.

Night came at last, and with it came Miss Keep's tea-table, at which Mr. Peckcraft seats himself, and gloomily sips his tea while meditating on the uncertainty of life, and especially a traveller's life, and wondering what if he should never sit at this table again? The thought came suddenly, and Mr. Peckcraft was so horrified at the bare probability of such a thing, that Miss Keep, who sat opposite him at table, noticed the cloud which came over his features and said:

"Will you tell us, Mr. Peckcraft,
What has happened unto you?
For the sad look on your features
Shows us you are feeling blue."

Mr. Peckcraft replied that nothing very serious had occurred, only that he was to undertake a business journey on the morrow, and being unaccustomed to such things, he was regretting the necessity which forced him to it. He did not say where he was going, but merely added that he should be absent through the day and possibly one night.

On hearing these words, Miss Keep is so overcome with surprise that she can only express it by clasping both hands, and turning her eyes up to the ceiling, gazes intently for one minute at a fly who had taken lodgings there for the night; then, recovering herself, finished her tea in an abstracted mood, and spoke not another word on the subject.

On the following morning, Mr. Peckcraft descends from his bedroom, and repairs to the parlour, where he finds Rosa and Miss Keep. Telling the ladies that he has only time to reach the station, he bids them good-bye, assuring Miss Keep that he shall return by the next day at farthest; whereat that lady replies that she sincerely trusts he *will* return safe, for they shall worry about him all the time he is gone, and finishes by adding a verse for the occasion:

"Though absent, still within my heart
Your welfare will be seated deep,
And though we should be miles apart,
A steadfast friend, you'll find Miss Keep."

And fortified by this comforting assurance, the old gentleman once more utters a farewell and departs on his journey.

Arriving safely at Cloisterham, he proceeds at once to the Crozier, and having made his presence known to Datchery through the aid of the Deputy and a porter, who had been employed to bear the intelligence of his arrival, was soon joined by Datchery and Joe Sloggers.

Mr. Peckcraft does not recognize in the faces of the new-comers a resemblance to the one he has come to see; but when Joe Sloggers advances and, holding out his hand, says:

"I hope you have not forgotten Eddy, Mr. Peckcraft," the old gentleman recognizes the voice and the smile that accompanies it, and shakes the proffered hand heartily.

"It is only a trifle more than one year since we met, Edwin," observes Mr. Peckcraft, "but you have changed greatly in that time, my boy, and I cannot understand it. I can see the same expression of the features when you speak or smile, which was always so like your father, but when in repose, your face is not that of the Edwin of old. Pray tell me the cause."

"All in good time, dear friend," is the response of Edwin Drood—for he it is—"but first allow me to present to you the gentleman whom you have been inquiring for here, my dear friend, Mr. Datchery—Mr. Peckcraft." While the two gentlemen are shaking each other by the hand, Edwin adds, "Please pardon me if I leave you for a moment," and disappears from the room, to return, in a very short time, and fill Mr. Peckcraft with surprise at his changed appearance. The dark, rough, scrawny face that had left the room a moment before, had given place to the clear and handsome countenance of the young man of one year ago, while the rough, uncouth clothing which had hung so loosely about his person, had been replaced with a neat and tasty suit.

Mr. Peckcraft holds up his hands in surprise, and ejaculates:

"God bless me, Ned, what does this mean? Do you want me to believe that you have lost your senses, or that I have lost mine?"

"Neither the one or the other," responds Edwin, good-naturedly; nor would I have you part from your senses, just now, on any account, for we have too much need of your assistance in a matter that concerns myself and various others."

Mr. Peckcraft, not knowing what reply to make, says nothing, but looks as though he would like an explanation, whereupon Datchery interposes a word:

"Mr. Peckcraft, permit me to explain the situation by illustrating: If we three, sitting in this room, should discover a rat, and each corner of the room offered opportunity for his escape unless it was guarded, one corner, of course, would be left open; now what should you say we would most desire under those circumstances?"

Edwin laughs heartily as Datchery pauses for a reply, and declares the illustration an apt one.

Mr. Peckcraft, still a little in the dark, ventures to reply that perhaps an additional person as guard would not come amiss.

Datchery, rubbing his hands together, bestows an approving smile on the speaker as he rejoins:

"You've hit it exactly, dear sir; we have found ourselves in just the position I have described, and so have sent for you to make up a requisite number."

"Ah! I think I understand now," Mr. Peckcraft ventures; "you want me to help you and Edwin to surround an enemy, that you may capture him. Who may the person be, and do I know him?"

He addresses Edwin, who replies:

"The person is my uncle, John Jasper, and that answers both your questions. It's a long story," continues Edwin, "and will occupy some time in the telling, but as it is quite interesting, I think you will not grudge the time. I think we had better repair to my room, however, lest we may be discovered or overheard by Mr. Jasper, who, as yet, is ignorant of my whereabouts, and who, until within a few days, supposed me a corpse in one of the church-yard tombs." This last remark causes still more surprise on the part of Mr. Peckcraft, and he is all impatience to listen to the recital of Edwin's narrative. They leave the parlour where they were seated, and make their way to the room where Datchery has been in the habit of spending so much of his time during his stay in Cloisterham, and always coming and going from it in a stealthy manner; why, the reader will now understand.

Securing the door, they are soon seated, and Edwin proceeds with his narrative:

"During the last Christmas holidays, I visited this place for the purpose of coming to some definite settlement of affairs concerning my marriage with the young lady to whom—you will remember—I was betrothed, and who was betrothed to me—our respective fathers doing that business for us almost before Pussy—Miss Bud—and I were born."

"God bless my soul!" interrupts Mr. Peckcraft, "I had forgotten all about that affair. Strange I didn't remember it when she told me her name. Why Edwin," he explained, "I've only just left Miss Bud, and—but I must not interrupt you; go on with what you were saying. I'll explain after you get through."

Edwin's curiosity was now excited by what the other had said; but he was content to wait, and so continued:

"Though we liked each other very well then—Rosa and I—we were satisfied that we should make a failure of it as husband and wife; so, there being nothing binding on either side, we being free to carry out the line as laid down by our fathers, or not, as we pleased, we pleased not, and decided accordingly."

"And a very wise decision to arrive at," remarks Mr. Peckcraft, with an approving nod.

Edwin continued to state that he had been the guest of his uncle while in Cloisterham, and that he and Neville had quarrelled on Rosa's account, the details of which are already familiar to the reader. He then proceeded to give the details connected with the supper at the Gate House on the memorable night that had been fraught with so much misery to many hearts.

"Every thing passed off splendidly," resumed Edwin, "and Jack did every thing in his power to make the occasion a happy one. I attached no importance to it at the time, but it has come back to me since as being remarkable, that always when I glanced at Jack he was looking steadily at me, as if his mind was constantly upon me. His looking at me so steadily became almost an annoyance, so that once when I caught his eye, I said to him: 'Dear Jack, if I were a woman I should think you had fallen desperately in love with me, and wanted me to read it in your eyes. As I am not a woman, however, I think your attention must be attracted to me from something unusual in my personal appearance to-night; so please tell me what it may be?'

"He laughed in his quick, nervous way, and said he was not aware of anything unusual about me to attract his attention, but that, as I was so soon to leave him, he must feast his eyes upon me then, for on the morrow he should not have an opportunity.

"About midnight we prepared to separate, when young Landless looked from the window and said it was a fearful night, and would it not be a grand sight to see the river during such a storm? I agreed with him, and proposed that we all go down.

"Jasper said we two might go if we liked, but we must excuse him, as he had seen it often, and it would afford him no interest. He could not be persuaded, so we left him alone and started for the river.

"We chatted on various unimportant subjects till we arrived at a place where we could view the scene at its best, and, after lingering there a half hour, it might be, retraced our steps, Mr. Landless on his way to Mr. Crisparkle's, and I to Jack's lodgings. Our conversation while returning had been upon the subject of young Landless taking a farewell of Cloisterham on the morrow, as he said he had determined to do so for the reason that he should be better off elsewhere, and he meant to locate in some place where he was unknown, and there remain till he had acquired some trade or profession that would enable him to make a name for himself in the world. I became so interested in what he said, and had so much advice that I wanted to give him,—having had, perhaps, more experience than he, that we had passed the Gate House, and reached the Minor Canon's almost before we knew it. I stopped a moment there, and, after a little further conversation, during which I had made him promise that if any thing like misfortune should overtake him as time passed on, he should communicate with me, that I might be of service to him, we finally shook hands, and, bidding each other farewell, he entered the house, and I turned in the direction of Jack's lodgings. The rain had ceased falling then, but the wind blew a perfect hurricane, and, muffling my coat-collar about my face to protect myself from the blast, I walked briskly forward, and was just in front of the Cathedral, when I realized that I had been struck a terrible blow upon my head. It was only an instantaneous realization, however, for I staggered and fell in an unconscious state, and remembered nothing further till I found myself in a close apartment—the sides, top and bottom being all stone—and, had I not recognized a familiar face, I should certainly have thought this to be my tomb, and should not have been surprised to have found myself enveloped in a shroud. The individual who was present saw that I was conscious of what was going on about me, and took a bottle from his pocket, which he held to my lips, telling me to take a good long draught. I did so, and in a few moments had recovered so far as to remember the stinging blow that I had received before consciousness left me, and I had good cause to remember it, too, for I became gradually sensible of great pain in my head, and, when attempting to get upon my feet was so weak that I could not do so. I sank back again upon the bed which my companion had improvised, which consisted of a woolen blanket spread upon the floor and an old coat for a pillow. As I lay back again upon the pillow, my companion addressed me, saying:

"''Taint often as Durdles has to do the doctors' work for 'em in this here way. They don't generally leave anything for Durdles to work on except their tomb-stones. If Durdles gits you out of this here fix, he's goin' to put a sign out, and have it read—Durdles, Stone-mason and Physician. Yer see I'll have this advantage over the professional chaps, that if Durdles' patients dies, he knows how to put 'em in a snug place; but when theirs knock off the handle they have to come to Durdles after all; so comin' to Durdles fust will save 'em some trouble at last.'

"Of course, I did not understand the man's words; and whispered —for I was so weak that I could not speak a loud word—I whispered, and asked him to tell me where I was and what all this unusual state of things meant.

"He held his forefinger close to my face, and shaking it in a slow and impressive manner, asked me if I had got so far recovered as to remember Mr. Jasper. I owned that I remembered him perfectly.

"'Very good,' he answers; 'it's all along of that there worthy as you finds yerself here.'

"The man then proceeded to tell me, in his peculiar phraseology, but which I will not attempt, how it all came about that I was in such a place, while the man, whom I had supposed loved me as he would his own brother, had every reason to believe himself my murderer.

"It appeared that Durdles, who is a rather eccentric person, and spends the greater part of his nights in the open air, took it into his head, on this particular night, to see if the violence of the gale would injure the great tower of the Cathedral, and had stationed himself in a safe position to witness a catastrophe, should one occur. He had no idea of the time that had elapsed while he waited there, but admitted that, feeling a little chilled, he took a pretty good quantity of a certain liquid that he carried with him, and which must have caused him to fall asleep. On returning to a conscious state, the first thing that he heard was the sound of approaching footsteps, and just as the footsteps had reached the place where he lay concealed, and after they had gone a little beyond, he perceived the form of another person hurry past him with the greatest speed, and when passing him he distinctly heard the person mutter—'He would not be warned; God help him!'

"The next thing that he heard was a heavy blow and, a moment after, a sound as of some one falling to the ground, and then all was still again. His first impulse was to hasten from the place of his concealment, and learn what it all meant, but he had scarcely thought of doing so when he heard footsteps, and became aware that some one was apparently making efforts to drag some heavy body towards where he lay, so he kept still and waited to see the end of this singular affair. He had not long to wait, for in a moment, and just as the storm clouds were parted for an instant, so that the moon's rays rendered objects visible, he discerned the features of my uncle Jack, and saw that he was dragging me towards the church-yard.

"Waiting till he could safely do so, Durdles followed cautiously after, and, crouching behind a stone to escape detection, watched the proceedings.

"Dragging me along with all the haste that was possible, Jack finally reached the monument which belongs to a Mr. Sapsea, and which had only a few days before been the scene of Mr. Durdles' labors—he having placed an inscription thereon. On gaining this spot, Jack took from his pocket a key and, unfastening a door which opened the tomb, he dragged me inside, where he left me, and then, locking the door of the vault, took himself off with rapid steps, leaving Mr. Durdles the most astonished man in Cloisterham."

"In Heaven's name," interrupts Peckcraft, "was Mr. Jasper crazy, that caused him to do such a strange deed as this?"

"Patience, sir," replies Edwin, "you shall learn the cause as I proceed."

"And before you proceed further," interrupts Datchery, "if agreeable, I propose that we order a rum punch to strengthen our stomachs, for I believe that Mr. Peckcraft, more especially, will stand in need of something strengthening and cheering to counteract the effect which I know the balance of this narrative will have upon his nerves—not to say temper."

No objection being raised to this proposal, the punch was ordered, and in a few moments a tray, on which was deposited glasses and a good sized bowl of steaming punch, was brought in, and Mr. Datchery proceeded to dish out the glasses. After the health of each had been drank, and an extra one to the health of Durdles, they were ready to listen once more to the narrative, and Edwin continued:

"Durdles thought it a little strange that Mr. Jasper had in his possession a key which gave him access to this tomb, for there was but one that he had ever seen or knew of, and that one belonged to Mr. Sapsea, and was at that moment in the pocket of Durdles.

"Waiting a little time, until he was satisfied that Mr. Jasper had really left the neighbourhood, Durdles entered the tomb, and found me still unconscious. He was satisfied that the man who had placed me there intended that I should die there, and he decided to remove me to a place where I should be safe from further harm, and, if he succeeded in saving my life, to tell me what he had seen and done, and leave the rest with me. Perceiving that my coat and waistcoat were both gone, I learned that Jack had taken them away. I cared nothing for the loss of the clothing, but the waistcoat pocket held a locket containing Rosa's picture, and a ring that I was to carry to London the next morning, and place in the hands of Rosa's guardian, the loss of which caused me great distress.

"For the knowledge of my uncle's further proceedings after he had left me a prisoner, Mr. Durdles was indebted to a boy who is known as Deputy, whose business it was,—a special contract having been made months before,—to stone Mr. Durdles home when he was so far gone with intoxication as not to know enough to go unless reminded. So it chanced that on the night in question the boy had been watching and waiting for his employer to get on his feet and be stoned, when *he* also became a witness of Jack's proceedings. With a cunning natural to him, he waited till my uncle had turned to leave the church-yard, and then followed him.

"Keeping as near to him as he safely could, and not be discovered, this boy kept Jack in sight, who, after continuing his way along the western end of the Cathedral, turned in that way, and entered a side-door, leading to the crypt. Most boys of Deputy's years would have been too timid to follow further, but this boy had pluck; and, furthermore, from being so often in Durdles' company, had a thorough knowledge of all the intricacies connected with the place.

"On entering the crypt, Jack's first proceeding was to light a lantern; and, as he threw its rays in every direction, to assure himself that he was not observed, the boy was obliged to be extremely cautious lest he should be detected. Evidently feeling secure from observation, Jack made his way, with great caution, to a part of the crypt which Mr. Durdles says, has not been used since he can remember, and probably not for a century. On reaching the spot, my uncle placed his lantern on the ground, and displacing some litter or loose earth which had concealed it, raised a stone slab, disclosing a vault beneath. This done, he proceeded to remove from the pockets of the clothing which he had taken from me, everything of value; then dropping the clothes into the vault, he replaced the slab, scraped the loose earth over it again, and made his way out of the crypt as he had entered it, Deputy still following, having taken the precaution to notice certain objects which would serve as guides to help him to find the spot again.

Still keeping Jack in sight, the boy followed him from the Cathedral to the Weir, where he saw him throw something into the water; then, hastily retracing his steps, he proceeded directly to the Gate House, and ascending the postern stair, was seen no more that night.

The boy then made his way back to the Cathedral, in search of Durdles, whom he met just as that person had started for his home to obtain some few articles which he thought I should stand in need of.

"The boy related to Durdles what he had seen; when the latter charged him to say nothing of the occurrence, and promised he should be well rewarded. As soon as I had recovered from the effect of the assault, I was informed of the whole particulars, and thinking it would be a good plan to let this precious uncle of mine believe that he had succeeded in his villainy, I charged Durdles to say nothing of the occurrence, but to feign total ignorance of what he knew, and gave him a slight idea of a plan I had formed for punishing, far more than any legal measure could, the guilty man.

"Still another object I had in thus deciding was to learn, from observation, what could be my uncle's motive in this attempt to put an end to my life. Of course he had a motive, or he never would have undertaken such a cold-blooded act, and I felt sure that I could best learn motive by observing how he would proceed now that he supposed me dead.

I had instructed Durdles to obtain for me a suit of rough clothing as a disguise, and, after donning this apparel, what with Durdles's cutting my hair short, and using a preparation that would give my face a darker colour, I felt that I should be pretty safe from being identified by Jack, should I happen to meet him. We then left the place of my concealment, and proceeded directly to the Crozier, where I engaged lodgings for an indefinite period. There I remained, watching Jack at such times as I thought I could glean anything of his purpose, and after a few weeks became satisfied that the rascal's object was to get rid of me, that he might make love to Rosa. I was so angry when I first discovered this, that I was determined to wait no longer, but present myself before him, and accuse him of the damnable treachery of which he had been guilty. The very day that I had decided on for carrying out my plan, Durdles came to me and said that a gentleman who had been wronged by Mr. Jasper, was stopping at Cloisterham, and as he felt sure that the said gentleman could be of service to me, he (Durdles) had returned the confidence reposed in him by this gentleman, and had confided to him my place of concealment; and, if I would like to see him, he would call on me within an hour. As I could see no harm that would arise from an interview with the stranger, I consented, and as a consequence this gentleman"—motioning Datchery—"and I have become the best of friends.

"I told Mr. Datchery what I proposed to do, and, after telling me the wrongs he had suffered at Jack's hands, he begged that I would be patient and wait a little before I revealed myself. I consented, and have not regretted it, for I believe my uncle has suffered far more than he would, had I shown myself at that time."

Edwin ceased, and for a moment each was silent. Datchery waited for Mr. Peckcraft to speak, but the latter had become so absorbed in the narrative, that he was hardly aware that it was finished. Furthermore, Mr. Peckcraft, from doing everything in a methodical manner, had allowed his mind to pass through various stages of excitement, during the past two hours, until it had attained a fiery heat, and from clenching his hand and holding it before his face, he had got to placing it against his nose, and withdrawing it to repeat the operation, in a very suggestive manner; and it was evident that, had Mr. Peckcraft's nose really been John Jasper's, the eyes above them might have seen, if they did not resemble shining lights. Seeing him thus abstracted causes Mr. Datchery to enquire:

"How do you find yourself now, dear sir?"

Thus interrogated, Mr. Peckcraft manages to find words, and replies:

"I find myself wondering how a man, holding the relations which Mr. Jasper held to this boy, could be so thoroughly depraved as to attempt such an atrocious piece of villainy as that to which I have just listened. But," he added, rising from his chair, and approaching Edwin, "let us shake hands in congratulation of your narrow escape, my boy," and shakes hands with Edwin, and then with Mr. Datchery and then they are seated again, while the latter once more addresses the old gentleman:

"Do you suppose, Mr. Peckcraft, that you could have patience to listen to the recital of another piece of that rascal's villainy, which will match the one you have just heard, only that it is of a little different character?"

There being a few swallows of punch left in Mr. Peckcraft's glass, he proceeds to dispose of it, and then makes answer:

"I don't suppose I can *lose* any more patience, for I have lost all I had while sitting here, and I am prepared to hear anything bad about this man now that can be told of him. If agreeable, please relate the wrongs he has done you, and be assured you have my sympathies beforehand."

Thereupon, Mr. Datchery observes that the punch will hold out to afford them another glassful all round, though it's a little cold; but, after he had finished his story, they would order in another bowl, and so start fresh, the better to help them in determining the course they should pursue looking to John Jasper's punishment. While thus speaking, he was engaged in dealing out the remaining punch, and, this done, they are once more seated and listening to the story of Mr. Datchery's wrongs, and with which the reader is already familiar, and finished by telling them the child was now in Cloisterham.

"I left her but a few hours since," he adds, "or rather I left the house where she has found a home and friends, but did not dare trust myself to see her, fearing that should she resemble my dead sister—her mother—the sight of her would so far make me forget myself, that I should seek Jasper instantly and tear him to pieces!"

"And very natural—though, between ourselves, a little bloodthirsty—such feelings are to be sure," rejoins Mr. Peckcraft, in a soothing tone. "But it don't benefit any body in the end for a man to take the law into his own hands, however much we may think to the contrary when our blood's up. Nine times out of ten the guilty wretch has sympathy, while his victim, the really innocent man, is condemned and regarded by society as the worst of the two."

"And do you suppose that I will be satisfied with any punishment that the law, whose wheels turn backward or forward with the heaviest purse of gold, may inflict on this man?" asks Datchery, in a tone of indignation.

"My dear sir," answers Mr. Peckcraft mildly, "I certainly did think there was no other proper course to pursue. Perhaps I am wrong. Pray tell me what you propose as a substitute?"

"I have sworn to have this villain's life," exclaims Datchery, in savage tones, and smiting his hands, "and, by heaven, I will! I have abstained from laying hands on him, and have controlled my feelings, all this time, because I wanted to kill him by piecemeal! I wanted to worry him and torment him, as does a dog the rat he has in his power, before I dealt the fatal blow which would end his miserable career!"

In his excitement the speaker has paced the room with rapid step; but after a little he is calmer, and Mr. Peckcraft, in a tone of sympathy, replies:

"I honor you, Mr. Datchery, for your devotion to your dead sister. As I said before, your feelings are natural, because they are produced by the excitement caused by the memory of that sister's wrongs; but when the excitement has subsided, when you realize that the blood of this man, on your hands, will not bring your sister back to life, but will, on the contrary, bring your own within the pale of the gallows, you will agree with me, that I am correct in saying that his punishment should be inflicted by the same power that provided a penalty for his crimes."

"Pardon me, Mr. Peckcraft," rejoins Datchery, in a tone of sadness, as he takes the other's hand. "Pardon me, if I have appeared rude, or, in my excitement, have said aught to wound your feelings. I do not doubt you mean kindly by counseling a legitimate punishment for this wretch's misdoings, but I shall never be able to agree with you, or change my plans concerning him in any particular. I shall revenge my sister's wrongs with my own hands. No, my darling Bess," he cried, and raising his eyes Heavenward, "I will avenge your wrongs! By the memory of your infant face, that smiled upon me from the cradle; by the memory of your girlhood's sunny days, when all the world was a garden spread out before your fancy; by the memory of that kiss of sisterly love and affection which your dear lips imprinted on mine, when last we parted; by the memory of that Heaven-born gift, a sister's love, and, more than all, by the memory of your maiden honor, I *swear* that this man's life shall end by my hands, *unless the Almighty shall interpose some obstacle!*"

The earnestness with which Mr. Datchery delivered these words, convinced his hearer that any further attempt to turn him from his purpose, would prove futile; so, after a short silence, Mr. Peckcraft said:

"I will not continue the subject, sir, for it is plain that nothing can turn you; but I must emphatically decline to assist in any way, towards the accomplishment of what I deem,—pardon the word,—a crime."

"Nor shall I ask your assistance," answers Datchery, "or that of any living creature; nor would I part with one jot of my vengeance under any circumstances; I will perform that work alone, asking the assistance of no man. Our friend here," pointing to Edwin, "sent for you on business exclusively pertaining to his own affairs, and I only wait for that to be finished, before balancing my account. I will leave you alone together now, that you may make such arrangements as you see fit, having that end in view, and Mr. Drood can follow me at his leisure. I thank you for your counsel, and appreciate your kindness and sympathy, but my work is before me. I have sworn to accomplish it, and trust you will not betray the confidence I have reposed in you."

"Rest assured, sir," is Mr. Peckcraft's reply, "that I do sympathize with you deeply, and will never do aught which shall prove an injury to you."

And thus avoiding a direct promise to the other's request, the two shake hands cordially, and Datchery returns to the Gate House, telling Edwin, at parting, that he shall expect him in an hour.

Being thus left to themselves, Edwin proceeded to give Mr. Peckcraft the details of the service he wished that gentleman to perform on his behalf. The principal thing was to obtain from Jasper certain papers and memoranda connected with his guardianship of Edwin. Besides this, he was to inform Jasper that he was in the land of the living, and not far from Cloisterham. "I do not think," remarked Edwin, "that he will be greatly surprised to learn that I am alive, for I have every reason to believe that he is certain of that now, but I think he will be astonished when he learns that I am so near him." He then instructed the old gentleman on other points connected with the intended inteview with Jasper, all of which will transpire in another chapter.

As it was now midnight, and there being nothing more of importance to communicate, Edwin took leave of his old friend, promising to see him the next day.

When Mr. Peckcraft had put on his night-cap that night, and put himself into bed, the strange bed-room and the strange stories he had heard, set him to thinking of the time, when a boy, he had read a book filled with stories of fiction, but not one of which was, in his opinion, more remarkable, taken all in all, than this Cloisterham Night's Entertainment.

CHAPTER XXXVIII.

MR. PECKCRAFT'S INTERVIEW WITH JASPER FORCES THE LATTER TO A DETERMINATION, BUT WHICH HE CHANGES ON ACCOUNT OF A DETERMINATION ON THE PART OF MR. FOPPERTY PADLER.

The Almighty has wisely ordained that great calamities shall not come suddenly and without warning upon his children, and hence, on the eve of some terrible misfortune or distressing intelligence, we have a foreboding of evil, which prepares us the better to bear the shock, as the mariner, before a storm, takes in his sails and prepares his vessel in advance for the coming tempest.

On that same night, when the scene at the Crozier Inn, as described in the previous chapter, was taking place, John Jasper was seated alone in his lodgings, with a foreboding of evil upon him which he could not shake off, try as hard as he would.

His frequent trips to London have ceased since his last interview with Mr. Grewgious concerning Rosa's abduction, and he has settled into a state of melancholy and despair, which he cannot drive away.

In consequence of this depressed state of mind, he has almost constant recourse to the use of opium; and the pale, haggard face, the sunken eyes, and the black circle about them, tell what terrible havoc the drug is having upon him, mentally and physically.

He has smoked, to-night, almost incessantly, but has only succeeded in bringing himself to that nervous condition which produces still darker forebodings of evil; hence his mental sufferings are intense. At last he starts in his chair like a man who has just been roused from some fearful nightmare, and gazing eagerly about the room, as though expecting to behold some dread phantom, leans back in his chair again, and mutters:

"Merciful God! am I to suffer thus forever more? Is there to be no end? Shall I have no rest except in the grave? Pshaw! John Jasper, you are a fool to think of graves so soon!" He presses his hands to his head as he ceases; then starts suddenly from his chair, and paces the room, with moody brow. "But what can this shadow be," he continues, "that haunts me by night and day? I would not mind it through the day, if it would keep away at night. One good night's sleep would recompense me for a week of tortures, but even that is denied me. Since that day when I learned that my nephew was not in the tomb of that egotistic fool, where I supposed him until then, I have rested easy, knowing that, in all probability, he was living, and I not a—well, that's the word—murderer. But where is he? Ah! that's it. Could I but see him, and have one hour's conversation with him, I think I could die willingly. I must leave Cloisterham. I'll go to-morrow. I don't know why I've delayed so long."

He threw himself into a chair as he ceased speaking, and appeared to meditate; at last he broke out again:

"To-morrow, farewell Cloisterham! Happy thought! why have I not considered it before. In some town far removed, among other scenes and faces, I'll soon forget the misery of the past year, and be a man again. My profession will give me support, go where I will, and, if necessary, I can assume another name. But what," he asks, interrupting the current of his thoughts, as he once more places his hands to his head, while his eyes have a wild look; "what is this strange sensation which I feel at times, that it seems as though moulten lead were being poured upon my brain? I cannot understand it. It must be that I need sleep." He looks at his watch, and ejaculates: "Just midnight. Well," he adds, in a weary tone, "I'll get me to bed and try to sleep." He takes the candle in his hand, and ascends to his sleeping-room. He is soon disrobed, and, extinguishing the light, throws himself upon the bed, and buries his face in his hands, as though dreading to encounter some fearful object. Hour after hour, he turns and tosses in a restless manner, perspiring from every pore and wishing for the light of day, for he then can sleep. So as daylight comes, and the first rays of morning enable him to discern surrounding objects, the miserable man forgets his sufferings for a little time, and just when Cloisterham is rubbing its eyes open, and preparing for another day of care and toil.

The Christmas holidays have come again, and on this particular morning the sun never shone brighter, nor the air, with its frosty, bracing touch, never seemed more invigorating than it does to-day. Still the wretched man sleeps on—a fitful, feverish sleep, it is true, but, nevertheless, to him most welcome. Thus sleeping, he has a vision. He seems to be walking in a peaceful, pleasant lane, and hears the birds sweetly carolling in the branches of the trees which overhang the road on either side. On reaching a certain point in the lane, he beholds a terrible Creature near him, whose like he had never before seen, and which seemed to be awaiting his approach. On reaching this object, he discerns, lying upon the ground near by, his nephew, Edwin Drood, apparently asleep and unconscious of his presence. As he gazes upon the sleeping form, the Creature opens its mouth, and, in a sweet, musical voice—so different from what he had expected to hear from such a horrible object—says: "Be sure and crush him as you pass. He only is the one that lies between you and earthly happiness." Then the creature places in his hand a ponderous club and points at the sleeping man. The dreamer acts upon the advice of the Creature, and, with one blow, crushes the skull of the sleeping man where he lay. Then, without stopping to look at his victim the second time, he hurries from the spot. A few moments after, his ears are greeted with a mocking laugh, and, on turning to perceive from whence it comes, he discovers by his side the Creature who had prompted him to do the dreadful deed. While he gazes upon it, the face seems to change, and gradually assumes the features of his fellow-lodger, Mr. Datchery.

With a shriek, he bounds from the bed, covered with perspiration and trembling from head to foot, and, when fully conscious, the first sound that greets his ear is a succession of double-knocks at his sitting-room door below stairs.

Trembling with doubt and fear as to the purpose which a visitor may have in thus summoning him at so early an hour, the wretched man hurriedly proceeds to dress himself, and betakes him to the door of his sitting-room.

On opening it, he encounters the person of Tope. That gentleman apologizes for thus disturbing him, but assigns as a cause that a stranger had requested him to show the way to Mr. Jasper's rooms. Thereupon the stranger himself steps forward from the passage where he had been standing during Tope's efforts, and discloses Mr. Peckcraft, who bows in a formal manner, and begs to know if he can have a private interview.

Mr. Jasper does not recognize his visitor, but bids him enter, nevertheless, and Mr. Tope departs, while Mr. Peckcraft enters the room and takes the seat which Jasper proffers him. Though not entirely recovered from his agitation, and, notwithstanding that his face shows signs of present apprehension, Mr. Jasper endeavours to assume a calm exterior, and, after a few common-place remarks, Mr. Peckcraft observes in a careless tone:

"I have not given you my name, as I had a curiosity to know if you would recognize me without it. I see that you do not recognize me, so will help to quicken your memory by informing you that I am Mr. Peckcraft, formerly the partner in business of your deceased brother-in-law, Mr. Drood."

Had John Jasper suddenly beheld Mr. and Mrs. Tope flying above the Gate House, after the sportive manner of martens, he would not have felt or shown any more surprise than he did at this announcement. He sat staring at his visitor, several moments, before uttering a syllable in reply, and then faintly enquired what had brought the gentleman to Cloisterham.

"Oh," is the pleasant rejoinder, "I came to see you."

"And how did you learn that I was here," anxiously enquires Jasper.

"By asking those who knew," is the answer, given in a sharp tone. Before Jasper, who is about to proceed, has an opportunity of speaking, his visitor continues:

"Give me your earnest attention, Mr. Jasper, to what I have to say. You knew me pretty well, some years ago, as being a man who never practiced deception, and who could never beat about the bush, when it was possible to get inside of it. I believe I have not changed materially, during the years since we last met. I have called to see you on a matter that affects you most deeply. Do not interrupt me, I beg," as Jasper makes an attempt to reply; "wait till I have performed the unpleasant business which brought me, and then say what you will.

"I will not ask you," continues Mr. Peckcraft, "where is the son of a dead man, whose interests were intrusted to your hands, and whom you took an oath to watch over and protect during his minority. I do not ask because I want to spare you the sin of a falsehood which you would utter by telling me that you did not know."

Mr. Jasper knits his brow, and, turning suddenly towards his visitor, seems about to make some angry reply, but thinks better of it, and contents himself with tapping his chair in a nervous manner with the tips of his fingers.

"I will only say," Mr. Peckcraft adds, "that I have seen Edwin Drood within the past hour, and that he is alive and well."

If Mr. Peckcraft could have known beforehand what was to be the effect of his last sentence, it is more than probable he would never have uttered it. John Jasper bounds from his chair as though a bullet had pierced his heart, and glares savagely upon the old man before him. Then comes a reaction; his whole frame quivers like an aspen, and he settles back into his chair with a face more colourless than is natural, if possible, and, while perspiration stands in great drops upon his forehead, he buries his face in his hands, and, giving utterance to a low moan that seems to come from a breaking heart, he gasps aloud:

"Oh, my God! My worst fears are realized; I am lost! lost! lost!"

Though greatly disturbed by the miserable man's emotions, Mr. Peckcraft waits for him to recover his composure, and then resumes:

"For your wickedness—for any act of injustice which you have committed against the dead or the living,—which, sooner or later, will bring its own punishment,—I do not come to upbraid you. My errand is of a far different nature. I come to you on behalf of the young man whom you have so deeply wronged, and who, with charity in his heart for your sins, has sent me to warn you of danger which is hanging over you."

The speaker paused for a moment, and the other raised his head as though to speak, but the words died upon his lips, and the old gentleman proceeded:

"I will first transact the business which I am directly interested in. By virtue of certain conditions pertaining to your guardianship, which authorize me to take control of all matters connected therewith, in the event of your proving faithless to your trust, I demand that you place in my hands all papers, memoranda, accounts, and everything of value now in your possession that bear reference to the affairs of Edwin Drood."

It may have been that the knowledge which Mr. Peckcraft had imparted, of Edwin Drood's disposition to forgive his uncle, was why

Mr. Jasper assumed a far different air from that which he had shown at the beginning of this interview. Apparently self-possessed now, and carrying withal a look of defiance on his features, he advances to a secretary as the old gentleman finished speaking, and took therefrom a package, which he handed his visitor, saying:

"You will find the desired documents here, sir; anticipating some such visit as this a long time since, I collected them into one parcel, and as all necessary explanations are given in writing, there will be no occasion for us to go over them."

Mr. Peckcraft places the package in his pocket, coolly thanking the other meanwhile, and then, after a brief silence, resumes:

"As I was saying, Mr. Jasper, your nephew desired me to come to you on his behalf, as he felt it his duty to warn you of impending evil. He knew it would not be pleasant to your feelings, nor to his, to come himself; and, possessing the noble spirit of his father, he has overlooked the wrongs you have done him, and wishes you to have time to repent, and be a better man before you die. So please consider that it is *him* who addresses you now and not me, for, I tell you plainly, could I have my way, you should be transported before you were a month older."

This seems to nettle Mr. Jasper not a little, and, opening his eyes quite wide as he gazes at the speaker, he ejaculates, in a sarcastic tone:

"Indeed?"

Mr. Peckcraft, without noticing this, however, proceeds:

"Your nephew pities you, and would have you repent and be a better man, before you are brought to that bar before whom we must all come, judged by a Judge whom no cunning barrister can influence by specious arguments; a Judge in whose heart equity is as firmly fixed as the stars in the firmament,—in whose sight all men are equal,—and who, having the power to read the inmost thoughts of men's hearts, can never err in His judgments."

The heart of Jasper is touched; he does not utter one word, however, but seems content to hear the other out without interruption. So, after a moment, Peckcraft continues:

"I have come to warn you that your life is in danger, and that you had better go away from here to some quiet place, where you are unknown, and devote the balance of your life to repentance, that God will forgive you the dreadful sins which you have committed. You had better go as soon as possible; do not delay an hour. I warn you that if you do not take my advice in this, you will be a dead man before another sun rises!"

This was something that Jasper had not anticipated,—danger to his own life,—and he is evidently incredulous, for he replies in a scornful tone:

"Do you think me a child, then, to be easily frightened with such absurd statements as these?"

Mr. Peckcraft is not disturbed by this manifest doubt on the part of the Music Master, but mildly returns:

"I beg that you will not impute to me a wish to deceive you, Mr. Jasper. Surely a knowledge of your own deeds should warn you that there is a possibility of the danger to you I have mentioned; and when you reflect that your nephew can have no motive but that of a friendly one in thus advising you, you must see the importance of acting upon that advice. Is it not better for you to seek some distant spot, where you will be safe from those who may be disposed to inflict upon you legal punishment for the acts you have been guilty of, than to remain and suffer in consequence?"

"You talk in riddles, sir," is Jasper's answer, given in a careless tone, and turning to look out of window at some passing object, the better to impress Mr. Peckcraft with the unconcern he felt. "Pray, will you please inform me what the crime you mention consists of?"

Mr. Peckcraft's better feeling leaves him at this display of callousness on the part of Jasper, and rising from his chair, he walks to where Jasper is seated, and standing before him with a dignified mien, and in a voice of sternness, answers:

"John Jasper, I came here to-day to save you trouble, and to advise you, for your own sake, of the danger which threatens you. I told you at the start that I did not wish to utter one word that would be unpleasant for you to hear. I should not have done so, but the contempt with which you receive the advice I have offered, and the thorough depravity which you display, convinces me that you are unworthy of any respect, and that it is no mercy to spare your feelings. Where is Edwin Drood?"

"Really," is the reply, given with a pleasant smile, "who should know that so well as you, since, as you said a moment before, you have seen him within an hour?"

"And who should know so well as you, John Jasper," continues the old gentleman, now thoroughly excited, "that had the attempt upon his life, made a little less than a year ago, succeeded, that you would have sat here to-day, a murderer!"

"Liar!" thundered Jasper, rising from his chair, and trembling with rage; "Ha, ha! I can see through the plot now, which you and my precious nephew have contrived between you to ruin me, because I revealed my love to Miss Bud, when I supposed he had deserted her and all of us, by taking himself off, nobody knew whence. But you shall be made to suffer for this abuse, sir. You forget that there is not one particle of proof to warrant you in making such a base charge as this against me."

"As for your epithet, Mr. Jasper," replies the old gentleman calmly, "I will only say that such language is worthy of the man who uttered it! But let me assure you that what I have said can be easier proven than you are aware of."

"Another lie!" retorts Jasper, "as base as the first."

"If any evidence is necessary," continues the other, without noticing the interruption, "to convict you of the attempt upon your nephew's life, it is ample, and that you may be sure of. I do not care to wrangle with you, however; only disregard the warning I have given you, and you shall be convinced. A few words more, and I will leave you: Edwin Drood lives, notwithstanding your efforts to the contrary. He does not wish that you should be harmed for the wrong you did him. He desired me to ask of you to instantly depart from this place, as I have before suggested; for, though he could never forgive you, he could not forget that you were the same flesh and blood of the mother who bore him, and he would not have you become a victim to the revengeful powers of a man who has sworn to have your life. Oh, you may smile, but you will learn that there is truth in every word I utter. Edwin Drood lives, thank God! but the woman whose innocence you took advantage of, years ago, and the price of whose love for you was death, had a brother who is nearer to you at this moment than you think; while the child—your child—the fruit of your unholy passion, is here also—receiving the love and care of strangers, which it was your duty to bestow upon her, but which you have neglected to do, because you possess a cruel heart, and are so thoroughly selfish that, in my opinion, you would see your own mother starve before you would trouble yourself to prevent it!"

The speaker steps to the piano, where his hat has been placed, and, taking it in his hand, moves towards the door, and, with his hand upon the latch, concludes what he has to say:

"Notwithstanding your insolence, I cannot leave you without once more urging upon you that your safety lies in leaving Cloisterham at once. I hope you will profit by what I have said. You cannot overcome the perils by which you are surrounded except by instant flight. Heed my words," concludes the old gentleman, raising his hand in an impressive manner, "and delay not; within two hours the brother of the woman you so foully wronged years ago, will stand before you; and then, God help you, miserable man!"

He leaves the room as he closes the sentence, leaving Jasper gazing upon the spot where he had stood, and inwardly repeating the parting words, "God help you, miserable man!"

He rises from his chair, repeating dreamily the words, which seem to cling to his memory above everything else. He consults his watch, and finds it most time for morning service. His mind still intent upon the fact that morning service is near at hand, he is startled by hearing a knock at his door, and is undecided whether to open it or not. What if it were the brother, come to carry out the horrid design of which Mr. Peckcraft had warned him! He does not stir to answer the knock, but sits, trembling with fear and distrust, until the knock is repeated, and then he recognizes it as Tope's, and hastens to answer the summons. He discovers Tope, as he expected, who hands him a sealed note, and, declining Jasper's invitation to enter and sit with him a while, takes his departure. On reaching an angle in the passage, just as Jasper is studying the handwriting to ascertain, if possible, who was the writer, Tope stops, and peeping curiously at the Music Master, shakes his head in a mournful manner, and mutters: "Whatever it is, I don't know. My orders is to not let him inside the Cathedral again, and I hope he wont try to see if I'll obey 'em, because, being the Verger, and expected to do the heavy work, I should feel it my duty to obey orders, and poor Mr. Jasper would make it wus for himself. But whatever is it all about?"

Meantime Jasper has entered his room, closed the door, and, seated in a chair, is reading the message just brought him, which is as follows:

MR. JASPER—*Sir:* It is my duty to inform you that, acting under the advice of the Dean, and being also painfully aware of facts that warrant me in writing this, I have to inform you that your services as Choir Leader in Cloisterham Cathedral will cease on and after this date, and you will please govern yourself accordingly. You will please communicate by letter the amount due you, and it will be paid forthwith. I have a decided objection to any personal interview.

I am, sir,

SEPTIMUS CRISPARKLE.

Could he have read aright? It cannot be that the Minor Canon has addressed such a letter as this to him. Yet here is the Minor Canon's handwriting. He is not deceived in that. He reads the note the second time, and then it drops from his hand, while he falls to meditating as to the course he must pursue. He rises suddenly from his chair, as though to carry out some plan which had just presented itself, and ascends to his sleeping-room.

Seating himself at a table, he proceeds to pen a few lines addressed to Mrs. Tope, stating that he is going to London and will not return for several days. She is to take good care of his effects during his stay, and need not be surprised should he not return for several weeks.

Should he not return in one week, she is to consider his apartments as vacated, and can let them to other parties if she desires, and is to keep what he leaves in the way of personal effects till he comes or sends for them. This last she is to do as a special favor to him. Then placing a few articles of wardrobe in a small travelling bag, he arranges his toilet, and, placing the note where it will be seen by the Verger's wife, puts on his hat, and, with carpet-bag in hand, descends to his sitting-room, casts one look of mingled love, hate, and despair upon the picture of Rosa as it hangs there in its old place upon the wall, and quits the room which has been to him an abode of happiness and misery combined, but which will know him no more from this time forth.

He descends by the postern stair, and proceeds cautiously and with soft footsteps, that he may not attract the attention of his fellow-lodgers. Reaching the Gate House entrance, he proceeds in the direction of the water, intending to depart from Cloisterham by that road, as being more retired, and so less likely to meet those who will recognize him.

He turns his head every few moments, as though he felt that he was being watched, and then quickens his steps, changing the travelling-bag from one hand to the other in a nervous manner.

He meets a number of people before he turns off from the High Street, and it may be imagination, but he fancies they turn out for him, and seem to fear lest they should brush against him as they passed. Once or twice he turns to look after those he passes, and they are always looking back after him, as if he were an object of special interest to them. As he is about turning into a narrow thoroughfare from off the High Street, he is seized with a desire to view once more the old gray towers of the Cathedral, under whose shadow he has dwelt for so long a time; so stops for a moment, for that purpose, before proceeding further on the road which will hide it from his gaze. While he is thus occupied, and just as he is about to turn away, a hand is laid upon his shoulder, and so suddenly that he starts and turns pale with surprise and terror. He recovers in an instant, however, for he recognizes Fopperty Padler, to whom he says:

"Fopperty, you really startled me. I am leaving Cloisterham for a few days, and I was indulging in some foolish fancies that always come upon me on such occasions, that perhaps I was looking for the last time upon the old Cathedral and its surroundings. It's a long time since I have seen you. How is Bessie?"

The black eyes of the other go out of sight, and the black brows come down. Then the black brows go up to their place, and the black eyes make their appearance, and fasten themselves upon the face of the Music Master, while he makes answer:

"You must not go from Cloisterham quite yet, Mr. Jasper. I was in search of you. You must go with me to a person as wants to look at ye." He lays his hand upon Jasper's arm, as though he meant to enforce his request, should the other decline.

Mr. Jasper wants to know who the "person" is.

"Bessie," is the reply; "she's been very sick, and the doctor says she can't get well; she wants to see ye, and I've come now to fetch ye."

"Your mother is taking care of her, I suppose," is Jasper's rejoinder; "I don't see how it will benefit her, seeing me; I can't make her better, and time with me just now is valuable. I shall return in a few days, and I'll go and see her then."

At this remark, Fopperty's eyes were gone so long behind his eyebrows that Jasper expected to see them appear at the back of his head. They return, however, after a time, and he proceeds to inform his companion that he (Mr. Jasper) will go with him (Mr. Padler) to see the child this blessed minute, or the next blessed minute will see him (Mr. Jasper) with a face upon him that his own mother would not recognize. Not caring to risk an encounter with the irate Fopperty, the Music Master bade him lead the way, which, as he supposed, was at Fopperty's house. He was somewhat astonished when, instead, his companion took him to the house of Uncle Sol Brobity, where, in a few moments, he finds himself waiting for that gentleman to convey him into the presence of his neglected child, who was slowly dying, but happier for knowing it than he could ever be, living or dying.

CHAPTER XXXIX.

WHILE THE DAWN APPEARS TO OTHERS, JASPER'S NIGHT COMES ON.

On that night following the day which had brought such grief to Helena Landless, and sorrow to the hearts of her friends, caused by the untimely taking off of Neville, the Minor Canon departed for Cloisterham, to make such arrangements as had been decided upon for the funeral and burial of the young man. So overcome with sorrow, was

Helena, that she could not bear to speak of the sad ceremony, but left all with the Minor Canon and Mr. Grewgious.

If Mr. Crisparkle had any previous doubt as to the nature of his feelings towards Helena, the sympathy which filled his heart at witnessing her grief, banished all such doubts, and caused him to realize how dear she was to him, and how much his own happiness depended upon hers. Thus it is that the tenderest affections of our nature grope blindly in the dark, until some great misfortune opens the door and throws light upon their pathway.

Doing all in his power to comfort her, and offering such consolation as affection and sympathy can suggest, he leaves her in the tender care of Rosa and her guardian, and being assured by the latter that he will remain with them until he, the Minor Canon, returns, the latter departs with a sad heart, on his homeward journey.

So absorbed with grief was he, that he had entirely forgotten the appointment previously made with the Puffer, and it is probable that he should have returned to Cloisterham without bringing it to mind, had he not been startled by a voice near him, as he was seated in the waiting room, saying "a good evenin' to your Reverence." On looking around to see whose voice it is, he is reminded of the appointment, and as there are several persons seated near him, he rises, and bidding her follow him, leads the way to a more retired spot, and tells her to sit beside him.

"I had entirely forgotten you," he said, after they were seated, "and if you had not made yourself known, should have gone home without you. Have you been long waiting?"

"A good hour," is the reply, "but that's nothing; I'd 'a waited for a whole day out, though, for that matter, and then not been tired, seein' as it's so near the blessed minute, that's to give me my reckonin' with that devil's child up there," pointing in the direction of Cloisterham.

A short silence follows, and then the Minor Canon:

"It surprises me not a little, that you have waited so long before exposing yourself to this man, and taking legal measures to punish him for the wrongs he has done you. Are you quite certain, after all, that you are not mistaken,—that this Mr. Jasper is really the person whom you seek?"

"Lord love ye, deary, do you think there's any mistake with you, that you're the Minor Canon of Cloisterham Cathedral? Mistaken! Do you think I've carried that face in my memory for eight long years, and then didn't know it when I see'd it? I'd good cause to know it, God knows! He'll have good cause to know mine, when I see him next. Curse him! My poor Bess, my poor Bess!" and burying her face in her hands, she sways back and forth, muttering unintelligible words, while tears trickle through her fingers, as she thinks of her dead child. Deeming it prudent to abstain from further reference to the subject, Mr. Crisparkle does not reply; after a short pause, she continues:

"Ye thinks it funny, as I'd not done somethin' before, to punish this man. The punishment I've waited for, is a punishment as the laws can't give me. If I thought now, as the laws would take this punishment out o' my own hands, I'd go back to-night to my hidin' place, and stay eight years longer, or, till I was sure I could deal him the blow with my own hands. Don't prevent me in this, dear sir," she adds, in a beseeching tone. "Don't try to save him. I've been so patient, dear sir, till now, that seein' myself so near the end, and not reachin' it, would make my head a belfrey," she lays her hand upon his arm, and gazes into his face with such a look of mingled entreaty and fear, lest he will throw some obstacle in her way, that he feels it necessary to assure her, that so far from hindering her, he will do all in his power to help her," and telling her that the train is ready, they enter a coach, and are soon steaming off to their destination.

Arriving safely, they proceed to the house of the Minor Canon, who, deeming it important that his mother should be made aware of the presence of the visitor, has the fact of his arrival instantly made known to her; consequently, they have only been in the house a few moments, before the good lady joins them and hastens to give her son a welcome kiss; after which he explains to her the presence of the Puffer, and begs that everything may be done, to make her feel at ease. He then briefly recounts to her the sad news of Neville's death.

If a genuine mantel ornament, in the shape of a China Shepherdess, had its face accidentally sprinkled with water, that China Shepherdess would have been a perfect representation of Mr. Crisparkle's mother on receiving the news of Neville Landless' death, and the wretched condition in which he had left the almost broken-hearted Helena.

"Poor thing!" she ejaculates, "poor thing, I hope it will not kill her. I'll tell you what, Sept.; we must have her come to live with us. I'll be a mother to her, Sept. Perhaps if I tell her so that will help to comfort her, and that she will feel slightly recompensed for the loss of her brother. What do you say, my dear boy? Don't you think this a sensible idea? I'm sure I do, and trust that she will consent to share our home. Poor child, poor child! I only wish I was with her this minute. What do you say, Sept?"

Her expressing a desire to become a mother to Helena had led the Reverend gentleman's thoughts to a future when perhaps she would have a legal claim to that relationship, and he was wondering if the good old lady would feel as willing then, as now, to receive her as a daughter, considering that Helena would hold the first place in his heart, which had so long been filled by this same good mother.

His mother repeats her last sentence, and he returns answer:

"Just like my dear mother, and what can I say, except that I love and honor the noble nature that prompts this suggestion. We will see what can be done. But we need a little rest before the day fairly sets in, and the grey dawn is just breaking; so please show our guest to her room; and, by-the-way, mother, dear, if you have any dress in your wardrobe which will serve for what she now wears, I wish you would place them at her service, for I do not wish that she should be recognized while she remains here. Am I right in this?" addressing the Puffer, who to him replies that she will be satisfied with whatever he thinks best; and then they retire to their different apartments, to obtain that rest which they will stand in need of to enable them to carry out their labours during the day which has dawned upon them.

Two hours sleep satisfies the Minor Canon. Then he hastily proceeds to dress himself, and, without waiting for breakfast, hurries off in the direction of the Gate House. A moment later and he is closeted with Datchery,—Joe Sloggers being absent, as he often is now, killing time in any way he can, and waiting impatiently for the time to arrive when Datchery is prepared to come out boldly and make himself known to Jasper, so that he (Edwin) can make himself known to Rosa.

The object of Mr. Crisparkle in calling upon this gentleman is to inform him that the Puffer is an inmate of his house, and that she is desirous of making her home with a Mrs. Padler, who has her grandchild in trust; whereat Datchery returns answer that the child is not at Mrs. Padlers's now, but is in better hands; that Mr. Brobity has adopted her, and that she now has a good home. Perhaps, he thought, Mr. Brobity could accommodate the Puffer for a short time; at any rate, it would do no harm to enquire. So the Minor Canon hastens to ascertain without delay. Returning to his own house, he finds the Puffer waiting impatiently for him, and, conducting her through a private way at the back of the house, which connected with the High Street, the better to escape observation on the part of Jasper, they are soon at Uncle Sol's door, and being admitted, are in a few moments in earnest conversation with Mr. Brobity.

Explaining to the satisfaction of that gentleman the circumstances which have led to their asking for the old woman a shelter beneath his roof for a short time, he willingly grants the request, and so it is arranged that she is to remain there. She is to be very cautious about going out of doors, lest she may be recognized by Jasper, and Uncle Sol tells her that as a recompense for this deprivation, a stroll in his garden every day will do her good, and she is welcome.

Delighted at the success which had attended this matter, the Minor Canon proceeds to London again that night, and arriving at Miss Keep's, imparts to the expectant ones the particulars of his mission, and that Mr. Datchery desires, as a favour to him and as an act of justice to the dead, that they will postpone the burial in Cloisterham until the man who had been instrumental in Neville's death shall have received the reward he so richly merits; and further stating, that were the burial to take place just at this time, the ends of justice would be likely to suffer defeat.

Aside from some inconvenience which would result from this plan, there could be no serious objection under the circumstances; so it was agreed to by Helena. Thereupon, Mr. Grewgious calls to mind an old acquaintance in the undertaking way who can help him in this matter, and to him he applies. Within the next two days the body of Neville Landless has been deposited in a London receiving tomb, and by the advice of both Grewgious and the Minor Canon, Rosa and Helena proceed to Cloisterham,—arriving at night to avoid observation,—where they intend to remain until such time as the body of Neville can be placed in the church-yard of Cloisterham Cathedral.

After the Puffer had taken up her abode in the house of Uncle Sol, Bessie,—who had instantly recognized her as the person whom she had met in the street some months before, and for whom she had at that time conceived an affection which she could not explain,—took great delight in passing many an hour daily in her society.

As the summer passed away and cold weather came on, Uncle Sol could not disguise from himself the fact that the child was failing in health, and her visits to the garden became less frequent. She was forced to content herself with gazing upon her pets from the window; and when she did not accompany him, Uncle Sol would bring her a bouquet to recompense her for the disappointment.

She was never happier than when the Puffer would come and sit with her and talk with her about her mother, and tell her how much she looked like her when a child, before troubles came upon them,—though she was always careful to suppress from her the nature of those troubles.

If the child had, at such times as these, a desire to know something of her father, that desire was never mentioned, nor did her grandmother ever allude to him. Perhaps an intuitive feeling that the subject would cause pain, was the reason why both had refrained from mentioning it. At all events, it was never spoken of.

On the night preceding the morning when John Jasper was called upon by Mr. Peckcraft, Bessie was seated in her room, in company with Uncle Sol, his mother, and the Puffer. The child had complained more than usual through the day of a terrible pain through her chest, and had experienced great difficulty in breathing. The doctor had been summoned, and had given her such relief as was in his power; but, when he took his leave, beckoned Uncle Sol to follow him, and confided to the old gentleman the alarming intelligence that the child was in a dangerous condition, and that no earthly power could save her. She might, he said, live many weeks, or she might drop away within an hour. At the best, her time was short, and they need not be surprised if her death should occur at any moment. Nearly distracted at what he had heard, Uncle Sol did not return to the child's room for quite a little time; he did not wish that she should know, by reading in his face, the anxiety that he felt in consequence of this sad intelligence. After a little, however, he re-entered the room, and, assuming a cheerful expression, spoke encouragingly of her recovery, telling her how happy they would be when the flowers had blossomed, and they should take their rambles amongst them as in days past.

The child did not reply, but sat gazing from the window as though she did not hear his words.

He turns to look upon her as he ceases speaking, and observes that her eyes are fixed intent upon the blue sky, as though she were striving to behold Heaven's gate above and beyond the ethereal curtain which hides it from mortal view. She sits so still and is so intent upon her thoughts, wherever they may be, that he is alarmed, and is about to take her hand just as she turns her face to his. He observes that her eyes are filled with tears, and asks her if she did not hear his last remark, and she replies:

"Dear Uncle Sol, do not attempt to build up hopes for me that can never be realized. It is not that I am ungrateful to you for thus striving to encourage me with a prospect of happy days in future; it is not that the kind heart which is striving to hide from me the danger that is so soon to fall upon me is unappreciated. Oh, no; it is because I want you to know that I am not afraid to die. I welcome death, as I would deliverance from a cell where I had been confined from all my friends. Why, Uncle Sol," she exclaims, a heavenly light shining in her eyes as she clasps her hands with an ecstatic impulse; "only think of it! I am going to see darling mother. She'll come to meet me. She'll fold me in her arms, and I shall feel her dear kisses on my lips, as I often do in my dreams, and never leave her again. Oh, Uncle Sol, who would *not* die to realize such bliss as that will be to me?"

Smothering the sobs that rend his breast, and hastily wiping away the tears that fall down his face, the old man begs that she will not talk of dying—she will live many years yet—he knows she will. They will have many a merry run in the garden in years to come, and she will laugh, then, to think how near she once thought herself to Death's door.

Bess shakes her head sadly and murmurs: "It can never be, Uncle Sol! We have watched and tended our pets together for the last time; and it is better so. In the world to which I am going, you will also go. It is our Creator's wish that I go first—only that difference—but the same in the end; you will come some time. When I'm gone, Uncle Sol, remember this—that, while you are watching and caring for the little garden yonder, I'll plant a garden there," pointing upwards, "whose flowers shall bloom perpetually—whose fragrance no earthly plant can equal, and whose colours are beyond compare. I'll devote every moment to that Heavenly garden, Uncle Sol, so that it may delight you with its wondrous beauty, in return for the happiness you have bestowed upon a poor, friendless little girl, when you permitted her to share this earthly garden with you. You'll deserve it, Uncle Sol; so I know I shall be permitted to do this. Noble souls, like you, will be doubly welcomed there, and by no one will you receive more welcome than from this unfortunate little girl who feels her life fast leaving her, and who throws her arms about your neck, and kisses your dear, good face."

He folds her in his arms when she leaves her chair and comes towards him, and thus they sit in silence for several minutes.

The only one, since her mother's death, that she ever loved, he is the idol of her heart for his kindness to her, as she is the idol of his for her affection and dependence upon him for what little she had enjoyed during her short life.

After a brief silence, Uncle Sol asks her if she has really no dread of death.

"I do not fear to die," is the reply, in a tone of calmness. "True, I have sometimes wondered if the way was long that would lead to where dear mother stood awaiting me, and have thought at such times that I would like to hold some loving hand in mine till I had reached the spot where she stood; but, when I remember that, after I have slept I wake and see the light at once, and recognize the friends about me, I gather courage again and have no fear that I shall not find a shining light to guide me safely on."

Thus they continue to converse until the night comes, and now she is surrounded by Uncle Sol, his mother and the Puffer. She had come to feel so weak as night approached, that she was now in bed, while the others are seated near her, listening to words from her which causes them to wonder, coming as they do from so young a child.

She has been silent for several moments, apparently thinking of some important subject, when she suddenly exclaims:

"I want to see my father! I must see him! Be sure and do not let me die without seeing him!"

At this singular request, coming so suddenly, and the person to whom she alludes being so far from the thoughts of all, they are struck with astonishment, and for a moment return no reply.

The Puffer looks inquiringly at Uncle Sol, to read in his face if he will gratify this wish, while Uncle Sol, with his eyes cast down, appears to be considering whether it is best to do so. As no previous conversation between Bess and either of the others has ever occurred in which the name of Jasper was mentioned concerning the ties which existed between them, they are puzzled to know why she should express a desire to see him now, and to gratify his curiosity in this respect, Uncle Sol asks her what she knows about her father.

A sad smile plays upon her face for a moment, and then she replies:

"Do not think me ignorant as to who he is, because I have not mentioned him before. He is the man with the black eyes and pale face, whom I have seen a few times at Mrs. Padler's, and a great many times in my dreams. Please try to have him found, and brought here to my room, for I shall be the happier for seeing him before I go there," pointing heavenward.

Feeling confident that any interview she might have with Jasper, would be a painful one, and that his presence would also prove unpleasant to them all, Uncle Sol strove to impress upon her that she must be mistaken in supposing that Mr. Jasper was any kin to her.

"What real cause, dear Bessie, have you for believing such a thing possible? This man has never treated you as a father would treat a child? Then what should cause you to believe him your father?"

She remains silent for a moment, and then answers:

"Who tells the flowers that they get their life from the sun? and yet they turn to it for that support, which they must obtain from its rays to enable them to live. Why does the sunflower, growing at the porch-door, turn its face to the east in the morning, waiting to greet the sun, and then follow it all the livelong day, gazing full upon it as it sinks into the west at night. The same power who gave that knowledge to the flowers tells me that my father is the one I speak of. Do not deny me this wish, Uncle Sol. It may be the last I shall ask, and it will make me happy. Pray, have him brought to me if he can be found."

Her face wears such a look of entreaty as she gazes up into his, that he has not the heart to refuse her. He tells her that to-morrow her father shall be brought, if he can be found.

She seems so pleased at this, that the old man is glad he has made the promise. Then she tells them that she thinks she can go to sleep now; so they prepare to leave her alone. Uncle Sol selects a little flower from the bouquet upon her table, and brings it to her to hold in her hand, as has been her habit every night since she came to live with him. He stoops down to impress upon her lips the good-night kiss, and she throws her arms about his neck and tells him that she loves him better than anything else on earth; and that if she has any regret that she cannot live, it is because of the pain that her loss will occasion him.

His heart is too full to reply. He only tells her that she is his dear child, and that everything shall be done for her comfort that he would do, were she truly his own little daughter. Then, kissing her again, he leaves to sleep and sunny dreams. That night, when all is quiet through the house, a soft footstep might be heard upon the staircase, and an old man could have been seen, bearing in his hands an easy chair, which he places outside and near the door of the child's apartment. There he seats himself, and through the live-long night listens eagerly for any sound that may indicate the need of some one hastening to her side. The night passes away; the morning comes and discloses the face of the midnight watcher to be that of Uncle Sol, who, carefully leaving his post, descends the stairs, gains the street, and hastens in the direction of the lodgings of the Padlers. He proceeds directly to their rooms, and is admitted by Fopperty.

On being seated, Uncle Sol informs Fopperty of the wish expressed by Bessie: that John Jasper may be brought to her side; on hearing which Fopperty asks the old gentleman if he thinks it prudent to grant her request.

"Yes," is the reply; "I have promised it, and have called here this morning to ask that you see Mr. Jasper within a few hours and conduct him to my house. He may refuse to come, in anticipation of an unpleasant scene; and I shall be sorry, should he so refuse, for the dear child will be keenly disappointed. Still, we cannot force him."

"You tell me that Bessie will feel bad if she don't see him?" observes Fopperty, thoughtfully.

"I think it would cause her great pain," is the answer.

"Then you may depend that he'll be there," is the emphatic rejoinder

"Unless he refuses," suggests Uncle Sol.

"And if he refuses," replies Fopperty, excitedly, "and will not come willingly, I'll bring him in small pieces, and be d—d to him—mark that!" and the speaker rubs his hands together very hard, as he utters the latter sentence, thereby intending to convey to his hearer an idea of the grinding process by which he purposes to reduce the body of Mr. Jasper into very small pieces indeed.

"Very good, Fopperty; I leave it with you, and hope you will succeed in bringing him without having recourse to the alternative which you have mentioned."

Mr. Brobity then takes his departure, and leaves the other to perform his task at such time as he is ready, with what result the reader is already aware.

We left John Jasper seated in the parlour of Mr. Brobity, while Fopperty goes in quest of the old gentleman, who soon joins the Music Master, to whom he introduces himself, and begs of the new comer that he will treat the child tenderly, for she is sick unto death, and he should feel very sad to have anything occur to render her more unhappy than she now is. Then beckoning Mr. Jasper to follow him, they proceed to the chamber of the child.

Bessie, who has had her bed placed by the window so that she may occupy it and still look out upon the garden which is so dear to her, does not seem to hear them as they enter, but is looking from the window in a thoughtful mood. Mr. Brobity places a chair for the new comer, and then, stepping gently to the bedside of the child, said:

"My dear child, the person whom you desire to see is here."

She turns her face slowly toward the spot where Jasper is seated, and, with her eyes full upon his, says, in gentle tones:

"You were kind to please a poor little girl, who has not long to stay in this world, by coming to see her, as she desired."

Why does he return her gaze, and look so steadily upon her, but return no answer? Why does his face turn pale, as though he were looking upon a being from the other world, and why does his hand tremble so violently as he wipes the perspiration from his brow that has gathered there in great drops?

Does he recognize in her pallid face and attenuated features the semblance of a woman, who, years ago, lay upon the death-bed which he had made for her, and who had such confidence in his love for her, —a love that his craven heart had never held,—that she died trusting in him, and murmuring his name,—the name under which he had deceived her,—with her last breath?

The voice of the child starts him from his abstraction, when she speaks again, and asks him if there is no spark of love in his heart for her, now that she is about to die.

Why does his gaze become more fixed upon her as she utters these words, and why does he remain dumb, with no power to answer her? Does his mind revert to another scene of years ago, when a dying woman looked upon him as this child does now, with affection and forgiveness in her face, and faintly asked him, as this child has, if he loved her better now that she was dying?

What is this Something that stands beside the child as she lies there returning his gaze, and waiting for him to reply? This Something seems to have come within a moment, and has placed itself there by the bedside with noiseless step, and stands in the attitude of a Protecting Form. The others do not notice it. He can discern no features when he looks for them; and yet he feels that Its gaze is turned on him. How can this be, that nothing can be seen about it that bears the likeness of a human face, and yet It is piercing him through and through with Its eyes? What is this Something standing thus, a sombre, shadowy form, which does not move,—only making Its presence known to him?

He strives to answer the child, but the consciousness of Its gaze always upon him causes the words to die upon his lips. He feels a strange sensation come upon him—he has realized it often of late, but never so intense as now—as though his brain was on fire, and the veins in his body were filled with molten lead,—and so he sits and looks at Bess, but does not move or speak.

Finding that he does not reply, the child beckons Uncle Sol to her side, and begs him to raise and support her in a sitting position. The old man tenderly performs the wish, and she once more addresses the miserable wretch who still gazes silently upon her:

"I should not have troubled you to come to me now, had I not felt that my days on earth were few, and that it was a duty I owed my Heavenly Father—who has prepared for me in Heaven, what you never provided for me on earth—a home,—to tell you that you have my forgiveness for the wrongs you have done me while living. I felt that I should die happier to have told you this with my own lips. I do forgive you, and I have prayed God to forgive you and make you a better man."

How can the Sombre Something look more earnestly into his face now, and he not see the eyes with which It looks, nor see aught that indicates a face about It?

"When I have gone to Heaven, I will still pray that you may repent of the sins you have committed, and will, if I am permitted, come back to earth and help you to be strong in overcoming the temptations that may surround you. I know not why it is, but, though you have treated me so cruelly, I love you dearly, and pity you."

She ceases, and seems to expect that he will reply now, and his lips moving, would indicate that he is trying to return some answer, but again he fails to utter one word.

He feels again the eyes of the Sombre Something fixed upon him, and a strange fancy comes upon him that his body is a fountain filled with boiling blood, whose seething jets will continue to mount to his brain until they have burned away its substance! Still he sees the Sombre Something yet present, and regarding him with the same earnest expression upon Its imperceptible face.

Both the child and the old man observe how strangely he acts, but can assign no cause. "Why do you not speak to me?" resumes Bess. "You would not have your child die without one word of affection from your lips. Think of the years of coldness and neglect through which I have lived. You would hardly refuse the dying child of a stranger a kind word or a tender kiss. How can you, then, refuse to grant your own child a like boon? Oh," she added in pleading tones, and holding her arms out to him, "will you not fold me to your heart and love me? Think how happy dear mother will be to know, even at this late day, that you have some affection for your child! Do not look so strangely at me. Let me realize, before I die, the happiness of feeling father's kiss upon my lips."

In God's name, what is the Sombre Something doing now! How can It thus grow to such proportions, that It slowly and carefully envelopes the dying girl, as with a shadowy mantle, and all the time never takes Its eyes from his.

No wonder they look upon him,—the old man and child,—and think it strange he does not answer, but stares so wildly at something which they cannot see.

"Father," the child continues in pleading tones, "I have told you why I sent for you to come to me. If there is no love or natural affection in your heart for me, at least tell me that there is one—even if only one—little spark for darling mother. I know how great was her love for you; oh, who could know better, when in my dreams I've seen such grief and sadness in her face, that the sight of it could never be forgotten. And yet, that sadness all gave way to a look of love, when she spoke of you; even when it was you who had brought such bitter woe upon her young life."

He does not see the child now, though looking where she lies, but hears the voice uttering the words he understands. The Sombre Something with Its shadowy, misty form, holds the place where he first beheld the child, and It looks upon him still; but now, he fancies, with a sorrowing, pitying expression on the face he cannot see.

"It seemed to me," the child continues, "that there might be one little drop of love in your heart for dear mother, and so I thought it would afford you some comfort to know, that as I was soon to join her, I could be your messenger to bear to her some loving word or kindly token of the past; or, failing that, a kiss upon my lips for her, and I would guard it with such care, that not a breath should take it from me, till I had borne it safely to her in Heaven."

The Sombre Something seems to approach him now. As It comes nearer, It seems to grow in size, until he can see nothing but It. The blood from the boiling fountain now shoots its scalding, burning torrents, with redoubled force. The Presence is almost upon him, and now he perceives that It has arms, for they are raised as though to embrace him. He rises from the chair, while his eyes are nearly started from their sockets. He feels the touch of the arms as they encircle him, and at that same moment the fountain shoots, with redoubled force, its liquid heat upon his brain.

They see him now place his hands upon his temples; they see him, an instant after, take the chair in his hands and dash it upon the floor, as though he was braining some imaginary foe. Then they hear him give vent to one wild, horrid scream, and he and the Sombre Something, which he will never shake off in this world, dash down the stairs at a frightful pace, and into the open street! Heaven has interposed the obstacle which Datchery had named as the only power which could stay the hand of vengeance, for John Jasper is a raving maniac!

With his hands still pressed to his temples, the raving man dashes blindly through the thoroughfare, and in a few moments comes in contact with a stone post, and falls violently to the pavement. Several men, near by, hasten to his assistance, and endeavour to place him upon his feet, but their efforts are fruitless,—he only falls again to the ground, still uttering those frightful screams. A crowd have collected now, and among the number is Durdles, on his way to Minor Canon Corner. He carries in his hand a hammer, and under his arm has something tied up in his handkerchief, which might have been thousands of pounds in bank-notes, from the concern which he manifests for its safety, but which, in reality, is nothing more than a select party, of bread and cheese, keeping company with a thick-set and very dark-complexioned bottle, filled with Durdles' Elixir—speaking after the manner of Durdles—but which the civilized world denominates gin.

Two of the men have raised and are supporting the wretched Jasper between them, and one of them, appealing to Durdles, cries out:

"In God's name, what shall we do with him now?"

If Mr. Durdles had returned that they might take him to the devil, he would have expressed the thought which was uppermost in his mind at that moment; but, thinking better of it, he rejoins:

"If this 'ere chap was aught to Durdles, he'd have him carried into some one of these 'ere houses till a doctor could be fetched. That's what Durdles would do."

At that moment a woman cries out to them from a window of the nearest house, to bring him inside, which is soon done, notwithstanding the raving man's struggles to free himself, and he is soon placed upon a bed. Some person, in the meantime, having hastened for a physician, one soon making his appearance, who, after viewing the struggling wretch, shakes his head gravely, and tells them that some one must notify the Choir Leader's friends at once, for that the man has lost his reason, and the sooner he is placed in an asylum the better.

On hearing this, the voice of a boy, proceeding from behind the group, was heard to exclaim:

"Jarsper hain't got no friends, he hain't! Nobody'll miss 'im either —'cept the Topeses and the Kin-free-der-el."

Observing Durdles in the crowd, the physician motioned him, and whispered him to hasten to the Minor Canon and tell him what had occurred, and ask him to repair at once to the scene.

Thought Mr. Durdles, as he wended his way along the High Street, on his way to Minor Canon Corner, "It's my opinion that if Durdles had first made the acquaintance of Mr. Jasper as a stiff 'un, instead of a deep 'un, Mr. Jasper would been a deal the gainer by it. But his time hadn't come. There's allers a time for everything." This last caused Mr. Durdles to remember that it's about his time for lowering the bottle under his arm; so, stepping into a neighboring area, he hastens to lighten the bottle of a portion of its contents, and then hastens to enlighten Mr. Crisparkle.

CHAPTER XL.

AN OLD FRIEND REVEALS HIMSELF, AND AN OLD ADAGE PROVES TRUE.

Edwin Drood, having learned, with disappointment and regret, from Mr. Peckcraft, the particulars of the interview between the latter and John Jasper, and the spirit with which his uncle had received the warning which had been given him at that time, determined to no longer conceal his identity, but to come out boldly and assume his true character, and leave Jasper to his fate and Datchery. He had also determined to avoid a meeting with Jasper, if possible, for such a meeting could benefit neither of them, and might end in bloodshed. Had Jasper not been his relative, he would have felt differently; but his heart recoiled at the thought of shedding the blood of a man who was the son of his mother's father—almost his own flesh and blood—villain though he had proved himself.

Although he did not admit to himself that he had any selfish reason for thus hastening to throw off his disguise, it was nevertheless true; for he was desirous of visiting Rosa,—whom he knew to be then at the Minor Canon's,—at the earliest moment, that he might ascertain if her feelings towards him were different from what they were at their last interview; to learn if her heart had changed towards him as his had towards her, during the troubles which had fallen upon them in the past year, and if she regarded him now with more tender feelings than those of sisterly affection.

After his interview with Mr. Peckcraft, and when he had bade that gentleman farewell,—as he was stepping into the omnibus on his way to the station, he had exacted a promise from him (Mr. Peckcraft) that he would call on Mr. Grewgious, and beg him to come to Cloisterham the day following,—he hastens to join Datchery at the Gate House. On his arrival he imparts to Datchery the resolution he has formed, of calling that morning at the Minor Canon's, and begs that he, Datchery, will bear him company.

"To say the truth, my dear fellow," returned Datchery, "I am in no frame of mind to encounter the society of ladies. I have a work laid out for to-day, which, though terrible in its nature, is far more pleasant to me than would be the society of the fairest woman in all England."

While his face wears a stern look as he utters these words, a deep-drawn sigh tells that his heart is sad, notwithstanding his assertion that his task is a pleasant one, and he paces the floor for a few moments in silence. His companion watches him with an expression of sympathy upon his face, and waits patiently for the unhappy man to recover himself. Finally, halting before the cupboard, and opening the door, he gazes silently upon the score which is affixed there, and seems to gather strength at the sight of it, for a moment after he is seated calmly by his companion.

Calmer than he would have been had he known that at that moment the man whose life he claimed was skulking away from the Gate House, to escape the vengeance of man, forgetting that the vengeance of the Almighty, which was so soon to overtake him, could not be warded off.

"Now, see here, my dear friend," Edwin begins, assuming a cheerful tone, "don't you think that, were you to leave this man to his fate, as I have done, he would be punished far more than he would be were he to lose his life by your hand? And then, again, is his life worth as much as yours, do you think? For it must be a life for a life, you know, if you kill him. I cannot bear to think," continues Edwin, sadly, "of a noble heart like yours being thrown into the balance with such a one as his, when, in all that is pure, noble, and generous, a thousand lives like his could not recompense the world for the loss of one like yours." The young man had spoken earnestly, for he was determined, if possible, to change the resolution which Datchery had formed to shed the blood of this man, knowing that in the end he (Datchery) would be the happier.

"To a man who has worked for all the time which I have to accomplish an end," replies Datchery, mournfully, "and who, now that the accomplishment of that end is so near at hand, is happier than he has been before for many a year, your words sound strange. Perhaps it is natural that you should plead for him, however, considering the relation he bears you; but, were he your father even, I would not change my purpose for all the pleadings which you could utter. I could never lose sight of the fact that a grave is made in a distant church-yard, whose tenant was dearer to me in life than any living creature,—that she lies there because she was deceived and wrecked by this man,—and that her voice cries aloud from the grave for vengeance!"

Mr. Datchery had uttered these last words with such earnestness and determination, that the young man was convinced how utterly impossible it would be to change his purpose; but the reflection that Mr. Datchery had cast upon his motives, by intimating that kindred ties had influenced him in striving to turn Datchery from his vengeance, wounded Edwin's feelings deeply, and he felt it his duty to assure his companion that he was in error. Hence he replies:

"My dear friend, I am sure you do me injustice when you hint that my pleadings for this man's life are actuated by any respect I entertain for him. Surely, his attempt upon my life ought to be sufficient evidence that he is entitled to no interposition from me. I assure you I was only thinking of your happiness and safety when I spoke of this matter, for I feel such great friendship for you that I should never cease to regret you had placed your life in jeopardy by taking that of this creature whom I have the misfortune to be connected with by ties of blood. I wish I had the power to make you feel as I do about this matter, and could convince you of the fact that, by permitting this man to go unharmed he would suffer ten—yes, a thousand—times more living, than from any violence you might inflict upon him. But do not harbour a thought that I would sue for *him;* no, it is for your happiness alone that I sue,—not his life."

Datchery grasps his young friend's hand, and assures him that he has no doubt he speaks truly.

"But," he continues, "my life is pledged to the fulfillment of this end. I should feel that I was recreant to my dead sister's honour, were I to even think of staying the hand of vengeance. Let us say no more about this. My mind is fixed. *Unless Heaven interposes some obstacle to prevent it,* John Jasper must die by my hand!"

Finding that no persuasion could turn the speaker from his purpose, and that he was determined to inflict punishment upon his sister's betrayer with his own hand, Edwin did not attempt to press the point further, but changed the theme by reverting to the subject which was uppermost in his mind when the conversation first began—namely, a visit to the Minor Canon in his true character, with Mr. Datchery to accompany him.

"I will not say more now, dear friend, concerning this unpleasant subject, but will leave it, hoping that you will think over what I have already said, and that your better judgment will convince you I am right. Let us return to what will be a far pleasanter theme to me, and speak of a visit to Mr. Crisparkle's."

Mr. Datchery is cool now—more like the Datchery of old. He seats himself at the window, and looks thoughtfully out for a moment before replying; then makes answer:

"Be it as you wish, my dear fellow, I will not object if you desire it, though, as I told you before, I am hardly in a state of mind to be in the society of ladies. I will waive that objection, however, and will accompany you, for I shall derive pleasure in witnessing the happiness of others, even if I cannot participate in it, and I know beforehand how happy you will be when you are brought in the presence of the woman you love, and from whom you have been separated for so long a time. In consenting to accompany you, I am also influenced by the fact of your kindness and self-sacrifice in assisting me to carry out the various tortures which have been inflicted upon John Jasper, and which would not have been so complete had you not, by your isolation, led him to suppose he was your murderer. Yes, let us go at once, and let us thank God that you can behold the friends from whom you have so long been separated, and who had given you up as lost to them forever. Oh, that a like blessing was in store for me! Oh, that I could behold her alive, and witness the joy displayed upon her face, which Miss Bud will show when she takes you by the hand! But that can never be. God! I feel as though I could not wait a moment till I have my hands about that man's throat, and have strangled him to death!"

The unhappy man rises hastily from his seat, and in his agitation, paces the floor for a few moments; then seats himself again, and says:

"Had this craven wretch only been guilty of attempting my sister's life, and failed, as in your case, I might find it in my heart to forgive him that, and let him go. Even had he been her murderer, I might have remained satisfied to leave him to the law and Heaven's punishment. But to destroy her, soul and body—to first ruin the casket and then crush the gem which it contained—it is too dreadful to think of! Oh, my God! give me patience, and let me not lose my reason—at least till I have my enemy dead at my feet!"

Poor Dick Datchery's heart is so full that he gives way to a flood of tears—God knows, were it not for tears at such times, our hearts would lack the only weapon with which to parry the stroke of Death—and Edwin is so greatly affected at his friend's grief, that it is several moments before he can find words to comfort the weeping man at his side.

Laying his hand on Datchery's shoulder, and speaking in earnest tones, he says: "Do not entertain the terrible thought, that your sister is lost, soul and body. No, no! the soul is a jewel no living mortal can destroy! It is the only thing direct from the hand of God, which we inherit! It can never be harmed, for it is a part of God himself. Our bodies may die and decay, but our souls, even though they become tarnished from contact with earthly things, shall be made as pure as snow again, when they have parted from the bodies which hold them; and they shall return again, to that loving Father from whence they came, in all their God-like purity!"

Datchery seizes the hand of the speaker, as he ceases, and thanks him for his words of encouragement.

"I believe you're right after all," he adds, "for it does stand to reason that God would not destroy, nor allow his creatures to destroy a man's soul. Yes, you must be right; our bodies belong to earth, our souls to Heaven. You have made me happier for the thought, my boy, and I thank you."

At the suggestion of Edwin, they prepare to visit the Minor Canon, and in a few minutes are on their way to that gentleman's house, which they reach soon after. They are met at the door by Mr. Crisparkle, who, seated at his sitting-room window, has observed their coming, and who has recognized, in the companion of Datchery, the form and features of Edwin Drood.

They have hardly reached the door, before the Reverend gentleman opens it, and taking Edwin by the hand, throws his arms about his neck, and actually kisses him upon the cheek, in the exuberance of his joy.

"I'm so happy, my dear boy," he exclaims, "I'm so happy, I cannot express it! Datchery," (who had been a silent spectator all this time,) "Datchery," grasping his hand, "you are welcome. I thought I could control my feelings a trifle, when you brought him, but you see I was mistaken. We were speaking of you this very morning,—the young ladies and I,—and Miss Bud was wondering if you had changed any, and when you would be likely to call; so it's no wonder after all, that you are here, for you know the old saying: The devil, etc.; but, come right in. We'll sit down in my study and have a quiet chat by ourselves, before joining the ladies, for I don't suppose I shall have a chance to put in a word edgeways, when you get where they are," and leading the way to his study, the Minor Canon (dear fellow) stops at about every third step to ask some question, or, to once more shake hands with the young visitor. It was quite amusing to the others, when, in his excitement, he would seize by mistake the hand of Datchery, for that of Edwin, and then discovering his error, which he did in an instant, would grasp Edwin with the other hand, as though no mistake had been made after all; and so they reach the study of the Minor Canon. The hearty welcome, and genial, happy manner of Mr. Crisparkle, has imparted to Datchery some of its spirit, for the latter is feeling much better in his mind than when he left the Gate House, and he joins in the conversation with as much interest as though no thorn of misery were rankling in his breast.

Although the Reverend gentleman had heard from Datchery nearly all the particulars connected with the attempted murder and subsequent escape of Edwin, he could not be satisfied till he had heard all over again from the young man's lips. After the narrative is concluded, Edwin intimates that he should be glad to meet the young ladies.

"I don't know," he continues, "whether my meeting with Pussy will be any more demonstrative on her part than it was a year ago, at the Nuns' House, but I do know that mine will be. Poor Rosa! I don't wonder now she didn't like me, knowing my uncle for the villain he has proved himself."

Then they discuss the method by which it is best to announce the young man—whether the Minor Canon had better go down and tell them first that he is here, and so prepare them for the meeting, or whether to come upon them suddenly.

"Perhaps it is better to announce me first," Edwin says; "Pussy may think it's my ghost, if I come upon her suddenly, and faint away. I shouldn't like her to do that, you know."

The Minor Canon don't think so, for the reason that Edwin was expected, and they were looking for him daily. He is in favour of taking them by surprise, just for the fun of the thing.

So it is decided, and they descend to the sitting-room together.

An old-fashioned but cozy sitting-room is that, wherein are seated the mother of Mr. Crisparkle, in company with Helena and Rosa. The former is attired in those emblems of mourning which indicate a recent visit from that dread messenger, whose approach is seldom welcome, and who is never satisfied to depart as he comes—alone—but must seize upon some one to bear him company to his pale abode.

It is evident that the topic of their conversation has been of Neville, for they all wear sad faces, and Helena is weeping and sobbing violently. Her companions are offering words of comfort and consolation, which, after a time, tend to calm the grief-stricken girl, and the conversation is resumed by Helena, broken occasionally by sobs:

"I cannot bear to think of him, lying there in a London churchyard, and I so far removed from him that I cannot daily visit his resting-place. If the funeral cannot soon take place, and his remains consigned to their final resting-place in Cloisterham church-yard, I must return to London and remain till that ceremony can be performed. God knows, I should be lonely enough were he buried here; but now, when he is so far away, I feel that I have lost him entirely, and, I am sure, if he can look back and see us so far from him, he'll think we have deserted him indeed. Poor Neville—poor boy!"

Then the China Shepherdess—kind of heart as kind of face—replies:

"Child, he will know that it is all for the best, and that, to a certain extent, necessity compels the present arrangement. Sept. tells me that a few days, at the farthest, will see those plans perfected which shall remove all obstacles to the burial. In fact, he is to call upon Durdles to-day, to have every thing in readiness at a moment's notice. Only have patience for a short time, and all will be well."

She has seated herself by Helena's side while speaking, and, taking her hand tenderly in her own, presses her lips affectionately upon the brow of her bereaved charge.

Then Rosa, assuming a cheerful air, endeavours to dispel the sadness of her friend by telling her that she must dry her eyes and be just as cheerful as she can, for there's no knowing when Eddy may come, and when he does she wants him to see her (Helena) at her best, for who knows but what he will fall in love with her, she is so handsome and looks so noble when she is herself; and then adds that she wouldn't blame him if he did, for if she, Rosa, were a young man, she is sure she should do the same thing.

Although Rosa uttered these words for the purpose of directing Helena's mind into a more pleasant channel, she could not help wishing in her heart that Edwin would come at that moment, so that such a result, which would prove a sad blow to her, would be less liable to happen; and that thought led her to wondering if Edwin Drood had really any affection for her now. He had told her once—the last time they had met, too—that he and she both would be happier to remain as brother and sister, and, in fact, she thought so then herself. Was it likely that he had changed his mind now, when they had not met for nearly a twelvemonth? But then she had changed hers, when she had lost him, as she supposed, forever. How had the parting affected him?

Just then, footsteps are heard ascending the stairs, and a moment after a tap at the door is answered by Mr. Crisparkle's mother, who cries "Come in."

The door opens. Enter Minor Canon, trying to appear unconcerned, as if there was nothing unusual going on, but making a miserable failure of it, as they can all see a world of fun and jollity expressed in every feature of his face; following the Minor Canon comes Datchery, who is regarded with some curiosity, he being to a certain extent a stranger to them,—and last of all comes Edwin Drood, looking very pale and feeling very nervous in anticipation of the emotion which his presence will occasion Rosa; while she does not stir one step, nor move a muscle of her face, but stands with one hand clasped in the other, and both pressed tightly to her bosom, as she stares upon him like one who is looking at the dead.

The Minor Canon is the first to break silence, and says:

"Ladies, a gentleman of whom you have all heard but did not know, Mr. Datchery." A pause. Then, "Ladies, a gentleman of whom you have not only heard, but whom you all know, Mr. Edwin Drood!"

Edwin and Rosa had not heard the Minor Canon's words. They had stood with their eyes riveted upon each other's faces, and both so motionless that it seemed as though they feared to move, lest they should break the spell which showed them to each other, and find it all a dream at last.

While the Minor Canon was uttering the last sentence, his eyes never left the faces of the two, while the others were as deeply interested as he.

Rosa is nearly overcome with agitation. She thought she was going to be so strong, and now she is so weak. It might have been that had not these two read in each other's eyes, during that earnest gaze, the secret of each other's heart, their meeting would have been more demonstrative, the better so that neither should witness the other's disappointment.

But that one look spoke more to them than volumes could have done! Rosa is the first to break the silence. Her bosom rising and falling with the emotion that fills her breast, and holding out her hands to Edwin Drood, while tears of joy fall down her cheeks, she murmurs in a trembling voice,

"Eddy!"

"Pussy!"

Regardless, nay, unconscious, of the presence of those standing near them, they are in an instant folded in each other's embrace; nestling closer to his breast, as though she feared, even now, that it was only a dream, and that he would vanish from her arms did she not hold him closer, she murmurs:

"Thank God. It is not a delusion!"

Gently raising her face to his, and looking into her eyes, with a world of love in his, he tells her that it is a reality indeed.

"I am alive and well, darling, and, God helping us, we will never part again! Our fathers could look into the future, after all, and, notwithstanding we tried so hard to go contrary to their last wishes, affliction came with its sharp teeth, and, tearing away the weeds of frivolity that hid our hearts from us, disclosed that which we should never have known else—that we could love each other dearly. Thus have we proved true the old adage, that afflictions are sometimes necessary to make us know our own hearts. No doubt our fathers, even now, are looking down upon us, and, with their hands clasped in each other's, are bestowing upon us their blessings." Then added, raising his eyes reverently, "and God grant that we may deserve them always!"

"Amen," is the response of the Minor Canon, who felt it his duty to say something, and thought this a very favourable opportunity; whereat they dry their eyes, and Edwin conducts Rosa to a distant corner of the room. On being seated, Rosa has an idea that she has not been quite so womanly as she ought to have been, and whispers Edwin if he thinks she has behaved silly?"

It is at this moment that a servant announces Durdles, who desires to see Mr. Crisparkle; whereupon that gentleman leaves the room, to return again in a few moments, and beckons Edwin to follow him; then, leading the way to another room, they are a moment after listening to Durdles' account of Jasper's affliction.

Filled with surprise at the startling intelligence, they determine to repair at once to the scene, and, after the Minor Canon has returned to the company above stairs and informed them that he and Edwin will be absent, on a matter of business, for a short time, and exacting a promise from Datchery that he will entertain the ladies during their absence, he again joins Edwin, and together they hasten to the bedside of the miserable Jasper, whom they find in the grasp of two strong men, from whom he is violently struggling to free himself. A moment after they enter the room he becomes less violent, and begs of them to save him from some terrible object which he fancies is approaching to destroy him.

"Will no one keep it off?" he cries, striving to release himself from those who are holding him. "Do you not see it there," he continues, staring wildly at Edwin, "looking at me with eyes that burn into my brain! Look there! See how it watches to spring upon me unawares! There! there! it's moving towards me now! Why do you not seize it where it stands! Don't let it come nearer," he cries, in a beseeching tone, "or it's arms will clasp me, and it's hot breath will strangle me!" Then he grows furious again, and exclaims, "Will no one help me? See how it raises its arms now! Hold it! hold it! Oh, God! too late, too late!" and then with one wild shriek he struggles and plunges madly to free himself from those who are holding him.

"This is too terrible," Edwin whispers the Minor Canon, turning his face from the sufferer; "let us depart; we cannot help him, and the sight of such misery unfits me."

Mr. Crisparkle is only too glad to act upon the suggestion, and begging of the physician to do all in his power to aid the miserable man, and have him placed at once in the Cloisterham Asylum, which is about a mile from the Precincts, they return to the house of the Minor Canon.

They find the ladies and Datchery awaiting their coming with no little impatience, and with some curiosity to learn the cause of their absence; but, as both Edwin and the Minor Canon had decided that it was better to say nothing about it at present, their curiosity is not gratified.

Shortly after, Edwin and Datchery depart for the Gate House, but not before they have promised to return and pass the evening with those they leave behind.

As they approach the Cathedral, and just as they have reached the elms that skirt its front, they hear a hackney-coach approaching at a rapid pace, and as it passes them they are startled at hearing frantic screams proceeding from the inside. The curtains being drawn, they cannot distinguish the occupants, but Edwin knows that one of them is a madman, and that he is no other than his relative, John Jasper, on his way to the asylum.

Mr. Datchery looks at Edwin and quietly remarks:

"The individual possessing those lungs would make a valuable acquisition to Bedlam."

"You are nearer the truth than you imagine," responds Edwin mournfully; "a most fitting place for him, I must confess."

"How do you know that?" Datchery asks, with some curiosity.

"Because I know the man, and know that he is already on his way to a private mad-house."

"Oh," observes Datchery carelessly, "and may I ask who the unfortunate creature may be?"

"One who will never more have power to injure you or me," Edwin answers, impressively; "one who has sinned deeply, but who is now suffering more than you or I could ever tell. That man is my uncle, John Jasper!"

Datchery starts with surprise and lays his hand upon his companion's arm, as though he was about to interrupt him, but the other proceeds:

"John Jasper; the man who, but for this Divine interposition, would have been instrumental in placing the mark of Cain upon your brow, but which, thank God, is spared you."

Edwin then proceeded to give his companion a detailed account of the terrible visitation which had befallen Jasper, together with the fact that it came upon him during his interview with the child.

By the time the story was told, they had reached the Gate House, and are seated in Datchery's lodgings. When Edwin had concluded, his listener said:

"It is better as it is. Bessie has been the instrument through whom it was brought about, and I feel now that my dead sister's wrongs are avenged. I must visit the child at once, and learn more of the particulars of that interview. By the way," he adds, after a moment, and approaching the cupboard door, "the account being settled, even though it was by proxy, I must wipe off the score; but it is a little singular that it should be settled so differently from what I had planned, which proves true another old adage, that man proposes, but God disposes."

And so, poor Datchery, you have learned the lesson which all of us, at some period of our lives, have to learn: that notwithstanding we feel so confident in our own abilities to carry out the ends we have in view—laying our plans, and rearing about them what to us seem strong defenses for their support; bringing to our aid such cunning agents as seem to us essential to our success—but finding, after all, that there is a Power above, before whom all earthly defenses must crumble away, and before whose strength all earthly plans, which have consumed years in their development, are scattered, in the twinkling of an eye, to the four winds of Heaven.

Oh, that man would learn to rely upon that Great Heart—that Mighty Power. Then would he realize how insignificant is his judgment compared with that of our dear Creator, and have patience to wait for Divine justice and blessings which, in the end, will surely come!

CHAPTER XLI.

TREATS OF VARIOUS SUBJECTS WHICH LEAD THE READER TO THAT TURN IN THE ROAD WHERE HE MUST SAY FAREWELL.

If there be any among those who read these pages who have never felt the grief that comes from seeing some loved one stricken with the hand of death, they cannot realize the agony which that day brings. when all that is mortal is to be consigned to its last resting-place, and the dear form is hid from their sight forever! Even after death has touched our loved ones with his cold hand, it is some consolation—poor, indeed, but nevertheless welcome—to feel that their familiar faces are still where we can gaze upon them, and imprint upon their cold lips the kisses which, in life, were given back again.

If, then, there be those reading these lines who have not experienced the agony which comes on that sad day, they cannot realize the wretchedness which filled the heart of Helena Landless when her brother was brought from London, to be placed in the church-yard of Cloisterham Cathedral.

Three days had elapsed since the terrible blow which had befallen Jasper, and, there being no further need of delay, arrangements had been perfected for the funeral to take place.

The Minor Canon having given orders to Durdles to prepare the grave, that gentleman had acted accordingly, and prided himself a good deal on the workmanship thereof.

Cloisterham was in nowise behind the times in possessing among its inhabitants a certain few, who are always on the alert when it comes to their ears that a funeral is in perspective; and, that they may never let an opportunity pass of being present on such occasions, watch the church-yard with eager eyes for a new grave which may be under way, that they may not be taken by surprise, and miss an opportunity of being present at the ceremony.

Hence Durdles finds himself surrounded by several lookers-on, while Neville's grave is being made, who evince some curiosity concerning it.

"Somebody dead?" asks one of the Curious-Inexorables.

"Durdles don't make these kind o' houses for livin' folks, he don't," is the abrupt answer.

"When's the funeral to be, Mr. Durdles?" perseveres the Curious-Inexorable, in a conciliatory tone, as who would say, "Mr. Durdles is competent to answer this, and he only." But Durdles, being familiar with the habits of the Curious-Inexorable, is not to be cajoled, and answer makes:

"Durdles don't have his say *when*, he don't; Durdles will make your bed, but you may occupy it when you're ready; it's all the same to Durdles."

But Durdles takes a pride in his work, and, after it is finished, affirms to those about him that "that one can't be beat."

"Let me tell you that there one is done by rule and measurement. It's Durdles' Best. That there one is exactly five foot deep from top to bottom, and won't vary a shovel's thickness 'twixt either end. It's what no man in London can equal. Durdles tells you that."

And now the hour has come—the wretched hour, that is to witness the final scene of all—the hour which must come to every mortal! The hour has come when the body of Neville Landless must be consigned to the earth, from whence it sprang—dust to dust; ashes to ashes—to rest in the peaceful company of the dead.

Although the Curious-Inexorables had known but a little time before, that the sad ceremony was to be performed, the news, even in that short time, had passed almost throughout the quaint old town. When they learn who the dead man is, they who remember him are struck with wonder, recalling, as they do, the brief space that has elapsed,—only one short year,—since he came to dwell in their midst, filled with young life and vigor; and some there be, who whisper among them, how uncertain is life, and how true the saying, that "in the midst of life we are in death."

Comes Mr. Tope, with slow and mournful step, to open the Cathedral door, through which the dead and the living are soon to enter. The step of Mr. Tope may well be termed "Tope's Own." He has practiced it on every occasion of this kind for twenty years, and it is the only thing connected with his professional duties on which he prides himself.

Comes the solemn cortegè, approaching the Cathedral from whose lofty tower the deep tolling of the bell is heard, and whose deep notes are echoed far away, until they seem like the voices of angels mourning in sympathy with the bleeding hearts who are following the loved one to the grave.

The service over, the little group of mourners return to the house of the Minor Canon, where Helena, almost wild with grief, receives such loving care and consolation as Rosa and the Minor Canon's mother can bestow upon her.

John Jasper's old lodgings at the Gate House had been deserted since the day that he was bereft of reason; and on the day following the funeral of Neville, Edwin, in company with Datchery and Mr. Crisparkle, visited the apartments for the purpose of placing Jasper's effects into a compact shape, and storing them in a loft at the top of the building, so that should the Choir Leader recover his reason at an early day, they would be kept safe for him. They had not the faintest idea that anything of interest would be found, which bore upon the events of the past twelve months; but, on opening the small drawer of a secretary in his sleeping room, they discovered a diary, about which was tightly wound a long black scarf, the same which Jasper wore on the night when he and the two young men had met together, for the last time on earth.

On running over the pages of this diary, they discovered that some valuable information could be obtained therefrom, and it was decided to wait till evening, before they examined it minutely, and then to have it read aloud in the presence of all interested.

"I think we are under some obligation to two other parties," said Mr. Datchery, "and that it is, therefore, our duty to invite them to be present at the reading of this infernal record. I refer to Durdles and his shadow, Winks. I am anxious that they should be present, for the reason that it has always been a great mystery to Durdles to know how John Jasper obtained the key to Mr. Sapsea's monument, which enabled him to use that sanctuary of the dead for such a villainous purpose, and I have no doubt the mystery will be solved when the contents of this Diary are brought to light."

There being no objection to this, Mr. Datchery sallies forth in quest of the two personages mentioned, and proceeds in the direction of the stone-mason's quarters as being the most likely place to find him, or obtain information of his whereabouts.

He had not proceeded more than half the distance when he descried the figure of a woman approaching him, and as she came nearer, he observed that it was no other than the mother who bore him, and known in this narrative as the Princess Puffer.

On that night, when she had the interview with Datchery and the Minor Canon, she had given a sketch of her life and the troubles which had befallen her, and her son had recognized her by the story, when he would never have suspected who she was by her features, so great had been the change which had taken place in her during his long separation from her. He had great difficulty in restraining himself from throwing his arms about her and revealing himself to her then and there, but decided that it would be better to wait the course of events before reawakening a love for one whom she no doubt had despaired of seeing again on earth; and a love that would, perhaps, only have possession of its object for a few weeks at the longest, should he meet with disaster and death in the cause which led him here.

She has come up to him now, and with her old cough still upon her, and which she has practiced for so long that it would seem to have become settled upon her, she says:

"A good day to ye, Mr. Datchery," and is proceeding on her way, when he calls out to her that he would like a few moments' conversation with her if she has the time to spare.

She stops suddenly at hearing this, and replies, in an impatient tone:

"Does ye think an old 'ooman has no business, that needs her seein' to, that she is to be stopped at every turn by them as takes a fit to hinder her? Well, what does ye want with me?"—this last as she has approached close to him, and looks eagerly into his face.

"I have no wish to interfere with your business, my good woman, and I won't detain you but a moment, if you do not desire to remain."

He pauses, as though at a loss how to proceed, and then continues:

"You have not forgotten, perhaps, that, a few months since, you related to the Reverend gentleman yonder, and myself, something of your history, and, in the course of your narrative, mentioned that you were the mother of two children. Am I correct?"

"I'll not dispute ye," is the careless reply.

"You only spoke of a daughter though, you may remember, as having been the cause of your leading the life which you then led. Will you tell me about the other child?"

"It's little good my tellin' of ye about 'tother one, for he's been gone so long that, never knowin' where he was, it's wiser to believe him dead than livin'. He was always good to his mother, and his sister Bess was his idol; he must be dead, or he'd a' search'd me out long ago."

"And what if he had known where you were for many months, but did not let you know it, lest he might destroy your happiness almost as soon as he had made it?"

"I'd say as it was not like him, and wouldn't believe a word on it," is the emphatic reply.

Mr. Datchery turns his head to conceal a smile, and then continues:

"What if he should come to you, and tell you that he had known all about you for ever so long a time; that he had known all about your sufferings and hardships while pursuing a villain who had brought all these troubles upon you?"

She heaved a great sigh at these words, and says she would be the happiest woman in England, old or young, and that it was cruel of him to tantalize an old woman thus who had but a short time to live at the best,—and fell to weeping.

"And what," pursued Datchery, "if I should say that I knew Capt. Tranders had kept you under his eyes for weeks and months, when you did not know that he was on the face of the earth,—much less, close by you all the time."

She ceases mourning now, and with a puzzled expression upon her face,—half serious, half curious,—exclaimed:

"Good God! dear gentleman, what does ye mean by that?"

"Just what I say, that your lost boy is near you; that he loves you with as much affection to-day as when he parted from you, ten years ago, and longs to hold you in his embrace and devote the balance of his days to your happiness."

He removes his hat quickly, and snatches from his head the wig that has so long been his disguise in Cloisterham, and looking lovingly into her astonished eyes, exclaims:

"Mother, do you know Henry—do you know your boy now?"

"Henry!" she exclaims. "Praise God! My boy is alive!" and in the excitement of the moment, they are locked in each other's embrace, not stopping to consider the publicity of the scene—or, if they did, caring nothing.

What sight is there more beautiful than the meeting between a mother and her child, after an absence of years, or even days? How forcibly are we reminded of that Heavenly Parent who sends his children to dwell away from him on earth for a brief period, and then calls them home, to greet them with the affection of a God instead of a mortal; and if we are happy in meeting our earthly parents, after an absence, how much happier we must be when we return to the dear Parent of us all, who watches over us, day and night, with a love that no mortal tongue can express.

The Puffer has soon recovered from the effects of her joy at beholding her son, and they have only separated from each other's embrace, when a voice, addressing the Puffer, from the opposite side of the way, cries out:

"Ain't yer gettin' wild in yer old age—yah! ain't the Mayor a-comin' right along behind yer, and won't 'er Royal 'ighness ketch it from Mr. Sap-sea-a," closing with a sing-song voice, and evidently not recognizing Datchery, for he winks at that gentleman in a very mysterious manner, as who would say, I caught you, but if you'll stand something handsome, I'll keep still.

Datchery, looking in the direction mentioned by the boy, sees Mr. Sapsea approaching in a stately manner and apparently oblivious to everything about him, as all truly great men are, or should be.

Not caring to enter into explanations at the present time, Datchery hastily replaces his wig, which the Deputy did not observe, and hence, when he looks again towards the Puffer and her companion, is so astonished to find Datchery standing there, that he gives a shrill whistle, and cries out excitedly:

"One, tother, or both on 'em's the devil!" and falls to dancing and whistling.

Mr. Sapsea by this time has nearly reached them, and happening to bring his eyes down just at that moment on a level with the boy's head, perceives that he is dancing,—yes, actually dancing!—in his path. For a moment the great man was nearly overcome at this mark of disrespect, but suddenly remembering that King Solomon tolerated such things, and being reminded furthermore, that the said king was rated a very wise man,—therefore a man of mind,—stopped short in his—we were about to say walk,—perhaps floating would be better,—and gazed upon the urchin in a very benign manner indeed.

Mr. Sapsea's thoughts having descended from the Realms of Vain-Gloriousness, and Mr. Sapsea, in consequence, realizing that he is still sojourning with common minds upon the face of the earth, is the cause of Mr. Sapsea's turning his eyes over the way and discerning the Puffer and her son; and it must be that the great man is filled with a spirit of condescension to-day, for he crosses over directly he sees them and holds out his hand to Mr. Datchery.

Hastily bidding his mother farewell, and promising to call at Mr. Brobity's very soon, when they will arrange for the future, the old lady departs on her way, while Mr. Datchery addresses the gentleman before him, saying:

"I am very glad to have met your Honor, for meeting your Honor now has suggested a thought which might not have occurred to me else. Are you disengaged this evening?"

Although Mr. Sapsea knew directly the question was put that he could answer in the negative, the Supreme Representative of a class of Supreme Jackasses thought that it would never do to reply at once, as great men are expected to have a multiplicity of engagements on hand for all times; so with his thumbs tucked into his waistcoat, and his eyes closed in a meditative way, standing on his heels and toes alternately, he finally answers that he *thinks* he is not engaged.

This important point being settled, Datchery asks if it would be agreeable for his Honor to pass the evening with a select number of acquaintances at Mr. Crisparkle's.

Mr. Sapsea returns that it will afford him pleasure; but, at the same time, with an air of saying, "It's a great condescension on my part, Mr. Datchery, but I'll be there."

"I take it for granted," the great man adds, "that this gathering is one of the—Elevating sort. No commonplace affair, I presume, but one in which Elevated Ideas serve to combine instruction with pleasure. No topic will prevail, I trust, which might be regarded—un-English!"

Again the Supreme Representative inserts his thumbs under his waistcoat, and poises alternately upon his toes and heels, as though conscious of having said something very great indeed.

It chanced at that moment that both gentlemen, casting their eyes over the way, discovered Deputy, with his thumbs tucked under his braces, gazing into the air, and trying to look very consequential and wise, in imitation of the great man.

Without appearing to notice the boy's comical appearance, Datchery calls to him. Deputy obeying the summons, Datchery says:

"Winks, I want you to perform a mission for me."

"What is it?" asks Deputy, promptly.

"I want you to seek Mr. Durdles, and ask him to call at my lodgings this evening, at seven o'clock, precisely."

"Then—E—don't—go—then—I—shy—
Widdy widdy, Wake-cock *warnin!*"

And bawling the last word in the face of Mr. Sapsea, the boy once more places his thumbs under his braces, and walks off very majestically indeed, after the manner of Sapsea, who must have felt highly complimented, judging from the way he stared at Deputy as the latter departed.

After Deputy had left them, Mr. Sapsea remarks:

"I often think, sir, of the terrible fate which came upon Mr. Jasper; but he was a singular person, sir, a very singular person. Although a close observer of human nature, sir—limited, it is true, to the confines of our City, which, though not extensive, affords opportunity for deriving a pretty accurate idea of the world, when viewed by a Superior Mind—I must confess that *I* was greatly deceived in that man. You may think that I am mistaken—you may say it was impossible—when I tell you that Mr. Jasper deceived Me, but it is true."

Whatever Mr. Datchery thought he kept to himself, but this is what Mr. Datchery said:

"How does your Honor account for Mr. Jasper's obtaining access to your deceased wife's tomb?"

"I have no idea, sir; I cannot account for it, and so I doubt the statement. If it is so, it is beyond my Power to explain it; and if I cannot explain it, of course it will never be made plain."

"Ah, well," rejoins Datchery, "we may know some time; but I have an engagement, and you will excuse me if I bid you good morning. I shall feel happy, the balance of the day, anticipating the pleasure of meeting your Honor this evening, at the Minor Canon's." And, with a formal bow, the speaker leaves the Presence.

When Edwin Drood first appeared in the streets of Cloisterham, after throwing off his disguise, those who saw him were greatly astonished, and more especially those who had supposed him to have been foully dealt with. Among the latter class was Mr. Sapsea, who felt no little chagrin that the missing man had turned up again, inasmuch as he, Sapsea, had always protested that murder had been done, and that Neville Landless was the guilty party. This living contradiction to his assertion, however, would tend to lessen him as a prophet in the eyes of Cloisterham, which thought was a very galling one indeed.

It having come to the ears of Mr. Sapsea that the monument erected to the memory of a Sapsea,—and which, in its owner's estimation, should pass for the eighth wonder of the world,—had been used as a place of concealment by the guilty party in that sad affair which had nearly cost Edwin his life, Mr. Sapsea was filled with indignation, and refused to credit any such statement.

For this reason Mr. Datchery had invited the Great Mind to be present at the reading of Jasper's private Diary, as, from some statements which he (Datchery) had noticed upon one of its pages, he felt assured that Mr. Sapsea would learn something of interest to him.

CHAPTER XLII.

THE HAVEN BEING REACHED, WE BID OUR FELLOW-TRAVELLERS FAREWELL.

On the afternoon of that same day, when Mr. Datchery had revealed himself to his mother, a mournful scene was being enacted at the house of Uncle Sol Brobity.

The family physician had been seen to enter and leave a great many times within a few hours, and the neighbours had declared among themselves, while shaking their heads in a significant manner, that somebody must be very sick there, or Dr. Leggoff wouldn't be so busy. Some more bold than the others, in their desire to satisfy their neighbours that it was no mystery to them, had gone so far as to state, that Uncle Sol had been struck with paralysis, in consequence of the deaf old lady—his mother—replying to a question the first time,—a thing she had not done in forty years,—and that only the doctor's constant attendance would save his life.

But while conjecture was rife outside, inside there was no uncertainty, for each member of Uncle Sol's family knew that Bess was failing very fast, and the doctor had assured them that she would not live to see the morning's light.

"With heavy hearts, and loving hands, the old man and the Puffer administer to the child's comfort; flitting with noiseless step about the room where she lies, or, passing about the house with the same cautious step, lest they may disturb her, and so hasten the dread moment, which they know must come at last."

They are seated now, at the bedside of the child, and as they look upon her lying there, with face so pale, and such a patient look upon it, the silent watchers cannot choose, but think that even Death will do her reverence, touching her so gently with his icy hand, that not a pang will change the features, which now bear the semblance of an angel-face from Heaven.

A few days after the child had come to live with Uncle Sol, she had spied a picture hanging upon the wall of the sitting-room,—a common print enough, but which had struck her fancy,—and she had begged Uncle Sol to have it placed in her room, which request was granted.

The picture represented a stately tree with heavy foliage, while countless buds could be seen in various stages of development, a few of which, seemed on the point of blossoming. In fact, one of the buds had burst, and a little hand had pushed itself out from the blossom, as though in search of some other hand, which it thought to clasp. Above the tree was represented an angel, with a heavenly light about its face, and who, with outstretched arms, was in the act of clasping the little hand just protruded from the blossom; while clinging to the angel's neck, was already a little child, that was to be borne away to Heaven.

This picture, hanging in her room, was almost the last thing that faded from the sight of the child as she fell asleep at night. While she lies so calm and peaceful now, her eyes are fixed upon the picture, as though it were the theme of her meditations.

So very quiet is she, not speaking or noticing them for so long a time, that Uncle Sol, in gentle tones, asks if there is aught they can do, to make her more comfortable.

For a moment she does not reply. Then, slowly removing her eyes from the picture, as though reluctant to leave it, she takes the old man's hand in hers, and tells him that she is as happy and comfortable now, as she can be. Then she whispers him, how thankful she feels towards him, for all the kindness he has shown her, and says God has been good to her, to give her such a dear friend as he, to be with her when her eyes must close forever. Then, in a loving way, smoothing the hand of the old man, which she holds in her own, she tells him how glad she is, to know that some kind hearts are to be found in the world; that all are not selfish and bad, as she always thought before she knew him.

From that she seemed to wander, and spoke of things that they used to talk of months before, when they took their walks in the garden together. After a little, she spoke of the picture, and begged Uncle Sol to tell her if he was sure that one bud, which she pointed out, had not grown larger, as if it were preparing to blossom.

He tells her that it is imagination; that the bud has not changed; and laughingly asks her if it would not be strange if a picture could assume life. But she still persists that she can see it change; the bud is larger than it was an hour ago, and the angel's hand has gone nearer that bud than it ever was before.

The bright sun of a December afternoon has cast its rays in at the window now, and the Puffer hastens to close the shutter to keep it out, but the child entreats to have it opened, for she desires that everything shall be bright about her to-day; and, furthermore, it may be that the sun's rays, entering the room, will help the bud to blossom sooner, and it cannot blossom too soon for her. So the sun's rays once more nestle by the bedside, reflecting a golden light upon the picture hanging near. With a happy smile as she beholds it, the child, still clasping the hand of her aged friend, closes her eyes and falls into a quiet sleep, which lasts for nearly an hour. Then she wakes, and Uncle Sol, who has not left her side, observes a change in her looks, and feels that very soon he must bid her good-bye forever. So affected is he, that, almost before he knows it, the tears are standing in his eyes; observing which, the child strives to comfort him by telling him he is doing wrong to grieve for her now; that he might well feel sad to know that she must live and suffer; but it should be a happy thought to know that she was so soon to be in Heaven with her mother, who had been so long awaiting her. A deathly pallor now comes upon her face, and so they gently bathe her brow, thinking she is faint. This revives her for a moment, and she looks eagerly at the picture as before.

Starting suddenly into a sitting posture, she points at the picture, and begs them to see how the bud has grown since they last spoke of it. The sun's rays have nearly reached it now, and she tells them that she is sure that the bud has opened a very little, and that she can see little fingers which she knows are meant for hers, just peeping from the blossom. They do not reply to her, for they know she wanders now, but they watch her lips carefully, to catch every word she utters, knowing that she can say but little more to them.

With loving hands they lay her gently back upon the pillow, but she does not remove her eyes from the picture which has so much interest for her now.

A moment more and she faintly murmurs:

"Good-bye, dear Uncle Sol; think of me when I'm gone, as tending a garden above, which you will share with me when you come! And you, dear grandmother, must place one kiss upon my lips for darling mother, and I will bear it safely to her. Look!" she cries, gazing intently upon the picture; "Look! the bud is open now. The little hand has reached that of the angel's! What makes it so dark? Has the sun gone down? The light about the angel's face is brighter than it was, and the face shines like gold! Now the light is brighter! Yes, it was my hand; and oh! the angel gazes on my face with such a tender love within its eyes, that, as I look upon them, I know it's darling mother come to lead her weary little girl to Heaven!"

With a happy smile upon her face, the child sank back upon her pillow, and when they glanced at the picture on the wall, and saw that the rays of the setting sun reflected full upon it, they turned their eyes upon the child again, and knew, although a smile was on her face, that her young life had fled.

And now the day has become another thing of the past, and, joining its innumerable predecessors, is only to be remembered, like other days that have passed away, by the events that were born during its light, whether for good or evil. Intelligence of the child's death has been conveyed to Mr. Datchery, and in turn imparted by him to his friends, and the news has cast a gloom upon them all.

In view of the melancholy event, Edwin suggests that they postpone the meeting at the Minor Canon's till some future time, but Datchery is averse to any different arrangements being made, and, in consequence of this determination, Mr. Peckcraft and Mr. Grewgious, who have come up from London to hear the Diary read, in company with Datchery and Edwin, leave the Crozier Inn just at twilight, and proceed to the Minor Canon's.

They find Mr. Sapsea and the members of the Reverend gentleman's family awaiting them, and the whole company have just got comfortably seated, when a servant announces Mr. Durdles, who is presently standing in their midst, looking as though he felt exceedingly uncomfortable,—which no doubt he did, considering that his habits were of the misanthrophic kind, and that, as he asserts at all times, he prefers to associate with stiff 'uns, for the reason that they ain't so partic'lar, and he don't have to stand on ceremony with 'em. The Minor Canon notices his embarrassment, and, greeting him kindly, places a chair and begs he will make himself at home.

Whereupon Mr. Durdles takes the proffered chair, and, seating himself, leans back against the wall in a very free-and-easy way, saying that he hopes this business is to be done lively, for he has things to look after before he sleeps that can't be put off.

After a little, Mr. Datchery rises from his seat, and takes from his pocket the Diary, whose contents they have assembled to hear read, and, placing it upon the table, he addresses Mr. Crisparkle:

"Reverend sir, before we proceed with the business which has brought us together, I desire to say a few words which will explain our object to those who, as yet, are ignorant of it—more especially the ladies. An individual, whose name had better not be spoken, but who is well known to all of us,—and, to our sorrow,—has, through the instrumentality of our Heavenly Father, been fearfully punished for the many crimes of which he has been guilty.

"While most of us know the nature of his offences, none of us could ever know the details, were it not that, while disposing of his effects, by those who had a legal right to do so, a certain memoranda was found, and which now lies on yonder table, that will afford some insight as to the manner in which this man has succeeded, the past year, in bringing so much misery upon innocent people. It would seem that this Diary was one in which he kept nothing else but that which pertained to matters connected with the disappearance of his nephew, Mr. Drood, and dates from the arrival of that gentleman at Cloisterham, one year ago. It will, therefore, prove interesting, as clearing up some points that have lain in the dark, and which we have assembled to hear read. A good portion of the memoranda we already know; that, of course, can be passed over. Will you, my dear sir," addressing the Minor Canon, "be pleased to read aloud those passages which you will find marked with pencil?" and passes the Diary to the Reverend gentleman, who draws his chair nearer the table, and, from John Jasper's Diary, reads:

"Ned came to-day. My hell in perspective, I suppose, will now be realized. His love for Rosa is but a drop of water, while mine is an ocean. But that will matter nothing. It is not affection, but duty, with them. My God! must I stand quietly by and see my idol taken from me! Have I no power to prevent this marriage?"

Here the Minor Canon turns over three or four pages, and reads again:

"Ned and I talk confidentially to-day. He admits that he has no love for Rosa, but still will marry her, because she was his father's choice. Great Heavens! and I love her so madly that I could sacrifice my soul's salvation for her! I wish that one of us three were dead—I have given him warning to-day, as far as I dared, but he will not observe it—I shudder to think what will be the result of all this."

At the termination of this last sentence Rosa, who is seated near Edwin, quickly takes his hand in hers, as though to protect him from some unseen danger; smiling at her fears, he whispers her that she has no cause for apprehension now; that the worst is over.

Referring to the next marked passage of the Diary, the Minor Canon continues:

"In view of what may occur, I must obtain the good opinion of all who may be a help to me in time to come, so visited Mr. Sapsea to-day for the first time, and found him what I expected—a fool with much flesh on his bones and few brains in his head; a man who, knowing absolutely nothing, strives to convince his fellows that he knows everything. I remember several persons with this egotistical nature, and they were in most cases constructed physically like Mr. Sapsea—very ponderous and heavy. Possibly they are of some benefit to the world,—perhaps society needs dead weights,—if so, the Sapseas fill their mission admirably. Durdles happened in while I was there. Something about the departed Mrs. Sapsea's monument. An idea is suggested by meeting him here. Would it not be well for me to make myself familiar with the Cathedral crypt, and if possible to mark the key to Sapsea's monument, so that I can identify it from others which Durdles carries, and obtain a duplicate? I decided that it would, and so, with two other keys I strike the Sapsea key so hard that a dent is made upon its wards, and I shall know it if I have occasion to use it."

Mr. Sapsea, during the reading of the last item, folds his arms in a very consequential way, and looks sternly into the faces of the company with an air of saying:

"If any person here would like to endorse those sentiments, I shall be happy to order my slaves to instantly confine that person in the deepest dungeon within my castle walls."

No notice, however, being paid to the irate Mind, the Minor Canon proceeds with another extract:

"My plans for preventing Ned's marriage are hardly matured when a quarrel takes place between he and young Landless, which helps me to see my way clear for perfecting a scheme that will enable me to ask Rosa to be my wife. I shall undertake this the more readily from knowing that the black fool is jealous of Ned, and, by throwing suspicion on him, shall get rid of them both at one stroke."

"The Sapsea Tomb will answer my purpose admirably. My visit to the crypt with Durdles enabled me to obtain the key, and while he was in a drunken stupor I explored the surroundings alone, and saw enough to satisfy me that it can be made available in disposing of Ned—poor fellow! Why would he not heed my warning?"

"Durdles pointed out the spot where was deposited a quantity of quick lime; this will prove useful. But there will be time enough to take the body from the Tomb, and destroy it, after the excitement attending the disappearance has partly subsided."

The Minor Canon paused at this point, and a shudder ran through his listeners, as they thought of the dreadful death which Edwin had so narrowly escaped.

Mr. Sapsea, however, did not shudder. The height of Jasper's wickedness had been reached, in the estimation of the great man, when the Diary spoke of him, and he could conceive of nothing which would equal the enormity of such a—to him—crime!

Mr. Grewgious, who has been an attentive listener thus far, whispers Mr. Sapsea at this point that it's a wonder the Heavens did not fall and crush the man who could thus calmly plan such a diabolical outrage.

Mr. Sapsea returneth answer that no doubt something of the kind ougth to have befallen Jasper, and no doubt would, had he been located in any other place than Cloisterham, which city contained Mind that could not be spared from the earth; by which he intended his hearers to infer that, out of respect to him (Mr. Sapsea), the Heavens could not have been prevailed upon to fall under any circumstances.

The Minor Canon, selecting another extract, proceeds:

"I wish this opium habit had never fixed itself so firmly upon me. The awaking from it is terrible. A horrible vision last night. Saw Bessie Tranders as plainly as when she lived. Poor girl! I have thought of her often of late. I must destroy those Renlaw letters to-night. They may prove troublesome, should their contents be seen by others. I must see her child before long. I suppose the Padlers have her yet. Fopperty may prove useful to me, too, ere long. He is a crafty fellow, and will do anything for money, though I don't know that he would take life. To-morrow night is Christmas-Eve. Ned and young Landless take supper with me. Every thing is progressing finely. How I wish it was all over."

The reading, thus far, had seemed so like the living over of the miserable days, that Helena, unable to restrain her feelings, burst into convulsive tears and sobs, and declared that she could not listen further to this record of Jasper's villainy. They do all in their power to comfort her, and, after a little time, she is calm again, and Mr. Crisparkle continues:

"John Jasper—murderer! These are the words, formed of letters of fire, that are burning constantly before my eyes. Oh, fool that I have been! Rosa's guardian has called upon me to-day, and told me that which convinces me that my crime was unnecessary—that Ned and Rosa had abandoned the path laid out for them, and that both were free to seek other loves. Great God! why could not I have known all this before? Too late, too late! I am a fool to keep this Diary. I'll burn it to-morrow. It may prove my ruin. Oh, my poor boy, I could weep tears of blood for what I have done. But stay; I must not let this misery blind my judgment. Young Landless may prove, after all, the greatest obstacle I have yet had to encounter. Rosa may have learned, through his sister, that he loves her; I must accuse him, by inuendoes, of being the author of this crime, and follow him till he is either convicted of it, or until I drive him from the country."

"I remember, very well, the time he speaks of in connection with myself," interrupted Mr. Grewgious. "I watched him closely, then, and felt sure, from his behaviour, that he was the guilty man. A long life in the legal surroundings of my profession has taught me that, no matter how thick or how high these villains rear their walls of defence, the breach is always made from the inside, and themselves the ones who first dislodge the foundations of their hiding places."

Edwin suggests that the Minor Canon abstain from reading further, as he must be fatigued; but that gentleman declares he is so interested that he will not stop till he has finished the contents of the Diary. He then proceeds with the reading:

"If any suspicion lurks in the bosom of Mr. Crisparkle towards me,—and I feel sure that there does at times,—the entries which I took the precaution to enter upon my Diary concerning the danger which I thought threatened Ned, long before the act was committed, and the subsequent entry, wherein I swore to devote my life to the destruction of the murderer, and inserting a clause whereby I declared I would never discuss the mystery with any living creature,—thus relieving myself of the annoyance of being obliged to converse on a subject which is tormenting every hour of my life,—have blinded him, I feel sure, and have proved a barrier which will ward off any suspicion that might otherwise attach to me when he hears that I have offered myself to Rosa, and by so doing revealed a passion that might have led me to make way with the poor boy."

The Minor Canon stops here to inform his hearers that Jasper was correct in his estimate as to how far these entries would blind him. That if he felt suspicious of Jasper's guilt, which he declared was often the case, his mind would instantly revert to the passages spoken of in the Diary, and he then felt that he was doing the guilty man an injustice.

"Heaven must have prompted him to keep this Diary," he added, "that it might fall into our hands, and make plain to us those things which otherwise we should never have known."

Then, referring to another marked page of the Diary, he reads the following extract:

"I am refused by Rosa, and treated by her with scorn and contempt: so now my life must be devoted to the destruction of the black fool whom she, I feel sure, has given her heart to."

The next entry has the following:

"Have arranged with Fopperty to take up his residence at the same house where she has been placed by her guardian; hoping thereby to gain information which will lead to the whereabouts of young Landless. Meantime, I have concluded to have her abducted, and shall immediately put the plan in operation."

Edwin looks inquiringly at Rosa, to signify that he would be pleased to learn the particulars of that outrage, which had never been explained in detail to him. Rosa promises to tell him all about it at some other time, and the Minor Canon continues with the reading:

"Met Slanduce to-day—the very man, of all others, I was the most anxious to see. He has promised to obtain possession of Rosa, and have her secure in his house within three days. I think he will succeed."

The next extract reads thus:

"Everything is favorable to my plans. Rosa is now in my power, and she shall either marry me, or remain a prisoner with Slanduce till her death. I'd rather see her dead than the wife of another man. I shall go to London to-day and see the opium mixer! After which I go to Slanduce's, and learn how fares my darling idol."

Then follows another extract, within a few days of the date of the last, telling of the escape of Rosa, and his annoyance that it should have happened. The last entry was evidently written in a desponding mood, and closes thus:

"What is to be the result of all these miserable failures? I feel like a man who is groping about in a dark room, filled with wild beasts, not one of which can be seen, and never knowing when they will spring upon him. Well, I cannot more than die. Something terrible is to befall me very soon, I know, for dark forebodings fill my mind when I am awake, and terrible dreams are with me when I sleep. This Diary I *must* destroy; but not now. I'll wait till I am sure that danger is imminent, for I derive some pleasure in referring to its pages, in that they tell me of plottings that have made bleed the hearts of those I hate. I'll place it with the scarf, and lock them both together—fitting company for each other. I had not the nerve to use my hands about Ned's throat; this shawl must do that work, and it was well done. A fearful storm to-night. I'll place the Diary with its black companion, and leave them for a time to keep each other company."

The Minor Canon takes a long breath, and says, with an air of relief, "That's all."

Datchery remarks: "It is evident that the Diary left off on the night when so much damage was done the church-yard and Precincts by the terrible storm he speaks of. The great mystery is cleared up, now, as to the manner in which he obtained entrance into the Sapsea monument, and it is no wonder that Mr. Sapsea was deceived by the cunning means which this villain took to obtain the key."

Mr. Sapsea rises majestically, and prepares to take his leave. They notice that the great mind is annoyed at something, and does not appear so completely confident of his own powers as is his wont. He feels it incumbent upon him to say something, however, and, in the pompous tone which is so natural to him, proceeds:

"Ladies and gentlemen:—The reading of the remarkable document, which we have just listened to, shows a depravity that I, for one, did not suppose could exist in the heart of any man who claims to be an Englishman. In fact, having listened to every word with an unprejudiced Mind—if I may be allowed the expression, with an Enlarged Mind,"—he waits a moment, that they may have time to digest the parenthetical sentence, and then, fearing that they may not quite grasp it, repeats, "Enlarged Mind,—I have arrived at a conclusion. Perhaps you may wonder that I *have* arrived at a conclusion so much in advance of others here assembled; perhaps, knowing my superiority in grasping subjects which common minds stagger at when they attempt them, you will *not* wonder. But whichever way you consider it, I repeat that I have arrived at a conclusion, which is, that the whole matter is so mixed and complicated, and, above all, that there is such an outrageous attempt, on the part of this man Jasper, to drag me down from my high position,—a position which, all will admit, is far above the common herd,—that I have decided it to be the most un-English—I repeat it—un-English business that I ever heard of in my life."

Having delivered himself of this remarkable production, Mr. Sapsea bows with a great deal of politeness, and with much dignity stalks out of the room on his way home.

Perhaps it may be as well at this time, as we shall not have the honour of his presence again, to inform the reader that Mr. Sapsea lived to a good old age, and never once saw the outside of Cloisterham.

Why should he? He had no business to take him thence, and certainly he had no need to go away for any other purpose. There was nothing in the world, and we had almost said out of it, that he did not know; and feeling convinced of this, he had no other desire than to live like some mammoth shell-fish, with Vain-gloriousness for his shell, content to occasionally raise the hard covering with which he was developed, and astonish the beholder with the wonderful richness of his mind.

He wrote his own epitaph long before his death,—an event of which he was sometimes in doubt, it being a question in his mind whether the grim messenger would ever pluck up courage enough to summon him,—and though it was not transcribed upon the monument during the life of the great man (he often wished it could be), it was framed and hung upon his parlour wall, to the great admiration of those who called on him at any time to obtain a favour. The epitaph was worthy of the Great Mind from which it emanated, and was as follows:

"Here lies
HON. THOMAS SAPSEA,
The possessor while living of an
ENLARGED MIND,
Which comprehended all things at a glance.
Notwithstanding that Nature had bestowed upon him
MENTAL GIFTS
Which are seldom granted to mortals, he was not unmindful of the
ignorance of his fellow-men, and strove to impress them at
all times with the
POWERFUL MENTAL RESOURCES
of his Nature.
The Almighty will welcome the entrance into Heaven of such a Mind,
and must find it much easier to govern the Planetary System
than before.
Ye who Read!
Pray that one such mind may exist on Earth during
each successive Age."

As every neighbourhood possesses one such Mind,—and in some neighbourhoods there are a great many of them,—it is but fair to presume that the request which terminates Mr. Sapsea's epitaph has been religiously complied with, and that the prayers of those readers have been granted in every instance.

CHAPTER XLIII.

CONCLUSION.

When a traveller has undertaken a long journey by public conveyance, and forms the acquaintance of some fellow-passenger at the start, in whose company he remains for a long distance, until one or the other reaches his destination, it often happens that they become interested in each other, and that a curiosity is felt, for years after, to learn how each succeeds in life, and if they are prosperous, or otherwise.

The author—taking it for granted that some such feelings exist in the breasts of his readers, and that they have a like curiosity to know what success attended those whose fortunes they have followed through the pages of this narrative, and from whom they are about parting company—takes pleasure in being able to impart the desired information.

When her period of mourning had expired, Helena gave her hand to the Rev. Septimus Crisparkle, and it would be difficult to tell which was the happiest in consequence, the Reverend gentleman himself, or the dear old China Shepherdess, his mother.

On the same day a similar ceremony took place between Rosa and Edwin, and although the occasion was a merry and happy one, its festivities were marred, to a certain extent, by the absence of Mr. Grewgious, who promised to be present, and whom they waited for up to the last moment; at which time the post brought a note from him, in which he stated that he was suffering from an attack of ague (they never knew him to be troubled with it before), and so they must not feel hurt if he only sent his blessing. Could they have read the old man's heart as easily as they read his letter, they would have known better why he excused himself, and that it was because the sight of Rosa, giving her hand away, would remind him of another Rosa, whose hand he had, many years ago, fondly hoped would be his, but had hoped in vain.

The interest which had been retained in the firm of Drood & Peckcraft by Edwin's father, until such time as the son should reach his majority, afforded him an opportunity to enter into active business life at once, after his marriage, and the business is still conducted under the old firm name, though the elder member is getting pretty well along in years, and leaves the management mostly to his young associate, only occasionally proffering such advice as his riper judgment enables him to give.

Captain Tranders (Datchery) and his mother live with Rosa and Edwin. The Captain, having some little capital lying idle, invested it with an old friend with whom he was acquainted in his sea-faring days, and who carried on the business of a ship-chandler, and the business proved a very prosperous one.

Dear old Mr. Grewgious comes often to see his ward, and though he has never told them why the sight of their happiness at times causes tears to fall down his cheeks, they more than suspect that he is reminded of a point in his life when he looked forward to domestic bliss with the woman who was a counterpart of Rosa, but whom fate had decreed should belong to another. They often urge him to make his home with them, but he always refuses, and declares that his habits are so very Angular that he could never exist out of his own chambers, and should not live a year, were he to change his present mode of life.

The Padlers, mother and son, returned to London, Fopperty entering the employ of Captain Tranders, and proves a very useful auxiliary in the business.

The portrait of Rosa, which had hung for so long a time upon the walls of Jasper's room, at the Gate House, was presented to Mr. Grewgious, and it was a little strange, (though no doubt he had good reason for so doing,) that he loaned it to his friend, Mr. Tartar, that he might hang it up in the Admiral's Cabin; and there it held a conspicuous place for many years, to the great delight of the Commander of that gallant craft, which floated in the imaginary waters of the Beanstalk Country.

Whether the fact of Deputy's passion for stoning everything he saw, led Mr. Durdles to believe that the young gentleman would prove a success as a stone-mason, is not positively known. Certain it is, however, that by dint of much persuasion, he did prevail upon the boy to apprentice himself to him (Durdles), and the result was highly satisfactory to both parties in the end, as Deputy turned out as good a workman as his master, and, in a few years, became a partner in the business.

Miss Twinkleton's name still holds its place on the brass plate outside the gate of the Nuns' House, and Miss Twinkleton still holds her place on the other side as principal of that Seminary for Young Ladies, still assisted by Miss Tisher, whose chronic sigh, and weak back, remain the same as they did from time immemorial.

Shortly after Rosa's marriage, the post brought her a most delicate little missive; on opening it, she found it to contain a short note, expressing kindest wishes for Rosa's future happiness, and also a neat little circular advertisement of the Seminary. It was some time before Edwin or Rosa could understand the object in sending this latter document, but after a little, they concluded Miss Twinkleton had an eye to the future; and if, at some distant day, a daughter should need the advantages of a Seminary, the said circular might serve as a reminder of the proper place to apply.

The Topes still continue to occupy the same positions as when they were first introduced into these pages. Mr. Tope, never being quite able to understand how all the events of the past year were brought about, is very reticent when Jasper's name is mentioned, while Mrs. Tope does not hesitate to act as Jasper's Champion, declaring that Mr. Jasper got along very well till the white-headed lodger came, who she had no doubt had bewitched him to do as he did, and that Mr. Jasper was an "abused man, poor fellow!"

Mr. Luke Honeythunder still holds the exalted position of Champion of the Heavy Weights in the Philanthropic Ring. As a counter with his right on the Reverend Septimus Crisparkle's body,—which he confidently expected would send the Reverend gentleman to grass,—he addressed a short note to the mother of the Reverend gentleman a few days after his marriage, in which he stated that he (Mr. Honeythunder) had always prophesied young Landless would die young, but he had never imagined that such a terrible fate awaited his sister as a marriage with the Minor Canon, and hoped he (Mr. Honeythunder) would never come in contact with either of them; all of which created a great deal of merriment at Mr. Crisparkle's breakfast table, on the morning of its reading.

Mr. Bazzard finished his tragedy in due time, but it proves to be a Thorn of Anxiety indeed to him, lest his name should appear as an author. Hence he kept the MSS. under lock and key, and Mr. Grewgious was the only person that ever had the privilege of hearing it read. The latter gentleman endeavoured, a great many times, to persuade the author to offer it to some manager, for he knew it would prove a success at the start, but Mr. Bazzard emphatically objected, declaring that all the fame which he might derive from being known as an author, would never recompense him for the misery he should endure by having ridicule cast upon his work by those who, having no brains of their own, seek to obtain notoriety by destroying the productions of other people's.

Mr. Stollop remained in the employ of the new firm for a few months, but was never able to reconcile himself to Edwin, whom he regarded in the light of a dire enemy for marrying Rosa, and shortly retired. He did not assign any cause for leaving the firm, only saying that it was better for the peace of mind of all parties that he should make a change. Before taking final leave, however, he placed in Edwin's hands a note, which he desired that gentleman to open in exactly half an hour from the time he (Stollop) left it. Complying with the request, they found it to contain the reasons for his discontent, beginning with a Shakespearean quotation, varied to suit the present occasion:

"He never told his love,
But let concealment, like a rose in the bud,
Prey on his pale and classic cheek,"

and ending with another familiar quotation, slightly changed:

> "I lately knew a dear Gazelle,
> That I would have to share my lot;
> But some one, who I will not tell,
> Stepped in, and knocked it all to pot."

As green-grocers are frequently seen to emerge from what was known in these pages as the Billickin Mansion, with countenances expressive of a high state of excitement, and carrying in their hands certain documents which resemble bills and accounts, it is fair to presume that that excellent lady continues to occupy those quarters to the present day.

If Father Time, in his skirmishing about Silver Square, has succeeded in making Miss Keep seem a little older than when we first saw her, that is the only change that can be perceived in her. There is the same methodical arrangement in everything about her, and she still gratifies her passion for rhyming on every possible occasion.

Rosa's marriage affording the good lady an excellent opportunity for displaying her talent in this direction, she composed some lines on the subject. As she desired to present them to Rosa in the neatest possible form, a professional penman was employed to copy them, with instructions to ornament the capitals with all the flourishes at his command, which was done, and in due time the document passed into the hands of the young bride. Lest this effusion should be lost to the world, it may be well to place it on these pages:

"THE OAK AND THE IVY.

> "Come, my Muse, and help me tell
> What I feign would say in rhyme,
> Of one who loved the Muses well,
> Yet loved her Edwin all the time.
>
> "Misfortune's clouds obscured her life,
> And troubles came on every side;
> The world looked dark and full of strife,—
> She felt she could not stem the tide.
>
> "But see! the clouds begin to rise!
> And sunshine shoots athwart the green;
> Edwin appears, with lover's sighs,
> And changed is all the dismal scene.
>
> "Who is the Oak, so stately and tall?
> Who is the Ivy, that clings so fast?
> The first is Edwin, who never shall fall,
> While Rosa, the Ivy, shields him from the blast.
>
> "So may their journey, through this vale
> Of Mud and Scattered Roses,
> Prepare their souls to take the sail
> Which leads to the Heavenly Muses!"

The sunniest spot in Cloisterham Church-yard holds all that is mortal of Bessie. Beneath a bed of violets—her favorite flower while living—she sleeps. Her aching bosom is at rest, and never more shall know the sorrows of earthly life.

As holy beings can see and hear (and who that have lost dear ones will not gladly hail it as a truth?) how happy must her spirit be to see that white-haired old man, in the spring and summer time, daily visiting her grave, keeping the flowers above it free from grass and weeds, and looking fresh and bright. No wonder, is it, that the birds linger longer about this spot than any other, and that in the bright, cloudless summer days, the bees dwell longer there to gather golden food, as though 'twere sweeter. There is not, in all the church-yard round a fairer spot, than Bessie Padler's grave.

Every year does the old man devote such time as is needed to keep this little bed in perfect order. "It makes her happy to see me doing this I feel sure," he would say; "I know she sees me, though I cannot see her, and I also know, that in that home beyond the stars, a little angel-hand is preparing a far more beautiful flower-bed for me, than you or I can imagine; so that, while I am cultivating flowers here to decorate the spot where only her dust reposes, but which, in time, must perish—(not while I live, though)—she is rearing a floral garden there, whose beauty and perfume can never fade or die!"

Datchery endeavoured to prevail upon Uncle Sol to employ some one to help him in his work, but the old man always refused, saying, that the care of her grave was the only pleasure left him in the world.

A year had passed since John Jasper was bereft of reason. The Christmas days are come again, and on Christmas eve, a black-eyed, black-haired man, with a haggard face and attenuated form, approaches Cloisterham from the main road. Although a light snow has fallen through the day, and still continues, the man is in his stocking feet, and his only covering consists of a shirt and trousers. Although the lateness of the hour (it is nearly midnight) would preclude the possibility of his meeting with any one, he stops at every sound of the winds, as they moan through the elms which skirt the road, and crouches beneath the hedges. Thus he continues on his way till he reaches the city. The moon, shining through the clouds, renders objects quite visible, and, casting his eyes upon the grim old Cathedral tower, looking in the moonlight like some mammoth goblin, the man continues towards the church-yard, seeming to know the grounds quite well, as he passes hastily through the paths, until he reaches the grave of Bessie Padler.

Then he kneels down by its side, and, with a wild light in his eyes, clasps his hands, in an attitute of devotion, above his head, and murmurs in a subdued voice, broken occasionally by sobs:

"The vision told me to kneel upon your grave, dear child, and ask you to intercede for the wretched man, who is not fit to live, and is not fit to die! You forgave me ere you died, Bess. I remember that—oh, how well! Ask God to forgive me, Bess, and take my spirit hence to dwell with you. You are an angel now, Bess, and can read my heart, and can behold how full of repentance it is for my misdeeds! While you are asking forgiveness for me, dear Bess, I'll lay me down to rest upon your grave. I'm very cold. Don't be long, dear child!" The voice grows indistinct as he repeats, hardly above a breath, "dear child." Then lays him down by the graveside, and, with his arms thrown across the mound, as though he would embrace it, heaves one long sigh, and so glides down the silent river that leads to the realms of eternity!

The Christmas Morning ushers in a bright, clear sky. The Christmas Morning sun, rising in regal splendor, throws its beams on tree and house-top, gilding the old Cathedral Tower till it resembles a golden pile. As the sun's warm rays cause the light snow to melt and fall in water-drops, one could almost fancy that they were tears of joy, in that the world was again permitted to behold the light of another blessed Christmas Day.

Making his way slowly along the unbeaten paths, comes Uncle Sol, bearing in his hand a wreath of green leaves to lay upon his darling's grave. When he has reached the spot, he discovers the body of the dead man lying there, but does not recognize it, as the snow has nearly hidden it with its mantle of white.

Observing some men passing near the church-yard, the old man calls to them for assistance, and they soon join him. One of the men proves to be an attendant at the mad-house, and he tells his companions that the man lying there is Mr. Jasper, who had escaped from his confinement during the previous night, and that he, the attendant, has been seeking him, high and low.

The others look astounded at hearing this; and one of them, who remembers how Jasper attempted his nephew's life, whispers his neighbour, as they look again upon the dead man's form:

"His was a wicked life, but he could not have had a purer winding-sheet," and might he not have added, that perhaps its purity had washed away his sins?

www.ingramcontent.com/pod-product-compliance
Lightning Source LLC
LaVergne TN
LVHW020914110826
845150LV00004B/667